CAMBRIDGE LIBRARY COLLECTION

Books of enduring scholarly value

History

The books reissued in this series include accounts of historical events and movements by eye-witnesses and contemporaries, as well as landmark studies that assembled significant source materials or developed new historiographical methods. The series includes work in social, political and military history on a wide range of periods and regions, giving modern scholars ready access to influential publications of the past.

Ta Tsing Leu Lee; Being the Fundamental Laws, and a Selection from the Supplementary Statutes, of the Penal Code of China

The sinologist George Thomas Staunton (1781–1859) learned Chinese as a child and accompanied his father on a trip to China in 1792 where, though the Ambassador's page, he was the only member of the delegation who could speak to the emperor in Chinese. A career in the East India Company's Canton factory followed, and he translated many texts between Chinese and English, including this penal code, published in 1810, which was its first translation into any European language. The 'Fundamental Laws' was the legal code of the Qing Dynasty (1644–1911), and contained more than 1,000 statutes. Staunton organised his translation of a selection of the laws into seven divisions: general, civil, fiscal, ritual (religious), military, criminal, and public works. He also includes an appendix with translations of edicts regarding matters such as punishment, making this compendium an invaluable guide to the complex legal regime of the Qing Dynasty.

Cambridge University Press has long been a pioneer in the reissuing of out-of-print titles from its own backlist, producing digital reprints of books that are still sought after by scholars and students but could not be reprinted economically using traditional technology. The Cambridge Library Collection extends this activity to a wider range of books which are still of importance to researchers and professionals, either for the source material they contain, or as landmarks in the history of their academic discipline.

Drawing from the world-renowned collections in the Cambridge University Library and other partner libraries, and guided by the advice of experts in each subject area, Cambridge University Press is using state-of-the-art scanning machines in its own Printing House to capture the content of each book selected for inclusion. The files are processed to give a consistently clear, crisp image, and the books finished to the high quality standard for which the Press is recognised around the world. The latest print-on-demand technology ensures that the books will remain available indefinitely, and that orders for single or multiple copies can quickly be supplied.

The Cambridge Library Collection brings back to life books of enduring scholarly value (including out-of-copyright works originally issued by other publishers) across a wide range of disciplines in the humanities and social sciences and in science and technology.

Ta Tsing Leu Lee

Being the Fundamental Laws,
and a Selection from the
Supplementary Statutes,
of the Penal Code of China

EDITED AND TRANSLATED BY
GEORGE THOMAS STAUNTON

CAMBRIDGE UNIVERSITY PRESS

Cambridge, New York, Melbourne, Madrid, Cape Town,
Singapore, São Paolo, Delhi, Mexico City

Published in the United States of America by Cambridge University Press, New York

www.cambridge.org
Information on this title: www.cambridge.org/9781108045865

© in this compilation Cambridge University Press 2012

This edition first published 1810
This digitally printed version 2012

ISBN 978-1-108-04586-5 Paperback

This book reproduces the text of the original edition. The content and language reflect
the beliefs, practices and terminology of their time, and have not been updated.

Cambridge University Press wishes to make clear that the book, unless originally published
by Cambridge, is not being republished by, in association or collaboration with, or
with the endorsement or approval of, the original publisher or its successors in title.

嘉慶十年新鐫

大清律例重訂
輯註通纂

遵照嘉慶六年奉
部頒行續纂并增修近年條例

比引條例督
捕則例附後

工本浩繁每部發
價番鏹三兩六錢

Mutlow sculp.

Fac-simile of the Title page of the latest edition of the
TA TSING LEU LEE
Published in the Year 1805, the 10th of the reigning Emperor Kia King.

see page lxiii. *note.*

TA TSING LEU LEE;

BEING

THE FUNDAMENTAL LAWS,

AND A SELECTION FROM THE

SUPPLEMENTARY STATUTES,

OF THE

PENAL CODE OF CHINA;

ORIGINALLY PRINTED AND PUBLISHED IN PEKIN,
IN VARIOUS SUCCESSIVE EDITIONS,
UNDER THE SANCTION, AND BY THE AUTHORITY, OF THE SEVERAL
EMPERORS OF THE *TA TSING*, OR PRESENT DYNASTY.

TRANSLATED FROM THE CHINESE;
AND ACCOMPANIED WITH AN APPENDIX,
CONSISTING OF AUTHENTIC DOCUMENTS, AND A FEW OCCASIONAL NOTES,
ILLUSTRATIVE OF THE SUBJECT OF THE WORK;

BY SIR GEORGE THOMAS STAUNTON, BART. F.R.S.

Mens, et animus, et confilium, et fententia civitatis, pofita eft in *LEGIBUS*.
CICERO PRO CLUENTIO.

LONDON:
PRINTED FOR T. CADELL AND W. DAVIES, IN THE STRAND.
1810.

Strahan and Preston,
Printers-Street, London.

TO

JOHN BARROW, ESQ. F.R.S.

&c. &c. &c.

IN TESTIMONY OF SINCERE REGARD AND ESTEEM,

THIS VOLUME IS INSCRIBED,

BY

HIS OBLIGED AND ATTACHED FRIEND,

THE TRANSLATOR.

TRANSLATOR's PREFACE.

IN undertaking the work which is now submitted to the eye of the Public, the Translator was not unconscious of the difficulties and disadvantages he would have to contend with in so novel an attempt. He was however encouraged to proceed by the persuasion that the work was in itself amply deserving of the labour which it might be necessary to bestow upon it; that the intrinsic value, the unquestionable authenticity of the materials, and the general importance and curiosity of the subject, would fully compensate those particular defects and imperfections which, in an undertaking of this nature, were foreseen to be unavoidable, and, upon the whole, make amends for the too concise and almost obscure brevity of the text, in some places, its tedious and uninstructive prolixity in others, and its general unsuitableness for translation into an English idiom. Under all circumstances he flattered himself, that a faithful version of the Fundamental Laws of the Penal Code of China might, with the addition of some supplementary matter, not only prove interesting as far as regards its immediate subject, but likewise afford a more compendious and satisfactory illustration, than any other Chinese work that could have been selected, of the peculiar system and constitution of the Government, the principles of its internal policy, its connection with the national habits and character, and its influence upon the general state and condition of the people in that country.

To account for the limited and defective nature of our information upon these interesting subjects, notwithstanding the number and variety of the literary communications concerning the Chinese empire, which we already possess in Europe, through the medium of the European languages, it will be requisite to advert particularly to the circumstances under which these communications have been made, and to the sources from which they have, for the most part, been derived.

It will not be necessary, in the course of this enquiry, to trace back the subject to any very remote period. It is well known that the Empire of China, bounded on one side by the ocean, and on the other by ranges of inaccessible mountains, or vast and seemingly impervious deserts, continued, until about the commencement of the 13th century of our era, to be effectually secluded by these natural barriers from any direct and regular intercourse with the rest of the inhabited globe. The various inquisitive and enlightened nations, which successively flourished in ancient times, both in Western Asia and in Europe, scarcely appear to have even suspected its existence.

In the mean while, however, the people who, at a remote period of antiquity, first colonized this fertile and extensive region, were gradually emerging from primeval barbarism. Without either receiving assistance, or encountering opposition, from their less fortunate neighbours, they slowly but regularly advanced upon the strength of their own internal resources and local advantages, nearly, if not entirely, to their present state of civilization and improvement.

The commencement of the 13th century is the period at which the Chinese first submitted in a body to the sway of a foreign conqueror; and although the dynasty, established by the successful invaders, was not of any long duration, it must have had a material, and even in some degree a permanent effect, upon the relations between China and contemporary Powers; more especially, as this revolution in the East was, it will be perceived, at no considerable interval of time,

seconded

seconded in the West, by the fortunate era of the restoration of letters, and of the introduction of the most important of the improvements in navigation in modern Europe.

As a new spirit of curiosity and enterprize had been thus excited, and means apparently adequate to its complete gratification discovered, it might naturally be supposed that one of the first objects would have been that of taking advantage of the additional facilities which seemed to have been afforded for a communication with the Chinese empire; that the early accounts, however vague and imperfect, which had been given by casual travellers, of its extent, magnificence, and political importance, would have soon led, in the ordinary course of events, to an intimate acquaintance and a regularly established intercourse with that remote and recently discovered, but, at the same time, highly interesting portion of the civilized world.

At the end, however, of several centuries, these expectations are still but very imperfectly realized. This Great Empire, too well assured of the competency of its own natural and artificial resources, to be induced to seek, and, if not too powerful, at least too distant and compactly united, to be liable to be compelled to enter into alliances and close connections with the Powers of Europe, has never as yet, except in a precarious and limited degree, admitted of any species of intercourse with them. It continues to this day wholly regardless and independent of those nations of the West, whose general superiority in policy and in arms has triumphantly extended their power and influence over almost every other existing society of mankind.

A considerable portion of the intercourse which actually subsists between China and the Nations of Europe owes its origin, as is well known, to the influence of religious motives; and was established under rather favourable auspices, by the indefatigable zeal and appropriate talents of the early missionaries of the Catholic church. These ecclesiastics, having been for the most part of the Society of Jesus, were not wanting in the fagacity, or neglectful of the policy, which had, on fo many other occafions, crowned the projects of their fociety with fuccefs. It is difficult indeed to fay how far, under fuch circumftances, even the moft ancient of the inftitutions, upon which the fabric of the Chinefe government is founded, or the moft deeply rooted of the prejudices and attachments, by which it continues to be fuftained, could have withftood their powerful and undermining influence, had they not happened to have loft the fupport and countenance both of the head of the Catholic church, and of their refpective temporal fovereigns.

The confequent extinction of their order having fubverted the fyftem of politics, which until then the Miffionaries in China had fuccefsfully obferved, having caufed the adoption of a plan of converfion more ftrict, and probably more orthodox, but, in the fame proportion, more unaccommodating to the prejudices of the people, and more alarming to the jealoufy of the government, and having alfo, generally fpeaking, thrown the profeffion into lefs able hands, the caufe of Chriftianity and of Europe neceffarily loft much of its temporary luftre and influence. In addition to this unfavourable change of circumftances, the French revolution has fubfequently had the effect of confiderably reducing both the amount of the funds which fupport, and the number of the labourers who cultivate the Chriftian vineyard in China; under which accumulated difadvantages the intercourfe with Europeans, as far as the Miffionaries are concerned, it will eafily be conceived, muft of late years, in fpite of every exertion, have been gradually on the decline.

Although, among the few Miffionaries whom the Emperor of China ftill retains in his fervice at Pekin, and among the larger number who are clandeftinely employed in maintaining and propagating the Chriftian faith in the provinces, there are, no doubt, many amiable and refpectable, and perhaps even fome learned men, they can fcarcely be

expected

expected to make any material addition, under their prefent difficulties, to the ftock of ufeful and valuable information which Europe has already derived from the fame quarter.

The literary labours of the Miffionaries, confifting of original defcriptions and of tranflations, are, however, already numerous and extenfive. Their works feem, at firft fight, to have been penned with fuch diligence, and formed upon plans fo comprehenfive, as to promife fatisfaction on every fubject connected with the Chinefe empire, in which European curiofity can be interefted. But, on a clofer examination, we find reafon to lament that their attention had not been more directed to the objects that were principally defirable, and we begin to fufpect that their fituation, or fome other circumftances, muft have had a tendency to difqualify them from reprefenting thofe objects with all the accuracy and fidelity of difinterefted and impartial obfervers. At the fame time, it is impoffible to conceive any fet of perfons more advantageoufly placed for the purpofe of collecting and communicating the information that was moft required. Having devoted themfelves to a refidence for life among the people of that empire, it was naturally one of their firft objects to acquire a knowledge of their manners, habits, and language. The active duties of their profeffion neceffarily led them to cultivate the favour of the rich, to conciliate the affections of the poor, and to affociate generally with every clafs of the inhabitants. As they appeared exclufively in the character either of artifts or of men of fcience, they were in no danger of becoming objects of jealoufy to any rank, or to any party; they had generally a free communication with every department of the court and of the government, and at times were admitted to a familiar intercourfe even with the fovereign himfelf.

It is, however, to be recollected, on the other hand, that, with the Miffionaries, fcience and literature were objects only of a fecondary confideration, infinitely inferior in their eftimation to that facred

caufe

cause in which they were united, which they were bound to support, and to which all others were to be made subservient; that they were persons who had all of them professedly renounced the world, and who, having abstracted themselves accordingly from its various pursuits, had been in great measure incapacitated from acquiring that particular experience which is necessary towards appreciating the merits and characteristic features of other countries, by the most obvious and indispensable of tests, a comparison with their own. It was also inevitable, that persons thus situated should be, generally speaking, under the influence of a strong pre-disposition in favour of a people, for the sake of whose conversion they had renounced their country, and devoted their lives; and of a government, from whom, at one period, they had received extraordinary kindness and indulgence, and upon the continuance of whose protection the success of their future undertakings was foreseen almost entirely to depend.

Although having, personally, access to all the principal objects of curiosity, and chief sources of information, and possessing sufficiently the requisite talents of description, we too often find that a want of substantial impartiality and discriminating judgment in their writings, has tended to throw a false colouring on many of the objects which they delineate, and has sometimes produced those inconsistencies by which errors and misrepresentations of this description are often found to contribute to their own detection.

In like manner, although an intimate knowledge of the language of China enabled the Missionaries to explore and illustrate the antiquities of the empire, by the perusal and translation of the obscure and disputed texts of its most ancient poets, historians, and philosophers, an extreme anxiety to place these productions in the most favourable and pleasing light, has led them, in some instances, to engraft so much of the European character and style upon the Chinese originals, that the authenticity of their versions has, however unjustly, been in those cases more than suspected.

Other

Other works again, such as the Chinese press abundantly affords, concerning the present state of the empire, its civil, political, and legal institutions, they have, it must be acknowledged, in great measure neglected, either as comparatively unimportant in their estimation, or as insufficient and ill-suited for conveying those highly favourable ideas, with which they seem themselves to have been impressed, of the character of the Chinese people, and the principles of the Chinese government.

By the foregoing observations, it is by no means intended to detract from the real merits of the learned and pious writers of this class, either by denying, that they have afforded to the European world a vast collection of useful and interesting information, or by asserting, that they have, in any particular instances, been guilty of wilful deception or misrepresentation. It is merely wished to point out some of the causes which render it unsafe to rely implicitly on their authority, to state the particular bias under which they wrote, and to notice some of the effects of which that bias was necessarily productive.

The communications between European states and the dominions of China, which a spirit of commercial enterprize gave rise to, although they have been, at times, of considerable importance to several of the Continental nations, and are at present, with respect to Great Britain, of such a nature and extent, as to be very essentially contributive to her national prosperity, yet they did not, until a very late period, produce any fruits deserving of particular notice, either to science or literature.

With the exceptions of the Travels of Mr. Bell of Antermony, and the Translation of a Chinese Novel, by an obscure hand, but illustrated by the name of its Editor, scarcely any thing of importance respecting China, derived from a commercial origin, appeared in England until the period of the Embassy of the late Earl of Macartney. His Lordship's mission was certainly an important step towards obtaining a more accurate and

intimate

intimate knowledge of the Chinese empire. That empire was, on that occasion, in some degree laid open to the view of persons, whose talents and judgment were worthy of their country, and of an enlightened age; and who, it was natural to expect, would be disposed to describe the country and its inhabitants, as they really found them, and to state the opinions they might be led to form on the different objects which occurred, with candour and sincerity. — If, in estimating the credit due to their impartiality, some allowance for the national prejudices of Englishmen should be deemed requisite, the tendency of those prejudices would, at all events, be very dissimilar to that of the bias which had influenced their predecessors in the same field of enquiry. When also it is considered that, in passing rapidly over the narrow path to which they were confined, the opportunities of observation must have been comparatively few and limited, it will justly be deemed a subject of pride and satisfaction, and a very material addition to the immediate advantages which that expedition produced to this country, that it has, in so short a time, and under such unfavourable circumstances, been the means of throwing an entire new light upon, and of correcting and extending our ideas of that extraordinary and interesting empire; that, in short, if it has not led to the discovery of a new world, it has, as it were, enabled us to recover a portion of the old, by removing, in a considerable degree, those obstacles by which our contemplation of it had been intercepted.

The short residence in China of Lord Macartney's Embassy, although it scarcely afforded any opportunity of either confirming or disproving the various geographical, historical, and statistical details, with which we had been furnished by the Missionaries, was amply sufficient to discover that the superiority over other nations, in point of knowledge and of virtue, which the Chinese have long been accustomed to assume to themselves, and which some of their European

historians

historians have too readily granted them, was in great measure fallacious; their knowledge was perceived to be defective in those points in which we have, in Europe, recently made the greatest progress, and to which we are therefore proportionately partial. Their virtues were found to consist more in ceremonial observances, than in moral duties; more in profession, than in practice; and their vices, when traced and discovered upon occasions where they were the least expected, seemed to deserve a more than ordinary degree of reprobation.

The first impressions occasioned by a discovery, that the Chinese people and government were in many respects the converse of that which, agreeably to the most authentic accounts, they might have been expected to be found, were naturally unfavourable.

But if the English visitors at the court of Pekin had been permitted to remain any considerable time, and with a sufficient degree of freedom in the interior of the empire, they might gradually have acquired a more direct and extensive knowledge of the governors and of the governed in China; they might, by constant and familiar intercourse with the several classes of the inhabitants, have learned more of their manners, habits, and ordinary conduct, and have been enabled to judge of, and to characterize, their influencing motives on different occasions, upon surer grounds.

If they had possessed equal opportunities with the missionaries, who preceded them, of exerting their judgment upon the Chinese character, though they certainly would not have coincided in all their sentiments and opinions, they might, perhaps, have found something to compensate the evils they had justly reprobated and lamented, and they might even have at last determined, that a considerable proportion of the opinions most generally entertained by Chinese and Europeans of each other was to be imputed either to prejudice, or to misinformation;

tion; and that, upon the whole, it was not allowable to arrogate, on either side, any violent degree of moral or physical superiority.

In regard to the diffusion of knowledge among the natives, they might not indeed meet with such illustrious instances as those of a Newton, a Locke, or a Bacon; nor even, perhaps, generally, find any tolerable proficiency in the sciences, which in Europe the writings of those great men have contributed so much to advance and to establish; but, nevertheless, such a sufficiency, in all ranks and conditions, of the information essential or most useful to each; such a competency and suitableness of the means to the end, as might, upon a general view of the whole population, fairly entitle the Chinese to be put in competition with some, at least, of the nations of Europe, in respect to all the essential characteristics of civilization.

The virtues of the Chinese, although very inferior, no doubt, to their professions, and of a lower order than those which Christianity has happily implanted, or invigorated, in the European world, they might also have found as little alloyed, either with the sanguinary or the selfish vices, as among any people for whose guidance the salutary light of revelation has not yet penetrated.

Even the crime of infanticide, for instance, which has been considered such an indelible stain upon the Chinese character, might be found to admit of some extenuation, if it was discovered to be rarely if ever practiced, except in the anguish of hopeless poverty, or in cases of such unhappy and defective formation, as might be conceived to render life a painful burden. The criminality of the Chinese, in this respect, might also be safely contrasted with the legalized cruelty and unnatural indifference of Roman fathers under similar circumstances, Passing from the people to the government, the obvious and undeniable defects of the latter might justly be compared with the acknowledged corruptions and imperfections of those of Europe; and it might

perhaps

perhaps be found, upon a general view, that the happiness of the people was not more frequently neglected or interrupted, upon the one system than upon the other.

There would still, no doubt, remain, both in the habits of the people, and the principles of the government, some exceptionable traits, which are happily not to be exactly paralleled in Europe; but, on the other hand, some very considerable and positive moral and political advantages might be found peculiar to the Chinese; attributable to the system of early and universal marriage, except indeed, as far as that system may be considered to conduce to the misfortune of a redundant population; to the sacred regard that is habitually paid to the ties of kindred; to the sobriety, industry, and even intelligence of the lower classes; to the almost total absence of feudal rights and privileges; to the equable distribution of landed property; to the natural incapacity and indisposition of the government and people to an indulgence in ambitious projects and foreign conquests; and lastly, to a system of penal laws, if not the most just and equitable, at least the most comprehensive, uniform, and suited to the genius of the people for whom it is designed, perhaps of any that ever existed.

The foregoing conjectures respecting the degree of estimation in which the Chinese government and people will be held by the other civilized nations of the world, when the veil is more completely withdrawn, which has hitherto intercepted their view, and balked their curiosity, although they neither have been nor can be verified, under present circumstances, by adequate personal enquiry, yet their reasonableness and probability may even now be investigated with advantage, and tried upon almost every point, by the interesting evidence which the Chinese, in their own numerous and respectable literary productions, have themselves afforded.

After making every allowance for national partialities, prejudices, and defects, whatever they may be, it will generally be found, that the best and most authentic information of the state of any country, having pretensions to civilization, is contained in the works of the natives, and in the vernacular language.

Although the character of the Chinese government, in common with that of those of all other Asiatics nations, necessarily prevents the press from becoming, in any confiderable degree, a vehicle for the investigation of political questions, or for the introduction of innovations of any kind, yet there are no previous licenses demanded, or restrictive regulations enforced; nor in the case of publications upon ordinary subjects, any checks whatever imposed upon their number or variety. On the contrary, the encouragement given to pursuits which are purely literary, has always been considered as one of the remarkable features of Chinese policy. These pursuits are professedly the sole channel of introduction to political advancement in the state, to offices, rank, and honours of almost every description. With the prospect of such rewards, the number of competitors in the paths of literature must necessarily be infinite; and, in point of fact, the first rudiments, at least, of literary knowledge, are almost universally diffused among the natives of every class and denomination. — Through the concurrence of these causes the productions of the press in China not only open a wide field of investigation to the literary and philosophical enquirer, but are, in a much greater degree than could otherwise have been expected, calculated to supply that species of information which the present system of our intercourse with the Chinese, affords so little prospect of obtaining by personal communication.

It is not, indeed, to be expected, that an acquaintance with Chinese literature, however intimate, can materially add to our present stock of theoretical knowledge upon natural and philosophical subjects; and in respect to the Ethics and Antiquities of the Chinese, it may perhaps be considered that the translations already effected by the Missionaries afford a sufficient specimen: but there are many other objects of research, which surely are neither uninteresting nor unimportant. As men of science, we have yet much to learn respecting the arts, which, with the advantage of long and uninterrupted experience, and a proportionate degree of practical skill, are successfully cultivated by an eminently industrious and ingenious people. As men of letters, we have yet to comprize, within the circle of our philology, the various branches of a new species of Belles Lettres, contained in a highly refined and most singular language; we have, lastly, as statesmen and philosophers, to examine more closely, and to dive more deeply into the principles, operation, and consequences, of the civil policy, characteristic laws, and general system of a government and constitution, not indeed the best or the purest, but certainly the most anciently, and, if we may judge from its duration, the most firmly established, and the most conformable to the genius and character of the people, of any of which mankind has had experience.

The great, and indeed almost the only obstacle, which exists to inquiries of this nature, is the circumstance of the literature of China being buried in a language by far the least accessible to a foreign student of any that was ever invented by man. Among the languages of Europe, several agree to a considerable extent, even in their phraseology, and all are connected by various analogies. The languages of the Asiatic nations are indeed radically different from those Europe, and their study is, to Europeans, proportionately difficult; but in one point at least, all the written languages of the world coincide, that of the Chinese only excepted. — In all, ideas are expressed by a combination of letters, representing, not the ideas themselves, but certain

particular

particular sounds with which these ideas, either by accident or convention, have become identified. It is exclusively in the Chinese language, that the seemingly visionary scheme of a philosophical character, immediately expressive, according to an established and received classification, of the ideas as they arise in the mind, under an entire disregard of the sounds employed to give them utterance, has ever been generally adopted as the universal medium of communication; a plan of which it may justly be said, that the practice is no less inconvenient and perplexing, than the theory is beautiful and ingenious.

Experience has nevertheless in various instances proved, that these difficulties, however great, are by no means insurmountable, even by ordinary zeal and application. It is also to be considered, that they would be more seriously felt by those, by whom the first steps should be taken towards introducing and recommending the knowledge of the Chinese language in this country, than by those who might afterwards follow in the same path of literature. The modes of acting and thinking peculiar to a people who have scarcely ever been placed in circumstances tending in any respect towards an assimilation with the rest of mankind, especially when conveyed in a language whose style and idioms are frequently as little conformable to our received notions of propriety, as they are reconcileable to our ordinary rules and distinctions of grammar, cannot indeed be expected to prove in any form of translation, altogether agreeable to the taste of European readers. It seems requisite that the students in this branch of oriental literature should become numerous, that its peculiarities should be traced and explained by a more correct knowledge of the people themselves, and that the minds of the readers should be somewhat habituated to them, as they already are in a considerable degree, to the peculiarities in the style and idioms of other Eastern languages. Yet, even in the present state of our knowledge of the Chinese people, and of our political relations with the Chinese empire, it is not unreasonable to hope, that communications derived from

authentic

authentic sources in the original language, may have some effect in drawing attention to, and exciting an interest in, the hitherto neglected literature of that country;— it is necessary indeed, that the work selected should, in one essential point at least, be unexceptionable, however defective in others; that its translation should combine as many advantages, and as few objections as possible, and in particular, that the excellence of the matter, should render the manner in which it was expressed a consideration of comparatively little importance.

Among the multifarious publications of the Chinese, ancient as well as modern, which are still extant, and hitherto untranslated into any European language, the *Ta-Tsing-Leu-Lee*, or Imperial Code of Penal Laws, certainly ranks with those of the first class, in respect to the importance of the subject of which it treats, and the pre-eminence of the authority by which it was originally established, as well as, at different periods down to the present time, successively sanctioned and confirmed. As in this work also, the two very desirable qualities of a comparatively simple style, and a compendious form, happen fortunately to be united, its contents are certainly, in many respects, less difficult of access, than those of most other publications of a similar extent in the Chinese language and character.

It has justly been observed by Mr. Gibbon, that " the laws of a " nation form the most instructive portion of its history." But the laws of the Chinese, if taken in the most comprehensive sense of the term, framed, as they have been, by the wisdom and experience of a long series of ages, and suitably provided, as they are, for the government of an empire, unparalleled in the history of the world, in extent and population, must, it will readily be imagined, be proportionally numerous and complicated. They are also, which is still more embarrassing, generally intermingled in such a degree with details concerning the ancient history and actual condition, of the civil, political, and ceremonial institutions of the empire, that individual works on these

subjects

subjects are sometimes extended to the extraordinary length of upwards of an hundred volumes, and the aggregate is, of course, enormous in proportion.

From such a vast and heterogeneous mass of materials, to attempt any thing like a compendious illustration of the true spirit and character of their legal institutions, would be a very presumptuous, if not absolutely a hopeless undertaking. The *Ta-Tsing-Leu-Lee*, however, happily renders, in this respect, any such laborious and indefinite research unnecessary, as, in fact, no selection could be made, however judiciously, that would not be superseded by the authority, as far as it extends, of the authenticated compendium.

The Chinese government, according to one of the fundamental principles of its constitution, is, it is to be observed, divided into several distinct, though not altogether independent, branches or departments. The civil and military establishments, the public revenue and expenditure, the national rites and ceremonies, the public works, and the administration of public justice, are each of them regulated by a particular code of laws and institutions; but the laws of the empire, in the strictest and most appropriate sense of the term, and which may be denominated Penal Laws, by way of contradistinction, are the peculiar and exclusive province of the last of these departments. All regulations which are either directly penal, by the denunciation of punishment in the event of disobedience, or indirectly, by their coercive operation, have evidently a distinct character, though necessarily connected, more or less, with every branch of that constitution which is upheld and protected by their sanction.

Accordingly, the *Ta-Tsing-Leu-Lee*, although originating with one, treats indirectly and incidentally of all the branches of the Chinese constitution; and the information it thus imparts, upon a comparatively reduced scale, of the administration of the civil and military affairs of the empire, of the public revenue and public works, and of the

the ceremonial inftitutions and obfervances, though not altogether fo clear or fo comprehenfive, as it might have been in a work having thefe for its profeffed objects, will not, probably, to a European reader, be the leaft acceptable of its contents.

In China, the fucceffion of a new line, or dynafty of princes, has been, as it muft be in moft regular and profeffedly abfolute monarchies, invariably attended, not only with an entire diffolution of the government, but nominally, at leaft, with an abrogation of the conftitution eftablifhed by the preceding family; though in moft cafes the neceffity muft already have been apparent of afterwards rebuilding the fabric of fimilar materials, and upon fimilar principles. None, therefore, of the laws and inftitutions now in force in the Chinefe empire, bear a more remote date than that of the laft Tartar conqueft: notwithftanding which, this code, as well as indeed almoft every thing in which the Chinefe people is concerned, carries with it, it is important to remark, an internal evidence of the antiquity of its origin and prototype, not lefs convincing and unqueftionable, perhaps, than the moft folid monuments, or the beft authenticated records by which the paft periods of the exiftence of any nation are at prefent attefted.

A confiderable portion of the intereft, to which enquiries into the prefent ftate of the Chinefe empire are entitled, neceffarily depends upon the credibility of its extraordinary pretenfions to antiquity; and thefe pretenfions have, it muft be acknowledged, been fometimes difputed as not fufficiently fupported, either by remains or veftiges, actually exifting in China, of very remote ages, or by the corroborative teftimony of any other than their own native hiftorians. It may be proper, therefore, to ftate in this place, fome of the grounds upon which the fubftantial accuracy and authenticity of the accounts given us in thefe refpects by the Chinefe themfelves, are neverthelefs affumed as points, which may now be confidered as almoft beyond the reach of controverfy.

It is, in the first place, a material consideration, that although the annals of the Chinese, like those of almost all other nations, are prefaced with incredible, and confessedly fabulous accounts of their primitive state, and of the circumstances which attended their first establishment, yet the period at which that part of their history which is professed to be authentic commences, early as it is, is completely reconcileable with the data concerning the re-peopling of the world, which we derive from the inspired writings.

As, therefore, no direct objection can be maintained on this ground to the antiquity claimed by the Chinese, it seems impossible by any indirect objection, drawn from the want of specific external or internal evidence, to resist the inference, that a people, whose written language, consisting of symbolical characters, is founded on the most ancient of principles, and the frame of whose government is essentially conformable to the patriarchal system of the first ages, must have segregated themselves (if the expression may be allowed) from the rest of mankind before the period at which the symbolical was superceded by the alphabetical character, and the patriarchal, by other systems and forms of government.

We do not indeed recognize in the Chinese constitution, which the lapse of so many ages has refined and consolidated, and which has been necessarily moulded to the various purposes of a great and powerful monarchy, that original form of the patriarchal government which subsisted in detached families, and among wandering tribes, in the rude and simple ages of antiquity.

But there is every reason to consider the foundation to be the same in both cases. The vital and universally operating principle of the Chinese government is the duty of submission to parental authority, whether vested in the parents themselves, or in their representatives, and which, although usually described under the pleasing appellation of filial piety, is much more properly to be considered as a general rule

of

of action, than as the expression of any particular sentiment of affection. It may easily be traced even in the earliest of their records; it is inculcated with the greatest force in the writings of the first of their philosophers and legislators; it has survived each successive dynasty, and all the various changes and revolutions which the state has undergone; and it continues to this day powerfully enforced, both by positive laws, and by public opinion.

A government, constituted upon the basis of parental authority, thus highly estimated and extensively applied, has certainly the advantage of being directly sanctioned by the immutable and ever-operating laws of Nature, and must thereby acquire a degree of firmness and durability to which governments, founded on the fortuitous superiority of particular individuals, either in strength or abilities, and continued only through the hereditary influence of particular families, can never be expected to attain. Parental authority and prerogative seem to be, obviously, the most respectable of titles, and parental regard and affection the most amiable of characters, with which sovereign or magisterial power can be invested, and are those under which, it is natural to suppose, it may most easily be perpetuated.

By such principles the Chinese have been distinguished ever since their first existence as a nation; by such ties, the vast and increasing population of China is still united as one people, subject to one supreme government, and uniform in its habits, manners, and language. In this state, in spite of every internal and external convulsion, it may possibly very long continue.

In conclusion of the subject of the antiquity of the Chinese it may be sufficient to answer the objections arising from the want of external evidence and internal monuments, by one or two general remarks.

The peculiar site of the region inhabited by the Chinese has been already noticed. The variety of soil and climate which it comprehends, its fertility and productiveness, are equally well known. Under

such

such circumstances the Chinese were neither necessitated by want, nor tempted by curiosity, to cross those barriers of sea and land to which they owed so much of their internal security and prosperity. Having no natural enemies to contend with, they soon lost that warlike character which their primitive ancestors might have possessed in the wilds of Tartary. The art of navigating ships at a distance from land, and the adventurous pursuits of trade with foreign nations, being wholly unnecessary to them, they generally despised as well as neglected.

With little opportunity of becoming generally acquainted with the state of the rest of the inhabited world, and with the unfavourable and uninviting specimen of it, which the wretchedness and barbarism of their immediate neighbours presented, it was almost impossible that they should not look back with peculiar complacency upon their own undisputed superiority, and gradually acquire much of that high degree of national vanity and arrogance for which they are remarkable.

Thus the Chinese, although they certainly became at a very early period a rich, populous, and, comparatively, an enlightened nation, have not been at any time enterprizing, warlike, or commercial, and therefore have been in fact deficient in those qualities which, of all others, are the most conducive to the extension of the fame of any people among distant countries.

The want of ancient monuments, were it even without exception to be admitted, might, in great measure, be accounted for by the proneness to decay of all their buildings, owing to the unsubstantial system and principles of their architecture; but they have at least one monument of antiquity, which, in point of magnitude and extent, certainly eclipses those of all other nations and ages.

There are, perhaps, few facts in history more incontestably proved than the construction, in the third century before the Christian era, of the great wall which still continues to separate and form a barrier between China and that tract of country, now denominated Chinese Tartary.

This stupendous effort of human labour is not indeed, viewing its object, any proof of the bravery, nor viewing its inefficacy, any proof of the sagacity, of the nation which produced it, but it will not be denied to be a decisive evidence that the Chinese formed even at that remote period a considerable empire, were united under a strong and regular government, and certainly in no very low state of civilization.

This digression relative to the antiquity of the Chinese empire, as far as it may be inferred from general considerations, has been conceived necessary to the introduction of the few following remarks, applicable more particularly to the origin and history of their laws, such as they now appear to us in the code of the present dynasty.

On this subject it is to be presumed the Missionaries might have given us ample and authentic details, as they expressly inform us (Memoires sur les Chinois, vol. viii. p. 220.) that there exists in China an " Histoire des Loix de Chine, en 74 volumes, en remontant de " dynastie en dynastie, jusqu'a *Yao* et *Chun*;" which emperors are universally admitted by the Chinese to be the founders of their laws, if not also of their monarchy. In the numerous quartos however, which are occupied by the translations of Moyriac de Mailla, the compilations of Du Halde and Grosier, and the miscellaneous work entitled " Memoires concernant les Chinois," very little is to be found concerning the laws which can be considered in the light of historical deduction, and that little, it is to be regretted, is in a great measure contradictory, or loose and inconclusive.

In the Memoires sur les Chinois, vol. i. p. 180, it is stated that " Les interpretes du *Chou-King* s'accordent assez à dire qu'il n'y avoit " point de supplices sous le regne de *Yao*, et qu'ils n'etoient pas néces- " saires. La vertu et la douceur de ce bon prince suffisoient, disent- " ils, pour empêcher les fautes, ou du moins en prévenir les suites. " Son exemple persuadoit l'amour de la vertu, et conservoit l'inno- " cence des mœurs publiques." Yet it is admitted in the same page,

that

that the affociate and fucceffor of the abovementioned monarch, and the emulator of his virtues, was fuppofed by fome of the commentators to have eftablifhed the following terrible punifhments, which equal in feverity any thing which is even now recognized, and in ordinary practice in China:—" 1. Une marque ineffaçable fur le " front : 2. l'amputation du bout du nez : 3. l'amputation du bout " des pieds : 4. la caftration : 5. la mort."

Thefe commentators are indeed imagined to have been miftaken; but in page 20, of the 3d volume, and 56, of the 4th volume of the fame work, the fact is re-afferted without any other refervation than that, although fuch laws had really been eftablifhed at the period ftated, the innocence and virtues of the people were fuch, that many centuries elapfed before it became neceffary to enforce them.

The truth, it is moft probable, lies between the two extremes; and while we may agree with the Miffionaries, that the practice of fuch cruelties in the ordinary adminiftration of juftice is improbable, and inconfiftent with the high character which is given of the wifdom of the fovereign and the mildnefs of the people at that era, we fhall fcarcely be fo extravagant as to fuppofe that punifhments, and even fevere ones, could have been at any time, altogether unneceffary.

The notices which are interfperfed throughout the above works, of the alterations and improvements which afterwards took place in the fyftem of the Chinefe penal law, under the princes of the feveral fucceffive dynafties, contain unfortunately, as has been obferved, nothing precife or circumftantial; and all the information, which, in addition to the communications of the Miffionaries, the Tranflator of the prefent work feels himfelf juftified in offering as authentic, is comprifed in a fhort note, attached to the Chinefe original.

The firft regular code of penal laws is, in that note, attributed to a perfon named LEE-QUEE, and is denominated after him, LEE-QUEE-FA-KING. It feems to have been fimple in its arrangement and conftruction,

ftruction, having been confined to fix books only, two of which appear to have been introductory, the third relative to prifons, the fourth to the adminiftration of the police, the fifth to the leffer or mifcellaneous offences, and the fixth to all the great and capital crimes againft public juftice.

The character of *Lee-Quee*, as well as the age in which he lived, are left in great meafure to conjecture; but there is reafon to infer that the code which bears his name, was firft put in force under the dynafty of *Tſin*, which fucceeded to the throne of China B. C. 249; but it is evident, from the flight mention that is made of this perfonage, that fo far from having been a legiflator, he was not even a compiler of any confiderable celebrity.

There can in fact be little doubt, that the principal characteriftics, not only of the code publifhed by *Lee-Quee*, but alfo of that in force at this day, originated at periods far more remote than that under confideration; but a new compilation, at leaft, of the Chinefe laws muft neceffarily have formed a part of the plan of that celebrated Emperor of the race of *Tſin*, who is faid to have been fo ambitious of the reputation of having been the actual founder of the monarchy, as to have fought it by a vain and abfurd attempt at the deftruction of all the books, records, and other exifting memorials, of preceding ages.

The Chinefe note already quoted likewife defcribes, generally, the alterations and enlargements which took place in the plan and divifions of the code upon the fucceffive elevation to power of each of the feveral dynafties of *Han*, *Wee*, *Tſin*, *Tſe*, *Swee*, *Tang*, *Sung*, *Yuen*, and *Ming*, until it affumed, fhortly after the acceffion, A. D. 1644, of the dynafty of *Tſing*, now reigning, that form in which it ftill continues to be promulgated and obferved throughout the empire.

Having thus been able to trace back the prefent code with certainty, to confiderably remote fources, it will not be deemed extraordinary that, as even in our European codes, although the ftructure is comparatively

paratively of a recent date, it is often rendered intricate and inconvenient from an adherence to a plan, which, owing to its antiquity, is in some places altogether inapplicable to the state of things as they at present exist; and yet, out of respect to its origin, is only cautiously, and perhaps awkwardly, modified, instead of being wholly set aside or fundamentally altered, as often as new circumstances and events had rendered it expedient. Another, and a no less considerable source of obscurity, is, it must be acknowledged, the very artificial and complex construction of the code itself; however much the ingenuity of the contrivance, and the labour bestowed in the adaptation of the means to the end, may at the same time be deserving of being admired.

It may indeed be almost invariably remarked, in respect to the institutions of civilized, and particularly anciently civilized, nations, that although the ends of substantial justice may in general be really consulted, it is almost in vain to expect to find a suitable provision for the attainment of those ends by the shortest and simplest means. This desideratum, however its attainment may be held out in the speculations of theorists, seems to be reserved to be accomplished by the wisdom of future ages. How far, in the formation of the laws of the Chinese, the ends of substantial justice are even consulted, there must, also, no doubt, be some variety of sentiment. There are certainly many points upon which these laws are altogether indefensible. We shall look in vain, for instance, for those excellent principles of the English law, by which every man is presumed innocent until he is proved guilty; and no man required to criminate himself. Such maxims the Chinese system neither does nor indeed could recognize. But it will scarcely escape observation, that there are other parts of the code which, in a considerable degree, compensate these and similar defects, are altogether of a different complexion, and are perhaps not unworthy of imitation, even among the fortunate and enlightened nations of the West. It is sufficiently obvious, indeed, that the intrinsic merits

of

of any code of laws, which is not profeſſed to be, either the reſult of the meditations of a philoſopher, or the untried theory of a legiſlator, but which, on the contrary, actually is in force, forms the baſis of the government of a nation, and as ſuch, has been fairly ſubmitted to the important teſt of experience, are not to be eſtimated by any imaginary ſtandard of perfection. Such a Code can be juſtly compared only with thoſe other codes of law, whoſe practicability and expediency have already been tried by a ſimilar ordeal; and in making the eſtimate, the conſideration of thoſe local circumſtances and peculiarities, upon a conformity to which, the excellence of the national laws in every country ſo greatly depend, is certainly leaſt of all to be omitted.

This is, upon the whole, very juſtly deſcribed, as well as happily illuſtrated, by the Preſident de Monteſquieu, in his "Eſprit des "Loix;" and is ſo important to the right underſtanding of the laws of the extraordinary people under conſideration, that the following ſhort quotation from that work, it is hoped, will not be unacceptable.

" Les loix politiques et civiles de chaque nation," he obſerves, " doi-
" vent être tellement propres au peuple pour lequel elles ſont faites, que
" c'eſt un très grand haſard ſi celles d'une nation peuvent convenir à
" une autre. Il faut qu'elles ſe rapportent à la nature et au principe
" du gouvernement qui eſt établi, ou qu'on veut établir; ſoit quelles
" le forment, comme font les loix politiques; ſoit qu'elles le main-
" tiennent, comme font les loix civiles. Elles doivent êtres relatives
" au *phyſique* du pays, au climat glacé, brûlant ou tempéré; à la qua-
" lité du terrain, à ſa ſituation, à ſa grandeur; au genre de vie des
" peuples, laboureurs, chaſſeurs, ou paſteurs: elles doivent ſe rappor-
" ter au degré de liberté que la conſtitution peut ſouffrir; à la religion
" des habitans, à leurs inclinations, à leur richeſſes, à leur nombre, à
" leur commerce, à leurs mœurs, à leurs manieres. Enfin, elles ont
" des rapports entr'elles; elles en ont avec leur origine, avec l'objet du
" legiſlateur,

"legiflateur, avec l'ordre des chofes fur lefquelles elles font établies
"C'eft dans toutes ces vues qu'il faut les confiderer."

To this may be added, from the high authority of Sir William Jones, the more concife and equally appropriate remark which he makes on the fame fubject, in his Preface to the Laws of *Menu*; "That the beft "intended legiflative provifions would have no beneficial effect, even "at firft, and none at all in a fhort courfe of time, unlefs they were "congenial to the difpofition and habits, to the religious prejudices, "and approved immemorial ufages, of the people, for whom they "were enacted."

After expreffing a wifh, that the reader fhould form his judgment of the Chinefe Laws by thefe criteria, it feems preferable to refer directly to the tranflation of the Code itfelf, and to the illuftrations fubjoined to it, than to attempt in this place any detailed anticipation of its peculiarities and characteriftics. A few general obfervations refpecting their application and practice, may, neverthelefs, until clearer lights can be thrown on the fubject by clofer and more capable obfervers, be of fome utility, in as much as they may contribute to that juft conception of the facts themfelves, without which the moft accurately drawn conclufions would, of courfe, be nugatory.

It may be noticed, in the firft place, that although the ingenious M. Pauw, in his Philofophical Refearches, has not exceeded the truth in obferving, that " les principaux refforts du gouvernement Chinois " font le fouet et le batôn;" neither thefe, nor any other corporal punifhments, are in fuch univerfal ufe, or adminiftered with fuch undiftinguifhing feverity, as has fometimes been imagined.

Thus, in a book of drawings, copied apparently from Chinefe originals, and publifhed in England under the title of " *Punifhments of* " *China;*" the fancy of the painter has given, in fome inftances, a reprefentation of cruelties, and of barbarous executions, which it would

be

be very erroneous to suppose have a place in the ordinary course of justice, although something of such a nature may, no doubt, have been practised heretofore under some tyrannical and sanguinary Emperors; and even perhaps in the present age, upon some particular and extraordinary occasions.

Thus, also, although every page of the following translation may seem at first sight to bear testimony to the universality of corporal punishments in China, a more careful inspection will lead to a discovery of so many grounds of mitigation, so many exceptions in favour of particular classes, and in consideration of particular circumstances, that the penal system is found, in fact, almost entirely to abandon that part of its outward and apparent character.

The acts which the laws of China enforce, and those which they prohibit, are indeed, in some cases, such as are more usually left in Europe to the decision of custom and individual feeling; but, in a country in which the laws have not in any considerable degree, the active concurrence, either of a sense of honour, or of a sense of religion, it may perhaps be absolutely requisite that they should take so wide a range. Experience may have dictated the necessity of their interfering in this direct manner in the enforcement of all those national habits and usages, whose preservation, as far as they are of a moral or prudential tendency, must undoubtedly be of essential importance both to the security of the government and to the happiness of the people.

Another object which seems to have been very generally consulted, is that of as much as possible combining, in the construction and adaptation of the scale of crimes and punishments throughout the Code, the opposite advantages of severity in denunciation and lenity in execution.

The excessive severity of the punishments actually inflicted in cases of treason, rebellion, breach of duty to parents and husbands, and in some others, is scarcely any exception to this rule; as, even in such instances, the execution of the law is lenient in comparison to its literal and *prima facie* interpretation. One considerable inconvenience, indeed, results from this system: in consequence of its adoption, although the place intended to be assigned to each transgression against the laws, in the general scale of criminality, is certainly very readily discoverable by the number of blows of the bamboo, or by the extent of the punishment, in other respects, nominally denounced against the transgressor, the punishment which he is in any particular case actually liable to suffer, is rarely if ever to be ascertained without various references and considerable research. The sections of the Chinese Code may thus, perhaps, not unaptly be compared to a collection of consecutive mathematical problems, with this additional circumstance of perplexity, that a just and entire comprehension of each section individually, requires a general knowledge of those that follow, no less than of those which precede it.

With all its defects, however, and with all its intricacy, this Code of Laws is generally spoken of by the natives with pride and admiration; all they seem in general to desire is, its just and impartial execution, independent of caprice, and uninfluenced by corruption.

That the laws of China are, on the contrary, very frequently violated by those who are their administrators and constitutional guardians, there can, unfortunately, be no question; but to what extent, comparatively with the laws of other countries, must at present be very much a matter of conjecture; at the same time, it may be observed as something in favour of the Chinese system, that there are very substantial grounds for believing, that neither flagrant, nor repeated acts of injustice, do, in point of fact, often, in any rank or station, ultimately escape with impunity.

The foregoing observations have either had relation to the peculiar subject of the original of the present work, or to the circumstances which

which have been conceived to render it not altogether unworthy of the attention of the learned and curious in Europe.

It ſtill remains for the Tranſlator to explain in what manner, and to what extent, it has been his endeavour to transfuſe the original Chineſe text into the idiom of the Engliſh language. And this he feels it his duty to do more fully and circumſtantially than if he had been purſuing a well known and beaten track, which might not only have juſtified a greater degree of confidence, but have likewiſe rendered explanations for the ſatisfaction of his readers leſs neceſſary.

In reſpect to the plan, the moſt obvious conſideration which occurred, at the very commencement of the undertaking, was, that a tranſlation at length, of every thing contained under the title of *TA-TSING-LEU-LEE*, a work occupying, in ſo conciſe a language as the Chineſe, no leſs than 2906 octavo pages, was, if not abſolutely impracticable, certainly altogether inexpedient.

If, in order to reduce the work into a compendious form, the Tranſlator had permitted himſelf the liberty of making an abſtract or abridgment of the text, he might, at the ſame time have endeavoured to have adopted a more ſyſtematic arrangement, a more pleaſing ſtyle, and a more harmonious phraſeology; but he was ſenſible that he ſhould in the ſame proportion have impaired the two recommendations moſt eſſential to the value of the work, its authenticity, and its originality. He, therefore, determined upon a ſelection, not, indeed, according to any conjectural eſtimate of the ſuperior importance of any particular part of the Code over another, but according to the rule, which, by the diviſion of the laws into fundamental and ſupplementary, the Code itſelf afforded.

The *Leu*, or Fundamental Laws, are thoſe of which the Penal Code, upon its formation ſoon after the acceſſion of the preſent dynaſty, appears originally to have conſiſted, and which, being, at leaſt nominally, permanent,

nent, are reprinted in each succeffive edition, without either alteration or amendment.

The *Lee*, or Supplementary Laws, are the modifications, extenfions, and reftrictions of the Fundamental Laws, which, after undergoing a deliberate examination in the Supreme Councils, and receiving the sanction of the Sovereign, are inferted in the form of claufes, at the end of each article or section of the Code, in order that they might, together with the Fundamental Laws, be equally known and obferved They are generally, however, revifed every fifth year, and fubjected to fuch alterations as the wifdom of government determines to be expedient.

Under thefe two denominations, the whole body of Chinefe Penal Law is comprehended; but the number of documents which poffefs the force of laws without the name, muft, under a government in which every authenticated expreffion of the will of the Prince bears that character, neceffarily be unlimited.

Each article of the Fundamental Laws is alfo accompanied by a familiar Expofition, or rather Paraphrafe, which bears the name of the Emperor *Yong-tching*; and the whole of the text is further illuftrated by extracts from the works of various commentators: Thefe appear to have been exprefsly written for the ufe and inftruction of the magiftrates, and accordingly form a body of legal reference, directly sanctioned for that particular purpofe by government.

Thefe extracts have not indeed been found to convey, on all occafions, that ample and fatisfactory information which was at firft expected from them; but this will not appear very extraordinary, when it is confidered, that the perfons whom they were defigned to inftruct, are exclufively natives, and, therefore, probably the leaft in want of an explanation upon thofe very points, which to a foreigner are neceffarily the moft perplexing.

Still

Still, however, the Tranflator has derived from a perufal of this part of the original work confiderable advantage; and when other fources of information failed to difpel the obfcurity of which the concifenefs of the text was fometimes productive, a reference to the expanded and explanatory form of expreffion, adopted in the paraphrafe of the Emperor *Yong-tching*, was often found to fupply every thing that was wanting to its complete elucidation.

Throughout the work, the Tranflator's firft object, and that which he has endeavoured to keep conftantly in view, has been to convey the full meaning of each article or paragraph fucceffively, in appropriate, and, at the fame time, intelligible language; in other words, to draw as juftly as poffible, the middle line between the unfaithfulnefs and and inaccuracy of a free, and the ungracefulnefs and almoft ungrammatical obfcurity of a clofe verfion.

He is very fenfible that his beft efforts cannot have wholly protected him from occafional deviations from the courfe which he has prefcribed to himfelf; but he trufts he fhall meet with the excufe, if not alfo with the approbation, of the reader, in entertaining in every doubtful cafe, a difpofition to prefer the latter of the oppofite alternatives. — He is, at the fame time, not unconfcious, that the prefervation of the ftyle and form of expreffion obferved in the original, is in itfelf, in this cafe, of little importance: that it is the nature and principles of the *laws*, not thofe of the language of the Chinefe people, which it is properly the object of his work to illuftrate. Under this impreffion, he has readily fubmitted to the neceffity, whenever it occurred, of altering the order of words, and the conftruction of fentences; he has feldom fcrupled to fupply the want of a fynonimous expreffion, by a definition; he has even ventured to embody in words thofe ideas which, though forming an integral

part

part of the sense of the text, were yet left, by a sort of ellipsis, to be understood by implication and inference.

It is, lastly, proper to notice, that in some few instances, the text has been found so obscure, and its construction so recondite, that no effort of attention was adequate completely to reconcile the apparent sense of the words, when considered individually, with their collective meaning, such as it was unanimously declared to be, by the most intelligent of the natives whom the Translator had an opportunity of consulting.

There is, certainly, something in the figurative or poetic style, with which the Chinese, on some occasions, embellish their writings, that a foreigner can scarcely ever hope to fathom, by any ordinary means of analysis or investigation; but, fortunately, instances of this kind are so rare in the Penal Code, that they form only a very trifling exception to the general style of the work, which, on the contrary, is remarkable for its concisenefs and simplicity, and as familiar, as the subject and the use of technical phraseology would permit. So peculiarly difficult, indeed, is the figurative and poetic style of certain compositions of the Chinese, that one of the most distinguished among the Missionaries, for his talents and knowledge of the language, declares in his preface to a translation of an Imperial poem, which he entitles "Eloge de Mougden," that without a reference occasionally to the Mantchoo Tartar translation of that work, he never could have accomplished his undertaking.

In regard to terms, more or less peculiar to the Chinese, such as in a work of this nature would necessarily be of constant occurrence, the Translator might easily have relieved himself from every responsibility, by retaining in each case the original Chinese expression; but, considering that the very sounds of the language are strange and unpleasing to European ears, and, in fact, but very imperfectly capable of

being

being reprefented by any European alphabet, he has conceived it would on every account be moft defirable to reduce the untranflated words into as fmall a compafs as poffible, explaining the remaining few in notes in the margin; and remarking generally, with regard to the reft, that, as in the cafe of the words *Emperor*, *Tribunal*, and the like, they are approximations to the truth, whofe ambiguity, if any, the context is generally fully fufficient to remove.

The Tranflator may be allowed to remark, that the choice of his fubject was originally influenced by circumftances, in fome degree accidental. It firft occupied his attention in confequence of his having been perfonally a witnefs to many of the unneceffary provocations, groundlefs apprehenfions, and embarraffing difcuffions, of which, fince the firft commencement of our prefent important commercial and national intercourfe with the people of China, falfe or imperfect notions of the fpirit of their laws have been, but too often, the occafion: and although the tranflation of every part of the work did not promife, in this point of view, to be of equal utility, he always found it, at the leaft, a gratification to curiofity, and a not uninterefting employment of leifure hours: it is only, however, very recently, and in compliance with the perhaps too partial fuggeftions of thofe to whofe perufal the Tranflator has had the pleafure of fubmitting the manufcript, that he has allowed himfelf to believe it might prove not altogether unworthy of the attention of the Public at large.

He was fenfible that on this occafion it was his firft duty to affure himfelf of the fubftantial accuracy of his tranflation. But it was, at the fame time, his anxious wifh to render it, preparatory to its publication, as little exceptionable in other refpects, as a due regard to that primary object would admit. It therefore affords him a peculiar pleafure to be able in this place to acknowledge the valuable fuggeftions which, to this end, two of his friends in particular have kindly contributed;

both

both of them diſtinguiſhed as men of letters, the one with the addition of being pre-eminent in his profeſſion of the law, and the other in reſpect to his ſuperior knowledge of the Chineſe empire, and his ardent zeal to promote and extend its relations with Great Britain, for the mutual benefit of both countries.

In making this declaration, however, it is far from the Tranſlator's wiſh to avail himſelf of theſe reſpectable ſanctions for the protection from cenſure of a work, for which he muſt of neceſſity be ſolely reſponſible; nor can he pretend to have had, in this country, the advantage of that particular aſſiſtance, which an acquaintance with the language of the original could alone have placed his friends in a ſituation to afford him.

In order to give as much of that ſpecies of illuſtration, which an undertaking of this nature more particularly requires, an Appendix is ſubjoined, conſiſting, firſt, of tranſlations of ſome of the moſt intereſting of the Chineſe official documents in the Tranſlator's poſſeſſion, which happened to be either connected with or in any way applicable to the ſubject; ſecondly, of tranſlations of ſome of the moſt remarkable among the ſupplementary laws or clauſes; and laſtly, of occaſional remarks and notices upon particular paſſages, which occurred in the courſe of the work, but which could not have been conveniently inſerted in the margin.

Still, however, the Tranſlator is ſenſible, that, after every endeavour to render the following work as complete as poſſible, it muſt yet, in many points, be unavoidably defective; but he at the ſame time feels encouraged by the aſſurance, that his readers are too well acquainted with the nature of the undertaking, and the peculiar circumſtances connected with it, to entertain expectations founded upon a reference, either to the excellent treatiſes upon our own laws by Blackſtone and others, or even to the accounts which we poſſeſs of the laws of many foreign, but at the ſame time more eaſily acceſſible, countries. Being

alſo

also almost the first essay at translation from a Chinese original into the English language, he trusts that even in that point of view it will not be deemed undeserving of indulgence.

His own wishes will be gratified in their full extent, if he can be considered to have succeeded in giving, through the medium of an authentic work, containing incidental notices upon the manners, customs, civil and religious habits, national characteristics, and moral principles of the Chinese, a just idea of the spirit, and a sufficiently extended specimen of the substance, of the coercive and penal laws by which the government of that vast empire has so long been maintained and regulated.

TABLE OF CONTENTS.

PRELIMINARY MATTER.

No		PAGE
I.	ABSTRACT of the Title-page of the Edition of the Penal Code printed and published in China in 1799, the 4th year of the Reign of the present Emperor KIA-KING	lxiii.
II.	Original Preface to the Penal Code, by the Emperor SHUN-CHEE, the first of the present Dynasty	lxv.
III.	Prefatory Edict of the Emperor KAUNG-HEE, (otherwise, but improperly, CAMHI,) the second of the present Dynasty	lxvii.
IV.	Prefatory Edict of the Emperor YONG-TCHING, the third of the present Dynasty	lxix.
V.	Table I.—Scale of Punishment of Offences against public and private Property	lxxi.
VI.	Table II.—Scale of pecuniary Redemption of necessarily redeemable Punishments	lxxii.
VII.	Table III.—Scale of pecuniary Redemption in such Cases as are not legally excluded from the Benefit of general Acts of Grace and Pardon	lxxiii.
VIII.	Table IV.—Degrees of ordinary Punishment	lxxiv.
IX.	Table V.—Specification of the ordinary Instruments of Punishment and Confinement	*ibid.*
X.	Table VI.—Degrees of Relationship and of Mourning	lxxv.

FIRST DIVISION,—*General Laws.*

BOOK I.

PRELIMINARY REGULATIONS.

Section		Page
I.	DESCRIPTION of the ordinary Punishments	1
II.	Offences of a treasonable Nature	3
III.	The Privileged Classes	5
IV.	Offences of Persons entitled to Privilege	7
V.	Relations of Persons entitled to Privilege	*ibid.*
VI.	Offences committed by Officers of Government, how investigated	9
VII.	Offences committed by Officers of Government in their public Capacity	10
VIII.	Offences committed by Officers of Government of a private and personal Nature	11
IX.	Offenders who are not liable to Banishment	12
X.	Offenders of the Military Class	13
XI.	Mitigation of Punishment	*ibid.*
XII.	Officers of Government, when removed without being disgraced	14
XIII.	Offences committed by Officers of Government previous to their Elevation	15
XIV.	Degraded Officers of Government liable to the same Obligations as private Individuals	16
XV.	Relations of Exiles	17
XVI.	Extent of an Act of Grace or General Pardon	18
XVII.	Effect of an Act of Grace on the Condition of Offenders in Exile	19
XVIII.	Indulgence to Offenders for the Sake of their Parents	20
XIX.	Offences of Astronomers	21
XX.	Offences of Artificers, Musicians, and Women	22
XXI.	Offences of Persons already under Sentence of Punishment	23

TABLE of CONTENTS.

Section		Page
XXII.	Indulgence to Offenders in confideration of their Age, Youth, or Infirmities	23
XXIII.	Plea of Age and Infirmities how to be conftrued	25
XXIV	Reftitution and Forfeiture of Goods	ibid.
XXV.	Offenders furrendering voluntarily	27
XXVI.	Offenders charged with feveral Offences	29
XXVII.	Proceedings in Cafes where all the Parties to an Offence have efcaped	ibid.
XXVIII.	Offences of Members of public Departments and Tribunals, committed in their official Capacity	30
XXIX.	Errors and Failures in public Proceedings	31
XXX.	Diftinction between Principals and Acceffaries	32
XXXI.	Proceedings relative to Offenders who have abfconded	34
XXXII.	Relations mutually affifting and concealing each other	ibid.
XXXIII.	Punifhment of Deferters	35
XXXIV.	Offences committed by Foreigners	36
XXXV.	Proceedings in Cafes where the Laws appear contradictory	37
XXXVI.	Rules relative to the Increafe and Diminution of Punifhments	38
XXXVII.	Extent of the Privilege and Diftinction of Imperial Rank	39
XXXVIII.	Relations in the firft Degree	ibid.
XXXIX.	Participators in Offences	40
XL.	Refponfible Superintendants	41
XLI.	Divifion of Time	ibid.
XLII.	Laws relative to the Priefthood	42
XLIII.	Execution of new Laws	43
XLIV.	Determination of Cafes not provided for by any exifting Law	ibid.
XLV.	Place of temporary and perpetual Banifhment	44
XLVI.	Place of extraordinary or military Banifhment	45

SECOND

TABLE OF CONTENTS.

SECOND DIVISION, — *Civil Laws*.

BOOK I.
SYSTEM OF GOVERNMENT.

Section		Page
XLVII.	Hereditary Succeſſion	49
XLVIII.	Great Officers of State not authorized to confer Appointments	51
XLIX.	Officers of Government not allowed to ſolicit hereditary Honours	52
L.	Supernumerary Officers of Government	ibid.
LI.	Tranſmiſſion of official Diſpatches	54
LII.	Partiality in the Examination of Candidates for Degrees	55
LIII.	Relative to Officers of Government diſmiſſed for Miſconduct	56
LIV.	Officers of Government quitting their Stations without leave	57
LV.	Officers of Government to proceed to their Deſtinations without Delay	58
LVI.	Attendance of Officers of Government at Court	59
LVII.	Irregular Interference of Superiors with ſubordinate Magiſtrates	ibid.
LVIII.	Cabals and State Intrigues	60
LIX.	Combination and Colluſion between provincial Officers and Officers of the Court	62
LX.	Addreſſes in favour of Great Officers of State	ibid.

BOOK II.
CONDUCT OF THE MAGISTRATES.

LXI.	Due Knowledge of the Laws	64
LXII.	Non-Execution of an Imperial Edict	65
LXIII.	Deſtroying or diſcarding Edicts and Seals of Office	ibid.
LXIV.	Errors and Informalities in public Documents	67
LXV.	Neglecting to make ſuch Reports to ſuperior Officers as are by Law required	68

LXVI.

TABLE OF CONTENTS.

Section		Page
LXVI.	Officers on detached Service not reporting their Proceedings	70
LXVII.	Delay in expediting the Edicts of Government	71
LXVIII.	Examination of official Records	72
LXIX.	Re-examination of outstanding Articles of official Records	73
LXX.	Transfer or Exchange of official Duties prohibited	74
LXXI.	Alteration of the Contents of an official Dispatch	ibid.
LXXII.	Use of the official or public Seal	76
LXXIII.	Omitting to use, or imperfectly using, an official Seal	ibid.
LXXIV.	Employing the Sanction of Seals of military Offices upon civil Affairs	77

THIRD DIVISION,—*Fiscal Laws.*

BOOK I.

ENROLMENT OF THE PEOPLE.

Section		Page
LXXV.	Families and Individuals to be duly enrolled	79
LXXVI.	Families and Individuals to be registered according to their Professions	82
LXXVII.	Privately founding religious Houses, and privately entering into the Order of Priesthood	83
LXXVIII.	Rule of Succession and Inheritance	84
LXXIX.	Regulations concerning stray Children	85
LXXX.	Impartiality in the Levy of Taxes and personal Services	86
LXXXI.	Impartiality in the Allotment of personal Services	87
LXXXII.	Evasion of personal Service	88
LXXXIII.	Supernumerary Persons exercising district Authority, prohibited	ibid.
LXXXIV.	Evasion of personal Service by Concealment or Desertion	89
LXXXV.	Selection of the Guards and Attendants of Prisons	90
LXXXVI.	Personal Services of Labourers and Artificers, required beyond the legal Extent, or for private Purposes	91
LXXXVII.	Individuals deserting, or prematurely separating from their Families	92

TABLE OF CONTENTS.

Section		Page
LXXXVIII.	Younger and inferior Branches of a Family difpofing of the Property without Leave	92
LXXXIX.	Care of the Aged and Infirm	93

BOOK II.

LANDS AND TENEMENTS.

XC.	Fraudulent Evafion of the Land-Tax	94
XCI.	Perfonal Vifitation of Lands fuffering from any Calamity	96
XCII.	Lands of the Nobility and Officers of Government	98
XCIII.	Fraudulent Sale of Lands and Tenements	99
XCIV.	Officers of Government reftricted from purchafing Lands within the Limits of their Jurifdiction	100
XCV.	Law of Mortgages	101
XCVI.	Sowing and tilling Lands belonging to others	102
XCVII.	Uncultivated and neglected Lands	103
XCVIII.	Deftroying or damaging the Harvefts, and Articles connected therewith	104
XCIX.	Taking away, without Leave, the Fruit growing in Gardens or Orchards	105
C.	Mifapplication of the Boats or Carriages of Government	106

BOOK III.

MARRIAGE.

CI.	Marriages how regulated	107
CII.	Lending Wives or Daughters on Hire	110
CIII.	Regard to Rank and Priority among Wives	ibid.
CIV.	Ejecting from Home a Son-in-Law	111
CV.	Marriage during the legal Period of Mourning	112
CVI.	Marriage during the Imprifonment of Parents	114
CVII.	Marriages between Perfons having the fame Family Name	ibid.
CVIII.	Marriages between Perfons related by Marriage	115
CIX.	Marriages with Relations by Blood, or with the Widows of fuch Relations	ibid.

TABLE OF CONTENTS.

Section		Page
CX.	Marriages of Officers of Government into Families subject to their Jurisdiction	116
CXI.	Marriage with absconded Females	117
CXII.	Forcible Marriage of a free Man's Wife or Daughter	ibid.
CXIII.	Marriage with Female Musicians and Comedians	118
CXIV.	Marriage of Priests of *Foe* or *Tao-ſſe*	ibid.
CXV.	Marriage between free Persons and Slaves	119
CXVI.	Law of Divorce	120
CXVII.	Giving in Marriage unlawfully	122

BOOK IV.

PUBLIC PROPERTY.

CXVIII.	Regulations concerning Coinage	124
CXIX.	Periods established for collecting the Revenues in Kind	125
CXX.	Fairness and impartiality in collecting the Revenues in Kind	126
CXXI.	Concealing or wasting the Proportion of exciseable Articles set apart for the Use of Government	127
CXXII.	Vicarious Contributors to the Revenue	128
CXXIII.	Premature Discharges or Quittances for Taxes due to Government	129
CXXIV.	Suppression and Misapplication of contingent Excess of Revenue	131
CXXV.	Privately lending or employing the public Revenue	132
CXXVI.	Privately lending or employing public Property	133
CXXVII.	Receipt, Transfer, and Expenditure of the Revenue	ibid.
CXXVIII.	Misconduct of supernumerary Revenue Officers	135
CXXIX.	Fraudulent Appropriation of public Property	ibid.
CXXX.	Revenue Officers reciprocally answerable for each other	136
CXXXI.	Responsibility of Revenue Officers in Cases of Theft.	137
CXXXII.	Responsibility of Receivers and Distributors of public Property	138
CXXXIII.	Established Regulations observed in the Receipt and Issue of public Stores	139
CXXXIV.	Vexatious Proceedings on the Occasion of the Receipt and Issue of public Stores	140
CXXXV.	Purity of the precious Metals payable to Government	ibid.

TABLE of CONTENTS.

Section		Page
CXXXVI.	Refponfibility for the Damage or Lofs of public Stores	141
CXXXVII.	Regular Tranfmiffion of public Stores from the inferior to to fuperior Jurifdictions	142
CXXXVIII.	Rule of Forfeiture and Reftitution	144
CXXXIX.	Intermediate Charge of public Property	145
CXL.	Concealment or Denial either of Property under Sentence of Forfeiture, or of Families under Sentence of Servitude	ibid.

BOOK V.

DUTIES AND CUSTOMS.

CXLI.	Duty on Salt	148
CXLII.	Superintendants of Salt-Duties to receive no intermediate Profits	153
CXLIII.	Prefervation of Salt-Laws from Neglect	ibid.
CXLIV.	Smuggling of Tea	154
CXLV.	Smuggling of Allum	155
CXLVI.	Evafion of Duties, or Smuggling in general	ibid.
CXLVII.	Merchant Veffels having falfe Manifefts of their Cargoes	156
CXLVIII.	Arrears of Duties and Cuftoms to be paid within the Year in which they are due	ibid.

BOOK VI.

PRIVATE PROPERTY.

CXLIX.	Ufury	158
CL.	Dilapidation of Property in Truft	161
CLI.	Loft and forgotten Property	ibid.

BOOK VII.

SALES AND MARKETS.

CLII.	Licence of commercial Agents	163
CLIII.	Valuation of Merchandize	164

Section		Page
CLIV.	Monopolizers and unfair Traders	164
CLV.	Falſe Weights, Meaſures, and Scales	165
CLVI.	Manufactures not equal or conformable to Standard	167

FOURTH DIVISION, — *Ritual Laws.*

BOOK I.

SACRED RITES.

CLVII.	Adminiſtration of ſacred Rites	169
CLVIII.	Deſtroying Altars and ſacred Terraces	172
CLIX.	Provincial ſacred Rites to be conformable to the Ritual Code	ibid.
CLX.	Care of the Tombs of diſtinguiſhed Perſonages	173
CLXI.	Diſhonouring celeſtial Spirits by unlicenſed Forms of Worſhip	174
CLXII.	Magicians, Leaders of Sects, and Teachers of falſe Doctrines	175

BOOK II.

MISCELLANEOUS OBSERVANCES.

CLXIII.	Preparation of Medicines and Proviſions for the Emperor	177
CLXIV.	Charge of the Imperial Equipage and Furniture	178
CLXV.	Poſſeſſion and Concealment of prohibited Books and Inſtruments	179
CLXVI.	Tranſmiſſion of Imperial Preſents	180
CLXVII.	Obſervance of Feſtivals and Days of Ceremony	ibid.
CLXVIII.	Due Performance of appointed Ceremonies	181
CLXIX.	Officers of Government to addreſs the Emperor in Succeſſion, according to their Rank	ibid.
CLXX.	Vexatiouſly detaining Officers of Government from the Imperial Preſence	ibid.
CLXXI.	Addreſſes on public Affairs	182
CLXXII.	Monuments raiſed by Officers of Government to commemorate their own Actions	183
CLXXIII.	Honorary Attendance on Superiors in Rank	184
CLXXIV.	Official Meſſengers contemptuouſly treating Officers of Diſtricts	185

CLXXV.

TABLE OF CONTENTS.

Section		Page
CLXXV.	Sumptuary Laws relative to Dress and Habitations	185
CLXXVI.	Dress and Conduct of the Priests	186
CLXXVII.	Neglect to observe and note the celestial Appearances	187
CLXXVIII.	Conjurors and Fortune-tellers prohibited from Prophesying public Events	ibid.
CLXXIX.	Evading the Duty, and concealing the Occasion of Mourning	188
CLXXX.	Officers of Government neglecting their Parents	189
CLXXXI.	Regulations concerning Funerals	190
CLXXXII.	Regulation of Country Festivals.	191

FIFTH DIVISION, — *Military Laws.*

BOOK I.

PROTECTION OF THE PALACE.

CLXXXIII.	Unauthorizedly entering the Imperial Temple	193
CLXXXIV.	Unauthorizedly entering the Imperial Palace	194
CLXXXV.	Imperial Guards failing to do their Duty	195
CLXXXVI.	Imperial Retinue failing in their Attendance	196
CLXXXVII.	Trespass upon the Imperial Roads	197
CLXXXVIII.	Rules concerning Labourers within the Palace	198
CLXXXIX.	Labourers in the Palace remaining after the Conclusion of their Work	ibid.
CXC.	Irregularity in passing through the Gates of the Imperial Palaces	199
CXCI.	Examination of the Certificates or Passports of Persons having Employments in the Palace	200
CXCII.	Shooting or throwing missile Weapons towards an Imperial Palace	202
CXCIII.	Soldiers and Officers on Guard to be always armed	ibid.
CXCIV.	Convicted Persons and their Relations not to be employed near the Imperial Presence	203
CXCV.	Intrusion into the Space allotted for the Imperial Retinue	204
CXCVI.	Passing through Gates leading to an Imperial Palace	205
CXCVII.	Scaling the Walls of fortified Places	206
CXCVIII.	Regulations concerning the Gates of Cities	ibid.

TABLE OF CONTENTS.

BOOK II.
GOVERNMENT OF THE ARMY.

Section		Page
CXCIX.	Unauthorizedly employing military Force	208
CC.	Military Operations to be regularly reported	210
CCI.	Expreſſes upon military Affairs	212
CCII.	Betraying the Secrets of the State	213
CCIII.	Application for and Tranſmiſſion of military Supplies	214
CCIV.	Errors and Failures in military Operations	215
CCV.	Military Officers and Troops not taking the Field according to their Inſtructions	ibid.
CCVI.	Soldiers ſerving by Subſtitutes	216
CCVII.	Officers on the Field of Battle unfaithful to their Truſt	217
CCVIII.	Connivance at the Depredations of the Soldiers	218
CCIX.	Exerciſe and Diſcipline of the Troops	220
CCX.	Exciting and cauſing Rebellion by oppreſſive Conduct	221
CCXI.	Clandeſtine Sale of Horſes taken in Battle	ibid.
CCXII.	Clandeſtine Sale of military Arms and Accoutrements	222
CCXIII.	Deſtroying and caſting away military Arms and Accoutrements	223
CCXIV.	Poſſeſſion of prohibited Arms and Accoutrements	224
CCXV.	Relaxation of, and Abſence from military Duties	ibid.
CCXVI.	Princes and Hereditary Nobility employing the Troops of Government	227
CCXVII.	Deſertion from military Service	228
CCXVIII.	Favour to be ſhewn to the Relations of Officers and Soldiers deceaſed	230
CCXIX.	Regulations of the nocturnal Police	ibid.

BOOK III.
PROTECTION OF THE FRONTIER.

CCXX.	Croſſing a Barrier without a Licenſe	232
CCXXI.	Granting or obtaining Paſſports or Licenſes under falſe Pretences	233
CCXXII.	Vexatious Treatment of Travellers at the Barriers	235
CCXXIII.	Aſſiſting and favouring the Eſcape of the Wives and Daughters of Deſerters	236

Section		Page
CCXXIV.	Examination and Detection of suspected Persons	237
CCXXV.	Illicit Exportation of Merchandize	238
CCXXVI.	Employment of Bow-men upon private Services	239

BOOK IV.

MILITARY HORSES AND CATTLE.

Section		Page
CCXXVII.	Responsibility of the Charge of Government Cattle	241
CCXXVIII.	Breeding of Horses	242
CCXXIX.	Examination of Animals to be purchased by Contract	243
CCXXX.	Exercise of the Veterinary Art	ibid.
CCXXXI.	Improper Usage and Neglect of Cattle	244
CCXXXII.	Neglecting to break in and exercise the Horses of Government	245
CCXXXIII.	Killing Horses, horned Cattle, and other Animals	ibid.
CCXXXIV.	Vicious and dangerous Animals	248
CCXXXV.	Concealment of the Increase of Animals belonging to Government	249
CCXXXVI.	Privately lending the Animals belonging to Government	250
CCXXXVII.	Public Messengers using the Horses of Government without Authority	ibid.

BOOK V.

EXPRESSES AND PUBLIC POSTS.

Section		Page
CCXXXVIII.	Conveyance of Government Orders and Dispatches	252
CCXXXIX.	Intercepting Addresses to Government	254
CCXL.	Post-houses to be kept in Repair	255
CCXLI.	Post-soldiers to be employed on no other Service	256
CCXLII.	Express-messengers delaying upon the Road	ibid.
CCXLIII.	Express-messengers exceeding the Allowances of Horses and Equipage fixed by Government	257
CCXLIV.	Express-messengers exceeding the fixed Allowance of Money and Provisions	259
CCXLV.	Express-post to be reserved for important Dispatches	260
CCXLVI.	Dilatoriness in Transmissions and Removals connected with the public Service	261

Section		Page
CCXLVII.	Occupation of the principal Apartments in Post-houses	262
CCXLVIII.	Transmission of private Property by Government Post-horses	ibid.
CCXLIX.	Officers and others compelling the Inhabitants of their District to carry their Palanquins	263
CCL.	Families of deceased Officers to be removed at the public Expence	264
CCLI.	Hiring Substitutes, and entrusting to them an allotted personal Service	ibid.
CCLII.	Conveyance of private Property at the Charge of Government	266
CCLIII.	Privately lending the Post-horses of Government	267

SIXTH DIVISION, — *Criminal Laws.*

BOOK I.

ROBBERY AND THEFT.

CCLIV.	High Treason	269
CCLV.	Rebellion and Renunciation of Allegiance	272
CCLVI.	Sorcery and Magic	273
CCLVII.	Sacrilege	274
CCLVIII.	Stealing Edicts and Ordinances of Government	ibid.
CCLIX.	Stealing Seals and Stamps of Office	275
CCLX.	Stealing from an Imperial Palace	ibid.
CCLXI.	Stealing the Keys of the Gate of a Fort or City	ibid.
CCLXII.	Stealing Military Weapons and Accoutrements	276
CCLXIII.	Stealing Timber from a Burying-Ground	277
CCLXIV.	Embezzlement of public Property	ibid.
CCLXV.	Theft of public Property	279
CCLXVI.	Robbery,—Highway Robbery	280
CCLXVII.	Rescue from Prison	281
CCLXVIII.	Robbing in open Day	283
CCLXIX.	Stealing in general	284
CCLXX.	Stealing Horses and other domesticated Animals	285
CCLXXI.	Stealing Corn or other Produce in the open Field	286

TABLE of CONTENTS.

Section		Page
CCLXXII.	Stealing from Relations or Connexions	287
CCLXXIII.	Extorting Property by Threats	288
CCLXXIV.	Obtaining Property under false Pretences	289
CCLXXV.	Kidnapping, or the unlawful Seizure and Sale of free Persons	290
CCLXXVI.	Disturbing Graves	293
CCLXXVII.	Unauthorizedly entering a Dwelling-house by Night	297
CCLXXVIII.	Harbouring Thieves and Robbers	ibid.
CCLXXIX.	Rules by which the Accessaries to a Theft and the Accessaries to a Robbery are distinguished	299
CCLXXX.	What constitutes a Theft or a Robbery, and what an Attempt only	300
CCLXXXI.	Defacing or destroying the Marks with which Thieves had been branded	301

BOOK II.

HOMICIDE.

CCLXXXII.	Preconcerted Homicide; Murder	303
CCLXXXIII.	Murder of an Officer of Government	304
CCLXXXIV.	Parricide	305
CCLXXXV.	Killing an Adulterer	307
CCLXXXVI.	Widows killing their deceased Husband's Relations	ibid.
CCLXXXVII.	Murder of three or more Persons in one Family	308
CCLXXXVIII.	Murder, with the Intent to mangle and divide the Body of the Deceased for magical Purposes	309
CCLXXXIX.	Rearing venomous Animals, and preparing Poisons	310
CCXC.	Killing with an Intent to kill, and killing in an Affray	311
CCXCI.	Depriving of Food or Raiment	312
CCXCII.	Killing or wounding in Play, by Error, or purely by Accident	313
CCXCIII.	A Husband killing his culpable Wife	315
CCXCIV.	Killing a Son, Grandson, or Slave, and attributing the Crime to an innocent Person	316
CCXCV.	Wounding mortally or otherwise, by shooting Arrows and similar Weapons	317
CCXCVI.	Wounding mortally or otherwise by Means of Horses and Carriages	318

TABLE OF CONTENTS.

Section		Page
CCXCVII.	Practitioners of Medicine killing, or injuring their Patients	319
CCXCVIII.	Killing or wounding by Means of Traps or Springes	320
CCXCIX.	Occasioning the Death of an Individual by violent and fearful Threats	321
CCC.	Compromising and concealing the Crime of killing an elder Relation	322
CCCI.	Neglecting to give Information of, or to interfere and prevent a violent injury which is known to be intended	323

BOOK III.

QUARRELLING AND FIGHTING.

CCCII.	Quarrelling and Fighting between Equals in ordinary Cases	324
CCCIII.	Periods of Responsibility for the Consequences of a Wound	327
CCCIV.	Quarrelling and Fighting within the Imperial Palace	329
CCCV.	Striking or wounding an Individual of the Imperial Blood	330
CCCVI.	Striking ordinary and extraordinary Officers of Government	ibid.
CCCVII.	Subordinate Officers of Government striking Persons who are their Superiors both in Rank and Jurisdiction	332
CCCVIII.	Co-ordinate or independent Officers of Government striking each other	333
CCCIX.	Officers of Government striking their Superiors in Rank, but not in Jurisdiction	ibid.
CCCX.	Resisting and striking any Person employed officially by Government on public Service	334
CCCXI.	Disciples and Apprentices striking their Masters	335
CCCXII.	Unlawful Detention and Imprisonment	ibid.
CCCXIII.	Slaves and free Persons assaulting and striking each other	336
CCCXIV.	Slaves striking their Masters	338
CCCXV.	Wives striking their Husbands	341
CCCXVI.	Striking a Relation not within any of the four Degrees	343

Section		Page
CCCXVII.	Striking a Relation in the 2d, 3d, or 4th Degree	344
CCCXVIII.	Striking a Relation in the 1st Degree	345
CCCXIX.	Striking a Father or Mother, paternal Grandfather or Grandmother	346
CCCXX.	Wives ſtriking their Huſband's Relations	349
CCCXXI.	Striking a Wife's Children by her former Huſband	351
CCCXXII.	Widows ſtriking the Parents of their deceaſed Huſbands	ibid.
CCCXXIII.	Striking in Defence of a Parent	351

BOOK IV.

ABUSIVE LANGUAGE.

Section		Page
CCCXXIV.	Abuſive Language between Equals	354
CCCXXV.	Abuſive Language to an Officer of Government	ibid.
CCCXXVI.	Abuſive Language between Officers of the ſame Tribunal	355
CCCXXVII.	Abuſive Language from a Slave to his Maſter	356
CCCXXVIII.	Abuſive Language to an elder Relation	ibid.
CCCXXIX.	Abuſive Language to a Parent, paternal Grandfather or Grandmother	357
CCCXXX.	Abuſive Language from a Wife to her Huſband's Relations	ibid.
CCCXXXI.	Abuſive Language addreſſed by a Widow to her deceaſed Huſband's Parents	358

BOOK V.

INDICTMENTS AND INFORMATIONS.

Section		Page
CCCXXXII.	Irregularity in preſenting Informations	359
CCCXXXIII.	Anonymous Informations	360
CCCXXXIV.	Neglecting or declining to receive Informations	361
CCCXXXV.	Informations which muſt be transferred to the cognizance of others	364
CCCXXXVI.	Falſe and malicious Informations	ibid.
CCCXXXVII.	Informations againſt Relations	371
CCCXXXVIII.	Diſobedience to Parents	374

TABLE OF CONTENTS.

Section		Page
CCCXXXIX.	Informations presented by Criminals under Confinement	374
CCCXL.	Exciting and promoting Litigation	375
CCCXLI.	Informations on Subjects affecting Civil as well as Military Affairs	376
CCCXLII.	Informations and Prosecutions on the Part of Officers of Government	377
CCCXLIII.	False Accusations of Offences punishable with extraordinary Banishment	378

BOOK VI.

BRIBERY AND CORRUPTION.

CCCXLIV.	Accepting a Bribe	379
CCCXLV.	Pecuniary Malversation	382
CCCXLVI.	Receiving Money corruptly by way of Reward	384
CCCXLVII.	Contracting for and agreeing to accept a Bribe	ibid.
CCCXLVIII.	Offering a Bribe	385
CCCXLIX.	Extortion of Loans, and unfair Sales	386
CCCL.	Extortion and other corrupt Practices of Persons in the Families of Officers of Government	388
CCCLI.	Extortion and other corrupt Practices of Great Officers of State	ibid.
CCCLII.	Levying extraordinary Contributions on the Plea of public Service	389
CCCLIII.	Suppressing the Discovery of stolen Goods	390
CCCLIV.	Receiving Presents from the higher hereditary Nobility	391

BOOK VII.

FORGERIES AND FRAUDS.

CCCLV.	Falsification of an Imperial Edict	392
CCCLVI.	Falsification of verbal Orders	394
CCCLVII.	Falsely and deceitfully addressing the Sovereign	395
CCCLVIII.	Counterfeiting any official Seal, or the Imperial Almanac	396

TABLE OF CONTENTS.

Section		Page
CCCLIX.	Counterfeiting the current Coin of the Realm	397
CCCLX.	Impoftors pretending to be Officers of Government	398
CCCLXI.	Impoftors pretending to be Great Officers of State	399
CCCLXII.	Officers of State, and others belonging to the Court, interfering without Authority	401
CCCLXIII.	Pretending to difcover Prognoftics	ibid.
CCCLXIV.	Pretending Sicknefs or Death	ibid.
CCCLXV.	Seducing Perfons to tranfgrefs the Laws	403

BOOK VIII.

INCEST AND ADULTERY.

CCCLXVI.	Criminal Intercourfe in general	404
CCCLXVII.	Conniving at or confenting to a criminal Intercourfe	405
CCCLXVIII.	Inceft or criminal Intercourfe between Relations	406
CCCLXIX.	Accufing an elder Relation of Adultery	407
CCCLXX.	Criminal Intercourfe between Slaves or Servants and their Mafter's Wives	ibid.
CCCLXXI.	Criminal Intercourfe between Officers of Government and Females under their Jurifdiction	408
CCCLXXII.	Criminal Intercourfe during the Period of Mourning	409
CCCLXXIII.	Criminal Intercourfe between free Perfons and Slaves	ibid.
CCCLXXIV.	Officers of Government frequenting the Company of Proftitutes and Actreffes	410
CCCLXXV.	Strolling Players	ibid.

BOOK IX.

MISCELLANEOUS OFFENCES.

CCCLXXVI.	Defacing or deftroying public Monuments	411
CCCLXXVII.	Care of Soldiers, and of Labourers for the Public, when fick	ibid.
CCCLXXVIII.	Gaming	412
CCCLXXIX.	Eunuchs	ibid.
CCCLXXX.	Making illegal Propofals	413
CCCLXXXI.	Compromifing Offences, and withdrawing them from the Cognizance of the Magiftrates	415

CCCLXXXII.

Section		Page
CCCLXXXII.	Accidental House-burning	415
CCCLXXXIII.	Wilful and malicious House-burning	417
CCCLXXXIV.	Theatrical Representations	418
CCCLXXXV.	Transgression of Standing Rules and Orders	419
CCCLXXXVI.	Improper Conduct not specifically punishable	ibid.

BOOK X.

ARRESTS AND ESCAPES.

CCCLXXXVII.	Duty of Police Officers	420
CCCLXXXVIII.	Criminals resisting the Police Officers	421
CCCLXXXIX.	Prisoners escaping or rising against their Keepers	422
CCCXC.	Returning or escaping from a Place of Banishment	423
CCCXCI.	Delaying the Execution of a Sentence of Banishment	425
CCCXCII.	Jailors and others suffering their Prisoners to escape	426
CCCXCIII.	Privately assisting and concealing Criminals	428
CCCXCIV.	Periods allowed for the Pursuit of Thieves and Robbers	429

BOOK XI.

IMPRISONMENT, JUDGMENT, AND EXECUTION.

CCCXCV.	Securing the Persons of Prisoners	431
CCCXCVI.	Imprisonment and Procedure against unaccused and unimplicated Persons	433
CCCXCVII.	Delay in executing the Sentence of the Law	435
CCCXCVIII.	Ill Treatment of Prisoners	436
CCCXCIX.	Allowing Prisoners sharp Instruments	ibid.
CCCC.	Encouraging and exciting Prisoners to make groundless Appeals	438
CCCCI.	Supply of Food and Clothes to Prisoners	439
CCCCII.	Indulgence in consideration of the Rank and former Services of Prisoners	440
CCCCIII.	Prisoners committing Suicide	441
CCCCIV.	Torture not to be used in the judicial Examination of Children or of the Aged	ibid.

TABLE of CONTENTS.

Section		Page
CCCCV.	Confronting Offenders and their Associates	442
CCCCVI.	Examination of Offenders to correspond with the Charges against them	444
CCCCVII.	Prosecutors not to be detained after a Trial is concluded	445
CCCCVIII.	Offenders recriminating upon innocent Persons	ibid.
CCCCIX.	Pronouncing and executing an unjust Sentence	447
CCCCX.	Reversal of a false Judgment	450
CCCCXI.	Execution of Judgment	451
CCCCXII.	Examination of the Body in Cases of Homicide	452
CCCCXIII.	Infliction of Punishments in an illegal Manner	453
CCCCXIV.	Proceedings against Offences committed by superior Magistrates	455
CCCCXV.	Laws, Statutes, and Precedents which are to be observed in passing Sentence	ibid.
CCCCXVI.	Prisoners upon Trial, at Liberty either to plead guilty or to protest against their Sentence	456
CCCCXVII.	Misapplication or Disregard of an Act of Grace and Pardon	457
CCCCXVIII.	Offending designedly, in the Expectation of Impunity through an Act of Grace and Pardon	ibid.
CCCCXIX.	Services to be performed by temporarily banished Offenders	458
CCCCXX.	Punishment of Female Offenders	459
CCCCXXI.	Execution of Criminals without waiting for the Emperor's Ratification	460
CCCCXXII.	Execution of a Sentence by a false Construction of the Laws	461
CCCCXXIII.	Clerks of Tribunals altering the Statements of Informers	462

SEVENTH

SEVENTH DIVISION, — *Laws relative to Public Works.*

BOOK I.

PUBLIC BUILDINGS.

Section		Page
CCCCXXIV.	Ordering public Works without sufficient Authority	463
CCCCXXV.	Unnecessary and unserviceable Works	464
CCCCXXVI.	Public Works and Manufactures to be conformable to Rule and Custom	465
CCCCXXVII.	Misapplication of public Stores	466
CCCCXXVIII.	Misapplication of the public Looms	467
CCCCXXIX.	Working Silks or Stuffs according to prohibited Patterns	ibid.
CCCCXXX.	Irregularity in the Supplies of raw Materials, and in the Issue of manufactured Goods	468
CCCCXXXI.	Due Preservation and Repair of public Buildings	ibid.
CCCCXXXII.	Officers of Government not residing in the Habitations allotted to them	469

BOOK II.

PUBLIC WAYS.

CCCCXXXIII.	Damaging Embankments of Rivers	471
CCCCXXXIV.	Neglecting duly to repair and maintain Embankments	472
CCCCXXXV.	Encroaching on public Highways	473
CCCCXXXVI.	Repair of Roads and Bridges	ibid.

lviii

TABLE of CONTENTS.

APPENDIX.

No.		Page
I.	TRANSLATION of the Teftamentary Edict of KIEN-LUNG, the late Emperor of China	477
II.	Tranflation of the Edict of the reigning Emperor KIA-KING, by which the Death of his Father, the Emperor KIEN-LUNG, was firft officially made public	483
III.	Note of the Tranflator; containing the Titles of omitted Articles of Preliminary Matter	486
IV.	Note of the Tranflator; relative to the introductory Table of Degrees of Relationfhip and Mourning	487
V.	Tranflation of the Supplementary Claufes to Section I. entitled "*Defcription of ordinary Punifhments*"	488
VI.	Note of the Tranflator upon Section II. entitled "*Offences of a treafonable Nature*"	490
VII.	Note of the Tranflator upon Section III. entitled "*Privileged Claffes*"	ibid.
VIII.	Note of the Tranflator; containing fome Remarks upon the Hiftory of *Ho-chung-tong*, the favourite Minifter of the Emperor KIEN-LUNG	491
	Tranflation of an Imperial Edict, in which various Articles of Impeachment againft the Minifter *Ho-chung-tong* are exhibited	493
	Tranflation of an Imperial Edict, announcing the Sentence of Condemnation paffed upon the Minifter *Ho-chung-tong*, and upon fome of his Relations and principal Adherents	498
	Tranflation of an Imperial Edict, declaratory of a general Amnefty in favour of all other Perfons who might have been connected with or influenced by the faid Minifter	502
IX.	Tranflation of an Imperial Edict, extracted from the Pekin Gazette, containing a Statement of the Grounds upon which a Sentence of Death had been paffed upon *Quay-lung*, Viceroy of the Province of *Sechuen*	504

TABLE OF CONTENTS.

No.		PAGE
X.	Translation of an official Statement of Charges exhibited by the Sub-Viceroy of *Quang-tung*, against sundry Officers of that provincial Government	509
	Translation of an Imperial Edict containing the Emperor's Decision upon the said Charges	513
XI.	Note of the Translator; containing some Remarks upon the Application of the Laws of China to the Case of British Subjects trading to and residing at Canton	515
	Translation of an Edict of the Governor of *Hiang-shan*, addressed to the Chinese and Portuguese Inhabitants of Macao, in consequence of the Refusal of the Portuguese to deliver into the Hands of the Chinese Magistrates a European charged with the Murder of a Chinese	517
	Translation of an Imperial Edict issued on the occasion of two Russian Ships visiting the Port of Canton, in order to open a Trade by Sea with the Chinese Empire	518
	Translation of an Extract of an Edict of the Viceroy of *Quang-tung* and *Quang-see*, issued on the occasion of an English Vessel having been stranded on the Coast of China	520
	Translation of an official Statement of the Trial and Sentence of an English Seaman, charged with having struck a native Chinese, so as to occasion his Death	521
XII.	Translation of an Imperial Edict issued on the Receipt of an Address recommending the Establishment of Colleges in the several Districts of Tartary	525
	Translation of an Extract from the Clauses annexed to Section LXXVIII. entitled " *Rule of Succession and Inheritance*"	ibid.
XIII.	Note of the Translator on the Nature of the ordinary Tenure of Land in China, in relation to the Subject of Section LXXXVIII. entitled " *Younger and inferior Branches of a Family disposing of the Property without Leave*"	526
XIV.	Extract of a Letter from a Missionary at Pekin, containing some Account of the Effects of an Inundation in the Province of *Pe-che-lee*	528
	Extract of a Letter from a Chinese Christian, containing some Observations on the general State of the Population in the Province of *Shan-see*	ibid.

No.		Page
XV.	Abstract of some of the principal Clauses annexed to Section XCV. entitled " *Law of Mortgages*"	529
XVI.	Translation of an Imperial Edict, containing the Sentence of certain military Officers convicted of the Crime of embezzling public Stores	530
XVII.	Note of the Translator on the high Rate of the legal Interest of Money in China; in reference to the Subject of Section CXLIX. entitled " *Usury*"	ibid.
XVIII.	Translation of an Imperial Edict, containing the Emperor's Sentence upon divers Persons convicted of embracing, or of endeavouring to propagate the Christian Religion in China	532
	Translation of an Imperial Edict, containing Animadversions upon the Contents of certain Chinese Books, descriptive of the Tenets of the Catholic Church	535
XIX.	Translation of an Imperial Edict, issued on the occasion of an Attempt to assassinate the present Emperor	537
XX.	Translation of an Extract from the Pekin Gazette, containing an official Report of certain Operations of the Chinese Imperial Forces on the occasion of a Rebellion in the Province of *Sechuen*	540
XXI.	Translation of two of the Clauses annexed to Section CCXXV. entitled " *Illicit Exportation of Merchandize*"	543
XXII.	Translation of the Clauses annexed to Section CCLIV. entitled " *High Treason*"	544
XXIII.	Translation of the Clauses annexed to Section CCLV. entitled " *Rebellion and Renunciation of Allegiance*"	545
XXIV.	Translation of the Clauses annexed to Section CCLVI. entitled " *Sorcery and Magic*"	548
XXV.	Translation of the most material among the Clauses annexed to Section CCLXIII. entitled " *Stealing Timber from a Burying-ground*"	550
XXVI.	Translation of the first seven Clauses annexed to Section CCLXIV. entitled " *Embezzlement of public Property*"	552
XXVII.	Translation of the Clauses annexed to Section CCLXV. entitled " *Theft of public Property*"	553
XXVIII.	Translation of the Clauses annexed to Section CCLXVI. entitled " *Robbery—Highway Robbery*"	554

TABLE OF CONTENTS.

No.		PAGE
XXIX.	Translation of the Clauses and Commentary annexed to Section CCLXXXII. entitled "*Preconcerted Homicide—Murder*"	560
XXX.	Translation of an Extract from a Volume of Chinese Law Reports, containing the Trial, Revisal of Proceedings, and final Sentence, in the Case of an Offender charged with Homicide by Gun-firing	563
XXXI.	Translation of another Extract from the same Collection of Law Reports, containing the Trial, Revisal of Proceedings, and final Sentence, in the Case of a Master charged with the Murder of his Servant	566
XXXII.	Translation of the Clauses annexed to Section CCCLXVI. entitled "*Criminal Intercourse in general*"	569

I.

TA TSING LEU LEE;

OR

THE LAWS AND STATUTES

OF

THE DYNASTY OF TSING,

A NEW EDITION,
PRINTED AND PUBLISHED IN THE FOURTH YEAR OF THE REIGN OF *KIA-KING*,
OF
THE ENTIRE CODE OF FUNDAMENTAL LAWS AND SUPPLEMENTARY STATUTES;
WHICH, AFTER HAVING BEEN REVISED AND COMPLETED, WAS, IN THE SIXTIETH YEAR OF THE REIGN OF *KIEN-LUNG*, PROMULGATED IN ITS PRESENT FORM, BY THE SUPREME COUNCIL OF STATE IN THE DEPARTMENT OF PUBLIC JUSTICE.

TO WHICH IS ADDED,
THE EXPLANATORY COMMENTARY ANNEXED TO THE FUNDAMENTAL LAWS, BY THE EMPEROR *YONG-TCHING*; AN EXTENSIVE COLLECTION OF ADJUDGED CASES AND A VARIETY OF USEFUL NOTES AND OBSERVATIONS DERIVED FROM THE MOST APPROVED SOURCES.

NOTE.—The above is an Abstract of the Title-Page to the Edition of the original Chinese Work, printed in the Year 1799, from which the Fundamental Laws, translated in the following Pages, have been extracted. — A still later Edition, exactly similar in respect to the Fundamental Laws, but containing a greater Number of Supplementary Statutes, and a different Selection of illustrative Notes, has likewise been occasionally consulted.

The Title-page of the later Edition may be translated as follows: " Recently engraved
" in the 10th Year of *KIA-KING*, a new Edition of the Laws and Statutes of the great
" Dynasty of *TSING*; comprising, agreeably to the universal Compendium promulgated
" by the Supreme Court of Judicature on the 6th Year of *KIA-KING*, all the Additions
" and Alterations which have been made of late Years in the supplementary Statutes;
" also compendious Abstracts from the various Commentaries, and an Appendix, con-
" sisting of two Books of additional supplementary Statutes. The whole carefully
" revised and examined; and each Copy sold for three *leang* six *tsien* of silver."

II.

ORIGINAL PREFACE

TO

THE CHINESE PENAL CODE

BY

THE EMPEROR *SHUN CHEE*,

THE FIRST OF THE PRESENT DYNASTY.

WHEN we contemplate the progressive establishment of our dominions in the East*, by our Royal Ancestors and immediate Predecessors, we observe that the simplicity of the people originally required but few laws; and that, with the exception of crimes of extraordinary enormity, no punishments were inflicted besides those of the whip and the bamboo.

Since, however, the Divine Will has been graciously pleased to entrust us with the administration of the Empire of China, a multitude of judicial proceedings in civil and criminal cases, arising out of the various dispositions and irregular passions of mankind in a great and populous nation, have successively occupied our Royal attention. Hence we have suffered much inconvenience, from the necessity we have been almost constantly under of either aggravating or mitigating

---

* The princes of the family now on the throne of China, do not date their origin from any remote period. Their ancestors were not established at Mougden in Mantchoo or Eastern Tartary, before the year 1616; but they made a rapid progress from that period. In 1644, during the troubles and internal commotions which prevailed in China, under a declining dynasty, they obtained possession of the Chinese capital, and in the course of a few years completed the conquest of the whole empire.

the erroneous sentences of the magistrates; who, previous to the re-establishment of a fixed Code of Penal Laws, were not in possession of any secure foundation, upon which they could build a just and equitable decision.

A numerous body of magistrates was, therefore, assembled at the capital, by our command, for the purpose of revising the Penal Code, formerly in force under the late dynasty of *Ming* *, and of digesting the same into a new Code, by the exclusion of such parts as were exceptionable, and the introduction of others, which were likely to contribute to the attainment of justice, and to the general perfection of the work.

The result of their labours having been submitted to our examination, we maturely weighed and considered the various matter it contained, and then instructed a select number of our Great Officers of State, carefully to revise the whole, for the purpose of making such alterations and emendations as might still be found requisite.

As soon as this object was accomplished, we issued our Royal authority for the impression and publication of the work, under the Title of " *Ta tsing leu chee kiay foo lee*," or the General Laws of the Imperial Dynasty of *Tsing*, collected and explained, and accompanied by supplementary clauses.

Wherefore, officers and magistrates of the interior and exterior departments of our empire, be it your care diligently to observe the the same, and to forbear in future to give any decision, or to pass any sentence, according to your private sentiments, or upon your unsupported authority.

Thus shall the magistrates and people look up with awe and submission to the justice of these institutions, as they find themselves respectively concerned in them: the transgressor will not fail to suffer

---

* The Dynasty of *Ming* succeeded that of *Yuen*, or the Mongol Tartars, in the year 1568.

a strict

a strict expiation for his offences, and will be the instrument of deterring others from similar misconduct; and, finally, the government and the people will be equally secured for endless generations in the enjoyment of the happy effects of the great and noble virtues of our illustrious progenitors.

Dated the 5th Moon, of the third year, of *Shun-Chee*, A.D. 1647.

III.

PREFATORY EDICT

OF

THE EMPEROR *KAUNG-HEE*,

(OTHERWISE, BUT IMPROPERLY, *CAMHI*,)

THE SECOND OF THE PRESENT DYNASTY.

THE chief ends proposed by the institution of punishments in the empire, have been to guard against violence and injury, to repress inordinate desires, and to secure the peace and tranquillity of an honest and unoffending community.

Laws have accordingly been enacted, numerous, as well as particular in their application, and subsequently varied and augmented at different times, as circumstances were found to require, but without ever losing sight of those principles of affection and benevolence, of which our Illustrious Predecessors, who laid the foundation of these institutions, were invariably observant.

The people being, however, gradually seduced, by their irregular desires, to disregard the penalties to which an infringement of the laws exposed them, to become the disciples of violence and iniquity, and to oppress those whom they found weak and defenceless, it became necessary to devise new regulations, and to strengthen those which already existed, by the denunciation of severer punishments.

Nevertheless, offences against the laws are again frequent, and evil propensities toward irregularities and crimes, do not appear to have been in any considerable degree repressed.

Those crimes which are either committed against, or lead to a forfeiture of the lives of our subjects, have been the objects of our most serious consideration, and their frequency is, to us, a source of much disquietude.

It is, therefore, our pleasure, that all the additional statutes of a recent promulgation, whereby those crimes which formerly were not punished with death, have been rendered capital; or where the penalties of transgression have been in any other manner altered or augmented, shall be taken into consideration and revised by the ministers of state, the inspectors general, and the presidents of the six supreme tribunals, in order that these magistrates may be enabled to make a due report to us upon their fitness and efficacy.

Dated the 14th of the 9th moon of the 18th year of *Kaung-hee*, A.D. 1679.

IV.

PREFATORY EDICT

OF

THE EMPEROR *YONG-TCHING*,

THE THIRD OF THE PRESENT DYNASTY.

SINCE the period of our Acceſſion to the Imperial Throne of our Anceſtors, the criminals who, at different times, have been awaiting their ſentence in confinement, have not failed to ſhare our Royal compaſſion and conſideration. — The reports of all the caſes adjudged by the provincial magiſtrates, and requiring our ſanction to their deciſion, have been examined by us with the moſt ſcrupulous attention, leſt they ſhould contain any flaw or incongruity which might invalidate the reſults. — We have alſo conſidered that among our various inſtitutions, the Code of Penal Laws is the moſt varied and complicated in its conſtruction; and that, therefore, unleſs clear and invariable rules are pointed out, the magiſtrates muſt, in ſome inſtances, unavoidably take upon themſelves to aggravate or mitigate the puniſhment due to criminals, according to their own diſcretion; in which caſes, they muſt conſtantly be liable to commit great errors, and even flagrant injuſtice.

With the view of preventing as much as poſſible, all ſuch abuſes, we ſubmitted the Penal Code to the reviſion of the members of our Imperial college, and have ſince attentively conſidered their written obſervations thereon, annexing, at the ſame time, to each article, the mark of our approbation or diſſent. In conſideration, however, of the vaſt mportance of a work which is to guide and inſtruct the magiſtrates in all judicial

proceedings,

proceedings, it is our pleasure, that the nine principal officers of state, revise, examine, and correct the results of all these operations, so as most effectually to fulfil our design of adapting the penalties of the laws in a just proportion to the crimes against which they are denounced.

Dated the 27th of the 5th moon, of the third year of *Yong-tching*, A.D. 1725.*

---

* In addition to these three Prefatory Edicts, two state papers issued in the names of the late Emperor *Kien-lung*, and the reigning Emperor *Kia-King*, have been inserted in the Appendix, No. I. and No. II. and although not directly connected with the subject of the Code, will, it is hoped, be found illustrative of many parts of it, and otherwise not uninteresting. The remaining articles of Preliminary Matter, which, in the original, precede the Table of Contents, have been omitted here, as not essential to the work, but their several titles will be found in the Appendix, No. III.

It has not been conceived necessary, or even desirable, to introduce, in the course of these occasional notes, any detailed references to the remarks of preceding writers. This has not, however, prevented the Translator from speaking generally, on one occasion, (page 318.) of the valuable work of Mr. Barrow; or on another, (page 107,) of the interesting translation published by the Bishop of Dromore; or, lastly, from taking the present opportunity of noticing the short, but excellent remarks on Chinese Literature, which we owe to the learned and judicious author of the *Horæ Biblicæ*. And with respect to the works of the Missionaries, although the Translator of the present work was aware that he should not be justified in recommending an implicit reliance upon them, he has been happy to refer generally to the vast fund of curious and important information upon China, which, notwithstanding this reservation, the above class of writers must be admitted to have afforded. With regard to the work, which, as far as it extends, perhaps stands the highest in point of authority of any that has been written on the subject of China, the Translator feels naturally a delicacy in saying any thing.—He has, however, the satisfaction to reflect, that the *Authentic Account of the British Embassy* does not, at this day, require any new arguments or testimony, to confirm it in its place in the public esteem.

V.

TABLE I.*

SCALE of Punishment Offences against Public and Private Property.						
	Pecuniary Malversation.	Theft.	Bribery for a lawful Object.	Bribery for an unlawful Object.	Theft of Public Property.	Embezzlement of Public Property.
	Amount in oz. of Silver†	Ditto.	Ditto.	Ditto.	Ditto.	Ditto.
20 Blows with the bamboo	1 or less					
30 ——	1 to 10					
40 ——	20 —					
50 ——	30 —					
60 ——	40 —	1 or less	1 or less			
70 ——	50 —	10 —	10 —			
80 ——	60 —	20 —	20 —	1 or less / 1 to 5 oz	1 or less / 1 to 5 oz	1 or less
90 ——	70 —	30 —	30 —	10 —	10 —	1 to 2,5
100 ——	80 —	40 —	40 —	15 —	15 —	5.
60 —— and 1 year's banishment	100 —	50 —	50 —	20 —	20 —	7.5
70 —— and 1½ —— ——	200 —	60 —	60 —	25 —	25 —	10.
80 —— and 2 —— ——	300 —	70 —	70 —	30 —	30 —	12.5
90 —— and 2¼ —— ——	400 —	80 —	80 —	35 —	35 —	15.
100 —— and 3 —— ——	500 — and upwards	90 —	90 —	40 —	40 —	17.5
	Dist. lee.					
100 —— and perpet. banish. 2000	——	100 —	100 —	45 —	45 —	20.
100 —— and —— —— 2500	——	110 —	110 —	50 —	50 —	25.
100 —— and —— —— 3000	——	120 —	120 —	55 —	55 —	30.
Death,—to be strangled		Upwards of 120 oz.	Upwards of 120 oz.	80 or 120 If an inferior Officer.	80 in extreme Cases.	
Death,—to be beheaded						80 in extreme Cases

* This Table is an abstract of the principal articles of the laws specially provided for the protection of public and private property. The subject is fully explained in the body of the code, (1st and 6th Book of the VIth Division,) but the advantage of this Table consists in its exhibiting the whole in a summary way, and upon a single inspection. Thus, it appears without reference, that whoever is guilty of any species of pecuniary malversation, to the extent of 20 ounces of silver, shall, generally speaking, be liable, at the least, to a punishment of 40 blows: that whoever is guilty of a theft of private property, or of receiving a bribe for an object in itself lawful, to the same extent, is punishable with 80 blows: that whoever is guilty to the same extent of a theft of public property, or of receiving a bribe for an object in itself unlawful, is punishable with 60 blows, and banishment for the space of one year: and, lastly, that whoever is guilty of embezzling so much of the public property, will be punishable with 100 blows, and perpetual banishment to the distance of 2000 *lee*.

† The value of the *Leang*, or Chinese ounce of silver, according to the established rule of exchange at Canton, is 6s. 8d. or the third part of a pound sterling.

VI.

TABLE II.*

SCALE of the Pecuniary Redemption of necessarily redeemable Punishments.											
	If well able to pay.		if not altogether destitute.		If aged, or under Age.		Females in certain Cases.		Killing or wounding accidentally.		Females in general.
											Days confine^t.	Dec. of oz.
	oz.	dec.	oz.	dec.	oz.	dec.	oz.	dec.	oz.	dec.	20 and 105
10 blows with the bamboo	—	2.5	—	3	—	7.5	—	1	—	—	
20 — . . .	—	5	—	4.5	—	1.5	—	2	—	3.5.4	25 and 135
30 — . . .	—	7.5	—	6	—	2.2.5	—	3	—	3.3.2	30 and 165
40 — . . .	1	—	—	6.5	—	3	—	4	—	7.9	35 and 195
50 — . . .	1	2.4	—	9	—	3.7.5	—	5	—	8.8.7	40 and 225
60 — . . .	3	—	1	2	—	4.5	—	6	—	—	50 and 3
70 — . . .	3	5	1	3 5	—	5.2.5	—	7	—	—	55 and 3375
80 — . . .	4	—	1	5	—	6	—	8	1	4.1.9	60 and 375
90 — . . .	4	5	1	6.5	—	6.7.5	—	9			
100 — . . .	5	—	1	8	—	7.5	—	110	1	774	
1 year's Banishment -	7	5	3	6	1	5	1	7.5	3	548	
1½ ——————— -	10	—	5	4	1	8.7.5	1	1125	—	—	
2 ———————	12	5	7	2	2	2.5	1	15	5	322	
2½ ———————	15	—	9	—	2	6.2.5	1	1875	—	—	
3 ——————— -	17	5	10	8	3	—	1	2250	7	097	
4 ———————	20	—	14	4	4	—	—	—	—	—	
5 ——————— -	25	—	18	—	4	—					
	See.										
Perpetual, ——— dift. 2000	—		—		—		1	30000	—		
———, ——— 2500	—		—		—		1	3375	—		
———, ——— 3000	—		—		—		1	375	10	645	
Death,—to be strangled	—		—		—		1	45	12	42	
Death,—to be beheaded											

* Upon the subject of this Table, see Note, page 24.

VII.

TABLE III.*

SCALE of pecuniary Redemption in such Cases as are not legally excluded from the Benefit of general Acts of Grace and Pardon, and which, though not necessarily redeemable, have, by an Edict of the 8th Year of the Emperor *KIEN-LUNG*, been made redeemable upon Petition.

Rank of the Offender.	Sentence.	Pecuniary Commutation in ounces of silver.
An Officer above the fourth Rank	Death by Strangulation or Decollation.	12000
———— of the fourth Rank		5000
———— of the fifth or sixth Rank		4000
———— of the seventh, or any inferior Rank, or a Doctor of Literature		2500
A Graduate or Licenciate		2000
A private Individual		1200
An Officer above the fourth Rank	Perpetual Banishment.	7200
———— of the fourth Rank		3000
———— of the fifth or sixth Rank		2400
———— of the seventh, or any inferior Rank, or a Doctor of Literature		1500
A Graduate or Licenciate		1200
A private Individual		720
An Officer above the fourth Rank	Temporary Banishment, or Blows with the Bamboo.	4800
———— of the fourth Rank		2000
———— of the fifth or sixth Rank		1600
———— of the seventh or any inferior Rank, or a Doctor of Literature		1000
A graduate or Licenciate		800
A private Individual		480

* This Table has, by mistake, been referred to in pages 19 and 24, as a part of the 5th article of the Appendix.

VIII.

TABLE IV.

DEGREES OF PUNISHMENT.

Degrees.	Nominally.	Reduced.	Inflicted with the Bamboo	In Breadth at its Extremities	Weight not to exceed.
1	10	4 Blows			
2	30	5 —	*Che Tſun*†	1½ *Tſun* by	1½ *Kin* ‡.
3	20	10 —	5 5 in length	1 *Tſun*.	
4	40	15 —			
5	50	20 —			
6	60	20 —			
7	70	25 —			
8	80	30 —		2 *Tſun* by	
9	90	35 —		1¼ *Tſun*.	2 *Kin*.
10	100	40 —			
			Together with Baniſhment		and to the Diſtance of
11	60	20 —	For one year - - -		500 *lee*, or about 50 leagues
12	70	25 —	For one year and a half - -		500 — — —
13	80	30 —	For two years - - -		500 — — —
14	90	35 —	For two years and a half - -		500 — — —
15	100	40 —	For three years - - -		500 — — —
16	100	40 —	For life - - -		2000 — 200 —
17	100	40 —	For life - - -		2500 — 250 —
18	100	40 —	For life - - -		3000 — 300 —
19	Death, by Strangulation.				
20	Death, by Decollation.				

IX.

TABLE V.

SPECIFICATION of the ordinary Inſtruments of Puniſhment and Confinement.

THE BAMBOO.

A ſtraight poliſhed piece of bamboo, the branches cut away, and reduced to the length, breadth, and weight above deſcribed; and when uſed, to be held by the ſmaller end.

---

* This Table is explained in the firſt ſection of the Code, and in the Appendix, No. V.

† *Che* and *Tſun* are Chineſe meaſures of length, uſually denominated at Canton *Covids* and *puntos*. The *Che* (of which the *Tſun* is the tenth part), which is in ordinary uſe throughout the empire, exceeds the Engliſh foot by rather more than half an inch; but the *Che*, uſed at Canton for the meaſurement of goods in trade, is ſomewhat longer, being 14 inches and 625 decimals.

‡ The *Kin* exceeds the Engliſh pound weight by one-third.

THE *KIA*, OTHERWISE, BUT IMPROPERLY, CANGUE.

A square frame of dry wood, three *Che* long, and 2 *Che* 9 *Tsun* broad; and weighing in ordinary cases 25 *Kin*.

THE IRON CHAIN.

The greater and less criminals shall all be confined by an iron chain, 7 *Che* long, and weighing 5 *Kin*.

THE HAND-CUFFS.

The hand-cuffs shall be made of dry wood, and 1 *Che* 6 *Tsun* long, by 1 *Tsun* in thickness, and shall be used to confine capital offenders of the male sex only.

THE FETTERS.

Iron fetters, weighing one *Kin*, shall be used to confine all such offenders as are destined to banishment or capital punishment.

X.

TABLE VI.

DEGREES OF RELATIONSHIP, AND OF MOURNING.

THE mourning for the nearest among relations in the first degree, shall be worn for three years, and shall be made of the coarsest hempen cloth, without being sewn at the borders.

The mourning for other relations in the first degree shall be worn for three or five months, and be made of middling hempen cloth, sewn at the borders.

The mourning for relations in the second degree, shall be worn for nine months, and be made of coarse linen-cloth.

The mourning for relations in the third degree, shall be worn for five months, and be made of middling coarse linen-cloth.

The mourning for relations in the fourth degree, shall be worn for three months, and be made of middling fine linen-cloth.

The full mourning for three years, shall be worn

By a son, for his father or mother.

By a daughter, for her father or mother, when living under the parents' roof, although affianced to her intended husband, or although once married, if afterwards divorced and sent home.

By a son's wife, for her husband's father or mother.

By a son and his wife, for his father's substituted first wife *; for the wife of his father substituted in the place of his mother, and for the wife of his father, who nursed him.

By an inferior wife's son and his wife, for his natural mother, and for his father's first wife.

By an adopted son and his wife, for his adopted parents.

By a grandson and his wife, for his paternal grand-parents.

By a wife, whether the first or inferior one, for her husband †.

* That is to say, for the one among his father's wives, who upon the death of the first or principal wife, takes her place.

† See the Appendix, No. IV. It may be proper, in order to prevent any misconception, to remark generally, in this place, that in whatever part of the translation degrees of relationship or mourning are mentioned, it is always to be understood to be in reference to Chinese, and not to European tables of alliance and consanguinity.

THE PENAL LAWS OF *CHINA*.

FIRST DIVISION,
General Laws.

BOOK I.
PRELIMINARY REGULATIONS.

SECTION I. — *Description of the Ordinary Punishments.*

THE lowest degree of punishment is a moderate correction inflicted with the lesser bamboo, in order that the transgressor of the law may entertain a sense of shame for his past, and receive a salutary admonition with respect to his future, conduct. Of this species of punishment there are five degrees:

| The first
The second
The third
The fourth
The fifth | nominally a punishment of | 10 blows,
20 blows,
30 blows,
40 blows,
50 blows, | of which only | 4 blows
5 blows
10 blows
15 blows
20 blows | are to be inflicted. |

The second degree, or division of punishment, is inflicted with the larger bamboo, and is subdivided in the following manner:

The first		60 blows,		20 blows
The second	nominally a	70 blows,	of which only	25 blows
The third	punishment of	80 blows,		30 blows — are to be inflicted.
The fourth		90 blows,		35 blows
The fifth		100 blows,		40 blows

The third division in the scale of punishments is, that of temporary banishment, to any distance not exceeding 500 *lee**, with the view of affording an opportunity of repentance and amendment. Of this species of punishment there are also five gradations: namely,

Banishment for
- 1 year, and 60 blows
- 1½ years, and 70 blows
- 2 years, and 80 blows
- 2½ years, and 90 blows
- 3 years, and 100 blows

with the bamboo, reduced as above.

Perpetual banishment, the fourth degree of punishment in the order of severity, is subdivided as follows; and is reserved for such of the more considerable offences whereupon the life of the criminal is spared by the mercifulness of the laws:

100 blows with the bamboo, and perpetual banishment to the distance of
- 2000 *lee.*
- 2500 *lee.*
- 3000 *lee.*

The fifth and ultimate punishment which the laws ordain, is death, either by strangulation, or by decollation.

All criminals capitally convicted, except such atrocious offenders as are expressly directed to be executed without delay, are retained in prison for execution at a particular period in the autumn; the sentence passed upon each individual being first duly reported to, and ratified by, the Emperor.

To this section of the fundamental laws a supplement is annexed, consisting of eighteen clauses †.

---

* Ten *lee* are usually estimated to be equal to three geographical miles, but the proportion varies a little in the different provinces of the empire.

† See Appendix, No. V.

SECTION II. — *Offences of a treasonable Nature.*

I. *Rebellion*, is an attempt to violate the divine order of things on earth; for as the fruits of the earth are produced in regular succession under the influence of the presiding Spirit, so is their distribution among the people regulated by the Sovereign, who is the sacred successor to the seat of his ancestors: resisting and conspiring against him is, therefore, an unspeakable outrage, and a disturbance of the peace of the universe.

II. *Disloyalty*, is evinced by an attempt to destroy the imperial temples, tombs, or palaces; for as the imperial temples and tombs are intended to perpetuate the memory, and to receive the remains, of former Sovereigns, so the imperial palaces, being designed for the use of the reigning monarch, are equally sacred and inviolable.

III. *Desertion*, is a term which may be applied to the offence of undertaking to quit, or betray the interests of, the empire, in order to submit or adhere to a foreign power, and may be considered as exemplified in the case of betraying a military post, or exciting the people to emigration.

IV. *Parricide*, is the denomination under which the murder of a father or mother, of an uncle, aunt, grandfather or grandmother, is comprehended, and is a crime of the deepest dye; for such a violation of the ties of nature, which are constituted by the Divine Will, is in every case an evidence of the most unprincipled depravity.

V. *Massacre*, is held to be the murder of three or more persons in one family, and comprehends other crimes sanguinary and enormous in a similar degree.

VI. *Sacrilege*, is committed by stealing from the temples any of the sacred articles consecrated to divine purposes, or by purloining any article in the immediate use of the Sovereign: similar guilt is incurred by counterfeiting the imperial seal, by ministering to the Sovereign improper medicines, or, in general, by the commission of any error or negligence, whereby the safety of his sacred person may be endangered.

VII. *Impiety*, is discoverable in every instance of disrespect or negligence towards those to whom we owe our being, and by whom we have been educated and protected.—It is likewise committed by those who inform against, or insult, such near relations while living, or who refuse to mourn for their loss, and to shew respect for their memory, when dead.

VIII. *Discord*, in families, is the breach of the legal or natural ties which are founded on our connexions by blood or marriage; under this head may be classed the crimes of killing, wounding, or maltreating any of those relations or connexions to whom, when deceased, the ceremony of mourning is legally due *.

IX. *Insubordination*, is the rising against, or murdering, a superior magistrate by an inferior; or any insurrection against the magistrates in general, by the people.

X. *Incest*, is the co-habitation, or promiscuous intercourse, of persons related in any of the degrees within which marriage is prohibited †.

---

* The nature and extent of these connexions is in some degree shewn in the preliminary part of the code, and also occasionally in some of the subsequent sections, and in the Appendix.

† See the division of the code, intitled, *Marriage*, and also the division, intitled, *Incest and Adultery*.

The crimes here arranged and diftributed under ten heads, being diftinguifhed from others by their enormity, are always punifhed with the utmoft rigour of the law; and, when the offence is capital, it is excepted from the benefit of any act of general pardon; being likewife, in each cafe, a direct violation of the ties by which fociety is maintained, they are exprefsly enumerated in the introductory part of this code, that the people may learn to dread, and to avoid the fame *.

No claufe to this fection.

Section III.—*The Privileged Claffes.*

I. *The Privilege of Imperial Blood and Connections.*—Becaufe the members of the auguft family of the Sovereign, who rules by the appointment of Heaven, are entitled to peculiar reverence in the adminiftration of the laws with regard to them; therefore, this privilege fhall extend to all the relations of His Imperial Majefty, who are defcended from the fame anceftors; to all the relations in the firft, fecond, third, and fourth degrees of His Imperial Majefty's mother and grandmother; to all the relations of His Imperial Majefty's confort, the Emprefs, within the firft, fecond, and third degrees; and, laftly, to all the relations of the confort of the hereditary Prince, within the firft and fecond degrees only.

II. *The Privilege of long Service.*—This clafs comprehends all thofe ancient fervants of the crown, who are zealoufly attached and have been honourably diftinguifhed.—Such perfons are entitled to privilege, becaufe the Emperor has exalted them, and becaufe the length of their fervices is a teftimony of their unalterable fidelity.

III. *The Privilege of illuftrious Actions.*—Thofe are entitled to privilege under this clafs, who purfue the enemy to the diftance of 10,000 lee, cut off the head of the general of the hoftile army, tear

* See Appendix, No. VI.

down his standard, and break his sword; or who, having brought multitudes to surrender themselves to the Imperial authority, restore peace and tranquillity to the age; and, lastly, those who by their talents and exertions shall extend the boundaries of the empire. Such deeds of valour shall be commemorated on tablets of stone.

IV. *The Privilege of extraordinary Wisdom.* — Those who are eminent for their wisdom and virtue are entitled to privilege, because by the advice of such men the administration of government is brought to perfection. *Kia Yee* has said, that the wise and good man may be afflicted with misfortunes, even unto death, without being subject to humiliation or disgrace.

V. *The Privilege of great Abilities.* — Great abilities are rare; the actions of the able are superior in value even to the words of the wise. — From those who have the talent of commanding armies, and of conducting the different departments of the state, the sovereign selects the best and most efficacious ministers of his power.

VI. *The Privilege of Zeal and Assiduity.* — This privilege is due to those who, by night and by day, are zealously and assiduously engaged in the performance of their civil or military duties; and to those who discharge any distant and arduous employment with distinguished honour.

VII. *The Privilege of Nobility.* — This privilege is to be enjoyed by all those who possess the first rank in the empire; all those of the second, who are at the same time employed in any official capacity whatever; and all those of the third, whose office confers any civil or military command.

VIII. *The Privilege of Birth.* — The Emperor esteems and protects those who are distinguished for their wisdom and eminent services, even to the second and third generation *.

No clause.

* See Appendix, No. VII.

SECTION IV.—*Offences of Perfons entitled to Privilege.*

When any perfon entitled to privilege has committed an offence againſt the laws, a diſtinct ſpecification thereof ſhall be laid before the Emperor, and it ſhall not be lawful to try or examine ſuch perſon, until the receipt of His Majeſty's expreſs commands for that purpoſe— The Emperor's commands having been received, the trial and examination of the offender ſhall be inſtituted, and a report made of the whole of the proceedings, for the information and final deciſion of His Imperial Majeſty.

Neverthelefs, if any privileged perſon commits an offence of a treaſonable nature, he ſhall not have the benefit of his privilege as provided by this law.

Five clauſes.

SECTION V.—*Relations of Perfons entitled to Privilege.*

When the father, mother, paternal grandfather or grandmother, wife, ſon, or grandſon of any perſon entitled to privilege, as belonging to one of the eight claſſes before mentioned, commits an offence againſt the laws, a diſtinct ſpecification thereof ſhall be laid before the Emperor, and it ſhall not be lawful to try or examine ſuch offender, until the Emperor's expreſs commands are received for that purpoſe.

The trial and examination having taken place, conformably to the Emperor's orders, a report of the whole of the proceedings ſhall be tranſmitted to the court, for the information and final deciſion of His Imperial Majeſty.

In the caſe of perſons privileged by their royal blood or illuſtrious ſervices, their paternal grandfathers and grandmothers, uncles, aunts,

and

and coufins, as alfo their fons-in-law and nephews; and moreover the father, mother, or wife of an officer of government of the 4th or 5th rank, and the fons or grandfons, if inheriting their rank, fhall, in each cafe, although their offences fhall be inveftigated by the magiftrate of the diftrict, not be finally condemned to any fpecies of punifhment, except by a decree of His Imperial Majefty.—— Neverthelefs, no diftinction fhall be made in favour of thofe perfons in cafes of treafon, rebellion, rapes, robberies, murders, or bribing for unlawful purpofes.

When any of the relations of privileged perfons, not being themfelves privileged, or their flaves, fervants, ftewards, tenants, and fuch like, avail themfelves of the authority and credit of their lords, mafters, or relations, to opprefs and injure the people, or to infult and refift the magiftrates, they fhall be punifhed one degree more feverely than in ordinary cafes of fimilar offences, but the privileged perfon fhall not be implicated in any judicial proceedings without a fpecial reference being had on the fubject to His Imperial Majefty.

When the tribunals of government undertake the inveftigation and trial of offenders fo connected with privileged perfons, if fuch perfons interpofe their influence and authority to interrupt the courfe of juftice, and prevent the offenders from anfwering the fummons of the magiftrate, the proper officer in the department in which fuch interpofition takes place, fhall lay a true and faithful report thereof before the Emperor, by whom alone the punifhment to be inflicted for fuch offence can be determined.

One claufe.

Section VI. — *Offences committed by Officers of Government, how investigated.*

When any officer of government at court or in the provinces commits an offence against the laws in his public or private capacity, his superior officer shall, in all cases of importance, draw up a distinct specification thereof for the information of the Emperor, and it shall not be lawful to proceed to try the offender without the express sanction of His Majesty.

The trial and examination having taken place conformably to the Emperor's orders, His Majesty shall be again advised by a due report of the result, after which a rescript of one of the supreme * tribunals shall be sufficient authority for passing and executing the sentence which the laws require.

When any officer of government is injuriously treated by his superior, he shall be at liberty to submit a faithful statement thereof in accusation of such superior, to His Imperial Majesty; but if he should have been previously accused of any offence by his superior, he shall not be permitted to recriminate in any manner, but must confine himself to the subject of the allegations preferred against him †.

Five Clauses.

---

* The supreme tribunals or departments in which the general administration of the empire is conducted are six in number, and correspond to the six principal divisions of the code, to which the present is an introduction.

† A translation of the official report of the trial of the prime minister and favourite of the late Emperor, of a viceroy of the province of Se-chuen, and of a governor of the city of Canton, are inserted in the Appendix as examples of the mode of proceeding adopted in such cases; see Nos. VIII. IX. and X.

SECTION VII.—*Offences committed by Officers of Government in their public Capacity* *.

All civil and military officers of government, when convicted of any offence connected with the discharge of their public duty, and not of a personal nature, which offence in ordinary cases is punishable by the infliction of corporal chastisement, shall instead thereof be subjected to a fine or to degradation, according to the number of blows of the bamboo to which they are nominally liable.

Instead of nominally
- 10 blows, to forfeit one month's salary.
- 20 blows, to forfeit two months' salary.
- 30 blows, to forfeit three months' salary.
- 40 blows, to forfeit six months' salary.
- 50 blows, to forfeit nine months' salary.
- 60 blows, to forfeit one year's salary.
- 70 blows, to be degraded one degree of rank.
- 80 blows, to be degraded two degrees of rank.
- 90 blows, to be degraded three degrees of rank, but, as in the preceding case, to retain his situation.
- 100 blows, to be degraded four degrees, and to be removed from his situation.

Those persons who have official situations without being actually officers of rank in the government, shall not be exempt from corporal punishment, but may retain their employments †.

One clause.

---

* The titles of this and the succeeding section would bear no other translation than that which has been given to them, and it is therefore requisite to add in explanation, that it appears from the notes in the original that the offences denominated *private*, in fact comprehend almost all cases of direct criminality, whereas those denominated *public*, are cases of liability to punishment, solely from the official responsibility of the party implicated.

† Every officer of government from the first to the ninth rank, must be previously qualified by a literary or military degree, according to the nature of his profession; but the clerks

SECTION VIII.—*Offences committed by Officers of Government, of a private and personal Nature* *.

All civil and military officers of government, when convicted of any offence unconnected with their public functions, or although connected therewith, yet of a private and personal nature, which offence in ordinary cases exposes the offender to corporal punishment, instead of the punishment awarded by the laws in general, shall be subjected to a fine, or to degradation, in proportion thereto in the following manner:

Instead of nominally
- 10 blows, to forfeit two months' salary.
- 20 blows, to forfeit three months' salary.
- 30 blows, to forfeit six months' salary.
- 40 blows, to forfeit nine months' salary.
- 50 blows, to forfeit one year's salary.
- 60 blows, to be degraded one degree.
- 70 blows, to be degraded two degrees.
- 80 blows, to be degraded three degrees.
- 90 blows, to be degraded four degrees, and in this, as well as in the three last cases, to be removed from their situations
- 100 blows, to be degraded entirely, and dismissed from the service of Government.

Those persons who have official situations below the rank of officers of government, shall not be exempt from corporal punishment, and if such punishment amounts to 60 blows or upwards, they shall be dismissed.

Two clauses.

---

clerks and other inferior attendants in the employ of government are not considered to have any rank, or to be permanently distinguished from the rest of the community.

* The distinction between the offences treated of in this and in the preceding section has been already stated, and is also further illustrated in some of the subsequent sections of the code, in which examples occur of each kind.

SECTION IX.—*Offenders who are not liable to Banishment.*

All the subjects of the empire, who are enrolled under the Tartarian banners*, when found guilty of committing any offences which render them liable by the laws in general to a corporal punishment, shall receive the whole number of blows specified; but the chastisement shall be inflicted with the whip instead of the bamboo: when guilty of offences punishable, in ordinary cases, with banishment, they shall, instead thereof, be confined with the *cangue* or moveable pillory † for a number of days, proportioned to the length of the banishment in ordinary cases, in the following manner:

Instead of banishment	for 1 year	-	to wear the cangue for	20 days.
	for 1½ years	-		25 days.
	for 2 years	-		30 days.
	for 2½ years	-		35 days.
	for 3 years	-		40 days.
	for 4 years	-		45 days.
Instead of perpetual banishment	distance 2000 lee			50 days.
	distance 2500 lee			55 days.
	distance 3000 lee			60 days.
Instead of the perpetual military banishment	to a remote station			70 days.
	to a more remote station			75 days.
	to a still more remote station			80 days.
	to the most remote station			90 days.

---

* All the Tartars who have obtained settlements within the limits of China, since the accession of the present dynasty, are enrolled for military service, and liable to be called upon to serve the Emperor under the banners to which they are severally attached. The enrolment or mode of registering the native Chinese in their several districts and provinces as prescribed by their laws, is the subject of the first book of the third division of this code.

† The instrument here mentioned (termed by the Chinese *Kia*) is described in the preliminary part of the code.—Among the plates in the folio volume of the account of the embassy of the Earl of Macartney, there is one representing an offender undergoing this species of punishment.

SECTION X.—*Offenders of the Military Class*.

All persons of the military class committing offences against the laws, shall undergo a corporal punishment in the ordinary manner, and when condemned to the punishment of temporary banishment, shall suffer the same during the term specified by the laws, but after the expiration thereof, shall be sent back to their proper station and service. When condemned to perpetual banishment, they shall be detached and appointed to serve at the military station which is nearest to the place of their destined banishment; but if condemned to the extraordinary military banishment, the law shall be executed in the usual manner.

No clause.

SECTION XI.—*Mitigation of Punishment.*

There are various considerations which shall be admitted in mitigation of punishment. When more persons than one are engaged in the commission of an offence, the original contriver shall be punished as the principal offender, and the rest one degree less severely, being considered only in the light of accessaries. In the case of an offender surrendering himself to the officers of justice upon hearing that an accusation is intended, such offender shall be entitled to a mitigation of punishment to the extent of two degrees. When an unjust sentence of acquittal is pronounced designedly, the law-officer or clerk of the court † in which such faulty sentence originates, provided he is able to recover the offender who had been unlawfully liberated, shall, in consideration,

* This class comprehends those who are liable to serve as well as those actually serving in the army.

† The constituent members of a court of justice, or criminal tribunal, are more distinctly stated in a subsequent part of the code, and are only noticed in this place in illustration of the subject of the section.

of such recovery be punished less severely by one degree; the deputy or executive officer of the court, if not intentionally concurring in the unjust sentence, shall be punished six degrees less than the expounder of the law or clerk of the court; one degree of mitigation being by virtue of his office, and the other five degrees because he did not offend against the laws designedly*.

If the unjust sentence was not wilful, the punishment thereof shall, in the case of the clerk of the court, be reduced three degrees; and if the unjust sentence had not been executed, four degrees. In the case of the deputy of the court, there shall be another reduction, making, in the whole, five degrees. In the case of each of the assessors of the court, another reduction, making six degrees; and, lastly, in the case of the presiding officer, another, making, in the whole, seven degrees:—thus one case is exemplified in illustration of all others of complicated mitigation to be attended to in the infliction of punishment.

No clause.

SECTION XII.—*Officers of Government, when removed without being disgraced.*

Such officers of government as, after the expiration of the appointed period of their respective functions †, are either removed to another office, or cease to be employed, shall not lose or forfeit any portion of the rank they held by virtue of any of their former offices.

---

* The law in these respects is explained at large in Section CCCCIX.

† The civil appointments in China are generally conferred for three years, at the end of which the appointments may be renewed, but the changes (in the higher departments especially) are generally more rapid; so much so, that a new edition is found requisite every three months of the Imperial Court Kalendar, which is a list of the civil and military appointments of the empire, filling six closely printed duodecimo volumes.

The same rule shall be observed upon their obtaining leave to retire on account of age, infirmity, or the death of relations; and also generally in the case of the removal or dismissal of inferior officers of the minor departments or tribunals, unless the honorary rank of their families is, in consequence of the circumstances of the case, expressly taken away at the same time.

Likewise all persons who have received honorary distinctions on account of the elevation and employment of their children or descendants, shall be held equal to them in rank.—Wives shall forfeit the rank derived from their husbands, in the event of a divorce; but this circumstance shall not deprive them of any rank derived from their children, with whom, notwithstanding such divorce between the parents, the original connection shall be held to subsist.

When any of the persons aforesaid commit offences against the laws, they shall be tried, examined, and punished according to the same regulations as those officers of government who are actually in employ.

One clause.

SECTION XIII.—*Offences committed by Officers of Government previous to their Elevation.*

All officers of government who are convicted of offences committed previously, but charged against them subsequently, to their elevation or coming into office, shall be permitted to redeem themselves from punishment, provided the offence is of a public and not of a personal nature.

All officers of government who, after their promotion or removal, are convicted of any public offence, committed previous to such promotion or removal, shall be fined or degraded according to the law concerning such offences, when committed by officers of government,

provided

provided that the offences would not in ordinary cafes have been puniſhable more ſeverely than with 100 blows with the bamboo, but, otherwiſe, the offenders ſhall be puniſhed in ſuch caſes according to the laws reſpecting perſons in general: if the party, diſcovered to have committed any offence of a public nature while in office, had, previouſly to ſuch diſcovery, been totally degraded and diſmiſſed from any poſt under government, he ſhall, in general, be excuſed from any further puniſhment for ſuch implied malverſation; but if the offence concerns a falſe return of receipts of revenue, or a deficiency or concealment of any government property, the magiſtrate, in whoſe department it lies, ſhall thoroughly and promptly inveſtigate the affair, ſo far as may be neceſſary to aſcertain the amount of property, whether in kind or value, which the offender is bound to replace or refund into the hands of government. If it is an offence of a private and perſonal nature, the laws ſhall take their ordinary courſe.—With reſpect to the clerks of all magiſtrates, and of the ſeveral tribunals or departments of public affairs, committing offences of a public or a private nature, under any of the preceding circumſtances, the laws ſhall be executed in the uſual manner.

One Clauſe.

SECTION XIV.—*Degraded Officers of Government liable to the ſame Obligations as private Individuals.*

All civil and military officers of government who have been degraded and diſmiſſed for any offence of a private and perſonal nature, ſhall likewiſe be deprived of the patent of rank granted to their families. In like manner, all the prieſts of *Foe* or *Tao-ſe* *, who ſhall have been convicted and puniſhed for any offence, ſhall be deprived of their licence, and diveſted of their ſacred character.

* See Section XLII.

All such degraded persons shall be replaced in the class of soldiers or citizens, from whence they were originally taken, and be liable to the customary demands of personal service in either capacity *.

Two clauses.

SECTION XV. — *Relations of Exiles.*

All the wives of banished criminals shall follow them into exile: the parents, grand-parents, children, and grand-children of exiles, shall be at liberty to follow them or not, according to their own choice; and when they desire it, a new settlement shall be given to them, at the place of banishment.—If the offenders die previous to the expiration of the term of banishment, their relations who had accompanied them, if desirous of returning to their original place of settlement, shall be allowed to do so.

Nevertheless, the relations of persons banished in consequence of being implicated in charges of treason, rebellion, poisoning, magic, or murdering three or more persons in one family, shall not be suffered to return to their original places of settlement, agreeably to the provisions of this law.

Eighteen clauses.

---

* It is not to be understood from this law, that there is in China any peculiar and indelible distinction of cast, as in Hindostan, but merely that every individual shall be liable to demands of personal-service for public purposes, agreeably to the nature of his calling or profession.—This is more fully stated in a subsequent division of the code, intitled, " Enrolment of the People."

SECTION XVI. — *Extent of an Act of Grace or General Pardon* *.

From the benefit of any general act of grace or pardon those offenders shall be excluded, who have been convicted of any of the ten treasonable offences before mentioned; of murder; embezzlement of government stores; robbery or theft; wilful house-burning; unlawful grave-opening; bribery, whether the object be lawful or unlawful; forgery and fraud; incest, adultery, and the like; kidnapping; swindling; exciting to commit murder; designedly deviating from justice in the denunciation of punishment against offenders; conniving at, assisting in, negociating, or conveying a bribe for the purpose of procuring a breach of the laws; and in general in all cases where the laws have been transgressed by premeditation and design.

On the other hand, an act of grace shall relieve all those from punishment, who have offended accidentally and inadvertently; such as accidentally killing or wounding any individual; accidentally setting fire to houses or other property; unintentionally or inadvertently wasting and occasioning the loss of government property, on the part of persons having charge of it.

Secondly; An act of grace shall extend to all those who are liable to punishment merely by implication, and in consequence of the guilt of others.

Thirdly; An act of grace shall, further, relieve from punishment all those, who are chargeable with public offences, not because they have personally and designedly committed them, but because such offences either of commission or omission, had taken place within the limits of their jurisdiction or responsibility.

* An act of grace to the effect here stated, is usually passed at the accession of a new Emperor, and also in honour of some particular anniversaries.

In all thefe cafes, an act of grace fhall have the effect of an immediate and unconditional pardon *..

Particular acts of grace or pardon, in which the offenders are defcribed by name, or in which the punifhment of certain offences is mitigated only, are not fubject to any of the limitations hereby provided.

Nine claufes.

Section XVII. — *Effect of an Act of Grace on the Condition of Offenders in Exile.*

When any offender condemned to perpetual exile is overtaken on the journey by the official notice of a general act of grace or pardon, it cannot take effect with regard to him, if the period legally allowed for reaching the place of his deftination had expired; as for inftance, in the cafe of an individual fentenced to be banifhed to the diftance of 3000 *lee,* he is fuppofed to travel at the rate of 50 *lee per* day, and therefore he muft have received the act of grace before he had been fixty days upon the journey, in order to be entitled to the benefit of it.—Neverthelefs, if the prolongation of the time appears not to have been wilful, and the caufe is duly certified by the proper magiftrate, whether from the roads being impaffable, from ficknefs, robbers, or other cafualties, this objection in point of time fhall be over-ruled.

If the offender, moreover, fhould have made his efcape previoufly to the receipt of the act of grace, he fhall not afterwards be allowed the benefit of it, but if he dies before he is retaken, his family and relations

---

* The offences enumerated as pardonable by an act of grace, are alfo redeemable at other times by a fine, upon a petition being made to that effect.—This regulation is not included among the fundamental articles of the laws, but is inferted in a note to the firft fection, under the authority of an act iffued the eighth year of the late Emperor *Kienlung.*—The particulars of this act, and of fome of the more material claufes to the firft fection, have been inferted in the Appendix, No. V.

shall be allowed either to return to their original settlement, or to obtain a new establishment at the destined place of banishment, according to their choice.

After the offender condemned to perpetual banishment reaches his destination, he shall no longer be capable of taking the benefit of any act of grace or general pardon, even although his offence may not have been such as already stated to be generally unpardonable.

Those who had only received sentence of temporary banishment, may, on the contrary, always have the benefit of any general act of pardon; and by such act, whenever it occurs, the execution of the remaining part of the sentence of such persons shall be remitted.

Two clauses.

Section XVIII. — *Indulgence to Offenders for the Sake of their Parents.*

When any offender under sentence of death for an offence not excluded from the contingent benefit of an act of grace, shall have parents or grand-parents who are sick, infirm, or aged above seventy years, and who have no other male child or grand-child above the age of sixteen to support them, beside such capitally convicted offender, this circumstance, after having been investigated and ascertained by the magistrate of the district, shall be submitted to the consideration and decision of His Imperial Majesty.

Any offender who, under similar circumstances, had been condemned to undergo temporary or perpetual banishment, shall, instead thereof, receive 100 blows, and redeem himself from further punishment, by the payment of the customary fine.

Sixteen clauses.

Section XIX. — *Offences of Astronomers* *.

All the members of the astronomical board † at Pekin, and other persons recognised as astronomers, or observers of the heavenly bodies, when convicted of offences punishable with temporary or perpetual banishment, shall only suffer 100 blows, and redeem themselves from further punishment by the payment of the customary fine; by which indulgence they are enabled to return to their profession.

Nevertheless, this regulation shall not extend to any persons who are under sentence of banishment for treason or rebellion; for poisoning, murdering, wounding, robbing, stealing, killing by magic, or for any such offences as may subject the party to the punishment of being branded.

Two clauses.

* This designation must of course be understood in a qualified sense, adapted to the low state of the science at present in China, owing to the ignorance and superstition of its professors, and the neglect or indifference of the government towards it. Still, however, this section of the laws, containing an exception expressly in favour of astronomers, and for securing to the state the benefit of their labours, is an honourable tribute to the excellence and utility of the science, and a proof that its cultivation is still considered in China an object of national importance.—It is also to be observed, that under the patronage of the enlightened Emperor *Kang-hee* the European missionaries at Pekin printed and published in the Chinese character several useful works connected with this science, some of which, particularly a beautiful edition of a table of logarithms, are at present in the library of the Royal Society.

† According to the Chinese imperial kalendar, this board, usually termed by the missionaries the Tribunal of Mathematics, consists of seven members, among whom three are Europeans, and the rest Tartars or Chinese, including the president, who is always a prince of the blood. There are also other boards or departments subordinate to the principal one, consisting, according to the kalendar, of seventy-five persons in the whole, all of whom are either Tartars or Chinese; but although the names of only three of the missionaries appear on the official list, all those who are retained in the service of the Emperor at Pekin, are employed according to their capacities, and are decorated with the buttons denoting official rank.

Section XX. — *Offences of Artificers, Musicians, and Women.*

All artificers and musicians * who are convicted of offences punishable with temporary banishment, shall, in the first instance, suffer the customary number of blows with the bamboo; but instead of being subsequently sent into banishment, they shall be detained during the legal period of such banishment at the tribunal † of the magistrate of the district, and employed for that time in the service of government.

This law shall not be considered to extend to such persons as are sentenced to be branded, or to be banished, either for stealing, or for any other more serious offence.

Women convicted of offences punishable with the bamboo, shall be suffered to retain a single upper garment, while the punishment is inflicted, except in cases of adultery, and the like, when they shall be allowed the lower garment only.

Moreover, when the offences committed by women are such as are usually punished also with temporary or perpetual banishment, that part of the sentence shall be always remitted upon payment of the

---

* Notwithstanding the simplicity and unimproved state of the Chinese music, it appears from the annals of the empire, that the art was anciently held in high estimation, and even at present the musical board is under the government of a prince of the blood, and is ranked with the other public offices at the capital.

With regard to artificers, it is probably considered necessary to secure their services, by an exception in their favour, in order to carry on with less interruption the various public works, the laws relative to which form the concluding division of this Code.

† The word *tribunal* has been employed in various instances, in which some other term more generally received in our language, such as board, office, council, committee, department, &c. would at first sight appear preferable, but the Chinese term for a court of justice being likewise applied to public offices in general, and the forms being similar in all cases, notwithstanding the difference of the business transacted, the above expression has been chosen in this and most instances, not only as sanctioned by former writers on China, but as more generally applicable than any other.

customary fine; but the corporal punishment, to the extent of 100 blows, shall be inflicted.

Two clauses.

Section XXI. — *Offences of Persons already under Sentence of Punishment.*

When any person, after having been charged with an offence, commits another offence before the infliction of the punishment due to the former, the punishment of the greater offence shall always supersede that of the lesser.

But if the offender had been already sent into banishment for the former offence, the punishment of the latter offence shall be inflicted according to the law in the usual manner, except in the case of a second sentence of perpetual banishment, when the latter shall be commuted for a sentence of extra-service for four years.

In like manner, a second sentence of temporary banishment shall prolong the period of service, but it shall never exceed four years on the whole.

When, after sentence of banishment or of corporal punishment, a further offence punishable with blows of the bamboo is committed, a proportionate punishment shall be inflicted to the full extent directed by law, in the usual manner.

Ten clauses.

Section XXII. — *Indulgence to Offenders in Consideration of their Age, Youth, or Infirmities.*

Any offender whose age is not more than fifteen nor less than seventy years, or who is disabled by the loss of an eye or a limb, shall be allowed to redeem himself from any punishment less than capital,

capital, by the payment of the eſtabliſhed fine*, except in the caſe of perſons condemned to baniſhment as acceſſaries to the crimes of treaſon, rebellion, murder of three or more perſons in one family, or homicide by magic or poiſoning, upon all of which offenders the laws ſhall be ſtrictly executed.

Any offender whoſe age is not more than ten nor leſs than eighty years, or who is totally diſabled by the loſs of both eyes or two limbs, ſhall, when the crime is capital, but not amounting to treaſon, be recommended to the particular conſideration and deciſion of His Imperial Majeſty.

In all caſes of robbery and wounding, which are not puniſhable capitally, when any perſons under the aforeſaid diſabilities are implicated therein, they ſhall always be liberated on paying the eſtabliſhed fine: in other caſes of a leſs ſerious nature, they ſhall not be held reſponſible in any manner whatever.

Offenders whoſe age is not more than ſeven nor leſs than ninety years, ſhall not ſuffer puniſhment in any caſe, except in that of treaſon or rebellion; but any perſon who ſhall be convicted of having inſtructed ſuch child or aged perſon in the commiſſion of any offence, ſhall ſuffer the ſame puniſhment as he would have been liable to, if he had actually committed the offence himſelf.

Eight clauſes.

---

* The amount of the fine is ſtated in the preliminary part of the code, but is ſo ſmall in each caſe as to be merely nominal, though the form is retained, probably in order to diſtinguiſh theſe caſes from others, in which the offender is entirely pardoned.—Several inſtances of diſtinctions of a ſimilar kind might eaſily be quoted from our own laws, and probably from thoſe of moſt other nations.

There are other caſes in which the fines are conſiderable in the amount, and levied under altogether different circumſtances.—They are deſcribed in the note to Section I. and XVI. and in the Appendix, No. V.

Section XXIII. — *Plea of Age and Infirmities, how to be construed.*

Whoever is ascertained to be aged or infirm at the period of trial for any offence, shall be allowed the benefit of such plea, although he may not have attained the full age, or laboured under the alleged infirmity at the time the offence was committed.

In any case of temporary banishment, the offender, on attaining the age, or becoming infirm as aforesaid, shall, in like manner, become thereupon entitled to the privilege of redeeming himself from further punishment.—On the other hand, the privilege of youth may be pleaded when the age of the offender, at the time of committing the offence, did not exceed seven, ten, or fifteen years, whatever may be his age at the subsequent period of trial.

No clause.

Section XXIV. — *Restitution and Forfeiture of Goods.*

In any case of an illegal transfer of property, in which both parties are guilty, or when any person is convicted of possessing prohibited goods, such goods or property shall be forfeited to the state:—But when any article of property has been obtained from an individual by violence, injustice, extortion, or false pretences, it shall be restored to the owner.

In all cases wherein the offender is liable to be punished in his property as well as in his person, if a pardon arrives after the execution of corporal punishment, but before the confiscation has taken place, or before the fine has been levied, the latter part of the sentence shall be remitted.—If however the amount to be levied by fine or confiscation, is actually received and appropriated before the notice of the general act of pardon arrives; or if the offence is connected with circumstances of a treasonable nature, the general act of pardon shall, in that particular case, have no effect.

Moreover, in any case of an available pardon arriving before the execution of corporal punishment, the property sequestrated on account of government, if not specifically appropriated, shall be restored, and the family of the offender, who may have been likewise held bound to government, shall be released from their responsibility.

If the offence arises from the unlawful possession of any property, and the property, the restitution of which is consequently claimed by government or by an individual, is still in existence, it shall be duly transferred, and, when of a productive nature, with all its produce. If, however, the unlawful possessor had wasted it, and afterwards died, his heirs shall not be compelled to make up the deficiency.

When the offence arises from circumstances of a different description, the fine shall be strictly levied, unless it be the wages of labour, in which case it shall be remitted.

In estimating the amount of the property and of the charges which are to be made good by the offender, the several articles shall be rated at the price they bore at the time and place in which they were unlawfully acquired.

The wages of labour shall be estimated at 8 *fen* 5 *lee* and 5 *hao**, for each man *per* day: the charges for the hire of horses, cattle, carriages, boats, and similar articles, shall be fixed at the current rate at the time and place in which such charges were incurred; provided always, that the total charge for the hire of any article, shall not, in any case, exceed its full value.

---

* That is to say, 0855 decimal parts of a *leang* or Chinese ounce of silver, whose estimated value is 6s. 8d. sterling. According to this computation, the wages of labour will be reckoned at rather less than seven-pence *per* day; it is probable however, that this is not an invariable rule, but subject to alteration at different periods according to circumstances.

The exact amount of the gold and silver * due to government, or to the individual owner, shall be made good agreeably to the original sums, as stated in the information, whatever part of such orignal sum may have been disposed of or wasted.

Eighteen clauses.

Section XXV. — *Offenders surrendering voluntarily.*

Whoever, having committed an offence, surrenders himself voluntarily, and acknowledges his guilt to a magistrate, before it is otherwise discovered, shall be freely pardoned; but all claims upon his property, on the part of government or of individuals, shall nevertheless be duly liquidated.

Moreover, if an offender, after having been charged with any particular offence, shall confess himself guilty of another and a greater offence before the magistrate; or in general, if, in the course of the investigation of the circumstances of any one alleged offence, it shall be discovered, without the application of torture, that the accused is guilty of other offences, he shall still only suffer punishment in proportion to the offence originally charged against him.

If the offender makes a timely confession of his guilt as aforesaid, through the intervention of another person, or if he is accused by, and through the ill-will of, his junior relations or dependants, he shall, in all cases not expressly excepted, receive full pardon.

If the voluntary confession of the offender is inaccurate and imperfect, he shall be liable to punishment for as much of the offence committed by him, as he had endeavoured to conceal; but in cases of a capital nature, the punishment shall always, upon making any timely confession whatever, be reduced one degree.

* The general currency in China is restricted to copper, but all accounts are kept in ounces, and the decimal parts of ounces, of silver.

If an offender does not confess his guilt until he is informed that a charge is prepared to be laid against him, or if he previously absconds, or takes refuge out of the empire, his punishment shall not be entirely remitted, but mitigated two degrees.

In all cases also of fugitives and deserters returning to their original places of abode, the punishment to which they are liable by law shall be mitigated no more than two degrees.

The remission of punishment, upon a timely and voluntary confession of guilt, shall not be allowed in those cases of injury to the person or property which cannot be repaired by restitution or compensation, or when the offence was known to the officers of justice while the offender was concealed, or in cases of clandestinely passing public barriers.

If the robber, thief, or swindler, repenting of his conduct, restores the plunder to the persons from whom he took it, or if the corrupt officer restores the amount of the bribe to the person from whom it was received, this restitution shall be deemed equal to a confession at a legal tribunal, and in the same degree entitle the offender to pardon.

If, having notice of an information intended to be laid against him, the offender then goes to the owner of the property, and makes restitution, he shall only be entitled to a mitigation of the punishment to the extent of two degrees; but if a repentant thief or robber is fortunate enough to be the means of bringing to justice his accomplices, he shall receive full pardon, and moreover be entitled to the reward that may have been offered for the discovery of such offenders. If, however, he should ever commit a second offence, the above privileges cannot be allowed in that or in any subsequent instance.

Eleven clauses.

Section XXVI. — *Offenders charged with several Offences.*

When any person is convicted of two or more offences, all the offences shall be estimated together, and punishment inflicted conformably to the extent of the criminality of the principal charge: the punishment of all the rest shall be considered as included in that of the first.—If the several offences are charged at different times, and the punishment of the first of the charges has been already inflicted, the latter charges shall not subject the offender to further punishment, unless of a more serious nature than the former, in which case the amount only of the difference between the legal punishments shall be inflicted.

In each separate case, however, the law shall be fully executed so far as respects the restitution of property to individuals, or the forfeiture of it to government; and also with respect to the branding of the offender, and his degradation from office.

No clause.

Section XXVII. — *Proceedings in Cases where all the Parties to an Offence have escaped.*

When all the parties to any offence have effected their escape from justice, if any individual amongst them surrenders voluntarily, and also delivers into custody one other more guilty than himself; or if, when the guilt is equal, the larger porportion of the party are delivered up by the smaller, those who thus voluntarily surrender themselves shall be pardoned, except in cases of killing, of wounding, and of criminal intercourse between the sexes.—When several persons are implicated in the guilt of one, who afterwards dies in prison, the punishment of those who are guilty by implication only, shall be thereupon reduced two degrees.

Moreover, when any offender obtains a remiſſion or mitigation of his puniſhment, or permiſſion to redeem himſelf from the ſame by a fine, either in conſequence of a voluntary ſurrender and confeſſion, by a general act of grace, or by a ſpecial edict of the Emperor in his favour, in all ſuch caſes the ſeveral perſons who may have become liable to puniſhment by implication in his offence, ſhall be pardoned or favoured to the ſame extent.

No clauſe.

Section XXVIII.—*Offences of Members of Public Departments and Tribunals committed in their official Capacity.*

In all caſes of officers of government aſſociated in one department or tribunal, and committing offences againſt the laws as a public body, by falſe or erroneous deciſions, and inveſtigations, the clerk of the department or tribunal ſhall be puniſhed as the principal offender; the puniſhment of the ſeveral deputies, or executive officers, ſhall be leſs by one degree, that of the aſſeſſors leſs by another degree, and that of the preſiding magiſtrate leſs by a third degree *.

---

* In tranſlating the titles of the conſtituent officers of a Chineſe tribunal or public board, it was impoſſible to find terms that were not in ſome point of view exceptionable, but thoſe that have been choſen will ſhew, that the arrangement is analogous to that adopted in ſuch of our own colonial governments, as are adminiſtered by a preſident, members of council, ſecretaries, and clerks. What is the moſt remarkable in this reſpect in China, is that the loweſt officer incurs the greateſt ſhare of the reſponſibility; but this being confined to offences by implication only, it will not appear ſo extraordinary that, when the meaſures or the deciſions of a board or tribunal are found to be reprehenſible without any offence being directly imputable to a particular individual, that member of the tribunal ſhould be ſubjected to the largeſt ſhare of the puniſhment, by whoſe ſuggeſtion and inſtrumentality, the buſineſs had been conducted, and whoſe inferior ſtation might be ſuppoſed to have enabled him to gain a more accurate knowledge of the circumſtances upon which the juſtice or injuſtice of the deciſion depended, than was likely to have been in the power of his ſuperiors.

Although there should be a vacancy in, or a want of any of the intermediate stations, the reduction of the punishment shall always take effect to the same extent *.

If in the case of any decision of a tribunal contrary to the laws, only one member of the court was guilty of the deviation from justice, knowingly and intentionally, his particular offence being of a personal nature shall be punished as such; while the others, being only guilty of an erroneous judgment, shall be punished more leniently, and according to the gradations prescribed above.

If an inferior tribunal reports its erroneous judgment to a superior, which superior, neglecting to examine and discover the error, confirms the same, the members of the superior tribunal shall be respectively liable to punishment less by two degrees than those of the inferior tribunal.

On the other hand, when a superior tribunal communicates its erroneous judgment to an inferior tribunal, if the members of the latter neglect to examine the same, and, having failed to discover the error, confirm it by their proceedings, they also shall be liable to punishment, though under a proportionate mitigation, in the case of each individual, to the extent of three degrees.

In all these cases, the scale of the punishments incurred shall commence with the clerks of the respective courts.

No clause.

SECTION XXIX.—*Errors and Failures in public Proceedings.*

Upon any error or failure in the public proceedings of an officer of government, if he discovers and corrects, or remedies the same, he shall be pardoned.—Also, in the case of error or failure in the proceed-

---

* As for instance; the presiding magistrates of these public boards or tribunals, in which from custom or accident, there may not be any assessors or deputies, shall, in every case of imputed delinquency, be punished three degrees less than the clerks, in the same manner as in those boards or tribunals which are constituted in the regular way.

ings of a public office or tribunal, if any one member discovers so as to correct or remedy the same, all the members shall obtain pardon. If however such error consists in an aggravation of the sentence of the law, and is not discovered until after the execution thereof, they cannot be entirely pardoned, but the punishment shall be mitigated three degrees.—If, on the other hand, the error consists in pronouncing too lenient a sentence, the parties shall be pardoned, although the error is not discovered until after the execution of the sentence, provided they do themselves discover and rectify their error.

An extraordinary delay in issuing public orders from any tribunal of justice or other public department, renders all the members liable to punishment; but if any one of them voluntarily interposes, and prevents any further delay from taking place, all the magistrates or officers of that tribunal or department shall be pardoned; but the clerk shall incur the full punishment, except he had himself acknowledged the impropriety of the delay which had taken place, and interposed to prevent its continuance; in which case, his punishment shall be reduced two degrees.

Five days shall be allowed to dispatch business of small importance; ten days for business of ordinary importance; and twenty days for business of high importance.

No clause.

SECTION XXX.—*Distinction between Principals and Accessaries.*

When several persons are parties to one offence, the original contriver of it shall be held to be the principal, and as such suffer the punishment required by the laws, in its full extent: the rest who followed, and also contributed to the perpetration thereof, shall suffer the punishment next in degree, under the denomination of accessaries.—When the parties to an offence are members of one family, the senior and chief member of that family shall alone be punishable; but if he be upwards of eighty years of age, or totally disabled by his infirmities, the punishment shall fall upon the next in succession.

When, however, the offence is a direct injury to the perfon or property of any indvidual, the feveral individuals fhall, as in all ordinary cafes, be punifhed as principals or acceffaries in the manner previoufly ftated.

When the relative fituation of the parties engaged in the commiffion of one offence, creates a difference in their liability to punifhment, the principals fhall fuffer as principals in the offence committed by themfelves, but the acceffaries fhall be punifhed as acceffaries in the offence of which they would themfelves have been guilty, had they been in the place of the principal. As for inftance: if a man engages a ftranger to ftrike his elder brother — the younger brother fhall be punifhed with ninety blows, and two years and a half banifhment, for the offence of ftriking his elder; but the ftranger fhall be only punifhed with twenty blows, as in common cafes of an affault.—Alfo, if a younger relation introduces a ftranger to fteal to the amount of ten *leang* or ounces of filver of the family property, he fhall only be punifhed as wafting, or difpofing of without leave, the family property to that extent, whereas the ftranger fhall be punifhed as in common cafes of theft.

When the law does not exprefsly declare, that the punifhment fhall be inflicted alike on all parties concerned, it is to be underftood, that one only is to fuffer as a principal, and the reft as acceffaries.— Neverthelefs, in all cafes of attempting to enter any of the imperial palaces, or to pafs the public barriers clandeftinely; avoiding the ftated and lawful fervices to government; committing adultery, and other offences of the fame nature; the parties fhall fuffer punifhment individually without any diftinction between principals and acceffaries, although the terms exprefsly including all parties equally, fhould be omitted.

One claufe.

SECTION XXXI. — *Proceedings relative to Offenders who have absconded.*

When, of two persons who have been parties to the perpetration of an offence, one has absconded, and the other, who is in custody, declares the former to have been the principal offender, and himself only an accessary, if there is no evidence to disprove the assertion, he shall be punished forthwith as an accessary. — If the offender who had absconded is afterwards taken, and thereupon contends that, on the contrary, the other was the principal offender, the matter shall be diligently investigated; and if the latter assertion is substantiated, the offender first seized shall suffer the remainder of the punishment due to him as a principal, and the rest shall each suffer according to the law, as accessaries.

If, after an offence is known to have been perpetrated, it can be proved by sufficient testimony, whether those who, being known to be implicated therein and, having absconded, are still at large, were principals or accessaries, it shall not be deemed requisite to confront all the offenders together, and they may therefore be tried and punished, as they are successively apprehended.

Four clauses.

SECTION XXXII. — *Relations mutually assisting and concealing each other*.*

All relations connected in the first and second degree and living under the same roof, maternal grand-parents and their grandchildren, fathers and mothers-in-law, sons and daughters-in-law, grandchildren's wives, husbands' brothers and brothers' wives, when mu-

* Concerning the degrees of consanguinity as distinguished by the Chinese, see the Table of Degrees of Mourning in the Preliminary Part of the Code, and also the Appendix thereto, No. IV.

tually affifting each other, and concealing the offences, one of another, and moreover, flaves and hired fervants affifting their mafters and concealing their offences, fhall not, in any fuch cafes, be punifhable for fo doing.

In like manner, though they fhould inform their relations of the meafures adopted for their apprehenfion, and enable them to conceal themfelves, and finally to effect their efcape, they fhall ftill be held innocent.

When relations in the third and fourth degrees affift and protect each other from punifhment in the manner here defcribed, they fhall for fuch conduct be liable to punifhment, but only in a proportion of three degrees lefs than would have been inflicted on ftrangers under the fame circumftances.

The fame offences committed by relations in ftill more remote degrees of kindred, fhall be punifhed within one degree of the extent of the punifhment inflicted in ordinary cafes.—Neverthelefs, none of the provifions of this law in mitigation or remiffion of the punifhment of harbouring, concealing, and affifting relations, fhall be pleaded, or have any effect, in cafes of high treafon or rebellion.

One claufe.

Section XXXIII.—*Punifhment of Deferters.*

When, in the frontier towns and other places of ftrength, any of the foldiers are difcovered to have formed a defign to defert and join the enemy, their commanding officer fhall take them into cuftody, and bring them for trial before his own immediate fuperior, who, having ftrictly inveftigated the charges, and gone through the evidence, fhall report the fame to the viceroy and fub-viceroy of the province: when the latter magiftrates have finally afcertained that there has been no partiality nor injuftice in the cafe, they fhall proceed, without further delay, to carry the sentence of the law into effect, and afterwards submit the whole of the proceedings to His Imperial Majesty.

When the army is in the field, and any of the soldiers openly attempt to desert, if they can be seized immediately and put to death, it shall be lawful to do so, in consideration of the urgency of the case; the provisions of this law may therefore, under such circumstances, be so far dispensed with, but it is still requisite to report faithfully all such transactions to the Emperor.

No clause.

SECTION XXXIV. — *Offences committed by Foreigners* *.

In general, all foreigners who come to submit themselves to the government of the empire, shall, when guilty of offences, be tried and sentenced according to the established laws.

The particular decisions however of the tribunal *Lee-fan-Yuen* † shall

---

* This section of the code has been expressly quoted by the provincial government of Canton, and applied to the case of foreigners residing there and at Macao for the purposes of trade. The laws of China have never, however, been attempted to be enforced against those foreigners, except with considerable allowances in their favour, although, on the other hand, they are restricted and circumscribed in such a manner that a transgression on their part of any specific article of the laws, can scarcely occur; at least not without, at the same time, implicating and involving in their guilt some of the natives, who thus, in most cases, become the principal victims of offended justice.—The situation of Europeans in China is certainly by no means so satisfactory on the whole as might be desired, or even as it may be reasonably expected to become in the progress of time; unless some untoward circumstance should occur to check the gradual course of improvement; it must be admitted, however, that the extreme contrariety of manners, habits, and language, renders some such arrangement, as that now subsisting for the regulation of the intercourse between the Europeans and the natives, absolutely indispensable, as well as conducive to the interests of both parties.—A translation of some Chinese official documents of a recent date, illustrative of the above remarks, is inserted in the Appendix, No. XI.

† This tribunal might be styled the office or department for foreign affairs, but its chief concern is with the tributary and the subject states of Tartary.

be guided according to regulations framed for the government of the Mongol tribes.

Three clauses.

SECTION XXXV. — *Proceedings in Cases where the Laws appear contradictory.*

When the law upon any particular case appears to differ from the general laws contained in this division of the code, the magistrate shall always decide according to the former, in preference to the latter. — When the offence, of which an individual is convicted according to one law, is at the same time in itself an evidence of designs, which are, by another law, more severely punishable than the act itself, sentence upon such an individual shall be pronounced and executed according to the latter instead of the former law. — If an offence is committed under aggravating circumstances, of which the offender himself is ignorant at the time, he shall be sentenced to suffer no more than the punishment due by law in ordinary cases.

As for instance: if a nephew, being educated at a distance from his uncle, and not knowing his person, strikes him in an affray, it shall be judged to be only an ordinary case of assault: — or if a thief steals any articles which are sacred or imperial, without knowing them to be so, it shall be adjudged to be an ordinary instance of theft, and not sacrilege. On the other hand, if the offence is committed under palliating circumstances, which legally reduce the amount of the punishment, the offender shall, at all events, have the full advantage thereof; as for instance, when a father strikes a person whom he supposes to be a stranger, but who was in fact his son.

No clause.

SECTION XXXVI. — *Rules relative to the Increase and Diminution of Punishments.*

When the sentence of the law is said to be increased, it is implied, that the punishment shall be inflicted more severely:—As for instance: a sentence of forty blows increased one degree, becomes a sentence of fifty blows: a sentence of one hundred blows increased one degree, becomes a sentence of sixty blows and one year's banishment; the next degree is seventy blows, and one year and a half's banishment:—a sentence of one hundred blows and three years banishment, when raised one degree, implies a sentence of one hundred blows, and perpetual banishment to the distance of 2000 *lee*; and when raised another degree, a sentence of one hundred blows, and perpetual banishment to the distance of 2500 *lee*.

When the sentence of the law is said to be diminished, it is implied that the punishment is mitigated: As for instance—a sentence of fifty blows diminished one degree is a sentence of forty blows:—one of sixty blows and one year's banishment diminished one degree, is one of one hundred blows: one of one hundred blows and three years banishment, diminished one degree, is one of ninety blows and two years and a half's banishment.

In the reduction of punishments, the two modes of inflicting death, and three kinds of perpetual banishment, shall be estimated in each case as only a single degree:—As for instance; if a sentence of capital punishment by strangling, or decollation, is mitigated one degree, the offender shall be banished perpetually to the distance of 3000 *lee*; if two degrees, he shall be banished for three years only.—In like manner, any sentence of perpetual banishment, when reduced one degree, shall only subject the offender to banishment for three years.

When the punishment is increased a degree in a specific case, the full extent required by law must be proved to warrant the same: as for instance; the increased punishment for bribery amounting to forty

leang

leang or ounces of silver, cannot be inflicted if the amount did not exceed thirty-nine ounces and ninety-nine decimal parts.

Moreover, whatever number of degrees the punishment is directed to be increased in certain cases, it cannot be rendered capital by construction, unless so especially provided; and if it is provided that, in certain cases, the offender shall be punished capitally, either by strangling or decollation, he must be executed in the manner stated, and not otherwise, under any circumstances of aggravation of the offence.

Three clauses.

Section XXXVII.—*Extent of the Privilege and Distinction of Imperial Rank.*

Whatever is stated in the laws concerning Imperial equipage, the Imperial presence, and the like, shall be considered to extend not only to the Emperor, but also to the Empress Consort, Empress Mother, and Empress Grandmother.—Also, all orders, instructions, and acts of any kind, termed Imperial, shall be understood to comprehend, beside those of the Emperor himself, those of the Empress Mother and Empress Grandmother, and of the Imperial Prince appointed to the succession *.

No clause.

Section XXXVIII.—*Relations in the first Degree.*

Whatever is declared in the laws to concern relations in the first degree, grand-parents or grand-children, shall likewise be understood to extend equally to great-grand-parents, and great-great-grand-parents,

* The last distinction of rank can only have been stated hypothetically, as such a nomination has never taken place under the present dynasty, except upon the resignation, or by the testamentary direction of the Emperor, published after his decease. One of the charges against the late and favourite minister *Ho-chung-tong*, was that of his having divulged to the present Emperor, previous to his elevation, the secret of the preference intended to be shewn him by his imperial father.

great

great-grand-children, and great-great grand-children, except in cases of constructive crimes, when the law shall be taken literally.

Also, the father's principal wife*, the father's wife substituted in the place of the principal wife after her death, the father's wife substituted in the place of the natural mother upon her death, and the adopted mother, shall all hold equal rank with the natural mother, and be understood to be referred to, in all laws in which the mother of the party concerned is only stated generally, except in the case of such mother having been divorced, or in the case of her killing, or attempting to kill, such son-in-law.

Also, except in cases of constructive offences, whatever the law states relative to the sons, shall be applicable to the daughters also.

No clause.

Section XXXIX. — *Participators in Offences* †.

Those, whom the law declares to be considered as participators in an offence, shall suffer the punishment incurred by it, without however including any circumstances of aggravation, which are personally applicable to the principal offender only; and in the case of capital offences, the participators in the offence shall only receive one hundred blows, and suffer perpetual banishment to the distance of 3000 *lee*: — they shall moreover not be liable to be branded for their participation in any offence so punishable.

In cases however of bribery and wilful connivance, all participators in the crime shall participate in the punishment, in its full extent,

---

* For an illustration of the legal distinction between the principal and inferior wives, see the division of the code entitled *Marriage*.

† This, as well as some other sections of the preliminary division of the code, are not so much declaratory of the law, as explanatory of technical phraseology, but being included among the fundamental articles, they could not, consistently with the general plan be omitted.

especially when the offence amounts to an act of treason or rebellion:—for wilful connivance in the latter crimes, the laws have expressly provided a particular punishment.

When it is declared that an offence shall be considered as an act of bribery, or theft, punishment shall follow according to the laws relating thereto, except that the branding shall not be inflicted, and the capital part of the sentence mitigated to perpetual banishment.—When, however, the case is referred directly to those laws, they shall be executed against the offenders in their full extent.

Section XL. — *Responsible Superintendants.*

All officers of government are considered by law to be the responsible superintendants of such charges and departments of public affairs and public justice, as may be placed under their authority and controul.—All those likewise, who have particular offices and charges in places and countries under the jurisdiction of others, and who have the particular government of treasuries, granaries, and prisons, even those who have only temporary and delegated authority therein, without being regularly established in such governments and appointments, shall, in every case, be considered the responsible superintendants within the extent of their offices.

No clause.

Section XLI. — *Division of Time.*

A day shall be considered to have elapsed when the hundred divisions are completed—(at present, according to the Imperial Almanac, the day consists of ninety-six divisions)*.—A day's work or labour shall, however, be computed only from the rising to the setting of the sun.

* This observation is taken from a note in the original.

A legal year shall consist of 360 days complete *, but a man's age shall be computed according to the number of years of the † cycle elapsed since his name and birth were recorded in the public ‡ register.

When the law speaks of several persons, three at least are to be understood; but when simply stating the circumstance of an agreement or combination, any number not less than two may be implied.

No clause.

SECTION XLII.—*Laws relative to the Priesthood.*

The *Tao-sse* and *Niu-quan* §, shall be subject in all cases to the established laws concerning the priesthood of both orders, and both sexes; the right and authority of the masters and superiors, and the duty of submission and subordination on the part of those who are legally ad-

---

* The civil year in China ordinarily consists of no more than 354 days, or twelve lunations, but an intercalary month is introduced as often as may be necessary to bring the commencement of every year to the second new moon after each preceding winter solstice.

† The most usual date employed by the Chinese, is the year of the reigning Emperor; but they have likewise, from a remote period of antiquity, computed time by cycles of 60 years, each year of such period being distinguished with a particular name, formed by a binary combination of ten initial, and twelve final, characters.

‡ As this mode of computation, which is generally in use among the Chinese, is not fully explained in the text, it may be proper just to point out its peculiar inaccuracy, which consists in its having always the effect of representing the age of the individual greater than it is in reality.—Thus a child born the last day of the year, will, on the following day, be described as two years old, being considered to have lived in two of the years in the cycle.

§ The priests and priestesses thus designated, and also those of *Foe*, have usually been described under the names of Bonzes and Bonzesses, which terms have probably been taken from the Japanese language, but the religion of the state in China cannot properly be said to have any priests whatever attached to its service, the Emperor and his ordinary magistrates always officiating in the sacred rites by law established, as in the ritual division of the code is particularly explained. The religious orders adverted to in this section are tolerated and regulated by government, but derive their support entirely from their own funds, or from occasional voluntary contributions.

mitted

mitted as apprentices or difciples, fhall be the fame as that eftablifhed between uncles and nephews in all ordinary cafes.

No claufe.

SECTION XLIII. — *Execution of New Laws.*

All laws, characterifed as, and intended to become, fundamental, fhall, in general, take effect and be in full force from the day on which they are publifhed, and every tranfaction fhall be adjudged according to the moft recent laws, although fuch tranfaction fhould have occurred previous to their promulgation. — Occafional ftatutes, which are modifications of the law, fhall not however operate in thofe cafes which were antecedent to their enactment; and when any period of days or years is affigned for the commencement of their operation, fuch period fhall be ftrictly obferved, except only in regard to ftatutes providing a mitigation of the ordinary punifhments, which fhall be conftrued to be immediately in force, in all cafes.

One claufe.

SECTION XLIV.—*Determination of Cafes not provided for by any exifting Law.*

From the impracticability of providing for every poffible contingency, there may be cafes to which no laws or ftatutes are precifely applicable; fuch cafes may then be determined, by an accurate comparifon with others which are already provided for, and which approach moft nearly to thofe under inveftigation, in order to afcertain afterwards to what extent an aggravation or mitigation of the punifhment would be equitable.

A provifional fentence conformable thereto fhall be laid before the fuperior magiftrates, and after receiving their approbation, be fubmitted to the Emperor's final decision.—Any erroneous judgment which may be pronounced in consequence of adopting a more summary mode of proceeding, in cases of a doubtful nature, shall be punished as a wilful deviation from justice.

One clause.

SECTION XLV.—*Place of temporary and perpetual Banishment.*

All persons sentenced to undergo temporary banishment, shall be removed to the distance of at least 500 *lee* from the place of their nativity, for the period specified in their sentence; which period shall be computed to commence from their arrival at the place of banishment, and from thence, at the moment the period expires, they shall be at liberty to depart.

The place of perpetual banishment shall likewise be regulated according to the distance prescribed in the sentence pronounced on the offender, and a permanent settlement shall be allowed him on such coasts, islands, or deserted and uncultivated districts, as circumstances may render most eligible for the purpose.—Those who are sentenced to the mitigated perpetual banishment, shall be settled at the distance of 1000 *lee* from the place of their nativity.—Temporary banishment is of five kinds, but in no case subjects the offender to be sent out of his native province.

Perpetual banishment is of three kinds, and, conformably to the sentence, the offender shall be banished to the nearer or more remote parts of the following provinces:

From		to	
	Pe-che-lee		Shen-see
	Kiang-nan		Shen-see
	Gan-wey		Shan-tung
	Shan-tung		Che-kiang
	Shan-see		Shen-see

From	Ho-nan	to	Che-kiang
	Shen-fee		Shan-tung
	Kan-foo		Se-chuen
	Che-kiang		Shan-tung
	Kiang-fee		Quang-fee
	Hou-pe		Shan-tung
	Hou-nan		Se-chuen
	Fo-kien		Quang-tung
	Quang-tung		Fo-kien
	Quang-fee		Quang-tung
	Se-chuen		Quang-fee
	Quei-cheu		Se-chuen
	Yun-nan		Se-chuen.

Forty-seven clauses.

Section XLVI.—*Place of extraordinary or military Banishment*.*

The several degrees of extraordinary or military banishment, are, the ordinary or 2000 *lee*; the distant or 2500 *lee*; the more distant or 3000 *lee*, and the most distant or 4000 *lee*; and conformably to the sentence, the offenders shall be perpetually banished in the manner hereafter provided; the settlement of those banished from Pekin being determined by the tribunal for military affairs, and of those banished

* Beside the several degrees of banishment described in this and the preceding section, a more severe punishment, of a similar description, has been introduced since the original formation of the code by the present dynasty, and amounts to transportation to, and slavery for life at, *Elee*, a government station in a remote province of Tartary, annexed by the late Emperor *Kien-long*, to the dominions of China. This species of punishment is either inflicted as a mitigation of the sentence in certain capital cases, or in aggravation of the punishment of crimes, whose frequency had increased, as stated in the Emperor *Kaung-hee's* introductory preface.—The numerous supplementary clauses annexed to the preceding section describe these regulations in detail.

from the provinces, by the different viceroys and fub-viceroys; due information and notice fhall alfo be given in the latter cafe to the faid tribunal, or fupreme board for military affairs, upon each occafion. The banifhment fhall, according to the fentence, be adjudged to one or other of the following provinces *:

From Pe-che-lee to Shan-tung, or Shan-fee, or Kiang-nan, or Hou-quang, or Shen-fee, or Che-kiang, or Kiang-fee, or Quang-tung.

From Kiang-nan to Hou-quang, or Shan-tung, or Che-kiang, or Shen-fee, or Che-lee, or Shan-fee, or Quang-tung.

From Shan-tung, to Teng-cheou-foo, or Che-lee, or Kiang-nan, or Shan-fee, or Che-kiang, or Shen-fee, or Quang-tung.

From Shan-fee to Shan-tung, or Kiang-nan, or Shen-fee, or Hou-quang, or Che-kiang, or Kiang-fee, or Quang-tung.

From Ho-nan to Shan-tung, or Shen-fee, or Hou-quang, or Che-lee, or Kian-nan, or Shen-fee, or Che-kiang, or Quang-tung.

From Shen-fee to Ning-hia-wey, or Ho-cheu-wey; or Che-lee, or Shan-fee, or Sing-tu-fee, or Shan-tung, or Hou-quang, or Kiang-nan, or Quang-tung.

From Che-kiang to Kiang-nan, or Shan-tung, or Hou-quang, or Che-lee, or Shan-fee, or Shen-fee, or Quang-tung.

From Kiang-fee to Shan-tung, or Che-kiang, or Hou-quang, or Quang-tung, or Che-lee, or Shan-fee, or Shen-fee, or Se-chuen.

From Hou-quang to Nang-yang-foo, or Kiang-fee, or Che-kiang, or Se-chuen, or Kiang-nan, or Shan-fee, or Shen-fee, or Che-lee, or Quang-tung.

* The enumeration which is here given of provinces and diftricts in China, may feem very unimportant, but being printed in the original Chinefe work, as a part of the fundamental law, it has been retained in its place, in conformity to the general rule of felection which the tranflator has prefcribed to himfelf, conceiving it to be (as already ftated in another place) the leaft liable to objection.

From Fo-kien to Che-kiang, or Kiang-fee, or Kiang-nan, or Quang-tung, or Hou-quang, or Shan-tung, or Che-lee, or Se-chuen.

From Quang-tung to Chao-cheu-foo, or Hou-quang, or Shan-fee, or Se-chuen, or Shan-tung.

From Quang-fee to Kiang-fee, or Hou-quang, or Se-chuen, or Shan-fee, or Shen-fee, or Che-kiang, or Quang-tung.

From Se-chuen to Yue-hee-wey, or Shen-fee, or Hou-quang, or Kiang-fee, or Shan-fee, or Che-kiang, or Quang-tung.

From Que-cheu to Se-chuen, or Kiang-fee, or Hou-quang, or Shen-fee, or Kiang-nan, or Che-kiang, or Shan-fee, or Quang-tung.

From Yun-nan to Quang-tung, or Hou-quang, or Shen-fee, or Kiang-fee.

Two claufes.

END OF THE FIRST DIVISION.

SECOND DIVISION,

Civil Laws *.

BOOK I.
SYSTEM OF GOVERNMENT.

SECTION XLVII. — *Hereditary Succeſſion* †.

EVERY civil and military officer of government, whoſe rank and titles are hereditary, ſhall be ſucceeded in them by his eldeſt ſon born of his principal wife, or by ſuch eldeſt ſon's ſurviving legal repreſentative, choſen according to the general rule here provided.

If ſuch eldeſt ſon, and all thoſe who might legally have repreſented him are deceaſed, or incapacitated to ſucceed to the inheritance by incurable illneſs or miſconduct, the ſon next in age, or his ſurviving legal repreſentative choſen as aforeſaid, ſhall be called to the ſucceſſion.

When there are neither any ſons, nor any legal repreſentatives of ſuch ſons, by the principal wife, capable of ſucceeding, the ſeveral ſons of the other wives, and their legal repreſentatives, ſhall be entitled thereto according to ſeniority; upon failure of whom, the ſuc-

---

* Laws relating to the adminiſtration of the civil government.

† Although titles deſcendible to the heirs male are occaſionally conferred in China by the Emperor, as a reward for eminent ſervices, they are reſumable by the Crown at pleaſure, and the poſſeſſors of them enjoy few, if any, excluſive privileges.—None of the hereditary dignities which exiſted previous to the Tartar conqueſt in 1644, appear to have been recognized by the preſent government, except that attached to the family of Confucius, whoſe real or ſuppoſed deſcendants are at this day diſtinguiſhed with peculiar titles of honour, and maintained at the public expence.

cession shall lastly devolve upon the sons of the younger brothers, taken in the order already mentioned. — Whoever enters upon the succession to an hereditary dignity, in violation of the order prescribed by this law, shall be punished for such offence with 100 blows and three years banishment.

When the claim of a son or grandson to the succession has been duly authenticated by the proper magistrate, it must be reported to the council of state, through which channel it will be submitted to the Emperor for ratification, and also for the authority to continue to the heir the emolument which may have been annexed to the dignity. —If the heir is a minor, he shall not be enrolled for public service at Court, until he attains the age of eighteen years.

When the family title is extinct for want of lineal male heirs to succeed to the hereditary dignities, the widow of the last possessor shall receive the emoluments annexed thereto, during her life.

If a stranger's child is educated and brought up in a family of rank, in order, by deceiving the magistrates, to obtain the inheritance, such supposititious heir shall receive 100 blows, and be sent into remote banishment; the emoluments annexed to the rank shall also cease from the time that such fraudulent intention was discovered. — Whoever instructs and instigates others to commit this offence, shall suffer the same punishment.

Those magistrates also, who connive at the fraud, and ratify the succession, shall be equally punished, as participating in the offence; but if really ignorant of the illegality of the transaction, they shall be excused.

If convicted at the same time of bribery, to such an extent as, according to law, is more severely punishable, the punishment of the greater offence shall, as in other cases, supersede that of the lesser.

Fifteen clauses.

Section XLVIII.—*Great Officers of State not authorized to confer Appointments* *.

All the appointments and removals of officers, whether civil or military, shall depend solely upon the authority of the Emperor.—If any great officer of state presumes to confer any appointment upon his own authority, he shall suffer death by being beheaded, after remaining in prison the usual time.

It is likewise hereby prohibited to appoint or remove any relations of the great officers of state, without an express order from the Emperor for that purpose, and a breach of this regulation shall expose the offender to the same punishment as that of the preceding.

Any officer of government employed at court, and receiving the Emperor's personal commands to undertake the performance of any service, or to resign or change his employment, whether the object be near or remote, if he make any excuse for not complying therewith, he shall receive 100 blows, and be rendered incapable of holding any office under government thenceforward †.

One clause.

---

* The viceroys and commanders-in-chief of provinces are constantly in the habit of filling up the various civil and military appointments under their respective jurisdictions, when they become vacant, but it is always done expressly by virtue of the authority conferred by the Emperor, and generally stated to be only *ad interim*, until His Majesty's pleasure is known.—The object of the law in this place appears to be to prevent any of the great officers of state, or principal nobility, from encroaching upon the royal prerogative, by forming a petty court or principality, dependent on themselves; an offence of this description was the subject of one of the leading charges against *Ho-chung-tong*, the minister and favourite of the late Emperor, an account of whose trial and condemnation is given in the Appendix, No. VIII.

† The punishments to which officers of government are stated in any particular instance to be liable, must always be understood to be subject to the modifications provided by the VIth, VIIth, and VIIIth Sections, and also by the clauses to the First Section, inserted in No. V. of the Appendix.

SECTION XLIX.— *Officers of Government not allowed to solicit hereditary Honours.*

When any officers of the civil department of government, who have not diftinguifhed themfelves by extraordinary and great fervices to the ftate, are recommended to the confideration of the Emperor, as deferving of the higheft hereditary honours; fuch officers, and thofe who recommend them, fhall fuffer death, by being beheaded, after remaining the ufual period in prifon.

Neverthelefs, thofe who are recommended to fuch honours in confequence of their being the lineal defcendants of diftinguifhed officers and magiftrates, who by their valour and exertions had averted national calamities, protected the empire, and contributed to the eftablifhment of the Imperial Family, fhall be free from any liability to the penalties of this law.

No claufe.

SECTION L. — *Supernumerary Officers of Government.*

In every public office and tribunal, whether at court or in the provinces, the number of officers to be regularly employed in each, is permanently eftablifhed by law*, and whoever fhall appoint, or caufe
to

---

* A detailed defcription of the manner in which the feveral public offices and tribunals are conftituted, and of their refpective powers and functions, in carrying on the bufinefs of government, does not form a conftituent part of the prefent work, although enough is ftated on the fubject, indirectly and incidentally, to afford, when confidered together, a fufficiently correct idea of the general fyftem.—To furnifh details of this kind, is one of the leading objects of another Chinefe work, entiled *Ta Tfing Hoey Tien,* or the Great general Code of the prefent Dynafty, and which may be confidered as the official account of the political conftitution of China in its feveral branches, though it has been defcribed in fome of the works of the miffionaries, rather improperly, as the legal code of the empire; and in terms, which excite more curiofity, than a tranflation of the work, if it could be executed, would be
likely

to be appointed any one fupernumerary officer, fhall be punifhed with 100 blows, and one degree more feverely for every three fupernumeraries fo appointed, as far as 100 blows and three years banifhment, beyond which degree the punifhment fhall not be increafed, unlefs the party fhall have been likewife convicted of bribery to fuch an amount as may, by law, aggravate the punifhment due to him.

Any perfon alfo, who employs, or caufes to be employed, more than the eftablifhed number of the clerks, or of the civil and military attendants of a tribunal or public office, fhall be punifhed with 100 blows and two years banifhment.

Any officer knowingly permitting one fuch fupernumerary to continue in the employ of government, fhall be liable to the punifhment of 20 blows, if the faid officer be a prefiding magiftrate; to 30 blows, if a deputy; and to 40 blows, if a chief clerk of fuch office or tribunal. — For every three fupernumeraries thus fuffered to remain in employ, the punifhment fhall be increafed one degree, to any proportionate extent, not exceeding the limit of 100 blows.

The fupernumerary fhall not in thefe cafes be liable to any punifhment. —If any perfons, who had formerly been officers or clerks in the fervice of government, interfere in any manner in the adminiftration of the public fervice, by writing orders, and pretending to poffefs authority, or by any other means extort money from and opprefs the people, they fhall, at the leaft, be punifhed with 80 blows, and fined 20 *leang* or ounces of filver, which fum fhall be paid to the perfon informing againft them; the corporal punifhment fhall, under any aggravating circumftances,

---

likely to gratify. See the *Memoires fur les Chinois*, vol. iv. page 220. and vol. viii. page 127. —Of this work, (*The Ta Tsing Hoey Tieng*) in which a comparatively fmall portion of curious matter is buried in a prodigious mafs of details of very inferior intereft, the tranflator is enabled to fpeak from fome degree of perfonal knowledge, having a copy in his poffeffion, confifting of 144 thin volumes, printed in the year 1764, the 29th of the reign of the late Emperor *Kien Lung*.

be as much more severe, as the laws in such cases provide.—Nevertheless, if the regular officers of government only hire the aforesaid persons occasionally to assist when necessary in collecting the duties, or in completing the registers of the people, their employment shall not be considered as a breach of this law.

Four clauses.

SECTION LI.—*Transmission of Official Dispatches.*

The official messengers who are employed in the several districts of the empire under the jurisdiction of the cities of the first, second, and third order*, for the transmission of dispatches relative to ordinary public business, or to the punishment of public transgressors, shall perform the services upon which they are respectively employed, within the periods which, with a due regard to the distance, and other circumstances, are in each case by law established. For one day's delay beyond the legal period, they shall be liable to a punishment of 10 blows, which shall be increased one degree, until it amounts to 40 blows, for every additional day's delay.—If the governing magistrates in any of the

---

* The Chinese empire is divided, in the first instance, into 18 provinces, which are governed either by a viceroy (*Tsong-too*), or a sub-viceroy (*Foo-yuen*), or by two such officers having a concurrent jurisdiction. Each province is subdivided into districts under the government of the magistrates of the several cities of the first order, and these governments are again divided into smaller jurisdictions, whose magistrates are governors of cities of the second or third in the empire.

According to one of the latest editions of the Chinese Imperial Court Kalendar, there are 11 officers bearing the title of viceroy, 15 that of sub-viceroy, 19 provincial treasurers, 18 provincial judges, and 17 provincial examiners for degrees; also 184 governors of cities of the first order, 212 governors of cities of the second, and 1305 of the third. These numbers are nearly the same with those stated in the authentic account of the British Embassy to China; but as the enumeration in the works of Du Halde and Grosier, differ from the above, and from each other, it was considered desirable to give these particulars from an authority that might be considered as decisive.

afore-mentioned districts and divisions of command, do not, when the administration of public affairs requires, send immediately the necessary orders and instructions to the officers subject to their authority, such neglect shall be punished with 100 blows.

The attention due to the repairing and inspecting of roads and bridges; to accidents and affrays; to the seizing of criminals; confiscation of property, and to any other such specific objects, being noticed and enforced elsewhere in this code, the neglect thereof is not to be punished as a breach of this general article.

Two clauses.

SECTION LII. — *Partiality in the Examination of Candidates for Degrees* *.

Whoever confers degrees of honour on persons who are not worthy, or who are under any disqualifications; and whoever, on the contrary, refuses at the proper time to confer such degrees upon those who are entitled to them by their merit, as well as duly qualified, shall be punished with 80 blows for a single instance of such offence, and one degree more severely, as far as 100 blows, for every

* These degrees have generally been considered as similar to those conferred upon students in European universities; but it is to be observed, that in China the examinations are not connected with any particular establishments or system of education, but conducted periodically by officers appointed by government, at each of the chief cities of the empire, and that they are, with few exceptions, open to all classes and descriptions whatsoever; the degrees also, instead of being merely literary, are, in fact, the sole regular channel of introduction to official employment, and consequently to rank and honours, in the empire.

With respect to the Tartars, these examinations are either wholly dispensed with, or very much relaxed in point of rigour, as well as conducted according to a different system. The Chinese are sometimes enabled, by the means of their wealth, to obviate a part of the difficulties attending their progress by an authorized commutation, but there is no reason to believe, that the legal enquiry into the qualifications of the candidates can in any instance be altogether evaded.—Those degrees which are partly obtained by purchase, although legal, are accounted less honourable. On this subject, see the Appendix, No. XII. containing a translation of an Imperial Edict, extracted from the Pekin Gazette of the 23d of April 1800.

two

two additional inſtances which may be proved upon inveſtigation. If the individual ſo improperly graduated is aware of his being ineligible, he ſhall be puniſhed as a participator in the offence, but otherwiſe ſhall be held innocent.

If the preſiding examiner of the merits of the candidates deſignedly makes a falſe report in any inſtance, by elevating or depreſſing their reſpective claims, the puniſhment of ſuch examiner ſhall be two degrees leſs than that of the officer who confers the degrees improperly*. If the report is erroneous, but not deſignedly falſe, the puniſhment ſhall be leſs by three degrees, but liable in all caſes to be increaſed whenever there is a conviction of bribery and corruption.

Seven clauſes.

SECTION LIII. — *Relative to Officers of Government diſmiſſed for Miſconduct.*

When any officer of government has been tried for an offence, condemned to loſe his employment, and rendered incapable of ſervice to the ſtate, none of the members of any public office or tribunal ſhall (regardleſs of ſuch conviction) become reſponſible for him, or take him again into employ.—Whoever employs ſuch convicted perſon, in violation of this law, ſhall be puniſhed with 100 blows; the ſame puniſhment ſhall likewiſe be inflicted on the party himſelf, and he ſhall continue, as before, incapacitated to enter the public ſervice.

When, however, an individual is diſmiſſed for inability, and not for corruption, or any other criminal practices, he may be employed whenever the officers into whoſe department he is to be received, having examined him, pledge themſelves that he is duly qualified.

Nine clauſes.

---

* It is evident from the gradations obſerved in puniſhing the miſconduct of theſe officers, that the department of the latter is of greater importance than the words ſeem to imply, but the text does not otherwiſe indicate the nature of their reſpective functions.

SECTION LIV. — *Officers of Government quitting their Stations without Leave.*

All civil and military officers, and their official attendants, whether at court or in the provinces, are prohibited from leaving their respective stations, except it be on account of sickness, or upon the public service, and shall be punished with 40 blows for every breach of this law.—If they should absent themselves for the sake of avoiding the execution of any unpleasant or difficult part of their duty, such as the collection of taxes, or the seizure of criminals, they shall be punished with 100 blows, as fugitives, and at the same time dismissed from their employments, as well as rendered for ever incapable of the public service. They shall, moreover, be liable to any aggravation of the punishment which may arise from the nature of the duty, the performance of which they had avoided.

As, for instance: if a civil officer, appointed to superintend the supplying of provisions to an army, should desert while the troops are in the field, the offence would be aggravated by the injury which might result therefrom to the state, upon such a critical juncture.

If, in ordinary cases, any officer or attendant of government is not on guard by day, or on watch by night, when it is his duty to be so, he shall be punished with 20 blows for such offence; but the punishment shall be increased to 40 blows in every instance of similar neglect, on the part of those who have the custody of granaries, treasuries, or prisons, or of any other places of similar importance.

It is only necessary to carry this law into effect, when no injury nor loss has ensued from the neglect above-mentioned, as in regard to the offence under such aggravated circumstances, particular punishments are elsewhere provided.

Two clauses.

SECTION LV. — *Officers of Government to proceed to their Destinations without Delay.*

When a change has been determined to be made in the administration of any department of the public service, the duty of the officer newly appointed, if at the court, shall commence from the delivery over of the charge; if in the provinces, from the receipt of the official order from the supreme council.—If, after such period, the newly appointed officer should, without assigning a sufficient cause, unnecessarily delay one day in proceeding to his station, he shall incur a punishment of 10 blows; for every further delay of ten days, the punishment shall be increased one degree, until it amount to 80 blows; but in all such cases, the offender shall still retain his new appointment.

Upon the arrival of a successor, the officer in possession shall, within the time, and in the manner prescribed by law, make up and close his several accounts relative to the collection of the revenue, and the execution of the laws against transgressors, that the said accounts may be delivered over to the officer appointed to receive them: when the same is concluded, if the officer who had delivered up his charge remains on the spot, without assigning a sufficient reason for so doing, more than ten days, he shall be punished for such delay two degrees less than is provided in cases of officers not proceeding in due time to their new appointments.

If an officer of government is detained by winds or other obstacles, is plundered by thieves, falls sick, or loses a parent, so as in any way to be prevented from proceeding to his destination, he shall make a due and circumstantial report thereof to the proper magistrates, that it may be ascertained by them whether the delay did not take place without sufficient cause, or with some sinister view; in either of which cases such misconduct shall be punished as the laws prescribe. — If the magistrates receiving the report are guilty of any improper partiality or collusion, they shall be equally punishable.

Five clauses.

Section LVI. — *Attendance of Officers of Government at Court.*

When an officer of government belonging to any of the interior departments, whatever may be his rank, does not present himself at court within due time; or, if belonging to a provincial government, he does not present himself at head-quarters; or lastly, when an officer of government, in either case, after having obtained a leave of absence, does not return to his station as soon as his leave of absence is expired; he must give sufficient reason for such omission, without which he will be punishable with 10 blows for one day's delay; and one degree more severely for every further delay of three days, until the same amounts to 80 blows; but the transgression shall not occasion the dismissal or degradation of the party offending.

No clause.

Section LVII. — *Irregular interference of Superiors with subordinate Magistrates.*

When any public measure originates in a superior court or tribunal, it shall be put upon record, and a period fixed for its execution:—A mandate shall then be issued, or a special messenger dispatched, to the inferior tribunals for their information and guidance.

If the officers of such inferior tribunals should afterwards be convicted of any error or delay in the execution of their duty, they shall be punished according to the laws; but if the superior magistrate unnecessarily interferes with, or supersedes, the determinations of an inferior tribunal, by sending for any of the clerks or members thereof, or by sending to them any of his own officers, by which interference or superseffion the due course of justice is impeded, the superior magistrate shall be punished with 40 blows, and the inferior magistrate who consents to, and concurs therein, or permits the clerks to receive such irregular instructions, shall be liable to the same punishment.

Nevertheless, in all serious criminal or intricate revenue cases, in which interference or consultation is requisite, it shall be lawful to summon the attendance of the members of the inferior tribunals; but they shall be dismissed immediately upon the termination of the inquiry.—If unnecessarily detained three days, the superior shall be punished with 20 blows, and one degree more severely, as far as 50 blows, for every additional three days detention *.

No clause.

Section LVIII.—*Cabals and State Intrigues.*

Whoever, with malicious design, provokes and excites by artful language any person, as yet innocent of a capital offence, to commit murder, shall for such offence suffer death, by being beheaded after the usual period of confinement.

If any great officer of state is convicted of a crime, which according to the laws is deserving of death, and any of the inferior officers of govern-

---

* How far the inferior tribunals of justice, and other departments of government, are connected with, and subject to, the authority of their respective superiors, will be best understood by a reference to particular instances; and partly with this view, a translation of the official reports of some remarkable legal proceedings have been introduced into the Appendix, each of which will be specifically referred to in its proper place.

As the investigation of all capital cases must pass through every step, from the tribunal of the lowest magistrate, to the throne of the Emperor; and as there is, generally speaking, a right of appeal through the same channel in all cases, whether civil or criminal, partiality and injustice could, according to such a system, scarcely ever escape detection and punishment, if the interference and collusion above adverted to, did not, whenever it takes place, render the appeal hopeless, and the repetition of the investigation nugatory.

ment, by artful reprefentations, endeavour to conceal his guilt and fcreen him from punifhment, in order to gain his good-will, they fhall likewife fuffer death, by being beheaded after the ufual period of confinement

If any of the officers about the court cabal and combine together, in order to impede and obftruct the meafures of His Imperial Majefty's government, all the parties to fuch cabal, without diftinguifhing between principals and acceffaries, fhall be beheaded after the ufual period of confinement; their wives and children fhall become flaves, and their fortunes fhall be confifcated*. — If the fupreme court of judicature, or any other fubordinate court of juftice, fhould refrain from carrying the laws into effect, in compliance with the wifhes of any fuperior magiftrate, and fhould unjuftly aggravate or mitigate the punifhment of offenders agreeably to the dictates of fuch fuperior, the offence fhall be confidered to come within the penalties of this law.

On the other hand, if the officers of any inferior court fhould difregard fuch unlawful interpofition, and, drawing up a faithful report thereof, as well as of any attempt that may have been made at fubornation, lay the fame perfonally before the Emperor, the punifhment fhall fall upon the fuperior magiftrate only, and the complainant fhall not only be pardoned for any previous compliance with unjuft commands, of which he might have been guilty, but rewarded with the whole of the confifcated property of the offender.

If the complainant is an officer of government, he fhall be raifed in rank two degrees; if not an officer of government, he fhall receive a fuitable office or, if not defirous of office, a further reward, inftead thereof, fhall be given to him of 2000 *leang* or ounces of filver.

No claufe.

* See the Laws relative to Treafonable Offences in general, in their proper place.

Section LIX. — *Combination and Collusion between Provincial Officers and Officers of the Court.*

Any combination and collusion between the officers of the several tribunals of justice throughout the empire, and the officers of the court in the immediate attendance on His Majesty, the object of which may be either, the betraying the secrets of the State, unwarrantable pretensions to offices of power and emolument, or joint addresses to the Sovereign for private and unlawful purposes, shall subject all the parties guilty of such an offence, to suffer death, by being beheaded after the usual period of confinement. — Their wives and children shall be perpetually banished to the distance of 2000 *lee*, and at the place of banishment, be allowed to form new establishments.

Nevertheless, when the connexion and intercourse between such parties shall have arisen merely from their relationship to each other, and without any view to the unwarrantable objects above stated, this law shall not be put in force.

No clause.

Section LX. — *Addresses in favour of Great Officers of State.*

If an officer belonging to any of the departments of government, or any private individual, should address the Emperor in praise of the virtues, abilities, or successful administration, of any of His Majesty's confidential Ministers of State, it is to be considered as an evidence of the existence of a treasonable combination subversive of government, and shall therefore be investigated with the utmost strictness and accuracy: the cause and origin of these interested praises of persons high in rank and office being traced, the offending party shall suffer death, by being beheaded,

beheaded, after remaining in prifon the ufual period.—His wives and children fhall become flaves, and his property fhall be confifcated.

If the confidential minifter or great officer of the crown, to whom the addrefs related, was privy to the defign, he fhall participate in the punifhment of the offence; but otherwife, fhall be excufed *.

One claufe.

* The feverity of the law in this, and in the fections immediately preceding, is probably grounded upon fome confiderations which are not explained in the text; but it is obvious, that the punifhments are not directed fo much at the acts themfelves, as at the treafonable motives they are fuppofed to indicate.

END OF THE FIRST BOOK OF THE SECOND DIVISION.

BOOK II.

CONDUCT OF THE MAGISTRATES.

Section LXI. — *Due Knowledge of the Laws.*

THE laws and ftatutes of the empire have been framed with deliberation, are fanctioned with appropriate penalties againft tranfgreffors, and are publifhed to the world* for perpetual obfervance.

All the officers and others in the employ of government ought to ftudy diligently, and make themfelves perfect in the knowledge of thefe laws, fo as to be able to explain clearly their meaning and intent, and to fuperintend and enfure their execution.

At the clofe of every year, the officers and other perfons employed by government, in every one of the exterior and interior departments, fhall undergo examination on this fubject before their refpective fuperiors, and if they are found in any refpect incompetent to explain the nature, or to comprehend the feveral objects, of the laws, they fhall forfeit one month's falary when holding official, and receive 40 blows when holding any of the inferior, fituations.

All thofe private individuals, whether hufbandmen, or artificers, or whatever elfe may be their calling or profeffion, who are found capable of explaining the nature, and comprehending the objects, of the laws, fhall receive pardon in all cafes of offences refulting purely from accident, or imputable to them only from the guilt of others, provided it be the firft offence, and not implicated with any act of treafon or rebellion.

* Literally, " to the Heaven-under," an expreffion fomething analogous to our epithet of fublunary, and here applied with Afiatic amplification to the Chinefe empire.

Whosoever, in the employ of government, fraudulently perverts or misconstrues, or presumptuously changes, abrogates or confounds the law upon any case, so as to produce disturbance and insurrection in the country, shall suffer death by being beheaded, after the usual period of imprisonment.

No clause.

SECTION LXII. — *Non-execution of an Imperial Edict.*

Whenever an Imperial Edict is issued on any subject, whoever wilfully omits the execution of any thing that is commanded therein, shall be punished with 100 blows. — In the case of the edict of the Imperial prince elect, the punishment shall be the same. — A failure in any such respect, from neglect or inadvertence, shall be punished three degrees less severely.

Moreover, any one who delays or postpones the execution of an Imperial edict for one day, shall be punished with 50 blows, and one degree more severely as far as 100 blows for each additional day of delay.

No clause.

SECTION LXIII. — *Destroying or discarding Edicts and Seals of Office.*

Whoever designedly discards or destroys an Imperial edict, or the official seal of any tribunal or department of state, shall suffer death, by being beheaded, after the usual period of confinement. — Whoever wilfully discards or destroys an edict issued by any individual officer, or by a tribunal of government, shall be punished with 100 blows, or as much more severely as the criminality of the motive may lawfully require; and if the edict destroyed or discarded concerned the affairs of war, or the supply of the army in the field with provisions, the offence shall be punished with death, and the offender strangled, after the usual period of confinement. — If the superior officer of the offender is privy to the offence, and does not take cognizance of it, he shall be considered as equally guilty, and participate in the full extent of the punishment, excepting only a reduction of one degree in capital cases. — When he is not aware of the offence having been committed, he shall be altogether excused. — Destroying, in any of the foregoing instances unintentionally, but through inadvertence, is punishable three degree less severely than the wilful offence; and if it can be clearly shewn, that the discarding or destroying was the unavoidable consequence of fire, water, or thieves, the punishment shall be remitted altogether.

Whoever loses an imperial edict, or a seal of office, shall be punished with 90 blows and two years and a half's banishment: if an edict of an officer of government, with 70 blows only; but in case such edict concerns the affairs of war, or supplies for the army, the punishment shall be increased to 90 blows and two years and a half's banishment.

Immediately upon ascertaining such a loss to have occurred, the payment of the salary of the offending party shall be suspended; but if he is able to recover the official document that was lost, within the space of thirty days, he shall be pardoned; if not able to do so within such period, the execution of his punishment shall not on any account be further delayed.

If an officer, having charge of government property, loses his books and registers, whereby error or confusion is introduced into the accounts of the revenue in store, he shall be liable to suffer 80 blows, but allowed a sufficient period to retrieve himself from such punishment by the recovery of the documents that were missing.

The clerks of all public offices, upon the expiration of their respective terms of service, shall deliver over to their successors, all the books of official accounts, with a distinct record in each case of the actual balance,

and

and of the state of the accounts in each department at the time when the transfer of the charge takes place, and any failure or neglect in these respects shall be punished with 80 blows.—The deputy or executive officers of the several tribunals or public boards, shall be liable to similar punishment, if they do not likewise ascertain and verify the state of each of the several accounts, whenever any such transfers are effected.

Five clauses.

Section LXIV.—*Errors and Informalities in public Documents.*

Whoever, in addressing the Emperor, irreverently, or inadvertently, makes use of His Imperial Majesty's appellative, or that of any of his Imperial predecessors, shall, for such offence, be punished with 80 blows:—if the same is introduced improperly into any public document, not addressed as aforesaid, the punishment shall be limited to 40 blows.—Whoever assumes for himself or others, any one of such sacred appellatives, thus employing it as the name of a private individual, shall be punished with 100 blows:—Nevertheless, it shall not be considered as a violation of such sacred names, if in any case the sound only is imitated *, or if only one of the characters of the name is employed †.— If any mistake or error is committed in the statements or suggestions contained in an address to His Majesty, the consequence whereof may be injurious to the public service; as, for instance, writing " inexcusable" instead of " excusable," writing " 10 stone weight" instead of " 1000 " stone weight ‡," the offender shall be punished with 60 blows.

* The choice of sounds in the Chinese language is confined within such narrow limits in comparison to that of written words or characters, that any accidental agreement in the former respect, is not sufficient to produce an equivoque, and therefore not deemed in these instances an act of disrespect to the Sovereign or His Imperial Family.

† Personal appellatives generally consist of two words or characters, and family names of one only.

‡ The difference between the character expressing 10 and that expressing 1000 is not more than a single stroke of the pencil.

If a similar error occurs in a report to any of the supreme courts, the punishment shall amount to 40 blows; and if in any official documents of an inferior description, to 20 blows. — Nevertheless, such errors as are of a trifling nature, and do not so materially alter the sense of the record, as to impede the public service, shall be excused, and therefore excepted from the operation of this law.

No clause.

Section LXV. — *Neglecting to make such Reports to superior Officers as are by Law required.*

When offences are committed by persons entitled to privilege by law, if the officer of government, to whose department it belongs to take cognisance thereof, does not report such offences to the Emperor, or if he does not specify the privilege to which the offending party is entitled, it shall be held to be a capital offence, but punished only with five years banishment, as ordered in other capital offences of a miscellaneous nature*.—When offences are committed by civil or military officers, the sentence upon whom requires the Emperor's ratification before it can be legally executed, any omission to lay the same before the Emperor shall be punished with 100 blows, or as much more severely as the circumstances of the case may authorize by other laws specifically applicable thereto.—The neglect to report to the Emperor any circumstance of military affairs, concerning the revenue, legislation, selection of magistrates, punishments, public calamities, or any extraordinary circumstances which by law it is requisite to report to His Majesty, shall be punished with 80 blows.—Similar

---

* The cause of certain offences, which are punished in each case with five years banishment, being denominated capital offences of a miscellaneous nature, is not explained in the text, but it is probable that this form of expression is retained for no other purpose, than that of preserving a nominal uniformity, with a pre-established system in the adjustment of punishments, which in these instances is practically abandoned.

neglect to report to a superior magistrate, what by law ought to be reported, shall be punished with 40 blows.

Whoever, after having made a due report according to the laws, either to his immediate superior in office, or to the Emperor, proceeds notwithstanding to execute the laws upon the case, without waiting for the arrival of further instructions, shall be liable to the same punishment, (capital cases excepted) that the law would have awarded had no report whatever been made.

When any tribunal or department of government addresses the Emperor upon affairs of state, the members thereof shall report collectively their judgment on the case, agreeably to the laws applicable thereto, and, the statement of the same being clearly drawn up, all those who were parties to the deliberation thereon, shall affix their names.

If, in such a report, the circumstances of any important affair of state are aggravated, palliated, or otherwise misrepresented, so as to mislead His Majesty, and fraudulently to obtain his royal orders conformably to such false statement, (although the deception should not be discovered until an indefinite time after the orders were carried into effect), the authors thereof, whenever the truth is brought to light, shall be beheaded. — Upon any visitation from the superior magistrate, the officers of the inferior tribunal shall, previous to any joint decision upon official business, state the circumstances fully and in due order, together with the arguments for or against any proposed arrangement, which, being duly registered and authenticated by the signature of the parties, shall remain as an evidence of their proceedings, for reference upon any future investigation.

If the inferior magistrate brings forward any improper proposal, and by a false or inadequate explanation thereof, obtains, or pretends to have obtained, the consent of his superior, such conduct shall be punished according to the law against a false interpretation of the

orders

orders of government, and as much more severely as the circumstances of the case may authorize.

Two clauses.

Section LXVI.— *Officers on detached Service not reporting their Proceedings.*

Whoever, when detached upon any particular service by an Imperial mandate, does not render an account of such of his proceedings, upon the result of which other business may be depending, shall be punished with 100 blows.

When detached on service by a mandate of any tribunal or department of government, and failing to render an account of the proceedings undertaken in consequence, the punishment shall likewise be 100 blows, provided military or other affairs of much importance are depending; if only ordinary affairs are depending, the punishment shall be limited to 70 blows.

If any person, acting under such especial authority, exceeds the limits of his commission, and encroaches upon the province of others, he shall be punished with 50 blows.— If the individual employed under an Imperial mandate, does not deliver up his powers or credentials within three days after his return, he shall be punished with 60 blows, and one degree more severely, as far as 100 blows, for every additional delay of two days, until such token of his resignation.

In like manner, when acting under any government commission specially issued by a public office, and not restoring or resigning the same within the above period after his return, such individual shall be punished with 40 blows, and one degree more severely as far as 80 blows, for each additional three days delay.—— In all cases, if the offence punishable by this law, is connected with any aggravating circumstances,

cumstances, the punishment shall be increased to any extent that the laws applicable thereto may warrant.

No clause.

SECTION LXVII. — *Delay in expediting the Edicts of Government.*

When an edict or authentic act of any public office or tribunal is neglected to be expedited, the clerk of such office or tribunal shall be punished, for one day's delay, with 10 blows; and one degree more severely, as far as 40 blows, for each three days further delay. — The deputies of the tribunal, being the immediate superintendants of the clerks, shall be liable to punishment only less by one degree; but the superior members thereof shall not be held responsible.

When any public board or tribunal receives a report upon official business from a subordinate department, the officers of the former shall proceed forthwith to examine into, and deliberate upon the proposals therein submitted to their decision, and having determined on the expediency of confirming, or rejecting the same, they shall issue their orders accordingly. — If, on the contrary, they reply equivocally and indistinctly, instead of giving any decision, so that the questions are repeatedly proposed and remanded, and the public service thereby materially injured and delayed, the officers of the superior tribunal shall be punished with 80 blows, for every such attempt to avoid the responsibility which is attached to the performance of their public duty.

In like manner, if the officers of an inferior tribunal receive orders relative to a measure which is fit and practicable, and yet, instead of carrying it into effect, they, under pretence of doubts on the subject, refer it again to the consideration of their superiors, their punishment shall be the same as that provided in the case last stated.

Eight clauses.

Section LXVIII. — *Examination of official Records.*

The records of all such public offices as have a specific command, and a public seal, shall be regularly examined; and if the adjustment of one or two articles is found in any case to have been unnecessarily retarded, the clerk of the office shall be punishable with 10 blows, if from three to five articles; with 20 blows, and one degree more severely, as far as 40 blows, for each five additional articles unadjusted.

The deputies of the tribunals of cities of the three several orders, and the superintending officers over granaries, treasuries, river police, and others, shall be punishable in such cases respectively less by one degree.

When any part of the records is found to be erroneous, or is kept back from examination; if in respect to one article only, the clerk of the office shall be punished with 20 blows; if in respect to two or three articles, with 30 blows; and one degree more severely, as far as 50 blows, for every three erroneous or suppressed articles, in addition to the number last mentioned.

The deputies of the tribunals of cities of the three several orders, and the superintending officers of granaries, treasuries, river-police, and others, shall be punishable, in each case, less by one degree. — Moreover, the presiding officers or governors of such cities, whenever it is found that from one to five articles are erroneous, or kept back from examination, shall forfeit one month's salary, and another month's salary, as far as three months, for each additional five articles so kept back or erroneous. — If such incorrectness or suppression of the articles of the records is practised from criminal motives, such as, suppression of the receipts of revenue, aggravation or palliation of offences, and the like, the punishment of such misconduct shall be proportionably increased according as the laws, applicable to such cases, direct.

Four clauses.

Section LXIX.—*Re-examination of outstanding Articles of official Records.*

Those officers in whose province it lies to re-examine the recorded transactions of the several tribunals and departments of government, shall inspect all such of the proceedings in the judicial and revenue departments as had been reported to have been found at the original examination unnecessarily in arrear or erroneous. — Whatever, in the revenue department, is found, at the expiration of an interval of a quarter of a year, still erroneous or defective, shall be charged against the magistrates of the several offices, and subject them to punishment according to the proportion which the erroneous and defective matter bears to the remainder of the proceedings—if one-tenth only, to 50 blows, and one degree more severely, as far as 100 blows, for every further tenth part erroneous or defective.

If, in the judicial department, they find at the end of the quarter, any case unadjusted or not corrected, which might and ought to have been adjusted or corrected, the responsible magistrate shall be punished with 40 blows, and the punishment shall be increased one degree for each additional month's delay, as far as 80 blows at the utmost, unless it happens to be a case of bribery, liable to severer punishment, in which event the latter shall supersede the former.

When any article is suppressed or kept back, for the purpose of avoiding the result of the re-examination, such suppression, if of one article only, shall be punished with 40 blows, and one degree more severely for each additional article so suppressed, as far as 80 blows at the utmost, except it be a case affecting the revenue, when the suppression, in the case of one article only, shall be punished with 80 blows, and one degree more severely for each additional article suppressed, as far as 100 blows, or as much further as may be lawfully inflicted in consequence of a corrupt or criminal design being substantiated against the offender. — If any officer of government, after the errors or omissions of which he had been guilty are discovered, should fraudulently attempt to alter or interpolate the official records, the offence shall be punished as any ordinary falsification of an official dispatch.

All those colleagues who assist in the commission of this offence, and their superiors who, having information of it, take no cognisance thereof, shall participate in the punishment. If unacquainted with the circumstances, or unconnected by office with the offending parties, they shall not be liable to punishment.

No clause.

Section LXX. — *Transfer or Exchange of official Duties prohibited.*

When it is the duty of an officer of government to investigate or report upon any affair, whether in its progress from inferiors to superiors, or from superiors to inferiors [*], if he employs any of his colleagues either to investigate the matter, or to address the Report of it, instead of doing both himself, he shall be punished with 80 blows; and if it be a case of previous neglect or omission, which it is thus attempted to repair by deputy, the punishment shall be increased one degree.—If, moreover, in any such case, a deviation from justice either by aggravation or extenuation should have been committed, the punishment shall be increased to any extent that the law, adapted to such circumstances, may authorize.

Three clauses.

Section LXXI. — *Alteration of the Contents of an official Dispatch.*

Whoever presumes to alter an official dispatch, by adding to, or taking from the sense and words thereof, shall be punished

---

[*] The regular course of proceedings in the several tribunals or courts of justice, is described in its proper place.

with 60 blows.—If such alteration is effected with the view to accomplish some unlawful purpose, not capitally punishable, the punishment incurred thereby shall, in consequence of such previous offence, be increased two degrees, but so as in no case to exceed 100 blows, and perpetual banishment to the distance of 3000 *lee.* —In any of the preceding cases, if the unlawful object had not been attained, the punishment shall be less by one degree.

If the unlawful object be in itself a capital offence, the previous minor offence shall not cause any aggravation of the sentence.—If the author of any official dispatch alters it himself, with a view to any unlawful purpose, he shall only be subject to the punishment to which such unlawful purpose renders him liable; except when such alteration is made to screen himself from the punishment of error or delay, for which offence he shall in such case be liable to receive 40 blows at the least.

If, in the course of transmitting, and re-issuing government orders upon judicial, revenue, military, or other important affairs, they are erroneously transcribed, or the emendations made in the originals omitted, the clerk of the office or tribunal guilty thereof shall be punished with 30 blows, and the deputy of the tribunal shall be punished one degree less for his neglect of revisal.

If the alteration affects any orders for the employment of troops, or concerns the amount of supplies to be forwarded to the army, or to the frontier stations, the clerk and deputy who are responsible for the same, shall respectively receive 80 blows for such neglect; but if it is a case of wilful misconduct, and the alteration is made for any unlawful purpose, the punishment shall be rated according to the scale already exhibited in the case of altering an official dispatch.—In general also, the non-execution of the unlawful purpose shall be considered so far to extenuate the offence, as to reduce the punishment one degree.—If, however, such deviation, whether wilful or not, should be the cause of the failure of any military operations, the person principally responsible shall be beheaded, after the usual period of confinement. — The deputy, being considered as an accessary, shall, in such case, receive 100 blows, and be banished perpetually to the distance of 3000 *lee*. — When, however, any official dispatch, or other document, is erroneously copied by mere accident, and does not concern the administration of military affairs, or of the judicial or revenue departments, but regards only the ordinary routine of business, the responsible parties shall not be held liable to punishment.

No clause.

Section LXXII. — *Use of the official or public Seal.*

In every department and tribunal of government, whether at court or in the provinces, the seal of office shall remain in the custody of the presiding magistrate or officer, and one of the magistrates or officers who are assessors, having stamped or affixed the impression of the seal upon the records of their joint official proceedings, the members shall then individually subjoin their signatures. — When all the assessors are absent from necessity, or engaged on other public service, the deputy may be employed to authenticate the documents, by affixing the seal of office. — Otherwise a punishment of 100 blows shall follow any deviation from this law.

No clause.

Section LXXIII. — *Omitting to use, or imperfectly using, the official Seal.*

When a public document is issued under the official authority of any of the departments of government, with only a confused and imperfect impression of the public seal, those who are responsible for the

sealing

sealing thereof, shall be punished with 60 blows; and if they should, in any similar case, altogether omit to employ the public seal, the punishment shall amount to 80 blows.—If such unauthenticated or imperfectly authenticated document should in any manner concern the operations, or the supply with stores and provisions, of the troops in the field, the responsible parties shall be punished with 100 blows; lastly, if in consequence of such neglect, those to whom the public document is addressed, doubt its authenticity, and hesitate to comply therewith, so as to occasion the failure of any military operation then depending, the principal offender (being the clerk of the office where the neglect originated), shall suffer death by being beheaded at the usual period; and the other officers implicated therein shall suffer 100 blows, and be banished perpetually to the distance of 3000 *lee*.

Employing the seal of office in an inverted position shall be considered equivalent to the offence of impressing it imperfectly, and shall be punished accordingly.

Three clauses.

SECTION LXXIV.—*Employing the Sanction of the Seals of military Offices upon civil Affairs.*

All generals, commanders of troops, colonels of regiments, and other military officers, have their respective seals; but, if instead of referring the power and authority confided in them by those seals, to the authenticating of military orders, and the direction of the movements and distribution of the cavalry and infantry under their authority, they presume to give official answers to petitions, to grant passes for goods, by which the revenue may be injured, or in any manner pretend to give instructions on affairs exclusively under the civil jurisdiction, the clerks and deputies in the departments of such officers shall

shall receive 100 blows in each case, and be for ever excluded from the public service.

The misconduct of the presiding officers shall be reported to the Emperor, and punished agreeably to His Majesty's decision.

One clause.

END OF THE SECOND DIVISION.

THIRD DIVISION.

Fiscal Laws.

BOOK I.

ENROLMENT OF THE PEOPLE.

SECTION LXXV. — *Families and Individuals to be duly enrolled.*

WHEN a family has omitted to make any entry whatever in the public register, the head or master thereof, if possessing any lands chargeable with contributions to the revenue, shall be punished with 100 blows; but if he possess no such property, with 80 blows only; and the family shall in the former case be registered as accountable for future public service, according to the amount of its taxable property, and in the latter, according to the number of male individuals of full age of which it consists.

When any head or master of a family, has among his household strangers who constitute, in fact, a distinct family, but omits to make a corresponding entry in the public register, or registers them as members of his own family, he shall be punished with 100 blows, if any such stranger possesses taxable property, and with 80 blows if he should not possess any; and in all cases, the register shall be duly corrected, by the insertion of a description of such strangers as a distinct family.

If the person harboured without making any corresponding entry, or represented falsely as a member of the family, is not a stranger as in the last case, but a relation, possessing a separate establishment, the punishment of the head or master of the family so offending,

offending, shall be less than as aforesaid by two degrees; the person harboured and concealed shall be liable to the same punishment, and be registered separately in the legal manner, as well as held accountable to the public service conformably thereto.

Nevertheless, such uncles, younger brothers, nephews, and sons-in-law, who had never formed separate establishments, shall be exempted from the obligation of a separate entry, prescribed by this law.

If any person guilty of omitting to register his family, is in the service of government, and registered as such, the omission shall be punished only according to the number of individuals of full age omitted, as the record of any one person is equivalent to the record of the family.

If any head or master of a family omits to enter in the public register any of the males belonging thereto, who have attained the full age of sixteen, or if he falsely represents any individuals thereof to be under age, aged, infirm, or decrepid, so as to evade their liability to the public service, he shall suffer the punishment of 60 blows, when the number of persons does not exceed three, and be punished one degree more severely for every addition of three persons to the number so omitted or falsely represented, as far as 100 blows at the utmost *.

Moreover, any head of a family omitting to make entry of from three to five males under the aforesaid age, shall be punished with 40 blows, and the punishment shall be increased one degree as far as 70 blows, for every additional five persons under age, who may have been so omitted.

In all cases the individuals found to have been omitted in the register, shall be duly entered, and if of full age, made accountable to the public service.

* In the Chinese commentary annexed to the text in the original, it is stated that the first entry shall be made of children when they attain the age of four years, but the period of liability to public service appears to be only between the ages of sixteen and sixty. Besides the ordinary registers of the people, one of a more comprehensive nature is occasionally effected, comprising persons of both sexes, and of all ages.

Neglecting

Neglecting to enter, or making a false entry of, a stranger, shall be punished in the same manner and proportions; and the stranger availing himself thereof shall be liable to equal punishment, as well as compelled to make entry and perform service, as a member of the family to which he really belongs *.

The head or responsible inhabitant of the division, through whose neglect and inadvertency, one or more families, as far as five, have evaded the insertion of their names in the public register, shall be punished with 50 blows; and one degree more severely, as far as 100 blows, for every additional five families so omitted to be inserted.

In like manner, when the names of any individuals are omitted to be inserted in the registers, the aforesaid responsible inhabitant shall be punished with 30 blows, when the number omitted does not exceed 10; and one degree more severely for every additional 10 omitted, as far as 50 blows at the utmost.

When the omission amounts to 10 families, the governor, deputy and clerk of the district, shall be liable to the punishment of 40 blows, for their negligence in allowing the same; and their punishment shall be greater by one degree as far as 80 blows for every additional 10 families so allowed to be omitted.

When the omission amounts to 10 individuals, the said magistrates and clerks shall be liable to 20 blows for their negligence in allowing the same; and their punishment shall be greater by one degree for every additional 30 individuals omitted, as far as 40 blows at the utmost.

When any of the preceding parties wilfully connive at such omission, they shall be punished as severely as the principal offenders; and if they are found guilty of receiving money, as the price of their connivance, they shall suffer any contingent aggravation of punishment,

* In this case, the family of the stranger is supposed to have been duly registered elsewhere, though the individual stranger, being absent from his family, had been omitted.

to which they may become liable from the amount thereof, according to the law againſt receiving a bribe for an unlawful purpoſe.

If, however, the officiating magiſtrates and clerks ſhall have three times ordered a reviſal of the cenſus of the people, and iſſued competent inſtructions and authority for ſuch inveſtigation to the head inhabitants of diſtricts, the ſaid head inhabitants ſhall alone be reſponſible for any ſubſequent omiſſion which may afterwards be diſcovered.

All caſes of wilful connivance are, at the ſame time, manifeſtly to be excepted.

Two clauſes.

SECTION LXXVI. — *Families and Individuals to be regiſtered according to their Profeſſions.*

All perſons whatſoever ſhall be regiſtered according to their accuſtomed profeſſions or vocations, whether civil or military, whether poſt-men*, artiſans, phyſicians, aſtrologers, labourers, muſicians, or of any other denomination whatever; wherever a military employment is repreſented as a civil one, or an artiſan endeavours to paſs himſelf as a mere labourer, or when any other device is employed to leſſen the individual's liability to the public ſervice, ſuch individual ſhall be puniſhed with 80 blows, and the magiſtrate who negligently conſents to ſuch omiſſion, irregularity, or confuſion in the entries on the public regiſter, ſhall be equally puniſhable.

Whoever falſely repreſents himſelf to belong to any military eſtabliſhment in garriſon, or in the field, and thereby evades all public ſervice whatever, ſhall receive 100 blows, and be ſent into the ulterior and perpetual military baniſhment.

Twenty-two clauſes.

* See the laſt Book of the Diviſion of Military Laws, entitled, " Expreſſes and Public " Poſts."

SECTION LXXVII. — *Privately founding religious Houses, and privately entering into the Order of Priesthood*.

No religious houses of the sects of *Foe* and *Tao-se*, except those which have been heretofore lawfully constituted and established, shall be privately maintained, appropriated, or endowed, whether upon a new, or in addition to an old foundation, or in any other manner whatsoever.

Whoever offends against this law shall receive 100 blows; if a priest, he shall be divested of his sacred character, and perpetually banished beyond the frontier:—if a priestess, she shall become a slave to government; and in general all the real and personal property belonging to any such illegal foundation shall be confiscated.

Whoever submits to the tonsure †, and joins a religious community as a priest or priestess, without having previously obtained a government licence, shall be punished with 80 blows, and be replaced in the class of ordinary citizens. When the offence is committed through the instigation of the head of the family, such head of the family shall bear the punishment thereof. The members and governors of religious communities, who illegally admit such persons, shall also suffer the punishment decreed by this law ‡.

Six clauses.

* See Section XLII. relative to the religious orders among the Chinese.

† The priests of the sect of *Foe* closely shave every part of the head; those of the sect of *Tao-se* wear their hair, but in a different manner from the natives in general.

‡ It is provided by the third clause to this section, that persons desirous of contributing to the foundation of a new temple, or other religious building, shall be allowed to apply for permission to the viceroy of the province, in order that their desires may be submitted to the consideration of His Imperial Majesty.

Section LXXVIII.—*Rule of Succeſſion and Inheritance.*

Whoever appoints his heir and repreſentative unlawfully, ſhall be puniſhed with 80 blows *.—When the firſt wife has completed her fiftieth year, and has no children living, it is allowed to appoint the eldeſt ſon by the other wives to the inheritance; but if any other than the eldeſt of ſuch ſons is ſo appointed, it ſhall be deemed a breach of this law.

If a perſon, not having ſons himſelf, educates and adopts the ſon of a kinſman, having other ſons, but afterwards diſmiſſes ſuch adopted ſon, ſuch perſon ſhall be puniſhed with 100 blows, and the ſon ſhall be ſent back to, and ſupported, as before, by the adopting parents.

Nevertheleſs, if the adopting parents ſhall have ſubſequently had other ſons, and the natural parents, having no other, are deſirous of receiving their ſon back again, they ſhall be at liberty ſo to do.

Whoever aſks for, and receives into his houſe as his adopted ſon, a perſon of a different family name, is guilty of confounding family diſtinctions, and ſhall therefore be puniſhed with 60 blows; the ſon ſo adopted ſhall, in ſuch caſes, always be returned to his family.—In like manner, whoever gives away his ſon to be adopted into a family of a different name, ſhall ſuffer the puniſhment decreed by this law, and receive ſuch ſon back again. Nevertheleſs, it ſhall be lawful to adopt a foundling under three years of age, and to give the child the name of the family into which it is adopted; but ſuch adopted child ſhall not be entitled to the inheritance upon failure of the children by blood.

If the relative appointed to the inheritance, on failure of children, is not the eldeſt in ſucceſſion, it ſhall be deemed a breach of this law;

---

* See the rule of ſucceſſion to Hereditary Dignities in the ſecond diviſion to the code, and alſo the abſtract of the clauſes annexed to this law, in the Appendix, No. XII.

the relative fo appointed fhall be fent back to his place in his own family, and the lawful heir appointed in his ftead.

Whoever brings up in his family, as a flave, the male or female child of a freeman, fhall be punifhed with 100 blows, and the child fhall regain its freedom.

Eight claufes.

SECTION LXXIX. — *Regulations concerning ftray Children.*

Whoever receives and detains the ftrayed or loft child of a free perfon, and, inftead of prefenting to the magiftrate, fells fuch child as a flave, fhall be punifhed with 100 blows, and three years banifhment. Whoever fells fuch child for marriage or adoption into any family, fhall be punifhed with 90 blows and banifhment for two years and a half. — Whoever fo difpofes of a ftrayed or loft flave, fhall fuffer the punifhment provided by this law, reduced one degree.

The perfon unlawfully fold fhall not in any of the above cafes be fubjected to any punifhment in confequence, but returned to his family or right owner.

If any one receives and detains a fugitive child, and, inftead of prefenting it to the magiftrates, fells fuch child for a flave, he fhall be punifhed with 90 blows, and banifhment for two years and a half. — Whoever fells any fuch fugitive child for marriage or adoption, fhall fuffer the punifhment of 80 blows and two years banifhment; in each of thefe cafes, the punifhment fhall be lefs by one degree, when the fugitive is found to be a flave.

All fugitives fo difpofed of fhall fuffer punifhment one degree lefs than that inflicted on the feller, except when the previous offence of the fugitive fhall have been the greateft, in which cafe the feverer of the two punifhments to which he is liable, fhall be inflicted.

Whoever,

Whoever, inftead of felling, retains for his own ufe as a flave, wife, or child, any fuch loft, ftrayed, or fugitive child, or flave, fhall be equally liable to be punifhed as above mentioned; but if only guilty of retaining the fame for a fhort time, the punifhment fhall not exceed 80 blows.

When the purchafer, or the negociator of the purchafe, is aware of the unlawfulnefs of the tranfaction, he fhall fuffer punifhment one degree lefs than that inflicted on the feller, and the amount of the pecuniary confideration fhall be forfeited to government; but when he or they are found to have been unacquainted therewith, they fhall not be liable to punifhment, and the money fhall be reftored to the party from whom it had been received.

Whoever falfely claims a free perfon as his flave fhall be punifhed with 100 blows and three years banifhment; if falfely claiming fuch perfon as his wife or child, with 90 blows and banifhment for two years and a half; if falfely claiming the flave of another perfon, with 100 blows only.

One claufe.

SECTION LXXX.—*Impartiality in the Levy of Taxes and perfonal Services.*

In all diftricts, where the taxes in money and in kind, and the extraordinary and mifcellaneous perfonal fervices to be required from the people, are eftimated and apportioned, due regard fhall be had in each cafe to the extent of the family in point of numbers and to its ability to contribute, according to which the members thereof fhall be rated in the fuperior, middle, or inferior clafs, of inhabitants.

If the poorer inhabitants are compelled to perform the fervices from which thofe who are rich are excufed, or any other fuch unjuft partiality

tiality is discoverable in the conduct of the officers of government, it shall be lawful for the injured poor to appeal and complain thereof to the tribunal of the immediate superiors of such officers, whence they may repeat the appeal to the several superior tribunals in succession. — The officer and his official agents, who shall be convicted of any such breach of this law, shall, each of them, be punished with 100 blows, and the unjust or partial arrangement shall be annulled. The officers of any tribunal where such an appeal shall have been refused a hearing, shall be punished with 80 blows; and if they shall appear to have been bribed to make such refusal, they shall be punished as many degrees beyond 80 blows, as the law against bribery to commit an unlawful act, may warrant or require.

Five clauses.

SECTION LXXXI. — *Impartiality in the Allotment of personal Services.*

All persons who, being engaged in providing personal services of labourers and artificers for government agreeably to the laws, do not duly provide, and impartially allot the same, shall be punished with 20 blows when there is a deviation in respect to one individual; and one degree more severely for every additional five individuals whom it may concern, as far as 60 blows at the utmost.

If such persons as are engaged to perform the required services delay, or fail in the execution of their engagements; or if the required services having been performed, they are still detained by the magistrate beyond the lawful period, the offending party shall be punished with 10 blows for one day, and one degree more severely for every additional three days delay, as far as 50 blows at the utmost.

No clause.

Section LXXXII.—*Evasion of personal Service.*

All citizens who, not being obliged to labour for their own support, place their unemployed sons, grandsons, brothers, or nephews, in the suite of an officer of government, in order to evade the performances of the personal services due by them to the state, shall (being masters of families) be punished with 100 blows; the officer of government conniving at such evasion, shall be liable to the same punishment, or, in the event of his having received a bribe, to such greater punishment as he might be liable to, for taking a bribe to such an amount, for an unlawful purpose. — The person so placed in the suite of an officer of government, shall not suffer corporal punishment, but be sent into the less remote military banishment.

When any of the superior and distinguished magistrates are guilty of such connivance, they shall be tried according to this law, but the sentence shall not be considered final until it has been submitted to, and approved by, the Emperor.

No clause.

Section LXXXIII. — *Supernumerary Persons exercising district Authority prohibited.*

In all districts of the empire, 100 families shall form a division, and shall consult together, in order to provide a head and ten assessors, who are to attend successively, in order to assist in the collection of the taxes, and duly to ascertain the performance of all other public duties and services.

If there are any other persons who, falsely assuming authority under the characters of deputies, assistants, and the like, create disturbances and harass the people, they shall be punished with 100 blows and banished.

The elders, who are to be appointed to these offices, shall be chosen among the most respectable persons of maturer age who belong to the district, and no person shall be eligible to, or accept, the said offices, who has ever held any civil or military employments, or who has ever been convicted of any crime. —Whoever accepts the same, in defiance of this law, shall be punished with 60 blows, and dismissed; the officer of government, who sanctions such undue appointment, shall be punished with 40 blows, at the least, and eventually suffer such further punishment as he may be liable to, in consequence of being guilty of receiving a bribe for an unlawful purpose.

One clause.

Section LXXXIV. — *Evasion of personal Service by Concealment or Desertion.*

All persons and families, who shall remove to a neighbouring district or city, in order to conceal themselves, and avoid rendering any personal service, shall be punished with 100 blows, sent back to, and compelled to serve at, the place of their original settlement.

The head of the district, and the superintending magistrates and clerks, if guilty of conniving at the departure of such persons; and all those in the neighbouring district who may have harboured and concealed them, shall be held to be participators in the offence, and punished accordingly.

Moreover, if the head man of the neighbouring district, knowing of the removal thereto of such persons, does not inform against and detain them; if the magistrate of the district to which they belong, does not issue letters of advice to the other magistrates, for the purpose of procuring their return; and lastly, if, after the issue of such letters, the magistrate of the district to which such persons have removed, declines to send them back, and protects them in defiance of the law, each of those officers shall be punished with 60 blows.

Any labourer, artificer, or other individual, who, during the period of his engagement to render personal service to the state, shall absent himself for one day, shall be punished with 10 blows, and one degree more severely for every additional five days absence, as far as 50 blows at the utmost.

The superintending magistrate and his clerks, when they connive thereat, shall be considered as participators in the offence, and be also liable to any contingent aggravation of punishment which may arise from the law against bribery for an unlawful purpose.

If the offence shall not appear to have been committed through the connivance of the magistrate and clerks, they shall still be liable to suffer the punishment of 20 blows, if five men escape; and to be punished one degree more severely, as far as 40 blows at the utmost, for every additional five men so offending: in the case of any number less than five, they shall be excused.

Three clauses.

SECTION LXXXV. — *Selection of the Guards and Attendants of Prisons.*

The guards and attendants of prisons shall be selected from among the most trust-worthy and experienced persons in the employ of government; and any person who, after having been so selected, shall not attend, but name a substitute to perform his duty, shall be punished with 40 blows for such offence.

No clause.

SECTION LXXXVI.—*Personal Services of Labourers and Artificers required beyond the legal Extent, or for private Purposes.*

All officers of government holding magisterial situations, or superintending public works, who shall compel persons under their jurisdiction to serve as labourers or artificers for any private purpose, beyond the distance of 100 *lee* from their houses, or who shall employ such persons in their private concerns for a considerable time at their own houses, shall be punishable in the following manner: In the case of ordinary magistrates so offending, they shall be punished with 40 blows, when one individual is unlawfully employed; and one degree more severely, as far as 80 blows, for every additional five individuals concerned; in the case of superintendants of public works, the punishment shall in every instance be more severe by two degrees. Each individual employed as above, shall receive a compensation of 8 *fen* 5 *lee* 5 *hao per* day*. Temporary services, however, required on the occasion of mourning, or of a festival, or under any other such accidental circumstances, shall not be deemed an infringement of this law.

In general, not more than 50 persons shall be employed on any kind of service at one time, or any individual detained thereon beyond a period of three days; and whenever these limits are transgressed, it shall be always considered and punished as a case of private service.

No clause.

---

* ,0855 decimal parts of a *leang*, or ounce of silver, and equivalent to nearly seven pence sterling.

SECTION LXXXVII. — *Individuals deserting, or prematurely separating from, their Families.*

Sons or grandsons who form to themselves a separate establishment from their parents and grand-parents, and also make a division of the family property, shall, provided such parents and grand-parents personally prosecute, be punished, on conviction, with 100 blows.

Also, the sons of the same parents, who shall form to themselves separate establishments, and divide their respective proportions of the inheritance, previous to the expiration of the lawful period of mourning, shall be punished with 80 blows, provided they are convicted upon an information laid by an elder relation in the first degree, and provided that they had not been expressly directed to do so in the last will of their parent deceased.

One clause.

SECTION LXXXVIII. — *Younger and inferior Branches of a Family, disposing of the Property without Leave.*

Any younger and inferior member of a family, living with the others under the same roof, who applies to his own use, or otherwise disposes of, the joint family-property without permission, shall be punished with 20 blows, if the value amounts to 10 ounces of silver, and one degree more severely as far as 100 blows, for every additional 10 ounces value.

An unjust or partial division of the patrimony between the elder and younger branches of a family, upon their separation, shall likewise be punished agreeably to the tenor of this law *.

Two clauses.

* On the subject of this and the preceding section, see the Appendix, No. XIII.

Section LXXXIX. — *Care of the aged and infirm.*

All poor destitute widowers and widows, the fatherless and childless, the helpless and the infirm, shall receive sufficient maintenance and protection from the magistrates of their native city or district, whenever they have neither relations nor connexions upon whom they can depend for support. — Any magistrate refusing such maintenance and protection, shall be punished with 60 blows.

Also, when any such persons are maintained and protected by government, the superintending magistrate and his subordinates, if failing to afford them the legal allowance of food and raiment, shall be punished in proportion to the amount of the deficiency, according to the law against an embezzlement of government stores *.

Six clauses.

* Agreeably to the tenor of this law, there are at Pekin, and in other parts of China, certain establishments for the support and education of foundlings, and for the maintenance of the aged and destitute; but the sacred regard which is habitually paid by the Chinese to the claims of kindred, operates more effectually and extensively in the relief of the poor, (except in the seasons of scarcity and distress from accidental causes), than almost any legal provision could be expected to do in so vast and populous an empire.

END OF THE FIRST BOOK OF THE THIRD DIVISION.

BOOK II.

LANDS AND TENEMENTS.

Section XC. — *Fraudulent Evasion of the Land-Tax.*

WHOEVER fraudulently evades the payment of the land-tax, by suppressing or omitting the register of his land in the public books, shall be punishable in proportion to the amount of the chargeable land omitted, in the following manner:—When the unregistered land amounts to one *meu**, and does not exceed five *meu*, with 40 blows; and for every additional number of five *meu* so suppressed, the punishment shall be increased one degree, until it arrives at the limit of 100 blows. The unregistered lands shall be forfeited to the state, and the arrears of the land-tax (computed according to the period during which it had been unpaid, the extent of the land, and the rate at which it would have been lawfully chargeable), shall be at the same time discharged in full.

When the land is entered in the register, but falsely represented, as unproductive when productive, lightly chargeable when heavily chargeable; or if the land is nominally made over in trust to another person, in order to exempt the real proprietor from personal service,

---

* A considerable difficulty has been experienced in estimating the exact extent of the division of land, called by the Chinese *meu*, owing to the various modes of admeasurement practiced in China at different periods, and by different classes of people; but from a comparison of several accounts given in original Chinese works, it appears certain that the legal measure at present consists of 240 square *Poo* or paces; that each *poo* is equal to six *che*, and that a *che* exceeds the English foot by rather more than half an inch.—According to this computation the *meu*, or Chinese acre, may be roughly estimated at a 1000 square yards of our measure.

the punishment, whether corporal or arising out of the payment of the arrears of the tax, shall be inflicted in the manner and according to the scale above stated; but instead of a forfeiture of the lands, the register of them shall simply be corrected, and the assessment and personal service of the real proprietor be established agreeably thereto.

When the land is thus illegally made over in trust, the person who undertakes the trust shall suffer equal punishment with the person who grants it.

If the head inhabitant of the district is privy to any breach of the law, but does not take cognizance of it, he shall be equally punishable with the original transgressors.

When any families or individuals return to the district and calling to which they originally belonged, and there happens to be a deficiency of resident population, in proportion to the extent and productiveness of the ancient allotments of lands therein, they shall be allowed to contribute to the cultivation thereof, in proportion to their capacity; and upon a due representation being laid before the magistrates, an allotment of unoccupied lands shall be made to them; and according to the entry thereof in the public registers, they shall thenceforwards be liable to the land-tax, and to personal service.

If any such individuals claim in their representations an excessive share of the unoccupied lands, so that they are afterwards unable to cultivate what is granted to them, they shall, when such excess amounts to three *meu*, and does not exceed ten *meu*, be liable to a punishment of 30 blows, and be punished one degree more severely for every further excess of ten *meu*, until the punishment reaches the limit of 80 blows; the excess shall moreover be forfeited back to the state.

When applications of this nature are made to the magistrate in any district where the cultivating population is already sufficient or excesfive, a part of the unoccupied lands in the nearest vicinity shall be allotted to the applicants, in proportion to their means of keeping up the cultivation.

Five clauses.

Section XCI.—*Personal Visitation of Lands suffering from any Calamity* *.

In all districts wherein the Lands have suffered from a temporary calamity, as from excessive rain, the overflowing of waters, excessive drought, unseasonable frosts, flights of locusts, and the like, the customary assessments shall be proportionally reduced, or remitted altogether; all representations on this subject the magistrates shall be obliged to receive; and if they fail to take cognizance thereof, both by reporting the same to the tribunals of their superiors, and by personally inspecting the injured lands; or if the magistrate of the superior tribunal does not dispatch an officer of government, under his immediate orders, to examine into and verify the facts reported to him by his inferiors; in all such cases, the omission shall be punished with 80 blows.

If the officer of government employed in the first visitation, or the officer employed in the re-examination, does not himself personally attend on the spot; or if although, he does personally attend, he afterwards, instead of making a faithful report, grounded on a diligent investigation, negligently trusts to the representations of the head

---

* A remission of a part or of the whole of the regulated amount of the assessment of the land-tax; and, at the same time, a prompt distribution of a supply of grain from the public stores, are the means most usually employed by the government to alleviate the distress, which a deficient harvest, whenever it occurs, must, in an empire depending solely on its own productions for the subsistence of a population already for the most part redundant, necessarily occasion. In the Appendix, No. XIV., some account of one or two recent instances of this kind is inserted.

head inhabitant of the diſtrict, or his deputies, and thereupon deſcribes as productive what is ſterile, and as ſterile what is productive, or in any other manner extenuates or exaggerates the circumſtances of the caſe, ſuch a ſtatement muſt neceſſarily be founded upon fraud or colluſion, and, while it deceives the government, it muſt in an equal degree injure the people; the offender ſhall, therefore, be puniſhed with 100 blows, deprived of his office, and rendered incapable of afterwards holding any rank or office under government. The amount likewiſe of the taxes, which in conſequence of ſuch miſconduct had been either improperly levied, or cauſeleſsly remitted, ſhall be eſtimated, and conformably thereto a reference ſhall be made to the law concerning pecuniary malverſation in general, in order that, if the puniſhment authorized by the latter prove the greateſt, it may be inflicted in preference to that hereby provided. — The head inhabitant of the diſtrict, and his deputies, ſhall be liable to puniſhment in an equal degree, when participating in the foregoing offence, in the manner above ſtated; and if they are further convicted of bribery, they ſhall be liable to any aggravation of the puniſhment which may ariſe from a reference to the law againſt bribery for an unlawful purpoſe.

Nevertheleſs, if the incorrectneſs of the report of the inſpecting magiſtrate be merely imputable to an error, or to inadvertence in aſcertaining the limits, neither the officer of government, nor his clerks, nor the head inhabitant of the diſtrict, nor his deputies, ſhall be liable to puniſhment, when the error does not exceed ten *meu*; from ten to twenty *meu*, the puniſhment ſhall amount to 20 blows, and be encreaſed one degree for each additional extent of incorrectneſs of twenty *meu*, until it arrives at the limit of 80 blows; and this offence not being deemed of a private or perſonal nature, ſhall not ſubject the magiſtrates to a loſs of their rank or offices.

If, on any ſuch occaſion, an individual, or head of a family, repreſents his productive lands to be unproductive, and falſely pleads loſs by any temporary calamity, he shall be punished with 40 blows when the misrepresentation exceeds one and is less than five *meu*; the punishment shall be increased one degree for every additional five *meu* so falsely represented, until it arrives at the limit of 100 blows, and the full amount of the customary assessment upon such lands shall be thenceforward strictly levied.

Seventeen clauses.

SECTION XCII. — *Lands of the Nobility and Officers of Government.*

All the lands and houses comprised in the estates of the nobility and officers of government, (except such as by the express direction and command of the Emperor, are exempted from taxation and personal service,) shall be duly reported by the respective tenants or stewards to the magistrates of the districts, and correctly entered on the public registers, that according to such entries they may be assessed and held accountable for personal services, as in all ordinary cases.

The tenant or steward of the land shall be responsible for the execution of this law, and if he neglects to comply with it, he shall be punished in proportion to the extent of the land omitted to be inserted in the register; that is to say, from one to three *meu* with sixty blows, and one degree more severely for every further omission of three *meu* in the register, provided the punishment does not in any case exceed 100 blows, and three years banishment. The lands shall moreover be forfeited to the state, and the arrears of the tax discharged in full, agreeably to the extent, the time, and rate of legal assessment.

If the head inhabitants of the several districts, or the magistrates thereof, upon a visitation of such lands, make false returns, in order to obtain favour with the proprietors; or if they connive at the omissions in the regifters, of which the latter are guilty, they fhall equally participate in the punifhment. They fhall not, however, be punifhed under this law in any manner, for the offences of others, except when it is proved that they have thus actually connived at the fame.

No claufe.

Section XCIII.— *Fraudulent Sale of Lands and Tenements.*

Whoever fraudulently fells, exchanges, or profeffes himfelf proprietor of, the lands of other perfons; and whoever, by a fictitious agreement, without due pecuniary confideration, purchafes, or wrongfully takes poffeffion of, the lands or tenements of others, fhall be punifhed according to the extent of the land, or the number of the tenements in queftion; if not exceeding one *meu*, or one tenement, with 50 blows, and one degree more feverely for each addition of five to the number of *meu*, or three to the number of tenements, provided the punifhment do not in any cafe exceed 80 blows, and two years banifhment. — If, however, the lands or tenements in queftion are the property of government, the punifhment in each cafe fhall be proportionably greater by two degrees.

Whoever feizes by open violence the lands and tenements of government, or of individuals, (that is to fay, not only cultivated lands and inhabited houfes, but alfo burying-grounds, fifh-ponds, cane plantations, metal founderies, and the like,) fhall, without reference to the number or extent, receive 100 blows, and fuffer pepetual banifhment to the diftance of 3000 *lee*.

When any individual takes land, or the produce of land, under litigation or belonging to others, and upon the pretext of being the lawful proprietor thereof, prefents the fame to officers of government, or to other perfons having influence and authority, as a free gift or donation,

donation, the giver and receiver shall each be punished with 100 blows, and three years banishment.

In general; all lands which, by fraud or force, have been unlawfully obtained, together with the produce thereof reaped during the unlawful possession; secondly, the sums for which any such lands and produce may have been clandestinely sold; thirdly, all the unreaped produce remaining on such lands; and lastly, the amount of all the other advantages whatsoever derived from such lands, during the period of unlawful possession, shall severally become forfeitures, and be restored or repaid to whom they are due, whether to the state, or to private individuals.

When this law is transgressed by any of the privileged officers of government, the circumstances of the case shall be investigated, and the nature of the punishment to be inflicted shall be determined as in ordinary cases, but the latter shall not be carried into effect until the sentence is submitted to, and ratified by, His Imperial Majesty.

Nine clauses.

SECTION XCIV. — *Officers of Government restricted from purchasing Lands within the Limits of their Jurisdiction.*

The officers and clerks officiating in any of the departments of government, which possess a territorial jurisdiction, shall not, during the exercise of their authority therein, purchase, or hold by purchase, any lands or tenements within the limits of such jurisdiction; whoever is convicted of a breach of this law shall suffer 50 blows, and be removed from his office, but shall not be thereby rendered incapable of holding offices under government elsewhere; the lands and tenements so unlawfully held shall be forfeited to government.

Two clauses.

SECTION XCV. — *Law of Mortgages* *.

Whoever takes lands or tenements by way of mortgage, without entering into a regular contract, duly authenticated and affessed with the legal duty by the proper magistrate, shall receive 50 blows, and forfeit to government half the confideration money of the mortgage. —If the mortgager does not transfer to the mortgagee unreservedly the whole produce of the land upon which the taxes are charged and made payable to government, he shall be punished in proportion to the extent of the property, in the following manner: if from one to five *meu*, with 40 blows, and one degree more severely for each five additional *meu*, until the punishment amounts to 100 blows; the land so illegally mortgaged shall be forfeited to government.

If the proprietor of lands and tenements already mortgaged, attempts to raife money thereon by a fecond mortgage, the amount obtained upon such falfe pretences shall be afcertained, and the offender punished accordingly, as in the cafe of an ordinary theft to the fame extent, except that he shall not be liable to be branded.

The pecuniary confideration received by the fraudulent mortgager shall be restored always to the mortgagee, unlefs such mortgagee is himfelf privy to the unlawfulnefs of the tranfaction, in which cafe it shall be forfeited to government.

The faid mortgagee and the negotiator of the bargain, when either of them is acquainted with the unlawfulnefs of the tranfaction, shall

---

* The mode here defcribed of lending money upon landed fecurity, is a very ancient and frequent practice among the Chinefe, and though certainly a fpecies of mortgage, will be feen to be modified by fome peculiar regulations. This fubject has been already noticed by the miffionaries in the *Memoires fur les Chinois*, vol. iv. p. 386. but as it is connected with the interefting and difputed queftion of the nature of the tenure of lands in China, an abftract of fome of the more material claufes annexed to the law, have been inferted in further illuftration of it, in the Appendix, No. XV.

moreover

moreover receive the fame punifhment as the mortgager. In all fuch cafes, the firft and lawful mortgagee fhall remain in poffeffion.

If, after the period, fpecified in the deed by which any lands or tenements are profeffed to be mortgaged or pledged by the proprietor, is expired, the faid proprietor offers to redeem his property by the payment back of the original confideration upon which he had parted with it, it fhall not be allowed the mortgagee to refufe to comply; any inftance of fuch refufal fhall fubject him to the punifhment of 40 blows, and to the forfeiture of all the produce of the land which he may have reaped after the expiration of fuch period. Neverthelefs, this law fhall only have effect when the proprietor is really able at the expiration of the prefcribed period to redeem his lands, and not otherwife.

Ten claufes.

Section XCVI.— *Sowing and tilling Lands belonging to others.*

Whoever ploughs and fows the lands of another clandeftinely, that is to fay, without giving notice to the proprietor, fhall fuffer punifhment in proportion to the extent of the land illicitly cultivated; when not exceeding one *meu*, with 30 blows, and one degree more feverely in proportion to each additional five *meu*, as far as 80 blows.— If the land had not been previoufly under cultivation, the punifhment fhall be lefs in each cafe by one degree.

If the land of a ftranger is cultivated by force, that is to fay, in defiance of the proprietor, the punifhment fhall be one degree more fevere in each cafe.

If the land is the property of government, the punifhment of intrufive and unlawful culture fhall be further aggravated two degrees; and in general, the profit derived from the cultivation of the land fhall shall be forfeited either to the individual proprietor, or to the state, according to the circumstances of the case.

One clause.

Section XCVII.—*Uncultivated and neglected Lands.*

In every district of the empire, when the lands which have been entered on the public registers as liable to the land-tax, and as subjecting the proprietors to the demands of personal service, are, without any cause, such as inundation, drought, or other calamity, neglected and omitted to be duly cultivated; as, for instance, if the established mulberry, hemp, and other similar plantations are not duly kept up, the head inhabitant of the district shall be held responsible, and punished according to the relative extent of the uncultivated to that of the cultivated portion of the registered lands in his district.—If the unclutivated portion is one-tenth of the whole, he shall be punished with 20 blows, and one degree more severely, as far as 80 blows, for each additional tenth uncultivated. The presiding magistrate of the city of the third order, to which the district is subjected, shall likewise be punishable, but less severely by two degrees in each case than the head inhabitant. The assessors of the chief magistrate shall suffer punishment as accessaries to his offence.

The individual proprietor also, who suffers his land to remain uncultivated, or who neglects his mulberry, hemp, or other plantations, shall be punished according to the proportion which the neglected part bears to the whole of his registered property,—if it amounts to one-fifth, with 20 blows, and one degree more severely for every additional fifth left uncultivated.

His lands shall moreover be assessed with the land-tax in proportion to the amount of the produce they are judged capable of yielding, and the contribution shall be levied on the proprietor accordingly.

No clause.

SECTION XCVIII. — *Destroying or damaging the Harvests and Articles connected therewith.*

Whoever purposely destroys, or abandons to destruction, any implements or utensils of husbandry, cuts down timber trees, or in general, damages the produce of the land, shall be punished in proportion to the estimated amount of the damage, according to the law against theft to the same extent, except that he shall not be branded; — if the article or produce destroyed or damaged was the property of government, the punishment in such case shall be encreased two degrees.

When the articles or produce of the earth belonging to government are lost or destroyed by an inadvertence only, the punishment shall be three degrees less than in the case of a wilful offence to the same extent; but in all cases, the extent of the damage shall be estimated, and the offender compelled to replace the amount to government, or to the individual proprietor, according to the circumstances of the case. — When any private property is lost or destroyed through inadvertence, corporal punishment shall not be inflicted on the offender, but he shall, as already stated, replace the amount of the damage or loss sustained by the injured party.

Whoever destroys the tomb-stones, or the emblematical figures cut in stone belonging to tombs, shall be punished with 80 blows; whoever destroys the figures of domestic or drural eities shall be punished with 90 blows; and generally, whoever destroys or damages the houses,

houses, walls, or buildings of any kind belonging to others, shall be punished in proportion to the estimated expence of labour and materials necessary to replace the same, according to the law for the punishment of pecuniary injuries in general. — In all these cases, the damage shall be fully repaired by the offending party, whose punishment shall, moreover, be raised in each case two degrees, when the buildings damaged or destroyed had belonged to government. When, however, the buildings of government or individuals are damaged or destroyed inadvertently, the person who did the injury shall be liable to no other punishment beside the obligation to repair the damage, or re-place the value of the property he had destroyed.

One clause.

SECTION XCIX. — *Taking away, without Leave, the Fruit growing in Gardens, or Orchards.*

Whoever, without leave, takes away or eats the fruit growing in the grounds or gardens of another, shall be liable to punishment in proportion to the value thereof, according to the law concerning pecuniary injuries. — Destroying or damaging the fruit shall be punished according to the same scale; and if the fruit so eaten or destroyed is taken from grounds or gardens belonging to government which had been appropriated to the preparation of fermented or spirituous liquors, or of any articles of subsistence for the public service, the punishment shall be in each of such cases, two degrees more severe than it would have been otherwise.

If the person who has the charge of any such property of government, gives it away, or connives at its being taken away, he shall equally participate in the punishment of the receiver or consumer. If he appropriates the same to his own use, he shall suffer punishment in proportion to the amount, according to the law concerning the embezzlement of the property of government.

No clause.

SECTION C. — *Misapplication of the Boats or Carriages of Government.*

If any person having the custody of the property, or the superintendance over any of the departments, of government, applies to his own private use and advantage, or lends out to others, the carriages, boats, warehouses, mills, or other buildings or implements belonging to government; he, as well as the borrower of such articles, shall suffer 50 blows; and if an officer of government, the offender shall moreover forfeit to the state the estimated amount of the charge of the hire of the articles, to any extent not exceeding their value. The offenders shall likewise be liable to punishment in proportion to the amount of the aforesaid charge, one degree more severely than the law prescribes in ordinary cases of pecuniary injury, whenever such punishment, being greater, supersedes that hereby provided.

No clause.

END OF THE SECOND BOOK OF THE THIRD DIVISION.

BOOK III.

MARRIAGE*.

SECTION CI. — *Marriages how regulated.*

WHEN a marriage is intended to be contracted, it shall be, in the first instance, reciprocally explained to, and clearly understood by, the families interested, whether the parties who design to marry are or are not diseased, infirm, aged, or under age; and whether they are the children of their parents by blood, or only by adoption; if either of the contracting families then object, the proceedings shall be carried no further; if they still approve, they shall then in conjunction with the negociators of the marriage, if such there be, draw up the marriage-articles, and determine the amount of the marriage-presents.

If, after the woman is thus regularly affianced by the recognition of the marriage-articles, or by a personal interview and agreement between the families, the family of the intended bride should repent having entered into the contract, and refuse to execute it, the person amongst them who had authority to give her away shall be punished with 50 blows, and the marriage shall be completed agreeably to the

---

* The peculiar customs and usages which are adverted to in this book of the laws, will be found illustrated and exemplified in a pleasing manner, together with an interesting picture of domestic life in China, in an English translation of a Chinese novel, which was edited many years ago by the learned and ingenious Dr. Percy, Bishop of Dromore, under the title of " *Hau-Kiou-Choaan,* or the Pleasing History." — The translation of this little work, not having been edited by the translator, and having, in part, been taken from a Portuguese version, cannot be expected to be minutely accurate, though perhaps sufficiently so for the purpose in view, and the translator of the present work has had the satisfaction of ascertaining its authenticity, by a comparison with the Chinese original, of which he has a copy now in his possession.

original contract.—Although the marriage-articles should not have been drawn up in writing, the acceptance of the marriage-presents shall be sufficient evidence of the agreement between the parties.

If, after the female is affianced, but previous to the completion of the marriage, her family promises her in marriage to another, the person having authority to give her away shall be punished with 70 blows; if such promise is made after the first marriage is actually completed, (that is to say, the bride is personally presented to and received by the bridegroom) the punishment shall be encreased to 80 blows.

If the person who accepts such promise is, at the same time, aware of the existence of a previous contract or marriage, he shall participate equally in the punishment, and whatever marriage-presents he may have transmitted on the strength of such promise, shall be forfeited to government.—On the other hand, if ignorant thereof, he shall not be punishable, and the marriage-presents made by him shall be restored.—The bride shall remain with the bridegroom to whom she was first married or affianced, unless he declines, in which case he shall receive back the amount of his marriage-present, and the bride shall be transferred to the family of the bridegroom to whom she was secondly affianced.

If the family of the intended bridegroom, after having agreed as aforesaid, repents of the contract, and makes marriage-presents to another woman, the same punishment shall be inflicted, as in the cases already mentioned. The bridegroom shall be obliged to receive his originally intended bride; and the female, to whom he is secondly affianced, shall retain the marriage-presents made to her, and be at the same time at liberty to marry another person.

If either of the contracted parties, previous to the completion of the marriage, are guilty of theft or adultery; that is to say, have been convicted of offences of such a description, the law for punishing a breach of the contract as aforesaid shall not be enforced. If the family of the

the bride deceives the family of the bridegroom, fo as to induce them to contract a marriage, by indicating and leading them to expect a different perfon from the one actually named and defcribed in the contract, the giver away of the woman fhall be punifhed with 80 blows, and her family fhall reftore the marriage-prefents. If the family of the bridegroom is guilty of this offence, the punifhment of the contractor fhall be one degree more fevere, and the marriage-prefents fhall remain with the family of the bride. If fuch marriage, thus contracted through mifreprefentation, is not completed, the bride or bridegroom, whom the other party had been led to expect, fhall complete the marriage, inftead of the bride or bridegroom who had been deceitfully fubftituted; if the marriage under the aforefaid falfe pretences, had neverthelefs been completed, it fhall be fufficient that the parties be feparated.

Although the parties had been lawfully affianced to each other, and the marriage prefents delivered and accepted; yet if the bridegroom forcibly takes away his bride, previous to the period agreed upon, or if the bride is defignedly retained and refufed to the bridegroom, after fuch period is arrived, the contractor of the marriage in the latter cafe, and the bridegroom in the former cafe, fhall be punifhed with 50 blows.

If, while a junior relation is at a diftance from his family, and engaged either in trade, or in official employment under government, his grandfather, father, uncle, or fenior coufin, binds him by a marriage-contract, and he, being ignorant thereof, happens to contract and complete a marriage with fome other female during his abfence, fuch marriage fhall be held valid, and the contract made by his relations being therefore fet afide, the affianced female will be at liberty to contract another marriage. If however, fuch abfent junior member of a family had only contracted a marriage, he fhall relinquifh it, and in preference fulfil that contract of marriage which had been made for him by his relations, the female to whom he had perfonally contracted himfelf, being alfo freed from her engagement to him. — A breach of this

this law shall be punished with 80 blows, and compliance with these regulations shall be duly enforced by the magistrate of the district.

Four clauses.

SECTION CII. — *Lending Wives or Daughters on Hire.*

Whoever lends any one of his wives, to be hired as a temporary wife, shall be punished with 80 blows,—whoever lends his daughter in like manner, shall be punished with 60 blows; the wife or daughter in such cases, shall not be held responsible.

Whoever, falsely representing any of his wives as his sister, gives her away in marriage, shall receive 100 blows, and the wife consenting thereto, shall be punished with 80 blows.

Those who knowingly receive in marriage the wives, or hire for a limited time the wives or daughters of others, shall participate equally in the aforesaid punishment, and the parties thus unlawfully connected, shall be separated; the daughter shall be returned to her parents, and the wife to the family to which she originally belonged; the pecuniary consideration in each case shall be forfeited to government. Those who ignorantly receive such persons in marriage, contrary to the laws, shall be excused, and recover the amount of the marriage-presents.

One clause.

SECTION CIII. — *Regard to Rank and Priority among Wives*.*

Whoever degrades his first or principal wife to the condition of an inferior wife or concubine, shall be punished with 100 blows. Whoever

---

* The peculiar limitations under which polygamy is allowed in China require here some explanation, as it was impossible in translating the text, to distinguish by any terms strictly appropriate, the two modes of espousal which are established by the Chinese laws, and which are equally distinct in point of form as in their legal consequences.

The

ever, during the life-time of his first wife, raises an inferior wife to the rank and condition of a first wife, shall be punished with 90 blows, and in both the cases, each of the several wives shall be replaced in the rank to which she was originally intitled upon her marriage.

Whoever, having a first wife living, enters into marriage with another female as a first wife, shall likewise be punished with 90 blows; and the marriage being confidered null and void, the parties shall be separated, and the woman returned to her parents.

No clause.

Section CIV. — *Ejecting from Home a Son-in-law* *.

Whoever either ejects the husband of his daughter whom he had received into his house as his son-in-law, or receives into his house another person, as the husband of such daughter, shall be punished with 100 blows. The wife shall not be punished unless she had assisted

---

The first or principal wife is usually chosen for the husband by his parents or senior relations, out of a family equal in point of rank and to other circumstances to his own, and is espoused with as much splendour and ceremony as the parties can afford; and the bride, when she is received into the house of the bridegroom, acquires all the rights and privileges, which, under the degraded state of the female sex in Asiatic nations, can be supposed to belong to a lawful wife.

A Chinese may afterwards lawfully espouse other wives, agreeably to his own choice, and with fewer ceremonies, as well as without any regard to equality in point of family and connexions: these wives are all subordinate to the first wife, but equal in rank among themselves. In describing this connexion, the term *inferior wife* has been preferred to that of hand-maid, or concubine, as there are always certain forms of espousal, and as the children of such wives have a contingent right to the inheritance.

* It is remarked in a note in the original Chinese, that the bridegroom, who, instead of taking home his bride to his own house, lives with her at the house of her parents, by so doing, deviates from the established forms of espousal; but that having been once so received as a son-in-law, the law protects him in the right which he had acquired, of either remaining there with his wife, or taking her away with him to a separate establishment.

and

and concurred in the ejection of her husband, in which case she shall likewise suffer 100 blows. The person, moreover, who is secondly received as a son-in-law, if privy to the illegality of the transaction, shall participate equally in the punishment, and forfeit to government the marriage-present, but otherwise, shall be excused from the punishment and the forfeiture. When the first marriage had been contracted, but not completed, the ejection of the intended son-in-law shall be punished less severely by five degrees. — The woman shall belong to her first contracted husband, and live with him separately from her father and mother.

No clause.

SECTION CV. — *Marriage during the legal Period of Mourning.*

If any man or woman enters into an equal marriage during the legal period of mourning for a deceased parent, or any widow enters into a second and equal marriage within the legal period of mourning for her deceased husband, the offending party shall be punished with 100 blows.

If it is not an equal match, that is to say, if a man takes an inferior wife from a subordinate rank, or a woman connects herself in marriage as one of the inferior wives of her husband, the punishment attending a breach of this law shall be less by two degrees.

If a widow who, during the life of her husband, had received honorary rank from the Emperor, ever marries again, she shall suffer punishment as above described, and moreover lose her rank, as well as be separated from her second husband.

Whoever knowingly contracts marriage with a widow of rank, or with any widow during the legal period of mourning, shall suffer punishment in each case proportionably less by five degrees, and the marriage-present shall be forfeited to government; if ignorant of the illegality

illegality of his conduct, he shall be exempt from punishment, and recover the marriage-present, but still be separated from his wife, as in the cases already stated

Whoever marries on equal terms, during the period of legal mourning for a grand-father, grand-mother, uncle or aunt, elder brother or elder sister, shall suffer 80 blows, but the marriage shall nevertheless be valid.

The marriage of, or with, inferior wives within such period shall be excused.

Whoever within the period of mourning for a father, mother, father or mother-in-law, or for a husband, completes an intended marriage to which the parties had been previously affianced, shall be punished with 80 blows.

If a widow, after the expiration of mourning for her husband, is really unwilling to enter into a second marriage; and nevertheless, her parents, grand-parents, or the parents or grand-parents of her late husband, force her to marry again, the party so compelling his daughter or grand-daughter to marry, shall be punished with 80 blows. If the widow is so compelled by any other relation in the first degree, such relation shall be punished one degree more severely;—if in a more remote degree, two degrees more severely. Neither the widow nor her second husband shall in these cases be punishable. — If the marriage is only contracted, but not completed, the widow shall remain in her first husband's family, and be permitted to continue single, and the marriage present shall be returned;—if the marriage has been completed, the widow shall live with her second husband, but the marriage-present shall be forfeited to government.

One clause.

Section CVI. — *Marriage during the Imprisonment of Parents.*

Whoever marries a wife or a husband upon equal terms of espousal, having a father, mother, grand-father or grand-mother at the same time under confinement in prison for a capital offence, shall be punished with 80 blows; — whoever at such time receives in marriage, or becomes by marriage, a subordinate wife, shall suffer punishment less by two degrees.

Nevertheless, if any such person enters into the marriage state at such period, by the express command of his or her parent or grand-parent in prison, no punishment shall ensue, provided the usual feast and entertainment is omitted; otherwise a punishment of 80 blows shall still be inflicted.

No clause.

Section CVII. — *Marriage between Persons having the same Family-Name.*

Whenever any persons having the same family-name intermarry, the parties and the contractor of the marriage shall each receive 60 blows, and the marriage being null and void, the man and woman shall be separated, and the marriage-presents forfeited to government*.

No clause.

---

* The most usual term in the Chinese language for describing " the people or nation," is *Pe-sing*, or " the hundred names." Although the names of families in China are at present somewhat more numerous, they are very few in proportion to the immense population, and the restrictions imposed by this law upon marriage must therefore be often embarrassing and inconvenient, however little the choice and inclination of the parties themselves, may under any circumstances, be consulted.

Section CVIII. — *Marriage between Persons related by Marriage.*

In general all marriages between persons who through another marriage are already related to each other in any of the four degrees, and all marriages with sisters by the same mother, though by a different father, or with the daughters of a wife's former husband, shall be considered as incestuous, and punished according to the law against a criminal intercourse with such relations *.

A man shall not marry his father's or mother's sister-in-law, his father's or mother's aunt's daughters, his son-in-law's or daughter-in-law's sister, or his grandson's wife's sister, on pain of receiving 100 blows for such offence.

Whoever marries his mother's brothers or mother's sister's daughter, shall receive 80 blows, and in these as well as the foregoing cases, the marriage shall be annulled, and the marriage-present forfeited.

Two clauses.

Section CIX. — *Marriage with Relations by Blood, or with the Widows of such Relations.*

Whoever marries a female relation beyond the fourth degree, or the widow of a male relation equally remote, shall be punished with 100 blows. Whoever marries the widow of a relation in the fourth degree, or of a sister's son, shall be punished with 60 blows, and one year's banishment. — Whoever marries the widow of any nearer relation, shall be punished according to the law against incestuous connexions with such persons. Nevertheless, when the connexion had been broken by a divorce, or an intervening marriage with a stranger, the offence shall in general be only punished with 80 blows.

* The book of the laws referred to in this and the following section is contained in the criminal division of the code, and entitled, *Incest and Adultery.*

Whoever receives in marriage any of his father's or grandfather's former wives, or his father's sisters, shall, whether they had been divorced or re-married, in all cases suffer death, by being beheaded. Whoever marries his brother's widow, shall be strangled.

The foregoing cases, in general apply to first wives only, and the punishment of marrying the inferior wives of such relatives as aforesaid, shall be less in each case by two degrees.

Whoever marries any female relation in the fourth, or any nearer degree, shall be punished according to the law concerning incest, and all such incestuous marriages shall be null and void.

Two clauses.

SECTION CX. — *Marriage of Officers of Government into Families subject to their Jurisdiction.*

If any officer belonging to the government of a city of the first, second, or third order, marries, while in office, the wife or daughter of any inhabitant of the country under his jurisdiction, he shall be punished with 80 blows.

If any officer of government marries the wife or daughter of any person having an interest in the legal proceedings at the same time under his investigation, he shall be punished with 100 blows, and the member of the family of the bride, who gave her away, shall be equally punishable. The woman, whether previously married or not, shall be restored to her parents, and the marriage-present forfeited in every case to government.

If the officer of government accomplishes the marriage by the force or influence of his authority, his punishment shall be increased two degrees, and the family of the female, being in such a case exempt from responsibility, she shall, if previously single, be restored to her parents;

rents; and if previously married, to her former husband; the marriage-present shall not in either case be forfeited.

If any officer of government, instead of marrying the female himself in any of the above cases, gives her in marriage to his son, grandson, younger brother, nephew, or other person belonging to his household, he shall be liable to the same punishment as aforesaid, but neither the bride nor the bridegroom shall suffer for such offence.

When the marriage is a compensation for some unjust decision on a subject under the magistrate's investigation, the punishment shall be encreased as far as the law, applicable to such a deviation from justice, may authorize.

No clause.

Section CXI. — *Marriage with absconded Females.*

Whoever receives and marries a female criminal, who had absconded from the fear of punishment, shall, whether she had been previously married or not, be punishable to the full extent of the crime such female had committed, setting aside only the aggravation of two degrees to which she is liable from her being a fugitive, and with a reduction of one degree, when the offence of the female is of a nature to be punishable with death. The marriage shall moreover be annulled, and the parties separated, unless the female was previously single, and obtains the benefit of a special or general pardon. When the person marrying a criminal fugitive had been ignorant of the circumstance of her being such, he shall be excused.

No clause.

Section CXII. — *Forcible Marriage of a free Man's Wife or Daughter.*

Whoever, confiding in his power and influence, seizes by violence the wife or daughter of a free-man, and carries her away to make her

one

one of his wives, shall suffer death, by being strangled after the usual period of confinement.

If the female was single, she shall be returned to her parents or relations; and, if previously married, to her lawful husband.

Whoever, instead of marrying such female himself, gives her in marriage to his son, grand-son, brother, nephew, or other person of his household, shall be liable to the same punishment, and the parties shall be separated, as in the former case; but the husband, not being the contriver of the offence, shall not be punishable.

Four clauses.

SECTION CXIII. — *Marriage with Female Musicians and Comedians.*

If any officer or clerk of government, either in the civil or military department, marries, as his first or other wife, a female musician or comedian, he shall be punished with 60 blows, and the marriage being null and void, the female shall be sent back to her parents and rendered incapable of returning to her profession. The marriage-present shall be forfeited to government.

If the son or grand-son, being the heir of any officer of government having hereditary rank, commits this offence, he shall suffer the same punishment, and whenever he succeeds to the inheritance, his parental honours shall descend to him under a reduction of one degree.

No clause.

SECTION CXIV. — *Marriage of Priests of* Foe *or* Tao-ffe *.

If any priest of *Foe* or *Tao-ffe* takes a first or inferior wife, he shall be punished with 80 blows, and expelled from the order to which he belonged. The member of the family of the female who gave her

---

* See Section XLII. and LXXVII. relative to these orders of priesthood in China.

away in marriage shall be equally punishable; the marriage shall be null and void, the female sent back to her family, and the marriage-present forfeited to government; all the other priests of the same establishment who were privy to the offence, shall be subject to the same corporal punishment, but not to expulsion from their order; if ignorant of the offence having been committed, they shall not suffer punishment in any respect.

If a priest solicits a woman in marriage, under pretence of obtaining a wife for his relations or servants, and afterwards appropriates the female to himself, the offence shall be punished according to the law prohibiting incestuous intercourse and adultery.

No clause.

SECTION CXV. — *Marriage between Free persons and Slaves.*

If any master of a family solicits and obtains in marriage for his slave, the daughter of a free-man, he shall be punished with 80 blows; — the member of the family who gives away the female in marriage shall suffer the same punishment, if aware that the intended husband is a slave, but not otherwise.

A slave soliciting and obtaining a daughter of a free-man in marriage, shall also be punished in the same manner; and if the master of the slave consents thereto, he shall suffer punishment less by two degrees; but, if he moreover receives such free-woman into his family as a slave, he shall be punished with 100 blows.

Likewise, whoever falsely represents a slave to be free, and thereby procures such slave a free husband or wife, shall suffer 90 blows. In all these cases the marriage shall be null and void, and the parties replaced in the ranks they had respectively held in the community.

No clause.

Section CXVI. — *Law of Divorce.*

If a husband repudiates his first wife, without her having broken the matrimonial connexion by the crime of adultery, or otherwise; and without her having furnished him with any of the seven justifying causes of divorce, he shall in every such case be punished with 80 blows. Moreover, although one of the seven justifying causes of divorce should be chargeable upon the wife, namely, (1) barrenness; (2) lasciviousness; (3) disregard of her husband's parents; (4) talkativeness; (5) thievish propensities; (6) envious and suspicious temper; and, lastly, (7) inveterate infirmity; yet, if any of the three reasons against a divorce should exist, namely, (1) the wife's having mourned three years for her husband's parents; (2) the family's having become rich after having been poor previous to, and at the time of, marriage; and, (3) the wife's having no parents living to receive her back again; in these cases, none of the seven aforementioned causes will justify a divorce, and the husband who puts away his wife upon such grounds, shall suffer punishment two degrees less than that last stated, and be obliged to receive her again.

If the wife shall have broken the matrimonial connexion by an act of adultery, or by any other act, which by law not only authorizes but requires that the parties should be separated, the husband shall receive a punishment of 80 blows, if he retains her.

When the husband and wife do not agree, and both parties are desirous of separation, the law limiting the right of divorce shall not be enforced to prevent it.

If, upon the husband's refusing to consent to a divorce, the wife quits her home and absconds, she shall be punished with 100 blows, and her husband shall be allowed to sell her in marriage; if, during such absence from her home, she contracts marriage with another person, she shall suffer death, by being strangled, after the usual period of confinement.

If, previous to the expiration of a period of three years after a husband had deserted and been no more heard of by his wife, such wife, without giving notice at a tribunal of government, should likewise quit her home and abscond, she shall be punished with 80 blows; and the punishment shall be increased to 100 blows, if she should moreover presume to contract another marriage within such period.

In all the foregoing cases, the first wife only is intended to be adverted to, but the laws in every instance shall be applied in cases of the inferior wives, upon a reduction being made in the punishment to the extent of two degrees for each offence.

To render the act of the wife a second marriage, there must have been a person to give her away to the new husband, and a delivery of marriage-presents; otherwise, it is to be considered simply as a case of adultery.

If a female slave deserts from her master's house, she shall be punished with 80 blows, or with 100 blows if she contracts a marriage during such absence, and in both cases she shall be restored to her master.

Whoever harbours a fugitive wife or slave, or marries them knowing them to be fugitives, shall participate equally in their punishment, except in capital cases, when the punishment shall be reduced one degree. The marriage-present in all such cases is forfeited to government. When, however, the person harbouring or marrying the fugitive is really ignorant of her criminality, he shall not be subject to any punishment, and shall be even entitled to demand the return of the marriage-present.

In the foregoing cases, if the giver-away in marriage of a fugitive wife, in the absence of her lawful husband, is an elder relation in the first degree of such female, the punishment attending such unlawful marriage shall be solely inflicted on the relation, and the female shall suffer, without aggravation, the punishment to which she was liable as a fugitive.

If the giver-away in marriage of such female was any more remote elder relation, the relation shall still be punished as in the last instance, but the female and the person marrying her, shall likewise be punishable, as accessaries to the aggravated offence. If, in such cases, the proposal of the marriage is shewn to arise from the parties themselves, they shall be punished as principals, and the giver-away of the female as an accessary only; but the punishment of the latter, although in extreme cases nominally capital, shall never exceed 100 blows and perpetual banishment to the distance of 3000 *lee*.

Two clauses.

Section CXVII.—*Giving in Marriage unlawfully.*

In all marriages contracted contrary to law, if the giver-away of the bride, or the contractor of the marriage on the part of the husband, is the paternal or maternal grand-father, grand-mother, father, mother, paternal uncle or aunt, or paternal elder male or female cousin, the punishment denounced by law shall be solely inflicted on such relations, and the parties themselves shall not be held responsible.

When the giver-away of the wife, or contractor of the marriage as aforesaid, is a more remote relation of the party marrying, but is still the chief agent in procuring the unlawful marriage, he or she shall be punished as a principal, but the husband and wife shall likewise participate in the punishment of the offence, as accessaries.

If, on the contrary, the unlawful marriage contracted as above originated with the parties themselves, they shall be punished as principals in the offence, and those who contracted the match for them, as accessaries only.

When, according to the application of these rules, the parties to a marriage are punishable as principals with death, the law shall be carried strictly into effect; but, when the persons who contracted an unlawful

lawful marriage in behalf of others, are nominally liable to capital punishment, it shall be mitigated one degree; those, however, who are punished as their accessaries, shall still suffer as accessaries to a capital offence.

Moreover, if the husband and wife, in consequence of having been previously terrified and threatened by their elder relations, had entered into an unlawful marriage, which they had not themselves devised or originated; or if the husband was not twenty years of age complete, and the wife had never previously quitted her parent's roof, the contractors on each side of the unlawful marriage shall, under such circumstances, be alone punishable and responsible.

When any unlawful marriage has been only contracted, but not completed, the punishment of the responsible parties shall always be less by five degrees.

The negotiator of any unlawful marriage, knowing it be unlawful, shall suffer punishment within one degree of that inflicted on the responsible party, but otherwise shall be excused.

In general, in every case in which it is directed that an unlawful marriage shall be annulled, the parties shall be placed in the same condition as that in which they were previous to the marriage; and although any general act of pardon should intervene, and occasion a remission of the punishment denounced by law against them as public offenders, such pardon shall be no bar to the divorce.

In general also, when the party giving the marriage-present is, at the same time, aware of the unlawfulness of the transaction, such present shall be forfeited to government; but otherwise it shall be restored to the giver.

Three clauses.

END OF THE THIRD BOOK OF THE THIRD DIVISION.

BOOK IV.

PUBLIC PROPERTY.

SECTION CXVIII.—*Regulations concerning Coinage* *.

ACCORDING to the regulations concerning coinage, there are founderies and mints where the metal is prepared and caſt, and alſo proper ſtore-houſes in which the coin is depoſited until required for the public ſervice. The quantity of metal coined in the former, and the periods of its iſſue from the latter, ſhall be ſtrictly conformable to the deliberate reſolutions thereon of the ſupreme court for affairs of revenue, in order that the ſucceſſive ſupplies of coin for the uſe of the people may correſpond with their wants, and be regulated according to the market-prices of gold, ſilver, grain, and other articles in general uſe and conſumption.

Whoever, having authority in any of theſe departments, retains and accumulates the coin, inſtead of diſtributing it at due ſeaſons, ſhall be puniſhed with 60 blows.

---

* It is well known to be the policy of the Chineſe government to have no other currency than a ſmall coin of baſe metal, chiefly copper, of which the legal value is one thouſandth part of a *leang*, or Chineſe ounce of ſilver; the actual exchange ſometimes riſes above, and ſometimes falls ſhort of this rate, in conſequence of the intrinſic value of the coinage of different dates varying according to the relative proportions as well as total quantities of the metals employed, while the value of ſilver is alſo neceſſarily ſubject to fluctuation, as that of any other marketable commodity.

On account of the inconvenience which would attend the payment of large ſums in a coin of ſo low a denomination, and as paper currency is at preſent altogether unknown in the empire, ingots of pure ſilver, of one and of ten Chineſe ounces weight, (uſually caſt in moulds, and diſtinguiſhed with a peculiar ſtamp,) are moſt generally employed on ſuch occaſions, eſpecially in all payments to government; but it is to be obſerved, that of late, the European trade has introduced the Spaniſh dollar into ſuch extenſive circulation in many of the provinces of China, that, excepting the officers of the government, it is very generally known and received among the natives, and even at a rate beyond its intrinſic value, in conſideration of the apparent ſecurity againſt fraud, which is afforded by the impreſſion.

In

In no private dwelling of any foldier or citizen fhall any utenfils of copper, or chiefly of copper, be ufed, except mirrors, military arms, bells, and articles fpecially confecrated to religious purpofes; but whatever quantity of copper any individual may have in excefs, he fhall be permitted to fell to government at the rate of feven *fen*, (or hundreth parts of a *leang* or ounce of filver) for every *kin* weight of copper, or as much more or lefs as the ftate of the market and circumftances may authorize *.

Whoever buys or fells copper clandeftinely, or conceals the fame in his houfe, inftead of offering it for fale to government, fhall be punifhed with 40 blows.

Three claufes.

SECTION CXIX.— *Periods eftablifhed for colleƈting the Revenues in Kind.*

For the purpofe of receiving the impoft on the fummer harveft, confifting of wheat only, the granaries of government fhall be opened on the 15th of the 5th moon, and the whole of the impoft laid in by the clofe of the 7th moon †.

For the purpofe of receiving the impoft on the autumnal harveft, which is of grain in general, the granaries of government fhall be reopened on the firft of the 10th moon, and the whole laid in by the end of the 12th moon.

This law fhall not prevent the receipt of thofe impofts at an earlier period, provided an unufually early harveft fhould admit of it, but if the fummer impoft is, at the end of the 8th moon, or the autumnal

---

* A Chinefe ounce of filver being eftimated at 6s. 8d. fterling, the average value of copper will appear to be no more that $5\frac{6}{10}$ pence a *kin* weight, (exceeding the Englifh pound by one-third,) but this (if it is not indeed merely ftated at random) can only be confidered as applicable to the period of the original promulgation of the code.

† Refpeƈting the Chinefe mode of computing time, fee the note to the XLI. Seƈtion.

impoſt at the end of the 1ſt moon of the ſucceeding year, ſtill deficient, the magiſtrate of the diſtrict, the magiſtrate ſuperintending the collection of the revenue in grain, their reſpective clerks, the officiating head inhabitants of the diſtricts in which the collection has been deficient, and the landholders not duly contributing, ſhall all of them be ſeverally reſponſible, each in his proper degree, according to the proportion the deficiency bears in each particular caſe to the whole amount which was due, or which ought to have been collected or furniſhed. If one-tenth, the puniſhment ſhall amount to 60 blows, and the puniſhment ſhall be encreaſed one degree for every tenth deficient, as far as the limit of 100 blows.

If the magiſtrates, their clerks, or the head inhabitants, have been convicted of bribery, they ſhall be puniſhed as much more ſeverely as the law concerning bribery for unlawful purpoſes may authorize.

If the deficiency in the contribution is not made up within a twelvemonth after it was due, the land-holder and the head inhabitant ſhall reſpectively be puniſhed with 100 blows, and the magiſtrates and their reſpective clerks ſhall ſuffer puniſhment in the manner ordered and provided in the ſupplemental regulations.

Six clauſes.

SECTION CXX.—*Fairneſs and Impartiality in collecting the Revenues in Kind.*

The officers and attendants belonging to the granaries of government, when collecting the impoſts in grain, ſhall permit each of the contributors perſonally to attend and meaſure the proportions of grain for the delivery of which he is anſwerable; and all ſuch allowances ſhall be made ſuch contributors as are warranted by the particular regulations of the ſeveral provinces.

If the officer superintending the grain department, or the collector under his controul, refuses to receive fair measure from the contributing land-holder, and insists on shaking the grain into as small compass as possible, or piles the grain into a heap, instead of striking it at the upper edge of the containing vessel, he shall receive at the least a punishment of 60 blows, and be liable to any increase in the punishment not exceeding 100 blows, which, according to the estimated value of the overplus, may result from the application to this case of the law for punishing pecuniary injuries in general.

These laws, however, are only intended to be applied to the cases in which the excess exacted from the contributors is duly appropriated to the use and service of government. If the offender applies the excess so exacted to his own use and advantage, he will be liable to severer punishment, as an embezzler of the property of government.

If the superintending magistrate of the district is privy to the commission of this offence, and does not take cognizance of it, he shall be equally punishable, but shall not otherwise be held responsible. The excess of grain which may have been exacted, shall be restored to the respective contributors.

Three clauses.

Section CXXI.—*Concealing or wasting the Proportion of exciseable Articles set apart for the Use of Government.*

In all cases in which the land-holder or house-holder is allowed to deliver in himself the proportion of his goods settled at the examination of the excise-officer or collector, as in the instances of the silk-worm-feeder and the metal-worker; and, in general, when any individual is responsible for the delivery of any article whatever to government, if, after having received the official notice demanding the same, the contributor conceals, wastes, or appropriates to his own use, any part of the amount of the articles due by him to government, and attempts to deceive the magiftrate by alleging that fuch part had been loft or deftroyed by fire, water, or thieves, he fhall be punifhed in proportion to the eftimated value of the amount remaining due by him, according to the law againft theft in ordinary cafes; neverthelefs, the punifhment fhall not in any cafe exceed 100 blows and perpetual banifhment to the diftance of 3000 *lee*, and the offender fhall not be branded.

If the officers and clerks of the department are privy to the offence, they fhall fuffer equal punifhment with the offending party, but otherwife fhall not be held refponfible. The offence, not being confidered of a private and perfonal nature, fhall not fubject the magiftrates to lofe their offices, unlefs they are at the fame time convicted of bribery, which will render them liable to fuch aggravation of the fentence as may refult from the law againft bribery for an unlawful purpofe.

Among others, the poorer land-holders and houfe-holders, who, when employed according to cuftom in conveying or fuperintending the conveyance of government property, avail themfelves of fuch opportunities of committing any wafte or depredation, fhall be punifhable conformably to this law.

One claufe.

Section CXXII.—*Vicarious Contributors to the Revenue.*

Whoever undertakes to deliver to government the amount of the impoft due from another, fhall fuffer 60 blows, and fhall ftill, in behalf of the refponfible proprietor, deliver into the granary of government the whole amount originally due, and half as much more, by way of forfeiture *.

* The object of the enactment of this law, appears to be to prevent any perfon from deriving an intermediate profit from the collection of the revenue, as fuch profit muft neceffarily either reduce the receipts on account of government, or become an addition to the burthen fuftained by the contributor.

If the superintending officer of government himself undertakes this vicarious mode of paying the legal contribution, his punishment shall (exclusive of the payment and forfeiture) be two degrees more severe than that of any other individual in a similar case.

The penalties of this law shall not, however, extend to those poorer land-holders or house-holders who, in consequence of their respective shares of rice or wheat being individually less than the estimated share of one family, unite together, and appoint one to contribute for the whole.

If the vicarious contributor is guilty of any deception, or does not contribute sufficiently, he shall, moreover, be liable to punishment in the same manner as the ordinary contributors.

Two clauses.

SECTION CXXIII. — *Premature Discharges, or Quittances for Taxes due to Government.*

The contribution to the revenue payable into the treasuries in specie, or to be deposited in kind in the public granaries, must not fall short of the amount determined by law; and if, previous to the full satisfaction of the claims of government, the superintendant of the department, in concurrence with the superior officer commanding the district, grants a general acquittance to any inhabitant, all the officers of the several public boards thus concurring therein shall be punished, each in proportion to the total amount deficient, according to the law regarding an embezzlement of government stores to the same extent.

When an officer of government is dispatched to any quarter with special powers and instructions for the collection of duties and taxes, if, in conjunction with the magistrates of the revenue department, and of the district in general, he reports falsely or prematurely to his superiors that all the claims of government are satisfied, he, and those concurring with him, shall, in like manner, be liable to the penalties of this law.

If any of the offending parties shall have been bribed for this purpose, they shall be liable to any contingent aggravation of the punishment resulting from the law against bribery for unlawful purposes.

If the officer intrusted with the collection of the revenue grants the partial receipts or quittances which are issuable from his department, without having obtained the articles in quality and quantity conformable to his instructions, he shall be liable to punishment as an embezzler of them, in proportion to the deficiency in quantity or value; and if the contributing inhabitant accepts any such quittance when he is aware that he is not entitled to it, he also shall be liable to punishment, less by two degrees, but shall not be branded. Whatever sum he may be found to have given to procure such quittance, shall also be generally forfeited to government; this sum shall, however, be returned to the giver, if he was not aware of the quittance having, in consideration of it, been improperly granted to him, and in such case he shall not in any respect be liable to punishment.

All those officers who belonged to the same public boards with the offending parties, if privy to the offence, and neglecting to take cognizance of it, shall be considered as participators therein, and suffer equal punishment with the principals. Those who neither knew of the offence indirectly, nor officiated when it was committed, shall only be punishable and responsible as guilty of neglect of examination.

Ten clauses.

SECTION CXXIV. — *Suppreſſion and Miſapplication of contingent Exceſs of Revenue.*

In all the tribunals, public boards, treaſuries, and magazines of government, the amount of the revenue received in ſilver, and in kind, beyond the ſum or value at which ſuch branch of the revenue was computed, ſhall be diſtinctly and faithfully reported, and the ſeveral ſums or quantities ſhall be placed accordingly to the credit of government on the records. If the ſuperintendant of the department privately tranſfers the exceedings of any one branch of the revenue, to ſome other branch, the receipt of which had been deficient, and thereby deceives the government by the falſe ſtatements which are thus introduced into his accounts, he ſhall be liable to puniſhment according to the law concerning the embezzlement of the property of government, in proportion to the amount ſo transferred; and he ſhall, moreover, be required to make good that deficiency in the other branch of the revenue, which he had, by ſuch transfer, endeavoured to conceal.

In all deliveries of precious metals or piece-goods * into the interior or private imperial treaſury, the accounts ſhould be cloſed on the day of delivery, but if they are not then completed, the unexamined parcels muſt not be removed, and the parties delivering in the ſame ſhall attend at the examination of the goods and cloſe of the accounts, on the day following.

Whatever exceſs may appear upon a computation of the articles, ſhall be diſtinctly reported to the ſupreme court of revenue for their deciſion reſpecting it, and if the ſuperintendant of the department, upon his own authority, preſumes to ſuffer any part of ſuch exceſs, after having been once received, to be removed again from the treaſury, he ſhall nominally be puniſhable capitally, but actually ſuffer only the alleviated ſentence of five years baniſhment.

* Silk, cotton or woollen ſtuffs, which are received and regiſtered by the roll or piece.

The officer on duty at the gate of the interior treasury, by whose neglect or want of examination such articles had been permitted to be carried away, shall suffer 100 blows. The articles carried away, whether consisting of precious metals, or piece-goods, shall moreover always be returned.

No clause.

SECTION CXXV. — *Privately lending or employing the Public Revenue.*

If any superintending officer of government, having charge of a part of the produce of the revenue, whether in grain or the precious metals, borrows for his own use, or lends the same to others, although the acknowledgment and engagement in writing of the borrower should have been duly obtained, such superintendant shall be punished for every offence in proportion to the amount and value, according to the law concerning the embezzlement of the property of government.

If any other person borrows for his own use, or lends the produce of the revenues as aforesaid, he shall be punished in proportion to the amount and value, according to the law for punishing thefts committed upon the property of the state.

The original article taken away shall in every case in which it may be practicable, be recovered in behalf of government.

If any person, moreover, exchanges any of his own goods with those belonging to government, he shall, upon conviction, forfeit those goods, and be further punishable in proportion to the amount of the goods of government withdrawn by such exchange, according as by this law is already provided.

Six clauses.

Section CXXVI.—*Privately lending or employing Public Property.*

Any officer of government, who, having under his charge clothes, carpets, furniture, utenfils, porcelane, or other articles of a fimilar defcription, which are public or government property, employs, or lends the fame to be employed for private purpofes, fhall, as well as alfo the borrower, be punifhed with 50 blows; and if the articles are not replaced within ten days, their value fhall be eftimated, and the offending parties punifhed in proportion thereto, according to the law concerning pecuniary injuries and malverfation in general, reducing the punifhment in each cafe two degrees. The article borrowed muft be moreover exactly replaced; and if loft or damaged, the offending parties fhall not only be refponfible for the value thereof, but fhall be likewife punifhable according to the law applicable to the cafe of damaging or deftroying the property of government; that is to fay, if the damage was done by defign, the punifhment fhall, proportionably to the amount, be two degrees more fevere than in common cafes of theft; and in an encreafing ratio, as far as 100 blows, and perpetual banifhment to the diftance of 3000 *lee*. — If the damage was the refult of accident or inadvertence, the punifhment fhall in each cafe be three degrees lefs than when committed by defign, and in no cafe fhall it exceed 80 blows, and two years banifhment.

No claufe.

Section CXXVII.—*Receipt, Transfer, and Expenditure of the Revenue.*

In every public department and tribunal of the empire, the receipts and expenditures fhall be particularly fpecified, as well in the document preferved to commemorate the tranfaction, as in the document iffued to authorize the execution of it, upon which two documents
laid

laid together, the impreffion fhall be affixed of the official feal, one half upon each document.

When the receipt and expenditure is not conformable to the tenor of thefe documents or vouchers, each alleged appropriation of the public property or funds, that is found to be unauthenticated, fhall be difallowed in the adjuftment of the public accounts, and the fuperintendant of the department fhall be punifhed in proportion to the deficiency, according to the law relative to embezzlement, the afcending ratio of punifhment being, however, limited to 100 blows and banifhment to the diftance of 3000 *lee*, and the offending party not liable in any cafe to be branded.

If the authority iffued by any tribunal or department of ftate for the expenditure of the public money, or public property, is not fanctioned by half the impreffion of the official feal, but is merely a written order to the fame effect; or if, although the proper document is iffued, no document of the fame tenor, fanctioned with the other half of the official feal, is retained; or again, if the fuperintending officer of the treafury or ftore-houfe complies with a mere written order, without having any other authority legally authenticated in the manner above ftated; or laftly, if fuch fuperintending officer, after having received the neceffary authority, makes the iffue of money or goods required, without duly recording the fame on the regifters of his department; all fuch cafes fhall fubject the offenders to the penalties of a tranfgreffion of this law.

Neverthelefs, when His Majefty's troops are on their march, if the commanding officer makes the demand of provifion and other neceffaries in due form, fuch demand fhall be fufficient to warrant the iffue of the articles required at the different ftations through which he paffes; but the fuperintending officer of the feveral departments fhall not omit afterwards to make due report to their refpective fuperiors, of the amount and of the nature of the fupplies they had afforded.

Any

Any superintending officer, who refuses to comply in such a case with the demand made upon the stores under his control, shall be punished with 60 blows for the offence

Fourteen clauses.

Section CXXVIII. — *Misconduct of supernumerary Revenue Officers.*

If any one of the supernumerary attendants, who are hired occasionally for the public service, and employed in the treasuries, store-houses, public offices, or manufactories, should be guilty of appropriating to their private use, borrowing, or exchanging any part of the produce of the revenue, he shall incur the ordinary punishment of embezzlement; and, if the superior who hired him was privy to the offence, and also a participator in the advantages arising from the unlawful transaction, he shall be equally punishable; but if he did not actually receive a share of the profits arising from it, the punishment of the latter shall be proportionally less by one degree.

The officer who hired the supernumerary shall be liable to the same reduced punishment if, being privy to the offence, he takes no cognizance of it, or suppresses it, in his report to his superiors. If ignorant of the offence having been committed, as well as without advantage from it, he shall not be punished or held responsible.

One clause.

Section CXXIX. — *Fraudulent Appropriation of Public Property.*

If, in the distribution of the supplies for the army*, any of the officers, or official attendants belonging thereto, appropriate to themselves any portion of what had been destined to the public service, by

---

* Under this general term, the pay of the troops, as well as every other species of allotment to them, appears to be comprehended.

falsely assuming the names and authority of individual soldiers who have claims thereon, they shall be punished in proportion to the amount, according to the law in cases of theft in ordinary cases.

If they appropriate to themselves a portion of what had been destined to the public service, by making a claim for the same in the assumed names, or in behalf of soldiers who, having deserted, had ceased in fact to have any claims whatever, they shall be punished in proportion to the amount, according to the severer law, provided in cases of stealing public property; lastly, if any officer, personally entrusted with the distribution of stores to the troops, appropriates any part of the same to himself, he shall suffer punishment in proportion to the amount, according to the still severer law which is provided against the embezzlement of public property.

In none of these cases, however, shall the offender be liable to be branded*.

No clause.

Section CXXX.—*Revenue Officers reciprocally answerable for each other.*

All the officers, clerks, collectors, inspectors, receivers, and others attached to the revenue department, and having authority in the treasuries and store-houses of government, shall possess a reciprocal controul and right of inspection over each other's proceedings; and when any one individual is guilty of clandestinely applying to his own use, lending to others, or in any manner misusing the property of government, if those who are privy to the removal of the public property from the treasury or store-house, conceal the offence, instead of informing against the offender, or otherwise wilfully connive at the trans-

---

* See the Appendix, No. XVI. for a notice of an offence of this description, extracted from the Pekin Gazette of the 23d of April 1800.

action, they shall participate equally in the punishment, except in capital cases, when they shall be entitled to a mitigation in the punishment of one degree.

Those who did not connive at the offence, but might have prevented it had they been vigilant and diligent in examination, shall suffer punishment proportionate to the offence, under a reduction of three degrees below that of the actual offender, and the reduced punishment shall not exceed in any instance 100 blows.

In cases however of the superior officers making false and unauthenticated records, and granting unauthenticated and premature releases, particular regulations have been provided, and the inferior collectors, inspectors, and others in the department of the revenue, shall not be responsible for any such offence, unless convicted of having been privy thereto.

No clause.

Section CXXXI. — *Responsibility of Revenue Officers in Cases of Theft.*

When any individual goes out of a public treasury or storehouse, to which he is not actually belonging, if the guards on duty neglect to search his person and examine him, they shall be punished with 20 blows each; and if, in consequence of such neglect, a thief succeeds in carrying away with him any of the property of government, the said guards shall suffer punishment within two degrees of the severity of that to which the thief himself is liable. If a theft is committed at night, in consequence of the want of vigilance of those on guard, they shall each suffer punishment within three degrees of that to which the thief is liable.

The superintending officers, inspectors, and others, not immediately on guard, shall, in cases of theft, suffer punishment within five degrees of that of the thief, for the want of vigilance which is imputable to them, but the punishment shall not, in any such case of misconduct by implication only, exceed 100 blows.

In any instance however of wilful connivance, the punishment of those who connive shall be as severe as that of the thief, excepting only a reduction of one degree in capital cases.

For acts of robbery and open violence, which the officers and others on duty really had not power to resist, they shall incur no responsibility.

In cases of implied neglect, the officers of government shall retain their places, the offence not being of a private and personal nature; but in all instances of connivance and wilful concurrence they shall be degraded and dismissed.

Two clauses.

SECTION CXXXII. — *Responsibility of Receivers and Distributors of Public Property.*

When any of the officers or inferior attendants in charge of, or employed in, the several public treasuries and store-houses, have completed their respective periods of service, they shall still remain at their proper stations until their several accounts of receipt and expenditure have been audited by the superior officer in the revenue department, whose duty it is personally to ascertain that there is no incorrectness or deficiency; but after the audit has taken place, they shall be subject to no further detention.

The distribution of such articles as are by law allotted in certain shares and proportions, shall be effected under the immediate direction and authority of the superintending officers of the district and revenue department, and this duty shall not at any time be left to be performed by the officer of the treasury or store-house from whence the articles are to be issued, under the penalty of 100 blows for every such offence.

When any public treasure, or other property, has been sealed with the seal of an officer of the revenue, it shall not be lawful for any of the inferior officers or attendants of the department, to break open the same, without previously requesting the officer who originally affixed the seal to be present; and whoever offends against this regulation shall suffer 60 blows, and shall be responsible for the deficiency that may be imputable to his interference.

No clause.

SECTION CXXXIII. — *Established Regulations observed in the Receipt and Issue of Public Stores.*

If the officers having charge of the treasuries and store-houses of government, and superintending the receipts and deliveries of public stores, issue fresh goods when they ought to have issued such as had been laying on hand, or receive goods of an inferior quality, when they ought to have been of superior quality; or if the superintending officer purchasing or hiring goods for the public service, does not pay the stipulated sum immediately, or stipulates for more or less than the market price or rate of hire of the goods in each case, the amount of the excess above, or of the deficiency below, what was fairly due, shall be estimated, and the offending party shall be proportionably liable to punishment according to the law applicable to the cases of pecuniary malversation in general and he shall moreover replace to government, or to the individual sufferer, whatever may have been improperly withheld.

The penalties of this law shall extend to all those who, being entrusted with the payment and distribution of salaries and wages, discharge the same in advance, instead of waiting until they regularly become due.

If the superior officer is privy to the commission of any such offence on the part of his inferiors, and takes no cognizance of it, he shall participate equally in the punishment, but shall not be in any manner responsible, unless acquainted with the fact.

Two clauses.

Section CXXXIV.—*Vexatious Proceedings on the Occasion of the Receipt or Issue of Public Stores.*

If the officers and clerks of government, entrusted with the superintendance of the receipt and collection, or the issue and distribution, of the public property, instead of promptly collecting and promptly distributing it, in any manner vexatiously detain and maliciously obstruct the claimants and contributors, they shall be liable to 50 blows for the delay of one day, and every addition of three days delay shall aggravate the punishment one degree, as far as 60 blows and one year's banishment.

The door-keepers who detain and impede persons attending for the purposes aforesaid, shall be punished according to this rule, and in the same proportion.

If the officer on duty does not collect from the contributors, and distribute to those entitled to receive, in the same order and succession as that in which they attend his office or tribunal for the purpose, he shall suffer the punishment of 40 blows.

Three clauses.

Section CXXXV.—*Purity of the Precious Metals payable to Government.*

Whoever has the charge of receiving and collecting the taxes due to government, or the proceeds of goods sold on account of government, and payable in precious metals, shall be answerable for the delivery of the same in no other than perfectly pure bullion, whether gold or silver.

If the gold or silver delivered on these accounts into any of the public treasuries contains an admixture of alloy, the superintending officer, his clerks, and the assay-master, shall be respectively punishable with 40 blows, and shall be made jointly responsible for the deficiency in value of the bullion received.

If guilty of wilfully receiving alloyed silver or gold, with a corrupt view to private advantage, they shall further be liable to the punishment of an embezzlement of public property to the extent of the deficiency; when merely conniving at such fraud, they shall be punishable as in a common case of pecuniary malversation to the same amount.

No clause.

Section CXXXVI.— *Responsibility for the Damage or Loss of Public Stores.*

If those who have the charge of the public treasuries and storehouses, or of any collection and depôt of public property, do not place and arrange the stores according to the established rules, or omit to expose them to the sun and the air at proper times and seasons, by which omission and neglect the property entrusted to them is damaged or destroyed, the loss shall be estimated and the responsible parties punished in proportion to the amount according to the law concerning pecuniary malversation in general, and they shall be required moreover to make good to government the amount of the loss sustained.

Nevertheless, should sudden and unexpected rain penetrate the building, or fire be communicated to it from without, or thieves and robbers break in, so that from any of these causes damage or loss arises to the property under charge, if the superintending officer deputes a proper person to ascertain the nature and extent of the damage, and makes a clear and correct report thereof to his superiors, he shall be pardoned, and excused from his responsibility to make good the deficiency.

On the other hand, if the superintending officer, having been guilty of any fraudulent disposal, loan, or transfer of the public property, takes advantage of the subsequent circumstance of an accidental loss by fire, water, or thieves, to falsify the registers of his office by attributing the whole loss and deficiency to such accident, and then makes a report of the case conformably to such false record, in order to deceive his superiors and screen himself, he shall be liable to punishment in proportion to the amount of the total damage and deficiency, according to the law concerning embezzlement.

If those who are associated with him in office are privy to, but take no notice of, such criminal proceeding, they shall be equally punishable, but otherwise shall not be held responsible.

One clause.

Section CXXXVII. — *Regular Transmission of Public Stores from Inferior to Superior Jurisdictions.*

The taxes levied and collected in the several districts of the empire, the supplies purchased, and the several kinds of warlike stores prepared and manufactured for the army, having been delivered into the charge of the several governments of cities of the second and third orders and having by them been transmitted in regular routine, and under the conduct of proper officers, to the governors of cities of the first order to whose jurisdiction they belong respectively, if those governors do not immediately take the further transmission of the articles under their charge, and issue the necessary orders, as well as depute the proper persons under their authority to superintend their conveyance and delivery to the treasurers of the respective

spective provinces, the president, deputy, and clerks of every government thus neglectful, shall suffer a punishment of 80 blows, but the offence shall not be deemed of a private or personal nature.

In like manner, if the provincial treasurers do not immediately take charge of all the public property thus received, and adopt proper measures for effecting its conveyance to the supreme court for all affairs of revenue the president, deputy, and clerks of the treasurers' offices, shall be equally punishable as the other officers in the preceding instances *.

From the penalties of this law, exception is necessarily made in all such cases wherein a slower mode of transmission than ordinary is especially directed.

If those officers with whom the transmission of such produce of the revenue towards its destination begins, or those who afterwards superintend and accompany the same, with the attendants who are employed in effecting the package, re-package, and transfer of the goods, do not place and dispose them according to the established regulations, in consequence of which deviation or omission a loss or damage ensues, the extent of such loss or damage shall be estimated, and the offence punished in proportion to the amount, according to the law concerning pecuniary malversation or injury to property in general; the offending parties shall likewise make good the deficiency.

If, however, in a conveyance by water, accidents should ensue from the winds and waves, upon sudden and unexpected bad weather, or at any time fire should be communicated from without, or thieves break in and steal, then, provided the superintending officer, immediately after ascertaining the circumstance, makes a faithful report

* These regulations obviously regard only the surplus revenue, or that which is not required for the service of the provinces in which it is collected. The total amount of the revenue collected in the Chinese empire has been stated at about 66,000,000l. and that of the surplus, remitted to Pekin, at about 12,000,000l. and these sums are probably not far from the truth, though on such a subject, the accuracy of the information which, in the present state of our relations with China, is likely to be accessible to Europeans, must be in some degree questionable.

thereof, and of the extent of the loſs or damage that has been ſuſtained, to his ſuperior, and provided that the officer who ſhall have been thereupon deputed by ſuch ſuperior to examine into the truth of the ſtatement, confirms its accuracy and fidelity, the reſponſible parties ſhall become free, both from liability to puniſhment, and from the charge of making good the deficiency; but ſhould there prove to have been any deception or malverſation committed, then, whatever the cauſe of loſs or damage may have been, the offending party ſhall be liable to puniſhment in proportion to the full amount, according to the law reſpecting embezzlement.

If the officers with whom the tranſmiſſion of the produce of the revenue begins, do not tranſmit the identical goods or articles received from the contributors, but purchaſe other goods or articles to ſubſtitute in their room, the difference between the value of the articles tranſmitted and thoſe withdrawn, ſhall be eſtimated, and the offence puniſhed in proportion to ſuch difference, according to the law concerning the embezzlement of public property.

Nineteen clauſes.

Section CXXXVIII. — *Rule of Forfeiture and Reſtitution.*

If any officer in pronouncing judgment in a caſe of property illegally holden, orders it to be reſtored to the original proprietor, when it ought, conformably to the laws, to have been forfeited to the ſtate, or directs a forfeiture of it to the ſtate, when it ought by law to have been reſtored to the proprietor, he ſhall for ſuch falſe judgment be puniſhed in proportion to the amount of the property illegally awarded according to the proviſions of the law againſt pecuniary malverſation in general, but the puniſhment ſhall not in any of theſe caſes exceed the limit of 100 blows.

Two clauſes.

SECTION CXXXIX. — *Intermediate Charge of Public Property.*

In all cases of public property which had been issued from the treasuries and store-houses of government to be delivered over, or paid away, to certain persons, but not yet received by such persons; and in all cases of private property, which, being destined to the service of government, has been received for that purpose, but not actually deposited in the public treasuries or store-houses, the goods shall be considered in the former case still to preserve, and in the latter case, already to have acquired, the character of public property.

Any fraudulent loan or misapplication thereof shall therefore subject the holder of the goods, in proportion to the amount misapplied, to the full punishment provided by law in the case of directly embezzling any other kind of public property. — Upon the same principle, the fraudulent application of such property, if imputable to persons who have not the charge thereof, shall be punished as an ordinary theft of public property.

One clause.

SECTION CXL.—*Concealment or Denial, either of Property under Sentence of Forfeiture, or of Families under Sentence of Servitude.*

The enslaving of the families of offenders, and the forfeiture of their real and personal property, shall not take place except in cases of treason, rebellion, or some other of the ten treasonable offences, or where it is by law expressly ordered and provided; and if any officer of government passes such sentence of forfeiture unauthorizedly and unjustly, he shall be punished as in the case of passing a wilfully unjust sentence of perpetual banishment. — If the sentence was only pronounced, but not executed, the punishment shall be less by one degree.

If those who are to give an account of the number of persons in a family under lawful sentence of perpetual service, and also of the real and personal property of such family which is by law forfeited to the state, are guilty of any deception or concealment, they shall be punished in the following manner:

In the first place, if they do not give a true and faithful account of the number of persons in such family, they shall be punished in the same manner as is provided in an ordinary case of suppressing the number of persons in the record of a family in the public register.

In the second place, if they do not give a true and faithful statement of the forfeited lands of the said family, they shall be punished according to the law for punishing those who falsely report the extent and value of their lands, to avoid duly contributing to the revenue. If they falsely report the amount of the houses, cattle, and miscellaneous articles under sentence of forfeiture, they shall be further punishable in proportion to the value of the property suppressed and falsely reported, according to the law concerning pecuniary malversation and injury to property in general; but the punishment shall not, in any of these cases, exceed 100 blows.

All such of the family, and such portions of their possessions, as were attempted to be concealed in evasion of the sentence of the laws, shall be in the former case held accountable to the service, and, in the latter case, forfeited to the use, of government, as previously provided and directed; but the punishment of misrepresentation shall be inflicted solely on the individual who made the false return.

If the head inhabitant of the district, from a partiality in favour of those under condemnation, confirms the false report, and if the magistrate knowing it to be false connives at it, they shall be equally punished

punished with the individual with whom the falsehood originated, and the punishment, instead of being limited to 100 blows, shall be regularly encreased in proportion to the amount in question, according to the law above referred to.

If such officer or head inhabitant shall have been bribed to connive on the occasion, he shall be subject to any contingent augmentation of punishment, which may be found proportionate to the amount of the bribe, agreeably to the law against receiving bribes for unlawful purposes.

When, on the other hand, a false report is accepted as correct, not through wilful connivance, but through inadvertence and defect of examination, the punishment shall be three degrees less than that to which the false reporter is liable, and shall not in any case exceed 50 blows.

Eight clauses.

END OF THE FOURTH BOOK OF THE THIRD DIVISION.

BOOK V.

DUTIES AND CUSTOMS.

SECTION CXLI. — *Duty on Salt* *.

I. WHOEVER, not having a licence, engages in a clandestine traffic in salt, that is to say, possesses any quantity however small of this article for sale, shall be punished with 100 blows, and banished for three years.

If such smuggler of salt is moreover provided with offensive weapons, the punishment shall be aggravated one degree, so as to amount to perpetual banishment to the distance of 2000 *lee*. — If he falsely accuses, and recriminates upon, innocent persons, his punishment shall be encreased three degrees, whereby the place of his perpetual banishment will be removed to a distance of 3000 *lee*; if lastly, he resists the officers of justice employed to take him into custody, he shall suffer death by being beheaded, after the usual period of imprisonment.

Not only the article itself, but likewise the carriage or the vessel by which it is conveyed, and the horses or cattle by means of which it is drawn or transported, shall be forfeited to government.

---

* The salt trade in China, the duties upon which form a considerable branch of the revenue, is a regulated monopoly, carried on by a limited number of merchants, to whom licences are granted by the Crown, and whose proceedings are at the same time subjected to the inspection and control of public officers especially appointed to that service, in each province. — The merchants who enjoy this monopoly, as well as those who have the exclusive privilege of trading with foreigners, rank very high in point of opulence and respectability:—the chief salt merchant of Canton is at present considered to be the richest subject in the province, and the next to him in wealth is, probably, a merchant, now retired from business, but who till lately held the principal station among those engaged in the foreign trade, and who acquired nearly the whole of his extensive fortune in the course of his transactions, and those of his family, with the English East India Company.

The

The guide or conductor, the agent for the sale, the harbourer of the smuggler, and the consignee of the salt, shall be respectively punished with 90 blows and two years and a half banishment, as accessaries.

Whoever carries, lets out beasts of burthen to carry, or furnishes any other means of conveying, this article without a licence, shall suffer the punishment of 80 blows and two years banishment.

If any person, although not bound by his office so to do, gives information of, and seizes any smuggled salt, he shall obtain the whole amount of the forfeiture as his reward. — In like manner, if one of a party of smugglers of salt surrenders himself, and gives information to government, he shall not only be pardoned, but rewarded with the whole amount of the forfeited article. — Even if a single smuggler voluntarily surrenders himself, he shall be pardoned.

The magistrates, in taking cognizance of any case of smuggled salt which may be brought under their consideration, shall confine their investigation to the examination of the goods seized, and of the offences committed by the smugglers in custody. — They shall not listen to any charges the smugglers may allege against others, whether in recrimination upon their accusers or otherwise. — Any magistrate who disregards this restriction, shall be punished as in an ordinary case of wilful deviation from justice, in determining the punishment of offences.

II. Whoever, being engaged and employed in a licensed and established salt-work, delivers out of the establishment annually a greater quantity of salt than is permitted and specified in the licence, or boils down salt brine clandestinely for private sale, shall be prosecuted, and punished in the same manner as the unlicensed dealer; and all those who, being privy to, connive at this unlawful transaction, or assist in the unlawful disposal of the goods, shall be subject to an equal participation in the punishment by law provided.

III. When-

III. Whenever a married woman is guilty of any breach of the regulations of the salt-trade, if her husband or sons are at home, and privy to the offence, they shall suffer the punishment attending the breach of the law, instead of the woman; but if the husband is absent from home, and the sons are of a tender age, the woman alone shall be punished, and (according to the laws concerning females,) that part of the sentence, which consists of some degree of banishment, shall be commuted for the proportionate fine.

IV. Whoever purchases for use any salt that he knows to have been prepared without a licence and sold clandestinely, shall be punished with 100 blows; but if he so purchases the salt in order to sell it again, he shall be punished with 100 blows and three years banishment.

V. The superintendants of the salt-duties, and the several officers of the civil and military departments, who may at any time be charged with the pursuit and seizure of clandestine and illicit traders, shall immediately deliver such of the offenders as they may have seized, into the custody of the superior courts of the treasurers of the provinces, not being themselves empowered by the laws to examine into their offences; but if any of the superior courts, in collusion with the subordinate magistrates, suffer such offenders to escape from trial and deserved punishment, such conduct shall render them (the members of such courts) punishable in an equal degree with the original offenders: and if such a collusion is the consequence of bribery, they shall experience any aggravation of the punishment which may result from the application to the case of the laws against bribery for unlawful purposes.

VI. The superintendants of the salt-duties, and the several officers of the civil and military boards or tribunals, who may at any time be charged with the pursuit and seizure of clandestine and illicit traders, shall station in convenient places within the limits of their jurisdictions, and

and especially near salt-works established according to law, a sufficient number of revenue and police officers to prevent and put a stop to all such smuggling and clandestine proceedings, as are hereby prohibited. If any instances of smuggling take place notwithstanding these regulations, the officer of the department, and those deputed by him to suppress such practices, shall upon the first occurrence of this nature be liable to be punished with 40 blows; upon the second, with 50 blows; and upon the third, with 60 blows; but this not being deemed an offence of a private and personal nature, the persons guilty of it shall not be deprived of their offices and employments. On the other hand, if those officers wilfully connive at any act of smuggling, or if any commanders of troops suffer their soldiers to carry on any such illicit traffic, they shall suffer the same punishment as the smugglers, and be deemed, moreover, guilty of, and liable to, the consequences of a private and personal offence, the punishment of which will again be subject to any further aggravation that may result according to law, upon a conviction of bribery. If the revenue officer employed upon this duty, suppresses the discovery of smuggled salt and appropriates the amount to his own use, instead of delivering it up to his superior officer's tribunal, he shall be punished with 100 blows and three years banishment. If such revenue officer falsely charges an innocent person with smuggling, his punishment shall be aggravated three degrees, and accordingly amount to a punishment of 100 blows and perpetual banishment to the distance of 3000 *lee*.

VII. Upon the removal of salt licenced by government, a regular permit shall be made out, expressing the quantities of salt in each bag, the allowance for tare, and the total amount of the salt intended to be removed; at each custom-house on the route, the quantity of the article shall be ascertained to be conformable to the permit, by weighing and examining some of the bags taken promiscuously; if it is discovered that the quantity transported exceeds the amount stated in the permit,

permit, the offenders shall be punished as in any ordinary case of unlicensed trade in the same article. If the salt-merchant conveys the salt through an unusual route, by which means the examination of the officers of government in the intervening stations is evaded, and their certificates consequently found to be wanting upon the permit, such merchant shall be punished with 90 blows, and the goods sent back to the stations where they had not but ought to have been examined, that the regular inspection may take place; the merchant will be further contingently liable to an aggravation of his punishment if upon such inspection taking place, the salt in his possession is found to exceed the amount specified in the permit.

VIII. The salt merchants and traders shall always transport the licenced salt for sale, in the exact quantities and proportions specified in their respective permits or licences; if the salt is sold in one place, while the permit is deposited in another, and therefore cannot be produced on demand, they shall be liable to all the penalties of a clandestine sale. If within ten days after having sold off the whole of any quantity of salt for which a permit has been granted, the salt merchant does not deliver up such permit to the proper officer of government in the district, he shall be liable to a punishment of 40 blows; and if he makes use of such expired permit, to colour and legalize the sale of any additional quantity of salt, he shall be held liable to the several pains and penalties denounced against the clandestine sale of this article in ordinary cases.

IX. In all cases of the transportation of salt licenced by government, whether from the manufactory to the store-house, or from one store-house to another, if military weapons are carried for defence, or if any other vessels than those belonging to government are employed, it shall be deemed a clandestine trade, and punished accordingly.

X. If any salt merchant, having submitted the salt for which he held a licence to the inspection of the officers of government, that it might

be

be ascertained to be agreeable thereto, afterwards adulterates it with sand or earthy matter, and in such state exposes his goods for sale, he shall be punished with 80 blows.

XI. If any person takes the salt which the government licence expresly declared to be saleable only in a particular district or quarter of the country, and conveys it for sale to any place not described in the licence, he shall be punished with 100 blows; the person who knowingly purchases the article shall be punished with 60 blows, but shall not be liable to such penalty, if ignorant of the illegality of the transaction. The goods thus conveyed for sale contrary to the terms of the licence, shall be forfeited to government.

Twenty-two clauses.

Section CXLII. — *Superintendants of Salt Duties to receive no intermediate Profits.*

If any of the officers or clerks of the tribunals and departments, having the administration of the laws respecting salt, and the collection of the salt duties, take upon themselves under assumed and fictitious names the payment of the duties intermediately, by purchasing or otherwise procuring salt licences through the authority and influence of their several offices, and thus appropriate to themselves those profits which ought to have been enjoyed by private individuals of the community, they shall be punished with 100 blows and three years banishment. Their property in salt, and the licences for vending it, shall both be forfeited upon conviction.

No clause.

Section CXLIII. — *Preservation of the Salt Laws from Neglect.*

All the wholesale merchants who purchase salt licences from government, shall personally receive their respective portions of the article at the public works where it is prepared: if inftead of fo doing, they difpofe of their licences to others at advanced prices, fo that in the end, the falt regulations are evaded and counteracted, the feller and purchafer of the licence fhall in each cafe be punifhed with 80 blows, and the negociator of the fale or of the transfer of the licence, fhall fuffer the punifhment next in degree. The purchafe-money received for the fale of the licence by the feller, and the falt obtained by the purchafer of the licence, conformably to the tenor thereof, fhall equally be forfeited. The retail venders of falt, who receive and difpofe of the article at the different markets on behalf of the wholefale dealer, are not however by any means to be confidered as coming within the fcope of this law, unlefs they fhould likewife engage in the trade as principals.

No claufe.

Section CXLIV. — *Smuggling of Tea**.

Whoever is guilty of a clandeftine fale of tea, fhall be liable to the fame penalties as already provided in the cafe of a clandeftine fale of falt. Whoever, having poffeffion of a tea licence that had been acted upon, and noted accordingly by the officers of government to whom it had been prefented for examination, avails himfelf of fuch expired and cancelled licence, to collect upon the authority thereof a frefh fupply from the the tea plantations, fhall be liable to all the penalties of fmuggling tea in the ordinary manner.

Six claufes.

---

* The regulations comprifed under this head relate folely to the home confumption. The laws framed for the government of the foreign trade, being for the moft part of recent date, are not contained among the original inftitutions, and their application being alfo confined within narrow limits, they are not defcribed at any length even in the fupplementary part of the penal code.—Some official documents connected with the fubject of foreign intercourfe will be found in the Appendix, No. XI.

Section CXLV.—*Smuggling of Allum.*

Whoever clandestinely manufactures allum and exposes it to sale, shall be subject to penalties similar to those already provided in the case of salt. In all places and situations which are found to yield a supply of this article, the amount, and the extent of the duty to be levied thereon, shall be ascertained and determined upon fixed principles, and private individuals shall not be allowed to bring it to sale without previously purchasing licences for that purpose from government.

No clause.

Section CXLVI.—*Evasion of Duties, or Smuggling in general*[*].

All merchants and dealers who defraud the revenue, by not duly contributing the amount of the rated and established duties on their merchandize, shall be punished with 50 blows, and forfeit half the value of the goods smuggled to government; three-tenths of such forfeiture shall in general be given to the informer, but no such reward shall be allowed when the smuggled goods are discovered and ascertained, by the regular officer on duty.

Whoever conveys goods through a barrier or custom-house station, without taking out the regular permit, shall be liable to all the or-

---

[*] The rigour of the laws against smuggling has been latterly encreased by several statutes and government edicts; and an instance occurred at Canton in the year 1801, in which a Chinese merchant was condemned to pay a fine of one hundred times the legal duty, upon some goods that had been attempted to be smuggled from the ship for which (according to the custom of the port) he had undertaken to become security.—It is to be observed, however, that this enormous fine was afterwards remitted, and that the sentence to that effect was only passed by the officiating magistrate provisionally, though recommended, at the same time, to the consideration of the Emperor as an exception to the established laws, which the peculiar circumstances of the case, and the frequency of the offence had rendered expedient.

dinary penalties of smuggling. The permit shall be drawn out conformably to the statement made of the quantity and quality of the goods; agreeably to which likewise, the duties shall be levied.

Whoever, lastly, purchases cattle without a stamped contract, shall be liable to punishment according to this law, and forfeit half the value to government.

Two clauses.

SECTION CXLVII. — *Merchant Vessels having false Manifests of their Cargoes.*

All large trading vessels which navigate the seas, shall on their reaching their destined port, deliver in to the officers of the custom-house, a full and true manifest of all the merchandize on board, that the duties payable thereon may be duly assessed. If the country merchant, or agent for the goods at the creek or reach where the vessel remains, makes no report, or makes a false and defective report, he shall be punished with 100 blows, and the whole amount of the goods not reported, or omitted in the report, shall be forfeited. The individual who receives on shore such goods as had not been duly reported, shall be equally punishable.

The person who gives information of a breach of this law, shall receive a reward of 20 *leang* or ounces of silver.

No clause.

SECTION CXLVIII. — *Arrears of Duties and Customs to be paid within the Year in which they are due.*

The whole of the arrears of duties and customs for which any individual has rendered himself liable to government in the course of the year, either for salt or tea licences granted to him, or upon any other grounds whatsoever, shall be finally discharged before the end of such year;

year; and if the demands of government are not liquidated by the time specified, the defaulter of one-tenth of his dues shall be punished with 40 blows, and the punishment shall be inflicted one degree more severely for every additional tenth in respect to which any individual is deficient in his quota of contribution; the punishment shall not however exceed 80 blows at the utmost, but such defaulter, besides being punished, shall continue to be held responsible for his arrears.

If the superintendants of the salt and tea duties, the superintending officers at the barrier custom-houses, and the collectors of every other description of duties and customs, are not active and diligent in the performance of the business of their several departments, so that the produce of the revenue in consequence of evasion or the non-payment of arrears, is in any one year less by one-tenth than in the years immediately preceding, they shall be liable in every such case to a punishment of 50 blows, and for every further defalcation of a tenth in the produce, there shall be an augmentation of one degree in the punishment, as far as the limit of 100 blows; the superintending officers shall likewise be held answerable for the ultimate discharge of all such arrears.

If the contributions due to the revenue are correctly made by the parties liable thereto, but fraudulently omitted to be entered in the registers of the revenue by the officers and clerks in that department, with the view of lending out to others, or applying to their private use and advantage, such omitted portions of the revenue, the said officers and clerks shall be liable to punishment in proportion to the amount so omitted, according the law in any ordinary case of the embezzlement of public stores.

Three clauses.

END OF THE FIFTH BOOK OF THE THIRD DIVISION.

BOOK VI.

PRIVATE PROPERTY.

Section CXLIX. — *Usury*.*

WHOEVER lends his money or other property of value, in order to derive a profit from such transaction, shall be limited to the receipt of an interest on the amount or value of the loan, at the rate of three *per cent. per* month; and, whatever the period of years or months may be, upon which interest is due at the day of repayment, no more shall be received or demanded, than the original sum lent, and the lawful interest thereon, to any amount not exceeding the principal.

Whoever transgresses this law, shall be punishable at the least with 40 blows, and as much more severely as may be proportionate to the amount of the excess of interest according to the law concerning pecuniary malversation in general; the punishment shall not however in any case exceed 100 blows.

Any superintending officer or clerk of a tribunal or department of government, lending money or other property of value to the people under the jurisdiction of such tribunal or department, in order to derive a profit and advantage from such loan, shall be punished with 80 blows, although he should have taken no more than the lawful interest; but if the interest derived from the transaction is excessive, he shall be liable to such aggravation of his punishment, as may render it proportionate to the amount of the excess, conformably to the law against receiving a bribe for a purpose not in itself unlawful; that is

---

* See Appendix, No. XVII.

to say, if, the half sum of the several excesses of interest received from different persons, by an officer having a regular salary, amounts to 30 *leang* or ounces of silver, the punishment in each case shall be encreased to 90 blows. But in the case of an inferior officer, not having such regular salary, the encrease of punishment shall only take place, when the said half sum amounts to 40 ounces of silver.

In both cases, the punishment shall be subject to a further encrease of one degree for every addition of ten ounces value to the amount of the corrupt transaction, until it attains the extreme limit of 100 blows and perpetual banishment to the distance of 3000 *lee*. In both cases likewise, the excess of interest extorted from the borrower shall be refunded.

On the other hand, if the debtor does not fulfil his agreement with the creditor, both in respect to the repayment of the principal, and the payment of the lawful interest, he shall be liable to punishment according to the following scale.

If three months after the stipulated period, he falls short of the amount due to his creditor by five *leang* or upwards, he shall be liable to a punishment of 10 blows, and to an encrease of punishment at the rate of one degree for every additional month of delay, as far as 40 blows.

If three months after the stipulated period he falls short of the amount due to his creditor by fifty *leang* or upwards, he shall be liable to a punishment of 20 blows, and to an encrease of punishment at the rate of one degree for every additional month of delay, as far as 50 blows.

If, lastly, three months after the stipulated period, he falls short of the amount due to his creditor, by 100 *leang* or upwards, he shall be liable to a punishment of 30 blows, and to an encrease of punishment at the rate of one degree for every additional month of delay, as far as the limit of 60 blows; and in this as well as in the preceding cafes, the debtor fhall continue refponfible for the amount of the principal and intereft lawfully due.

If a creditor whofe debtor has failed to fulfil his agreement, inftead of applying for redrefs at the tribunal of the magiftrate of the diftrict, relies on his own power and authority, and attempts to reimburfe himfelf by feizing violently the cattle, furniture, or other property of fuch debtor, he fhall be punifhed with 80 blows; the aforefaid punifhment may however be redeemed by the payment of the eftablifhed fine, provided the creditor is not found to have feized more in value than was actually due to him. On the other hand, if the eftimated value of the property fo unlawfully feized, exceeds the principal and intereft due, the excefs fhall fubject the offender to a punifhment as much greater than 80 blows as may be found to be proportionate to the amount thereof, according to the law concerning pecuniary malverfation in general; fuch excefs in the amount or value of the feizure, fhall moreover be returned to the debtor.

If a creditor accepts the wives or children of his debtor in pledge for payment, he fhall be punifhed with 100 blows; and one degree more feverely, if he is afterwards guilty of criminal intercourfe with the fame.

If the creditor feizes and carries off by force his debtors wives or children, he fhall be punifhed two degrees more feverely than in the cafe of receiving them in pledge by mutual agreement; and, laftly, if he is guilty of a criminal intercourfe with the females fo feized, he fhall fuffer death by being ftrangled, after the ufual period of imprifonment.

All perfons fo unlawfully transferred, feized, or detained, fhall be reftored to their refpective families, and the debt originally due in any fuch cafe, fhall not afterwards be recoverable by the creditor.

Eight claufes.

SECTION CL. — *Dilapidation of Property in Truft.*

If an individual who is entrufted with the goods or live-ftock of another waftes or confumes the fame, without authority from the proprietor, he fhall be punifhed in proportion to the value, one degree lefs than is provided by the law concerning pecuniary malverfation in general, and the extreme extent of the punifhment fhall be limited to 90 blows, and banifhment for two years and a half.

If fuch truftee fhould moreover deceitfully allege the death of the cattle, or the lofs of the money or other property fo intrufted to him, he fhall be punifhed in proportion to the amount or value, one degree lefs than is provided by law in cafes of theft, but fhall not be branded, nor fuffer more than 100 blows and three years banifhment, however confiderable the amount or value deficient.

In all fuch cafes the truftee fhall be obliged to reftore the property committed to his care, or its full amount and value, to the right owner.

Neverthelefs, if he can bring fatisfactory evidence of the deftruction or lofs of the goods by fire, water, or thieves, or of the ficknefs and death of the live ftock, he fhall be thereby totally freed from punifhment, as well as from pecuniary refponfibility.

All incidental circumftances of fraud, or fraudulent fale of entrufted property, of which an offender againft this law may be proved guilty, fhall be moreover taken into confideration in aggravation of his punifhment, conformably to the laws fpecially applicable in fuch cafes.

One claufe.

SECTION CLI. — *Loft and forgotten Property.*

Whoever finds any loft and forgotten goods fhall, within five days time, deliver up the fame to the magiftrate of the diftrict. If it is then

then afcertained to have been public property, the entire amount fhall be retained by government, but otherwife remain to be claimed and identified by the owner, to whom half fhall be reftored, and the remaining half allowed as a reward to the finder. If no perfon proves a claim to the property within thirty days, the finder fhall then receive back and retain the whole.

If the finder of any loft and forgotten goods, does not deliver up the fame to a magiftrate within the five days already ftated, he fhall be punifhed in proportion to the amount or value, according to a fcale grounded upon that eftablifhed by the law concerning pecuniary malverfation in general; that is to fay, if it proves to be public property, he fhall fuffer the full extent of the punifhment provided by that law, otherwife, a proportionate punifhment lefs in each cafe by two degrees; half of the private property, the difcovery of which had been unlawfully fuppreffed, fhall be forfeited to government, and the other half reftored to the owner, when an owner can be found; but if none, then the whole fhall be retained by government.

If any perfon, by digging in private or public ground, difcovers articles which had been buried and concealed in the earth, and to which no owner can be found, he fhall be at liberty to retain the fame for his own ufe, faving and excepting all ancient utenfils, bells, facred vafes, feals of officers of government, and other fuch extraordinary and uncommon articles as it is not befitting the people in general to poffefs; all which, within thirty days after the difcovery, muft be delivered up to government, on pain of receiving a punifhment of 80 blows for omitting to do fo, and ftill continuing to be refponfible for the furrender of the goods to government.

No claufe.

END OF THE SIXTH BOOK OF THE THIRD DIVISION.

BOOK VII.

SALES AND MARKETS.

SECTION CLII.—*Licence of Commercial Agents.*

IN every city, public market, and village district, where there is a commercial agent stationed and authorized by government, and in every sea-port and reach of a river, at which there are ship-agents, customarily stationed and authorized in the same manner, these agents shall be selected from such of the inhabitants as are from their wealth enabled to sustain the pecuniary responsibility attached to the situation; a regularly authenticated licence shall be granted to them by the officer of the district, and they shall be required to keep an official register of the ships and merchants that successively arrive, describing their real names and references, and also the marks, numbers, quality and quantity of the goods imported or introduced into the market; which register shall be submitted to a monthly examination at the board or tribunal of the officer of the district, that he may act accordingly.

Whoever privately takes upon himself the business of such agency without the licence of government, shall suffer a punishment of 60 blows, and forfeit to government the amount of his profits arising therefrom.

If the officers of government, or any of the established agents, connive at such illegal assumption of power, they shall be respectively punished with 50 blows, and dismissed from their employments.

Six clauses.

Section CLIII. — *Valuation of Merchandize.*

The valuation and appraisement of goods and merchandize, shall be effected by the commercial agents, after due consideration, and upon fair and equitable terms; any deviation on their part from such terms, either by enhancement or depreciation of value, shall subject the agent to a proportionate punishment according to the law concerning pecuniary malverfation in general.

If the difference between his appreciation of the goods and their real value is converted by such agent to his own benefit and advantage, he shall then be liable to the severer punishment provided by the law in cases of theft, except that the part of the sentence which requires the offender to be branded, shall, in these cases, be remitted.

If the commercial agent estimates the amount of a fine or forfeiture to which any offender is liable, more or less than is conformable to the just execution of the laws, he shall be liable to suffer according to the scale of punishment, which officers of government are subject to, by the law concerning a wilful deviation from justice in pronouncing a judicial sentence.

If, lastly, the agent has been induced by a bribe to estimate falsely the price of goods, or the amount of forfeitures, he shall be liable to a punishment as much more severe than that already provided, as may be found to correspond to the amount of the bribe, according to the law against bribery for an unlawful purpose, committed by officers who have not regular salaries.

One clause.

Section CLIV. — *Monopolizers and unfair Traders.*

When the parties to the purchase and sale of goods do not amicably agree respecting the terms, if one of them monopolizing, or otherwise using

using undue influence in the market, obliges the other to allow him an exorbitant profit; or if artful speculators in trade, by entering into a private understanding with the commercial agent, and by employing other unwarrantable contrivances, raise the price of their own goods, although of low value, and depress the prices of those of others, although of high value, in all such cases the offending parties shall be severally punished with 80 blows each for their misconduct.

When a trader, observing the nature of the commercial business carrying on by his neighbour, contrives to suit or manage the disposal or appreciation of his own goods in such a manner, as to derange, and excite distrust against, the proceedings of the other, and thereby draws unfairly a greater proportion of profit to himself than usual, he shall be punished with 40 blows.

The exorbitant profit derived from any one of the foregoing unlawful practices, shall, as far as it exceeds a fair proportion, be esteemed a theft, and the offender punished accordingly, whenever the amount renders the punishment provided by the law against theft more severe than that hereby established and provided. The offender shall shall not however be branded as in the ordinary cases of theft.

Eight clauses.

Section CLV.—*False Weights, Measures, and Scales.*

Whoever procures false measures, or false weights and scales, and makes use of them in the public market; and whoever adds to, or takes any thing away from, those measures, weights and scales which have been issued and sanctioned by government, shall be punished with 60 blows. The same punishment shall likewise be inflicted on the artificer of such articles.

If any measures, weights, or scales, not made according to the established rules, are issued under the sanction of government, the officer who issued, and the artificer who made them, shall alike be punished with 70 blows. The inspecting officers, if privy to, and conniving thereat, shall be equally punishable; but if only guilty of neglecting to examine and compare such articles with the standards established and provided, their punishment shall be less by one degree.

If any measures, weights, or scales are made use of in the public market, which, however exactly conformable to standard, have not been examined, compared and duly stamped by the officers or government, they shall be held to be unlawful, and the person employing them shall be accordingly punishable with 40 blows.

If the officers and others in the employ of government in the public treasuries and store-houses, make any alteration in the measures, weights, and scales issued or sanctioned by government, whereby more or less than the just amount of any article is received in contribution to the revenue, or issued upon the public service, they shall be punished with 100 blows at the least, and as much more severely, as the law respecting pecuniary malversation may proportionably to the amount of such aforesaid deviation, be found to authorize.—If however the consequent excess of receipts, or amount of short deliveries, has been converted by the offender to his own private use and advantage, his punishment shall be inflicted in proportion to the amount, according to the severer scale established by the law concerning the embezzlement of public property.

The artificer employed in effecting such fraudulent alteration in the measures, weights or scales issued or sanctioned by government, shall be punished with 80 blows.

The superintending officer having immediate jurisdiction over the department of the offender, shall be equally punishable, when-

ever

ever, being privy to, he takes no cognizance of such transgression; when it is imputable to his inattention and neglect only, his punishment shall be less than that of the original offender by three degrees, and in no case exceed 100 blows.

No clause.

SECTION CLVI. — *Manufactures not equal or conformable to Standard.*

If a private individual manufactures any article for sale, which is not as strong, durable, and genuine, as it is professed to be, or if he prepares and sells any silks or other stuffs of a thinner or slighter texture and quality, narrower, or shorter, than the established or customary standard, he shall be punished with 50 blows.

One clause.

END OF THE THIRD DIVISION.

FOURTH DIVISION,

Ritual Laws.

BOOK I.

SACRED RITES.

SECTION CLVII. — *Adminiſtration of Sacred Rites.*

ALL the officers of government whoſe province it is to ſuperintend the grand Imperial ſacrifices and oblations to Heaven and Earth, and to the ſpirit preſiding over the productions of the earth and the generations of mankind*; and thoſe likewiſe who have the direction of the ſacred rites which are performed in the temple of the Imperial

---

* Whether theſe, and ſome other ſimilar terms employed by the Chineſe, are intended to imply the exiſtence of as many diſtinct objects of worſhip, or are in fact only deſcriptive of the different characters and attributes of one ſupreme Being, recognized and adored as ſuch, is a queſtion upon which even the miſſionaries, to whom the inveſtigation of the principles of the national or ſtate religion in China muſt have been an object of peculiar intereſt, were for a long time divided. The latter opinion was always ſtrenuouſly ſupported in the writings, and countenanced by the practice of the Jeſuits; but the former, though in a great meaſure incompatible with the pleaſing notions which have been entertained of the purity of this moſt ancient part of the Chineſe religious ſyſtem, appears at preſent to prevail, or at leaſt to be tacitly acknowledged in all the forms of inſtruction adopted in China by the teachers of Chriſtianity. The phraſes conſidered to be of queſtionable meaning are carefully excluded, and the Deity is addreſſed by the native converts under no other title than *Tien Chu* or " Maſter " of Heaven," a term or combination of words, previouſly unknown in the Chineſe language, but thus introduced by Europeans, in the idea that any other would be liable to abuſe or miſconception.

Family, shall prepare themselves for every such occasion by abstinence; they shall bind themselves to the performance of such abstinence*, by solemn vows; and previous to making these vows, they shall announce the intended sacrifices and oblations in the manner by law established.

If they do not by such preparatory declaration of the day appointed for the sacred rite, give sufficient notice to the tribunals and public boards the members of which are officially required to assist at the ceremony, they shall be punished with 50 blows; and if, in consequence of such omission, the solemn proceedings are in any respect irregularly or imperfectly conducted, the punishment shall be encreased to 100 blows.

When, after the regular notice has been duly given, any imperfection or irregularity occurs in the administration of the sacred rites, all the individuals to whom such imperfection or irregularity is attributable, shall be subject to the last mentioned punishment.

If any individual of the intended assemblage † of officers of government for the performance of sacred rites, having had the Imperial command to prepare himself by abstinence duly communicated to him, takes the oath of abstinence, but afterwards violates it, either by mourning for the dead, visiting the sick, taking cognizance of capital offences, or partaking of public feasts, he shall in all such cases forfeit one month's salary.

If the superintendants of the rites are aware that any individual of the intended assemblage, has it incumbent on him to mourn for a relation within the four degrees, or was ever convicted of an offence

---

* The sense in which the term abstinence is employed is explained in a subsequent paragraph of this section.

† Literally " The one hundred officers of government," but meaning no more than a considerable assemblage of persons, varying in number according to circumstances.—In the same manner, when the expression " ten thousand" occurs in the Chinese language, it does not generally imply any precise number, but merely a great or an indefinite multitude.

punishable

punifhable with 50 or more blows of the bamboo, or with banifhment, they fhall not permit fuch perfon to affift at the ceremony, on penalty of forfeiting themfelves the aforefaid one month's falary.

The fuperintendant of the rites, if ignorant of the caufe of mourning, or former mifconduct, of a member of the affemblage, fhall not be liable to the penalty; but it fhall be levied on thofe who, being fubject to fuch difabilities, do not make known the fame.

Moreover, all thofe officers of government fhall be liable to the fame forfeiture, who, after having taken the oaths of abftinence, do not pafs the night apart from their families, if on duty in the provinces, or at their official apartments, if on duty at court.

If the animals, precious ftones, filks, grain, and other articles introduced in the grand facrifices and oblations, are not of the quality, and in the ftate prefcribed by the ritual regulations*, the fuperintendants fhall be punifhed with 50 blows; if an article of any kind is wanting, the punifhment fhall be encreafed to 80 blows, and if any one of the altars is wholly unprovided, the punifhment fhall be further encreafed to 100 blows.

If the officer of government having the charge of the animals referved for facrifice at grand folemnities, does not rear and feed them in the manner, and according to the practice by law eftablifhed, fo that any one of them becomes lean, or is otherwife injured, he fhall fuffer 40 blows, and be liable to a punifhment proportionally greater by one degree, as far as 80 blows, for every addition of one to the number of animals fo circumftanced. — When any one or more of thefe animals die in confequence of fuch neglect, the punifhment fhall be further encreafed one degree.

* The code of ritual regulations which, in this divifion of the Penal Laws, is frequently referred to, is, as might be expected from the national character and peculiar habits of the Chinefe, extremely voluminous; and the fubject likewife occupies a very confiderable portion of the great Chinefe work already noticed under the title of *Ta-tfing-hoey-tien.*

The same punishments and penalties shall likewise be inflicted in any cases of a breach of the regulations established respecting the intermediate and inferior sacred and imperial rites, as far as the circumstances correspond.

Two clauses.

Section CLVIII.—*Destroying Altars and Sacred Terraces.*

Whoever destroys or damages, whether intentionally or inadvertently, the altars, mounds, or terraces consecrated to the sacred and imperial rites, shall suffer 100 blows, and be perpetually banished to distance of 2000 *lee*. — Whoever destroys, or occasions any damage to, the gate or entrance to such consecrated ground, shall suffer punishment less by two degrees; that is to say, 90 blows and two years banishment.

Whoever discards, or destroys any articles, however trifling their value, which are consecrated to the service of sacred and imperial rites, shall suffer 100 blows, and be banished for three years; the punishment shall be less by three degrees in cases of losing or destroying such articles inadvertently; that is to say, 70 blows and banishment for one year and a half.

When the value of such articles is so considerable as to subject the offenders, conformably to the law against losing or destroying the property of government, to severer punishment than that hereby provided, such severer punishment shall be inflicted accordingly.

Two clauses.

Section CLIX.—*Provincial Sacred Rites to be conformable to the Ritual Code.*

Within the limits of the jurisdiction of each city of the first, second, and third order, the local genii, the genii of the hills, the rivers,

rivers, the winds, the clouds, and the lightnings, alfo the ancient holy Emperors, enlightened Kings, faithful minifters, and illuftrious fages, fhall all be feverally honoured and commemorated by the oblations and other holy rites which the ritual code prefcribes.

The fuperintendants of the feveral diftricts fhall not fail to erect fuitable monuments in honour and commemoration of thefe divine and holy perfonages, with tablets defcribing their names and titles, and the days on which facrifices and oblations are appointed to be made to them *.

Thefe tablets fhall be affixed in clean places near to running ftreams; and if the facred rites which are thus publicly announced, are afterwards neglected when the day appointed arrives, the officers and others belonging to the board or tribunal refponfible for the performance thereof, fhall incur the punifhment of 100 blows.

On the other hand, any officer of government who commemorates, or performs facred rites to the honour of, any fpirit or holy perfonage, to whom neither honours nor oblations are decreed by the laws of the ritual code, fhall be punifhed with 80 blows.

No claufe.

Section CLX.—*Care of the Tombs of diftinguifhed Perfonages.*

The fepulchral monuments of ancient Emperors and princes, and alfo the tombs of faints, fages, faithful minifters, and other illuftrious individuals, fhall be carefully preferved by the officers of the diftrict in which they are fituated; and no perfon fhall prefume, on pain of receiving a punifhment of 80 blows, to feed cattle, cut wood,

* Thefe monuments, commonly, but improperly, termed triumphal arches, are defcribed in Mr. Barrow's Travels in China, p. 35., and a reprefentation of one of the moft confiderable of the kind, is given in one of the plates in the folio volume annexed to the account of the Britifh Embaffy.

or guide the plough in the places, where the remains of such distinguished personages are deposited.

No clause.

SECTION CLXI. — *Dishonouring Celestial Spirits, by unlicensed Forms of Worship.*

If any private family performs the ceremony of the adoration of Heaven and of the North Star, burning incense for that purpose during the night, lighting the lamps of Heaven, and also seven lamps to the North Star, it shall be deemed a profanation of these sacred rites, and derogatory to the Celestial Spirits; the parties concerned therein shall accordingly be punished with 80 blows.

When the wives or daughters are guilty of these offences, the husbands and fathers shall be held responsible.

If the priests of *Foe* and *Tao-sse*, after burning incense and preparing an oblation, imitate the sacred Imperial rites, they also shall be punished as aforesaid, and moreover be expelled from the order of priesthood.

If any officers of government, soldiers, or citizens, permit the females belonging to their families to go abroad to the temples of priests, in order to burn incense in token of worship, they shall be punished with 40 blows; but when widows, or other women not under the guardianship of men, commit the same offence, the punishment shall fall on themselves.

The superior of the temple, and the porter at the gate, shall likewise be equally punishable for admitting them.

One clause.

SECTION CLXII. — *Magicians, Leaders of Sects, and Teachers of false Doctrines.*

Magicians, who raise evil spirits by means of magical books and dire imprecations, leaders of corrupt and impious sects, and members of all superstitious associations in general, whether denominating themselves *Mi-le-fo*, or *Pe-lien-kiao*, or in any other manner distinguished, all of them offend against the laws, by their wicked and diabolical doctrines and practices.

When such persons, having in their possession concealed images of their worship, burn incense in honour of them, and when they assemble their followers by night in order to instruct them in their doctrines, and by pretended powers and notices, endeavour to inveigle and mislead the multitude, the principal in the commission of such offences shall be strangled, after remaining in prison the usual period, and the accessaries shall severally receive 100 blows, and be perpetually banished to the distance of 3000 *lee*.

If at any time the people, whether soldiers or citizens, dress and ornament their idols, and after accompanying them tumultuously with drums and gongs, perform oblations and other sacred rites to their honour, the leader or instigator of such meetings shall be punished with 100 blows *.

If the head inhabitant of the district, when privy to such unlawful meetings, does not give information to government, he shall be punished with 40 blows.

The penalties of this law shall not however be so construed as to interrupt the regular and customary meetings of the people, to in-

---

* As this prohibitory clause describes nothing more than what is frequently and openly practised in every part of the empire, the law in this respect must be either considered as obsolete, or as an article retained for the purpose of enabling the magistrates to control and keep within bounds these popular superstitions, though it may have been found dangerous or unavailing to attempt to suppress them altogether.

voke the terrestial spirits in spring, and to return thanks to them in autumn*.

Eight clauses.

---

* As the Catholic Christians in China have been estimated at upwards of 200,000, and have been very frequently objects of the attention of the government, sometimes encouraged, but much oftener severely persecuted, some specific notice in this place of the Christian sect, might naturally have been expected: but, whether on account of its comparatively small importance in the eyes of the Chinese, or from some hesitation which may still exist about pronouncing on its character a decisive and irreversible judgment, the subject is in this code entirely passed over in silence. — To make up in some degree for this defect of information on the interesting question of the present disposition of the Chinese government towards the Christian religion (at least in the form and under the appearance given to it by the Roman Catholic missionaries), a translation has been inserted in Appendix, No. XVIII. of two Imperial Edicts, which are expressly declaratory of the law on this subject, and were issued to the public as late as the year 1805.

END OF THE FIRST BOOK OF THE FOURTH DIVISION.

BOOK II.

MISCELLANEOUS OBSERVANCES.

SECTION CLXIII. — *Preparation of Medicines and Provisions for the Emperor.*

IF any phyſician inadvertently prepares and mixes the medicines deſtined for the uſe of His Imperial Majeſty, in any manner that is not ſanctioned by eſtabliſhed practice, or does not accompany them with a proper deſcription and directions, he ſhall be puniſhed with 100 blows. If the ingredients are not genuine and well choſen, as well as carefully compounded, the phyſician ſhall be puniſhed with 60 blows.

If the cook employed in preparing the Imperial repaſts, introduces any prohibited ingredients into the diſhes by inadvertence, he ſhall be puniſhed with 100 blows.

If any of the articles of liquid or ſolid food are not clean, he ſhall be puniſhed with 80 blows. If they are not genuine and properly ſelected, with 60 blows; and laſtly, if the cook does not aſcertain the quality of the diſhes by taſting, he ſhall be puniſhed with 50 blows.

The ſuperintending and diſpenſing officers ſhall in each caſe reſpectively, be puniſhed two degrees leſs ſeverely than the cook and the phyſician.

If either the ſuperintending or diſpenſing officer, or the cook, introduces into His Majeſty's kitchen any unuſual drug, or article of food, he shall be punished with 100 blows, and compelled to swallow the same.

If the superintending or dispensing officers are aware of the cooks or others in the Imperial kitchen committing offences of this nature, and do not report the same to the Emperor, they shall participate equally in the punishment. When such offences have been overlooked through the neglect of the officer on guard at the gates, or the officers about the Emperor's person, they also shall participate equally in the punishment; and in every case, the circumstances immediately after they are discovered, shall be submitted to His Majesty's notice and decision.

One clause.

Section CLXIV. — *Charge of the Imperial Equipage and Furniture.*

Whoever, having charge of the Imperial equipage, or of any other articles destined for Imperial use, does not attend to their repair and preservation in the manner prescribed by the established rules, shall be punished with 60 blows: — Whoever having such charge, presents to the Emperor any articles for his Imperial use, in an improper manner, whether by omitting to present what is necessary, or by presenting what ought not to be presented, shall be punished with 40 blows. — Whoever, having charge as aforesaid, does not duly exercise and examine His Majesty's horses and carriages, so as to ascertain that they are sound, and fit for the service of His Majesty, shall be punished with 80 blows.

Moreover, if any such person should appropriate to his own use, lend for the use of others, or wilfully discard or destroy, any part of His Imperial Majesty's equipage, or any article whatsoever destined in
like

like manner for the immediate use of His Majesty, shall be punished with 100 blows and three years banishment.

When any of the aforesaid articles are lost or destroyed, not wilfully, but inadvertently, either through idleness or neglect, the punishment shall be less by three degrees.

If His Imperial Majesty's pleasure boats and vessels are not found and in good order, the artificer shall be punished with 100 blows.

If the said vessels are not likewise in every other respect kept in good repair, or if they are not properly supplied with poles and planks, the punishment shall amount to 60 blows, and be inflicted on the person in charge, or on the artificer, according as the fault shall be found to be imputable to the one, or to the other.

The superintending officer and dispensing officer of the department, shall each be liable to punishment proportionably less than that inflicted on the artificer or person in charge, by two degrees.

All offences punishable according to this law, shall however be made known immediately on discovery to His Majesty, and the sentence only executed so far as is conformable to His Imperial pleasure.

No clause.

SECTION CLXV.—*Possession and Concealment of prohibited Books and Instruments.*

Any private householder or master of a family, who secretly keeps in his possession celestial images, instruments for explaining and pourtraying the celestial bodies, astrological books, books for calculating good and bad fortune, or other books which are prohibited; or portraits and representations of former Emperors and Kings, official seals cut in gold or in gems, or any other similar articles which private individuals cannot lawfully use or possess, shall, if he does not voluntarily surrender up the same to government, be punished with 100 blows, and be held answerable for the payment of a fine of 10 *leang* or ounces of silver, which sum shall be bestowed as a reward on the informer.

The aforesaid articles shall in every case be forfeited to government.

No clause.

Section CLXVI. — *Transmission of Imperial Presents.*

When His Imperial Majesty is pleased to make presents of dresses or other articles to the officers of His Majesty's government, if the officer deputed to execute His Majesty's commands, does not perform in person the duty assigned to him, but on the contrary transmits the Imperial presents to be delivered by other hands, he shall be punished with 100 blows, and be rendered incapable of holding any employment in the public service.

No clause.

Section CLXVII. — *Observance of Festivals and Days of Ceremony.*

Upon all solemn court festivals, and other occasional public solemnities, appointed for the receipt with due honour of Imperial orders and communications, the officer having the superintendance of this department shall give sufficient previous notice, on pain of receiving a punishment of 40 blows, whenever he omits the same. — All those, on the other hand, who after having received sufficient notice, nevertheless perform their functions imperfectly or improperly upon such occasions, shall be liable to similar punishment.

No clause.

Section CLXVIII. — *Due Performance of appointed Ceremonies.*

If any of the officers of government who affift at the facred and Imperial rites, who attend the vifitation of the Imperial tombs, or who are prefent at the folemnity of a public audience given by the Emperor, miftake, or in any manner deviate from, the eftablifhed ceremonial of the day, they fhall forfeit one month's falary; and if thofe who are appointed to prefide over the ceremonies overlook any fuch miftake or deviation, they fhall be liable to the fame penalty.

One claufe.

Section CLXIX. — *Officers of Government to addrefs the Emperor in Succeffion according to their Rank.*

When any of the officers of government in waiting, or in the train of His Imperial Majefty, are fpoken to, or queftioned collectively, by His Majefty; the firft in rank fhall come forward and fpeak in reply firft, and the others fucceffively according to their order of rank; if any one violates this order, by coming forward and fpeaking, before or after his turn, he fhall forfeit one month's falary.

No claufe.

Section CLXX. — *Vexatioufly detaining Officers of Government from the Imperial Prefence.*

If any officer of government, or other perfon who is entitled to the honour of being prefented to His Imperial Majefty, is vexatioufly detained and impeded upon unwarrantable pretexts by the fuperintendant of the ceremonies, inftead of being forthwith introduced by him

to

to the Imperial prefence, fuch fuperintendant fhall, upon conviction of having fo done by malicious defign, be condemned to fuffer death by being beheaded after confinement in prifon for the ufual period.

All the great officers of ftate who are privy to this offence without making any enquiry into it, fhall be punifhed as equal participators in the guilt, but if ignorant thereof, fhall be fubject to no punifhment or refponfibility whatever.

No claufe.

Section CLXXI. — *Addreffes on Public Affairs.*

Whatever is erroneous in the general adminiftration of public affairs, whatever is beneficial or injurious to the foldiers and people, and, in general, whatever tends to the acquifition of a public benefit or the prevention of a public injury, fhall be enquired into, and the refult perfonally communicated to the Emperor, by the officers of the fix fupreme tribunals or departments of ftate.

The cenfors*, the viceroys, and the deputy viceroys, fhall likewife reprefent faithfully and unrefervedly whatever appears to them advifeable to communicate on thefe fubjects.

If any officer of government at court, or in the provinces, of high or low rank, is aware of any impropriety in the proceedings of the board or tribunal of which he is a member, he fhall fully and diftinctly ftate to his fuperior officer whatever may be requifite and pro-

---

* The board or tribunal of the cenforate has the power of infpecting and animadverting upon the proceedings of all the other public boards and tribunals in the empire, and even on the acts of the fovereign himfelf, whenever they are to be conceived to be cenfurable, but it may eafily be imagined that in a government profeffedly abfolute, the power afcribed to the cenfors in the latter cafe, muft be little more than a fiction of ftate, inftead of operating as a real and effective influence and control.

It muft however be admitted that, from other circumftances peculiar to the conftitution and adminiftration of the Chinefe government, fome of which it is hoped this work may be found to elucidate, there are probably few regular and nominally abfolute monarchies, in which both the perfonal conduct and public meafures of the fovereign are neceffarily fo much under the united influence of laws, cuftoms, and public opinion.

per to be submitted on the subject to His Imperial Majesty, to whom the same shall be faithfully reported in order to be decided upon according to his royal pleasure. Those who, although privy to, take no notice of, and connive at such proceedings, during months and years, shall, if at court, be liable to an investigation of their conduct in such instances, by the censors; but by the viceroys and deputy viceroys, if their connivance should have taken place in any of the provincial departments. When found guilty, they shall be punished according to the law in ordinary instances of omitting to make due report upon public affairs to superiors, or to His Imperial Majesty.

In all representations to the Emperor, the facts, and the reasoning that is grounded upon them, must be stated simply and candidly; each article must be brought forward and explained separately; and all empty phraseology and unnecessary repetition must be avoided.

If any officer of the state, prompted by unprincipled ambition, addresses the Emperor in artful terms, and, upon colourable pretexts, solicits places and employments, he shall be punished with 100 blows. If in such address he falsely criminates any officer or public board immediately entrusted or connected with the administration of civil or military affairs, and if he moreover borrows the sanction of an official seal and envelope, in order to procure the address to be received, both the lender and borrower of such official seal and envelope, shall be beheaded.—The offence is however ranked among those denominated miscellaneous, and the punishment is reducible accordingly to banishment.

One clause.

SECTION CLXXII.—*Monuments raised by Officers of Government to commemorate their own Actions.*

If any officer of government during the period of his administration, presumes to raise within the limits of his district, public monuments
displaying

displaying inscriptions in honour of himself, when he had in fact performed no service to the state worthy of such commemoration, he shall be punished with 100 blows.

If an officer sends any person to his superior to solicit his sanction to the elevation of honorary monuments as aforesaid, upon the pretext of services falsely alleged to have been performed by him, he shall be punished with 80 blows, and the person who undertakes to convey the request under such circumstances shall suffer punishment less by one degree. The monuments undeservedly raised, shall be destroyed, and the inscriptions effaced.

No clause.

Section CLXXIII.— *Honorary Attendance on Superiors in Rank.*

When the superior officers of government, or other officers charged with a special mission by the Emperor, are proceeding through any part of the empire, if any of the officers or members of the several tribunals and departments of government in the districts through which they pass, proceed beyond the walls of their respective cities, either to meet them when approaching, or to accompany them when departing, they shall be punished with 90 blows.

Whoever authorizes and allows such honorary attendance to be paid him, instead of taking cognizance of it as an unlawful procedure, shall be equally punishable.

Six clauses. *

---

* By the fourth clause it is enacted that any soldier or citizen shall be punishable with 50 blows, who does not make way when he meets a civil or military officer of government on the public road, or who, if on horseback, does not dismount on such an occasion.

In respect to this law and others of the same description it may be remarked, that however degrading and oppressive they may appear in the eyes of a European, they are in China intimately connected with, and indeed no more than the natural consequence of the peculiar

Section CLXXIV. — *Official Messengers contemptuously treating the Officers of Districts.*

When any officer or attendant of government is dispatched upon a message or mission relative to the public service, if instead of conducting himself with civility and decorum, he contemptuously treats, either the military officers, who protect, or the civil officers, who govern the district, he shall be punished with 60 blows. If inferior officers are guilty of such misconduct, they shall be punished with either 70 or 80 blows, according to the nature of their ordinary employment in the public service.

One clause.

Section CLXXV. — *Sumptuary Laws relative to Dress and Habitations.*

The houses, apartments, carriages, dress, furniture, and other articles used by the officers of government, and by the people in general, shall be conformable to the established rules and gradations. Accordingly any individual who possesses such articles for use, contrary to these rules and gradations, shall, if an officer of government, be punished with 100 blows, deposed from his office, and rendered incapable of future service; if a private individual is guilty of this offence, the master of the family in which the article is used, shall be punished with 50 blows. In both cases the offending party shall be required to alter and rectify the article in the manner the regulations prescribe. The artificer shall also in both cases be liable to 50 blows, unless he should have surrendered himself voluntarily, in which case he shall be pardoned, but not in any case rewarded.

---

liar character and genius of the people.—In a country where forms and ceremonies are so closely interwoven with all the real business and pursuits of life, it is not felt to be either harsh or tyrannical, that they are thus enforced and regulated by the highest public authority.

If any person possesses for use, articles absolutely prohibited, such as silk stuffs representing the Imperial Dragon (*Lung*), or the Imperial Phœnix (*Fung-whang*), he shall, whether an officer of government, or a private individual, be punished with 100 blows and three years banishment; the officer of government thus offending shall moreover be deposed and rendered incapable of future service. The artificer shall be punished with 100 blows, and the prohibited goods shall be forfeited to government. — Whoever gives information of the commission of this offence, shall receive a reward of 50 *leang* or ounces of silver; even the manufacturer of the goods, if he gives information, shall not only be pardoned for his share in the offence, but also receive the above reward *.

Sixteen clauses.

SECTION CLXXVI. — *Dress and Conduct of the Priests.*

All persons licenced to enter into religious orders as priests of *Foe* or *Tao-sse*, shall nevertheless continue to visit their parents, to sacrifice and make oblations to their ancestors, and to mourn for their recently deceased relations, in the same manner as is by law required from the people in general, on pain of receiving a punishment of 100 blows, and being obliged to renounce their religious orders.

All persons in priest's orders shall wear stuffs and silks of a single colour, and of a simple pattern; they shall abstain from the use of

---

* The law, which in this place enforces, what in other countries is usually governed only by custom or caprice, is, no doubt, frequently evaded by the private and domestic luxury of individuals; it is however certain that, generally speaking, the pleasure which the possessor of superior wealth may be supposed to derive from the display of it, a Chinese, whatever his situation, is in great measure, if not wholly, precluded from enjoying.

At the same time there is nothing which leads to a belief that the law of extraordinary severity mentioned in the description of China compiled by the Abbé Grosier from the writings of the missionaries, for punishing with death those who wear pearls, has any existence either in theory or in practice.

damasks, and flowered or variegated stuffs, on penalty of receiving a punishment of 50 blows, of being excluded from their order, and forfeiting all such dresses to government.

Nevertheless the *Kia-sha*, and other ceremonial vestments exclusively worn by the priests shall not be considered to come within the scope of this regulation.

No clause.

Section CLXXVII. — *Neglect to observe and note the Celestial Appearances.*

Whatever concerns the science of the celestial bodies, such as the sun, the moon, the five planets, the twenty-eight principal and other constellations; and also the observation of the celestial appearances, such as eclipses, meteors, comets, and the like, being the province of the officers of the astronomical board at Pekin, if they neglect duly to observe, and mark the times of the celestial appearances, in order to report them to His Imperial Majesty, they shall be punished with 60 blows for such omission.

One clause.

Section CLXXVIII. — *Conjurors and Fortune-tellers prohibited from prophesying Public Events.*

It shall not be allowed to conjurors and fortune-tellers to frequent the houses of any civil or military officers of government whatever, under the pretence of prophesying to them impending national calamities or successes, and they shall upon every such offence suffer a punishment of 100 blows. This law shall not however be understood to prevent them from telling the fortunes and casting the nativities of individuals by the stars in the usual manner.

No clause.

SECTION CLXXIX. — *Evading the Duty, and concealing the occasion, of Mourning.*

If a son on receiving information of the death of his father or mother, or a wife, receiving information of the death of her husband, suppresses such intelligence, and omits to go into lawful mourning for the deceased, such neglect shall be punished with 60 blows, and and one year's banishment. If a son or wife enters into mourning in a lawful manner, but previous to the expiration of the term, discards the mourning habit, and forgetful of the loss sustained, plays upon musical instruments and partakes of festivities, the punishment shall amount for such offence to 80 blows.

Whoever on receiving information of the death of any other relation in the first degree than the above-mentioned, suppresses the notice of it, and omits to mourn, shall be punished with 80 blows; if previous to the expiration of the legal period of mourning for such relation, any person casts away the mourning habit, and resumes his wonted amusements, he shall be punished with 60 blows.

When any officer or other person in the employ of government, has received intelligence of the death of his father or mother, in consequence of which intelligence he is bound to retire from office during the period of mourning; if, in order to avoid such retirement, he falsely represents the deceased to have been his grand-father, grand-mother, uncle, aunt, or cousin, he shall suffer the punishment of 100 blows, be deposed from office, and rendered incapable of again entering into the public service.

On the other hand, if any officer of government falsely alleges the pretext of mourning, while his parents are still living, or after they are so long dead that the period of mourning had expired, he shall be liable to the same punishment as in the opposite case last mentioned.

If either of the foregoing misrepresentations should be designed to effect any criminal purpose, the offender shall be liable to any aggravation of the punishment which may be conformable to the law, applicable to the case under such circumstances.

If, previous to the expiration of the lawful term of absence in consequence of the loss of a parent, any officer or other person in the employ of government, returns to, and resumes his office or command, he shall be deprived thereof, and punished with 80 blows. If the superior officers of the same department are aware that the return of the mourner is premature, and nevertheless permit him to resume his functions, they shall be equally punishable; but if not aware of the fact, they shall not be responsible.

Those officers of government, who hold remote and important stations and commands, shall not be bound by the above regulations on the arrival of the intelligence of the death of their parents, as the line of conduct they are to pursue on such occasions will always be determined by express orders from the Emperor.

Four clauses.

SECTION CLXXX. — *Officers of Government neglecting their Parents.*

If any person, in order to hold an office under government, absents himself from a father, mother, paternal grandfather, or grandmother, who is either upwards of 80 years of age, or totally disabled by any infirmity, while such near relation has no other male offspring above sixteen years of age, to perform the duties of filial piety; or if, on the contrary, any person being in office, solicits permission to retire to his family, upon a falsely alleged pretext of the age or infirmity of any such near relation as aforesaid, the offender, in either of these opposite cases, shall suffer a punishment of 80 blows.

Whoever

Whoever plays on mufical inftruments, or partakes of feafts at home or abroad, while her hufband, or his or her father, mother, paternal grandfather or grandmother, are in confinement upon a charge of a capital offence, fhall alfo be liable to the aforefaid punifhment.

One claufe.

SECTION CLXXXI. — *Regulations concerning Funerals.*

When a family has loft any of its members by death, the furvivors muft not fail to be obfervant of the eftablifhed rites and ceremonies, and to fix a proper time for the interment of the deceafed; if, vainly feeking an aufpicious time and place, or upon any other pretext, any perfon detains the coffin of his relation unfeelingly expofed in his houfe, and fuffers it thus to remain for more than a twelvemonth unburied, he fhall be punifhed with 80 blows*.

Whoever, in compliance with the laft wifhes expreffed by a fenior relation, confumes his corpfe with fire, or commits it to the waters, fhall be punifhed with 100 blows. In the cafe of a corpfe of a junior relation, the punifhment fhall be lefs by two degrees.

When however a relation happens to die in a diftant country, and the children or grand-children are unable to bring the corpfe to be interred in the native diftrict of the deceafed, it fhall in fuch cafe be permitted to confume it by fire.

The family of the deceafed by whom the funeral obfequies are performed, fhall lay out, and afterwards partake of, the funeral meats; but the male and female branches of the family fhall by no means mix

---

* This law feems to have been required to check the abfurd confequences of a fuperftitious notion univerfally prevalent among the Chinefe, of an intimate connexion always fubfifting between the advantageous or difadvantageous mode and place of interment of perfons deceafed, and the future good or bad fortune of their furviving relations.

indifindiscriminately together, to eat meat and drink wine on such occasions; and if any master of a family permits this practice, he shall be punished with 80 blows for such misconduct. Any priests who thus misconduct themselves, shall be punished in the same manner, and moreover compelled to renounce their order.

Three clauses.

Section CLXXXII.—*Regulations of Country Festivals.*

Among the inhabitants of villages and country districts who associate together, there is an established rule of precedence and seniority at their solemn feasts, and there are certain forms prescribed; whoever disregards either the one or the other, shall be punished with 50 blows for his misconduct.

Two clauses.

END OF THE FOURTH DIVISION.

FIFTH DIVISION.

Military Laws.

BOOK I.

PROTECTION OF THE PALACE.

Section CLXXXIII. — *Unauthorizedly entering the Imperial Temple.*

ALL persons passing unauthorizedly and without sufficient cause, through the gate of the Imperial Temple, or of the inner enclosure of the Imperial burying-ground, shall be punished with 100 blows. — Those who pass through the gate of the hall of Imperial sacrifices, unauthorizedly and without sufficient cause, shall in like manner be punished with 90 blows. The offence of those who come to, but do not pass through, the gates aforesaid, is punishable in each case less severely by one degree. The officer on guard, who designedly permits such offences to be committed, is generally punishable in an equal degree.

If, however, the offence shall have been committed by the neglect, but without the concurrence, of the officer on guard, his punishment shall be less in each case by three degrees.

No clause.

SECTION CLXXXIV.—*Unauthorizedly entering the Imperial Palace.*

All perfons unauthorizedly paffing through any of the gates of the Imperial Citadel at Pekin, and entering therein, or into any of the Imperial gardens, fhall receive 100 blows.

All perfons unauthorizedly entering any of the Imperial palaces, fhall be punifhed with 60 blows, and one year's banifhment.

All perfons unauthorizedly entering any of the apartments in the actual occupation of the Emperor, or into his Imperial refectory, fhall fuffer death by being ftrangled, after remaining in prifon the ufual period.

Thofe who approach with an intent to pafs, but do not actually pafs, through the gates or entrances aforefaid, fhall be fubject to a proportionate punifhment, lefs in each cafe by one degree.

The apartments of the Emprefs, Emprefs-mother, and Emprefs-grand-mother, are protected by the laws in the fame manner as thofe of the Emperor.

All perfons who, not having been infcribed in the proper regifter, pafs or attempt to pafs through any of the gates or entrances aforefaid, by means of affumed names, fhall be punifhed according to this law.

All perfons who, having ftations and employments within the palace, either enter the fame previous to the infertion of their names in the proper regifters, or remain after their duty ceafed to require them, or do duty there out of their turn or order, fhall in each cafe be punifhed with 40 blows.

If any perfons, not having efpecial duty to keep guard within the palace, bring in with them any of the foldiers, or come armed with fharp weapons, they fhall fuffer death by being ftrangled after the ufual period of confinement.

All persons who under similar circumstances enter the Imperial citadel, shall be punished with 100 blows, and banished perpetually to the most remote frontier of the empire.

Those officers and soldiers on guard at the several gates, who consent or connive at the commission of any of the aforesaid offences, shall be held equally guilty with the party transgressing the law, except in capital cases, when the punishment shall be reduced one degree. Officers and soldiers by whose neglect, but without whose concurrence, such offences are committed, shall suffer the punishment provided by law, reduced three degrees; but they shall not in any case suffer more than 100 blows.

In respect to the last mentioned regulation, it is further provided that only those soldiers whose day it was to be on duty shall be liable to punishment, and that their punishment shall be one degree less than that of their superior officer, who in such cases is, in the contemplation of the law, the principal offender.

No clause.

SECTION CLXXXV.—*Imperial Guards failing to do their Duty.*

Every person who, after having been appointed to keep guard and to do duty at the gates of the Imperial citadel, or at the gates of any of the Imperial palaces, does not attend at his post when his turn arrives, shall be punished with 40 blows.

All persons who, in such cases, privately depute substitutes from among the other guards of the palace to supply their places, shall, as well as such substitutes, be liable to the punishment of 60 blows.

If any such substitute be a stranger, the punishment of both parties shall be encreased to 100 blows: in all cases of officers on duty so offending, the punishment shall be one degree more severe.

Persons quitting their posts after having taken charge of them, shall be punished under this law.

Persons appointed to keep guard at any of the gates of the Imperial city, and offending in the manner already stated, shall suffer a punishment less in each case by one degree. Persons appointed to keep guard at the gate of any other city, shall be liable to the punishments awarded by this law, reduced in each case two degrees.

The corporal or serjeant commanding the guard, if guilty of consenting or conniving at the offence, shall be liable to the same punishments as the original offender.

If the offence is to be attributed to his neglect, but not to his connivance or concurrence, his punishment shall be reduced three degrees; when, however, the individual absent had duly reported, and had alleged sufficient cause for his intended absence to his superior officer, it shall be considered as a sufficient justification and exempt all the parties from punishment.

No clause.

SECTION CLXXXVI.—*Imperial Retinue failing in their Attendance.*

If any of the persons immediately attached to the suite or retinue of the Emperor do not attend at the time appointed, or if they quit their stations before the period of their service had expired, they shall for the first day's absence be liable to a punishment of 40 blows, and for every additional three days absence, the punishment shall be encreased one degree, until it amounts to 100 blows.

If the offender is a civil or military officer, the punishment shall be encreased one degree, but not in any case exceed 60 blows and one year's banishment.

Any individual of the Emperor's retinue who deserts his post, during any of the Imperial journies or provincial visitations, shall be punished

punished with 100 blows and perpetual banishment to the most remote frontier of the empire.

If the offender is a civil or military officer of government, he shall suffer death by being strangled, after the usual period of confinement.

The corporal or serjeant of the guard conniving at or consenting to such desertion, shall be liable to the same punishment, except in capital cases, when his punishment shall be reduced one degree.

If the desertion happened without his consent, and is only attributable to his neglect, his punishment shall be three degrees less than in the preceding case, and not in any instance exceed 100 blows.

One clause.

SECTION CLXXXVII.— *Trespass upon the Imperial Roads.*

No person shall presume to travel on the roads or to cross the bridges which are expressly provided and reserved for the use of the Emperor, except only such civil and military officers and other attendants, as immediately belong to His Majesty's retinue, and who are in consequence necessarily permitted to proceed upon the side-paths thereof.

All other persons, whether civil or military officers, soldiers or people, who presume to travel on the roads or to cross the bridges aforesaid, shall be punished with 80 blows.

In like manner, those who shall presume to proceed upon any of the particular passages and pathways within the palace, which are expressly reserved for the Emperor, shall suffer the punishment of 100 blows; and the attendants on duty in the palace, who connive thereat, shall be equally punishable. But if the offence is merely attributable to their neglect, and not their consent or connivance, their punishment shall be reduced three degrees. When, in any of the foregoing cafes, the offence is only momentary, and not repeated, it fhall not be confidered requifite to carry this law into effect.

Two claufes.

Section CLXXXVIII.—*Rules concerning Labourers within the Palace.*

All labourers, meffengers, and other perfons, hired for any work or fervice within the palaces, treafuries, or other buildings, exclufively appropriated to His Imperial Majefty, fhall be provided with perfonal licences or paffports.

Any perfon attempting to introduce himfelf by means of a paffport or licence intended for another, and attempting to act as a fubftitute for fuch perfon, fhall, as well as the perfon transferring fuch licence or paffport, be liable to the punifhment of 100 blows.

The wages due to fuch perfon fhall alfo be forfeited to government.

No claufe.

Section CLXXXIX.—*Labourers in the Imperial Palace remaining there after the Conclufion of their Work.*

When labourers of any defcription are employed in the Imperial palaces, whether in the domeftic or ftate apartments, the officer of government who has the fuperintendance of their work, fhall give in an exact ftatement of the proper name and family name of each perfon to the officers on guard at the feveral gates, and alfo to the fuperior officers in waiting; when any fuch individual enters the palace for the firft time, his name and his perfon fhall be identified at the gate, and an exact notice taken of his figure and appearance.

In the courfe of the hour *Shin* (between three and five in the afternoon), the number of perfons, as well as the figure and appearance of each, having been found to correspond with the register, they shall all depart through the identical gates by which they had been admitted.

If any of them wilfully remain within the palace, contrary to this regulation, they shall be liable to the punishment of death by being strangled, after the usual period of imprisonment.

Whenever it is found that the list of labourers departing from the palace is deficient in names or number, it shall be the duty of the superintendants of the works, the officers and soldiers on guard, and those attached to the several gates, immediately to make a diligent search and enquiry, and also to give respectful intimation of the circumstance to His Imperial Majesty. All such officers and others who are privy to and guilty of concealing the fact, shall be liable to the same punishment as the offender himself, except in the case of his being convicted capitally, when the punishment shall be reduced one degree.

When such offence is committed without the knowledge and concurrence of the officers on duty, and is therefore to be attributed to their neglect only, the punishment with regard to them shall be reduced three degrees, and not in any case exceed 100 blows.

No clause.

SECTION CXC.—*Irregularity in passing through the Gates of the Imperial Palaces.*

If any persons who, (having obtained leave of absence, or having been appointed to quit the palace on duty,) cease to have their names registered at the several gates, nevertheless remain after their supposed departure; or if those who have been tried on any charges, and in consequence dismissed altogether from the service of the palace, unauthorizedly return thereto, they shall, whether their names had been struck

struck out or not from the regifters, in each cafe be punifhed with 100 blows.

When any of the guards of the palace are, in confequence of charges exhibited againft them, committed for examination and trial, if the commanding officer does not in the firft inftance take away the arms which had been allotted to fuch perfons, he fhall on his part be liable to the punifhment laft ftated.

All thofe who are regularly entered in the regifters as having fixed ftations within the palace, are, equally with other perfons, prohibited from paffing to and fro after dark. If going in, they fhall be punifhed with 100 blows; if going out, with 80 blows. But if going in without having been regiftered, the punifhment fhall be greater by two degrees: if moreover they are difcovered with arms in their hands, they fhall fuffer death by being ftrangled, after the ufual period of confinement.

No claufe.

Section CXCI. — *Examination of the Certificates or Paffports of Perfons having Employments in the Palace.*

When any perfon in the immediate fervice of His Majefty, or having any duty or fuperintendance within the palace, quits the precincts thereof, his certificate or paffport fhall be required of him by the officer at the outer gate, whofe duty it fhall alfo be to retain the fame, after having carefully identified the names, marks, and official ftamps thereof; the officer fhall likewife duly record whither the perfon quitting the palace is going, and upon what bufinefs. Every fuch perfon fhall moreover, previous to his departure, be perfonally examined by the officer on guard and his attendants, in order to afcertain that he does not illicitly carry away any public or private property. Upon the return of the perfon to his employment within the palace, he fhall again undergo go at the outer gate, previous to his certificate being returned to him, a similar examination. There shall also be a monthly examination of the registers, to ascertain how often each person has passed and re-passed during each successive interval.

If, in the course of examination, any person should be found to carry about him drugs of a suspicious nature, he shall be compelled to swallow the same.

If any person passing the gates presumes to refuse to submit to the required examination, he shall be punished with 100 blows and perpetual and remote banishment.

Any person who, without having His Majesty's express licence and authority so to do, carries arms and military weapons into the Imperial citadel, within which is the Imperial residence, shall be punished with 100 blows, and sent into perpetual and most remote banishment. If any person is detected carrying arms without authority as aforesaid, into any of the Imperial palaces, he shall suffer death by being strangled at the usual period; and the officer of the gate, as well as the officer on guard, who neglected to examine and prevent the passage of such person, shall be liable to the same punishment as the principal offender, excepting a reduction of one degree in capital cases*.

No clause.

---

* Notwithstanding the multiplicity and apparent rigour of the laws provided in this and other sections of the code, for ensuring the safety of the person of the Sovereign, the present Emperor, in the year 1803, very narrowly escaped assassination within the precincts of his palace, from the hand of a single, but desperate intruder. — The official report of the circumstances, which was published at the time, being illustrative of the law in this respect; and otherwise also, rather a curious and interesting document, a translation of it is inserted in the Appendix, No. XIX.

SECTION CXCII. — *Shooting or throwing missile Weapons towards an Imperial Palace.*

All persons who shall shoot arrows or bullets, or fling any bricks or stones, towards the Imperial temple, or towards any Imperial palace, whether a place of residence or appropriated to purposes of state only, with any apparent possibility of hitting such place or building, shall in each case suffer death by being strangled at the usual period: if towards the temple of Imperial sacrifices, the offender shall be punished with 100 blows and perpetual banishment to the distance of 3000 *lee*.

If any person within any of the buildings above-mentioned is wounded by such means, the offender shall, in every such case, be beheaded at the usual period.

No clause.

SECTION CXCIII. — *Soldiers and Officers on Guard to be always armed.*

All persons doing duty upon guard, by day or by night, shall constantly carry their arms about them, and are punishable with 40 blows upon any failure in this respect. If convicted of having been at any time absent from their station and duty, they shall be liable to 50 blows, and if passing the night elsewhere than at their appointed station, the punishment shall amount to 60 blows; if the offender is an officer of government, the punishment shall in each case be more severe by one degree.

If the corporal or serjeant of the guard connives at, and concurs in, the commission of the above offences on the part of the soldiers under his authority, he shall be liable to the same punishment; but if the offence takes place without his knowledge or concurrence, and is therefore attributable only to his neglect, his punishment shall be less by three degrees.

No clause.

SECTION CXCIV. — *Convicted Persons and their Relations not to be employed near the Imperial Presence.*

In all cases of persons living within the jurisdiction of the Imperial city, being condemned to die by the sentence of the law, their families, and all persons whatsoever who resided under the same roof with them, shall remove forthwith, and reside in future under another jurisdiction.

All such persons as aforesaid, all the other relations of persons who have suffered under the laws, and also all persons who have themselves undergone any species of punishment by the sentence of the law, shall be judged for ever incapable of holding any office near the person of His Imperial Majesty, or of being entrusted with the duty of guarding any of the Imperial palaces, the Imperial citadel, or the gates of the city of Pekin.

Any person who shall absurdly undertake any such office, concealing the previous circumstance by which he is disabled from so doing, shall be beheaded at the usual period.

Any officer of government who does not take proper care to ascertain that the person whom he trusts or employs as above-mentioned is free from such disability, or who knowing him to be under such disability, accepts his services in consideration of a bribe, shall be liable to the same punishment, and accordingly be beheaded.

Nevertheless, if any relation of a criminal who has suffered capital punishment, or any person who has himself undergone any less punishment by the sentence of the law, is, by an Imperial edict, expressly chosen to fill some one of the responsible situations above-mentioned, and the superior officer of the department lays before His Majesty a due report of the former trial and punishment of such person, or of his relations, as the case may be; this law in such case shall not be put in force.

No clause.

Section CXCV. — *Intrusion into the Space allotted to the Imperial Retinue.*

During the Imperial journies and visitations, all the soldiers and people shall carefully make way for the approach of His Majesty, excepting only those forming his retinue, namely, the officers and soldiers on guard in special attendance, and those immediately attached to his royal person. Any person who, notwithstanding, forcibly intrudes within the lines, shall be condemned to suffer death by being strangled; but the offence being ranked among the miscellaneous, the punishment may be mitigated to five years banishment*.

When His Majesty travels in distant places, and his retinue arrives at any place unexpectedly, it shall be sufficient for those who are unable to retire in time, to prostrate themselves humbly on the road side, until the retinue has passed them.

Any of the civil and military officers of government, who not belonging to the retinue, presume to enter within the lines without being summoned by His Majesty, or having other sufficient cause, shall be punished with 100 blows.

Any officer or soldier on guard belonging to the retinue, who designedly permits any person to pass the lines who is not entitled to do so, shall suffer tne same punishment as the original offender; but if the offence is committed merely through the neglect of such officer or soldier, the punishment shall in such case be less by three degrees.

Any person who is desirous of presenting a complaint of injustice, shall be suffered to prostrate himself for such purpose on the road, but always outside of the lines.

If any person should, nevertheless, suddenly force his way through the lines, in order to present a complaint, which afterwards proves

---

* See the note to Section LXV.

groundless, he shall be condemned to suffer death by being strangled, but the offence being ranked among those termed miscellaneous, the punishment may be mitigated to five years banishment. When, however, the complaint proves just, the intrusion within the lines shall be pardoned.

If any of the soldiers, or people living in the neighbourhood through which the Emperor is passing, do not confine their cattle, and such cattle through the neglect of the guards are suffered to come within the lines, the guards so in fault shall receive 80 blows; and, if by a similar accident any cattle rush into the Imperial citadel, the punishment of the guards, for not preventing the same, shall amount to 100 blows. The punishment of the persons to whom the cattle belonged shall be estimated according to the severer clause of the law relative to offences against propriety *.

Two clauses.

SECTION CXCVI. — *Passing through Gates leading to an Imperial Palace.*

The same laws shall be enforced in respect to persons passing the gates of the first and second barriers leading to any palace, as in respect to persons passing the gates of the Imperial citadel at Pekin, and the offence of entering through them unauthorizedly shall be punished with 100 blows. The passage through the inner gates styled *Ya-chang-men*, shall be subject to the same restrictions as the passage through the gates of the palace, and any person entering through the same unauthorizedly, shall be punished with 60 blows, and one year's banishment.

No clause.

* See Section CCCLXXXVI.

Section CXCVII.—*Scaling the Walls of fortified Places.*

All perſons guilty of ſcaling the walls of the Imperial citadel in Pekin, ſhall ſuffer death, by being ſtrangled at the uſual period. In like manner, the offence of ſcaling the walls of the Imperial city of Pekin, ſhall be puniſhed with 100 blows and perpetual baniſhment to the diſtance of 3000 *lee*.

The offence of ſcaling the walls of any city of the firſt, ſecond, or third order, or of any fort, ſhall be puniſhed with 100 blows; and, laſtly, that of ſcaling the walls of any officer of government's official reſidence, with 80 blows; in each caſe, the attempt to ſcale, if unſucceſsful, ſhall ſubject the offender to the puniſhment above provided, reduced one degree.

If the perſon guilty of ſcaling any of the walls aforeſaid, is concerned at the ſame time in the commiſſion of any other offence, he ſhall be made to ſuffer for that one among his offences, which by law is the moſt ſeverely puniſhable.

One clauſe.

Section CXCVIII.—*Regulations concerning the Gates of Cities.*

Any perſon ſhutting at the proper period, but inadvertently neglecting to bolt, the gate of any city or fortified place, ſhall be puniſhed with 80 blows; and the puniſhment ſhall be encreaſed to 100 blows, if guilty of opening or ſhutting ſuch gates at an improper time. In reſpect to the gates of the Imperial city of Pekin, the puniſhment ſhall be one degree more ſevere than in other caſes; but in general, if the opening or ſhutting any of the gates above-mentioned at an irregular time, takes place in execution of the public ſervice, and upon a preſſing emergency, the puniſhment provided by this law ſhall not be inflicted.

flicted. Those persons who, at the regular period of shutting the gates of the Imperial citadel at Pekin, neglect to bolt them, shall suffer 100 blows, and be sent into perpetual and very remote banishment: the person who opens or shuts such gates at an irregular time, shall be punished with death, by being strangled at the usual period.

Nevertheless, persons bearing an Imperial order on any occasion, may open or shut such gates at all times, without being liable to the penalties by this law provided.

No clause.

END OF THE FIRST BOOK OF THE FIFTH DIVISION.

BOOK II.

GOVERNMENT OF THE ARMY.*

SECTION CXCIX. — *Unauthorizedly employing Military Force.*

WHEN any of the general officers or commanders in chief of the cavalry or infantry, stationed for the protection and defence of the cities, fortified towns, military posts, and frontier encampments in the different parts of the empire, receive reports of symptoms of insurrection and revolt having appeared within the limits of their respective commands, they shall immediately dispatch proper persons to ascertain how far the reports are well founded, and how far the circumstances are of such a nature as to require the interference of military force.

If the result of the enquiry in any case, confirms the previous report, the commanding officer shall transmit a statement of the particulars to his immediate superior at the head quarters, that the same may be submitted to the consideration of His Imperial Majesty, whose sacred and royal orders on the subject shall, in ordinary cases, be requisite to sanction the adoption of the measure of assembling and detaching an efficient body of troops for the suppression of the insurrection, and punishment of the insurgents.

---

* As some account of the military operations of the Chinese, as given in the reports of their own general officers, may contribute in a considerable degree to illustrate the abstract which this book of the code contains of their martial laws, and be at the same time perhaps, a novelty not altogether uninteresting in itself, a translation has been inserted in the Appendix, No. XX. of a few extracts from the Pekin Gazette of the year 1800, relating to the proceedings of the Imperial army, on the occasion of a formidable rebellion, which raged at that period, in two or three considerable provinces of the Chinese empire.

If, in a cafe of no actual emergency, any commander of the forces, without tranfmitting a previous ftatement of the cafe to his fuperior, or, having tranfmitted fuch a ftatement, without waiting for orders in reply, upon the ftrength of his own authority, prefumes to iffue inftructions for the affembling of the infantry or cavalry within the limits of his command, fuch commander, and the officers of the fubordinate ftations and garrifons, who furnifhed him with troops conformably to his requifition, fhall each be fubject to receive 100 blows, and fent into perpetual and remote military banifhment.

On the other hand, if an enemy's force has already marched into any of the diftricts of the empire in order to make an attack; if open revolt or mutiny breaks out in any of the cities, or other military ftations; or if the condition and progrefs of the infurgents is in any manner fuch as to render it inexpedient to wait a return of the meffenger with orders from the fuperior officer, it fhall in all fuch cafes be lawful for the officer in command of the diftrict, to take inftant meafures for the affembling the troops belonging to the feveral ftations under his controul, and to employ them in any way that the exifting circumftances may render moft conducive to the defeat and apprehenfion of the infurgents. If the infurrection fhould have become fo confiderable in point of numbers and extent, as to render it expedient that the troops ftationed in neighbouring diftricts fhould co-operate in the meafures to be adopted againft the infurgents, it fhall be lawful for the commander of the forces to demand the aid of fuch troops, although beyond the limits of his ordinary command; but the feveral commanders of diftricts, affifting or requiring affiftance, fhall not fail in fuch cafes, immediately to acquaint their fuperiors with their refpective proceedings, for the information of His Imperial Majefty.

If, under fuch circumftances, the commanding officer of the diftrict in a ftate of infurrection, and the commanding officer of the neighbouring diftrict, whofe aid is required, do not affemble and difpofe of their forces as the cafe requires, or if they do not tranfmit information of their proceedings to their refpective fuperiors; or laftly, if the officers in the immediate command of the troops do not difpatch them according to the orders of their fuperior officers, the punifhment fhall be the fame as already ftated in the cafe of employing military force, without authority or neceffity.

The orders which any commanding officer of a diftrict may receive, to difpofe of and detach the forces under his controul, either from his fuperior military officer, or from the minifters of ftate, fhall not in ordinary cafes warrant their removal beyond the limits of the diftrict they are ftationed to protect, unlefs fuch orders are exprefsly ftated to be in obedience to the facred commands of the Emperor. In like manner the orders for the removal, promotion, degradation, or trial of any military officer on duty, fhall not be carried into effect, unlefs derived exprefsly from His Majefty's facred command; and whoever obeys any fuch orders, without the above fanction, fhall be punifhed in the fame manner as in the other cafes previoufly defcribed.

No claufe.

Section CC.— *Military Operations to be regularly reported.*

When any officer who commands a detachment or divifion of the forces on their march upon actual fervice, fubject to the orders of the general and commander in chief of the expedition, is directed to proceed againft any of the forts or other ftrong holds of the rebels, he fhall, immediately after having reduced the place, and accomplifhed the object of his deftination, difpatch a fwift meffenger with the intelligence to the commander in chief at head-quarters, and by him a correfponding communication fhall with equal expedition be made to the fupreme board for military affairs. The commander-in-chief fhall alfo draw up another special report of the event, for the purpose of its being laid before His Imperial Majesty.

If, on the other hand, the strength and numbers of the rebels are found to be so considerable, that the force destined to proceed against them by the commander in chief is inadequate to the service, the commanding officer of the detachment shall instantly transmit information of this state of affairs to the said commander in chief, that such a reinforcement of infantry and cavalry may be sent from head quarters, as may be necessary to ensure the defeat and apprehension of the rebels and insurgents. If the commanding officer of the detachment omits to give such information, the commander in chief shall determine and inflict such punishment as may be warranted by the circumstances of the case; but if a failure of the military operations of government in that quarter is the consequence of such omission, the extent of the punishment shall be determined according to the law which is expressly applicable to such a case, and elsewhere provided.

When any of the revolters and insurgents voluntarily surrender themselves to a detachment or division of the forces, the commanding officer shall immediately deliver them over to the custody of the commander in chief, that the latter may respectfully acquaint the Emperor with the circumstance, and solicit a declaration of His Majesty's pleasure respecting their future disposal.

If any such commanding officer rapaciously plunders the property of those who have voluntarily surrendered, and subsequently kills or wounds them; or if he oppresses them in such a manner that they are driven to desert, and either attempt or effect their escape, he shall be beheaded after remaining in prison the customary period. If he does not kill or wound them, or drive them to the said extremities by violence, the punishment shall be conformable to the law provided for cases of defraudation only.

No clause.

SECTION CCI. — *Expresses upon Military Affairs.*

Whenever any expresses, containing information and intelligence respecting military affairs, are received by the governors of the cities of the first and second orders, from the districts, stations, and governments, within the limits of their respective jurisdictions, the contents shall be reported in dispatches entrusted to the care of special messengers, to the viceroy, sub-viceroy, treasurer, judge, and other heads of departments in the province, and subsequently also to the commander of the forces in the district, and to the commander in chief in the province.

The commanders of military stations shall address their dispatches upon military affairs only to the commander of the forces of the district, the commander in chief, the viceroy, and the sub-viceroy.

When the intelligence arrives at the offices of the viceroy, sub-viceroy, commander in chief, and other military officers of the first rank, they shall, on the one hand, transmit a particular statement of the circumstances to the supreme board for military affairs, and on the other, address a respectful report of the case for the express purpose of its being submitted to the immediate consideration of His Imperial Majesty. If the aforesaid superior officers, after a joint deliberation on the subject, agree to suppress and conceal the intelligence, and, conformably to such agreement, make no timely report to the Emperor, they shall be severally punished with 100 blows, deprived of their offices, and rendered incapable of the public service. If the military operations then in progress are, in consequence of such concealment, erroneously or improperly conducted, the offenders shall suffer death, by being beheaded after the customary period of imprisonment.

No clause.

Section CCII. — *Betraying the Secrets of the State.*

When any person is in possession of important secrets of state, such as the intended distribution of the troops, and other measures taken, and arrangements made by the Emperor, or by the commander in chief, for the attack and reduction by surprise of any foreign tribes, or for the defeat and seizure of revolters and insurgents; if such person betrays or in any manner divulges such state secrets, so that they come to the knowledge of the enemy, he shall be beheaded after undergoing the customary imprisonment.

In like manner, if any person betrays or divulges the contents of the reports of generals of the forces, addressed to His Majesty from the frontiers, so that the enemy comes to the knowledge thereof, he shall be punished with 100 blows and banishment for three years; but, if in this or the preceding case, the offending party shall have been convicted of treasonable motives, he will be more severely punishable, as is elsewhere by law provided.

The first divulger of the secret shall always suffer the full punishment of the law, as the principal offender, and each of those who afterwards successively transmitted it, shall suffer the mitigated punishment of accessaries.

Whoever privately opens and reads any sealed government or official dispatch whatever, shall be punished at the least with 60 blows; but if it relates to any important military affairs, he shall be punished with 100 blows and three years banishment, as a divulger of state secrets.

If any of the officers of government holding employments and places immediately about His Majesty's person, divulge an important secret of the court, they also shall suffer death for the offence, by being beheaded after the usual period of imprisonment; and even if they divulge any secrets upon ordinary affairs, they shall be punished

with

with 100 blows, deprived of their places, and rendered incapable of the public service*.

Three clauses.

Section CCIII.—*Application for, and Transmission of Military Supplies.*

Whenever there is any deficiency of grain, specie, or military stores at any of the frontier stations, the commanding officer of the post shall send a messenger to give notice thereof to the treasurer of the province, and shall at the same time address official letters to the viceroy, sub-viceroy, and chief military officers of the province, requesting their sanction to the issue of a further supply. The chief authorities in the province shall make known the application for supplies, describing their nature and amount, to the supreme board in that department at Pekin, and through that channel information shall, lastly, be conveyed to the Emperor, conformable to whose orders, the supplies shall be issued and distributed.

If any unnecessary delay retards the progress of the application for, and issue of, the supplies in the different stages; if the Emperor is not informed of the application as soon as it is received; or if the officer stationed at the frontier does not duly and regularly make the application as often as is necessary, the individual failing to perform his duty, shall be punished with 100 blows, deprived of his situation, and rendered incapable of the public service.

If through the misconduct thus punishable, so great a deficiency in point of supplies is experienced at the period of a subsequent conflict with an enemy, that the military operations of government are in that instance rendered unsuccessful, the delinquents shall suffer death, by being beheaded after the usual period of confinement.

No clause.

---

* The first clause to this section denounces the punishment of perpetual banishment against those who betray the secrets of state, by clandestinely visiting and plotting with the members of foreign embassies.

Section CCIV. — *Errors and Failures in Military Operations.*

When the troops of government are on the point of taking the field upon any public service, if the supplies of arms, ammunition, stores, and requisite provisions of all kinds are not found to have been completed within the period previously determined, the officer of government who occasioned the delay, whether by a tardy transmission of the proper orders or a tardy execution of them, shall be punished with 100 blows.

If any such delay or neglect shall occasion a deficiency in the aforesaid articles when the troops are near to, and on the point of engaging the enemy; if the commanding officers of the troops who have received orders to co-operate on such occasions, lose time and wait the issue of events, instead of assembling their forces on the day, and at the place appointed; or lastly, if those who are entrusted with the orders or dispatches for assembling the troops, as aforesaid, do not execute their commissions in due time; any error or failure in the military operations that may arise from such causes shall subject the offending parties to the punishment of death, by being beheaded after the customary period of confinement.

No clause.

Section CCV. — *Military Officers and Troops not taking the Field according to their Instructions.*

When a certain number of military officers, together with the troops under their command, have been selected for the performance of any particular military service; as soon as the season approaches for the commencement of their operations, a day shall be fixed for their marching from their quarters, and after that period arrives any delay of a single day shall subject the offending party to a punishment of of 70 blows; and the punishment shall encrease at the rate of one degree for every further delay of three days, of which any individual is guilty.

If any one shall designedly wound or maim himself, or pretend sickness or infirmity, in order to evade his duty on such an occasion, the punishment shall be one degree more severe, and be encreased according to the number of the days of the delay, until it attain the limit of 100 blows. The offender shall still be compelled to join the army in the field, unless he has maimed himself in such a manner as to be unfit for service, in which case, his district shall be obliged to find a substitute.

After the troops have entered the destined field of their operations, whoever under any pretext absents himself a day beyond the period fixed for repairing to his station, shall be punished with 100 blows; and whoever absents himself for three days, under the like circumstances, shall, although no ill consequence to the military operations should arise therefrom, suffer death, by being beheaded after the usual confinement, and be executed under the immediate direction of the commander in chief; but if the offender is capable of redeeming his credit, by zealous exertions in the line of his duty, the commander in chief shall possess the discretionary power of remitting his punishment, and of deciding relative to his future disposal.

One clause.

SECTION CCVI. — *Soldiers serving by Substitutes.*

When any individual of the military profession, instead of personally joining the army when summoned, sends a substitute whom he has hired to assume his name, and serve for him, the substitute shall be punished with 80 blows, and the individual who hired him, with 100 blows; and the latter shall be compelled to take a station in the ranks instead of the former.

Any soldier of a garrison who hires a temporary substitute to personate and serve for him in his absence, shall, as well as such substitute, be liable to punishment within two degrees of the severity of that provided in the former case.

Nevertheless, if the son, grandson, nephew, younger brother, or other relation, living on the farm, or establishment of the person liable to serve, voluntarily offers himself without any pecuniary consideration, he shall be allowed to supply the place of the other, provided the individual declining service is really necessitated to do so, by age or infirmities.

The individual offering to serve shall address a statement of the case to the commanding officer, who, having verified and duly investigated the same, shall grant the other his discharge. If the persons of the medical profession who are held in requisition to attend and prepare medicines for the army, evade their duty by hiring itinerant quacks and ignorant persons, to personate them and serve in their stead, the substitute and the individual hiring him, shall each suffer the punishment of 80 blows; and whatever pecuniary consideration the former may have received from the latter, he shall forfeit to government.

One clause.

SECTION CCVII.—*Officers on the Field of Battle unfaithful to their Trust.*

If any general or other commanding officer entrusted with the charge of a city, fortress, or other military station, when it is attacked or invested by rebels or insurgents, suddenly deserts and flies from his post, instead of effectually maintaining and defending it; or if such general or commanding officer, having neglected the previous adoption of proper measures of defence and security, suffers the enemy to come upon him unawares, and take possession of such city, fortress, or military station, he shall in either case suffer death, by being beheaded, after the customary period of confinement. If, when the army is in the neighbourhood of the lines of the rebels or insurgents, the scouts and advanced guards stationed on the heights, do not take care to give timely notice of the enemy's motions; and if, in consequence of their neglect, the fortresses are taken, or the forces of government worsted by an unexpected attack, the scouts or guards shall, for such misconduct, be also liable to the punishment of death, by being beheaded after the usual period of confinement.

If the neglect of proper precautions on the part of the general, or of due communication of intelligence, on the part of the scouts or advanced guards, is not attended with the loss of any fortress, or with any other consequences directly injurious to the forces of government, but still enables the insurgents to advance beyond their former limits, and to ravage the country and plunder the inhabitants, the individual whose offence occasioned such misfortunes, shall be punished with 100 blows, and sent into perpetual and remote military banishment.

If, when the forces of government are drawn out to engage the enemy in a pitched battle, or to invest or assault the enemy's fortresses, any of the officers or soldiers set the example of giving way and retreating, they shall suffer death by being beheaded, after the usual period of confinement.

Three clauses.

SECTION CCVIII. — *Connivance at the Depredations of the Soldiers.*

Any commanding officer of troops in the field, or at a frontier station, who privately authorizes or instructs his soldiers to proceed beyond the limits of the territories under subjection, in order to seize and plunder the inhabitants, shall be punished with 100 blows, deprived of his office, and sent into the less remote military banishment.

If the superior authorities in the provinces authorize such conduct on the part of the military officers, they shall suffer punishment less by one degree; and if the civil officers in the station concur therein, they shall suffer punishment less by two degrees.

Those only who authorize the pillage shall be punishable, and therefore the soldiers, when warranted by the permission of their superiors, shall not be held responsible.

If, on the other hand, any of the soldiers go beyond the boundaries, and pillage the country, without any authority or licence to that effect from their superior officers, the ringleaders shall be punished with 100 blows, and the rest severally with 90 blows; if in the course of such unwarrantable proceedings, they should wound any of the inhabitants, their ringleader shall be beheaded, after the usual confinement, and the rest punished severally with 100 blows, and sent (as also the offenders in the former case) into remote military banishment. If, on these occasions, the immediate superior of the soldiers guilty of this offence, is chargeable with a neglect of proper discipline, he shall be punished with 60 blows, but retain his office.

Nevertheless, when any of the insurgents escape beyond the frontiers, this law shall not be construed so as to prevent the officers of garrisons in frontier stations from detaching parties of troops across the boundaries, to pursue and reduce such fugitive insurgents into subjection.

If at any time the troops are guilty of pillage within the boundaries of the empire, or of countries reduced to subjection, they shall, without any distinction between principals and accessaries, suffer death by being beheaded, after the customary confinement.

If the immediate superiors of the soldiers guilty of this offence are chargeable on such occasions with a neglect of proper discipline, they shall be punished with 80 blows, but retain their offices.

If the commanding and other officers of the troops are privy to their designs of pillaging the country and inhabitants, within or without the boundaries of the empire, and yet connive at, and permit such unwarrantable proceedings, they shall be liable to the same punishment as the soldiers, excepting only the customary reduction of one degree in capital cases.

Two clauses.

SECTION CCIX. — *Exercise and Discipline of the Troops.*

If the commanding officer of any military post or station, either upon the frontiers or elsewhere within the empire, does not preserve military law and discipline; if he does not constantly employ his troops in military exercises; if he does not keep the walls and fortifications in a state of repair; or lastly, if he does not provide an adequate supply, in proper condition, of clothes, armour, arms, and ammunition; he shall in every such case be punished with 80 blows, when it is the first offence, and with 100 blows, when it is the second offence.

If through a relaxation from the due severity of precautionary discipline, or an ill-judged exercise of military authority in dispensing rewards and punishments, the troops at length mutiny and desert to the enemy, all the officers who held commands over such troops, shall be punished respectively with 100 blows, their families degraded, and themselves dismissed into remote and perpetual military banishment.

If in consequence of the desertion or mutiny of the troops, any officer shall fly from his post, he shall suffer death by being beheaded, after the usual period of confinement.

One clause.

Section CCX.— *Exciting and causing Rebellion by oppressive Conduct.*

If any officer of government, whose situation gives him power and controul over the people, not only does not conciliate them by proper indulgence, but exercises his authority in a manner so inconsistent with the established laws and approved usages of the empire, that the sentiments of the once loyal subjects being changed by his oppressive conduct, they assemble tumultuously and openly rebel, and drive him at length from the capital city and seat of his government; such officer shall suffer death, after the usual period of confinement. If the rebellion does not extend so far as to occasion the loss of the government station, subject to the authority of such officer, the case shall be considered similar to that of a criminal neglect of discipline leading to mutiny, which is treated of in the preceding section; but the final decision upon the extent of the punishment due to the offender, shall remain with His Imperial Majesty.

Two clauses.

Section CCXI. — *Clandestine Sale of Horses taken in Battle.*

Whenever the troops of government take and secure any of the horses belonging to the enemy, the full number of the animals captured shall be reported to the superior officer on the spot; if any soldier sells such horses to private individuals, receiving goods or money in return, he shall be punished with 100 blows; if any officer of government is guilty of a similar offence, he shall receive the same punishment, and moreover be deprived of his office and command.

The purchaser shall also be punished with 40 blows; the horses, and the amount of the purchase-money, shall be forfeited to government.

When the purchaser is an officer or soldier of government, he shall not himself be punishable, but the amount of the money paid by him to the seller shall be forfeited; the horses shall likewise be forfeited when the purchaser is an officer having rank over, or a soldier of the same division with, the seller, as he is in such case supposed to have had an opportunity of knowing the illegality of the transaction.

One clause.

Section CCXII. — *Clandestine Sale of Military Arms and Accoutrements.*

If any soldier sells to a private individual the clothes, armour, swords, spears, flags, standards, or any of the other necessary military accoutrements delivered to his charge on the account of government, and actually receives a valuable consideration in exchange for the same, he shall be punished with 100 blows, and sent into remote and perpetual military banishment. If any military officer of government is guilty of a similar offence, he shall suffer the same number of blows, be degraded, and sent into the less remote military banishment.

The purchaser of the military accoutrements shall in these cases be punished with 40 blows, although it should be an article, not in itself prohibited; but if prohibited, he shall, in such case, be liable to greater punishment, according to the law against private individuals retaining possession of such articles; that is to say, according to circumstances, from 80 blows as far as 100 blows, and perpetual banishment to the distance 3000 *lee*.

The military accoutrements, as well as the purchase-money, shall in general be forfeited; but when the purchaser is an officer or soldier of government, such purchaser shall be liable to no punishment, and the

the forfeiture shall then be limited to the amount of the purchase-money received by the seller.

No clause.

Section CCXIII. — *Destroying and casting away Military Arms and Accoutrements.*

If, after the accomplishment and termination of any military service or expedition, the commanding officer does not, within the period of ten days, restore to the proper officer of government all the additional arms and accoutrements that had been entrusted to his charge for the public service, such defaulter shall be punished with 60 blows; the punishment shall be encreased as far as 100 blows, at the rate of one degree for each additional period of ten days, during which he retains possession of such articles.

If, after the conclusion of any such military service or expedition, the commanding officer wilfully casts away or destroys any one article belonging and necessary to the military equipment, he shall be punished with 80 blows, and one degree more severely for every additional article cast away or destroyed, until the number exceeds 20, when he shall be liable to suffer death after the usual period of confinement.

If, any such officer shall unintentionally lose, or inadvertently destroy, one or more of the articles aforesaid, the punishment shall be proportionately less by three degrees, than that inflicted for the wilful offence; and if in any of the preceding cases the offender is a private soldier, instead of being an officer, the punishment shall be further reduced proportionably, one degree.

The amount and value of the articles lost or destroyed shall be carefully ascertained in each case, that the offender may be required to make good the loss sustained by government.

When,

When, however, any such military stores or accoutrements had been lost or destroyed in actual service or in battle, no punishment shall be inflicted, nor any compensation for the loss required.

Two clauses.

Section CCXIV. — *Possession of prohibited Arms and Accoutrements.*

If any private individual secretly retains in his possession, armour for man or horse, shields, tubes for firing large cannon, Imperial flags and standards, or any other similar articles exclusively of military use, he shall be punished with 80 blows, though he should possess only one article, and one degree more severely for every additional article of the kind, in his possession. If he is likewise the maker or manufacturer of the articles, his punishment shall be proportionately more severe in each case, by one degree, as far as 100 blows, and perpetual banishment to the distance of 3000 *lee*.

If the articles are not completed so as to be fit for immediate use, neither the possessor nor manufacturer shall be liable to punishment, but they shall deliver up all such unfinished articles to government.

This prohibition does not comprise bows and arrows, slings, spears, or knives, or any of the instruments used in fishing or agriculture.

Seven clauses.

Section CCXV. — *Relaxation of, and Absence from, Military Duties.*

If any colonel or inferior officer of a regiment, or any serjeant of a particular troop, suffers or licenses the soldiers under his command to proceed under the pretext of buying or selling, to a distance of more than 100 *lee* from their station, or clandestinely to cultivate lands ; or if any officer or serjeant as aforesaid, shall require such soldiers to perform private services, which interfere with, and occasion a neglect of, his military duties and exercises, such officer or serjeant shall be punished in proportion to the number of soldiers so misemployed; that is to say, with 80 blows, if one man; and one degree more severely for each addition of three to the number misemployed, until the punishment amounts to 100 blows; in which case the offender shall be deprived of his office and command. If a bribe is given and received, in consideration of such a breach of discipline, the punishment shall be subject to such augmentation as may be warranted by the law applicable to all cases of bribery for unlawful purposes. The soldier who avails himself of any criminal relaxation of discipline, or consents to employ himself inconsistently with his military duty, shall be punished with 80 blows.

If any officer or serjeant dispatches a soldier beyond the frontiers, and in consequence thereof such soldier loses his life, or is taken and detained by rebels or enemies, the officer or serjeant shall be punished with 100 blows, degraded, and sent into perpetual and remote military banishment.

If the number of soldiers so lost to the service amounts to three or more, the officer or serjeant shall suffer death by being strangled, after the customary confinement.

If the commanding officer of the station or encampment, or the serjeants in his attendance, knowingly suppress and assist in the concealment of such circumstances, by concurring with the officer or serjeant in fault, in a fictitious statement to government of the natural death or desertion of the individuals who had in fact been lost to the service in the manner aforesaid, they shall, except as to forfeiture of life, be equally punishable with the original offenders.

In general, when the colonel, inferior officer, or serjeant of a regiment, authorizes or occasions a dereliction and neglect of military and exercises among the troops; if the commanding officer of the station or encampment avowedly consents to, or privately connives thereat, instead of taking cognizance of every such offence against military discipline; or if, when the commanding officer is guilty of authorizing or occasioning a dereliction of duty, the colonel, inferior officer, or serjeant of the troops, being acquainted therewith, does not complain of, and inform against him, the party directing, and the party conniving, shall be equally punished, in the manner already provided.

If, from the neglect to maintain authority by proper severity and strictness of discipline, the soldiers become licentious and transgress the law, in any of the aforesaid respects, although without express instruction or permission so to do; or if any such misconduct is permitted through inattention and want of investigation, although not designedly concealed or connived at, the extent of the punishment shall be apportioned in the following manner: The serjeant shall be punishable with 40 blows, when a single individual under his command transgresses; the centurion with the same, when five transgress; the colonel or commander of 1000 men with the same, when 10 transgress; and lastly, the commanding officer of the encampment or station shall be liable to be punished as above, when 50 transgress. 50 blows shall be the punishment of the serjeant when two transgress, of the centurion when 10 transgress, of the colonel when 20 transgress, and of the commander in chief, when 100 transgress.

The officers in such cases shall not forfeit their commands, nor suffer the punishment here stated, unless the full number of the soldiers under their respective commands are proved to have been transgressors.

If any military officer should employ a soldier in private domestic service, although without exempting or removing him from the discharge of his public duty, or from the performance of his military exercises,

exercises, he shall still be punished with 40 blows, and the amount of his punishment shall be progressively encreased as far as 80 blows, at the rate of one degree for every five men so illegally employed. He shall, moreover, forfeit the amount of the wages of such men, estimated at the rate of 8 *fen* 5 *lee* 5 *hao* (about seven-pence sterling) *per* man *per* day.

Nevertheless, the officer borrowing the services of his men only upon occasional mournings and rejoicings, shall be excepted from the penalties of this law.

One clause.

SECTION CCXVI. — *Princes and hereditary Nobility employing the Troops of Government.*

The princes and hereditary nobility shall not be permitted to call for the assistance of the officers or troops of government, or to dispatch them on any particular service, unless expressly authorized so to do, by an edict issued by the Emperor.

The first and the second offence of this kind shall, however, be pardoned; but the third shall be taken into cognisance by the magistrates, and reported for the decision of His Majesty.

If any military officers of government comply with such unlawful demands, or, when unengaged in actual service, serve and do honorary duty at the gate or palace of any prince or hereditary nobleman, they shall be all equally punished with 100 blows, degraded, and sent into remote and perpetual military banishment. Private soldiers committing this offence shall be punished in the same manner.

No clause.

Section CCXVII.—*Desertion from Military Service.*

If any officer or soldier selected for, and actually employed in, any military expedition or detached public service, deserts his post and station, whether in order to return to his home or to go elsewhere, he shall for the first offence be punished with 100 blows, and compelled to proceed to his original destination; for the second offence, he shall be punished with death, by being strangled, after the usual period of confinement.

Any person who is privy to the crime of desertion, and who harbours the deserter, shall, whether it is the first or second offence, be punished with 100 blows, and subjected to military banishment.

If either the head-inhabitant of the district of which the deserter is a native, or the head-inhabitant of the district in which he has concealed himself, is acquainted with the fact, but omits to give any information thereof to government, he shall be punished with 100 blows.

If, after the conclusion of any service in which the troops were engaged, any individual amongst them presumes to quit the ranks, and to return home before the rest of the army, he shall be punished five degrees less severely than in the last instance; that is to say, with 50 blows; but if, to avoid such punishment, he at such time deserts altogether, he shall be liable to suffer the punishment of 80 blows.

If any of the troops stationed at the Imperial city of Pekin are guilty of desertion, they shall be punished with 90 blows for the first offence; the troops employed to garrison any of the other cities or fortified stations in the empire, shall be punished with 80 blows for the first offence; for the second offence the troops of any garrison, whether of the Imperial city or of any other fortification, shall be punished with 100 blows, and sent into perpetual and remote military banishment. For the third offence they shall, in each of the above cases, suffer death, by being strangled, after the usual period of confinement.

In general, all persons harbouring or concealing deserters, knowing them to be such, shall be punishable in an equal degree, as partners in their guilt, excepting only the cases of remote banishment and capital punishment, upon all of which the harbourer of the criminal shall suffer only the punishment of the less remote military banishment.

If the head-inhabitant of the district in which the deserter is harboured is privy to the fact, but does not give information of it to government, he shall suffer punishment in proportion to that to which the harbourer of the deserter is liable, but less in each case by two degrees.

If the serjeant of any troop knowingly suffers his men to desert, his punishment shall be the same as theirs, except that it shall in no case exceed 100 blows, degradation, and the less remote military banishment.

During an interval, beginning on the day upon which any individual deserts from the army, and ending when an hundred days are expired, such deserter shall be freely pardoned, if he voluntarily surrenders himself to government; but after that period a voluntary surrender will only entitle him to a reduction in his punishment of two degrees. A voluntary surrender may be made at any military station, and the officer of the station shall have full power to accept the same, as well as altogether to remit, or partially to reduce the punishment of the deserter in consideration thereof, according to the circumstances of the case. Any soldier who deserts his own troop or battalion in order to enter into another shall equally be liable, according to the nature of the case, to all the several penalties of desertion.

Six clauses.

Section CCXVIII.—*Favour to be shewn to the Relations of Officers and Soldiers deceased.*

When any officers or soldiers are killed in battle, or die of sickness, their surviving relations shall be provided by government with present subsistence, and with the means of returning to their respective homes and families.

If the officers of any district, through which they have occasion to pass, detain them unnecessarily a single day, such officers shall be punished with 20 blows; and one degree more severely, until the punishment amounts to 50 blows, for every additional three days delay.

One clause.

Section CCXIX.— *Regulations of the Nocturnal Police.*

All persons in the Imperial city of Pekin are strictly prohibited from stirring abroad during the night, and whoever transgresses this law after the third bell of the first watch has sounded, (twelve minutes past nine in the afternoon), or before the third bell of the fifth watch has been struck (twelve minutes past five in the morning), shall be punished with 30 blows; whoever transgresses this law during the second, third, and fourth watches (from ten P. M. to four A. M.), shall suffer the severer punishment of 50 blows. In all other cities and fortifications of the empire, the same prohibitions shall be enforced, but the punishment attending a transgression of this article of the laws shall be less in each case by one degree.

From these restrictions, however, exception shall be always made in favour of persons stirring abroad at night upon public business, or upon private affairs of an urgent nature, such as sudden illness, women taken in labour, deaths, burials, and other similar emergencies.

On the other hand, if the patroles maliciously arrest and detain any persons before the striking of the evening bell, or after the striking of the morning bell*, falsely charging them with having violated the rules of the watch, they shall themselves undergo the punishment of the offence imputed to the person unjustly detained.

If any person who had really violated the rules, nevertheless refuses to surrender, and succeeds in making his escape from the patrole, he shall be punished with 100 blows. If in the scuffle, he strikes the patrole, so as to wound him in any degree, he shall suffer death, by being strangled, after the customary imprisonment; if he kills the patrole, he shall suffer death by being beheaded.

If at any time a scuffle of the same kind takes place between the patrole and any person whom he had seized and attempted to detain, contrary to the laws; in such case, the person seized and attempted to be detained, shall not be liable to suffer for any of the consequences of his resistance, otherwise than he would have done in an ordinary case of a scuffle or affray between equals.

One clause.

---

* It may be proper to explain, that it is not intended to be understood that a bell, according to the strict interpretation of the term, is employed in China to announce the successive periods of time; but merely that some article is used for the purpose, which, when struck, is capable of returning a sufficiently audible sound.

END OF THE SECOND BOOK OF THE FIFTH DIVISION.

BOOK III.

PROTECTION OF THE FRONTIER.

SECTION CCXX. — *Crossing a Barrier without a License.*

WHOEVER, without being provided with a regular licenfe or paffport, proceeds either by land or water-carriage, clandeftinely through any barrier ftation, fhall be punifhed with 80 blows; whoever, in order to avoid examination at the barrier, paffes it by any other than the cuftomary road, channel, or ford, fhall be punifhed with 90 blows.

Whoever in a fimilar manner paffes, without fubmitting himfelf to examination, any of the barriers or pofts of government at the frontiers, fhall be punifhed with 100 blows, and banifhed for three years.

If fuch individual proceeds afterwards fo far as to have communication with the foreign nations beyond the boundaries, he fhall fuffer death by being ftrangled, after the cuftomary period of confinement.

The examining officer of the ftation, when aware of the intentions of fuch offender and guilty of confenting thereto, fhall be equally punifhable, except that in capital cafes the fentence of death fhall be commuted for that of banifhment.

The refponfible officers of government, to whofe want of vigilance and examination a breach of this law is at any time attributable, fhall, in each cafe, fuffer a punifhment proportionably lefs by three degrees than the original offender, and in no cafe exceeding 100 blows.

The military attendants who were on guard on the day upon which the laws were thus transgressed, shall, proportionably to the nature of the offence, be punished one degree less in each case, than their superior officers.

Whoever fraudulently obtains leave to proceed through a barrier station, by presenting a licence intended for another person, shall be punished with 80 blows.

When the servants or inmate relations of any family commit this offence, the master of such family shall be held responsible, and punished accordingly. The examining officer of the station, if privy to the fraud, shall be equally punished as an abettor of the offence, but if not privy thereto, he shall not be held in any manner responsible.

Whoever clandestinely, or under cover of a licence granted for other purposes, leads or drives his horses or asses through any barrier station, shall be punished with 60 blows. If any person leading or driving such animals, avoids the barrier altogether, by bringing them to the opposite side by an unusual route, the punishment shall be encreased to 70 blows.

Nine clauses.

SECTION CCXXI.—*Granting or obtaining Passports and Licenses, under false Pretences.*

Whoever grants a passport to those to whom it ought not to be granted, such as exiles, and residents expressly settled by the laws; whoever applies for a passport under a feigned name, or pretending to be of the military, when belonging to the civil profession and *vicè versâ*; and lastly, whoever, having legally obtained a passport, delivers it over to a person for whom it was not intended, shall in every case be punished with 80 blows. If the officers of a government station through which any person, having a passport, takes his route, presume to renew the passport after it had legally expired; or if any civil or military board or tribunal, in compliance with the desires of an officer of government or other person of authority and influence, grant general letters of protection from examination inwards or outwards in favour of the goods of any person, the individual officer or the members of the tribunal, as the case may be, shall be punished with 100 blows.

Nevertheless, this law shall not be construed as a prohibition to renew the customary annual passports of any officer, clerk, or artificer of government, if applied for in proper time, at the office where it was granted originally. Any officers of government who attend to unwarranted and illegal applications for passports, and who, knowing them to be so, yet grant the passports requested, shall be liable to punishment in an equal degree with the persons applying for the same; but if the officer is not aware of the fraud intended, or if, as soon as aware thereof, he refuses to comply with the application, he shall not be liable to punishment.

Also, if any of the inferior officers and examiners exceed the limits of their authority, by granting such passports, they shall be punished in the same manner as in the last case of granting passports, when unlawfully applied for.

If any member of a public board or tribunal, authorized to grant passports or licenses, issues the same to any person, without correctly filling up in each document, the date, description, and other necessary remarks, and also making a record thereof in his office, he shall be punished at the least with 100 blows and three years banishment; and as much more severely as the law may assign, in the event of his having been influenced by bribery or any other corrupt motive.

No clause.

Section CCXXII.—*Vexatious Treatment of Travellers at the Barriers.*

On the arrival of any vessels in the inland navigation at a barrier station, the proper officers shall immediately examine them, and prepare the passports or clearances conformably to their cargoes and other circumstances, in order that they may with the least possible delay be free to proceed on their route: if, on the contrary, the said officers unnecessarily detain the vessels and passengers one day, they shall be punished with 20 blows, and one degree more severely as far as 50 blows, for every additional day of detention. When any money is extorted, the punishment shall be increased according to the law applicable to such case.

If any officer of government or other person, confiding in the strength of his influence and authority, when passing a barrier station, refuses to submit to the customary examination and verification of his passport, he shall be punished with 100 blows.

When there is any risk from winds or waves, the boatmen belonging to passage-boats shall not attempt to cross the ferries on pain of receiving punishment to the extent of 40 blows; but if they should have attempted to cross the water in despite of winds and waves, the officers of the customs shall not stop them in the middle of the current for the purpose of urging the demand for toll-money, on pain of receiving 80 blows. If in so doing they shall occasion the death or bodily injury of any person, they shall be liable to the same punishment as in cases of killing and wounding by design. If no demand of toll-money shall have been made as aforesaid, the death or injury any person may sustain by the destruction of the boat, shall be deemed accidental.

No clause.

Section CCXXIII.—*Affisting and favouring the Escape of the Wives and Daughters of Deserters.*

If any military officer or soldier upon guard in the Imperial city of Pekin, shall in any manner assist the wives and daughters of deserters in effecting their escape beyond the walls of the said Imperial city, they shall be sentenced to suffer death by being strangled, but the punishment shall be reduced to banishment as in the case of other offences termed miscellaneous. If any private individual is guilty of such an offence, he shall be punished with 100 blows.

If the military officers or soldiers of any ordinary city, garrisoned station, or plantation *, shall assist and favour the escape of the wives and daughters of deserters from such stations, they shall be severally punished with 100 blows and three years banishment; private individuals committing the like offence, shall suffer 80 blows.

When the offending party has been convicted of receiving a bribe to transgress the law, he shall be liable to such aggravation of his punishment, as may be conformable to the law against bribery for unlawful purposes. If the deserter himself had either implored or purchased the assistance of any person to effect the release of his wives or daughters, he shall be liable to that aggravation of the punishment due to him as a deserter, which may be the consequence of his being held an equal participator in the offence punishable by the present regulation.

If the officer on guard at the gate of the city or fortification, knowing the circumstances of the case, connives at, and permits the passage of such persons, he shall suffer punishment as an equal participator in the offence of forwarding their escape. When nothing more than a neglect of due examination is imputable to such officer, the punishment shall be proportionably less by three degrees, and in no case exceed 100 blows.

* This refers to the new colonies established in different parts of Chinese Tartary.

The punishment of the private soldiers of the guard shall, in each case, be one degree less than that of their commanding officer. Whoever assists the escape beyond the city walls, of the wives and daughters of persons not coming under the description of deserters, but otherwise held to be criminals, either by their own act or by implication, shall be punished with 80 blows, or as much more severely as the corrupt and culpable motive of affording such assistance may, conformable to any other existing law or statute, be found to deserve.

No clause.

SECTION CCXXIV.—*Examination and Detection of suspected Persons.*

If, in any of the chief barrier stations along the frontiers, or in any of the passes or other places of importance in the interior, there are plotters, seeking to carry out to strangers beyond the boundaries, the internal productions and inventions; or any spies, secretly introducing themselves from without, in order to give intelligence concerning the affairs of the empire; when persons of this description are discovered and brought before the tribunals of government, they shall be strictly examined, and as soon as they shall have been convicted, either of introducing themselves or others into the empire, or of having plotted the means of removing themselves or others out of the empire, they shall all, without any distinction between principals and accessaries, be condemned to suffer death by being beheaded, after the usual period of confinement.

If any of the examining officers of government at the different barrier stations through which such criminals shall have travelled, knowing their guilt, purposely conceal their arrival, and connive at their departure, they shall be held equally guilty, and suffer in the same

same manner, except that capital punishments shall be commuted for banishment. If no greater crime than want of vigilance and due examination is imputable to such officers, their punishment shall be limited to 100 blows, and that of the soldiers who were on guard on the day on which the criminals passed, to 90 blows *.

Eleven clauses.

Section CCXXV.—*Illicit Exportation of Merchandize.*

Whoever clandestinely exports to sea, or conveys for sale beyond the boundaries of the empire on the land-side, horses, cattle, iron-work capable of being wrought into military weapons, copper coin, silks, gauzes, or sattins, shall be punished with 100 blows: whoever with such unlawful design carries for hire, or places upon any beast of burthen, or upon any vehicle, any of the aforesaid articles, shall suffer the punishment next below that inflicted by law upon the exporter.

The goods clandestinely exported shall be forfeited, together with the carriages or vessels employed for their conveyance.—Three-tenths of the amount of the goods shall be given as a reward to the person informing against the offending party. Whoever exports by sea or land any military arms or accoutrements shall suffer death by being strangled after the usual period of confinement. If such exportation leads to the disclosure of any state affairs, the offender shall be beheaded.

* By the 11th clause to this section, it is provided with the view of more effectually preventing improper communications with foreigners by sea, that none of the small islands along the coast which are at any distance from the main land, shall be built upon or in any manner inhabited.—The absolute want of a competent naval force has however disabled the Chinese government from giving any effect to such a regulation, and these islands are at present the constant or chief resort, not only of fishermen, but also of the numerous pirates, by whom the unprotected coasts of China are infested.

If the governing or examining officers at the port or station are themselves parties in the clandestine exportation of such goods, or if they knowingly and purposely suffer such illicit exportation to take place, they shall suffer the same punishment as the exporter, excepting only, that in capital cases, the punishment shall be reduced to perpetual banishment.

If only a defect of vigilance and want of due examination is imputable to the governing and examining officers, their punishment shall be proportionably less than that of the exporter by three degrees, and never exceed 100 blows. The soldiers whose turn it was to be on guard at the time the clandestine exportation of the goods took place, shall likewise suffer punishment, but proportionably less than their superiors by one degree, being at the same time, however, subject, in cases of bribery, to be punished as much more severely as the laws applicable thereto require *.

Thirty-seven clauses.

Section CCXXVI.—*Employment of Bowmen upon private Services* †.

Whoever employs upon a private service any soldier of the corps of bow-men, shall be punished with 40 blows, and one degree more severely as far as 80 blows, for every three soldiers in addition to the

---

* In the several clauses annexed to this section of the laws, (a translation of one or two of the most remarkable of which is inserted in the Appendix, No. XXI.) various prohibitory and restrictive regulations are introduced against foreign intercourse generally, but those which particularly concern Europeans, are chiefly comprized in the occasional edicts of the emperors and of the provincial magistrates, a translation of some of which will be found in the Appendix, No. XI.

† It is explained in the commentary annexed to the original Chinese, that this law particularly relates to those soldiers, who are detached from the military department, to that of the revenue or of the police.—The term bow-men certainly does not convey the precise idea, and the bow and arrow are, in fact, the military weapons most generally in use among the Chinese.

number so illegally employed. The offender against this law shall likewise forfeit to government the estimated amount of the wages of the bow-men, at the rate of 8 *fen*, 5 *lee*, 5 *hao*, (about seven pence sterling) *per* man *per* day. The officer who grants the service of such men to any person, shall be subject to the same punishment as those who employ them.

No clause.

END OF THE THIRD BOOK OF THE FIFTH DIVISION.

BOOK IV.

MILITARY HORSES AND CATTLE.

SECTION CCXXVII. — *Responsibility of the Charge of Government Cattle.*

EVERY officer in charge of the rearing and feeding of the horses, horned cattle, camels, mules, asses, and sheep belonging to government, shall be responsible for an hundred head of animals, (that is to say, the following punishments are provided on a supposition of the number in charge being precisely one hundred, and therefore the following numbers shall vary and be more or less, in proportion as the total is more or less than one hundred;) and a strict and faithful report shall be made to government of the death, loss, or partial injury which occurs to any of them, that the neglect and mismanagement which, unless the contrary is proved, is in consequence imputable to the rearers and feeders, may be punished as hereafter provided.

Moreover, under whatever circumstances the animals die, the skin, the hair of the tail, and the bullock's tendons and horns, shall be duly delivered to the charge of the proper officer of government; the rearer and feeder, and all his assistants, shall severally be punished with 30 blows, when one horse, bullock, or camel dies; and one degree more severely for every three that die in addition to the number, until the punishment amounts to 100 blows; beyond which it shall encrease at the rate of one degree for each addition of 10 to the number of deaths, until the punishment amounts to 100 blows and three years banishment. The death of sheep shall subject the rearers and feeders to punishment proportionably less severe than in the case of horses by three degrees; and the death of mules and asses to a punishment less than in the case of horses, by two degrees.

When any of the aforesaid animals are brought forth dead, or die of old age, if they are thereupon duly submitted to the official inspection of the proper officers, the rearers and feeders shall be excused from punishment.

When any of the animals are lost, the rearers and feeders shall make up the full number or value; when any are maimed or injured so as to be unfit for use, the punishment of the responsible persons shall be proportionably less than in the case of the death of the animals by one degree, but they shall continue to be responsible for the full original number; the dead or maimed cattle shall be sold towards replacing the same with living and perfect animals.

One clause.

Section CCXXVIII.—*Breeding of Horses.*

The responsibility attending the charge and superintendance of breeding mares shall be estimated according to the produce of the several droves, consisting of 100 in a drove. Every year the breeder in charge of the animals shall be answerable for the production of one hundred foals from every three droves. If three droves yield no more in the year than 84 foals, the breeder shall be punished with 50 blows; if less than 74 foals, with 60 blows.

The superintending officer, being in such case held guilty of neglecting to attend and inspect this department, shall suffer punishment proportionably less than the breeder by three degrees. The officers of the tribunal at court, superintending this department, shall be also liable to punishment in these cases further reduced proportionably two degrees.

One clause.

Section CCXXIX.—*Examination of Animals to be purchased by Contract.*

In the examination and selection of horses, cattle, camels, mules, and asses to be purchased by contract for the use of government, if the officers do not report and estimate every animal truly and justly, they shall, in the case of one animal falsely described, be punished with 40 blows, and one degree more severely as far as 100 blows, for every addition of three to the number of animals described falsely.

In the case of the examination and selection of sheep, the punishment shall be proportionably less by three degrees.

Every excessive appreciation being injurious to government, and every inadequate appreciation being equally a hardship on individuals, the offenders shall be punishable in proportion to the amount of the deviation in either way, as much more severely as the law concerning pecuniary injuries and malversation is found to authorize.

In like manner also, if the difference between the true and the fictitious value of the animal, had been appropriated to the private advantage of the offender, the punishment shall be increased as far as the law concerning the embezzlement of stores, to the same amount and value, would have warranted.

One clause.

Section CCXXX.—*Exercise of the Veterinary Art.*

If the horses, horned cattle, camels, mules, or asses belonging to government are lean or diseased, in consequence of not having been managed and treated according to the approved and established practice, the farrier or veterinary surgeon shall be punished with 30 blows; and if any one animal dies in consequence of such improper treatment, the punishment shall be increased to 40 blows, and progressively one degree more, for every three additional deaths, until the punishment reaches the limit of 100 blows. With regard to sheep, the punishment of mismanagement shall be proportionately less in each case by three degrees.

No clause.

Section CCXXXI. — *Improper Usage and Neglect of Cattle.*

When the horses, horned cattle, camels, mules, or asses belonging to government are harnessed to draw vehicles, or otherwise employed on service, if the attendant places the harness improperly, so as to injure the back and neck of any of the animals by the yoke, and to produce a wound three *Tsun** in circumference, he shall be punished with 20 blows; and if the wound is five or more *Tsun* in circumference, the punishment shall be encreased to 50 blows.

If any of the aforesaid animals become lean from being ill-fed, the feeder, the superintendant, and his deputies, shall, whenever the proportion of lean cattle under the charge of each of them respectively, amounts to ten in an hundred, be severally punishable with 20 blows.

The punishment shall be progressively encreased as far as 100 blows, in the proportion of one degree for every additional tenth of lean animals. In respect to the care of sheep, the punishment in each similar case shall be proportionately less by three degrees.

The superior officers of the department shall be liable to similar punishment, according as one or more tenths of the superintendants of cattle under their authority are convicted of the above delinquency. The members of the supreme board for this department at court, shall

---

* The *Che,* of which the *Tsun* is a tenth, is equivalent to about twelve inches and a half of British measure.

be punishable, in the proportion of three degrees less than the last mentioned superior officers.

One clause.

SECTION CCXXXII.— *Neglecting to break in, and Exercise the Horses of Government.*

If any officer who has the charge and superintendency of the horses of government, suffers them to be rode by strangers, or does not attend to their being duly broke in and exercised, he shall, when the law is infringed in respect to one horse only, be punished with 20 blows, and one degree more severely for every addition of four horses, to the number of those insufficiently attended, until the punishment attains the limit of 80 blows.

No clause.

SECTION CCXXXIII. — *Killing Horses, Horned Cattle, and other Animals.*

Whoever clandestinely, that is to say, without the permission of government, kills his own horses or horned cattle, shall be punished with 100 blows: if his camels, mules, or asses, with 50 blows; and the horns and skins of the animals killed shall in each case be forfeited to government.

If the animals are killed by inadvertence, or die of disease, the owners shall not be held responsible.

Whoever designedly kills another man's horses or cattle, shall be punished with 70 blows, and banished for one year and a half; if he kills another man's camels, mules or asses, he shall be punished with 100 blows. In either case, the punishment shall be subject to increase

increase in proportion to the value of the animals killed, according to the scale provided by the law against theft in ordinary cases.

The same punishment shall be inflicted for killing animals belonging to government, except that the contingent increase shall be rated, not according to the law concerning ordinary theft, but according to the law concerning the theft of government property.

In the one case, the value of the animal killed shall be made good to the owner, in the other case, to government: the offenders shall not in either case be branded.

Any person who wounds any of the aforesaid animals, or kills any swine or sheep, shall, without making any distinction between public and private property, be punished, in the former case in proportion to the consequent diminution of the value of the wounded animals; and in the latter, in proportion to the full value of the animals killed, according to the scale provided by law against theft in ordinary cases. — The loss in every case shall be made good to the injured party, whether a private individual or government.

If there is no assignable diminution in the value of the animals wounded, the offender shall still be punished with 30 blows. If any one should, by inadvertence, kill or wound any such animals, he shall not be liable to punishment, but shall be obliged to make good the amount of the loss sustained by the proprietor of the animals.

The punishment of the accessaries to the offence of designedly killing or wounding any of the animals belonging to private individuals, shall be one degree less than that of the principal offenders; but in the case of killing or wounding the animals of government, the punishment shall be the same.

If any person designedly kills the horses, horned cattle, camels, mules or asses belonging to any of his relations within the four degrees, he shall suffer the reduced punishment provided in the case of an individual

clan-

clandestinely killing those belonging to himself; he shall however be further required in these cases, to make good the loss to the owner.

Whoever kills the sheep or swine belonging to his relations within the aforesaid degrees, shall be punished in proportion to estimated value of the animals slaughtered, according to the scale provided by the law concerning pecuniary injuries in general, but the punishment shall in no case exceed 80 blows. Designedly wounding, or inadvertently killing, animals belonging to relations, shall not be punished, but shall be subject to the obligation of making good the loss to the proprietors.

If any animals, whether they are government or private property, are suffered to feed upon such of the stores of private individuals or of government, as are likely from their nature, to occasion death or bodily injury to such animals, those who permit or are the cause thereof, shall be punished proportionately less by three degrees than in the case of designedly killing or injuring such animals; they shall moreover make good the loss to the owners; on the other hand, the owners of the cattle shall make good to the owners of the stores, the value of the amount consumed.

If the proprietor of private cattle, or the feeder of government cattle, designedly suffers the animals to feed upon private or government stores, he shall be punished with 30 blows; and as much more severely as may be adequate to the value of the amount of the stores consumed, according to the law concerning pecuniary injuries in general.

The punishment shall be less by two degrees in each case, when the proprietor or feeder of the cattle has suffered such trespass to be committed, through inadvertence only, but he shall be equally liable to make good the loss to the injured party.

The loss shall not however in such case be made good, when the trespassing animal is public property.

In all cafes of animals or their offspring, attempting or endeavouring to ftrike with their horns, or to kick or bite, the perfon who, being fo attacked, immediately kills or wounds the attacking animal, fhall, whether it be public or private property, neither be liable to corporal punifhment, nor even to any pecuniary refponfibility.

Four claufes.

Section CCXXXIV. — *Vicious and dangerous Animals.*

When horfes, horned cattle, or dogs are vicioufly inclined, either to kick or bite, or horned cattle to ftrike with their horns; if the owner does not fet a mark on them, and tie them up in the cuftomary manner, or if he does not kill his dogs when they become mad, he fhall be punifhed with 40 blows. If, in confequence of fuch negleft, any perfon is killed or wounded, the owner of the animal fhall be obliged to redeem himfelf from the punifhment of man-flaughter, or man-wounding, by the payment of the legal fine.

If any owner of fuch animals defignedly loofens them, or encourages them to attack, fo as to kill or wound any perfon, he fhall be punifhable proportionately lefs feverely by one degree than in the cafe of killing or wounding fuch perfon in an affray.

Neverthelefs, if a farrier or veterinary furgeon, hired to cure the difeafe of any animal, approaches without properly fecuring it, or if an indifferent perfon carelefsly ftrikes any animal, and is killed or wounded by it in return, the owner fhall not be refponfible.

Whoever, laftly, defignedly fuffers his dogs to kill or wound the animals of other perfons, fhall be punifhed with 40 blows, and compelled to make good the amount of the lofs, to the injured party.

No claufe.

Section CCXXXV. — *Concealment of the Increase of Animals belonging to Government.*

The rearers and feeders of the horses, mules, and asses of government shall report to the proper officer, every time that each animal produces a foal, within ten days after the birth. If, on the contrary, they suffer the period to elapse, and afterwards endeavour to conceal the produce, they shall be punished in proportion to the value of it, according to the scale provided by law in cases of theft, but the punishment shall in no instance exceed 100 blows, and perpetual banishment to the distance of 3000 *lee*; if they are further guilty of fraudulently selling or exchanging such produce, they shall be punished in proportion to the amount of the loss sustained by government, according to the scale established in the different cases of embezzlement, and which, when the goods embezzled equal or exceed 40 *leang* or ounces of silver in value, subjects the offender, nominally to the punishment of death by being beheaded, though in effect only to five years banishment, in consideration of the offence coming within the class of those termed miscellaneous.

If the superior officers, and the members of the chief board for this department at court, are privy to such fraudulent proceedings, and take no cognizance of them, they shall participate equally in the punishment; but otherwise, they shall not be held responsible. The purchasers or receivers in exchange of the produce, if privy to the fraud, shall be punished in the same manner as purchasers of stolen goods in ordinary cases, and forfeit their purchases to government.

Two clauses.

Section CCXXXVI. — *Privately lending the Animals belonging to Government.*

If any governor, superintending officer, or clerk in any department, privately takes to his own use, or lends out to others, the horses, horned cattle, camels, mules, or asses belonging to government, whether many or few, for a shorter or longer period; the lender and the person to whom the animals are lent, shall, at the least, be severally punishable with 50 blows. The period during which such animals are thus fraudulently employed shall at the same time be ascertained, that the amount of hire due to government may be calculated, and required from the offenders. Moreover, if the punishment proportionate thereto, according to a scale, raised one degree above that prescribed in ordinary cases of pecuniary injuries, exceeds 50 blows, the punishment shall be encreased accordingly.

The hire, however, of any animal, shall never be calculated so as to exceed its full value. If the animals die while thus employed contrary to law, the offenders shall be punished as in the case of a theft of goods of the same intrinsic value.

No clause.

Section CCXXXVII. — *Public Messengers using the Horses of Government without Authority.*

If any public messenger or other person so employed, makes a demand for the use of the horses of government at the different stations through which he passes, without being warranted to do so, or when he ought to have employed the ordinary post-horses, he shall be punished

punished with 60 blows; if demanding the use of the asses or mules of government, with 50 blows.

The officers or clerks of government who delivered the horses, asses, or mules, thus unwarrantably demanded, shall, in general, be liable to punishment less than as aforesaid by one degree; but the punishment in these cases shall never extend beyond those who were immediately parties to the illegal transaction.

No clause.

END OF THE FOURTH BOOK OF THE FIFTH DIVISION.

BOOK V.

EXPRESSES AND PUBLIC POSTS.[*]

Section CCXXXVIII. — *Conveyance of Government Orders and Dispatches.*

THE military post-soldiers charged with the transmission of government orders and dispatches, must proceed on their route at the rate of 300 *lee* in a day and a night: If through dilatoriness they exceed the time to the extent of three quarters of an hour, (an hour and a half European computation) they shall be punished with 20 blows; and the punishment shall increase by a progressive ratio of one degree for each additional delay of three-quarters of an hour, until it amounts to 50 blows.

Immediately that the dispatches of government arrive at any military post or station, the post-master shall not fail to forward them, whether many or few, under the charge of the soldiers who are placed under his jurisdiction for that purpose.

---

[*] The government-post in China, which is the subject of the several sections of this book of the Penal Code, though not professedly open to the people in general, is an establishment of considerable utility and importance, and carried to a degree of perfection, which in an empire so extensive, as well as so ill adapted, from the inequalities and intersections of the surface of the country, to an expeditious mode of internal communication, could scarcely have been expected.

Although the distance from Pekin to Canton by land exceeds 1200 English miles, government dispatches have been known to arrive in twelve days, and within a period of thirty days, answers and instructions have frequently been received by the magistrates from the court, even upon affairs of no extraordinary importance.

If, instead thereof, the post-master waits for subsequent dispatches, in order to forward them all at one time, he shall be punished with 20 blows.

If the military post-soldiers rub or tear the cover of a government dispatch entrusted to them, but not so as to break the seal thereof, they shall be punished with 20 blows, and the punishment shall increase progressively, in the ratio of one degree for every three additional covers so injured, until it amounts to 60 blows.

If the wrapper or cover is entirely destroyed, but the inner seal of the dispatch not broken, the punishment shall be fixed at 40 blows at the least, and encreased progressively as far as 80 blows, at the rate of two degrees for every additional wrapper or cover so destroyed.

If any one dispatch is suppressed or destroyed altogether, or the inner seal of it removed or broken, the punishment shall amount to 60 blows, and be encreased progressively as far as 100 blows for every additional dispatch so suppressed, destroyed, or broken open.

In the latter case, if the dispatches were secret, or concerned military operations, the punishment shall not be less than 100 blows, however small may have been the number of the dispatches destroyed or broken open; and the punishment shall be as much more severe than 100 blows, as may be warranted by any other article of the laws, which the offender had transgressed in the course of the same transaction.

If the post-masters do not report the misconduct of the military post-soldiers, they shall be liable to equal punishment; and if, having duly reported the same to the superior officers of government, those officers decline to take cognizance thereof, their punishment shall be proportionably less than the aforesaid, only by two degrees.

The post-master-general of each district shall diligently inspect and superintend the proceedings of all the post-masters and post-soldiers in his department; and the visiting officer and clerks shall personally visit and inspect all the stations once a month.

If the number of lesser offences, such as rubbing and tearing the wrappers of dispatches, or dilatoriness in forwarding them, which are overlooked or connived at by these officers, exceeds ten, the post-master-general of the district shall be punished with 40 blows, the clerks of the tribunal of the visiting officer with 30 blows, and the visiting officer himself with 20 blows.

When any greater offence, such as the suppressing, destroying, or breaking open of a dispatch, is overlooked and connived at, the post-master-general of the district shall be equally punishable with the post-soldier; the visiting officer's clerks one degree less; the visiting officer two degrees less; and the governors of cities of the first and second orders, when officiating as superior visiting officers, three degrees less.

Six clauses.

SECTION CCXXXIX. — *Intercepting Addresses to Government.*

When an officer of any greater or lesser provincial board or tribunal has dispatched, in the lawful manner, an address of information or complaint to His Imperial Majesty, if his superior officer intercepts the progress of such dispatch, by sending a messenger to any of the military stations through which it was to have been forwarded to court, with orders to detain and suppress it, the post-master and post-soldiers at the stations to which such orders were addressed, shall immediately wait on the governor of the district to report the circumstance, by whom information thereof shall be transmitted to the superior officer of the province, and by him again, to the supreme board at Pekin, the officers whereof shall, lastly, enter into a strict investigation of the circumstances of the transaction, and lay before the Emperor the final result;

result; if the charge is substantiated, the offender shall receive sentence of death, to be inflicted by beheading, after the usual period of confinement.

If the post-master and post-soldiers comply with such unlawful requisition, and conceal the fact when aware of its unlawfulness, they shall each of them be punished with 100 blows; the governor of the district shall be liable to similar punishment, if, after the post master or post-soldiers duly report the circumstance, he declines to take cognizance of it.

In like manner, if any superior officer intercepts the progress of any true and lawful dispatch addressed by his inferior to any of the supreme departments of state at Pekin, punishment shall be inflicted on the several parties proportionably less by two degrees.

Although this law is expresly designed to prevent superior officers from intercepting the complaints which may be brought forward against them by their inferiors, it shall equally apply to the case of inferiors attempting to intercept the transmission of the charges exhibited against them by their superiors.

No clause.

SECTION CCXL. — *Post-Houses to be kept in Repair.*

When any military station through which express posts are forwarded, falls into a decayed and ruinous state, if it is not put into good repair, and all the requisite appurtenances provided and completed; or when the establishment of post soldiers falls short of the full complement, if the vacancies are not filled up; or if weak and aged persons are employed on such a service, the post-master-general of the district shall be punished in each of the several cases with 50 blows, and the president and other members of the visiting and inspecting board or tribunal, shall each be punished with 40 blows.

One clause.

Section CCXLI. — *Post-Soldiers to be employed on no other Service.*

The officers and attendants of the several boards or tribunals of government, when travelling upon the public service, are not permitted, even on such occasions, to employ the post-soldiers of the stations through which they pass, either in transporting from place to place the property of government, or their own private baggage and travelling furniture.

For every offence against this law, they shall be liable to a punishment of 40 blows, and forfeit to government the amount of the wages of such soldiers at the rate of 8 *fen*, 5 *lee*, 5 *hao*, (about seven-pence sterling) *per* man *per* day.

No clause.

Section CCXLII. — *Express-Messengers delaying upon the Road.*

Any light-horseman dispatched upon ordinary business shall perform his duty within the time appointed by law conformably to the distance and other circumstances; if he exceeds the same by one day, he shall be punished with 20 blows, and his punishment shall be increased one degree, as far as 60 blows, for every addition of three days dilatoriness. If the dispatch concerns military affairs of importance, the punishment shall be proportionably greater in such case by three degrees.

If such delay occasions the failure and miscarriage of the military operations then in progress, the messengers shall suffer death, by being beheaded after due imprisonment. If the several post-horse-officers upon the road, or any of them, reserve the best horses, or upon any pretence refuse to grant them to the use of the express-messenger, and thereby occasion the delay which has been stated to be punishable by this law; the circumstances of the case shall be accurately investigated,

and

and if their guilt is substantiated, the messenger shall be released from his responsibility, and the punishment to which he would have been liable, shall be inflicted upon them only.

When an inundation or other unavoidable obstruction upon the road, shall have impeded the progress of the express-messenger, and occasion the legal period to be exceeded, all the responsible parties shall be excused.

If a light-horse express-messenger, charged with a government dispatch, mistakes the direction of it, and, having in consequen e conveyed it differently from its destination, does not afterwards rectify his error within the legal period of the proper delivery of the dispatch, the punishment, in ordinary cases, shall be proportionably less by two degrees than that in the case of an intentional delay; but in extraordinary cases affecting military operations of importance, the punishment of delay shall be the same, whether imputable to error or to design, but be inflicted solely on the party that occasioned it, whether the messenger himself or the post-horse officer on the road. On the other hand, if the delay arises from the express-messenger having been misguided by an improper and erroneous direction upon the cover of the dispatch, the punishment shall fall upon the person who wrote the direction instead of either of the former.

Three clauses.

SECTION CCXLIII.—*Express-Messengers exceeding the Allowance of Horses and Equipage fixed by Government.*

If any messenger or officer of government, dispatched upon express service with authority to make use of the post-horses and express-boats of government, employs one horse or one boat more than the proper number, he shall be punished with 80 blows; and for every additional horse or boat so employed, there shall be a proportionate incr ase of one degree in the punishment. If such officer or messenger employs horses, when it was lawful only to employ asses; or if he insists upon having the use of the best horses, when it was only lawful for him to have employed the middling or inferior sort, he shall be punished with 70 blows.

If, in disputing the matter with the post-horse officer upon the station, the messenger strikes or wounds him, the punishment shall be encreased proportionately in such case one degree; but if the blow or wound is attended with serious bodily injury, the punishment shall be rated according to the rule applicable to affrays in ordinary cases.

If the post-horse officer submits to, and complies with, the unlawful demand, he shall participate in the punishment attending the transgression of this law at the rate of one degree less in each case, than that on the express-messenger.

The above punishment shall be inflicted on, and confined to, the post-horse officer, when such officer gives middling or inferior horses to those messengers who are warranted in claiming the best; except he should happen not to have any of the best horses at his command, which circumstance shall excuse him, as well also as the other party, from punishment.

If the express-messengers quit the direct road, and thereby avoid the post-houses, or when passing the post-houses, if they do not exchange their horses for fresh ones, or their boats for a new set of boats, they shall be punished with 60 blows; and if by such deviation or omission they ride any of the government post-horses so as to occasion their death by over-fatigue, the punishment shall be more severe by one degree, and they shall forfeit to government a sum equal to the value of the horses.

If the messengers of government dispatched upon business of no extraordinary urgency, though without having been guilty of the deviation or omission here described, ride their horses to death, they shall forfeit to government a sum equal to the value of the horses, but not be liable in consequence to further punishment.

When

When, however, the messengers are dispatched upon urgent military affairs, or the next stations happen to be unprovided with the boats or horses required for their accommodation, neither the deviation, omission, or excessive riding, shall expose them to any pecuniary forfeiture, or corporal punishment, provided the justifying circumstances are properly substantiated.

Four clauses.

SECTION CCXLIV. — *Express-Messengers exceeding the fixed Allowance of Money and Provisions.*

If any officers or messengers travelling express upon public service, demand a larger supply of money or provisions on the road, than the laws authorize, they shall be punished in proportion to the amount or value of the excess, according to the scale provided by the law against receiving bribes for purposes not in themselves unlawful.

The officer of government who grants such excessive supplies, shall participate in the punishment due to this offence, at the rate of one degree less in each case, than the receiver.

If the officer or messenger travelling express, extorts by violence such excessive supplies, he shall be punished in proportion to the amount of the excess, according the severer scale provided by the law against bribery for unlawful purposes: but the officer from whom they are obtained, shall, in such cases, be excused.

One clause *.

* In this clause it is declared, that whereas all foreign embassies travelling through the empire, are duly supplied by government with every thing they require upon the road, the shop-keepers who clandestinely sell to, or buy from, such foreigners any article whatever, shall forfeit to government whatever they may have received for the same in exchange, and shall moreover be condemned to wear for the space of one month the *Cangue* or moveable pillory.

SECTION CCXLV. — *Express-Post to be reserved for important Dispatches.*

All the Emperor's orders relative to the disposition and employment of the military forces; all urgent communications of important military intelligence from the court to the frontier stations; and all addresses upon urgent military affairs from the several public boards and tribunals in the empire, to the Emperor, shall be forwarded by messengers riding express; whoever designedly omits to send dispatches of this nature to the post-houses, with instructions that they may be forwarded express, shall be punished with 100 blows; but if the omission occasions the failure and miscarriage of the military operations to which those dispatches relate, the individual so offending shall suffer death, by being beheaded, after undergoing the customary confinement.

All addresses announcing to the Emperor desirable public events, soliciting aid to provinces suffering from dearth or scarcity, or reporting extraordinary occurrences and calamities, shall likewise be forwarded express, as well as in general, all communications respecting the supplies required by the army, and other affairs of similar importance. — Whoever designedly omits to forward such dispatches in that manner, shall be punished with 80 blows, and be further responsible, as in the preceding case, for the contingent consequences of such omission.

On the other hand, those who designedly transmit to the express-post-houses, those government dispatches which, having relation to ordinary affairs only, were not intended to be forwarded by that mode, shall be punished with 40 blows.

No clause.

SECTION CCXLVI. — *Dilatoriness in Transmissions and Removals connected with the Public Service.*

In all cases of the public service requiring that the property of government in goods or cattle, or that prisoners or exiles, should be removed from one station to another, they are to be committed to the care of a particular person in the employ of government, who shall be responsible for the performance of this service within the period appointed by law; if through any dilatoriness he exceeds such period by a single day, he shall be punished with 20 blows, and be liable to a punishment progressively increased as far as 50 blows, at the rate of one degree for every three days further delay: any similar delay in forwarding the provisions and supplies of the army, when in the field, shall be punished two degrees more severely in each case, and the scale of punishment shall be carried on as far as 100 blows.

If, in consequence of such delay, the deficiency of the requisite supplies at the moment of engaging the enemy is so great, as to frustrate, and occasion the miscarriage, of the military operations depending thereon, the offender shall suffer death by being beheaded, after the usual confinement.

If the individual entrusted in ordinary cases with such charge, exceeds the period allowed for performing the service allotted to him, not intentionally, but from having misunderstood the written orders on the subject, and in consequence loses time by proceeding in a direction contrary to his real destination, his punishment shall be proportionally less, in each case, by two degrees; but if the charge concerns any military operations, the delay shall be attended with the same punishment, whether it be the result of inadvertence or of design.

If the mistake arose from the orders on the subject having been erroneously written, the punishment shall fall upon the writer thereof,

thereof, inftead of being inflicted upon the perfon fuperintending the removal of perfons or goods, on account of government.

Two claufes.

Section CCXLVII. — *Occupation of the principal Apartments in Poft-Houfes.*

If any meffengers or ordinary officers difpatched upon public fervice, prefume to occupy, or in any refpect to avail themfelves of the accommodation of the principal and moft honourable apartments in the poft-houfes, they fhall be punifhed with 50 blows; fuch principal apartments, including the chief hall of reception, being referved for the particular ufe and benefit of regular officers of government and other fuperior guefts.

No claufe.

Section CCXLVIII. — *Tranfmiffion of private Property by Government Poft-Horfes.*

If any of the officers or meffengers, difpatched upon the public fervice, and therefore entitled to employ on the occafion the poft-horfes of government, carry with them, befides clothes and neceffary accoutrements, any other articles of baggage weighing ten *kin* * or more, they fhall be punifhed with 60 blows; the punifhment fhall alfo be progreffively encreafed as far as 100 blows, for every additional 10 *kin* of weight.

When the mules or affes, inftead of the horfes of government are thus over-loaded, the punifhment fhall, in each cafe, be proportionably lefs by one degree.

* The *kin* is generally eftimated at one-third more than the Britifh pound.

The amount or value of the excess in weight of the property conveyed, shall be forfeited to government: If the animals thus overloaded are killed, the punishment of the offender shall be encreased as far as the law provided against such contingency authorizes.

One clause.

SECTION CCXLIX. — *Officers and others compelling the Inhabitants of their district to carry their Palanquins* *.

If any officers or clerks of a tribunal or other department of government, or any other officers or messengers, employ the inhabitants of the district to carry their palanquins, except as hereafter provided, they shall be punished with 60 blows, and the superintending officer of the district who connives at, or authorizes the same, shall suffer punishment less by one degree, as a participator in the offence.

If any private individuals, relying on their influence and riches, employ the labourers or cultivators of the soil to carry their palanquins, without paying the wages due for the labour, they shall be punished in the same manner. In every case they shall be obliged to make good the amount of the wages, at the rate of 8 *fen*, 5 *lee*, 3 *hao*, (about seven-pence sterling) *per* man *per* day.

---

* The Chinese sedan or palanquin is figured and described in the authentic account of the British Embassy. The sedan with two bearers, is the ordinary mode of conveyance by land, for almost every description of unprivileged persons. The sedan with four bearers is exclusively employed by officers of the government, and not allowed even to certain classes of persons who enjoy all the other honorary marks of distinction belonging to that rank. — Some of the great officers of state have the further privilege of being carried, upon particular occasions of ceremony, by eight bearers; but to His Imperial Majesty alone, is reserved the honour of being carried by sixteen.

Whenever the inhabitants have been regularly hired, and the wages of their labour duly paid, this law shall not take effect.

Two clauses.

SECTION CCL.— *Families of deceased Officers to be removed at the Public Expence.*

When any of the civil or military officers of the empire fall sick and die while in employ at their respective stations, their families, if not in possession of the means of returning to their native homes, shall be removed thither at the public expence; the officers of the several districts through which they have occasion to pass, shall appoint the escorting officers, provide a sufficient number of carriages, boats, porters, and horses for their conveyance, and issue rations of provisions from the public stores, in proportion to the number of individuals in each family; the quantities required being previously ascertained by personal investigation.

Any officer of a district, who neglects to provide for such families, and to superintend their progress homeward in the manner here directed, shall be punished with 60 blows.

One clause.

SECTION CCLI.— *Hiring Substitutes, and entrusting to them an allotted personal Service.*

If any person, being charged with the conveyance of government property, whether goods or cattle, or with the removal of prisoners and exiles, instead of personally performing such service, hires a substitute to perform his duty in his stead, he shall be punished with 60 blows; and if, in consequence of such substitution, any of the property

perty of government is injured or loft, or any of the prifoners efcape, he fhall fuffer punifhment as much more fevere as the law, particularly provided for punifhing the neglect of perfons in charge under fuch circumftances, may be found to prefcribe.

Whoever undertakes for hire or otherwife, to officiate as the fubftitute of another in any of thefe refpects, fhall participate in the punifhment of the offence, at the rate of one degree lefs in each cafe, than the perfon whofe office he undertakes to perform.

Whenever two or more perfons are jointly entrufted with the performance of any fuch fervice as above defcribed, if they mutually replace, and agree alternately to connive at the abfence of each other, they fhall be punifhed with 40 blows; and in cafe any bribes fhould have been given and received, as much more feverely as the law provided againft bribery for purpofes not in themfelves unlawful, may be found to prefcribe.

When any ill confequences enfue, fuch as the injury or lofs of the property, or the efcape of the prifoners entrufted to their charge, they fhall be condemned to fuffer a punifhment as much more fevere as may be conformable to the law particularly applicable under fuch circumftances; and in general, in all cafes of perfons jointly entrufted with any affair or duty, the party abfenting himfelf, and the party undertaking the vacant charge, fhall be equally punifhable, inftead of the punifhment of the acceffary being mitigated, as ufual in other inftances. The parties however fhall not be liable to the aggravation of punifhment, arifing from fraud or connivance, except as far as they are individually and perfonally privy to, or concerned therein.

One claufe.

Section CCLII. — *Conveyance of private Property at the Charge of Government.*

All thofe who, being engaged in the public fervice, have authority to employ, when travelling, the horfes, cattle, camels, mules, or affes belonging to government, but who do not come under the defcription of travellers licenfed to proceed by the exprefs poft, fhall, in fuch cafes, be reftricted from loading the animals with more than 10 *kin* weight of baggage, befide the clothes and cuftomary accoutrements about their perfons; if they exceed this allowance by five *kin* weight, they fhall be punifhed with 10 blows, and the punifhment fhall be progreffively encreafed one degree for every addition of ten *kin* weight, until it amounts to 60 blows.

All perfons authorized in the fame manner to employ in travelling, the carriages or boats which belong to government, fhall, in fuch cafes, confine themfelves to thirty *kin* weight of baggage; and if they exceed that limit by ten *kin* weight, they fhall be punifhed with 10 blows, and the punifhment fhall be progreffively increafed one degree for every addition of 20 *kin* weight, until it amounts to 70 blows.— For this offence, the mafters, and not the fervants, fhall be refponfible.

When the excefs of weight arifes from the amount of goods undertaken to be conveyed for another perfon, the proprietor configning his property to be fo conveyed, fhall participate equally in the punifhment denounced againft this offence; and in every cafe the goods thus illicitly conveyed fhall be forfeited to government.

The fuperintending officer of the diftrict fhall alfo participate in the fame degree in the punifhment, when he is privy to the commiffion of the offence, but not otherwife.

When, however, whole families are to be conveyed from place to place at the expence of government, as in the cafe of the return of

the

the relations of deceased soldiers, and of civil and military officers, the amount and weight of their baggage shall not be subject to any of the ordinary limitations hereby imposed.

Three clauses.

Section CCLIII.— *Privately lending the Post-Horses of Government.*

Any post-horse officer who employs for his private use, or lends out to others, the post-horses of government, and also, whoever borrows the same, shall, for each offence, be punished with 80 blows, and one degree less in the case of asses so employed.

The estimated sum due for the daily hire of such animals shall likewise become a forfeiture to government, and the punishment shall be subject to any contingent increase, which the scale provided by the law against pecuniary injuries, proportionably aggravated two degrees, may be found to prescribe.

No clause.

END OF THE FIFTH DIVISION.

SIXTH DIVISION,

Criminal Laws.

BOOK I.

ROBBERY AND THEFT.

SECTION CCLIV. — *High Treason.*

HIGH treason, is either treason against the state, by an attempt to subvert the established government; or treason against the Sovereign, by an attempt to destroy the palace in which he resides, the temple in which his family is worshipped*, or the tombs in which the remains of his ancestors are deposited.

All persons convicted of having been principals or accessaries to the actual or designed commission of this heinous crime, shall suffer death by a slow and painful execution †.

All

---

* That is to say, the temple in which certain ceremonies and oblations are performed periodically in honour of the Imperial family.

† This mode of execution is not noticed among the ordinary punishments, but is particularly described in one of the notes subjoined to the original text. It has been termed in the works of the missionaries, " cutting into ten thousand pieces," and appears to amount, at the least, to a licence to the executioner to aggravate and prolong the sufferings of the criminal undergoing the sentence of the law, by any species of cruelty he may think proper to inflict. It is however understood to be the ordinary exertion of the Emperor's pre-

rogative

All the male relations in the firſt degree, at or above the age of ſixteen, of perſons convicted as aforeſaid; namely, the father, grandfather, ſons, grandſons, paternal uncles, and their ſons reſpectively, ſhall, without any regard to the place of reſidence, or to the natural or acquired infirmities of particular individuals, be indiſcriminately beheaded.

All the other male relations at or above the age of ſixteen, however diſtant their relationſhip, and whether by blood or by marriage, ſhall likewiſe ſuffer death, by being beheaded, if they were living under the ſame roof with the treaſonable offender, at the time the offence was committed.

The male relations in the firſt degree, under the age of ſixteen, and the female relations in the firſt degree, of all ages, ſhall be diſtributed as ſlaves to the great officers of ſtate.

The property of every deſcription belonging to treaſonable offenders, ſhall be confiſcated for the uſe and ſervice of government.

The female relations of ſuch criminals, who ſhall have been previouſly married into other families, and alſo thoſe females who, although affianced to ſuch criminals, or to the ſons or grandſons of ſuch criminals, ſhall not have been taken home and married, ſhall always be excepted from the penalties of this law.

All perſons who, when privy to the commiſſion of, or to the intent to commit the crime of high treaſon, wilfully conceal and connive at the ſame, ſhall be beheaded.

Any perſon who ſhall apprehend, and deliver into the cuſtody of a magiſtrate, an offender againſt this law, ſhall be employed forthwith

---

rogative of mercy, to commute this terrible ſentence for the milder one of death, by ſimply ſevering the head from the body; but there are certainly ſome inſtances in which, with a view to public example, or from other cauſes, this law has been rigorouſly executed.

under

under government, according to his qualifications; or if already an officer in the employ of government, he shall be suitably promoted; and in every case he shall be rewarded with the possession of the whole of the confiscated property of the offender*.

Any person who shall give the information which may be requisite towards enabling the magistrates to bring such offenders to justice, shall be rewarded with the whole of the property, which may consequently be confiscated; but not entitled as in the preceding instance, either to employment or promotion in the service of government.

If any person who is privy to the intention to commit, or to the actual commission of the aforesaid crime of high treason, is guilty of neglecting to communicate to the magistrate of the district the information he possesses, he shall, although not expressly chargeable with any acts of connivance and concealment, be punished with 100 blows, and banished perpetually to the distance of 3000 *lee*.

If the relations of persons intending to commit the aforesaid crime shall, previous to the commission of any overt act, deliver them up to the officers of justice, those who are so delivered up, and their several relations, shall all of them, be entirely pardoned.

If the relations of persons actually guilty of any acts of high treason, voluntarily surrender them into the custody of the magistrates, such relations, and all other persons guilty by implication only, shall

---

* As this appropriation of the confiscated property of the offender, is an exception to the general rule noticed in a preceding paragraph, it is probably by no means the ordinary reward of the police officer on such occasions, but only of the person who volunteers his services, and who being the prosecutor and public accuser, thereby exposes himself to all the penalties of a false accusation, whenever the charges are not substantiated. — When the crime is public and notorious, or committed by persons high in rank or office, of whom the sovereign himself is generally the only avowed accuser, those who are instrumental in bringing the criminal to justice, merely in the course of their official duty, are not, it is conceived, intended to be benefited in the event of his conviction, any more than they would be liable to suffer, on the event of his acquittal. — For the punishment to which in different cases false accusers are liable, see Section CCCXXXVI.

be pardoned; but with regard to the principal offenders, the laws must be strictly executed.

Four clauses*.

SECTION CCLV. — *Rebellion and Renunciation of Allegiance.*

All persons renouncing their country and allegiance, or devising the means thereof, shall be beheaded; and in the punishment of this offence, no distinction shall be made between principals and accessaries.

The property of all such criminals shall be confiscated, and their wives and children distributed as slaves to the great officers of state. — Those females however, with whom a marriage had not been completed, though adjusted by contract, shall not suffer under this law; from the penalties of this law, exception shall also be made in favour of all such of the daughters of criminals as shall have been married into other families. — The parents, grand-parents, brothers, and grand-children of such criminals, whether habitually living with them under the same roof or not, shall be perpetually banished to the distance of 2000 *lee*.

All those who purposely conceal and connive at the perpetration of this crime, shall be strangled.

Those who inform against, and bring to justice, criminals of this description, shall be rewarded with the whole of their property.

Those who are privy to the perpetration of this crime, and yet omit to give any notice or information thereof to the magistrates, shall be punished with 100 blows, and banished perpetually to the distance of 3000 *lee*.

If the crime is contrived, but not executed, the principal shall be strangled, and all the accessaries shall, each of them, be punished

---

* A translation of the supplemental clauses annexed to this law, is inserted in the Appendix, No. XXII.

with 100 blows, and perpetual banishment to the distance of 3000 *lee*.

If those who are privy to such ineffective contrivance, do not give due information and notice thereof to the magistrates, they shall be punished with 100 blows, and banished for three years.

All persons who refuse to surrender themselves to the magistrates when required, and seek concealment in mountains and desert places in order to evade, either the performance of their duty, or the punishment due to their crimes, shall be held guilty of an intent to rebel, and shall therefore suffer punishment in the manner by this law provided. If such persons have recourse to violence, and defend themselves when pursued, by force of arms, they shall be held guilty of an overt act of rebellion, and punished accordingly.

Eight clauses*.

Section CCLVI.— *Sorcery and Magic.*

All persons convicted of writing and editing books of sorcery and magic, or of employing spells and incantations, in order to agitate and influence the minds of the people, shall be beheaded, after remaining in prison the usual period. If the influence of such acts shall not have extended beyond a few persons, the criminal shall be banished perpetually to the distance of 3000 *lee*; and generally, the punishment shall be proportionate to the nature of the case, and therefore more or less severe according to circumstances.

All persons who are guilty of retaining in their possession, and concealing from the magistrates, any books of the above description, shall be punished with 100 blows, and banished for three years.

Four clauses †.

---

* A translation of the clauses annexed to this law is inserted in the Appendix, No. XXIII.
† A translation of these clauses is inserted in the Appendix, No. XXIV.

Section CCLVII. — *Sacrilege.*

All perfons guilty of ftealing the confecrated oblations offered up by the Emperor to the fpirits of Heaven and Earth, or any of the facred utenfils, cloths, meat-offerings, and precious ftones ufed on fuch occafions, fhall, whether principals or acceffaries to the offence, whether previoufly entrufted or not with the charge of the faid articles, in all cafes, be beheaded.

The offence of ftealing articles prepared and defigned for confecration, but not actually confecrated or offered up as aforefaid, and alfo that of ftealing fuch confecrated articles and oblations, after they had ceafed to be applied to facred ufes, fhall be punifhed with 100 blows and banifhment for three years.

When the amount of the articles facrilegioufly ftolen is confiderable, they fhall be valued, and the punifhment inflicted on the offender fhall, at the leaft, exceed that awarded in ordinary cafes of theft by one degree.

The offenders in thefe cafes fhall be likewifed branded in the arm, in the manner defcribed in Section CCLXIV.

No claufe.

Section CCLVIII. — *Stealing Edicts and Ordinances of Government.*

All perfons guilty of having been principals or acceffaries to the crime of ftealing an Imperial edict, after it has received the impreffion of the great Imperial feal, fhall be beheaded.

The crime of ftealing the authenticated edict of any governing magiftrate or tribunal, or an edict of the Emperor, not yet authenticated by the impreffion of the Imperial feal, fhall be punifhed with 100 blows; the criminal fhall be moreover branded in the arm.—

When any corrupt motive is assignable, the theft shall be punished according to the most severe among the different laws applicable to the case. If the edicts stolen, concerned the collection of supplies for the army, or were connected with any military operations, the principals and accessaries shall be strangled.

No clause.

Section CCLIX. — *Stealing Seals and Stamps of Office.*

All persons guilty of having been principals or accessaries to the crime of stealing the official seal of any magistrate or tribunal, or any seal or stamp whatever issued by the Emperor, shall be beheaded.

The crime of stealing the official seals or stamps, of persons employed by the magistrates, or employed in public offices by the authority of the magistrates, shall be punished with 100 blows; the criminal shall be moreover branded in the arm.

No clause.

Section CCLX. — *Stealing from an Imperial Palace.*

All persons found guilty of having been principals or accessaries to the crime of stealing any articles from the Imperial palace, or from the private Imperial treasury, shall receive sentence of death by decollation, but this is one of the offences in which capital punishment is commutable for five years banishment.

One clause.

Section CCLXI. — *Stealing the Keys of the Gate of a Fort or City.*

All persons found guilty of having been principals or accessaries to the crime of stealing the key of the gate of the Imperial city, shall be sentenced to suffer 100 blows, and perpetual banishment to the distance of 3000 *lee*, but this offence shall be ranked among those in which the punishment of perpetual, is commutable for that of temporary, banishment.

The crime of stealing the key of the gate of any other city, or of any town, fortress or barrier station, shall be punished with 100 blows, and banishment for three years; that of stealing the key of a granary, treasury, or other government building or public office, shall be punished with 100 blows, and the thief shall be branded in the arm.

All persons who, having the charge of the key of a gate of a city or fortress, are convicted of having lost such key, or of having, on any pretext, suffered the same to be out of their possession, shall be punished with 90 blows, and banished for two years and a half.

One clause.

Section CCLXII. — *Stealing military Weapons and Accoutrements.*

All persons found guilty of stealing any of the ordinary military weapons and accoutrements, such as the common military dress, swords, and bows and arrows, shall be punished in proportion to the amount and value of the articles stolen, according to the law applicable to theft in ordinary cases; but those who steal any of the weapons and accoutrements which are exclusively military, and which it is therefore unlawful for the people in general to possess, such as coats of mail, breast-plates, and fire-arms, shall, at the least, be punished as severely as is provided by the law prohibiting the possession of such articles.

When soldiers in actual service are guilty of stealing arms and accoutrements of any kind from each other, they shall be punished according to the law against theft in ordinary cases, except that when the articles stolen are voluntarily surrendered to government, the punishment shall be less in each case, than it would have been otherwise, by two degrees.

One clause.

Section CCLXIII. — *Stealing Timber from a Burying-Ground.*

All the principals and accessaries to the offence of stealing, (that is to say, privately cutting down and removing,) any of the trees growing within the boundaries of the Imperial cemetery or burying-ground, shall be punished, at the least, with 100 blows and three years banishment.

The principal in the offence of stealing any of the trees growing in a private burying-ground, shall be punished, at the least, with 80 blows, and each of the accessaries thereto, with 70 blows.

If the value of the timber cut down and carried away is considerable, it shall be estimated, and the punishment increased in proportion to the result, to such an extent, as in every case to exceed by one degree that which would have been legally inflicted for an ordinary theft to the same amount and value.

Five clauses*.

Section CCLXIV. — *Embezzlement of Public Property.*

When any of the persons who are lawfully entrusted with the public property deposited in the treasuries and store-houses of government, are found guilty of having been concerned as principals or accessaries in the offence of embezzling any part thereof, they shall be punished according to the following scale, in proportion to the total amount embezzled at one time, without paying any regard to the number and ex-

* A translation of these clauses is inserted in the Appendix, No. XXV.

tent of the shares, into which the embezzled property may have been divided.

The offenders shall moreover be branded or marked in the arm between the wrist and the elbow, with the three following, words *tao quan* $\begin{Bmatrix} leang, \\ vo, \\ yn, \end{Bmatrix}$ stealer of government $\begin{Bmatrix} Grain, \\ Stores, \\ Silver, \end{Bmatrix}$ according as the case may be, each character being distinctly marked, and of the dimension of one *Tsun* and a half in the square.

Value less than	1	*leang* (ounce) of silver	80			
	1	- -	90	blows with the bamboo.		
	5	- -	100			
	7½	- -	60		1 year.	
	10	- -	70	blows and banish-	1½ years.	
Value ex-	12½	- -	80	ment for	2 years.	
ceeding	15	- -	90		2½ years.	
	17½	- -	100		3 years.	
	20	- -	100	blows and perpetual	2000 *lee*.	
	25	- -	100	banishment, dif-	2500 *lee*.	
	30	- -	100	tance	3000 *lee*.	
	40	- -	Death, by being beheaded *.			

Ten clauses†.

---

* In a note in the original Chinese it is stated, that in cases nominally punishable with perpetual banishment by this law, the offenders shall be banished for four years only; and that, in those nominally punishable capitally, the offenders shall, instead thereof, be banished for five years, unless the value of the property embezzled exceeds 100 ounces, and falls short of 1000 ounces, when the banishment of the offender shall be perpetual.— If the value exceeds the latter sum, it is again declared, that the offender shall be beheaded.

† For a translation of the clauses to this law, see the Appendix, No. XXVI.

SECTION CCLXV.—*Theft of Public Property.*

All persons found guilty of stealing, or attempting to steal, the property of government, deposited in the public treasuries and storehouses, shall be punished for their offences in the following manner:—

The principals in an attempt to steal, shall be punished with 60 blows, and each of the accessaries to such an attempt, with 50 blows.

If the theft is accomplished, the offenders, as in the preceding article, relative to the embezzlement of the same species of property, shall be punished in proportion to the total amount stolen at one time, and likewise branded in the arm, in the manner there described, but the scale of punishment shall be less severe, and as follows:—

Value less than	1 *leang* (ounce) of silver	70	} blows with the bamboo.			
Value exceeding	1	80				
	10	90				
	15	100				
	20	60	} blows and banishment for	1 year.		
	25	70		1½ years.		
	30	80		2 years.		
	35	90		2½ years.		
	40	100		3 years.		
	45	100	} blows and perpetual banishment to distance of	2000 *lee.*		
	50	100		2500 *lee.*		
	55	100		3000 *lee.*		
	80	Death, by being strangled*.				

Two clauses†.

---

* When the amount stolen does not exceed 100 ounces, it is provided, as in the preceding section, that the punishments of death and perpetual banishment shall be commuted for banishment, in the former case for five years, and in the latter for four years.

† For a translation of the clauses annexed to this law, see the Appendix, No. XXVII.

SECTION CCLXVI. — *Robbery — Highway Robbery* *.

All perfons found guilty of having been jointly concerned as principals or as acceffaries, in an attempt to feize the property of another by force, that is to fay, to commit a robbery, fhall be punifhed with 100 blows and perpetual banifhment to the diftance of 3000 *lee*; when a robbery is actually effected, all the individuals concerned in the commiffion thereof, fhall be beheaded, whether participators or not in the booty, and however fmall may be the total amount of the plunder.

If the contriver of the robbery does not actually contribute to the perpetration thereof, nor afterwards participate in the booty obtained, he fhall not fuffer death, but receive 100 blows, and be fent into perpetual banifhment at the diftance of 3000 *lee*. All other perfons who, although belonging to the gang or affociation, neither actively contribute to the perpetration of the robbery, nor afterwards partake of the booty, fhall be feverally difmiffed, after undergoing the punifhment of 100 blows.

Whenever ftupifying drugs, or other means, are previoufly employed in order to deprive the perfon intended to be plundered, of the ufe of his fenfes, and fuch perfon is thereby incapacitated from making any refiftance, this proceeding fhall be confidered as equivalent to an act of open violence, and although, in other refpects, merely a theft, fhall always be punifhed as a robbery.

If thieves, when caught in the act of ftealing, refufe to furrender, and continue their refiftance fo long as to kill or wound any perfon, they fhall be beheaded.

If, upon the occafion of a theft being committed, females are alfo violated, the theft fhall be punifhed as a robbery, but thofe of the

* See Section CCLXVIII.

party, who were guilty as acceffaries to the theft only, fhall not participate in the confequent aggravation of the punifhment of their companions.

A thief who, when purfued, cafts away the ftolen goods, but afterwards defends himfelf by force, and refufes to furrender, fhall be punifhed, according to the law in ordinary cafes of criminals not furrendering, with 70 blows at the leaft; but a thief who upon fuch an occafion wounds any perfon, fhall be ftrangled; and a thief who upon fuch an occafion, kills any perfon, fhall be beheaded.

Thirty-four claufes *.

SECTION CCLXVII.—*Refcue from Prifon.*

All perfons concerned as principals or acceffaries in the offence of forcibly refcuing, or attempting to refcue any lawful prifoner, fhall fuffer death by being beheaded, after confinement during the ufual period.

All perfons, relations as well as others, who are guilty of clandeftinely releafing any prifoner, fhall be punifhed with the fame degree of feverity as that to which the prifoner himfelf is liable, excepting the cuftomary reduction of one degree in capital cafes.

All thofe who are guilty of having made the attempt, though unfuccefsfully, privately to releafe a prifoner, fhall fuffer punifhment proportionately lefs than that to which the prifoner is liable, by two degrees. If thofe who make the attempt, are guilty of wounding any perfon, the principal offender amongft them fhall fuffer death by being ftrangled, after confinement during the ufual period; when guilty of killing any perfon, the principal among them fhall fuffer death by

* For a tranflation of fome of the moft material claufes annexed to this law, fee the Appendix, No. XXVIII.

being beheaded. In general, in all the cases of attempting to release a prisoner clandestinely, the punishment of the accessary shall be less than that of the principal by one degree.

In all cases of persons assembling in the public highways*, to oppose by force a servant of government, appointed by the magistrates to perform any official duty, such as the collection of the revenue, or the pursuit and seizure of offenders, the principal shall suffer the punishment of 100 blows and perpetual banishment to the distance of 3000 *lee*. If upon such an occasion the individual thus employed in the service of government is wounded, the principal offender shall suffer death by being strangled, after being confined during the usual period.

If, in this latter case, the number of persons riotously assembled amounts to ten or more, or if, whatever the number of persons assembled, the individual employed in the service of government is killed in the course of the affray, the principal among the offenders shall be beheaded, and as many of the others as are found guilty of having struck a mortal blow, shall be strangled. All the other accessaries, in this and in the preceding cases, shall suffer a punishment one degree less severe than that inflicted upon their respective principals.

When the master of a family assembles his household, in order to oppose the officers of government, he alone shall be punishable and responsible, unless his followers are guilty of striking so as more or less to wound, in which case they shall be punished as independent persons in ordinary cases.

Three clauses.

* It is stated in a note in the original, that the act of assembling in the public highways, is the particular circumstance of aggravation which distinguishes this offence from that of resisting, and refusing to admit the visits of the officers of justice and the revenue, in ordinary cases, which, under the head of Fiscal Laws, has been already noticed.

SECTION CCLXVIII. — *Robbing in open Day**.

All perfons found guilty of taking unlawful poffeffion of the property of others, in open day and by forcible means, fhall, however fmall the amount of the property fo taken, be punifhed with 100 blows and banifhment for three years.

If the value of the property in queftion is confiderable, it fhall be eftimated, and the punifhment of the offending parties fo far increafed, as to render it two degrees more fevere than it would have legally been, in a cafe of privately ftealing to a fimilar amount; but it fhall not in any cafe become capital, unlefs there are other aggravating circumftances.

When the individual plundered is likewife wounded, the principal offender fhall fuffer death, by being beheaded, after remaining during the ufual period in confinement.

The acceffaries to that fpecies of robbery which is in the contemplation of the law in this fection, fhall in all cafes be punifhed one degree lefs feverely than the principal offenders; and all the individuals concerned therein, principals as well as acceffaries, fhall be

---

* There is a perceptible difference in the meaning of the Chinefe expreffion at the head of this fection, and that at the head of fection CCLXVI., and which requires perhaps fome further explanation. It is ftated in a note in the original Chinefe, that although open violence is implied in the one inftance, as well as in the other, yet the former fection of the law is to be underftood to apply more particularly to thofe cafes, in which a number of perfons had, for the exprefs purpofe of committing a robbery, affembled together, and provided themfelves with offenfive weapons, all which circumftances of aggravation are in this latter fection fuppofed to be wanting; it is however added, that the magiftrates are not intended to be bound by this precife interpretation, but allowed to exercife a difcretionary power, in adopting the more or lefs fevere law, according as the circumftances of each particular cafe are, upon a general view, more or lefs atrocious.

The expreffion *open day* is alfo explained to imply nothing more than that the offence in queftion, is perpetrated openly, and without fear of obfervation.

branded in the lower part of the left arm, with the words *Tſiang to* ſignifying robber.

All perſons who take an opportunity to plunder in a caſe of fire or ſhipwreck; or who, in the latter caſe, contribute in any manner to the deſtruction of the veſſel, ſhall be puniſhed according to this law.

Thoſe who, in the caſe of an affray, or upon the occaſion of their being authorized and employed by government in the purſuit and apprehenſion of offenders, take an opportunity of ſtealing, ſhall be puniſhed as in ordinary caſes of theft, unleſs they are guilty of uſing force, in which caſe the puniſhment ſhall be proportionately increaſed two degrees, but the parties ſhall not be branded for the offence, nor liable, under any circumſtances, except thoſe of killing or wounding the individual plundered, to ſuffer capital puniſhment.

Twenty-four clauſes.

Section CCLXIX.—*Stealing in general.*

All perſons found guilty of an attempt to ſteal, ſhall be puniſhed with 50 blows.

When a theft is actually committed, that is to ſay, poſſeſſion obtained of the property intended to be ſtolen, all the parties concerned, whether ſharers or not in the plunder, ſhall be puniſhed in proportion to the amount of the largeſt ſum ſtolen from any one individual, according to the ſubjoined ſcale: The principal offender in each caſe ſhall ſuffer the full puniſhment therein ſtated, and the reſt ſhall be puniſhed one degree leſs ſeverely as acceſſaries. It is likewiſe always to be underſtood, that the puniſhment ſhall be eſtimated, not according to the ſhare of the plunder which any one of the offenders may receive or obtain individually, but, as above ſtated, according to the total amount of the ſum which they had been jointly concerned in ſtealing from any one individual: for example, if ten perſons jointly ſtole to the amount of of 40 ounces of silver in value, they would, although their respective shares would not exceed four ounces in value, be liable to suffer the full punishment of stealing forty ounces of silver, such being the value of the total amount stolen.

For the first offence, the individuals convicted of being concerned in a theft, shall be branded in the lower part of the left arm with the words *Tsie tao*, signifying thief; for the second offence they shall be branded again with the same words, in the lower part of the right arm; for the third offence, or for having defaced the said marks, they shall suffer death by being strangled, after remaining the usual period in confinement.

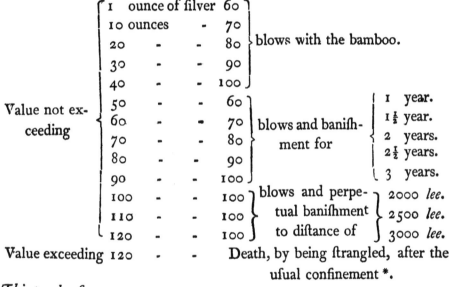

Thirty clauses.

SECTION CCLXX.—*Stealing Horses and other domesticated Animals.*

All persons found guilty of stealing the horses, horned cattle, asses, mules, sheep, fowls, dogs, geese, and ducks of private individuals,

* Although that part of the law in this place which states, that a theft shall in certain cases be punished with death, does not appear to have been expressly repealed, there is every reason to believe that it is never enforced.

shall

shall suffer, conformably to a valuation of the animals stolen, the ordinary punishment of theft.

When the animals stolen are the property of government, the punishment of the offending party shall be the same as in other cases of a theft of government-property to the same extent in value.

If any person steals a horse or a cow, and afterwards kills the animal, he shall be punished, at the least, with 100 blows and three years banishment; if the animal stolen and killed is an ass or a mule, the punishment shall not be less than 70 blows and banishment for a year and a half. In both cases, when the value of the animals stolen and killed is considerable, they shall be estimated, and the punishment of the thief so far increased beyond that already provided, as to render it one degree more severe than that of an ordinary theft to the same extent in value.

Fourteen clauses.

Section CCLXXI.—*Stealing Corn and other Produce in the open Field.*

All persons found guilty of stealing any kind of grain, fruit, or vegetables growing in the open fields, and not customarily guarded by any person, or by any contrivance, shall be punished according to the amount in value of the produce stolen, as in ordinary cases of theft, except that the offenders shall not be branded *.

All persons unauthorizedly taking away stones, timber, or brushwood, which although found in uncultivated places, had been cut or otherwise prepared for use, shall be punished in the same manner as is above provided.

Twenty clauses.

* When the fields in which a theft is committed are known to be usually watched and guarded by the proprietor, the offence is more severely punishable, according to a law in a preceding section, against " robbing in open day."

Section CCLXXII.— *Stealing from Relations and Connections.*

All persons found guilty of stealing from a relation by blood, or by marriage, in the first degree, shall suffer a punishment five degrees less severe than that which is legally inflicted in ordinary cases of theft to the same extent *.

In like manner, all persons guilty of stealing from relations, in the second degree, shall suffer a punishment four degrees less severe than that legally inflicted in ordinary cases: — In the case of stealing from relations in the third degree, the punishment of the offenders shall be three degrees less than in ordinary cases: — In the case of stealing from relations in the fourth degree, the punishment shall be two degrees less than in ordinary cases: — and, lastly, the punishment of stealing from any relation, in a more remote degree than the aforesaid, shall be but one degree less than in ordinary cases.

In general the punishment of the accessaries shall be one degree less severe than that of the principals in each case; but regard is always to be had, at the same time, to the relationship which such accessary bears, and not merely to that which the principal offender bears, to the person upon whom the theft is committed.

Persons stealing from their relations shall not, as other thieves, be subject to be branded for their offences.

In cases also of robbery among relations, that is to say, a violent as well as unlawful seizure of the property of a relation; when an elder relation is the offending party, a reduction in the punishment shall be allowed, similar to that already provided in cases of theft; but if the

---

* The mitigation of punishment provided by this law, in consideration of circumstances, which at first view appear to aggravate the guilt of the offender, is in fact easily reconciled with the general spirit of the code; as according to the Chinese patriarchal system, a theft is not in this case a violation of an exclusive right, but only of the *qualified* interest, which each individual has in his share of the family property.

offending

offending party is a junior relation, the punishment shall be the same as is inflicted in the ordinary cases of the commission of the same offence.

If the robbery is accompanied by the additional crime of killing or wounding the relation who is plundered, the offender shall suffer for the assault, or for the robbery, according as the one or other offence proves, under all the circumstances of the case, the most severely punishable.

If the junior of two relations residing together under the same roof, introduces a stranger to steal the property of his elder relation, he shall suffer a punishment two degrees more severe than that provided by law, for using and consuming, without permission, an equal amount of the joint family property, in ordinary cases*; but the punishment of a relation in this case, shall never be so far increased, as to exceed 100 blows. — The stranger thus introduced to steal, shall be punished one degree less severely than in ordinary cases of stealing, and not be branded.

If hired servants or slaves steal from their masters, or from each other, the punishment shall be one degree less severe than in ordinary cases of theft, and the thief shall not be branded †.

Five clauses.

Section CCLXXIII. — *Extorting Property by Threats.*

All persons who are guilty of extorting from any individual his property, by the use of threatening language, shall be punished one

---

* See Section LXXXVIII., under the head of Fiscal Laws.

† Notwithstanding the tenor of the last paragraph of this article, it is provided in one of the supplementary clauses, that the punishment of slaves guilty of theft, shall be, at the least, equal to that of thieves in general, and one degree more severe, when the offence is committed by them, in combination with strangers.

degree more severely than in ordinary cases of theft to the same amount, but shall not be branded.

A junior relation extorting the property of his senior by threats, shall be punished in the same degree, as if there had been no relationship whatever between the parties; but a senior relation guilty of extorting by threats, the property of his junior, shall have the full advantage of the mitigation of punishment which the law allows in ordinary cases of pecuniary differences between relations.

Eight clauses.

SECTION CCLXXIV.— *Obtaining Property under false Pretences.*

All persons obtaining public or private property, by any fraudulent means, or upon false pretences, shall be punished with the same degree of severity, as if guilty of stealing, to an equal amount, and under similar circumstances in other respects, but shall not be branded.

In all cases of a senior relation defrauding his junior, or a junior his senior, the punishment shall be as much less than in ordinary cases of fraud, as under circumstances of relationship, in instances of theft and other offences of a similar nature, has been already stated and provided.

When two or more persons are jointly intrusted with the custody of government or public property; if one of them fraudulently and upon false pretences, obtains from the rest, any part thereof for his own use, he shall be punished in the same manner as if he had been an embezzler to a similar amount of the public property under his own individual custody.

When the offence amounts to an attempt only, the punishment shall in each of the several cases, be less than is above provided, by two degrees.

In general, whenever any species of property is fraudulently obtained, whether by asserting falsely a claim to it, by deceiving the owner by a fabricated story, or by prevailing on the owner to trust the property on any pretence out of his possession, it shall be deemed an offence against this law, and punished accordingly.

Six clauses.

Section CCLXXV. — *Kidnapping, or the unlawful Seizure and Sale of free Persons.*

All persons who are guilty of entrapping by means of stratagems, or of enticing away under false pretences, a free person, and of afterwards offering for sale as a slave such free person, shall, whether considered as principals or as accessaries, and whether successful or not, in effecting such intended sale, be severally punished with 100 blows, and banished perpetually to the distance of 3000 *lee*.

All those who are guilty of entrapping, or enticing away any persons in the manner aforesaid, in order to sell them as principal or inferior wives, or for adoption, as children or grand-children, shall, if considered as principals, be punished with 100 blows, and three years banishment.

When the person who is attempted to be entrapped or enticed away, resists, and is wounded, the offender against this law shall suffer death, by being strangled, after the usual period of confinement.

When such person, in consequence of having resisted, is killed, the offender shall suffer death, by being beheaded, after the usual confinement.

In all of the preceding cases, except the first, the punishment of the accessaries shall be less severe than that of their respective principals, by one degree.

The persons kidnapped, or attempted to be kidnapped, shall not in any of the aforesaid cases be liable to any punishment, but shall be restored without delay to their respective families.

All such persons also, as receive the children of free parents, upon the faith of a promise to educate and adopt them as their own, and nevertheless sell them afterwards to others, shall be punishable according to this law, except in those cases in which it can be proved that a pecuniary consideration was given and received in the first instance.

When the persons enticed away, had not been deceived by any false pretences, but had yielded themselves up voluntarily, those who, under such circumstances, sell them as slaves, shall be punished with 100 blows, and three years banishment. Those who, under the same circumstances, sell such persons, as principal or inferior wives, or for adoption, as children or grand-children, shall be punished with 90 blows, and banished for two years and a half.

The persons who thus voluntarily submit themselves to be sold, shall be punished likewise; and their punishment shall be but one degree less severe than that of those who sell them.

When the sale of a person willing to be sold, is proposed, but not completed, the punishment of the several parties to the offence, shall be respectively less severe than in the case of an actual sale, by one degree.

When the persons kidnapped or enticed away are under ten years of age, they shall not be deemed capable of consenting thereto, and therefore held innocent of any participation in the offence of the kidnappers, who, under such circumstances, shall always suffer punishment according to the severer law.

The offence of entrapping and carrying off for sale, or persuading to come away voluntarily for the same purpose, the lawful slave of any person, shall be punished one degree less severely than that of kidnapping a free person under similar circumstances.

Any perſon who ſells his children or grand-children againſt their conſent, ſhall be puniſhed with 80 blows *.

Any perſon who in like manner ſells his younger brother or ſiſter, his nephew or niece, his own inferior wife, or the principal wife of his ſon, or his grandſon, ſhall be puniſhed with 80 blows, and two years baniſhment:—the puniſhment inflicted for the ſale of the inferior wife of a ſon or grandſon, ſhall be leſs ſevere than that laſt mentioned by two degrees. Whoever, laſtly, ſells his junior firſt couſin, junior ſecond couſin, or his grand-nephew, in the manner aforeſaid, ſhall be puniſhed with 90 blows, and baniſhed for two years and a half.

When, in any of the preceding caſes, the ſale had been effected with the free conſent of the party ſold, the puniſhment of the ſeller ſhall be leſs ſevere by one degree. In general alſo, when an unlawful ſale is only proved to have been propoſed, the puniſhment ſhall always be one degree leſs ſevere, than it would have been in the caſe of ſuch ſale having actually taken place.

The children, or junior relations, although conſenting to be thus unlawfully ſold, ſhall not in any caſe be liable to puniſhment for ſuch conſent, in conſideration of the obedience which is always due from them to their ſenior relations, and they ſhall therefore ſimply be reſtored, upon conviction, to their families.

Any perſon who is guilty of ſelling his firſt wife, or any relation of his in a more remote degree than thoſe already ſpecified, ſhall ſuffer

---

* Although it would appear from this reſtriction, that the power of a parent over his child, according to this code, is much leſs extenſive than that allowed by the laws of the ancient Romans, yet as the adoption of children, and the purchaſe of inferior wives or concubines, is a tranſaction of conſtant occurrence, and one in which the real parents lawfully may, and uſually do, receive a pecuniary conſideration, it can ſcarcely be denied that the ſale of children in China, is practically allowed.—The crime of infanticide, the exiſtence of which has been ſo often alleged as a ſtain upon the national character of the Chineſe, as well as upon their laws and government, will be noticed in another place. See Section CCCXIX.

the unabated punishment of seizing and selling free persons in ordinary cases.

If the harbourers, and purchasers of the persons kidnapped, are aware of the unlawfulness of the transaction, they shall suffer equal punishment with the kidnappers, excepting only the usual reduction of one degree in the punishment of participators in offences, in capital cases.

The person who becomes a party to the transaction, by making himself answerable that the sale shall be completed, shall, (if aware of its unlawfulness, and not otherwise) be punished one degree less severely than the principal offender. — When the purchaser is thus a participator in the offence committed, the pecuniary consideration given to the seller shall be forfeited to government, but otherwise shall be restored to the purchaser, in consequence of the sale being null and void *.

Fourteen clauses.

Section CCLXXVI. — *Disturbing Graves.*

All persons guilty of digging in, and breaking up another man's burying-ground, until at length one of the coffins which had been deposited therein, is laid bare and becomes visible, shall be punished with 100 blows, and perpetual banishment to the distance of 3000 *lee.*

Any person who, after having been guilty as aforesaid, proceeds to open the coffin, and uncover the corpse laid therein, shall be pu-

---

* From the length of this section, and also from some of the observations contained in the official report of the charges against the governor of Canton (see Appendix, No. X.) it is certainly to be inferred, that the abuses here adverted to, are not unfrequent. It is to be observed, indeed, that the slavery which is recognized and tolerated by the laws of China, is a mild species of servitude, and perhaps not very degrading in a country, in which no condition of life appears to admit of any considerable degree of personal liberty and independence.

nifhed with death, by being ftrangled, after undergoing the ufual confinement *.

Thofe who are guilty of digging in, and breaking up a burying-ground, but do not proceed fo far as to expofe any of the coffins, fhall be punifhed with 100 blows, and three years banifhment.

Thofe who on fuch occafions practice incantations, in order to call up the fpirit from the grave, fhall be confidered as acceffaries, and accordingly punifhed one degree lefs feverely than the principals.

The offence of ftealing a coffin from an old grave or burying-place, which had fallen in, or was broken down, as well as that of ftealing a coffin from above ground, fhall be punifhed only with 90 blows, and banifhment for two years and a half.

Breaking open an unburied coffin, and expofing the body to fight, is nominally a capital offence, but the punifhment fhall be limited to five years banifhment.

The offence of ftealing bricks, ftones, or other articles, from a burying-ground, fhall be punifhed according to the value of the articles ftolen, as in ordinary cafes of theft, but the offenders fhall not be branded.

A junior relation within the degrees of mourning, breaking up the grave of his elder relation, fhall be punifhed as in the ordinary cafes of the offence above ftated: but if he opens the coffin to fee the body, he fhall be beheaded, after remaining in prifon the ufual period. If he cafts away the corpfe, and fells the ground, he fhall be punifhed in the fame manner.— The purchafer of the ground and the negociator of the fale, if privy to the breach of the laws, fhall be punifhed each with 80 blows. The land fhall be reftored to the family, and the pur-

* This very long article, in fome of the provifions of which there is an apparent inconfiftency, is evidently connected with certain fuperftitious notions and practices of the Chinefe, and probably may alfo have been requifite to protect even the dead, from the vengeance and from the rapacity of the living.

chafe-money shall be forfeited, but all such of the relations as were not privy to the transaction shall be held to be exempt from responsibility.

An elder relation in the fourth degree, breaking up the grave and opening the coffin of his junior, shall be punished with 100 blows, and three years banishment. In the case of any nearer elder relation, the punishment shall be less severe by one degree. — A father breaking up the grave, and opening the coffin, of his son, or a grand-father that of his grand-son, shall be punished with 80 blows. — Nevertheless, if, in any of the preceding cases, the grave be broken open upon a sufficient cause, and the coffin removed with all due rites and ceremonies, the parties shall not be punishable. — Destroying, mutilating, or throwing into the water the unenclosed and unburied corpse of a stranger, is an offence punishable with 100 blows, and perpetual banishment to the distance of 3000 *lee*.

The offence of destroying, mutilating, or casting away, the unburied corpse of an elder relation, shall be punished with death, by being beheaded, after the usual period of confinement.

The punishment in the two last mentioned cases shall be reduced one degree, if the injury done to the corpse amounts only to the loss of the hair, or if the corpse, after being cast away, is found again.

If the offence is committed by an elder, instead of a junior relation, the punishment shall be one degree less severe, than in ordinary cases.

If a father destroys or casts away the corpse of his son, or a grand-father that of his grandson, he shall be punished with 80 blows.

But if a son destroys or casts away the corpse of his father or mother, a grandson that of his grandfather or grandmother; a slave or hired servant that of his master, they shall in each case, whether the corpse so cast away is afterwards recovered or not, be beheaded after the usual period of confinement.

If any person in digging the earth should discover an unclaimed body, and not immediately bury it, he shall be punished with 80 blows.

If any person having lighted a fire on the grave of a stranger to drive away foxes by the smoke, suffers the fire to communicate, so as in any manner to burn the coffin deposited underneath, he shall be punished with 80 blows, and two years banishment; but if the body is likewise consumed, the punishment shall be increased to 100 blows, and three years banishment;—if the party offending is a junior relation, the punishment shall be increased one degree; if a senior, abated one degree.

If a son, lighting a fire on the grave of his father or of his mother, for the aforesaid purpose; a grandson, on the grave of his grandfather or grandmother, a slave or hired servant, on that of his master, thereby burns the coffin, they shall, in each case, be punished with 100 blows, and three years banishment. If the body is burned likewise, they shall be strangled, after remaining in confinement during the usual period.

Any person who levels the burying-place of a stranger, in order to convert the ground to the purposes of agriculture, shall, although none of the coffins shall have been disturbed, be punished with 100 blows, and obliged to replace every thing in its former condition.

Any person who privately buries a corpse in another man's ground, shall be punished with 80 blows, and also be obliged to remove such corpse within a limited period.

Whenever an unclaimed corpse is found in any district or village, if the head or presiding inhabitant thereof, instead of reporting the same, in order that the corpse may be examined by the proper magistrate, of his own accord removes or buries it, he shall be punished with 80 blows; if the body is in consequence lost, he shall be punished with 100 blows.

If the body is destroyed or cast into the water, the principal in the commission of such an offence shall be punished with 60 blows, and one year's banishment. If the person who contrives, likewise carries the design into effect, he shall be banished perpetually. If the body is cast away, but not lost; or is injured, but entire, the punishment shall be reduced one degree.

Stealing the clothes belonging to a dead body, shall be punished according to their value, as an ordinary case of theft, but the offender shall not be branded.

Thirteen clauses.

SECTION CCLXXVII.—*Unauthorizedly entering a Dwelling-house by Night.*

All persons who unauthorizedly, and without lawful cause, enter the dwelling-house of a stranger by night, shall be punishable, at the least, with 80 blows. — If the master of the house at the moment of any such person entering, kills him, he shall not be punished for doing so; but if after having seized such person, he then kills or wounds him without necessity, he shall be punished but two degrees less severely than is provided by law in cases of killing or wounding in an affray; the punishment shall not however in any case exceed 100 blows, and three years banishment.

One clause.

SECTION CCLXXVIII.—*Harbouring Thieves and Robbers.*

Whenever any persons who are harbourers of robbers; that is to say, masters and proprietors of the customary habitations and retreating places of robbers, are discovered and found guilty of having likewise in any inftance contrived a robbery, and of having afterwards participated in the booty thereof, they fhall, although they had not perfonally affifted in the perpetration of the crime, be beheaded as principals.

It has already been provided by a preceding article of the laws, that all thofe who perfonally affift in the perpetration of a robbery, fhall, without making any diftinction between principals and acceffaries, be indifcriminately beheaded. When, however, the contriver of a robbery, and harbourer of robbers, neither gives any affiftance in effecting the robbery nor participates in the plunder after it is obtained, he fhall be punifhed only with 100 blows, and perpetual banifhment to the diftance of 3000 *lee*.

If the harbourer of the robbers, though not a contriver of the robbery, is privy to the defign, and either accompanies the robbers without participating in the booty, or participates in the booty without accompanying the robbers, he fhall be beheaded, without any diftinction being made between the cafes of principals and thofe of acceffaries.

If, in the laft cafe, the harbourer of robbers neither accompanies them, nor participates in their plunder, he fhall be punifhed with 100 blows only.

All harbourers of thieves, who contrive a theft, and afterwards receive a fhare of the booty, fhall be punifhed as principals in fuch theft, although they had not been perfonally engaged therein. If the plan is contrived at the moment previous to execution, the leader only fhall be efteemed a principal, and the harbourer of the thief an acceffary; he fhall likewife be deemed no more than an acceffary, if he affifts in obtaining without partaking of, or partakes of without affifting in obtaining, the plunder. If the harbourer of the thief neither affifts in obtaining, nor partakes of the plunder when obtained, his punifhment fhall be limited 40 blows.

If a number of individuals, meeting without any previous deliberation or contrivance, commit a theft or a robbery, the propofer and

leader

leader shall, in the case of a theft be esteemed the principal, and the rest only accessaries; but in the case of a robbery, no distinction shall be made, and accordingly, all the offenders punished alike.

All persons participating in property known to have been obtained by robbery or theft, or in any sum received as the purchase-money of a free person unlawfully sold, shall, at the least, be punished as accessaries to a theft to the same amount, but shall not be branded.

The offence of purchasing goods knowing them to have been stolen, shall be punished as an ordinary case of pecuniary malversation or unlawful acquisition of property.

Any person who, knowing any article of property to have been stolen, nevertheless consents to take charge of it, shall be punished one degree less severely than an unlawful purchaser. When, however, such purchaser and such consignee of stolen property, in any case are ignorant of its having been unlawfully acquired, they shall not be esteemed guilty, or anywise punishable, merely in consequence of their being implicated in a charge against others.

Seventeen clauses.

SECTION CCLXXIX. — *Rules by which the Accessaries to a Theft, and the Accessaries to a Robbery are distinguished.*

In all cases of persons concurring in a design to commit a robbery, if any of them do not afterwards actively engage therein, or only so far, as to commit a theft; and if the original contriver of the plan, although a partaker of the booty, is one of these, he shall be punished only as a principal in a theft. Those who, though they assisted therein, neither contrived the criminal enterprise, nor participated in the plunder, shall (except the leader, who shall still be deemed a principal) be esteemed accessaries; as also those who merely contrived the criminal enterprise, without either partaking of, or assisting in obtaining, the plunder.

All the others, who merely concurred in the first design, without having been the contrivers of it, assisting to carry it into execution, or profiting by it afterwards upon a division of the plunder, shall be punished with 50 blows each.

In cases of persons concurring in a design to commit a theft, if any of them in pursuance thereof, commit a robbery instead of a theft, the contriver of the original plan, although a partaker of the plunder, shall, if not an agent in obtaining it, be punished only as a principal in a theft, similar in amount to the robbery; and the other partakers, not being agents or contrivers, shall be punished as accessaries thereto. But all those who were actively engaged in the robbery, shall be punished as principals in such robbery, whether or not contrivers thereof, and whether participators or not in the booty.

No clause.

SECTION CCLXXX. — *What constitutes a Theft or Robbery, and what an Attempt only.*

In general an open and violent taking, constitutes a robbery, and a private and concealed taking, a theft; but the attempt is to be distinguished from the accomplishment of the criminal purpose, differently in different cases, in the following manner: — In cases of strings of copper-money, utensils, and other easily moveable articles of that description, possession must not only be obtained, but they must have been removed out of the place or apartment in which they were found, otherwise a theft or robbery of such articles is only to be considered as having been attempted. In the case of pearls or precious stones, and other small and valuable articles,

articles, it is sufficient that they are found on the person of the offender. On the contrary, in the case of large heavy articles of wood or stone, which the unassisted strength of man is not adequate to remove to any distance, they must not only have been displaced, but actually lifted upon the cart, or on the animal, provided for their removal.

In respect to horses, asses, mules, and cows, they must have been taken out of the stable; and also in respect to dogs, hawks, and animals of the like kind, there must have been some evidence of exertion on the part of the offender to make himself master of them, and of their having been, in consequence of such exertion, actually in his possession; thus, if one horse is stolen, and the rest follow, the thief is not responsible for more than the theft of one horse; but if he steals a mare, and the foal follows, his offence is to be deemed a theft of both the mare and the foal.

These observations are applicable to all the preceding cases in this book. In general, when there are circumstances to trace, and witnesses to give evidence of the overt act, but not of any actual possession of the goods, the offence shall always be punished as an attempt only. When actual possession is proved, the theft or robbery shall then be considered to have been completely carried into effect, and punished accordingly.

No clause.

SECTION CCLXXXI.—*Defacing or destroying the Marks with which Thieves had been branded.*

All convicted thieves are in ordinary cases branded with appropriate characters, as a warning to others, and a reproach to themselves, the impression impreffion of which it is equally neceffary to preferve undefaced, whether the offenders are permitted to return to their diftricts immediately after receiving a corporal punifhment, condemned to undergo temporary banifhment, or exiled perpetually. Therefore, when guilty of defacing the characters, fo as to render them illegible, they fhall be punifhed with 60 blows, and the characters fhall be branded anew.

Fifteen clauses.

END OF THE FIRST BOOK OF THE SIXTH DIVISION.

BOOK II.

HOMICIDE.

Section CCLXXXII. — *Preconcerted Homicide; Murder* *.

IN every cafe of perfons preconcerting the crime of homicide, whether with or without a defign, againft the life of a particular individual, the original contriver fhall fuffer death, by being beheaded, after the ufual period of confinement. All the acceffaries to the contrivance, who likewife contribute to the perpetration of the preconcerted homicide or murder, fhall fuffer death, by being ftrangled, after being confined until the ufual period.

The other acceffaries not actually contributing to the perpetration of the murder, fhall be punifhed with 100 blows, and perpetual banifhment to the diftance of 3000 *lee*. In thefe cafes, fentence is not to be pronounced finally, until the deceafe of the perfon mortally wounded.

When the wounds inflicted in confequence of a previous defign to commit murder, do not prove mortal, the original contriver of the deed fhall be ftrangled, after remaining in confinement the ufual period. The acceffaries contributing to the perpetration, fhall be punifhed with 100 blows, and perpetual banifhment to the diftance of 3000 *lee*. The other acceffaries fhall be punifhed with 100 blows, and three years banifhment.

* The diftinguifhing character of the crime which is the fubject of this fection, appears to be *previous contrivance*. In refpect to the crime of *killing, with an intent to kill*, noticed in Section CCXC, every idea of combination is there excluded, and the defign is fuppofed to have originated at the moment, or nearly fo, of its execution.

When a homicide has been preconcerted as aforesaid, but no blow struck, the original contriver shall be punished with 100 blows and three years banishment: —the accessaries to such contrivance shall be each punished with 100 blows.

The original contriver shall suffer punishment as a principal, though not otherwise contributing in any manner to carry the design into effect; but the accessaries to the contrivance who are not guilty of any subsequent overt act, shall suffer punishment less by one degree than those of the accessaries, who acted in some respects upon the contrivance, although they did not personally contribute to the perpetration of the deed.

Those who commit murder for the sake of plunder shall, as in the case of a robbery, all of them be beheaded, without any distinction whatever between principals and accessaries.

Eight clauses*.

Section CCLXXXIII. — *Murder of an Officer of Government.*

When an ordinary officer of government is guilty of designing to kill an officer invested with peculiar or extraordinary powers by the Emperor; when a private inhabitant of a district is guilty of designing to kill the governor or supreme officer of the same; when a private soldier is guilty of designing to kill his commanding officer; and, lastly, when an official attendant of a public office or tribunal, is guilty of designing to kill an officer of the fifth, or any superior rank: —in all these cases, if the individual entertaining such criminal design and contrivance, is the original contriver, he shall, though a blow had not been struck in execution thereof, be punished with 100 blows, and banishment to the distance of 2000 *lee*. If a blow is struck, so as more or less to wound, the principal offender shall be strangled; if

---

* A translation of these clauses is contained in the Appendix, No. XXIX.

the murder is actually perpetrated, all the parties thereto shall be beheaded. In the other cases the punishment of accessaries shall be one degree less severe than that of their respective principals. All persons not holding offices or rank under government, when capitally convicted under this law, shall be executed immediately; but the execution of officers of government shall not take place till after the usual period of confinement.

Accessaries to the contrivance, who are not guilty of any subsequent overt act; attendants of tribunals and public offices, guilty of designing to kill an officer of government of the sixth or any inferior rank; and, lastly, private inhabitants or soldiers, guilty of designing to kill any officers to whose jurisdiction they are not subject, shall only be punished as in ordinary cases *.

No clause.

Section CCLXXXIV. — *Parricide.*

Any person convicted of a design to kill his or her father or mother, grand-father or grand-mother, whether by the father's or mother's side; and any woman convicted of a design to kill her husband, husband's father or mother, grand-father or grand-mother, shall, whether a blow is, or is not struck in consequence, suffer death by being beheaded. In punishing this criminal design, no distinction shall be made between principals and accessaries, except as far as regards their respective relationships to the person against whose life the design is entertained. If the murder is committed, all the parties concerned therein, and related to the deceased as above-mentioned, shall suffer

* That is to say, in cases of a design to kill a stranger and an equal, under circumstances which are not legally considered either to palliate or to aggravate the guilt of such design.—The meaning however of an expression which occurs so frequently, must already have been apparent to the reader from the context.

death by a flow and painful execution. If the criminal fhould die in prifon, an execution fimilar in mode fhall take place on his body. The acceffaries more diftantly related, fhall be punifhed according to the law particularly applicable to the cafes of perfons fo related; and thofe acceffaries who are not related at all, fhall be punifhed as fimilar offenders would be in ordinary cafes.

The principal in a defign to kill any other fenior relation within the four degrees of connexion and confanguinity, fhall, if no blow is ftruck, be punifhed with 100 blows, and perpetual banifhment to the diftance of 2000 *lee*. The acceffaries to a defign to kill a perfon fo related to them, fhall be punifhed with 100 blows, and three years banifhment. If a blow is ftruck fo as to wound, the principal fhall be ftrangled, and the reft punifhed in the degree and proportion provided in ordinary cafes. If the intended murder is actually committed, all fuch of the principals and acceffaries, as are related as above defcribed, to the deceafed, fhall be beheaded.

The punifhment of entertaining a defign to kill a junior relation within any of the aforefaid degrees of connexion or confanguinity, fhall be two degrees lefs fevere than that elfewhere provided in the cafe of killing with an intent to kill, fuch junior relation. The punifhment of wounding with an intent to kill, fuch junior relation, fhall be lefs fevere than that of killing, by one degree; when the murder is actually perpetrated, the punifhment fhall be the fame as that already ftated to have been elfewhere provided *.

Any flave or hired fervant defigning to murder, or murdering his or her mafter, or any relation of his or her mafter, living under the fame roof, fhall be liable to the fame punifhment as has been provided in the cafe of a fon or grandfon being guilty of fuch a criminal act or defign.

Five claufes.

* See Section CCCXVII. in the following book, entitled, " Quarrelling and Fighting."

Section CCLXXXV.—*Killing an Adulterer.*

When a principal or inferior wife is discovered by her husband in the act of adultery, if such husband at the very time that he discovers, kills the adulterer, or adulteress, or both, he shall not be punishable. If in such a case, he does not kill the adulteress, she shall be punished according to the law applicable thereto, and afterwards sold in marriage. The money paid for her, shall be a forfeiture to government.

If there had not been an actual commission of adultery, but only such an intercourse as implied a design to commit that crime; or if the adulterer and adulteress had surrendered themselves to the husband; or if, lastly, they had removed from the apartment where the adultery had been committed, the husband who kills either of the guilty parties under any such circumstances, shall not be justified or protected by this law.

If the guilty wife shall contrive with the adulterer to procure the death of her husband, she shall suffer death by a slow and painful execution, and the adulterer shall be beheaded.—If the adulterer kills the husband, without the knowledge or connivance of the wife, she shall suffer death by being strangled.

Twenty-five clauses.

Section CCLXXXVI.—*Widows killing their deceased Husband's Relations.*

If any widow, whether married or not to a second husband, is guilty of killing her deceased husband's father, mother, grand-father or grand-mother, she shall suffer the same punishment as if guilty of killing the said relations, while such husband was still living;

the cafe of widows who had been divorced from their former hufbands, is the only one in which this law fhall not take effect.

A fervant or flave killing the perfon who had been, but was no longer his mafter, fhall only be punifhed as in ordinary cafes of murder, except in the inftance of a flave who had been manumitted by his mafter; where, the party being bound by fuch an obligation, fhall be liable to the aggravated punifhment, which is applicable to the cafe of flaves killing their mafters, and is elfewhere provided.

No claufe.

Section CCLXXXVII.—*Murder of three or more Perfons in one Family.*

Any perfon who is guilty of killing, by previous contrivance, intentionally but without premeditation, or in the courfe of a robbery or houfe burning three or more perfons, whereof none were guilty of capital offences, and all of whom were relations in the firft degree, or inmates of one family; and alfo any perfon who is guilty of mangling and dividing the limbs, and thus in a cruel and revengeful manner killing any individual, fhall, when convicted of being a principal offender, fuffer death by a flow and painful execution. The property of fuch principal offender fhall be forfeited to the ufe of the fuffering family, and his wives and children fhall be banifhed perpetually to the diftance of 2000 *lee*. Acceffaries, contributing to the perpetration of the crime, fhall be beheaded. The other acceffaries fhall be punifhed as acceffaries in ordinary cafes of murder. Where the original defign had been to kill one perfon only but from any fubfequent caufe three or more are killed, the original contriver, if not contributing to the execution, fhall be beheaded; and the individual who firft propofed upon the fpot, the killing of three or more perfons, fhall be executed as the principal, agreeably to this law.

Twelve claufes.

Section CCLXXXVIII.—*Murder, with an Intent to mangle and divide the Body of the deceased, for Magical Purposes.*

The principal in the crime of murdering, or of attempting to murder any person, with a design afterwards to mangle the body and divide the limbs of the deceased, for magical purposes, shall suffer death by a slow and painful execution. His wives, sons, and all the other inmates of his house, although innocent of the crime, shall be perpetually banished to the distance of 2000 *lee*.—The accessaries contributing to the perpetration of this crime shall be beheaded, and the other accessaries who neither contributed thereto, nor were inmates of the house in which the principal offender resided, shall be punished as accessaries in ordinary cases of murder *.

If the crime had been contrived, but no persons killed or wounded in order to carry it into effect, the principal offender shall be beheaded; and his wives and sons banished perpetually to the distance of 2000 *lee*. The accessaries contributing to any overt act, shall be punished with 100 blows, and perpetual banishment to the distance of 3000 *lee*. The other accessaries shall suffer the last mentioned punishment reduced one degree.

The head inhabitant of the village or district, when privy to the commission of, or the design to commit this crime, and not giving information thereof, shall be punished with 100 blows; but if really ignorant thereof, he shall not be liable to any punishment. All persons giving information by which such offenders are brought to justice, shall receive from government a reward of twenty ounces of silver.

One clause.

* As this law is only followed by one supplementary clause or statute, it is probable, that the attention of the government has not been frequently drawn to superstitious and sanguinary practices of the above description; but the case does not appear to be altogether an imaginary one, as two persons are recorded in a note in the original, to have been capitally convicted under this law, in the 14th year of *Kien-lung*.

Section CCLXXXIX. — *Rearing venomous Animals, and preparing Poisons.*

All perfons rearing venomous animals, or preparing drugs of a poifonous nature, for the purpofe of applying the fame to the deftruction of man, or inftructing others fo to do, fhall be beheaded, although no perfon is actually killed by means of fuch drugs or animals. The property of the perfon guilty of this crime, fhall be forfeited to government, and his wives and children, as well as the other inmates of his houfe, although innocent of the crime, fhall be perpetually banifhed to the diftance of 2000 *lee* *.

The relations and inmates of any family in which an individual has been poifoned by fuch drugs or animals, fhall not be liable to be fent into banifhment, unlefs privy to the circumftances which led to his death.

The head inhabitant of the village or diftrict, when privy to, and failing to give information of this crime, fhall fuffer a punifhment of 100 blows; but if really ignorant thereof, he fhall be excufed. Perfons giving the requifite information fhall receive from government a reward of 20 ounces of filver.

All perfons guilty of ufing magical writings and imprecations with a view to endeavour to occafion the death of any perfon therewith, fhall fuffer the punifhment of contriving a murder in ordinary cafes. If any perfon is killed by means of fuch proceedings, the offending parties fhall be punifhed as in the cafe of a contrived murder, actually carried into effect. All perfons ufing fuch magical writings and imprecations, in order to produce difeafe and infirmity in any individual, fhall fuffer a punifhment lefs by two degrees than that above provided; except

---

* It is probably fuppofed that the relations of the criminal, although innocent of the particular crimes imputed to him, muft have been familiarized to, and acquainted with his art, and that therefore they ought to be banifhed, as dangerous members of fociety.

in the case of a child against his parent, a grand-child against his grand-father or grand-mother, or a slave or hired servant against his master, each of whom for such an offence shall be beheaded.

In general, all persons guilty of poisoning with drugs, shall be beheaded. If in any case the poison shall have been administered without proving mortal, the offender shall be strangled.

All persons guilty of purchasing a poisonous drug for the purpose of killing, shall be punished with 100 blows, and three years banishment. Persons selling such drugs, knowing the object, shall suffer the same punishment as the purchasers; except in capital cases, where the punishment shall be reduced one degree. When the seller is really ignorant of the criminal object of the purchaser, he shall not be punishable.

One clause.

SECTION CCXC. — *Killing with an Intent to kill, and killing in an Affray.*

All persons guilty of killing in an affray; that is to say, striking in a quarrel or affray so as to kill, though without any express or implied design to kill, shall, whether the blow was struck with the hand or the foot, with a metal weapon, or with any instrument of any kind, suffer death, by being strangled, after the usual period of confinement.

All persons guilty of killing with an intent to kill, shall suffer death by being beheaded, after being confined until the usual period.

When several persons contrive an affray, in the course of which an individual is killed, the person who inflicts the severest blow or wound, shall be strangled, after the usual period of confinement. The original contriver of the affray, whether he engages in it or not, shall be punished at the least, with 100 blows, and perpetual banishment to the distance

distance of 3000 *lee*. The rest of the party concerned shall be punished with 100 blows each.

Twelve clauses.

Section CCXCI. — *Depriving of Food or Raiment.*

In every case of the offence of applying any substance capable of occasioning an injury to the nose, ears, or other natural outlets of the body of any person; and also in every case of depriving any person of his necessary food and raiment, so as in any instance to produce an assignable injury, the offending party shall be punished with 80 blows.

Not only those who strip others of their clothing in winter, and those who deprive of their food or drink the hungry and the thirsty, but also those who privately take away the ladder from a man who has ascended a height, or the bridle from a man on horse-back, shall be liable under this law to punishment for the consequences of such conduct. Whenever any of the natural faculties are permanently injured, the offender shall be punished with 100 blows, and three years banishment. If the injury amounts to absolute imbecillity and irremediable infirmity *, the offender shall be punished with 100 blows, and perpetual banishment to the distance of 3000 *lee*: moreover, half his property shall be forfeited for the support and indemnification of the sufferer. If the wound or injury sustained proves mortal, the offender shall suffer death, by being strangled, after remaining in confinement during the usual period.

Whoever is guilty of wilfully occasioning a snake, or other venomous animal to bite any person, shall be punished according to the

---

* The degree of injury which is in this place intended to be implied, could not be expressed in terms having as precise a meaning as those contained in the original, but in the first article of the next book, entitled, " Quarrelling and Fighting," an explanation is given in the text.

texten of the injury sustained, as in the case of wounding in an affray.

If the bite proves mortal, the offender shall be beheaded, after remaining in confinement during the usual period.

No clause.

SECTION CCXCII. — *Killing or wounding in Play, by Error, or purely by Accident.*

All persons playing with the fist, with a stick, or with any weapon, or other means whatsoever, in such a manner as obviously to be liable by so doing to kill, and thus killing or wounding some individual, shall suffer the punishment provided by the law in any ordinary case of killing or wounding in an affray; likewise any person who, being engaged in an affray, by mistake kills or wounds a by-stander, shall be punished in the same manner; that is to say, the person killing another in the manner above stated, shall suffer death by being strangled. If guilty of wounding only, he shall be punished more or less severely, according to the nature of the wounds inflicted.

Deliberately contriving, or simply entertaining an intention, to kill one particular person, but by mistake killing another, shall be punishable in the same degree as any ordinary case of intended homicide, and such offender shall accordingly be beheaded, after remaining in confinement the usual period.

If any person, knowing that a place resorted to in order to ford a river, is deep and full of mud, deceitfully represents it to be shallow and good ground; or, knowing that the planks of a bridge or ferry-boat are rotten, and therefore not trust-worthy, deceitfully represents the same to be good and secure, such person shall in either case be chargeable with the consequences, according to this law;—when, therefore, any individual is induced on the strength of such wilfully false information to cross the water, and is drowned, or in any manner injured by making such attempt, the offending party shall be deemed guilty of playing with the means by which he was aware an individual might be killed, and in consequence shall suffer the punishment provided by the law in the cases of killing or wounding in an affray.

All persons who kill or wound others purely by accident, shall be permitted to redeem themselves from the punishment of killing or wounding in an affray, by the payment in each case of a fine to the family of the person deceased or wounded.

By a case of pure accident, is understood a case of which no sufficient previous warning could have been given, either directly, by the perceptions of sight and hearing, or indirectly, by the inferences drawn by judgment and reflection; as for instance, when lawfully pursuing and shooting wild animals, when for some purpose throwing a brick or a tile, and in either case unexpectedly killing any person; when after ascending high places, slipping and falling down, so as to chance to hurt a comrade or by-stander; when sailing in a ship or other vessel, and driven involuntarily by the winds; when riding on a horse or in a carriage, being unable, upon the animal or animals taking fright, to stop or to govern them; or lastly, when several persons jointly attempt to raise a great weight, the strength of one of them failing, so that the weight falls on, and kills or injures his fellow-labourers:—in all these cases there could have been no previous thought or intention of doing an injury, and therefore the law permits such persons to redeem themselves from the punishment provided for killing or wounding in an affray, by a fine * to be paid to the family of the deceased or wounded person, which fine will in the former instance be applicable to the purpose of defraying the expence

---

* The fine is determined by the second clause annexed to this law, at twelve ounces of silver and forty-two decimals, or about 4*l.* 2*s.* 10*d.* sterling.

attending the burial, and in the latter, to that of procuring medicines and medical affiftance *.

Thirteen claufes.

Section CCXCIII. — *A Hufband killing his culpable Wife.*

If a wife ftrikes and abufes her hufband's father or mother, grand-father or grand-mother, and the hufband, inftead of accufing her before a magiftrate, kills her in confequence of fuch offence, he fhall be punifhed with 100 blows.

If a wife, having been ftruck and abufed by her hufband, in confequence thereof kills herfelf, the hufband fhall not be refponfible. When a wife, after her hufband's father and mother, grand-father and grand-mother are dead, is guilty of difrefpect to their memory only, or is charged with fome other fault not worthy of death according to the laws, if thereupon the hufband kills her, he fhall fuffer the punifhment of death, by being ftrangled, after the ufual period of confinement.

Two claufes.

* From this fection of the laws it clearly appears, that although a peculiar degree of ftrictnefs may exift in China in enforcing the punifhment of homicide in general, the commonly received notion of the rigour of the law being fuch, that no allowance is made even in cafes purely accidental, is totally without foundation.

Upon a late occafion, when one of our feamen at Canton was held refponfible for the murder of a native Chinefe, under circumftances indeed, of a peculiar nature, and by which for a time the Britifh interefts in China were very ferioufly involved, and all commercial intercourfe between the two nations fufpended, he was ultimately acquitted agreeably to the provifions of the law contained in this fection: — had it not been known at the time that fuch a law exifted, and had not the Chinefe government been almoft neceffitated as it were, by the firm, but temperate and judicious meafures adopted on the occafion by the Eaft India Company's reprefentatives, to apply it to that particular inftance, the forms of Chinefe juftice could not have been fubmitted to, without rifking unwarrantably the facrifice of the life of a Britifh fubject. See a tranflation of the Chinefe official report of the affair in the Appendix, No. XI.

SECTION CCXCIV. — *Killing a Son, Grandson, or Slave, and attributing the Crime to an innocent Person.*

Whoever is guilty of killing his son, his grandson, or his slave, and attributing the crime to another person, shall be punished with 70 blows, and one and a half year's banishment.

Any person attributing, previous to burial, the death of his father, mother, grand-father or grand-mother; and any slave in like manner, attributing the death of his master to a person innocent thereof, shall, if aware of the falsehood of the imputation, be punished with 100 blows, and three years banishment.

Any person in like manner falsely attributing to an innocent person the death of any other of his relations in the first degree, shall be punished with 80 blows, and three years banishment.

If the case concerns a more distant relation, the punishment shall be reduced at the rate of one degree for each degree of remoteness in the relationship.

Any person in like manner falsely attributing the death of his junior relation, or of any indifferent person, shall be punished with 80 blows.

If, in any of the preceding cases, an accusation should actually have been laid before a magistrate, the offence shall be punished according to the law against false and malicious accusations.

If by falsely attributing the crime of murder as aforesaid, any money or property is fraudulently extorted from the party accused, the offence shall be punishable as a theft, proportionably to the amount. If, in like manner, any money or property is extorted by actual violence, the offence shall be punished as a robbery in open day, but in neither case shall the offender be branded. The punishment inflicted shall moreover be always the severest applicable to the case, whether that of falsely attributing murder, or that of a theft or robbery.

Five clauses.

SECTION CCXCV. — *Wounding mortally or otherwise, by shooting Arrows and similar Weapons.*

All persons who causelessly shoot with a bow, either arrows or any other weapons, or throw bricks or stones, towards walled towns, places of trade, or any other places or buildings whatsoever which are the residence and habitation of man, shall be punished with 40 blows for every such offence, although no person shall have been struck or wounded thereby. — If any person is struck or wounded, the punishment shall be reduced one degree below that provided by the law in the case of striking or wounding in a similar degree in an affray; but no part of the property of the offender shall, as there provided, be forfeited to the use of the sufferer.

If any person is killed by such aforesaid act, the offender shall be punished with 100 blows, and perpetual banishment to the distance of 3000 *lee*.

Although, according to the general principle on which the laws are framed, the punishment ought be aggravated when the person killed is a relation of the offender, yet as the offender in the present case is not supposed to foresee the particular consequences of his offence, the relationship between the parties shall be disregarded. In all these cases however, ten ounces of silver shall be paid to the relations of the deceased to defray the expences of burial*.

No clause.

---

* See a translation of the report of a trial of an offender convicted agreeably to this law, in the Appendix, No. XXX., and also another in Mr. Barrow's Travels in China, p. 370.

SECTION CCXCVI.—*Wounding mortally, or otherwise, by means of Horses and Carriages.*

Whoever causelessly drives carriages, or rides horses with extraordinary speed, through streets, markets, military stations, or any other places of resort, and by so doing happens to wound any person, shall suffer the punishment provided by the law in the case of wounding in a similar degree in an affray, reduced one degree — If any person is killed, the offender shall be punished with 100 blows, and banished to the distance of 3000 *lee*.

Those who causelessly ride or drive as aforesaid in the open country, where people do not commonly resort, although they should happen, by so doing, to wound any person, shall not be punishable, unless the wound proves mortal, in which case they shall suffer 100 blows, and under all circumstances pay ten ounces of silver to the family of the deceased.

When any person proceeding with great speed upon urgent public business, either on horseback or in a carriage, happens by so doing to kill or wound any one, the case shall be deemed purely accidental, and the punishment redeemable accordingly, by the payment of a fine to the relations of the deceased.

One clause.

---

p. 370.—Although since the publication of that work, some points may have been placed, by the discovery of new facts, in a light somewhat different, so as perhaps to warrant in those respects an opinion rather less disadvantageous of the Chinese character, the general view which has been taken by Mr. Barrow, of the present state of the people and government of China, is so unquestionably just and excellent, his descriptions so happy, and the information interspersed throughout so various and interesting, that instead of quoting particular passages occasionally in illustration of the present work, the translator conceives that he shall contribute ultimately more to the satisfaction of the reader, by taking this opportunity of making one general reference to that valuable publication.

Section CCXCVII. — *Practitioners of Medicine killing or injuring their Patients.*

When unskilful practitioners of medicine or surgery * administer drugs, or perform operations with the puncturing needle, contrary to the established rules and practice, and thereby kill the patient, the magistrates shall call in other practitioners to examine the nature of the medicine, or of the wound, as the case may be, which proved mortal; and if it shall appear upon the whole to have been simply an error, without any design to injure the patient, the practitioner of medicine shall be allowed to redeem himself from the punishment of homicide, as in cases purely accidental, but shall be obliged to quit his profession for ever.

If it shall appear that a medical practitioner intentionally deviates from the established rules and practice, and while pretending to remove the disease of his patient, aggravates the complaint, in order to extort more money for its cure, the money so extorted shall be considered to have been stolen, and punishment inflicted accordingly, in proportion to the amount.

If the patient dies, the medical practitioner who is convicted of designedly employing improper medicines, or otherwise contriving to in-

---

* Strictly speaking, the art of Surgery is unknown in China, and the term is here employed merely to point out the distinction which the Chinese make in the medical profession, between external and internal operations.

It is a fact worthy of notice in this place, though not immediately connected with the objects of the present work, that notwithstanding the peculiar prejudices of the Chinese on the subject of medicine, and their general aversion to every species of innovation, more especially to that which is derived from the suggestions of foreigners, the benefits of Dr. Jenner's invaluable discovery of the vaccine inoculation, are at present enjoyed in a considerable degree by the natives of the southern coast of the Chinese empire, through the skilful and indefatigable exertions of Mr. Pearson, the principal surgeon of the East India Company's factory at Canton.—See that gentleman's interesting communication on the subject, in the Medical Journal for November 1808.

jure

jure his patient, shall suffer death by being beheaded, after the usual period of confinement.

No clause.

Section CCXCVIII.—*Killing or wounding by means of Traps or Springes.*

All persons, huntsmen by profession, digging pit-falls, and laying traps or springes in mountainous or desert places, where wild animals are supposed to haunt, but omitting at the same time to give warning thereof, by distinguishing each of such places by a flag-staff, and a small cord stretched across, at the height of a man's eye from the ground, shall be punished with 40 blows, although no mischief to any one should ensue.

If any person is hurt or wounded for want of such warning, the punishment of the responsible person shall be only two degrees less than that provided by law in the case of wounding in a similar degree in an affray.

If any person is killed, the offender shall be punished with 100 blows, and three years banishment, and shall moreover pay ten ounces of silver to the family of the deceased, to defray the expences of burial.

If such pit-falls are dug, and traps or springes placed, without the above prescribed warnings, in places cultivated and inhabited by man, the offending parties shall be punished according to the law against shooting with bows and arrows or other-weapons, against places so cultivated and inhabited.

No clause.

Section CCXCIX. — *Occasioning the Death of an Individual by violent and fearful Threats.*

Any person who, with a view to accomplish some object, such as a marriage-contract, the transfer of property, payment of debts, and the like, alarms another to such a degree by violent threats, that he kills himself in despair, shall, whenever reasonable grounds can be shewn to have existed for such extreme apprehensions on the part of the deceased, be punished with 100 blows.

Any officer of government who shall be guilty of such conduct, when not acting in execution of his public duty, shall be liable to the same punishment; and in every case the offender shall pay ten ounces of silver to the family of the deceased to defray the expences of burial.

If any person shall thus alarm with violent threats an elder relation in the first degree, so that such relation kills himself in consequence thereof, the junior so offending, shall suffer death, by being strangled, after the usual period of confinement.

Every similar offence against an elder relation in any of the more remote degrees, shall be subject to the punishment last mentioned, under a reduction of one degree for each degree of additional remoteness, in the relationship.

All persons guilty of alarming to death with violent threats, as above mentioned, in order to accomplish any object criminal and unlawful in itself, such as theft or adultery, shall, whether such criminal and unlawful object is, or is not attained, be punished with death, by being beheaded, after the usual period of confinement.

Eighteen clauses.

SECTION CCC.—*Compromising and concealing the Crime of killing an elder Relation.*

If, in the event of the murder of a grandfather, grandmother, father, mother, husband, or master of a family; the grandson, son, wife, slave, or hired servant, as the case may be, agrees to a compromise with the murderer, and conceals the crime, the party so offending shall be punished with 100 blows, and banished for three years.

In the event of the murder of any other elder relation in the first degree, being compromised and concealed by the junior relation, such junior relation shall be punished with 80 blows, and two years banishment; and in case of any relationship between the parties in a more remote degree, the punishment of the junior shall be reduced at the rate of one degree for each degree of additional remoteness.

An elder relation compromising and concealing the murder of a junior, shall, in general, be punished one degree less severely than such junior relation would have been, had the case been reversed.

Any person, lastly, who is guilty of compromising and concealing the murder of his son, grandson, wife, slave, or hired servant, shall be liable to the punishment of 80 blows. When any bribe is received in consideration of such compromise and concealment, the receiver shall be held guilty of a theft to the same amount, and the punishment shall be either that provided by law in the case of such a theft, or that already stated conformably to the circumstances of the compromise, whichever proves to be the most severe. The amount of the bribe shall be forfeited to government.

Compromising and concealing the murder of a stranger shall subject the offending party to the punishment of 60 blows; and when the offence is committed in consideration of a bribe, the punishment shall be be subject to such aggravation, as may be conformable to the law against receiving bribes for unlawful purposes.

One clause.

SECTION CCCI. — *Neglecting to give Information of, or to interfere and prevent a violent Injury which is known to be intended.*

When any person is aware that his comrade has contrived the means of inflicting a violent injury, and is desirous of executing such unlawful purpose, if he does not endeavour to prevent the design from being carried into effect, so as to preserve harmless the object of it; or, when unable so to do, if he does not, at least, after the crime is committed, give information thereof to a magistrate, he shall be punished for the omission with 100 blows.

No clause.

END OF THE SECOND BOOK OF THE SIXTH DIVISION.

BOOK III.

QUARRELLING AND FIGHTING.

Section CCCII. — *Quarrelling and Fighting between Equals in ordinary Cafes.*

IN all ordinary cafes of quarrelling and fighting, every perfon who ftrikes another with his hand or foot, but not fo as to produce any affignable hurt or wound, fhall be punifhed with 20 blows.

If a blow is ftruck with the hand or foot, and produces a hurt or wound; or is ftruck with a cudgel, or any other fimilar weapon, but produces no affignable hurt or wound, the punifhment, in either cafe, fhall amount to 30 blows. — If, in the latter cafe, any hurt or wound is occafioned by the blow, the punifhment fhall be increafed to 40 blows. — Whenever the part of the body ftruck, fwells or inflames, the injury received fhall be deemed a hurt or wound; in general alfo, when any blow is ftruck, otherwife than fimply by the hand or foot as aforefaid, that circumftance fhall always occafion an aggravation of one degree in punifhment. — A foldier ftriking with the back of his fword, fhall alfo be liable to the aggravated punifhment.

The offence of tearing away more than an inch (*Tfun*) of hair, fhall be punifhed with 50 blows. — If a blow has been ftruck in fuch a manner as to occafion blood to flow from the eyes or ears, or to be difcharged from the ftomach in confequence of fome internal injury, the offender fhall be punifhed with 80 blows. — In the cafe however of blood flowing only from the noftrils, or immediately from the part of the body where the blow was received, merely in confequence of the

fkin

skin upon such part having been broken, the punishment shall not be more severe than in the case of an ordinary hurt or wound above mentioned.

The offence of throwing filth and ordure on the head or face, shall also be punishable with 80 blows. — Breaking a tooth, a toe, a finger, or any bone in the body; wounding an eye, without totally destroying the sight; materially injuring and disfiguring the ears or nose; scalding with hot water; burning with fire; wounding with copper or iron needles; or filling up the mouth and nose with filth or ordure, shall in each case subject the offender to a punishment of 100 blows.

Breaking two teeth, two fingers, two toes, or tearing away all the hair of the head, shall in each case subject the offender to a punishment of 60 blows and one year's banishment.

Breaking a rib; wounding both eyes; striking a woman ninety days gone with child, so as to occasion miscarriage or abortion; or wounding in any case with the edge of a sharp instrument, shall subject the offender to a punishment of 80 blows, and two years banishment.

Breaking a leg or an arm, or the back-bone, or destroying one eye, is considered by the law to be an infliction of a permanent and irremediable injury, and shall subject the offender to the punishment of 100 blows and three years banishment.

Breaking both legs, both arms, or a leg and an arm; destroying both eyes; or doing any other injury which produces entire disability and incurable infirmity; cutting out the tongue so as to deprive the sufferer of the faculty of speech; or violently injuring a person of either sex, so as to incapacitate such person from becoming a parent, shall subject the offender, in each case, to the punishment of 100 blows, and perpetual banishment to the distance of 3000 *lee*; half the property of the offender shall also, in such cases, be forfeited to the support of the person injured.

In the case of a woman being violently injured, but not to the extent of rendering her incapable of becoming a mother, this law shall still be put in force, except in as much as respects the forfeiture of half the property of the offender. When there are more offenders than one, and they agree together to attack jointly, they shall be punished according to the severity of the blows respectively inflicted by them, except in the case of the original contriver, who, whether he joined in the attack or affray or not, shall always suffer, at the least, a punishment but one degree less severe than that which is inflicted on him who struck the severest blow. — In the case of an ordinary affray, no other persons shall be liable to suffer punishment in consequence of their being implicated therein, beside the original contriver, and such of the parties as may be convicted of actually striking a blow: but if any person is killed in the course of an affray, all the persons who were privy to and in any manner concerned in the same, shall, at the least, be liable to a punishment of 100 blows each.

If several persons jointly attack another, and in course of the affray, mortally wound him, the person who struck the last and severest blow, shall be esteemed the principal in the homicide: in those cases of promiscuous fighting, in which it is impossible to ascertain who struck the first blow, and who the last, who struck the lightest, and who the heaviest, the original contriver shall in general be esteemed the principal; and when there is no evidence of previous contrivance, the responsibility, as principal offender, shall attach to the person who first engaged in the affray, or commenced the quarrel.

In the case of a combat between two persons; and in the case of several persons engaging in an affray, and promiscuously striking and fighting each other, they shall be punished respectively, according to the blows duly ascertained, and proved by the examination of the effects, to have been received by their antagonists, except that the punishment of the person or persons who only return the blows received, and have the right and justice of the dispute on his or their side, shall be

reduced

reduced two degrees in confideration of fuch favourable circumftances: but this reduction fhall not take place in the inftance of ftriking an elder brother or fifter, or an uncle; or when inflicting, in any cafe, a mortal blow.

As for inftance; let *Kia** and *Yee*, be fuppofed to quarrel and fight, and that *Kia* deprives *Yee* of an eye, and *Yee* deprives *Kia* of a tooth; now the injury fuftained by *Yee* is the heavieft, and fubjects *Kia* to the punifhment of 100 blows and three years banifhment, whilft the leffer injury fuftained by *Kia* fubjects *Yee* to a punifhment of 100 blows only:—neverthelefs, if it appears that *Kia* only returned the attack, and had the right on his fide, his punifhment fhall be reduced two degrees, and accordingly amount to 80 blows and two years banifhment:—on the contrary, if *Yee* only returned the attack, and had the right in the difpute, his punifhment fhall be reduced two degrees, and amount to 80 blows only; the punifhment to which the antagonift is fubjected remaining in either cafe the fame as before: when the punifhment originally included a forfeiture of half the property of the offender, that penalty fhall not in any cafe, be reduced.

Eight claufes.

Section CCCIII.—*Periods of Refponfibility for the Confequences of a Wound.*

When any perfon is wounded, the magiftrates fhall diftinctly examine, and take evidence refpecting the wound, in order to afcertain the nature thereof, and the manner in which it was inflicted; which having done, they fhall according to the circumftances determine the period during which the offender is to be held refponfible for the con-

---

* *Kia* and *Yee* are names ufed merely by way of exemplification, in the fame manner as with us fometimes, the letters of the alphabet, or the fictitious names introduced into the proceedings of our civil courts of juftice.

sequences, that is to say, strictly bound both to provide medicinal assistance for the wounded person for such time, and also to answer for the contingency of his death, either on account of such wound, or from any external cause operating thereon, previous to the expiration of the period.

If the wounded person should die after the expiration of the period; or even within the period, provided he had recovered from the wound, and is clearly proved to have died from some other cause, the offender shall not be held guilty of a capital offence, but be punished according to the apparent nature of the wound inflicted, as stated in the preceding section.

If, on the contrary, the wounded person not only survives the period assigned, but by the aid of medicine entirely recovers within the same, the punishment of the offender for inflicting such wound shall be reduced two degrees.

Nevertheless, if any permanent injury, disability, or bodily infirmity remains, after a recovery from the immediate effect of the wound, the law shall be executed on the offender in its full extent.

When a wound has been inflicted with the hand or foot, or with any article which is not an ordinary weapon of offence, and the injury sustained is apparently not considerable, a period of twenty days responsibility shall only be required.

When a wound has been inflicted with a sharp instrument, with fire, or with scalding water, the period of responsibility shall be extended to thirty days.

When any bones are broken or dislocated, or the body or limbs violently injured; and when, in any case, the sufferer happens to be a woman with child, the period shall be extended to fifty days, in whatever manner the blow may have been inflicted *.

Seven clauses.

* According to one of the supplemental clauses annexed to this law, an intermediate period of forty days is established for cases of gun-shot wounds; the judicious application

SECTION CCCIV.—*Quarrelling and Fighting within the Imperial Palace.*

All perfons who are guilty of difputing and quarrelling within the precincts of the Imperial Palace, fhall be punifhed with 50 blows.

If they proceed fo far as to ftrike one another, or if the found of the voices of the difputants reaches to the apartments of His Majefty, the punifhment fhall be increafed to 100 blows.

If, as aforefaid, within the precincts of the palace, a cutting wound is inflicted, the punifhment of the offenders fhall be two degrees more fevere than in ordinary cafes. If the offence is committed in the prefence chamber, or in any of the Imperial halls of audience, the punifhment fhall be further aggravated one degree, but limited in all cafes fhort of homicide, to 100 blows and perpetual banifhment to the diftance of 3000 *lee*. As in every quarrel and difpute under thefe circumftances, both parties are confidered culpable, if the injury occafioned by the wound received by one of the offending parties is incurable or amounts to complete difability, the fufferer muft ftill redeem himfelf from his fhare in the punifhment ordained by this law, by the payment of the ordinary fine, and fhall not receive that portion of the property of the other offender, which is always granted in ordinary cafes of perfons fuftaining a fimilar injury.

One claufe.

---

of this particular law, it is worthy of notice, once very materially contributed to extricate the Eaft India Company's reprefentatives in China, from very ferious difficulties, and from the diftreffing alternative, of either ignominioufly facrificing the life of a Britifh fubject, or totally abandoning the important commercial interefts under their management.

SECTION CCCV. — *Striking or wounding an Individual of the Imperial Blood.*

Any person who strikes an individual of the Imperial Blood, although not one within any of the four degrees of relationship to the Emperor, shall be punished with 60 blows, and one year's banishment; slightly wounding such person, shall be punishable with 80 blows and two years banishment; inflicting a cutting wound, shall be punished two degrees more severely than in ordinary cases between equals, provided the punishment do not in any such case exceed 100 blows, and three years banishment.

If the individual of Imperial blood is related to the sovereign in the fourth degree, the punishment shall be aggravated one degree; and if more nearly related, the punishment shall be aggravated an additional degree for each degree of approximation in relationship, but in no case exceed 100 blows and perpetual banishment to the distance of 3000 *lee*, except the consequent injury amounts to total disability and incurable infirmity; when, in all such instances of injuries sustained by persons of Imperial blood, the offenders shall suffer death, by being strangled, after the usual period of imprisonment.

When in any of the preceding cases death ensues, the offenders shall be beheaded, after the usual confinement.

Two clauses.

SECTION CCCVI. — *Striking ordinary and extraordinary Officers of Government.*

Any ordinary officer of government striking an officer of government invested with extraordinary powers by the Emperor; any private inhabitant of a district, striking the governor or chief officer of the same; any private soldier striking his commanding officer; and, lastly, any

any official attendant of a tribunal ſtriking a preſiding officer who is at the ſame time, of the fifth, or of any rank ſuperior thereto, ſhall in every ſuch caſe be puniſhed with 100 blows, and three years baniſhment. If the blow produces a ſlight wound or bruiſe, the puniſhment ſhall be increaſed to 100 blows, and perpetual baniſhment to the diſtance of 2000 *lee*.

If the blow produces a ſevere cutting wound, the offender ſhall ſuffer death, by being ſtrangled, after the uſual period of confinement.

Any official attendant of a tribunal, (that is to ſay, a perſon having a civil or military office or command below the regular officers of government,) ſtriking a preſiding officer or magiſtrate below the fifth rank, ſhall be puniſhed according to the nature of the blow, in the proportion above ſtated, but with a reduction of three degrees in each caſe. — If the officer or magiſtrate who is ſtruck, is only an aſſeſſor of the tribunal, the puniſhment ſhall be further reduced one degree, and it ſhall be again reduced another degree, if he is the loweſt officer of ſuch tribunal. — Nevertheleſs, no reduction ſhall take effect ſo as to render the puniſhment leſs, than one degree more ſevere than in ordinary caſes.

In all the preceding caſes, when the injury ſuſtained produces entire diſability and incurable infirmity, the offender ſhall ſuffer death, by being ſtrangled; and when it occaſions the death of the ſufferer, the offender ſhall be beheaded, after having in either caſe remained in priſon until the uſual period of execution.

Officers of government not yet raiſed to any of the regular ranks, perſons having official employments immediately under the civil or military officers of government, ſoldiers, and private individuals, when ſtriking any civil or military officer of the third, or any rank ſuperior thereto, but to whoſe juriſdiction or command they were not ſubject, ſhall, in each caſe, be liable to a puniſhment of 80 blows, and two years baniſhment.

If guilty of wounding ſo as to bruiſe, the puniſhment ſhall be increaſed to 100 blows, and three years baniſhment. — If guilty of cutting and wounding, the puniſhment ſhall be further increaſed to 100 blows, and perpetual baniſhment to the diſtance of 2000 *lee*.

If the officer ſtruck or wounded as above, is of the fourth or fifth, inſtead of the third, or any ſuperior rank, the puniſhment ſhall, according to the caſe, be proportionably reduced two degrees; but neither in this, nor in the preceding caſes, nor in the caſe of the perſons above mentioned ſtriking or wounding an officer of government below the fifth rank, ſhall any reduction in the puniſhment operate ſo as to render it leſs, than two degrees more ſevere than in ordinary caſes.

Official meſſengers on duty, ſtriking or wounding the officer of government to whom they are diſpatched, ſhall be puniſhed as above ſtated, conformably to this law.

When the offender and the ſufferer belong to different diſtricts ſubject to diſtinct juriſdictions, the cognizance and trial of the offence ſhall always take place in the diſtrict of the latter.

Four clauſes.

SECTION CCCVII. — *Subordinate Officers of Government ſtriking Perſons who are their Superiors both in Rank and Juriſdiction.*

If in any court, tribunal, or public office of government, the deputies thereof, or the magiſtrates holding ſubordinate courts, tribunals, or public offices, ſtrike or wound the preſident of ſuch ſuperior court or tribunal, the puniſhment ſhall be leſs by two degrees, than that already provided in the caſe of the official attendant thereof committing a ſimilar offence. — If the aſſeſſors of ſuch tribunals and public offices ſtrike or wound the preſidents thereof, their puniſhment ſhall be fixed
according

according to a further reduction of two degrees below that of the deputies or fubordinates aforefaid, under fimilar circumftances.

Neverthelefs no reduction fhall take place fo as to render the punifhment lefs than one degree above that which is provided by the law in ordinary cafes between equals.

In each of the preceding cafes, if total difability and incurable infirmity are occafioned by the blows inflicted, the offender fhall fuffer death, by being ftrangled, after the ufual period of confinement. — If death enfues, the offender fhall be beheaded at the ufual period.

No claufe.

SECTION CCCVIII.—*Co-ordinate or independent Officers of Government ftriking each other.*

Any affeffor or deputy of a court, tribunal or government ftation, who ftrikes an officer of government, holding the prefidency of a fubordinate court, tribunal, or government ftation, fhall, without regard to the refpective rank of the parties, be punifhed as in ordinary cafes, between equals. — Likewife officers of government belonging to diftinct and independent tribunals, if of the fame rank, fhall, when ftriking each other, be punifhed as in ordinary cafes.

No claufe.

SECTION CCCIX. — *Officers of Government ftriking their Superiors in Rank, but not in Jurifdiction.*

Any officer of government below the regular ranks, or of the ninth, eighth, feventh, or fixth rank, ftriking an officer of government of the third, fecond, or firft rank, who is not at the fame time his commanding officer, fhall be punifhed with 60 blows, and one year's banifhment.

If a blow inflicted as aforesaid produces a cutting wound; if any one of the aforesaid officers of government strikes an officer of the fifth or fourth rank, who is not his commander; or if under similar circumstances an officer of the fifth or fourth rank, strikes an officer of the second or first rank, the punishment shall, in each case, be two degrees more severe than in ordinary cases: — but this aggravation of the punishment shall not extend to cases of wounds occasioning the entire disability or death of the injured party.

No clause.

Section CCCX. — *Resisting and striking any Person employed officially by Government on Public Service.*

All persons resisting and striking those who, under the authority of any public office or officer of government, are employed in collecting duties, or enforcing any legal and public services, shall be punished at the least with 80 blows: — all persons so resisting, and striking severe blows, causing a discharge of blood from the stomach, and the like, shall suffer a punishment two degrees more severe than that which would have been inflicted according to law in ordinary cases between equals: — but the punishment shall not, in any case, exceed 100 blows, and perpetual banishment to the distance of 3000 *lee*; unless the blows which are inflicted occasion, what the law considers a total disability and incurable infirmity, in which event, the offenders shall suffer death by being strangled, after the usual period of confinement:— if death ensues, they shall be beheaded.

These are the punishments to be inflicted in the different cases of resistance to lawful authority, employed in the collection of duties, or in the enforcement of any other services of a public nature: but if any such offender had been antecedently guilty of neglect or wilful delay, in discharging the former, or performing the latter, he shall be punished according

according to the law provided againſt thoſe who, after having been ſubjected to a criminal proſecution for their offences, reſiſt, and defend themſelves againſt the officers of juſtice.

No clauſe.

Section CCCXI. — *Diſciples and Apprentices ſtriking their Maſters.*

A knowledge of letters, of huſbandry, of arts and manufactures, and of commerce, cannot be acquired without regular diſcipline, and ſufficient apprenticeſhip, and gratitude is therefore due to thoſe from whom the neceſſary inſtruction has been received.

A diſciple of the literary claſs, is held to be bound in gratitude from the very commencement of his apprenticeſhip; but the diſciples of huſbandry or agriculture, of arts and manufactures, and of commerce, are only held to be thus bound, after having concluded their apprenticeſhips, and ſeverally entered into the profeſſions, the knowledge of which they had thereby acquired. They ſhall, accordingly, be liable to a puniſhment two degrees more ſevere than in ordinary caſes between equals, whenever they are guilty of ſtriking, in the latter three caſes, the perſons who have been, or in the firſt caſe, the perſons who either are, or have been, their maſters and inſtructors.

Neverthelefs, the puniſhment ſhall not be, in any caſe, capital, unleſs death enſues from the blows inflicted, and then the offender ſhall ſuffer the puniſhment of death, by being beheaded, after the uſual period of confinement.

Two clauſes.

Section CCCXII. — *Unlawful and forcible Impriſonment.*

All perſons who have quarrels and diſputes, ought to forbear from ſeeking redreſs otherwiſe than by complaining to the proper officer

officer of government, and fubmitting the juftice of their caufe to his decifion: — all thofe on the contrary, who, relying on their ftrength and power, feize, and carry away their opponents, and attempt in private houfes to confine and torture them, fhall, even if no affignable injury be actually inflicted, be punifhed with 80 blows. — If any fevere or internal injury is done to the individual fo feized, the offender fhall be punifhed according to the nature of the wounds inflicted, two degrees more feverely than in ordinary cafes. — If death enfues, the offender fhall be ftrangled at the ufual period.

If any perfon hires another thus to maltreat his opponent, the perfon fo hired fhall be deemed an acceffary, and fuffer punifhment lefs than that of his principal by only one degree.

If more than one perfon is hired, the chief agent among them fhall be the only one to be punifhed as an acceffary under this law.

Four claufes.

Section CCCXIII. — *Slaves and free Perfons affaulting and ftriking each other.*

A flave ftriking a free man fhall, proportionably to the confequences, be punifhed one degree more feverely than is by law provided in fimilar cafes between equals. — If the blow produces entire difability and incurable infirmity, the offender fhall be ftrangled. — If death enfues, the offender fhall be beheaded.

A freeman ftriking a flave, fhall, in like manner, be punifhed lefs feverely by one degree than in the ordinary cafes of the fame offence; but in the cafe of the death of a flave, in confequence of the injury received, and in the cafe of a flave having been killed defignedly, the offender fhall be ftrangled. — Slaves ftriking, wounding, or killing one another, shall be punished as already provided in ordinary cases between equals.

In cases of stealing, and other similar offences, between free persons and slaves, the law of diminution and aggravation of punishment shall not take effect.

Striking the slave of a relation in the third or fourth degree, but without producing a cutting wound, shall not be punishable. — If the blow produces any greater injury, short of occasioning death, the punishment shall be two degrees less severe than in ordinary cases. — Striking the slave of a relation in the second degree, shall be punished three degrees less severely than in ordinary cases. — If, in either case, the blow occasions death, the offender shall be punished with 100 blows, and three years banishment: — if the blow proves mortal, and has likewise been struck with an intention to kill, the offender shall suffer death, by being strangled. In the case of killing accidentally, no punishment shall be required.

Striking the hired servant of a relation in the third or fourth degree, but without producing a cutting wound, shall not be punishable.

If the blow produces any greater injury short of occasioning death, the punishment shall be one degree less severe than in ordinary cases: the punishment of striking the hired servant of a relation in the second degree, shall be two degrees less than in ordinary cases. — Killing by such blows, or intentionally killing, shall, in either of the cases last stated, subject the offender to the punishment of death, by being strangled, at the usual period.

Accidentally killing such hired servant, shall not render the person convicted thereof, liable to any fine or punishment.

The offence of assaulting and striking the hired servant of a stranger, shall subject the party guilty thereof, to the same punishment as is provided and inflicted in ordinary cases.

One clause.

Section CCCXIV. — *Slaves striking their Masters.*

All slaves who are guilty of designedly striking their masters, shall, without making any distinction between principals and accessaries, be beheaded.

All slaves designedly killing, or designedly striking so as to kill their masters, shall suffer death by a slow and painful execution.

If accidentally killing their masters, they shall suffer death, by being strangled at the usual period.

If accidentally wounding, they shall suffer 100 blows, and perpetual banishment to the distance of 3000 *lee*; not being allowed, as under similar circumstances in ordinary cases, to redeem themselves from such punishment by a fine *.

Slaves who are guilty of striking their master's relations in the first degree, or their master's maternal grandfather or grandmother, shall be strangled at the usual period. If more than one are concerned, the principal shall be strangled, and the rest suffer the punishment next in degree. — All slaves who strike so as to wound such persons, shall, without distinction between principals and accessaries, be beheaded at the usual period.

If accidentally killing, the punishment shall be two degrees less severe than in the case of intentionally striking such persons. — If accidentally wounding, the punishment shall be another degree less severe than in the case of intentionally striking. — All slaves who are concerned in the crime of designedly killing such persons, shall suffer death by a slow and painful execution.

---

* This part of the law, denouncing punishment even in cases which are admitted to have been purely accidental, is in some degree modified in the supplemental clauses.

A flave who is guilty of ftriking, or ftriking and flightly wounding his mafter's relation in the fourth degree, fhall be punifhed with 60 blows, and one year's banifhment: if guilty of ftriking his mafter's relation in the third degree, he fhall be punifhed with 70 blows, and banifhment for a year and a half: if guilty of ftriking his mafter's relation in the fecond degree, the punifhment fhall be 80 blows, and two years banifhment.

If a flave is guilty of ftriking any of his mafter's relations in the fourth degree, fo as to produce a fevere cutting wound, the punifhment fhall be one degree more fevere than it would have been if he had fo wounded a free perfon in ordinary cafes: in the cafe of a mafter's relation in the third degree, two degrees more fevere; and in the cafe of a mafter's relation in the fecond degree, three degrees more fevere.— If by thefe augmentations, the punifhment, in any cafe, becomes capital, the offender fhall be ftrangled at the ufual period; but if the wound occafions death, then, whether there was originally a defign to kill or not, all the flaves concerned fhall be beheaded.

If a hired fervant ftrikes his mafter, his mafter's relations in the firft degree, or his mafter's maternal grandfather or grandmother, he fhall be punifhed with 100 blows, and three years banifhment. — If he ftrikes in fuch a manner as to wound, he fhall be punifhed with 100 blows, and perpetual banifhment to the diftance of 3000 *lee*. — If he ftrikes fo as to produce a cutting wound, he fhall be ftrangled at the ufual period: if he ftrikes fo as to occafion death, he fhall, in the cafe of his mafter being the perfon ftruck, be beheaded immediately on conviction; in the other cafes, at the ufual period. If he defignedly kills any of the aforefaid perfons, he fhall fuffer death by a flow and painful execution. — If the killing or wounding is purely accidental, the punifhment fhall be two degrees lefs than that eftablifhed by the laws, in proportion to the confequences of blows, in ordinary cafes.

A hired servant who is guilty of striking, or striking and slightly wounding his master's relations in the fourth degree, shall be punished with 80 blows; if guilty of striking his master's relations in the third degree, with 90 blows; if guilty of striking those in the second degree, with 100 blows. — If striking and wounding so as to produce an internal injury, spitting of blood, and the like, the punishment of so striking his master's relations in the third or fourth degree, shall be one degree more severe than that provided by law in ordinary cases; and if guilty of so striking his master's relations in the second degree, the punishment shall be two degrees more severe than in ordinary cases; but shall not exceed 100 blows and perpetual banishment, unless death ensues; in which event, all the parties to the offence shall be beheaded at the usual period.

If, in the case of a slave having been guilty of theft, adultery, or any other similar crime, his master, or some one of his nearest relations in the first degree, or his master's maternal grandfather or grandmother, instead of complaining to a magistrate, privately beats to death such slave, the person who so offends shall be punished with 100 blows.

If any such person as aforesaid, beats to death, or intentionally kills a slave belonging to his family, who had not been guilty of any crime, the person so offending shall be punished with 60 blows, and one year's banishment; and the wife or husband, as well as the children of such deceased slave, shall be thereupon entitled to their freedom. The master, or relations of the master of a guilty slave, may however chastise such slave in any degree short of occasioning his death, without being liable to any punishment.

When a master, or some one of his relations as aforesaid, strikes a hired servant, the person so striking the servant shall not, whether

such

such servant merited or not his chastisement, be punishable, unless the blow produces a cutting wound; in which event also, the punishment shall be three degrees less than in ordinary cases. If death ensues, the offender shall be punished with 100 blows, and three years banishment.

If designedly killing such hired servant, the offender shall suffer death, by being strangled at the usual period. — Nevertheless, if a master, or his aforesaid relations, in order to correct a disobedient slave or hired servant, should chastise him in a lawful manner on the back of the thighs, or on the posteriors, and such slave or hired servant happens to die; or if he is killed in any other manner accidentally, neither the master nor his aforesaid relations, shall be liable to any punishment in consequence thereof*.

Seventeen clauses.

SECTION CCCXV. — *Wives striking their Husbands.*

If a principal or first wife is guilty of striking her husband, she shall be liable to the punishment of 100 blows; and the husband, if desirous thereof, may obtain a divorce by making application for the same to the magistrate of the district. If any such wife strikes so as to wound her husband, she shall be punishable three degrees more severely than in the case of striking in the same manner an equal in ordinary cases. — If the blow occasions, what is in the contemplation of the law, entire disability and permanent infirmity, the wife shall be

* A translation of the official statement of a case of a master convicted of the crime of killing his servant, extracted from a printed collection of Chinese law reports, is inserted in the Appendix, No. XXXI., and may contribute something to the illustration both of this particular section, and of the manner in which the laws in general are carried into effect in criminal cases.

strangled

strangled immediately after conviction. — If death ensues, the wife shall be beheaded immediately after conviction.

If any such wife designedly kills her husband by blows, poison, or other means, she shall suffer death by a slow and painful execution.

If any inferior wife strikes her husband, or her husband's first wife, the punishment shall, in each case, be one degree more severe than that of the first wife striking her husband.

If the augmentation renders the punishment capital, the offender shall be strangled; in the latter case, at the usual period; but in the former, immediately after conviction. — In the more atrocious cases, the punishment of the inferior wife shall correspond, and be equal in all respects to that of the first.

A husband shall not be punished for striking his first wife, unless the blow produces a cutting wound; in which case, complaint having been made by the wife to a magistrate, punishment shall be awarded two degrees less than in ordinary cases between equals; but it shall be duly ascertained, before punishment is actually inflicted, whether the parties are desirous or not of a divorce; because, in the latter case, the husband shall be allowed to redeem himself from punishment by a fine.

If the blows, whether struck with a previous intention to kill or not, should prove mortal, the husband shall suffer death, by being strangled at the usual period.

A husband who strikes and wounds any of his inferior wives, shall be punished one degree less severely, than in the case of a husband striking his first wife; if the blows struck by the husband as aforesaid prove mortal, he shall be punished with 100 blows, and three years banishment.

A first wife who is guilty of striking any of the inferior wives of her husband, shall be punished in the same manner as is already provided

vided in the cafe of a hufband ftrking his firft wife. — Accidentally killing in thefe cafes fhall not entail any fine or punifhment.

The offence of ftriking a firft wife's father or mother fhall be punifhed with 60 blows, and one year's banifhment; the offence of ftriking fo as to wound fuch perfons in any manner, fhall be punifhed two degrees more feverely than an equal offence in ordinary cafes; when the injury amounts to total difability and permanent infirmity, the offender fhall be ftrangled: if death enfues from the blows ftruck, either with or without a previous intention to kill, the offender fhall be beheaded at the ufual period.

Four claufes.

SECTION CCCXVI.— *Striking a Relation not within any of the four Degrees.*

In all cafes of affaulting and ftriking, which occur between relations of the fame name, but not within the degrees for which mourning is enjoined, a diftinction fhall be made between the junior and the fenior; and the blow ftruck by a junior fhall accordingly be punifhed one degree more, and that ftruck by a fenior one degree lefs feverely, than an equal offence would have been in ordinary cafes between equals:— Provided, neverthelefs, that fuch aggravation do not render any offence capital that previoufly was not fo. When the act of the offender is already by law a capital offence, it fhall be punifhed as provided in ordinary cafes.

No claufe.

Section CCCXVII. — *Striking a Relation in the second, third, or fourth Degree.*

A junior relation striking his senior in the fourth degree, who is also equi-distant from the parent stock, shall be punished with 100 blows: — if in the third degree, with 60 blows, and one year's banishment; and if in the second degree, with 70 blows, and banishment for a year and a half. — If the relation struck is not only elder but nearer to the parent-stock, the punishment shall be still severer by one degree. — In cases of striking so as to wound, the punishment shall be generally one degree more severe than in ordinary cases, but limited to 100 blows, and perpetual banishment, except when the wound produces permanent disability and infirmity, in which event the offender shall be strangled.

When death ensues, the offender shall be beheaded. If the deceased is an elder relation in the second degree, this sentence shall be executed immediately after conviction; but otherwise, not until the usual period.

A senior relation in the second, third, or fourth degree, shall not be liable to punishment for striking his junior, unless the blow should produce a cutting wound; and in severe cases, the punishment of a senior relation in the fourth degree, shall be reduced one degree; if in the third degree, two degrees; and if in the second degree, three degrees below that provided in ordinary cases of a similar offence between equals. — If the wound occasions death, the offender, in all the above cases, shall, whether killing with or without a previous design to kill, suffer death by being strangled. — Nevertheless, a person who strikes either his junior first cousin, his junior first cousin's children, or his grand-nephew or grand-niece by the brother's side, so as to occasion death

death, but without any direct intention to kill, fhall only be punifhed with 100 blows, and perpetual banifhment to the diftance of 3000 *lee*; if at the fame time guilty of defigning to kill, the offender fhall, in every fuch cafe, be ftrangled *.

Seven claufes.

SECTION CCCXVIII. — *Striking a Relation in the firft Degree.*

Any perfon who is guilty of ftriking his elder brother or fifter, fhall be punifhed, at the leaft, with 90 blows and banifhment for two years and a half; but if guilty of ftriking fo as to wound, with 100 blows and three years banifhment; if guilty of ftriking fo as to caufe a cutting wound, with 100 blows and perpetual banifhment to the diftance of 3000 *lee*. The offence of ftriking and in any manner wounding with a fharp-bladed inftrument fuch aforefaid relations, breaking a bone, or blinding an eye, fhall be punifhed (the offender being the principal, in this as well as in the preceding cafes,) with death, by being ftrangled. If the blow inflicted proves mortal, the principal, and all the acceffaries related as aforefaid to the deceafed, fhall be beheaded. — If a nephew ftrikes his paternal uncle or aunt, or a grandfon his maternal grandfather or grandmother, the punifh-

---

* As almoft every imaginable degree and fpecies of affinity by blood, or connexion by marriage, is diftinguifhed in the Chinefe language by a fpecific and appropriate term, it would have been impoffible, in many cafes, to convey in the tranflation the precife idea, without burthening the text with very tedious and unimportant definitions. It is hoped, however, that the general terms employed, will be deemed by the European reader fufficiently explanatory. — The nice and apparently trifling refinements which extend this book of the laws to an immoderate length, it might alfo, in many inftances, be more fatisfactory to have been juftified in omitting, but thefe details, however uninterefting in themfelves, are characteriftic of the general fyftem of the code, and could not have been retrenched without partially abridging the text, and thus deftroying the unity as well as impairing the authenticity of the tranflation.

ment shall, according to the consequences, be one degree more severe than in the case of striking an elder brother or sister. — If any person accidentally kills or wounds such of his relations, the punishment shall be two degrees less than that of killing or wounding an elder brother or sister, as already provided, and shall not be redeemable, as in other cases of accident, by a fine. — All the principals and accessaries to the crime of intentionally killing any person related as last mentioned, provided each of them is individually so related to the deceased, shall suffer death by a slow and painful execution. — Nevertheless, if the principal and contriver of the murder is a stranger, the accessaries thereto, related as above stated, shall only be punished as accessaries in ordinary cases. — The offence of wounding so as to kill a younger brother or sister, a brother's son or daughter, a grandson or grand-daughter by a daughter, shall, in each case, be punished with 100 blows and three years banishment.

The offence of intentionally killing such junior relations shall subject the offender to a punishment of 100 blows and perpetual banishment to the distance of 2000 *lee*: killing by accident, or wounding in any manner without killing such junior relations, shall not be attended with any punishment*.

Fourteen clauses.

Section CCCXIX. — *Striking a Father or Mother, paternal Grandfather or Grandmother.*

Any person who is guilty of striking his father, mother, paternal grandfather or grandmother; and any wife who is guilty of striking

---

* Notwithstanding this general exemption from punishment, it is provided by the sixth clause, that a senior relation striking his junior maliciously, and so as to occasion entirely disability and incurable infirmity, shall be punished but one degree less severely than already provided in the case of mortally wounding.

her husband's father, mother, paternal grandfather or grandmother, shall suffer death by being beheaded. — Any person who is guilty of killing such a near relation, shall suffer death by a slow and painful execution.

Any person who kills so near a relation, purely by accident, shall still be punished with 100 blows and perpetual banishment to the distance of 3000 *lee*. In the case of wounding purely by accident, the person convicted thereof, shall be punished with 100 blows and three years banishment: in these cases, moreover, the parties shall not be permitted to redeem themselves from punishment by the payment of a fine, as usual in the ordinary cases of accident.

If a father, mother, paternal grandfather or grandmother, chastises a disobedient child or grandchild in a severe and uncustomary manner, so that he or she dies, the party so offending shall be punished with 100 blows. — When any of the aforesaid relations are guilty of killing such disobedient child or grandchild designedly, the punishment shall be extended to 60 blows and one year's banishment*.

In the case of a mother-in-law or adopted mother so offending, the punishment shall be increased one degree beyond that provided in the pre-

---

* It is manifest from this article, that parents are not in any case absolutely entrusted with a power over the lives of their children, and that accordingly the crime of infanticide, however prevalent it may be supposed to be in China, is not in fact either directly sanctioned by the government, or agreeable to the general spirit of the laws and institutions of the empire. This practice, so revolting to the feelings of humanity, must certainly be acknowledged to exist in China, and even to be in some degree tolerated, but there are considerable reasons for supposing that the extent has been often over-rated; and at all events it does not seem allowable to lay any very great stress upon the existence of such a practice, as a proof of the cruelty or insensibility of the Chinese character. — Even the dreadful crime of a parent destroying its offspring, is extenuated by the wretched and desperate situation to which the labouring poor in China, to whom the practice of infanticide is admitted to be in general confined, must, by the universal and almost compulsory custom of early marriages, often be reduced, of having large and increasing families, while, owing to the already excessive population of the country, they have not the most distant prospect of being able to maintain them.

ceding case; but if the connexion had been previously dissolved by a divorce between the parents, or otherwise, the crime of killing, either with or without a previous design to kill, shall be punished with death, by being strangled. — If a father, mother, paternal grandfather or grandmother chastises a son's or grandson's wife, or an adopted child or grandchild, in a severe and uncustomary manner, so as to produce a permanent injury, they shall suffer the punishment of 80 blows.

If the chastisement produces total disability and irremediable infirmity, the punishment shall be increased to 90 blows, and in every such case, the adopted child and own child's wife shall be sent back to the family whence they were taken.

In the case of the wife, the marriage present shall be refunded, and ten *leang* or ounces of silver added to it by the offending party, towards the support of the sufferer; in that of the child, the two families shall raise jointly the sum requisite for that purpose. — If the blows given as aforesaid prove mortal, the offenders shall be punished with 100 blows and three years banishment: if the blows which proved mortal were struck with an intention to kill, the punishment shall be further increased to 100 blows and perpetual banishment to the distance of 2000 *lee*.

If, in any of these cases, the son's or grandson's wife was not the first or principal wife, the punishment shall be proportionably less in each case by two degrees, and the family shall not be compelled in any such instance, to concur in providing for the support of the wife, after she is restored to her family.

If a son or grandson abuses and strikes his father mother, paternal grandfather or grandmother, or a wife her husband's father, mother, paternal grandfather or grandmother; and such father, mother, grandfather or grandmother, in consequence, strikes or beats to death such child or grandchild; or if such child or grandchild being disobedient, his or her relations as aforesaid chastise him or her in a lawful and customary manner,

manner, and under such chastisement he or she accidentally and unexpectedly dies; or lastly, if by mere chance or accident any person is killed by any of his or her aforesaid near relations, the party convicted of homicide under such circumstances, shall not be liable to any punishment.

Nine clauses.

Section CCCXX.—*Wives striking their Husband's Relations.*

A principal or other wife striking any of her husband's relations in the first, second, third, or fourth degree, shall be punished in the same manner as the husband would have been, had he been guilty of striking such persons, except that, unless the blows occasion death, the punishment of the wife shall not exceed 100 blows and perpetual banishment. — If the blows occasion death, the wife shall, in the case of a senior relation, be beheaded at the usual period, and in the case of a junior relation, strangled at the usual period. — In the case of a principal wife, striking so as to kill her husband's brother's children, the punishment shall amount to 100 blows and perpetual banishment to the distance of 3000 *lee*; but in the case of killing such persons designedly, the punishment shall be that of death, by being strangled. — Any other wife than the principal, striking her husband's junior relations, shall (in exception to the foregoing rule) be punished as severely as is provided by the laws in ordinary cases between equals.

A senior relation in any of the four degrees, striking his junior relation's principal wife, shall be punished one degree less severely than in ordinary cases between equals. — If striking any of the inferior wives, the punishment shall be further reduced one degree.

Nevertheless, if death ensues, whether or not in consequence of a previous intention to kill, and whether the deceased had been or not a principal wife, the offender shall be strangled.

If a younger brother or sister strikes an elder brother's principal wife, the punishment shall be one degree more severe than in ordinary cases between equals.

If an elder brother or sister strikes a younger brother's wife; if an elder brother's principal wife strikes her husband's younger brother or sister, or younger brother's wife, the punishment shall, in each case, be one degree less severe than in ordinary cases; and when the wife who is struck is not the principal one, the punishment shall be further reduced one degree.

A man guilty of striking the husband of any of his sisters, or any of his principal wife's brothers, and a principal wife guilty of striking the husband of any of her husband's sisters, shall only be punished as in ordinary cases. — Nevertheless, within the limits of offences not capital, the punishment in the case of an inferior wife offending shall be one degree more severe than in that of the principal one, that is to say, one degree more severe than in ordinary cases between equals — If an inferior wife strikes any of her husband's other inferior wives' children, the punishment shall be two degrees less severe than in ordinary cases between equals; but if any such inferior wife strikes any of her husband's principal wife's children, the punishment shall be the same as in ordinary cases between equals.

If a principal wife's child strikes his or her father's inferior wife, the punishment shall be one degree more severe than in ordinary cases. — If a child of one of the inferior wive's should strike any other of the inferior wives, except its own mother, the punishment shall be further increased two degrees; these several augmentations shall not however have effect so as to render any punishment capital, that would not have been so in ordinary cases. — When death ensues, the punishment of such offenders shall be inflicted in the degree and manner provided in the case of similar offences committed between equals in ordinary cases.

Two clauses.

Section CCCXXI. — *Striking a Wife's Children by her former Husband.*

When any person strikes his wife's children by a former husband, he shall, if living with such children under the same roof, be punished two degrees, but if living separately, one degree only, less severely than in ordinary cases between equals.

Whenever in such cases, the blows struck prove mortal, the offenders shall suffer death, by being strangled at the usual period.

Any person striking his or her step-father, shall be punished with 60 blows, and one year's banishment.

In all aggravated cases, the punishment shall be one degree more severe if the parties live separately, and two degrees more severe than in ordinary cases, if they live under the same roof: but these augmentations shall not, in any case, render the punishment capital: — when death ensues, the offenders shall be beheaded, whether the deceased was struck with or without a previous intention of killing.

When the parties neither lived under the same roof at the time, nor had ever lived so previously, this law shall not take effect; and all reciprocal offences between them shall be punished as in ordinary cases between equals.

No clause.

Section CCCXXII. — *Widows striking the Parents of their deceased Husbands.*

Any principal or inferior wife striking her husband's father or mother, paternal grandfather or grandmother, after the death of such husband, and even after having entered into a second marriage, shall (except in the case of her having been divorced from such former husband)

husband) be liable to the same punishment for each offence, as if such former husband had been still living. — In like manner, any person striking his or her deceased son's widows, except as aforesaid, in the case of a divorce having taken place, shall, even after such wife had entered into a second marriage, only be liable to the punishment provided in the case of striking such a relation during the son's lifetime.

When however a divorce has taken place, the connexion between the parties and their relations is thereby totally dissolved, and all reciprocal injuries between them are accordingly punishable in the same manner as between equals in ordinary cases.

When a master strikes his former slave, or a slave his former master, the parties shall be punished as in ordinary cases between slaves and freemen, the connexion which had previously existed having been broken by the sale and purchase. — But if a master manumits or releases his slave, the original right and obligation not having been transferred to another, and the original connexion being still in some sense unbroken, the provisions contained in this law shall not take effect, and punishment shall therefore be awarded in all such cases in the same manner as if no manumission had taken place.

No clause.

SECTION CCCXXIII. — *Striking in Defence of a Parent.*

Whoever, upon perceiving a father, mother, paternal grandfather or grandmother, to be struck by any person, immediately interposes in defence of such near relation, and strikes the aggressor, shall, unless striking such a blow as to produce a cutting wound, be entirely justified and free from responsibility; and even if the wound inflicted by the individual who interposes under such circumstances is severe, he shall be punished punifhed lefs feverely by three degrees than in ordinary cafes; excepting only thofe inftances in which the blows ftruck prove mortal, when the punifhment fhall be the fame as in ordinary cafes. To entitle, however, any perfon to the benefit of this law, it muft always be ftrictly proved that the blows were inflicted on the impulfe of the moment, and actually in defence of fuch aforefaid relation.

If a fon or grandfon, upon the event of a father or mother, a paternal grandfather or grandmother having been murdered, inftead of complaining to the magiftrate, takes revenge by killing the murderer, he fhall be punifhed with 60 blows; fuch fon or grandfon fhall be however entirely juftified, if he kills the murderer upon the impulfe of the moment, and at the inftant that the murder is committed. — At the fame time, this law is not by any means to be pleaded in juftification of a fon or grandfon, who enters jointly into a quarrel or affray with his parents or grandparents; and accordingly the offenders in all fuch inftances fhall be punifhed either as principals, or as acceffaries, as the cafe may be, in the fame manner as they would have been in ordinary cafes:— And altho' it fhall be lawful to defend any of the aforefaid near relations, not only againft ftrangers, but alfo againft other relations lefs nearly connected, it fhall not be allowed to ftrike any of the latter relations in return, and all fons or grandfons who are guilty thereof fhall be punifhed in the ordinary manner according to the law in fuch cafes provided.

When any perfon kills the murderer of any of his other relations, inftead of lawfully complaining to a magiftrate, he fhall, if it appears upon the trial, that he was really actuated by no other motive befide that of revenging the death of fuch relation, only be punifhed with 100 blows.

Three claufes.

END OF THE THIRD BOOK OF THE SIXTH DIVISION.

BOOK IV.

ABUSIVE LANGUAGE.*

SECTION CCCXXIV.—*Abusive Language between Equals.*

IN ordinary cases, all persons guilty of employing abusive language shall be liable to a punishment of 10 blows; and persons abusing each other, shall be punishable with 10 blows respectively.

No clause.

SECTION CCCXXV.—*Abusive language to an Officer of Government.*

When any civil or military officer of a district addresses abusive language to a magistrate invested with especial powers by the Emperor; when any private individual addresses abusive language to the governor, or other superior officer having authority in his district; when any private soldier addresses abusive language to an officer having a command directly or indirectly over him; and lastly, when any person having a civil or military employment in any public office, or under any civil or military officer of government, addresses abusive language to an officer of government having authority over him, and being of the fifth or any superior rank; the offender in each of these cases shall be punished with 100 blows.

* It is observed in the Chinese commentary that " opprobrious and insulting language " having naturally a tendency to produce quarrels and affrays, this book of the laws " is expressly provided for its prevention and punishment." It is not however to be supposed that laws of this nature are often, or very strictly enforced.

Any person who, having a civil or military employment as in the case last mentioned, abuses an officer having immediate authority over him, but yet only of the sixth or of any still lower rank, shall be liable to a punishment of 70 blows only. — If the inferior officer of government who had been abused, was only the assessor or deputy of the tribunal or public office to which the person abusing him belonged, the punishment shall be further reduced to 60 blows: and in this, as well as in all the preceding cases, in order to convict the offender, it is necessary that the abusive language shall have been actually heard by the person to whom it was addressed.

Two clauses.

SECTION CCCXXVI. — *Abusive Language between Officers of the same Tribunal.*

If, in any government tribunal or public office, abusive language is addressed to the presiding member, by the deputy thereof, or by the presiding member of any government tribunal or public office which is subordinate, the punishment shall, in each case, amount to 80 blows, provided the presiding member who is abused is of the fifth or any still higher rank; otherwise the punishment shall be 50 blows only. — If the abusive language is addressed by the assessor of any tribunal or public office to the presiding member thereof, the punishment shall, agreeably to the distinction made in the preceding cases, amount to 60 or to 30 blows, according as such president is or is not of the fifth or any superior order of rank in the state.

In no case shall the offender be convicted, unless the abusive language had been actually heard by the person to whom it was addressed.

No clause.

Section CCCXXVII.—*Abusive Language from a Slave to his Master.*

A slave guilty of addressing abusive language to his master shall suffer death, by being strangled at the usual period.

If guilty of addressing abusive language to his master's relations in the first degree, or to his master's maternal grandfather or grandmother, he shall be punished with 80 blows, and two years banishment:— If addressing abusive language to his master's relations in the second degree, the punishment shall be 80 blows; if in the third degree, 70 blows; if in the fourth degree, 60 blows.

A hired servant addressing abusive language to his master, shall be punished with 80 blows, and two years banishment; if to his master's relations in the first degree, or maternal grandfather or grandmother, his punishment shall amount to 100 blows; if to his master's relations in the second degree, to 60 blows: if to the relations in the third degree, to 50 blows; and if to the relations in the fourth degree, to 40 blows.— In these cases, as well as others, the abusive language must have been heard by the person to whom it was addressed, and such person must always be the complainant.

No clause.

Section CCCXXVIII.—*Abusive Language to an elder Relation.*

Any person who is guilty of addressing abusive language to an elder relation in the fourth degree, equi-distant from the parent stock, shall be punished with 50 blows: if to a relation in the third degree, under similar circumstances, with 60 blows: and if to a relation as aforesaid, in the second degree, with 70 blows; but when such relation is also one or more generations nearer to the parent stock, the punishment shall be more severe, in each case, than above provided, by one degree.

Whoever addresses abusive language to his elder brother or sister, shall be punished with 100 blows: whoever abuses his paternal uncle or aunt, or his maternal grandfather or grandmother, shall be punished one degree more severely than in the case last mentioned: — but, as it has been stated in the preceding articles, the law can only be enforced when the person to whom the abusive language was addressed, actually heard it, and is himself the complainant.

No clause.

SECTION CCCXXIX.—*Abusive Language to a Parent, Paternal Grandfather or Grandmother.*

A child or grandchild who is guilty of addressing abusive language to his or her father or mother, paternal grandfather or grandmother; a wife who is guilty of addressing abusive language to her husband's father or mother, paternal grandfather or grandmother, shall in every case suffer death, by being strangled; provided always however, that the persons abused, themselves complain thereof to the magistrates, and had themselves heard the abusive language which had been addressed to them.

One clause.

SECTION CCCXXX.—*Abusive Language from a Wife to her Husband's Relations.*

A principal or inferior wife who is guilty of addressing abusive language to any of her husband's relations within the four degrees, shall be liable to the same punishment as her husband would have been for using towards such persons the same language.—An inferior wife abusing her husband or husband's principal wife, shall be punished with 80 blows.—A husband abusing his wife's father or mother, shall be be liable to a punishment of 60 blows; but in all cases such abusive language must, as already observed, have been heard and complained of by the parties to whom it was addressed.

There is no clause respecting abusive language addressed by a principal wife to her husband, as the interposition of the laws can scarcely be supposed to be necessary; yet if such a case should occur, the magistrates may lawfully award a punishment of 50 blows, according to the law respecting offences against propriety.

No clause.

SECTION CCCXXXI. — *Abusive Language addressed by a Widow to her deceased Husband's Parents.*

If any principal or inferior wife is guilty of addressing abusive language to her husband's father or mother, paternal grandfather or grandmother, after the death of such husband, and even after having entered into a second marriage, she shall (except in the case of her having been divorced from such former husband,) be liable to the same punishment for each offence, as if such husband were still living.

A slave addressing abusive language to his former master, shall only be punished as in ordinary cases, the connexion between the parties having been broken by the transfer to another master; but a slave addressing abusive language to the master who had manumitted or released him, shall be liable to the same punishment as he would have been if he had continued in such master's service.

No clause.

END OF THE FOURTH BOOK OF THE SIXTH DIVISION.

BOOK V.

INDICTMENTS AND INFORMATIONS.

Section CCCXXXII. — *Irregularity in presenting Informations.*

ALL the subjects of the empire, whether soldiers or citizens, who have complaints and informations to lay before the officers of government, shall address themselves in the first instance, to the lowest tribunal of justice within the district to which they belong, from which the cognizance of the affair may be transferred to the superior tribunals in regular gradation *. — Any individual who, instead of addressing himself to the proper magistrate within his district, proceeds at once to lay his complaint and information before a superior tribunal, shall be punished with 50 blows, although his complaint should be just, and his information correct.

It is however lawful to appeal to a superior magistrate, when the inferior officer of justice refuses to receive the information and complaint, or decides thereon unjustly; but not otherwise.

Whoever, in order to present an information, detains an officer of justice in his public progress; and whoever, for the same purpose, summons any officer of justice to his tribunal by beat of drum, shall be punished with 100 blows, if his information be false and complaint groundless; and if he should be likewise guilty of the crime of a false and malicious accusation against any person, he shall be punished as

* For an exemplification of the ordinary routine of judicial proceedings in the more serious criminal cases, see the official report of the investigation of charges against an English seaman, in the Appendix, No. XI.

much more severely as the law applicable to such cases of criminality may authorize.

Nevertheless, if his cause is found to be a just one, the irregularity of his proceedings shall be pardoned *.

Twenty clauses.

SECTION CCCXXXIII. — *Anonymous Informations.*

Any person who addresses and presents an information and complaint to an officer of government, containing direct criminal charges against a particular individual, without having inserted therein his (the informant's) proper name and family name, shall, although the charges should prove true, be punished with death, by being strangled at the usual period.

Whenever any such anonymous information or complaint is discovered, it shall be immediately burned or otherwise destroyed; and if the person who accidentally finds such a document, instead of so doing, presents it to a magistrate or some other officer of government, he shall be punished with 80 blows.

Any officer of government who, nevertheless, takes upon himself to act upon any such anonymous information and complaint, shall be punishable with 100 blows; and no person, whether accused justly or not, shall be liable to be in any case convicted or punished on the ground of anonymous charges.

---

* It appears from this and other articles of the code, that an appeal from the lower to the higher tribunals is allowed both in civil as well as criminal causes, not, as has been supposed, in criminal causes only; indeed there are no traces of any such distinction, as that of civil and criminal, in the jurisprudence of the Chinese; but it is probable, that as those causes which might be denominated *civil*, are, from the ordinary tenure of property and other circumstances, of comparatively small importance in China, they are not necessarily referred to the decision of the higher courts, and therefore, generally speaking, decided by the officers of the districts in which such disputes originate.

Every officer of government who has unlawfully acted as aforesaid, shall likewise be obliged to make a compensation of ten ounces of silver to each of the persons whom, on account of anonymous charges, he may have summoned to his tribunal.

According to this law, all those also shall be punished who, under assumed or forged names, pretend to give information to the officers of government of any undiscovered crimes or other secret and hidden transactions; or who, availing themselves of blank stamped papers belonging to others, fill them up with accusations, and prevail upon or bribe the soldiers or other attendants of tribunals, to deliver them to the sitting magistrates.

This law shall not however extend to those who may have prepared, or be in possession of, such anonymous informations, unless they shall likewise have been instrumental in their presentation to the officers of government; nor shall this law extend to those anonymous informations, which, although actually presented, merely contain general censure and abuse, without precise charges of crimes against particular individuals.

Three clauses.

SECTION CCCXXXIV. — *Neglecting or declining to receive Informations.*

When an information concerning a charge of high treason or rebellion is regularly presented to an officer of government, if he does not immediately receive and act thereon, that is to say, take measures for seizing the culprits, and preventing the progress of such disorders, he shall be liable to a punishment of 100 blows and three years banishment, although no evil consequences should ensue from his neglect: but if through his inattention, considerable numbers are suffered to assemble tumultuously, attacking fortified stations, ravaging the country, and distressing the inhabitants, such officer of government shall suffer death, by being beheaded at the usual period.

In like manner, any officer of government who declines to receive, and to act upon an information containing a charge of parricide, or of some other enormous crime of a private nature, shall be punished with 100 blows.

If the rejected information contained a charge of robbery, murder, or of any like offences, the officer of government shall be punished with 80 blows.

If the offence charged in the rejected information, was a breach of the laws against quarrelling and fighting, or of those concerning marriage and landed property, or concerning any other laws of the same class, the punishment of the officer of government for not receiving the same, shall be two degrees only less than that to which the accused person would have been liable, except that it shall not, in any of these cases, exceed 80 blows. — If such officer of government had been bribed by the accused party, he shall be punished proportionably to the amount of the bribe, according to the law against receiving a bribe for an unlawful purpose, whenever the punishment is greater than that provided by the law above stated.

When the accuser and the accused party belong to different districts and jurisdictions, the magistrates having authority over the latter, shall take cognizance of, and pronounce judgment upon the charges made in the district of the former, and if he should endeavour to excuse himself from such duty, he shall be punished according to this law.

When any cause comes before the tribunal of the viceroy, sub-viceroy, or ordinary or extraordinary judge in any province, which cause had either not been reported at all, or if reported, not finally judged and determined by the magistrate to whose jurisdiction it belonged, it shall be duly registered, and an entry made of the particulars thereof,

by

by the viceroy or other superior officer having cognizance thereof, in order that a certain limited period may be fixed for its final determination by the proper magistrate; and if, when such magistrate commits any mistake, or is guilty of any culpable delay, the viceroy and other superior officers connive thereat, instead of rectifying or accelerating the decision, as the case may require, they shall be liable to the same punishment as the inferior magistrates.

If, in any case of an official report, or of a criminal information having been laid before the proper officer or magistrate, such magistrate refuses to receive the same and act thereon, or if, after having received, he acts upon it unjustly and illegally, the officers and magistrates of superior tribunals are bound to take cognizance thereof in regular gradation and succession, and if the said superior officers excuse themselves from receiving and acting upon such appeals from inferior jurisdictions, or transfer the cognizance of them to a deputy, or send them back unexamined to the magistrates from whose tribunals the appeals had been made, they shall, in each case, be punishable under this law.

In general, every magistrate and tribunal shall, conformably to the extent of their powers and jurisdiction, not only receive and undertake to investigate, but also bring to a final issue and adjudication, each of the several criminal causes and questions on official business that lawfully come before them; and whenever they, on the contrary, depute or instruct other magistrates to continue any such investigations in their place and stead, the magistrates and members of tribunals so offending shall be liable to punishment, in the same manner as above provided.

Nine clauses.

SECTION CCCXXXV. — *Informations which muſt be transferred to the Cognizance of others.*

Whenever any information is laid before a magiſtrate, who is related by blood or by marriage to the accuſer or to the accuſed, who was educated by, or had ever ſerved under either party, or who, laſtly, had been habitually the enemy or public adverſary of either; in all ſuch caſes the magiſtrate muſt decline to act thereon, and ſhall therefore transfer it forthwith to another juriſdiction.

Any magiſtrate who takes cognizance of a cauſe under ſuch circumſtances, ſhall be liable to a puniſhment of 40 blows, although he ſhould have pronounced a juſt and impartial ſentence: — otherwiſe, he will be liable to the ſeverer puniſhment attending an intentional deviation from juſtice.

No clauſe.

SECTION CCCXXXVI. — *Falſe and malicious Informations*.*

Whoever lays before a magiſtrate a falſe and malicious information, in which ſome perſon is expreſsly charged with a crime puniſhable with any number of blows, not exceeding 50, ſhall ſuffer a puniſhment two degrees more ſevere than that which the accuſed would have merited had the accuſation been true. — If the crime falſely alleged was puniſhable

---

* The following long article, by which the reſponſibility of each individual for the truth of the charges he may bring forward publicly before a magiſtrate, is, in every imaginable caſe, preciſely determined, ſeems in great meaſure to correſpond in its object with the laws in force in European countries, againſt (what is denominated by us) wilful and corrupt perjury.

The Chineſe do not indeed ſpecifically puniſh the breach of an oath, becauſe although frequently introduced into the private inveſtigation and adjuſtment of diſputes, oaths are never required, or even admitted, in judicial proceedings.

with more than 50 blows, or with temporary or perpetual banishment, the punishment of the accuser shall be three degrees more severe than that to which the accused is rendered liable; but shall not, in these, or in any of the preceding cases, be so increased as to become capital.

When the accused person, having been condemned upon such false accusation as aforesaid, shall have proceeded to the place to which he had been sentenced to be either temporarily or perpetually banished; although he should have been afterwards speedily recalled on a discovery of his innocence, an estimate shall be made and verified before the magistrate, of the expences he may have incurred by his journey, that the false accuser may be compelled to reimburse him to the full amount; and the false accuser shall likewise be obliged to redeem, or re-purchase for him, any lands or tenements which he may have sold or mortgaged to defray such expences. — Moreover, if such unmerited banishment should occasion the death of any of the relations of the innocent person, who may have followed him to his destination, the false accuser shall suffer death, by being strangled; and besides the reimbursement aforesaid, half his remaining property shall be forfeited to the use of the innocent person. — When any person is falsely accused of a capital offence, and upon such accusation has been condemned and executed, the false accuser shall be either strangled or beheaded, according to the manner in which the innocent person had been executed, and half his property shall be forfeited as in the preceding instance.

If the execution of the sentence of death against the innocent person had been prevented by a timely discovery of the falsehood of the accusation, the false accuser shall be punished with 100 blows and perpetual banishment to the distance of 3000 *lee*, and moreover subjected to extra-service during three years.

If the false accuser is proved to be really so poor as to be unable to reimburse the innocent person to the amount of his expences, his punishment

punishment shall not be aggravated on account of such incapacity. — If the innocent person should in his complaint or appeal to the magistrates, attempt to aggravate the guilt of the false accuser, by falsely alleging the death of a relation, or upon some other pretext, he shall, in his turn, be liable to the punishment of a false accuser, and the offence of the former shall be punished only according to its real extent.

When any person accuses another of more offences than one, if the lesser charge proves false, and the greater true; or among charges of equal criminality, if one only proves true, and the rest false, the accuser shall, in both cases, be excused from the penalties and punishment of a false and malicious information.

When, on the other hand, any person accuses another of two or more offences, whereof the lesser only proves true; and when in the case of a single offence having been charged by one person against another, the statement thereof is found to exceed the truth; upon either supposition, if, the punishment of the falsely alleged, or falsely aggravated offence, had been actually inflicted in consequence of such false accusation, the difference (estimated according to the established mode of computation hereafter exemplified,) between the falsely alleged and the actually committed offence, or between the falsely alleged greater, and the truly alleged lesser offence, shall be inflicted on the false accuser: — but if punishment, conformably to the nature of the falsely alleged, or falsely aggravated offence, shall not have actually been inflicted, having been prevented by a timely discovery of the falsehood of the accusation, the false accuser shall be permitted to redeem, according to an established scale*, the whole of the punishment which would have been due to him in the former case, provided it does not exceed

---

* See the introductory table. — The fines, it will be perceived, are little more than nominal.

100 blows; but if it should exceed 100 blows, the 100 blows shall be inflicted, and he shall be only permitted to redeem the excess.

TABLE of Reference in Cases of false and malicious Informations.

Degree.	Actual Punishment.		Estimated Equivalent.
	Blows.	Banishment.	Blows.
1.	10	none	10
2.	20	none	20
3.	30	none	30
4.	40	none	40
5.	50	none	50
6.	60	none	60
7.	70	none	70
8.	80	none	80
9.	90	none	90
10.	100	none	100
11.	60	for one year	120
12.	70	for one year and a half	140
13.	80	for two years	160
14.	90	for two years and a half	180
15.	100	for three years.	200
16.	100	for life, distance 2000 *lee*	220 ⎫
17.	100	for life, distance 2500 *lee*	240 ⎬ or 240
18.	100	for life, distance 3000 *lee*	260 ⎭

Banishment for life shall be estimated at 240 blows, when compared with any of the inferior degrees of punishment.

The use of the foregoing table may be illustrated by the following examples:

1. When the alleged and real offence are both punishable with the bamboo; as for instance, alleging a blow producing a bruise, and punishable with 40 blows, when abusive language, which is punishable with 10 blows, had been the only offence committed.— The difference in this case is 30 blows, and shall be inflicted on the accuser, if the accused had actually undergone the aggravated punishment, but otherwise may be redeemed.

2. When

2. When the alleged offence is punishable with temporary banishment, and the real offence, with the bamboo only; as for instance, alleging a blow occasioning a fracture of a limb, or violent injury to the body, which offence is punishable with 100 blows and three years banishment, when in fact, only a bruise had been inflicted, which latter offence is punishable with 40 blows; the former punishment is in this case equivalent, according to the preceding table, to 200 blows, and the difference will therefore be 160 blows, equivalent (according to the same table) to 80 blows and two years banishment.

If in any such instance, the accused has been condemned to suffer, and had actually proceeded to undergo the aggravated punishment, the accuser shall be punished with 80 blows and two years banishment; otherwise he shall suffer 100 blows, and redeem the remaining 60 by the payment of a fine.

3. When the alleged offence is punishable with perpetual banishment, and the real offence with the bamboo only; as for instance, alleging a blow struck so as to break both thigh bones, which is punishable with 100 blows and perpetual banishment to the distance of 3000 *lee*, when only a bruise had been inflicted, which is punishable with 40 blows: now the latter punishment being generally estimated at 240 blows, the difference will be 200 blows, which, again is estimated to be equivalent to 100 blows and three years banishment; accordingly, if the accused had been condemned to suffer, and had actually proceeded to undergo the aggravated punishment, the accuser shall be punished with 100 blows and three years banishment; but otherwise he shall only suffer the 100 blows, and be permitted to redeem himself from the remaining punishment of banishment.

4. When the alleged and real offence are both punishable with temporary banishment; as for instance, alleging a theft to the amount to ninety ounces of silver, which offence is punishable with 100 blows and three years banishment, when it is afterwards proved that no more than fifty

fifty ounces had been ſtolen, which latter offence is puniſhable only with 60 blows and one year's baniſhment: ſince by the preceding table the former offence is equivalent to 200 and the latter to 120 blows, the difference will be 80 blows, and ſhall be accordingly inflicted on the accuſer if the accuſed had undergone the heavier puniſhment, but otherwiſe, be redeemable by the eſtabliſhed fine.

5. When the alleged offence is puniſhable with perpetual and the real offence with temporary baniſhment; as for inſtance, alleging the offence of ſacrilegiouſly digging up another man's burying ground, ſo as to lay a coffin bare, which offence is puniſhable with 100 blows and perpetual baniſhment to the diſtance of 3000 *lee*, when it afterwards appears on examination, that the ſacrilegious digging, not having been carried to the extent of laying bare any coffin, was puniſhable only with 100 blows and three years baniſhment; the former puniſhment being eſtimated at 240 and the latter at 200 blows, the difference will be 40 blows, and as ſuch ſhall be inflicted on the accuſer if the heavier puniſhment had been actually executed upon the accuſed, but otherwiſe, be redeemable by the ordinary fine.

6. Laſtly, when the alleged and real offence are both puniſhable with perpetual baniſhment, but to a greater diſtance in the former caſe than in the latter; as for inſtance, alleging a theft of one hundred and twenty ounces of ſilver, which is puniſhable with 100 blows and perpetual baniſhment to the diſtance of 3000 *lee*, when in fact, no more than one hundred ounces had been ſtolen, and the theft therefore puniſhable only with 100 blows and perpetual baniſhment to the diſtance of 2000 *lee*. In this caſe, by referring to the eſtimated equivalents of the ſeveral degrees of perpetual baniſhment in the table, as compared with each other, it will be found that the difference amounts to 40 blows; and therefore puniſhment to that extent ſhall be inflicted upon the accuſer,

if the accufed had actually undergone the aggravated punifhment; but otherwife fhall be redeemable as in the preceding cafes.

In every cafe, when an offence has been committed which is not capital, the perfon falfely alleging another offence which is capital, or falfely aggravating the offence committed, fo as to make it appear capital, fhall, in the event of the accufed perfon having been condemned and executed, fuffer death in the fame manner; in the event of execution not having been the confequence of fuch falfe information, the falfe accufers fhall be punifhed with 100 blows and perpetual banifhment to the diftance of 3000 *lee*; but not be liable to the extra fervice ftated in a fimilar cafe previoufly defcribed.

Moreover, no aggravated or exaggerated ftatement of an offence, on the part of the informant, fhall be confidered or punifhed as fuch, however much the offence may have been falfely alleged to be greater than it afterwards proves to be on examination, provided fuch exaggeration does not, according to the exifting laws, expofe the offender to a feverer punifhment: as for inftance; alleging the acceptance of a bribe to the extent of two hundred ounces, when one hundred and thirty ounces was the real amount of the bribe; now, becaufe the receipt of a bribe to any extent beyond one hundred and twenty ounces is equally punifhable with death by being ftrangled at the ufual period, the additional charge againft the offender of feventy ounces, does not in this cafe tend to aggravate his punifhment. — If the different charges are not made againft one and the fame, but againft different perfons, the truth of the charges againft one or more perfons fhall not be deemed any palliation of the offence of falfely accufing other perfons, and all fuch falfe accufations fhall be therefore regarded and punifhed as diftinct cafes.

When any of the magiftrates fuperintending the public tribunals are guilty of preferring falfe accufations, or any public officers having high judicial and minifterial powers, addrefs falfe accufations of each other

other to the Emperor, they shall be punished according to this law; and, in the latter case, the least punishment incurred, will be that provided by law in ordinary cases of a false statement being wilfully made in an addrefs to his Imperial Majesty.

If the relations of a prisoner, who had brought himself into that situation by his own misconduct, and who had therefore in fact suffered no injustice, groundlessly appeal and complain to the tribunals of government against his confinement and condemnation, they shall suffer a punishment three degrees less than that incurred by the prisoner, such reduced punishment being at the same time limited to the extent of 100 blows.

If any such justly condemned person, after having undergone the sentence of the law, whether of corporal punishment with the bamboo, or the same, together with the addition of subsequent banishment, should himself groundlessly complain of his having suffered injustice, and attempt to frame and exhibit before the public tribunals, charges of culpability against the magistrates and clerks who had tried and condemned him, his punishment shall be three degrees more severe than that of the crime which he falsely alleges against such magistrates and clerks; but nevertheless shall not exceed 100 blows, and perpetual banishment to the distance of 3000 *lee*.

If a person, justly condemned as aforesaid, brings forward a false accusation previous to the complete execution of his sentence of banishment, his punishment shall be further regulated according to the law provided for the cases of offences committed by exiles during the period of their banishment.

Twenty-three clauses.

SECTION CCCXXXVII. — *Informations against Relations.*

A son accusing his father or mother; a grandson his paternal grandfather or grandmother; a principal or inferior wife, her husband, or her

her husband's father or mother, paternal grandfather or grandmother, shall, in each case, be punished with 100 blows and three years banishment, even if the accusation prove true: the individuals so accused by their relations, if they voluntarily surrender and plead guilty, shall in each case also, be entitled to pardon.

In any of the above instances, if the charge should prove either in part or wholly false, the accuser shall suffer death by being strangled.

A junior relation accusing an elder relation in the first degree; a grandson accusing his maternal grandfather or grandmother, or an inferior wife accusing her husband's first wife, shall in each case suffer 100 blows, although the accusation should prove true. — In like manner, justly accusing an elder relation in the second degree, shall subject the accuser to be punished with 90 blows; an elder relation in the third degree, with 80 blows; and in the fourth degree, with 70 blows.

In the first of these cases, if the accused surrenders voluntarily, he or she shall be pardoned; in the other cases, the punishment shall be three degrees less than if the parties had been accused under the same circumstances by strangers. — In all these cases, if the accusation should prove to be false, the punishment of the junior relation accusing, shall be three degrees greater than when falsely accusing strangers in ordinary cases, except that such augmentation shall not in any case have the effect of rendering the punishment capital:—in cases of falsely accusing an elder relation beyond the fourth degree, the punishment shall exceed that provided in ordinary cases, by two degrees.

From the provisions of this law, an exception shall be made in favour of all those who justly accuse their relations of treason, rebellion, concealment of criminals, and the suppression or compromise of any of the greater offences against the state; and also in the case of the step-mother, mother in law, or natural mother killing the accuser's father; or the accuser's adopted mother killing his natural mother; or lastly in cases of

the

the accuser having been himself robbed or maltreated by a relation. — In all the cases herein excepted, it shall be lawful to complain to the magistrates.

When justly accusing a junior relation in the first or second degree, or a son in law, if the accused voluntarily surrenders and confesses his offence, he shall be pardoned.

In the case of a relation in the third or fourth degree, the punishment of the accused under the same circumstances, shall be reduced three degrees.

Falsely accusing a junior relation in the first degree, shall be punished three degrees less severely than in ordinary cases: in the second degree, two degrees less; and in the third or fourth degree, one degree less:—a husband falsely accusing his principal wife, or a principal wife falsely accusing any of the inferior wives of her husband, shall be only liable to the ordinary punishment reduced three degrees. — The slaves of any family accusing, whether truly or falsely, the master thereof, or any of his relations within the four degrees, shall be liable to the same punishment as the sons or grandsons in such family would have been, for accusing truly or falsely their elder relations within the same degrees of affinity.

When accusing such persons truly and justly, the punishment of hired servants shall be one degree less than that of slaves; but if falsely and unjustly, the same.

When slaves or hired servants are accused by their masters, or their masters relations, they shall not be entitled to pardon, as junior relations are stated to be in the preceding cases, although voluntarily surrendering themselves and acknowledging their offences.

A parent falsely accusing his child; a paternal or maternal grandfather or grandmother their grandchild, or grandson's principal or inferior wife; a husband his inferior wife, or a master his slave or hired servant, shall not, in any case, be punishable. — Although the mutual accusations of fathers

and

and mothers in law on the one hand, and of sons in law on the other, are generally to be judged according to the provisions of this law; yet, when the connexion between the parties shall have been dissolved by long separation, by a divorce between the husband and wife, or by the death of one of them; or lastly, by any offence in direct violation of the connexion originally subsisting between the parties, the laws shall be administered as in ordinary cases between strangers.

Three clauses.

Section CCCXXXVIII. — *Disobedience to Parents.*

All children and grand-children who are disobedient to the instructions and commands of their fathers, mothers, paternal grandfathers and grandmothers, or who do not adequately provide for their support and sustenance, shall be punishable with 100 blows.

This law shall nevertheless only be understood to apply to cases of wilful disobedience of lawful instructions and commands, and to cases of wilful neglect of maintenance, on the part of such children or grand-children as have the means thereof; and it shall be moreover necessary in each case, that the near relation so disobeyed or neglected, should personally complain of, and inform against the offender.

Three clauses.

Section CCCXXXIX. — *Informations presented by Criminals under Confinement.*

Criminals, while in confinement, shall not be allowed to present or prosecute informations against any person or upon any affair whatsoever, except only when the object is to make complaint of ill treatment against the officers or inferior persons belonging to the prisons; or to confess and give information upon other offences committed by themselves,

besides

besides those for which they are confined; or lastly, to give evidence against and accuse the partners of their guilt, in which cases their informations shall be received and acted upon in due course of law, as under ordinary circumstances.

Persons upwards of eighty or under ten years of age, persons totally and incurably infirm, and females, in all cases, are incapacitated from presenting and prosecuting any informations, excepting only such as concern the crimes of high treason and rebellion, or the impiety of their children or grand children, or such as concern designed murders, robberies, thefts, wounds, frauds, and the like, against themselves or persons living with them under the same roof. — On any other subjects the informations of such persons must be rejected, because in all ordinary cases they are entitled to redeem themselves from punishment by a fine, and therefore not deterred from making false accusations by the apprehension of the consequences to which, under the same circumstances, other persons would become liable.

All magistrates, therefore, who receive and act upon such unlawful informations, shall be punished with 50 blows for their misconduct.

One clause.

Section CCCXL. — *Exciting and promoting Litigation.*

In all cases of exciting and disposing others to inform and prosecute, the person who draws up the information for the prosecutor, and by any aggravation or extenuation deviates from the truth, shall be liable to the same punishment as the false accuser; except in a capital case, when his punishment shall be reduced one degree. — In the case of hiring any person to present and prosecute a false accusation, the person hired shall be liable to the same punishment as the

the false accuser, under the same mitigation in capital cases, as in the preceding instance.

If the person who is hired had received a reward in money, such reward shall be considered as a bribe for an unlawful purpose, and the punishment which is legally proportionate to such offence shall be inflicted, whenever it proves on comparison more severe than that by this law provided.

Nevertheless, if any one meets with a simple and uninformed person, who is unable to state the injuries and injustice which he has suffered; and consequently advises and instructs such person rightly and truly how to act upon the occasion, and moreover, without extenuating or aggravating the particulars, draws up an information for him in the legal and customary manner, the giver of such assistance shall not, under these circumstances, be in any manner punishable.

An adulterer who is guilty of advising and instructing the adultress to accuse her legitimate son of a neglect of his filial duty, shall be punished as a contriver of murder.

Ten clauses.

Section CCCXLI.— *Informations on Subjects affecting Civil as well as Military Affairs.*

In cases of homicide charged against persons enrolled in the military class, the commanding officer of the persons charged therewith shall assist and be present, when the civil magistrate of the district investigates and decides upon the case. of which he only has competent authority to take cognisance. — In all cases of adultery, robbery, frauds, assaults, breach of laws concerning marriage, landed property, or pecuniary contracts, and of any other the like offences, committed by or against individuals in the military class; if any of the people are implicated or concerned,

the

the military commanding officer and the civil magistrate shall have a concurrent jurisdiction; if not, the military officer in command shall examine and decide the case between the parties, at his own tribunal. — Whenever, in any of the preceding cases, the officers of a military tribunal interpose an undue influence and authority in order to impede the regular progress of judicial proceedings, and to protect the criminals belonging to their particular jurisdiction from merited punishment, the deputies administering in, and the inferior officers belonging to such tribunal, shall each be liable, at the least, to a punishment of 50 blows.

This law shall also extend to all military officers who exceed their powers by receiving and acting upon informations belonging of right to the civil jurisdiction.

Seven clauses.

SECTION CCCXLII. — *Informations and Prosecutions on the Part of Officers of Government.*

All officers of government of every description, including those having official situations without rank, when interested in any private causes respecting marriage, pecuniary contracts, debts, or the division of landed property, shall, instead of prosecuting or defending their suits personally, appoint a servant or other person belonging to their family to perform that service; and at the same time refrain from interposing their influence and authority by any official communication on the subject with the magistrates who have the cognizance of the affair.

40 Blows shall be the punishment of any breach of this law.

No clause.

SECTION CCCXLIII.—*False Accusation of Offences punishable with extraordinary Banishment.*

All persons falsely accusing others of offences punishable with any kind of extraordinary perpetual banishment, shall suffer banishment of the same kind and in the same degree: all officers of government pronouncing an unjust sentence of extraordinary perpetual banishment, shall be liable to the same punishment as provided in cases of an unjust sentence of ordinary perpetual banishment.

In the case of a false accusation of an offence punishable with the remote or extraordinary temporary banishment, it shall be estimated as two years banishment, and the punishment of the false accuser increased thereon, either three degrees or otherwise, according to the circumstances.

No clause.

END OF THE FIFTH BOOK OF THE SIXTH DIVISION.

BOOK VI.

BRIBERY AND CORRUPTION*.

Section CCCXLIV. — *Accepting a Bribe.*

ALL civil and military officers, and also all persons who have employments without rank under government, shall, when convicted of accepting a bribe for a lawful or for an unlawful purpose, be punished in proportion to the amount thereof, as stated in the subjoined table; and moreover be deprived of their rank and offices, if having any; and if not, of their actual employments whatever they may be. — Those who are not in the receipt of any salary, or of a salary not amounting to one stone of rice† *per* month in value, shall be punished less severely, in every case, by one degree.

---

* How far the various and seemingly appropriate provisions contained in this book of the code, against bribery in almost every shape which it can be supposed to assume, are reconcileable with the systematic corruption which, under the less odious name of presents, must be acknowledged to be but too prevalent in the various departments of the administration of public affairs and public justice in China, it is not easy to determine. — That flagrant acts, at least, of bribery do not always escape unpunished, appears from a note in the original Chinese, inserted in this place, and containing an abridgement of the official report of the trial of a governor of a city in the province of Pekin; who, in the 33d year of the Emperor *Kien-lung*, appears to have accepted a bribe of 7000 ounces of silver, which had been offered him as an inducement to stop certain proceedings in a case of disorderly conduct and contempt of court; but afterwards to have returned the money, on finding himself unable to accomplish the object for which it was given: — yet, at the close of a detailed investigation of the case, it is stated that he was finally sentenced to suffer death for his original acceptance of the bribe, by being strangled at the usual season.

† Supposed to be 120 *kin* or 160 pounds British weight.

Those who negociate, and through whose hands the bribe passes, if they are persons of the former class, shall be punished one degree less, and if of the latter class, two degrees less than the receiver; but, to which ever class they belong, they shall not be liable in any case to a greater punishment than 100 blows and two years banishment; if participating themselves in the bribe, they shall either suffer the punishment incurred by receiving a bribe themselves, or the punishment of negociating one for another, according as the one or the other is found, by a computation of the amount in each case, and a regard to the circumstances, to be the most severe.

When the object for which the bribe is received is unlawful, all the sums received by the offender from different persons, but charged against him at the same time, and in the same information, shall be added together and estimated as one bribe; and if, after punishment is inflicted, another instance of bribery is discovered, that offence, whether greater or less than the former, shall likewise entail a punishment proportionate to its amount.

When, on the contrary, the object for which the bribe is received is in itself lawful, though unlawfully sought after, all the sums received, and charged in the same information, shall be added together as in the former case, but only half the aggregate shall be referred to the scale of punishments in the annexed table, for bribes for purposes which in themselves are lawful.

TABLE

TABLE of Reference in cafes of regular Officers of Government being guilty of receiving Bribes.

When the Object is in itself lawful.

Amount received. Value in Ounces of Silver.	Punishment. Blows.	Banishment.
1 or less	60	none.
1 to 12	70	none.
20	80	none.
30	90	none.
40	100	none
50	60	for one year.
60	70	for one year and half.
70	80	for two years.
80	90	for two years and a half.
90	100	for three years.
100	100	for life, distance 2000 *lee*.
110	100	for life, distance 2500 *lee*.
120	100	for life, distance 3000 *lee*.
Upwards of 120		Death, by being strangled at the usual period.

When the Object is unlawful.

Amount received. Value in Ounces of Silver.	Punishment. Blows.	Banishment.
1 or less	70	none.
1 to 10	80	none.
10	90	none.
15	100	none.
20	60	for one year.
25	70	for one year and a half.
30	80	for two years.
35	90	for two years and a half.
40	100	for three years.
45	100	for life, distance 2000 *lee*.
50	100	for life, distance 2500 *lee*.
55	100	for life, distance 3000 *lee*.
80 and upwards.		Death, by being strangled at the usual period.

Persons who are not in the receipt of what is considered a regular salary from government, shall, when guilty of accepting a bribe for an unlawful object, be subject only to the punishment proportionally reduced one degree, below that already stated; but shall be punished with death, by being strangled at the usual period, when the amount of the bribe which they are found guilty of having accepted, exceeds in any degree 120 ounces.

In the case of a bribe being accepted to a similar extent, for a lawful object, the punishment of persons guilty thereof under those circumstances, shall never exceed 100 blows, and perpetual banishment to the distance of 3000 *lee*.

Fourteen clauses.

Section CCCXLV. — *Pecuniary Malversation.*

When any officers of government, or other persons, whatever may be their denomination, are guilty of receiving, appropriating, or expending any sum or sums unwarrantably, if the offence does not come under the description of a bribe to do any specific act, lawful or unlawful, the different sums received, appropriated, or expended unwarrantably, and charged against an offender at any one time, shall be added together, and half of the aggregate shall be the estimated amount of the unwarrantable transaction; according to which the offender shall receive punishment, as stated in the following table; but if the amount was not in any manner applied by the offender to his own benefit and advantage, he shall not lose his rank or employments. — The person who presented any sum which was thus unwarrantably received and disposed of, shall be punished five degrees less than the receiver.

TABLE of Reference.

Amount in Ounces of Silver.	Punishment.	
	Blows.	Banishment.
less than 1	20	none.
1 to 10	30	none.
20	40	none.
30	50	none.
40	60	none.
50	70	none.
60	80	none.
70	90	none.
80	100	none.
100	60	for one year.
200	70	for a year and a half.
300	80	for two years.
400	90	for two years and a half.
500 and upwards	100	for three years.

The provisions of this law are designed to comprehend every species of pecuniary over-charge, in cases of blows, theft, and the like injuries; presents of all kinds, made to civil and military officers upon taking charge of their governments, eatables only excepted; exaction of more than the just and due proportion of revenue, or (in an unfavourable season) of more than the people are fairly able to contribute; unnecessary and extravagant expenditure of public money, and of the labour of the people, although not conducive to the advantage or emolument of the offender. — If, in any case, the giver or receiver is implicated in any other manner by the transaction, his punishment shall always be measured and inflicted in conformity to the law, applicable to the greater and more severely punishable offence of which he may be found guilty.

No clause.

Section CCCXLVI. — *Receiving Money corruptly by way of Reward.*

All officers of government, and others having official employments, who, although not bribed in the firſt inſtance, afterwards receive ſums by way of reward for any tranſaction in their official capacity, ſhall, if there had been any thing unlawful in ſuch tranſaction, be puniſhed in the ſame manner as in a caſe of bribery to do an unlawful act; but if the tranſaction had been in itſelf lawful, then the receipt of a reward for it ſhall be puniſhed, as the receipt of a bribe to the ſame amount for the ſubſequent performance of any act in itſelf lawful.

The ſame diſtinction ſhall be made as heretofore, between perſons with and without regular ſalaries, and they ſhall, in both caſes, loſe their rank and employments; but the honorary diſtinctions which had been allowed by the Emperor ſhall not be taken away from their families.

The puniſhment of officers of government having high judicial and miniſterial ſituations, ſhall be two degrees more ſevere than that of ordinary officers, in this, as well as in the other caſes.

No clauſe.

Section CCCXLVII. — *Contracting for, and agreeing to accept a Bribe.*

All officers of government, and other perſons having official employments, contracting for, or agreeing to accept a bribe to do any lawful or unlawful act, but not having actually received the ſame, ſhall, upon competent evidence being had of the agreement, and the amount ſtipulated for, be puniſhed according to the law provided againſt receiving a bribe for a lawful or an unlawful act, rejecting the capital caſes, and further reducing the puniſhment in each caſe one degree: the conſequence thereof will be, that the puniſhment of this

offence

offence will not, in any cafe, exceed 100 blows and three years banifhment.

Neverthelefs, if the unlawful act be in itfelf an offence fubject by any other law to a more fevere punifhment than that incurred by the mere ftipulation for the bribe, the former punifhment fhall be inflicted inftead of the latter.

One claufe.

Section CCCXLVIII.—*Offering a Bribe.*

If an individual of any defcription whatever, having an affair to fubmit to the decifion of an officer of government, endeavours, by the offer of a bribe, to prevail on him to deviate from the law, he fhall be punifhed in proportion to the amount, according to the law concerning pecuniary malverfation in general; but if the attempt to procure the commiffion of fuch unlawful act, whether with a view to obtain an advantage, or to avoid an evil, is by law more feverely punifhable than the offer of a bribe, the punifhment fhall be eftimated according to the former offence, inftead of the latter.—Neverthelefs, if the officers of government, and others, having official fituations, vexatioufly and violently extort money as a bribe, which, in the firft inftance, had not been offered to them, the perfons complying and giving what was required fhall not be punifhed.

In all cafes, the amount of the bribe offered or received fhall be forfeited to government.

One claufe.

SECTION CCCXLIX. — *Extortion of Loans, and unfair Sales.*

When any superintending officers of government, or any other persons in official situations, avail themselves of the influence of their authority, or any private individuals, of their personal strength and resources, and by means thereof extort loans of the goods or money of the inhabitants of their districts, they shall be punished proportionately to the estimated value of the goods or money borrowed, according to the law against bribery to do an act which is in itself lawful; but when actual force and violence is used, the offenders shall be punished proportionately to the amount, according to the law against bribery for unlawful purposes. — In each case, the punishment of persons without salaries shall be less by one degree. — The articles borrowed shall be restored without reserve or delay, to the owners.

When persons in authority as aforesaid, lend their own money or goods to the inhabitants of their districts upon exorbitant interest, or buy or sell goods upon an unfair valuation, the unlawful advantage accruing from such transactions, whether by excess of interest, or buying at a lower rate, and selling at an higher rate, than the market allows, shall be estimated, and the offender punished as in the cases of bribery for a lawful object; but if the influence exerted amounted to compulsion, the punishment shall be rated as in cases of bribery for unlawful objects.

The articles lent or sold by the offenders shall be forfeited to government, and the articles borrowed or bought by them shall be restored to the owners.

If persons in authority do not, when purchasing articles from the inhabitants of their district, immediately pay the price thereof; or if they borrow from them, clothes, table or house furniture, and the like, without returning the same within one month, they shall suffer punishment proportionately to the amount, according to the law concerning pecuniary malversation; that is to say, corrupt transactions without direct bribery; and in all cases the goods delivered shall be immediately restored to the owners. — The same persons, when convicted of privately borrowing from the people, their horses, horned cattle, camels, mules, asses, carriages, boats, mills, houses or barns, and the like, shall be liable to the punishment of the law against pecuniary malversation, according to the estimated amount of the hire of such articles during the time that they were retained; which estimate shall, however, in no case, exceed the actual value of the articles.

The aforesaid persons, when guilty of accepting at any time, from the inhabitants of their district, presents consisting of the produce or manufacture thereof, shall be punished, at the least, with 40 blows, and the giver shall suffer punishment less than the receiver only by one degree. — If such presents are made and accepted with a view to any future and specific official transaction on the part of the receiver, whether a lawful or an unlawful one, punishment shall be inflicted as in the ordinary cases of bribery for similar purposes, already stated.

Nevertheless, all presents of eatables to such persons, when upon any official progress, and presents of all kinds, when made to them by their relations, on particular occasions, shall be excepted from the prohibitions and penalties of this law. — All persons, lastly, who when detached or sent upon government service, as messengers, or otherwise, on such occasions extort loans, buy or sell unfairly, or receive presents, shall be liable to the same punishments as are above provided in the cases of superintending officers, or others having official situations under government.

When abdicated or superseded officers of government are guilty of extorting loans, receiving bribes, and the like, from the inhabitants of the districts formerly under their jurisdiction, they shall suffer a punishment less severe by three degrees than that which they would, under similar circumstances, have incurred, had they been still in office.

Eight clauses.

SECTION CCCL. — *Extortion and other Corrupt Practices of Persons in the Families of Officers of Government.*

All persons belonging to the family of an officer of government, or of any individual having official employment under government, whether brothers, sons, nephews, slaves, or servants, shall, when guilty of extorting loans, receiving presents, unfairly trading, or otherwise unlawfully acting towards the inhabitants of the district or station in which their relation or master has a jurisdiction, suffer punishment less by two degrees than the master of the family would have incurred under similar circumstances; but in the case of receiving a bribe for any specific object, they shall be punished as the case may be, without any reduction, according to the different rules established in ordinary cases of bribery for lawful, and bribery for unlawful purposes.

The master of the family, if privy to the offence committed by the person belonging thereto, shall be punished in an equal degree; but if ignorant thereof, shall be excused.

One clause.

SECTION CCCLI. — *Extortion and other Corrupt practices of Great Officers of State.*

All such officers of government as are invested with judicial or ministerial situations, rendering them superior in rank and jurisdiction

tion to the governors of the cities of the firſt order, ſhall, when guilty of any corrupt tranſactions with the inhabitants of the country ſubject to their authority or influence, whether by receiving bribes or preſents, extorting loans, buying or ſelling unfairly, or committing any other ſimilar offences, be puniſhed two degrees more ſeverely than any inferior officers of government would have been under ſimilar circumſtances; except that ſuch augmentation of puniſhment ſhall not take place in capital caſes, or render any puniſhment capital that would not have been ſo otherwiſe.

No clauſe.

Section CCCLII. — *Levying extraordinary Contributions on the Plea of public Service.*

If any civil magiſtrate of a diſtrict, levies perſonally, or through the intervention of perſons in his employ, extraordinary contributions from the people, on the plea of public ſervice, without any expreſs orders or authority from a ſuperior officer for that purpoſe; or if any military officer attempts in any caſe to levy ſimilar contributions on the people, upon the plea of paying the troops, he ſhall, in each caſe, ſuffer at the leaſt, the puniſhment of 60 blows, although the contributions exacted ſhould not have been applied to any corrupt or private purpoſe; and if the ſum levied is conſiderable, it ſhall be eſtimated, and puniſhment inflicted in proportion to the amount according to the law againſt pecuniary malverſation in general:— But if the ſums contributed are converted by the receiver or collector to his own uſe, puniſhment ſhall be inflicted conformably to the law againſt bribery for unlawful purpoſes.

If, on the other hand, any ſuch contributions are raiſed without expreſsly alleging the falſe plea of public ſervice; then, although the amount

amount should be appropriated by the offender to his own use, the punishment shall only be rated according to the law against bribery for purposes in themselves lawful.

In these cases it shall not be considered as making any difference in the nature of the offence, whether the offender applies the sum contributed to his own use, or distributes the same in presents to others.

Two clauses.

Section CCCLIII. — *Suppressing the Discovery of Stolen Goods.*

When the police officers who are, by the authority of the superior magistrates, engaged in the pursuit and apprehension of criminals, recover any stolen or plundered effects, if they do not deliver up the same forthwith to government, they shall be punished with 80 blows; and if they appropriate the articles or sums of money so obtained, to their own use, they shall be further liable to the punishment of bribery for lawful objects, in proportion to the amount.

Upon estimating the guilt of the thief or robber, the plunder previously surrendered to government, shall be added to whatever had been subsequently recovered, but unlawfully retained by the officers of government; and if in consequence of such retention, an insufficient punishment had been inflicted on the offender, the remainder shall be executed afterwards.

In the case of ordinary soldiers and thief-takers offending against this law, the punishment, shall not, in any instance, exceed 80 blows.

One clause.

SECTION CCCLIV. — *Receiving Presents from the Higher Hereditary Nobility* *.

All military officers of government, whether stationed at court or in the provinces, are prohibited from receiving presents of gold, silver, silk-stuffs, clothes, wages, or board-wages, from individuals in any of the three principal ranks of hereditary nobility; upon any breach of this law they shall be deprived of their rank and employments, suffer the punishment of 100 blows, and be sent into the more remote perpetual banishment; for the second offence they shall suffer death.

The nobleman making the present shall be excused for the first and second offence; but upon the third offence, he shall be accused in due form, and the nature and degree of his punishment referred to the decision of the Emperor. — Nevertheless, when a nobleman of the rank above mentioned is invested by His Majesty with special powers to administer any department of the public service, and with a view to promote the execution thereof, makes presents, or allows wages to the civil or military authorities belonging to such department, neither the giver nor the receiver shall be liable to any punishment in consequence thereof.

No clause.

* The hereditary nobles alluded to, are, for the most part, Tartar chieftains, who altho' reduced to vassalage, may be supposed to be desirous of acquiring, by the means here described, a certain degree of power and influence in the state, independent of the crown, and therefore dangerous to the Imperial prerogative.

END OF THE SIXTH BOOK OF THE SIXTH DIVISION.

BOOK VII.

FORGERIES AND FRAUDS.

SECTION CCCLV. — *Falsification of an Imperial Edict.*

ALL the principals and accessaries to the crime of falsifying an Imperial edict; that is to say, pretending any document to be an Imperial edict which is not one, or adding to, or substracting from a real one, shall, in the event of such falsified document having been actually published and sent forth, be beheaded at the usual period; but if the same is only found prepared and ready for publication, the principal offender shall be strangled at the usual period, and the accessaries punished less severely by one degree. In either case the crime shall always be imputed to the framer or contriver, and not to the mere transcriber.

All persons who are guilty of an error or omission in engrossing an Imperial edict, shall be punished with 100 blows, and the accessaries thereto with 90 blows.

All persons guilty of the falsification of an edict of any one of the six supreme boards or councils of state, of the board of censors, of any of the commanders in chief of the Imperial armies, of the viceroys, sub-viceroys, or generals of provinces, or of the governors of any important frontier towns, whether by the forgery of the requisite marks and signatures, by the privately affixing of the official seal to a false document or to a blank paper, or by any other contrivance adequate to the said criminal purpose, shall, if such false document should

should have been actually sent forth and published as a real one, be strangled at the usual period, without any distinction being made between the principals and the accessaries; but if the falsified document was only prepared for publication, the punishment of the principal offender shall be one degree less, and that of the accessaries, two degrees less, than it would have been, had the said document been actually published.

The principal in the offence of falsifying an edict of any of the other important but subordinate public boards, such as the subordinate board of censors, that of the judges, and of the treasurers of provinces, and those of the governors of cities of the first, second, and third rank, shall be punished with 100 blows, and perpetual banishment to the distance of 3000 *lee*.

The principal offender in the falsification of the edict of any still lower public officer or public board, shall be punished with 100 blows and three years banishment; the accessaries thereto, one degree less, and there shall be a further reduction of one degree in both cases, if the false document was only prepared for publication, instead of being actually published.

In every case, if the falsification of an official document is contrived and executed with any unlawful and corrupt motive, such as is punishable by law more severely than the mere crime of falsification, the punishment so incurred shall be inflicted in preference to that by this law provided.

If the officer of government to whom any of the aforesaid pretended edicts are addressed, receives and acts upon the same, knowing them to be forged, he shall suffer the same punishment as the falsifier, with the exception only of one degree in capital cases: but if ignorant of the forgery, such officer shall be excused.

Three clauses.

Section CCCLVI. — *Falfification of Verbal Orders.*

All perfons who are guilty of delivering falfely any verbal orders of his Imperial Majefty, fhall, if principals in the offence, be beheaded at the ufual period; and if acceffaries thereto, fhall be punifhed with 100 blows and perpetual banifhment to the diftance of 3000 *lee*.

In like manner, thofe who are guilty of falfely delivering any verbal orders of the Emprefs or of the hereditary prince, fhall, if principals in the offence, be ftrangled at the ufual period, and if acceffaries, punifhed with 100 blows and perpetual banifhment to the diftance of 3000 *lee*.

All perfons who, under the influence of a corrupt motive, falfely deliver the verbal orders of an officer of a public board or tribunal of government of the firft or fecond rank, fhall, if fuch orders had been iffued upon the public fervice, in behalf of the public board, and for the information and guidance of the officers of fubordinate jurifdictions, be punifhed with 100 blows and three years banifhment. — In the cafe of falfely delivering, likewife under the influence of a corrupt motive, the verbal orders of any officer of a tribunal of the third or fourth rank under the fame circumftances, the punifhment fhall amount to 100 blows; and if of any officer of an inferior tribunal, to 80 blows; in each of thefe cafes, the punifhment of the acceffaries fhall be proportionably lefs by one degree.

If the offender had been bribed in any cafe to falfify the verbal orders entrufted to him to communicate, the amount of the bribe received fhall be afcertained, and the offender made liable to the punifhment of bribery with a lawful, or bribery with an unlawful object, according as the falfification of the orders had been defigned to effect a lawful or an unlawful purpofe.

In all cases, the most severe of the two or more punishments to which, from the application of different laws, the offender may be liable, shall be inflicted, and by including, supersede the others.

The punishments provided by this law, shall only be understood to affect the original false-deliverer or falsifier of the orders, and not be applied to any of the cases of subsequent false deliveries of the orders, through intermediate and innocent persons.

If the officer of government to whom any falsified verbal orders are officially addressed, receives and acts upon the same, knowing them to be false, he shall be liable to the same punishment as the person uttering the falsehood, with the usual exception only of a reduction of one degree in capital cases:— But if really ignorant of the falsehood thereof, he shall be excused. — If any of the officers of tribunals engaged in the trial of offenders, or in the collection of the revenue, after having received the Imperial commands to desist from the same in any particular instance, nevertheless continue such proceedings on pretence of acting as before under the Imperial authority, they shall conformably to the principle of this law, be beheaded at the usual period.

No clause.

Section CCCLVII. — *Falsely and Deceitfully addressing the Sovereign.*

If any individual makes a false and deceitful communication to the sovereign, either verbally or in writing, either in an ordinary address concerning the affairs of a particular department, or in an extraordinary one concerning public affairs in general, such individual shall be punished with 100 blows and three years banishment:— if in such address secrets of state, such as treason or rebellion, are alleged in cases where they do not exist, the punishment shall be more severe by one degree.

If any one, when engaged in a criminal investigation, or other judicial proceedings in obedience to the Imperial commands, makes a false and deceitful report thereof, he shall be punished with 80 blows and two years banishment, or as much more severely as he may appear to deserve, according to the law against an intentional deviation from justice, in pronouncing a judicial sentence.

No clause.

SECTION CCCLVIII.—*Counterfeiting any Official Seal or the Imperial Almanac.*

Whoever counterfeits the official seal of any officer or tribunal of government, the Imperial almanac, or the stamps which are used to authenticate the land or water permits which it is usual to issue for the conveyance of tea or salt through the empire, shall, if a principal in the crime of engraving such counterfeits, be beheaded at the usual period; and if an accessary, punished with 100 blows and perpetual banishment to the distance of 3000 *lee*.

Whoever seizes and delivers up such an offender to the officers of justice, shall be rewarded by government with fifty ounces of silver.

Whoever counterfeits custom-house stamps, or the official seals of persons not having the rank of regular officers of government, shall be punished with 100 blows and three years banishment; and any person who seizes and delivers up such an offender, shall be rewarded with thirty ounces of silver.

All the accessaries to their offences, as well as also all those who make use of such seals or stamps knowing them to be counterfeit, shall suffer the punishment next in degree.

If the counterfeiting of any seal is attempted, but not completed or perfected, the punishment for such an attempt shall in each case, be further reduced one degree. — All officers of government likewise, who knowingly acquiesce in and connive at such counterfeiting, or employment of counterfeits, shall suffer the same punishment as the original offenders, but the acquiescence of those who were ignorant of the fraud shall always be excused.

As the ancient characters, and all other marks whatever, which are used in, and which distinguish official seals and stamps, may be imitated upon divers materials besides the metals of which the genuine seals or stamps are composed, it shall be sufficient that the counterfeit resemble the original with apparent exactness, and that the legend thereon be the same; but if it be only a gross imitation, and the characters are not identically the same, it shall be considered as an attempt only, and the offender punished accordingly: — if no stamp at all is employed, but the characters and marks are merely drawn upon the paper, so as to resemble the impression of a seal, the offence shall not be considered to come within the meaning and intent of this law.

Four clauses.

Section CCCLIX. — *Counterfeiting the current Coin of the Realm.*

All persons who privately cast copper coin, that is to say, all the masters of private manufactories of copper coin, and the workmen employed therein, shall suffer death by being strangled, at the usual period: — Whoever is an accessary to this offence, and whoever purchases for use such copper coin, knowing it to be counterfeited, shall suffer the punishment of the principal offenders, reduced one degree.— Whoever seizes and delivers up any such aforesaid coiner, shall be rewarded with fifty ounces of silver by government. — If the responsible inhabitant of the village or district, in which such unlawful manufacture

facture and coinage is carried on, is acquainted therewith, and does not give information to government, he shall be punished with 100 blows; but if ignorant thereof, he shall be excused.

All those also who take an opportunity of clipping or filing down the current coin of the realm when it passes through their hands, in order to make a profit thereby, shall in like manner be punished with 100 blows. — Those moreover who contrive mixtures of copper, iron, quickfilver, and the like, in order to imitate and counterfeit gold or silver, shall be punished with 100 blows, and three years banishment: all accessaries to the offence, and those who purchase such imitations of gold or silver, in order to pass the same in trade, knowing them not to be genuine, shall suffer the punishment of the contrivers thereof, reduced one degree.

Those however who merely sell gold or silver below the standard weight or color, shall not, in consequence, be held liable to any of the penalties of this law.

Five clauses.

Section CCCLX. — *Impostors pretending to be Officers of Government.*

Whoever contrives a false deed or instrument of investiture, and therewith represents himself to be an officer of government; and whoever, having contrived such false deed, or obtained the genuine one of any officer deceased, pretends to invest any person therewith, shall suffer death, by being beheaded at the usual period.

The individual who accepts of such a deed of investiture, knowing it not to be genuine shall be punished with 100 blows, and perpetual banishment to the distance of 3000 *lee*; but if ignorant of the forgery, he shall be excused.

If any private individual, although not pretending to any such investiture as aforesaid, yet assumes the character of an officer of government,

ment in order to accomplifh a particular purpofe, or if he falfely pretends to have the authority of any officer or tribunal of government to arreft fome perfon; or, laftly, if he affumes the family name, and proper name, of any perfon actually in office, in order to accomplifh a particular purpofe under fuch affumed character, he fhall in each cafe be liable to 100 blows, and three years banifhment.

Whoever impofes himfelf on others as the fon, grandfon, brother, nephew, fervant, or authorized agent of any perfon in office, in order to carry any particular point with the inhabitants under the jurifdiction of fuch officer, by the influence of an affumed character, fhall receive 100 blows, and the acceffaries to the deception, 90 blows.

If the perfon guilty as aforefaid, fhould obtain or extort any money or goods from different individuals by means of his affumed character, the largeft of the fums fo received from any one perfon fhall be eftimated, and referred to the table of punifhments proportionate to any amount of a theft in ordinary cafes; the punifhment which refults conformably to the table (the branding excepted) fhall be inflicted, inftead of that already ftated, whenever it proves, by comparifon, the moft fevere. — All officers of government, who connive at, and concur in fuch impoftures, fhall be punifhed as impoftors themfelves (capital cafes only excepted), but if ignorant thereof, fhall be excufed.

Eight claufes.

SECTION CCCLXI. — *Impoftors pretending to be Great Officers of State.*

If any perfon falfely impofes himfelf on the officers of government and the other inhabitants of any of the provinces, as a great officer of ftate difpatched from court with extraordinary powers, or as a member of one of the fix fupreme tribunals or councils of ftate, of the tribunal of cenfors, or of any of the other principal boards or tribunals at Pekin; and upon the ſtrength of ſuch falſely aſſumed authority, inveſtigates the provincial affairs, deceives the provincial government, and influences in a dangerous manner the minds of the people, he ſhall be beheaded at the uſual period, even although he ſhould not have actually provided himſelf with any forged inſtrument of inveſtiture.

Thoſe who concur in, and connive at ſuch deception, and form a part of the ſuite of the impoſtor, and alſo thoſe officers of government who receive and countenance the impoſtor, knowing him to be ſuch, ſhall in each caſe be puniſhed with 100 blows, and perpetual baniſhment to the diſtance of 3000 *lee* : — But if the latter perſons have really been deceived themſelves, they ſhall be excuſed.

If any perſon, even without producing any forged or pretended powers, falſely aſſerts himſelf to be an officer of government diſpatched from court on public ſervice, and upon that plea, employs the poſt-horſes and other travelling equipage provided at different ſtations by the authority and for the uſe of government, he ſhall in ſuch caſe be puniſhed with 100 blows, and perpetual baniſhment to the diſtance of 3000 *lee* : — All acceſſaries to the offence ſhall ſuffer the puniſhment next in degree. — Thoſe officers of the public poſts, who, although aware of the impoſition, nevertheleſs provide what is demanded, ſhall ſuffer the ſame puniſhment; and although ignorant thereof, ſhall ſtill ſuffer 50 blows as a puniſhment for their neglecting to make a proper inveſtigation and inquiry. — When, however, the impoſtor produces apparently authentic powers, they ſhall be excuſed.

Two clauſes.

Section CCCLXII.—*Officers of State, and others belonging to the Court, interfering without Authority.*

If any one of the officers of government attached to the court, and employed near the person of the sovereign, proceeds privately to investigate state affairs in any part of the empire, pretending to have especial authority for that purpose; and thereby in a dangerous manner influences and agitates the minds of the people, he shall be beheaded at the usual period.

No clause.

Section CCCLXIII.—*Pretending to discover Prognostics.*

Whoever falsely asserts that he has discovered prognostics in the Heavens, shall be punished with 60 blows and one year's banishment; but whenever there are really any omens of a calamity, if the officers of the astronomical board fail to give a true and faithful notice thereof, they shall suffer a punishment two degrees more severe than that last mentioned.

No clause.

Section CCCLXIV.—*Pretending Sickness or Death.*

If any regular officer of government, any person employed by government in an inferior station, or any private individual, falsely alleges sickness or infirmity, as an excuse for not performing the more difficult parts of his duty, such as the collection of the revenue, and the pursuit and seizure of criminals, he shall be punished with 40 blows; and if the case is important, with 80 blows.—If any officer of government, or other person, who has been guilty of any offences against the laws, in the interim previous to the examination, wounds, or otherwise disables himself, in order to become entitled to an exemption from the question by torture, he shall be punished with 100 blows for such conduct; and if he further feigns death, in order to avoid dismission and disgrace, he shall be punishable with 100 blows and three years banishment.

In either case, if the offence, the investigation of which the offender endeavours to avoid, is more severely punishable; such punishment shall take place instead of that hereby ordained and provided.

If any officer of government, or other person, without having in view to evade any duty, or any impending investigation into his conduct, but merely in order to alarm and implicate others, wounds and disables himself, or procures himself to be wounded and disabled in the manner aforesaid, he shall be punished with 80 blows; and in every case of a person being hired or employed to inflict such wound, and thereby occasioning disability, such person shall suffer the same punishment. — If death ensues from such wounding, the person so hired or employed, shall suffer punishment one degree less severely than in cases of killing in an affray.

If any officer of government having authority to interfere in such cases, instead of so doing, advisedly connives at the deceptions practiced by the officer or other person who is subordinate to him; either by suffering such person to retire upon a false plea of indisposition, to evade the question by torture on the plea of his purposely acquired disability and infirmity, or to withdraw himself altogether from further examination and punishment, by feigning death; the officer so conniving, shall be equally punished with the person whose offence is connived at; but if really ignorant in any particular instance of the falsehood of the pretence, his acquiescence shall be excused.

Two clauses.

Section CCCLXV. — *Seducing Persons to transgress the Laws.*

All descriptions of persons who, having with fallacious words or arts seduced and instructed any individual to transgress the laws, or who, having prevailed on any individual to combine with them for any unlawful and criminal purpose, afterwards become informers, and seize, or direct others to seize and inform against, such offending individual, whether doing so with a view to injure the party so seduced and misled, or merely with a view to the profit or reward expected to accrue from his apprehension, shall be held equally guilty, and liable to the same punishment as the offender, in all cases except those of capital offences; in which the usual reduction shall be allowed of one degree.

Four clauses.

END OF THE SEVENTH BOOK OF THE SIXTH DIVISION.

BOOK VIII.

INCEST AND ADULTERY.

Section CCCLXVI. — *Criminal Intercourse in general.*

CRIMINAL intercourse by mutual consent with an unmarried woman, shall be punished with 70 blows; if with a married woman, the punishment shall be 80 blows.

Deliberate intrigue with a married or unmarried woman shall be punished with 100 blows.

Violation of a married or unmarried woman; that is to say, a rape, shall be punished with death by strangulation.

An assault with an intent to commit a rape, shall be punished with 100 blows, and perpetual banishment to the distance of 3000 *lee*. — In these cases however, the conviction of the offenders must be founded on decisive evidence of force having really been employed.

Criminal intercource with a female under twelve years of age, shall be punished as a rape in all cases.

In cases of criminal intercourse by previous agreement, or by any intrigue, the man and woman shall be esteemed equally guilty; and if any male or female child be the fruit of such connexion, it shall be supported at the expence of the father; the mother shall either be sold in marriage or remain with her husband, according to his choice; but if the husband is guilty of selling his wife in marriage to the adulterer, the parties to such an illicit agreement shall be respectively punished with 80 blows; the woman shall be sent back to her family, and the price paid for her, forfeited to government. — The woman upon whom a rape is committed shall not be liable to any punishment.

Persons aiding and assisting, or conniving at the meeting of the parties guilty of a criminal intercourse as aforesaid, shall suffer the punishment next in degree, as usual in the case of accessaries.

Persons discovering a criminal intercourse, and afterwards submitting to a compromise, by which the same is concealed, shall suffer the punishment due to the offenders, reduced two degrees.

A person charged with a criminal connexion, shall not be convicted unless positively proved to have been on the spot, where the fact was stated to have taken place.

When, however, a woman is found with child, she shall be liable to the penalties of this law, though the father should not be discoverable.

Twelve clauses*.

SECTION CCCLXVII. — *Conniving at, or consenting to a Criminal Intercourse.*

In all cases of a husband consenting to, or conniving at, the adultery of the principal or any other of his wives, the husband, the adulterer, and the adultress, shall each be punished with 90 blows.

Any individual compelling his principal or inferior wife, or any female educated under his roof as an adopted daughter, to engage in a criminal intercourse, shall be punished with 100 blows, and the adulterer or fornicator shall be punished with 80 blows; but the woman shall be considered innocent, and sent back to her parents or family.

Any person who consents to, or connives at the compulsion of his wives or adopted daughters in the manner aforesaid, or who compels

---

* The clauses annexed to this law contain an application of it, which, though necessary to be stated, is very properly perhaps, reserved for the supplement. — For a translation of three of these clauses see the Appendix, No. XXXII.

his own daughters, or the wives of his sons or grandsons, to engage in a criminal intercourse, shall be punished as above stated.

Any person who parts with his wife and transfers her to another for a pecuniary consideration, shall, as well as also the purchaser, and the wife, if consenting to the transfer, undergo the punishment of 100 blows, and the wife shall be sent back to her family. — The money paid for the transaction shall be forfeited to government.

If the wife and the person proposing the purchase, shall have combined together to oblige the husband to consent to a separation from her, and no corrupt motive be imputable to him in the transaction, he shall not be punished; but the wife, and the person whom she proposes to herself as a husband, shall be respectively condemned to suffer 60 blows, and one year's banishment: the banishment, in the case of the woman, shall be commuted for a fine, and she shall either remain in her first condition, or be sold in marriage, at the choice of the first husband.

If the case relates to any other wife except the first, the punishment of the parties shall be reduced in every instance one degree.

Persons aiding, assisting, or negotiating in the business, shall be punished one degree less severely than the principals.

When the husband discovers the wife to have committed adultery, and sells her in marriage to the adulterer, he shall be punished with 100 blows; the other parties, as already stated.

No clause.

Section CCCLXVIII. — *Incest; or Criminal Intercourse between Relations.*

A criminal intercourse between relations more remote than the fourth degree, or with the wives of such remote relations, shall be punished with 100 blows: — if a rape is committed, the offender shall be beheaded.

A criminal intercourse with relations in the fourth degree; with a wife's former husband's daughters, or with sisters by the same mother, but by different fathers, shall be punished with 100 blows and three years banishment.

When in such cases a rape is committed, the offenders shall be beheaded.

A criminal intercourse with a grandmother's sisters, cousins by the father's side, the wives of brothers or the wives of nephews, shall be punished with death by being strangled immediately upon conviction. — If a rape is committed, the party offending shall be beheaded.

A criminal intercourse with a father's or grandfather's inferior wife, with a father's sisters, or father's brother's wives, or the wife of a son or grandson, shall be punished with death, by being beheaded immediately upon conviction.

In general in the cases of inferior wives, the punishment shall be reduced one degree, unless otherwise provided.

Nine clauses.

Section CCCLXIX.—*Accusing an Elder Relation of Adultery.*

When a wife falsely accuses her father-in-law or her elder brother-in-law, of having obliged her to consent to an incestuous intercourse, she shall suffer death by being beheaded.

No clause.

Section CCCLXX. — *Criminal Intercourse between Slaves or Servants, and their Master's Wives.*

All slaves or hired servants who have been guilty of a criminal intercourse with their master's wives or daughters, shall be beheaded imme-

immediately after conviction: when guilty of a criminal intercourse with their master's female relations in the first degree, or with the wives of the male relations of their masters in the same degree, they shall be strangled after remaining in prison the usual period. In the above cases, the punishment of the woman, if consenting, shall be less, only by one degree. When guilty of a criminal intercourse with their master's more distant female relations, or with the wives of his more distant male relations, they shall be punished with 100 blows, and perpetual banishment to the distance of 2000 *lee*.

If guilty of committing a rape upon the latter persons, they shall be beheaded after remaining in prison the usual period: except in the cases of rape, the punishment of a criminal intercourse with any of the inferior wives, shall, generally speaking, be less than in the case of principal wives by one degree.

Three clauses.

Section CCCLXXI.—*Criminal Intercourse between Officers of Government and Females under their Jurisdiction.*

In all cases of civil or military officers of government and of their official clerks and attendants, being guilty of a criminal intercourse with any the wives or daughters of the inhabitants of the country under their jurisdiction, the punishment shall be two degrees more severe than in ordinary cases between equals;—they shall also be deprived of their offices and employments, and moreover rendered incapable of returning afterwards to the public service.

The woman, if consenting, shall be punished for such consent, only as in ordinary cases.

If such officers, or any of the persons serving under them, are guilty of having a criminal intercourse with a female convict who is under confinement in prison, they shall be punished with 100 blows and three

three years banishment: the female convict shall not suffer any aggravation of the punishment to which she had previously been liable: when in such cases violence is offered, the offending party shall be strangled.

Two clauses.

SECTION CCCLXXII.—*Criminal Intercourse during the Period of Mourning.*

All persons who, during the period allotted to mourning for a parent or husband; or who, being attached to either of the acknowledged sacred orders, in the characters of priests or priestesses, are guilty of any species of criminal intercourse, shall suffer punishment two degrees more severely than in ordinary cases between equals; the other party to any such criminal intercourse shall be punished only in the usual degree.

Two clauses.

SECTION CCCLXXIII.—*Criminal Intercourse between Free Persons and Slaves.*

A slave who is in any case guilty of a criminal intercourse with the wife or daughter of a freeman, shall be punished, at the least, one degree more severely than a freeman would have been under the same circumstances.

On the contrary, the punishment of a freeman for having criminal intercourse with a female slave, shall be one degree less than in ordinary cases.

When both parties are slaves, the criminal intercourse shall be punished in the same manner as in the case of free persons.

No clause.

Section CCCLXXIV.—*Officers of Government frequenting the company of Prostitutes and Actresses.*

Civil or military officers of government, and the sons of those who possess hereditary rank, when found guilty of frequenting the company of prostitutes and actresses, shall be punished with 60 blows.

All persons who are guilty of negotiating such criminal meetings and intercourse, shall suffer the punishment next in degree.

One clause.

Section CCCLXXV.—*Strolling Players.*

All strolling players who are guilty of purchasing the sons or daughters of free persons, in order to educate them as actors or actresses; or who are guilty of marrying or adopting as children such free persons, shall, in each case, be punished with 100 blows.

All persons who knowingly sell free persons to such strolling players, and all females born of free parents, who voluntarily intermarry with them, shall be punishable in the manner aforesaid.

The person who negotiates the transaction, shall in each case suffer the punishmemt next in degree; the money paid, shall always be forfeited to government, and the females shall be sent back to their parents or families.

Three clauses.

END OF THE EIGHTH BOOK OF THE SIXTH DIVISION.

BOOK IX.

MISCELLANEOUS OFFENCES.

SECTION CCCLXXVI. — *Defacing or Destroying Public Monuments.*

ANY person who is guilty of defacing or destroying any of the public monuments and buildings, which have been erected in honour and commemoration of particular individuals and events; and any person who defaces or destroys the inscribed tablets upon, or within the same, shall be punished with 100 blows and perpetual banishment to the distance of 3000 *lee*; the offender in these cases shall be moreover compelled to repair the damage.

One clause.

SECTION CCCLXXVII. — *Care of Soldiers, and of Labourers for the Public, when Sick.*

In all civil and military jurisdictions, where there are private soldiers attached to the government stations, or labourers employed in the public works; whenever such persons are suffering under any disease or infirmity, the officer in command shall duly communicate the circumstance to the officer whose province it is to furnish medicines and medical aid to the sick; if he fails to make such communication, or in the event of such communication having been made, if the proper officer does not provide sufficient medical assistance, the individual neglecting his duty shall be liable to the punishment of 40 blows; and this punishment shall be increased to 80 blows, whenever the sick person dies in consequence of such neglect.

No clause.

Section CCCLXXVIII. — *Gaming* *.

All perfons convicted of gaming, that is to fay, of playing at any game of chance for money or for goods, fhall be punifhed with 80 blows; and the money or goods ftaked, fhall be forfeited to government.

All thofe likewife, who keep gaming-houfes, fhall fuffer the fame punifhment, although not actually joining in the game; and the houfe appropriated to gaming, whether it is at the fame time, the ordinary habitation of the proprietor, or one exprefsly purchafed by him for the faid unlawful purpofe, fhall be forfeited to government. — A conviction however fhall not take place under this law, by implication, but only upon direct evidence againft the accufed parties.

All officers of government offending againft this law, fhall be punifhed one degree more feverely than other perfons; neverthelefs, a few friends playing together, for articles of food or drink, fhall not, in any cafe, be punifhed under this law.

Eighteen claufes.

Section CCCLXXIX. — *Eunuchs*.

No private individual, nor any officer of government, excepting only the princes of the Imperial family, fhall prefume to educate caftrated children, in order to their being employed as eunuchs in their domeftic eftablifhments; every breach of this law fhall be pu-

---

* There is probably no vice to which the Chinefe are more generally addicted than that of gaming, but it is, generally fpeaking, the vice of the lower claffes: a certain degree of difcredit is attached to every game which depends either partly or wholly on chance, and between the fharper and the honourable player the line does not feem to be very diftinctly drawn; perfons therefore in official fituations, or who value themfelves upon their reputation, are feldom known to engage in play, even within limits and under circumftances, which might be confidered to render it perfectly innocent and allowable.

nished with 100 blows, and perpetual banishment to the distance of 3000 *lee*: and the castrated children shall be sent back to the families whence they were taken, or to which they belonged *.

Four clauses.

Section CCCLXXX.— *Making illegal Proposals.*

Any regular officer of government, any person having an official employment under government, and any private individual, whatever his description may be, who is guilty of suggesting and recommending to persons in authority an illegal act, whether with a view to his own advantage, or to that of any other person, shall be punished, at the least, with 50 blows. — The officer or person in the employ of government, who assents to such suggestion and recommendation, shall be liable also, at the least, to the same punishment; if the illegal act shall have been carried into effect conformably thereto, his punishment shall be increased to 100 blows; and if the act of injustice thereby suffered or committed, is punishable by the law against an unjust decision more severely than by 100 blows, he shall be punished accordingly.

When the illegal act is suggested and recommended, not upon directly personal considerations, but in favour of a relation, or some other third person, the proposer shall, if the nature of the transaction renders the officer of government, or other person, who complies there-

---

* The number of eunuchs employed within the precincts of the Imperial palace has ever been considerable; and, from the access they must necessarily have at all times to the sovereign, in the capacity of his domestic servants, it is not improbable, that they may still continue to exert some degree of undue influence: it does not however appear that they are ever likely to enjoy under a Tartar dynasty, that exclusive and dangerous confidence, which, while the government was in the hands of native princes, was sometimes reposed in them.

with, liable to a severer punishment than that of 50 blows already provided, be punished in every such case, according to the rate of three degrees less severely than such officer or person in authority: the former is not supposed, in this case, to exercise any positive influence or controul, and therefore the latter, through the responsibility of his situation, is held to be guilty to a greater extent. In general, however, the punishment of the proposer shall be one degree more severe than that provided according to the reduced rate last mentioned, whenever the illegal act proposed regards his immediate interest.

If any officer of government makes, and strongly urges such illegal proposition to a person who is by his office or situation subordinate to him, the punishment of the former shall be increased beyond that in other cases provided, as far as 100 blows; and shall be subject to further aggravation agreeably to the law concerning an intentional deviation from justice; but in capital cases there shall, nevertheless, be a reduction in favour of the proposer of one degree. — If there should have been any act of bribery involved in the transaction, the punishment arising therefrom, in proportion to the amount, according to the law concerning bribery for unlawful purposes, shall, if the most severe, be inflicted in preference to any other which by this article of the laws has been provided.

In every case of recommendatory propositions, their illegality must entirely depend upon an implied desire and design of deviating from the laws.

If an act of bribery is proved, though committed without any such desire and design, the offenders will be punishable according to the law relative to the offer and acceptance of bribes, for purposes not in themselves unlawful. — If neither any pecuniary or valuable consideration had been given and received, nor the object of the proposition in itself illegal, the transaction must then necessarily be considered as innocent.

If any officer, or other person employed by government, disregarding the urgency and influence of his superior, refuses to assent to his illegal proposition, and instead of carrying his wishes into effect, informs against him at a still higher tribunal; such person, if an officer of government, shall be raised a degree of rank, or if not yet a regular officer, shall be raised one degree, as soon as he becomes one.

One clause.

Section CCCLXXXI. — *Compromising Offences, and withdrawing them from the Cognisance of the Magistrates.*

If any person agrees privately to overlook, and thus compromises, any offence against public justice, so that in the end it is illegally withdrawn from the cognisance of the magistrates, he shall be punished only two degrees less severely than the person whose offence was compromised; the punishment of such a compromise shall not however, in any ordinary case, exceed 50 blows.

The act of compromising an offence in cases of life and death, such as that of homicide; and in cases injurious to public morals, such as that of adultery, is punishable by other laws, and therefore the last mentioned limits are not in such cases to be regarded.

No clause.

Section CCCLXXXII. — *Accidental House-burning.*

Any person who accidentally sets fire to his own house, shall, at the least, be punishable with 40 blows; and if such fire should chance to communicate to any other buildings, public or private, the punishment shall be increased to 50 blows. — If such fire should occasion the death

death of any perſon, the puniſhment of 100 blows ſhall be inflicted: — In each caſe, the individual who was the cauſe of the accident, whether the maſter of the houſe, or not, ſhall be the only perſon reſponſible. — If the fire ſhould extend to any of the Imperial temples, or to the gates of the Imperial palace, the individual who was the occaſion of ſuch accident, ſhall ſuffer death, by being ſtrangled at the uſual period. — If it ſhould extend to any of the monuments conſecrated to the ſpirit of the earth, the puniſhment ſhall be leſs by one degree.

Any perſon who accidentally ſets fire to the monumental or other buildings within the precincts of the Imperial cemetery, ſhall be puniſhed with 80 blows and two years baniſhment; and if the conflagration extends to the burning of any of the trees within the ſame, the puniſhment ſhall be increaſed to 100 blows, and perpetual baniſhment to the diſtance of 2000 *lee*.

If any perſon ſhould accidentally ſet fire to a government reſidence, treaſury, or ſtore-houſe, ſuch perſon ſhall be puniſhed with 80 blows, and two years baniſhment; if the ſuperintendant thereof takes the opportunity of fraudulently appropriating to himſelf any of the property of government, his offence ſhall be puniſhed, as an act of embezzlement in ordinary caſes.

If any of the public buildings aforeſaid take fire from without, the perſon having the cuſtody thereof, ſhall be liable to a puniſhment three degrees leſs ſevere than that provided in the caſe of a ſimilar accident originating from within.

All perſons lighting fires within government treaſuries or ſtore-houſes, ſhall be puniſhed with 80 blows, although no miſchief ſhould enſue.

Thoſe alſo, who are entruſted with the care and ſuperintendance of palaces, treaſuries, or ſtore-houſes, or who have the cuſtody of criminals,

nals, fhall, from the moment that a fire is found to have accidentally commenced from within or without, attend diligently at their refpective pofts, and fhall be punifhed with 100 blows whenever guilty of deferting the fame upon fuch occafions.

Two claufes.

Section CCCLXXXIII. — *Wilful and malicious Houfe-burning.*

Any perfon who wilfully fets fire to his own houfe, fhall be punifhed with 100 blows; and if the fire fo kindled fhould communicate, in confequence, to any other building, or to any property ftored up for ufe, public or private, the punifhment fhall be increafed to 100 blows and three years banifhment. — If the perfon guilty of fuch wilful and malicious burning, fhould take the opportunity of purloining any goods or property, he fhall be beheaded at the ufual period; and if fuch burning fhould be the caufe of the death or fevere wounding of any perfon, the offender fhall be punifhed, at the leaft, according to the utmoft feverity of the law concerning intentionally killing or wounding.

All the acceffaries, as well as principals, to the crime of wilfully and malicioufly fetting on fire any refidence, either of an officer of government, or of any private individual, their own only excepted, or to the crime of, in the fame manner fetting fire to any government or private building, treafury, or ftore-houfe, in which public or private property of any kind is ftored and depofited, fhall be punifhed with death, by being beheaded at the ufual period.

To convict fuch offenders, it is neceffary that they fhould have been taken or difcovered on the fpot where the fire took place, and that the fact of their having been wilful incendiaries, be proved by the direct teftimony of competent witneffes.

The crime of wilfully and malicioufly fetting fire to empty and uninhabited buildings, or to grain and other property of the like kind, which is stacked and stored up in fields and open places, shall be punished one degree less severely than the crime last mentioned.

All the property of the offenders shall, in such cases, be sequestrated, and charged with the reparation of the loss or damage sustained, whether by private individuals or by government; and when such property does not prove sufficient, it shall be divided into shares proportionate to the respective losses of the individual proprietors and of government.

Slaves and hired servants offending against this law, shall be punished in the same manner as other individuals.

Two clauses.

Section CCCLXXXIV. — *Theatrical Representations.*

All musicians and stage-players shall be precluded from representing in any of their performances, Emperors, Empresses, famous princes, ministers, and generals of former ages; and shall be punished with 100 blows for every breach of this law. — All officers of government and private individuals likewise, who receive such comedians into their houses, and employ them to perform such prohibited entertainments, shall suffer the same punishment.

Nevertheless, by this law it is not intended to prohibit the exhibition upon the stage of fictitious characters of just and upright men, of chaste wives, and pious and obedient children, all which may tend to dispose the minds of the spectators to the practice of virtue*.

Two clauses.

* As the representations here described as prohibited, are in fact in China the favourite and most usual theatric exhibitions, this article of the laws must either be considered to have become obsolete, or to be enforced only so far as may be necessary to confine such exhibitions within the limits approved by government, and which may not be always the same, at different times, and under different circumstances.

Section CCCLXXXV.—*Transgression of Standing Rules and Orders.*

Whoever is guilty of a transgression of any standing rules and orders, shall, although such transgression is not specifically punishable by any existing law, be punished with 50 blows.

No clause.

Section CCCLXXXVI.—*Improper Conduct not specifically punishable* *

Whoever is guilty of improper conduct, and such as is contrary to the spirit of the laws, though not a breach of any specific article, shall be punished, at the least, with 40 blows; and when the impropriety is of a serious nature, with 80 blows.

No clause.

---

* This article has been sometimes referred to under the title of offences against propriety.

END OF THE NINTH BOOK OF THE SIXTH DIVISION.

BOOK X.

ARRESTS AND ESCAPES.

Section CCCLXXXVII. — *Duty of Police Officers.*

ALL perfons who, after having entered into the fervice of government as conftables, bailiffs, thief-takers, or in any capacity of that defcription, at any time allege pretexts for excufing themfelves from the duty of purfuing and feizing offenders; or do not actually purfue and feize thofe offenders, with the place of whofe retreat they are acquainted, fhall, in each cafe, be liable to the punifhment next in degree to that which is due to the offender, or to the moft guilty of the offenders, if there fhould be more than one, whom their neglect had occafioned to remain at large.

Neverthelefs, a period of thirty days fhall be allowed from the iffue of the orders of the magiftrate; during which, if more than one half of the offenders directed to be feized and brought to juftice, fhould be overtaken, or even any lefs proportion of them, provided fuch proportion includes the moft guilty, the original neglect and mifconduct of the refponfible police officers fhall be pardoned. — And this indulgence fhall extend to all the officers employed, although only one of them fhould have the merit of bringing the offender to juftice.

If, moreover, within the aforefaid interval, the offender or offenders fhould die, or furrender themfelves voluntarily, the failure of the police officers fhall likewife, in either cafe, be excufed. — And, in general, when any proportion whatever of the total number of the offenders fhall have died, or furrendered within the prefcribed period, the refponfibility of the officers of the police, fhall be meafured only according

ing to the number and criminality of thofe of the furviving offenders who are ftill at large.

In the cafe of fimilar neglect on the part of other perfons in the fervice of government, who may on particular occafions have been detached and employed in the purfuit of criminals, out of the regular line of their duty, the punifhment fhall be proportionably lefs by one degree, than that which the eftablifhed police officers would have incurred under the fame circumftances. Whenever it further appears, that the remiffnefs of thofe employed in the purfuit of criminals has been the effect of bribery, the perfon guilty of receiving bribes, fhall not have the benefit of the pardon held out to the reft on the condition of the feizure of the principal criminals within a limited period, and they fhall therefore fuffer punifhment to the full extent, to which the criminals at large are liable, capital cafes only excepted; or inftead thereof, the punifhment of accepting bribes for unlawful purpofes, according as the former or the latter is found in any particular cafe to be the moft fevere.

Ten claufes.

Section CCCLXXXVIII. — *Criminals refifting the Police Officers.*

Whenever a criminal, at any time after a difcovery has been made of his guilt, that is to fay, at any time after charges againft him have been legally prefented to, and received by an officer of government, takes flight, or without having taken flight, refifts and defends himfelf againft the police officers employed in the purfuit of him, his punifhment fhall be two degrees more fevere than that to which his original offence had rendered him liable, previous to this circumftance of aggravation; this aggravation of punifhment fhall not, however, take place in capital cafes, or render thofe cafes capital,

which

which would not have been so otherwise. If, in any of the preceding cases, an offender should strike the police officers so as to inflict a cutting wound, he shall be strangled at the usual period; and if he should kill any of them, beheaded.

All the accessaries in these cases shall suffer the punishment of the principal, reduced one degree.

If the criminal who resists, is armed with any weapons of defence, and the police officers kill him, in endeavouring to secure his person; or if the criminal escapes from their custody, or from prison, and is killed upon a renewal of the pursuit; or if, lastly, the criminal when driven to the last extremity, destroys himself; in such cases, the police officers shall in no wise be answerable for his death.

On the other hand, if a police officer at any time kills or severely wounds a criminal, who is not capitally punishable, and who had surrendered without resistance, either immediately, or as soon as overtaken; such police officer shall be punished according to the law against killing or wounding in an affray. — In the case of killing a criminal whose offence was capital, the punishment of the police officer shall not exceed 100 blows, unless it should appear that the homicide was the result of a previous contrivance and design.

Nine clauses.

SECTION CCCLXXXIX. — *Prisoners escaping, or rising against their Keepers.*

Whenever an offender in confinement quits his cell, and having contrived to release himself from his fetters and hand-cuffs*, escapes from prison, he shall suffer a punishment two degrees more severe than that to which he had exposed himself by his original offence; and if he takes the opportunity of releasing at the same time, any of the

* A particular description of these is given in the introductory part of the code.

other offenders, who were with him in confinement, he shall be liable to the punishment of the most guilty of those whose escape he had so assisted; provided, nevertheless, that in no case the punishment be increased beyond 100 blows, and perpetual banishment to the distance of 3000 *lee*, unless the offender contriving the means of escape as aforesaid, had been previously liable to capital punishment, in which case the sentence shall be executed without alteration.

If one or more offenders in confinement rise against their keepers, and thus forcibly effect their escape, they shall all suffer death, by being beheaded, whatever might have been originally the nature or degree of their offences.

It is hereby provided, at the same time, that those of the prisoners who had really no knowledge of, nor concern in the insurrection, shall not, in any respect, be made to participate in the punishment of the guilty.

Ten clauses.

Section CCCXC.— *Returning or escaping from a Place of Banishment.*

All offenders, who, after having been condemned to, and arriving at the place of their banishment, whether ordinary or extraordinary, temporary or perpetual, desert the same, and endeavour to effect their escape, shall, for the first day's absence, be punished with 50 blows, and for every additional three days absence, one degree more severely, as far as 100 blows; and as soon as retaken, shall be remanded to the place of their banishment; and if they had been sentenced thereto only for a limited period, such period shall recommence from their return after their last attempt to escape, instead of being computed from the original date of their condemnation.

An offender, also, who deserts and attempts to effect his escape at any time after the declaration of his sentence, but previous to his

his arrival at the place of his deſtination, ſhall be equally liable to the penalties of this law.

In the former caſe, the ſuperintendant at the place of baniſhment, and in the latter, the conductor of the offenders thither, ſhall be held reſponſible; and in any caſe of neglect by which one offender eſcapes, they ſhall be puniſhed with 60 blows; and one degree more ſeverely as far as 100 blows, for every additional individual who ſo eſcapes from their cuſtody.

One hundred days ſhall however be allowed for their retrieving themſelves from the conſequences of ſuch neglect, by retaking the offenders and producing them at the ſtations appointed for their baniſhment.

In theſe caſes, the puniſhment of the inſpecting or conducting officer, ſhall be leſs by three degrees than that of the ſuperintending or conducting ſoldier or conſtable.

The miſconduct of all the reſponſible parties ſhall however be pardoned, whenever, within the one hundred days above mentioned, the offenders die, ſurrender voluntarily, or are in any way whatever retaken.

On the other hand; if, in any inſtance, the offenders are deſignedly ſuffered to eſcape, the perſons guilty thereof, whether officers of government, or ſubordinate attendants of the police, ſhall undergo the identical puniſhment to which the releaſed offenders had been condemned. — If ſuch wilful breach of duty is the effect of bribery, the puniſhment ſhall be computed in proportion to the amount of the bribe, according to the law againſt receiving a bribe for an unlawful purpoſe, and inflicted inſtead of the former, whenever it proves the moſt ſevere.

Twenty-three clauſes.

Section CCCXCI. — *Delaying the Execution of a Sentence of Banishment.*

Whenever a sentence of banishment, ordinary or extraordinary, temporary or perpetual, has been regularly pronounced against any offender, the officer of government at whose tribunal the offender had been tried, shall, within the space of ten days, deliver over such offender, fettered and handcuffed in the lawful manner, to a competent guard, with full instructions, and properly authenticated powers, to conduct him to the place of his destination.

The causeless detention of an offender under sentence of banishment three days beyond the period stated, shall be punished with 20 blows; and punishment shall be increased as far as 60 blows, at the rate of one degree for every additional three days of causeless detention: — In all such cases of imputed neglect, the chief clerk of the court shall be deemed the principal offender *.

If an offender avails himself of the opportunity afforded by such causeless detention, to make his escape, the salary of the presiding magistrate shall be suspended until he is retaken, and the clerk of the court shall be banished during the same period.

The penalties of this law shall likewise take effect in the case of every causeless detention of offenders proceeding into banishment, attributable to those officers of government and others, in whose custody and under whose superintendance they happen to be, at any subsequent period, previous to their arrival at their destination.

When offenders under sentence of banishment are proceeding, in the usual way, to their destination, if the inspecting officers do not effectually provide for their safe custody, by fetters and handcuffs, and in the lawful manner; so that they are able to release themselves from

* Relative to the clerks of tribunals, see note, page 30.

such fetters or handcuffs, or in any other manner to effect their escape, they shall be liable to the same punishments as those already provided in the case of such escapes being attributable to the carelessness of the conductors.

In every instance of a bribe having been received for any such unlawful purpose, the law upon the case shall be consulted, and always preferred, whenever it is found to aggravate the punishment.

Three clauses.

SECTION CCCXCII. — *Jailors and others suffering their Prisoners to escape.*

Whenever any offenders escape from prison through the neglect of the jailors, the jailor who was principally responsible in the case, shall be punished only two degrees less severely, than the most guilty of the escaped offenders.

If any such offenders forcibly effect their escape by rising against their keepers or jailors, the punishment of the jailors shall admit of a further reduction of two degrees; and in either case, a period of one hundred days shall be allowed, within which, if they, or any other persons, retake the offenders, or if the offenders either die or surrender voluntarily, the previous neglect of the jailors shall be pardoned.

In the preceding cases, the punishment of the principally responsible individual of the directing board or tribunal of the prison, being the clerk thereof, shall, under a reduction of three degrees, be proportionate to that of the jailors.

If the inspecting officer of the prison had gone through the due and accustomed examination of the prisoners, each individually, and had personally ascertained them to have been fettered and handcuffed in the legal manner, and if he had finally given the necessary instructions

tions to the superintending magistrate and jailors respecting their safe custody, he shall not be responsible for their subsequent escape; but if he had omitted such visitation of the prisoners at the proper period, he shall, in the event of their escaping, suffer punishment, equally with the superintending magistrate of the prison.

When, in any case similar to the preceding, the prisoners had been wilfully and advisedly permitted to escape, the individual convicted thereof, whether a magistrate or a jailor, shall be punishable in an equal degree with the most guilty of the offenders so released and suffered to escape, capital cases only excepted, and not be allowed the benefit of a period of one hundred days, to redeem himself from punishment; nevertheless, when an offender has so escaped previous to condemnation, and, within the aforementioned period, is by any means retaken, dies, or surrenders himself, such circumstance shall have the effect of mitigating the punishment of the magistrate or jailor who had designedly permitted him to escape, one degree.

In any case of a bribe having been received as a consideration for such connivance, the law against bribery for an unlawful purpose, shall be referred to, and acted upon whenever it is found to aggravate the punishment.

Whenever thieves and robbers break into a prison from without, and, overpowering the keepers, carry off any of the prisoners by open violence, the penalties to which jailors and others are subjected by this law in all ordinary cases of prisoners effecting their escape, shall not take effect, and the responsible parties shall be accordingly excused.

The laws determining the responsibility of jailors and others in cases of offenders escaping from prison, shall moreover have the same force and application, in all similar cases of offenders escaping from their conductors, between the prisons and the tribunals of justice.

Fourteen clauses.

SECTION CCCXCIII. — *Privately affisting and concealing Criminals.*

If any person who knows that an information has been laid against an offender before a magistrate, and that orders are issued in consequence to pursue and apprehend him, receives notwithstanding such offender into his house, and there conceals him, instead of delivering him up to justice, or, knowing the premises, assists such offender to make his escape, by supplying him with clothes and provisions, or by indicating to him a place of retreat; such person shall, in all cases, except those of a relationship existing between the parties, suffer a punishment only less by one degree, than that incurred by the offender thus assisted, harboured, or concealed.

It is however provided, that the person harbouring an offender, shall be punishable only in proportion to such of the offender's criminal acts, as he must have been aware of at the time, and not in proportion to others, of which he may have been also guilty, and which may be alleged against him in the course of the trial. — In cases of persons harbouring known offenders previous to the issue of the warrant for their commitment, this law cannot take effect; but the person guilty of such an act may be punished according to the law applicable to cases of improper conduct not specifically punishable*.

All those likewise, who successively entertain and accommodate offenders in their flight, shall be liable to the penalties of this law, whenever they shall appear to have been acquainted with the premises aforesaid, but otherwise shall be excused.

All persons moreover, who, upon being informed of the measures taken by government for pursuing and overtaking a criminal, divulge and publish the same, so as defeat the object thereof, and enable the criminal to escape, shall be punishable in proportion to the guilt

* See Section **CCCLXXXVI.** among the miscellaneous offences.

of such criminal, under a reduction of one degree in each case, except that it shall still be in their power, by overtaking and personally delivering the criminal up to justice, previous to the final determination of his case, to obtain entire pardon; but if the criminal dies, surrenders, or is taken by any other means, within the same period, they shall only obtain a mitigation in their punishment of one degree.

One clause.

Section CCCXCIV. — *Periods allowed for the Pursuit of Thieves and Robbers.*

In ordinary cases of robbery, if the soldiers and attendants of the police, employed on the public service in the district in which the offence is committed, do not seize and bring to justice the robbers within one month, computed from the day on which the information was laid before the magistrates, such attendants and soldiers shall be punished with 20 blows; if unsuccessful at the end of two months, with 30 blows; at the end of three months, with 40 blows; and in the last case, the superintending magistrate shall likewise forfeit two months' salary.

If, in a case of theft, the police officers fail to seize and bring to justice the thieves, within the period of one month, they shall receive a punishment of 10 blows, if unsuccessful at the end of two months, a punishment of 20 blows; and at the end of three months, a punishment of 30 blows; and in the latter case, the superintending magistrate shall likewise be punished for the failure, by a forfeiture of one month's salary. When more than one robber or thief are charged in the information, it shall be sufficient that half the number are seized and brought to justice within the prescribed period, to exempt the

the responsible parties from the punishments and penalties aforesaid:— They shall, moreover, be exempt therefrom, when the plaintiff or party aggrieved, had neglected to lay his information before the magistrate within twenty days from the date of the commission of the offence.

In respect to the provisions of this law, thieves who have likewise committed murder, shall be considered in the same light as robbers.

Thirty clauses.

END OF THE TENTH BOOK OF THE SIXTH DIVISION.

BOOK XI.

IMPRISONMENT, JUDGMENT, AND EXECUTION *.

SECTION CCCXCV. — *Securing the Perfons of Prifoners.*

IF in any cafe of imprifoned offenders, the fuperintending magiftrate does not ftrictly confine thofe, who, according to the laws, ought to be ftrictly confined, fuch as all ordinary prifoners charged with offences punifhable with banifhment or death, and not privileged in confideration of their rank, tender youth, extreme age, or bodily infirmities; or if the fuperintending magiftrate does not confine with fetters and handcuffs, thofe who, by law, ought to be fo confined; or having fo confined, afterwards

* Although clofe imprifonment is not awarded by the Chinefe laws, as the ordinary punifhment of any fpecific offence, and is confidered in this book of the code, only as far as it is applicable and neceffary to the fafe cuftody of accufed perfons, between the period of their arreft and that of their conviction or acquittal; or that of condemned perfons between the period of their conviction and that of their execution: yet, in fome inftances, chiefly thofe of European miffionaries, capitally convicted during occafional perfecutions, a fentence of death has been, through the Imperial clemency, commuted for that of imprifonment during a limited period. The moft recent inftance of this kind is that of an Italian prieft of the name of Joakim, who has been releafed from the prifons of Canton, within the prefent year (1809), after undergoing three years clofe confinement, to which he had been fentenced, in confequence of having been unfortunately difcovered and apprehended, when on his way to join his brethren in the interior. — It does not appear that he has fuffered any very ferious hardfhips; but the report and edict, of which tranflations are given in the Appendix, No. X., clearly prove, that in the adminiftration of the prifons in China, very enormous abufes have at times been committed. — At the fame time, it is but juft to obferve, that it is not improbable there may be fome exaggeration in the fub-viceroy's report of thofe abufes, which he would naturally picture in ftrong colours, as an accufer, and alfo as one to whom the merit was due of the difcovery.

releases them, his punishment shall be proportionate to the guilt of the offenders in question, in the following manner:

In the case of an offender punishable with the bamboo only, the magistrate shall be liable to suffer 30 blows; with temporary banishment, 40 blows; with perpetual banishment, 50 blows; and if with death, 60 blows. — In the case of confining a criminal with fetters, who ought according to the laws to have been handcuffed, or *vicê versâ*, the punishment of the superintending magistrate shall, having regard to the circumstances already stated, be proportionably less by one degree.

If the governing magistrate of the prison, his official attendants, or the jailors, release any of the prisoners from their fetters and handcuffs, or permit them so to release themselves, they shall be equally liable to the penalties of this law, as the superintending magistrate would have been under similar circumstances.

Again, if the inspecting magistrate of the prison is privy to such a neglect of the laws, and does not notice the same to the superior jurisdiction, he shall be liable to the same punishment as those actually guilty of the neglect; but if unacquainted therewith, he shall not be responsible.

On the other hand, if any unnecessary severity is practised by the magistrates or officers aforesaid, by confining with particular strictness, or confining with fetters and handcuffs, any of the prisoners, without being legally required or authorized so to do, such misconduct shall be punished in every instance with 60 blows.

Whenever any of the aforesaid offences are found to have been the result of bribery, the legal punishment, proportionate to the amount thereof, according to the law against bribery for an unlawful object, shall be ascertained, and if it proves to be more severe than that provided by this law, it shall be inflicted in preference.

Seven clauses.

Section CCCXCVI.—*Imprisonment of, and Procedure against, unaccused and unimplicated Persons.*

All officers of government, and their official attendants, who, instigated by private malice or revenge, designedly commit to prison an unaccused and unimplicated individual, shall be punished with 80 blows; and if such false imprisonment should directly or indirectly occasion the death of such individual, they shall suffer death, by being strangled at the usual period.

The inspectors and governors of prisons, their official attendants, and the jailors, when privy to, and not giving information against, such illegal proceedings, shall be liable to the same punishments, except in capital cases, when a mitigation of one degree shall take place; but when unapprized of the illegality of the procedure, they shall not be liable to any punishment whatever.

When, in the examination of offences connected with the public service, any individuals are brought before the magistrates merely to give evidence; if such individuals, without being chargeable with any participation in the unlawful transactions under investigation, are inadvertently committed to prison, instead of being simply held responsible for their re-appearance, the superintending magistrate shall be subjected to the punishment of 80 blows, in every case of such persons dying, either directly or indirectly, in consequence of such irregular imprisonment.

But in all cases of imprisoning in the lawful manner persons who are actually charged with, or implicated in, any criminal transactions, the magistrates shall be entirely free from any responsibility for the consequences.

Moreover, all officers of government, and their official attendants, who, instigated by private malice or revenge, designedly examine with judicial severities, any unaccused and unimplicated person, shall, although they should not by so doing actually wound such person, be punished with 80 blows; if guilty of inflicting, by such procedure, any cutting or severe wound, they shall be punished according to the law against cutting and wounding in an affray in ordinary cases; lastly, if death ensues, the superintending magistrate shall be beheaded.

The assessors, and other officers of justice concerned in the transaction, shall, if aware of the illegality of their act, suffer punishment according to the same rule, except in capital cases, upon which they shall be allowed a reduction of one degree in the punishment. — When, however, they are really unconscious of the illegality of the transaction, and the blows with the bamboo, or the question by torture, although illegal, under the circumstances of the case, are administered by the official attendants in the customary manner, the said officers shall be respectively exempted from any participation in the punishment of the presiding magistrate.

Lastly, if in the course of proceedings connected with the public service, any of those persons, whom, although not personally implicated in an illegal transaction, it may have been requisite to examine, obstinately persist, after the charges have been clearly proved by evidence and corroborating circumstances, in denying or endeavouring to suppress the truth, in order to protect the guilty, it shall be lawful for the magistrates to administer the question according to the severities allowed by the laws applicable to extreme cases, and they shall not be punishable, even if the person so examined, and subjected to torture, should accidentally and unexpectedly die under the same.

Six clauses.

SECTION CCCXCVII.—*Delay in executing the Sentence of the Law.*

When any person in custody has been brought to trial, and the judicial proceedings instituted upon all charges legally exhibited against him, either in the peculiar jurisdiction of the courts of judicature at Pekin, or in any of those of the provincial tribunals of the several viceroys and sub-viceroys, are finally closed, upon its having satisfactorily appeared upon the trial, that nothing had been falsely alleged, or insufficiently investigated; then, provided it be a case in which the sentence, conformable to the laws, may be pronounced and executed without reference to the supreme authority, such sentence shall, within the space of three days, be pronounced and executed, as far as regards any corporal punishment to which the culprit may be liable. — And when the remainder of the sentence consists of temporary or perpetual banishment, the culprit shall, within the space of ten days, be dispatched towards the place of his destination. For a delay of three days beyond the period allowed by this law, the officers of the tribunal in which the affair had been investigated, shall be punished with 30 blows, and the punishment shall be increased as far as 60 blows, at the rate of one degree for every additional three days delay. — If in consequence of any unlawful delay of justice, an offender happens to die, either previous to the infliction of corporal punishment, previous to his departure conformably to his sentence of banishment, or previous to the execution of his sentence in any other respect, the officers of the tribunal shall, in the case of capital offenders, be punished with 60 blows; in a case of a sentence of perpetual banishment, with 80 blows; in a case of a sentence of temporary banishment, with 100 blows; and in a case of merely corporal punishment with the bamboo, with 60 blows, and one year's banishment.

Four clauses.

Section CCCXCVIII. — *Ill treatment of Prisoners.*

All jailors, and others having the care and custody of prisoners, when guilty of striking, wounding, or otherwise ill treating them, shall be punished in proportion to the injury done, according to the law against striking or wounding in ordinary cases of an affray. In all cases also, of the jailors or others suppressing any part of the government allowance of clothes and provisions, the deficiency shall be estimated, and the offence punished as an embezzlement of government stores to the same amount and value: and if any prisoner dies in consequence of such default in his allowance, the jailor or other attendant guilty thereof, shall suffer death by being strangled at the usual period.

If the inspecting and superintending magistrates of the prison, upon being made acquainted with the misconduct of the jailors, take no cognizance thereof, they shall, excepting the usual reduction of one degree in capital cases, equally participate in their punishment; and even when ignorant thereof, they shall still be liable to punishment according to the law respecting offences by implication*.

Twelve clauses.

Section CCCXCIX. — *Allowing Prisoners Sharp Instruments.*

All jailors and other attendants of prisons, who shall be found to have provided any of the prisoners with sharp weapons of metal, or with any other articles by means of which they might possibly kill or release themselves, shall be punished with 100 blows.

If any prisoners should, by such means so provided, effect their escape, or wound themselves or others, the punishment of the persons

---

* See Section CCCLXXXVI.

providing the said instruments or articles, shall be increased to 60 blows and one year's banishment. — If any of the prisoners should kill themselves therewith, the punishment of the persons guilty as aforesaid, shall be further increased to 80 blows and two years banishment; and lastly, if in consequence of having obtained such instruments, they rise against their keepers and effect their escape by force, or commit murder, the jailor or attendant who had provided the instruments, shall suffer death by being strangled at the usual period.

If, however, in any of the preceding cases of a criminal making his escape in consequence of being thus provided with the means thereof, the criminal should, before the judicial proceedings upon the case are finally closed, die, surrender himself, or by any means be retaken, the person punishable under this law, shall be allowed a reduction in his punishment of one degree.

In the case of such prohibited articles being supplied to a prisoner by a stranger, by a son to his parent, or by a slave or hired servant to his master, when in such a situation, the punishment shall be one degree less than that of the jailor would have been under the same circumstances.

Whenever the inspecting and superintending officers, and their clerks or assistants, are privy to, and yet take no cognizance of this offence, they shall be liable to the same punishment as the jailors and other immediate attendants of the prison, according to the circumstances, excepting only the usual reduction of one degree in capital cases.

If bribes had been received by the offending parties to such an extent as would, conformably to the law against bribery for an unlawful purpose, aggravate the punishment, the punishment shall be aggravated accordingly.

If the jailors and other responsible persons, although not actually chargeable with having supplied the means by which mischief might be effected, are not duly vigilant and attentive in guarding against

accidents,

accidents, and it happens in confequence that any of the prifoners fucceed in an attempt to deftroy themfelves, the jailors fhall be punifhable with 60 blows, the fuperintending officers and attendants with 50 blows, and the infpecting officers and their attendants with 40 blows.

No claufe.

SECTION CCCC. — *Encouraging and exciting Prifoners to make groundlefs Appeals.*

All officers, official attendants and jailors, belonging to prifons, who inftruct or encourage prifoners to appeal againft their fentence under frivolous pretexts, after their juft and lawful condemnation; or who affift them in communicating with others out of prifon for the fame purpofe, fhall, according to the nature of the defigned diminution of the prifoner's offence, or of the extent of the offence which wholly or in part is by implication imputed to the informer, be punifhed conformably to the law againft a fimilar intentional deviation from juftice in awarding judgment.

The punifhment of a ftranger, or of a relation of the prifoner, when offending in the fame manner, fhall be lefs than that inflicted upon the officers of the prifon when guilty, by one degree. — Moreover, the officers and attendants of prifons who fuffer, or connive at improper communications of this defcription between the prifoners and ftrangers, fhall, although fuch communications fhould not have the effect of increafing or diminifhing the punifhment of any perfon, be punifhed, at the leaft, with 50 blows; and, as in all the preceding cafes, when any of the parties have been bribed, the legal punifhment of fuch bribery fhall be inflicted in preference to any other, if it proves, on comparifon, to be more fevere than the punifhment otherwife provided.

Three claufes.

SECTION CCCCI. — *Supply of Food and Clothes to Prisoners.*

Whenever the individuals committed to prison, have no families or relations by whom they may be supplied with necessaries, the superior authorities shall be addressed for leave to supply them with clothes and provisions, and, whenever they are sick, with medicines and medical assistance; leave shall also be asked in favor of those who are not charged with capital crimes, that they may, when sick, be released from their fetters and handcuffs; and in favor of those who are only liable to a punishment of 50 blows or less, that they may, when sick, be let out of prison, upon sufficient security being given for their return; and lastly, in favor of those who are dangerously sick or incurably infirm, that their families may have free access to them.

Although it is not left at the option of the officers and attendants of the prisons to grant any of these indulgences, yet, if they do not solicit them in behalf of the prisoners when lawfully allowable, they shall suffer a punishment of 50 blows for such neglect; and if in the meanwhile any capitally punishable offender dies for want of such indulgence, the above neglect shall be punished with 60 blows; if any offender punishable with perpetual banishment dies, with 80 blows; if an offender punishable with temporary banishment dies, with 100 blows; and lastly, if any offender punishable with the bamboo only, dies for want of any of the said indulgences, the neglect of the officers of the prison shall be punished with 60 blows and one year's banishment.

If the inspecting officer of the prison is privy to the neglect of the others, and yet takes no cognizance thereof, he shall be liable to the same punishment.

When the officers of the prisons have duly solicited any such indulgences conformably to the laws, if the superior officer delays one day in complying with their lawful requests, he shall be punished with 10 blows and for every additional day of delay, one degree more severely, until the punishment amounts to 40 blows.

If, in consequence of such remissness or delay on the part of the superior officer, the prisoner dies; then, in the event of his having been a capital offender, such superior officer shall be punished with 60 blows; if he had been punishable with perpetual banishment, with 80 blows; if he had been punishable with temporary banishment, with 100 blows; and if with the bamboo only, with 60 blows, and banishment for the space of one year.

Nine clauses.

SECTION CCCCII. — *Indulgence in consideration of the Rank and former Services of Prisoners.*

All offenders in confinement, who had held the fifth or any superior rank among the officers of government, or who had at any time distinguished themselves by their public services, shall be allowed a free communication with their relations and connections while in prison, and such relations and connections shall likewise be freely permitted to accompany them, when undergoing a sentence of temporary or perpetual banishment. — If any such favourably considered offender falls sick and dies, either in prison, on his journey to, or after his arrival at the place of his banishment, the officer of government in whose jurisdiction such event takes place, shall immediately dispatch a messenger with information of the circumstances to the relations of the deceased, that they may in due form apply to the sovereign for leave to recover his body. — Every officer of government shall be liable to a punishment of 60 blows, who under such circumstances fails to comply with the provisions of this law.

No clause.

Section CCCCIII. — *Prisoners committing Suicide.*

In all cases of capitally convicted offenders, who, after having confessed their guilt, shall have been induced, under apprehensions of the consequent execution of their sentence, to instruct and employ their relations or near friends to kill them, or to hire some third person to kill them; the relation or friend hiring a third person, and the individual who strikes the blow, whether a relation, a friend, or hired stranger, shall suffer the ordinary punishment of killing in an affray, reduced two degrees: — but if the capitally convicted offender had confessed his guilt without having made such a request to his relations and friends, or had made the request without having confessed his guilt; in either case, the relation or friend hiring a person to kill, and the person killing, shall be punished according to the law in ordinary cases of killing and wounding in an affray, without any reduction.

In regard to either of the preceding cases however, it is provided, that if the party killing the prisoner or hiring another to do so, be the son or grandson, slave or hired servant, of such prisoner, he shall invariably be beheaded at the usual period, for so great an offence against piety or subordination.

No clause.

Section CCCCIV. — *Torture not to be used in the judicial Examination of Children or of the Aged.*

It shall not, in any tribunal of government, be permitted to put the question by torture to those who belong to any of the eight privileged classes, in consideration of the respect due to their character; to those who have attained their seventieth year, in consideration of their advanced age; to those who have not exceeded their fifteenth year, out of indulgence to their tender youth; and laſtly, to thoſe who labour under any permanent diſeaſe or infirmity, out of commiſeration for their ſituation and ſufferings. — In all ſuch caſes, the offences of the parties accuſed ſhall be determined on the evidence of facts and witneſſes alone; and all officers of government who diſregard the reſtrictions of this law, ſhall be puniſhed either according to the law againſt a deſigned, or the law againſt a careleſs aggravation of the puniſhment of an offender, according as the ſaid miſconduct on the part of the magiſtrate is attributable to deſign, or to inattention.

Moreover, in all caſes in which the circumſtances or connexion between the parties, produce a legal incapacity, or in the caſe of individuals arrived at eighty, or under ten years of age, or entirely and permanently infirm, it ſhall not be permitted even to require or to receive their teſtimony; every breach of this law in any tribunal of government, ſhall be puniſhed accordingly with 50 blows, and the clerk of the court eſteemed, as in all other caſes of miſconduct in a joint and official capacity, the principal offender.

No clauſe.

SECTION CCCCV. — *Confronting Offenders with their Aſſociates.*

All officers of government in whoſe tribunals the trial and inveſtigation of the charges againſt any offenders has commenced, ſhall ſtop their proceedings whenever any of the aſſociates or accomplices of ſuch offenders are aſcertained to be in the cuſtody of any other officers of government, in order that they may be confronted one with another; for which purpoſe the officer of government engaged in the inquiry, ſhall claim from the officers having any of the ſaid accomplices in cuſtody, their delivery and tranſmiſſion to his tribunal, by official letters to that effect, although their reſpective juriſdictions ſhould

be

be altogether independent of, and unconnected with each other; such official requests shall in general be complied with before the expiration of three days; beyond that period a delay of one day shall be punished with 20 blows, and there shall, for every additional day of delay, be an augmentation of one degree in the punishment, as far as 60 blows in the whole. — On all such occasions, the officer of government making the application ineffectually, shall accuse the other of delay, before the superior authorities to which he is subjected, in order that the offence of which he is guilty may be investigated, as well as his compliance with the said application enforced, according as the laws direct.

If the trial and investigation of the charges against such accomplices or implicated persons had actually commenced in the jurisdiction to which they belonged, previous to their being officially demanded on the ground of the necessity of confronting them with the other offenders at the same time under examination elsewhere, it shall be observed as a constant rule, that the prisoner charged with the lesser offence, be removed to the tribunal in which the prisoners charged with greater offences are under examination; but if the offences are similar in degree, then the few shall be transferred to the tribunal having within its jurisdiction the greater number; and if the numbers are likewise equal, then the prisoners last accused shall be removed to the jurisdiction in which the first accusation was made.

It is however provided, that if the distance between the aforesaid independent jurisdictions exceed 300 *lee*, (in which case it may be inexpedient to remove the prisoners on account of the risk of escape) each charge shall be examined and determined separately.

Every neglect of the provisions of this law, shall be punished with 50 blows; nevertheless, when the greater offenders have been actually transferred to the jurisdiction in which the lesser had been apprehended, or the many to the few, the firſt accuſed to the laſt accuſed, the officer of government receiving them ſhall not decline to undertake the trial at his tribunal, under the pretext of being under an obligation to refer them back again, according to this law, to their proper juriſdiction; he ſhall, however, give due information of the irregularity, to the ſuperior authorities over the officer who had been the occaſion thereof, that by ſuch ſuperior authorities the ſaid irregularity may be inveſtigated and puniſhed.

If, in any of theſe caſes, the magiſtrate, after the arrival of the priſoners at his tribunal, delays for one day to take cognizance of their offences, he ſhall ſuffer a puniſhment of 20 blows; and the puniſhment ſhall be augmented as far as 60 blows, at the rate of one degree for every additional day of delay.

Eleven clauſes.

Section CCCCVI. — *Examination of Offenders to correſpond with the Charges againſt them.*

Every trial and examination of a priſoner brought before a tribunal of government, ſhall, generally ſpeaking, be ſtrictly confined to the ſubject of the information laid againſt him; if, on the contrary, any preſiding magiſtrate urges an inquiry upon matters irrelevant thereto, in order in one way or other to fix guilt upon a priſoner, he ſhall be liable to puniſhment conformably to the law concerning magiſtrates deſignedly over-rating the guilt, and aggravating the puniſhment of offenders under examination: — The aſſeſſors of the tribunal, when they do not perſonally inveſtigate in this unlawful manner, ſhall not be anſwerable.

At the ſame time, it ſhall not be underſtood that this law forbids the examination of any criminal acts and circumſtances of which a diſcovery may have neceſſarily taken place, either in the courſe of ſecuring the

the person of an offender, or in the regular process of the inquiry into the charges for which he had been brought to trial.

One clause.

Section CCCCVII. — *Prosecutors not to be detained after a Trial is concluded.*

In all cases of trials and investigations of charges which have been duly laid before the tribunals of government, as soon as the facts alleged are fully substantiated, and confessed by the criminals themselves, the accusers and informants shall cease to be subject to detention or to examination; the presiding magistrate shall therefore dismiss them forthwith, and absolve them from all further responsibility. — If he should, on the contrary, designedly prolong the detention of such persons, for three days, he shall be liable to a punishment of 20 blows; and punishment, in these cases, shall be further increased, at the rate of one degree, as far as 40 blows, for every additional three days of detention.

Two clauses.

Section CCCCVIII. — *Offenders recriminating upon innocent Persons.*

All offenders who, while in durance, or under examination, maliciously charge with crimes any innocent persons, shall be liable to punishment to the same extent as false accusers in ordinary cases, and such punishment shall be inflicted instead of that to which the offenders thus recriminating were liable on account of their original offences, in the event of the former being more severe than the latter.

Nevertheless, if an offender, without entertaining a previous intention of recrimination upon any innocent person, should be required and compelled so to do, by the unlawful application of torture, the presiding magistrate shall be responsible for the same, according to the law concerning an intentional and unjust aggravation of the guilt of persons accused, as in ordinary cases.

In like manner, if a revenue officer engaged in the recovery of the amount of duties payable by a defaulter, at the same time urges and compels him to accuse an innocent person of a similar default, the amount of the excessive contribution to the revenue, which may be in consequence extorted, shall be ascertained, and restored to the injured party, while the magistrate shall be punishable according to the law relative to pecuniary malversation in ordinary cases.

If, moreover, in any of these cases, the magistrate detains the person, whom he had occasioned to be, or known to have been, falsely criminated by an offender, he shall be liable to the punishment of 20 blows, when such detention is continued for three days; and the punishment shall be increased as far as 60 blows, at the rate of one degree, for every additional three days of detention.

If, in the course of the trial and investigation of any offence, the witnesses and by-standers, in consequence of being under the influence of private partiality, or of other improper motives, do not, when examined, give true evidence of the facts, or designedly and falsely criminate any person, such false and prevaricating witnesses shall be punished two degrees less severely than is legally proportionate to the amount of the deviation from justice in the subsequent sentence of the offender; but if, in the case of the trial and investigation of the offences of foreigners, the official interpreters are found to be actuated by private motives, and therefore to interpret falsely, such interpreters shall suffer punishment to the full extent of the consequent deviation from justice.

No clause.

Section CCCCIX. — *Pronouncing and executing an unjuſt Sentence**

Whenever, by the authority of a tribunal of juſtice, confiſting of regular officers of government, and of official clerks, an unjuſt ſentence is wilfully and deſignedly pronounced and executed, whether by the acquittal and difmiſſal of a priſoner, who ought to have been condemned to the full extent of the charges againſt him; or by the condemnation and puniſhment (whether capitally, or otherwiſe,) of a priſoner, conformably to the full extent of the charges againſt him, who ought, on the contrary, to have been acquitted and difmiſſed; in every ſuch caſe, the member of the court who ſtands firſt in point of reſponſibility, ſhall ſuffer puniſhment equal in degree with that which was, when it ought not to have been, or was not, when it ought to have been, inflicted.

If the ſentence pronounced and executed by the authority of any tribunal, is not wholly unjuſt and groundleſs; but yet, in point of ſeverity, either falls ſhort of, or exceeds to a certain extent, that ſentence which the laws applicable to the circumſtances of the caſe would have juſtified, the amount of the deviation from a juſt and lawful ſentence ſhall be computed by eſtimating each ſix months of temporary baniſhment at 20 blows, and every augmentation of 1000 *lee* in the diſtance of perpetual baniſhment, as equivalent to one half year's temporary baniſhment; the amount thus computed, if it does not exceed 100 blows of the bamboo, ſhall be inflicted therewith on the officer of the court principally reſponſible; but if exceeding the ſame, ſhall be divided into two equal portions, one of which ſhall be

---

* This ſection of the laws is of very extenſive application, as is apparent from the frequent references made to it; theſe references will eaſily be diſtinguiſhed when they occur, though the context has not always admitted of the preciſe terms of the title being adhered to.

inflicted

inflicted corporally, and the other exchanged for banishment, according to the preceding computation.

Nevertheless, when any sentence of capital punishment, which is in any respect unjust, is wilfully and knowingly pronounced and executed, there shall be no deduction whatever in consideration of the prisoner being in some degree guilty, and the officer of the court principally responsible shall be punished with death, in the same manner as the unjustly condemned and executed prisoner. — Whenever the unjust sentence had not been pronounced wilfully, but through error, there shall be a reduction in each case, of three degrees in the punishment, if the injustice consisted in an aggravation; and of five degrees, if it consisted in a mitigation of the sentence.

In general, the clerk of the court shall be punished as the individual principally responsible; the executive or deputy officer shall suffer the punishment reduced one degree; the assessor or assessors of the court, reduced two degrees; and the presiding officer, judge, or magistrate, the same reduced three degrees.

If the unjust condemnation had only been pronounced, but not executed, or if the unjust acquittal had been pronounced, but the prisoner either not dismissed, or recovered after having been dismissed; or, lastly, if the natural death of the prisoner had prevented the execution of the unjust sentence of condemnation, or had prevented the subsequent pronouncing and executing of one that was lawful; in all such cases, the punishment incurred by a false judgment shall be reduced one degree.

The system of punishment in all imaginable cases of false judgment, will more distinctly appear, by a reference to the several examples in the following table.

An unjust sentence of capital punishment, if not executed, shall be deemed equivalent to an unjust sentence of perpetual banishment already

ready executed; but every unjuft fentence of capital punifhment which has been executed, fhall be punifhed with death.

Six claufes.

TABLE of EXEMPLIFICATION.																
	Grounds of Eftimate of Injuftice.				Sentence having been executed.								Sentence pronounced but not executed.			
	The Sentence having been unjuft, wilfully, or by Defign.															
	The Sentence which ought to have been pronounced and executed.		The Sentence which actually was pronounced.		Punifhment of the Clerk of the Court.		Punifhment of the Deputy or Executive officers of the Court.		Punifhment of the Affeffors.		Punifhment of the prefiding Magiftrate.		Punifhment of the Clerk of the Court.		Punifhment of the Deputy or Executive Magiftrate.		Punifhment of the Affeffors.		Punifhment of the prefiding Magiftrate.	
	Blows of the Bamboo.	Banifhment, temporary or perpetual.	Blows of the Bamboo.	Banifhment, temporary or perpetual.	Blows.	Banifhment.	Blows.	Banifhment.	Blows.	Banifhment.	Blows.	Banifhment.	Blows.	Banifhment.	Blows.	Banifhment.	Blows.	Banifhment.	Blows.	Banifhment.
Aggravated.	10	—	80	2 years	70	yrs. 2	60	yeₐrs 1½	50	yrs. 1	90	yr. —	60	yrs. 1½	50	yrs. 1	90	—	80	—
	80	—	60	1 year	40	—	30	—	20	—	10	—	20	—	10	—	—	—	—	—
	80	—	100	2500 *lee*	60	2	60	1	100	—	80	—	60	1	100	—	80	—	60	—
	60	1 year	90	2½ years	60	—	40	—	20	—	—	—	40	—	20	—	—	—	—	—
	70	1½ years	100	2000 *lee*	60	½	60	—	40	—	20	—	60	—	40	—	20	—	—	—
	100	2000 *lee*	100	3000 *lee*	—	1	—	—	—	—	—	—	—	—	—	—	—	—	—	—
Mitigated.	60	1 year	50	—	70	—	50	—	40	—	30	—	50	—	40	—	30	—	20	—
	90	2½ years	100	—	80	—	60	—	40	—	20	—	60	—	40	—	20	—	10	—
	100	3 years	70	1½ years	60	—	40	—	20	—	—	—	40	—	20	—	—	—	—	—
	100	2000 *lee*	40	—	80	2½	80	2	70	1½	60	1	80	2	70	1½	60	1	100	—
	100	3000 *lee*	80	2 years.	40	1½	40	—	20	—	—	—	40	—	—	—	—	—	—	—
The Sentence having been unjuft through Error.																
Aggravated.	10	—	80	2 years	90	—	80	—	70	—	60	—	80	—	70	—	60	—	50	—
	80	—	60	1 year	—	—	—	—	—	—	—	—	—	—	—	—	—	—	—	—
	80	—	100	2500 *lee*	80	—	60	—	40	—	20	—	60	—	40	—	20	—	10	—
	60	1 year	90	2½ years	—	—	—	—	—	—	—	—	—	—	—	—	—	—	—	—
	70	1½ years	100	2000 *lee*	20	—	—	—	—	—	—	—	—	—	—	—	—	—	—	—
	100	2000 *lee*	100	3000 *lee*	—	—	—	—	—	—	—	—	—	—	—	—	—	—	—	—
Mitigated.	60	1 year	50	—	10	—	—	—	—	—	—	—	—	—	—	—	—	—	—	—
	90	2½ years	100	—	—	—	—	—	—	—	—	—	—	—	—	—	—	—	—	—
	100	3 years	70	1½ years	—	—	—	—	—	—	—	—	—	—	—	—	—	—	—	—
	100	2000 *lee*	40	—	80	—	60	—	50	—	40	—	60	—	50	—	40	—	30	—
	100	3000 *lee*	80	2 years	—	—	—	—	—	—	—	—	—	—	—	—	—	—	—	—

SECTION CCCCX. — *Reverſal of a falſe Judgment.*

Whenever the tribunals of juſtice in the provinces, or in the capital, have occaſion to take cognizance of a caſe of falſe judgment, an accurate and faithful report of the circumſtances thereof, and of the extent of the injuſtice alleged, ſhall be laid before the Emperor, in order that a ſpecial commiſſion may be granted for trying the ſame. — When the falſehood of the accuſation if falſe, and the injuſtice of the ſentence if unjuſt, are ſatisfactorily proved, the inveſtigating magiſtrate ſhall, in the firſt inſtance, rectify the ſentence with regard to the accuſed and ſentenced perſon, and then proceed to decide upon the guilt incurred, and the puniſhment conſequently merited, either by the accuſer, or by the magiſtrate, according as the unjuſt ſentence had, or had not been conformable to the accuſation.

On the contrary, when any tribunal of juſtice groundleſsly reverſes a former judgment, and charges it, in a report to the Emperor, with injuſtice; the principal offender, among the members of ſuch tribunal, ſhall be liable, at the leaſt, to a puniſhment of 100 blows, and three years baniſhment; but if the conſequent falſe condemnation of the accuſer, or of the judging magiſtrate, be more ſeverely puniſhable, the puniſhment ſhall be eſtimated and inflicted according to the laws againſt ſuch a deviation from juſtice.

If the juſtly accuſed and condemned offender ſhall have been a party to ſuch undue reverſal of judgment, he ſhall be liable to the ſame puniſhment, as far as it may tend to aggravate that to which he was liable in the firſt inſtance; but if ignorant and unconcerned therein, he ſhall only ſuffer puniſhment conformably to the nature of his original offence.

Nine clauſes.

Section CCCCXI. — *Execution of Judgment.*

The trial and investigation of the offences of all prisoners in custody, shall be effected with clearness and precision, by the authorities to which they are respectively subject; those who are in a lawful manner convicted of offences punishable with banishment, temporary or perpetual, ordinary or extraordinary, shall be severally ordered to their destination, each conformably to his sentence, by the governor of the city or jurisdiction in which they were condemned. But in all cases of a capital nature, the trial and investigation of the alleged offence, shall be renewed, if at Pekin, by the courts of judicature; and if in the provinces, by the respective viceroys and sub-viceroys thereof; in order that it may be ascertained with more than ordinary care and deliberation, that no error nor injustice had been committed; when the sentence is thus confirmed, a final report of the circumstances and of the judgment pronounced, shall be transmitted for the information of His Imperial Majesty.

If the Imperial orders on the subject contain a warrant for the execution of the offender conformably to his sentence, an officer shall be specially appointed to carry the same into effect, and shall be liable to a punishment of 60 blows for any wilful delay on his part therein.

If, during the process of the final investigation, the offender retracts his confession, and appeals against his sentence, or his relations complain of the injustice thereof, in his name, the superior authorities are bound to take cognizance of such appeal; and if the complaint and appeal be found well grounded, they shall not fail to reverse such unjust sentence, and they shall likewise proceed criminally against the judges of the tribunal, in which it had been pronounced.

If the superior authorities refuse or neglect to inquire into, and to take cognizance of such lawful appeal and complaint of injustice, when duly brought forward to their notice, they shall be liable to punishment conformably to the law against an erroneously or wilfully unjust sentence, according as their guilt is found to be, upon an investigation of the circumstances, imputable to error or to design.

Fifty clauses.

Section CCCCXII. — *Examination of the Body in Cases of Homicide.*

Whenever an inquest is to be held on the body of any person deceased, in order to ascertain the nature of the wounds and of the injuries sustained by the same; if the magistrate in whose department it lies to perform such duty, does not proceed to examine the body immediately on the receipt of his instructions, in consequence of which omission, a change takes place in the corpse before it is visited; if, instead of attending the examination personally, he deputes any of the civil or military attendants of his tribunal, and thereby exposes himself to be deceived by a false report; if he allows the previous and subsequent examiners privately to compare, in order to agree in their reports; or lastly, if he does not examine carefully and minutely, or represents one thing instead of another, the slight for the severe, and the severe for the slight, so that his statement of the wounds and injuries being incorrect, the cause of death, and the other circumstances of the case cannot be distinctly traced and ascertained; in all such cases the magistrate presiding shall suffer a punishment of 60 blows, his deputy, a punishment of 70 blows, and the officiating clerk, a punishment of 80 blows: — The attendants likewise, who perform the manual part of the operation, shall be punished with 80 blows, if implicated in the offence.

When, in consequence of the insufficient or inaccurate examination of the body of any person deceased, the crime of the person accused of homicide

micide shall have been aggravated or palliated unjustly, the parties to the examination shall be punishable according to the law against either a wilful or an erroneous deviation from justice, as the case may be. — If any of the parties have been bribed to make such defective examination and consequently false report, they shall be liable to the punishment of bribery for an unlawful purpose, as far as such punishment exceeds that to which they were previously liable by this law, or by the law against an intentional or erroneous deviation from justice.

Eighteen clauses.

Section CCCCXIII. — *Infliction of Punishment in an illegal Manner.*

If, in any tribunal of justice, punishment is inflicted illegally, by the employment of the larger bamboo instead of the lesser, or otherwise, such a deviation from the law shall be punished with 40 blows; and if the punishment so illegally inflicted occasions death, the deviation shall be punished with 100 blows, and ten ounces of silver shall be forfeited to the family of the deceased, to defray the expences of burial.

In each case, the punishment of the attendant who inflicts the blows, shall be less by one degree.

If the attendant of the tribunal appointed to inflict the blows, contrives to strike in such a manner as not to touch the skin*, the number of such ineffectual blows shall be ascertained, and inflicted effectually, either on the attendant himself, or on the person under whose orders he acted, according as, by an investigation of the circumstances of the case, the contrivance is found to be imputable to the one or to the other.

* A deception of this kind is said to be frequently practised in favour of such offenders as are able to purchase it; the attendant in such cases contrives that the effect of each blow should be intercepted by the extreme end of the bamboo hitting the ground.

In all cafes in which a bribe has been accepted as an inducement to aggravate or mitigate the punifhment in the manner above defcribed, the parties to the deviation from the laws fhall fuffer the punifhment of bribery for an unlawful purpofe, whenever it exceeds that to which they were otherwife liable.

If a fuperintending officer of government on the occafion of any breach of civil or military duty, directs his official attendants to inflict chaftifement on a more vulnerable part, than is warranted by the law; or if he inflicts himfelf, or directs others to inflict, punifhment in a violent and unlawful manner, either with the large bamboo, with the hand, with the foot, or with any metal weapon, fo as to produce a cutting wound, the individual who inflicts, or caufes to be inflicted, fuch unlawful and unwarrantable chaftifement, fhall be punifhed for the confequences, only two degrees lefs feverely than is provided by law in ordinary cafes of fimilar injuries being inflicted in affrays between equals.

If, in fuch cafes, death enfues, the punifhment fhall be increafed to 100 blows, and three years banifhment, and ten ounces of filver fhall be, moreover, forfeited to the relations of the deceafed, to defray the expences of burial.

The punifhment of the perfon who inflicts, in obedience to orders, fuch irregular and unlawful chaftifement, fhall, in each cafe, be lefs fevere than that of his fuperior, by one degree.

Neverthelefs, when it fo happens, that immediately after the infliction of punifhment, on the upper part of the back of the thighs, and in a lawful manner, the culprit commits fuicide, or dies in any manner in confequence of the punifhment he had undergone, no perfon fhall be held refponfible for the fame.

One claufe.

Section CCCCXIV. — *Proceedings againſt Offences committed by Superior Magiſtrates.*

Whenever the preſiding officer of any provincial tribunal commits an offence againſt the laws, at the place of his official reſidence, or any extraordinary officer furniſhed with the commands of the Emperor, at the place of his official deſtination, the ſubordinate officers of government ſhall not in either caſe tranſgreſs the limits of their authority, by inquiring into the offence, but merely report the ſame to ſuch of the ſuperior authorities as have a juriſdiction over the offender. — In the caſe however of a charge of a capital offence, it ſhall be lawful for the ſubordinate magiſtrate to take the offender into ſafe cuſtody proviſionally, until inſtructions for further proceedings are received in reply from the ſuperior authorities; and in the mean while, the ſeals of office, and the keys of the priſons, treaſuries or ſtore-houſes under his juriſdiction, ſhall all be delivered over to the next in command.

This law ſhall apply to the caſe of any ſuperior officer, although he ſhould not happen to be the preſiding officer of his tribunal; and in general, the ſubordinate officer who in any inſtance neglects the proviſions of this law, ſhall be puniſhed at the leaſt with 40 blows.

No clauſe.

Section CCCCXV. — *Laws, Statutes, and Precedents, which are to be obſerved in paſſing Sentence.*

In all tribunals of juſtice, ſentence ſhall be pronounced againſt offenders according to all the exiſting laws, ſtatutes, and precedents applicable to the caſe, conſidered together, the omiſſion of which, in any reſpect, ſhall be puniſhed at the leaſt with 30 blows; when, however,

however, any article of the law is found to comprife and relate to other circumftances befides thofe which have occurred in the cafe under confideration, fo much only of the law fhall be acted upon, as is really applicable.

Thofe determinations of the punifhment of offences, which have been announced by the fpecial edicts of his Imperial Majefty, and carried into effect as conformable to the exigency of the cafe in particular inftances, without being declared to be defigned as a rule for future guidance, fhall never be confidered or received as precedents; and whoever wilfully or erroneoufly fo receives and confiders them, fhall be liable to the punifhment provided by law againft a wilful or erroneous act of injuftice.

Four claufes.

SECTION CCCCXVI. — *Prifoners upon Trial at liberty either to plead Guilty, or to proteft againft their Sentence.*

After a prifoner has been tried and convicted of any offence punifhable with temporary or perpetual banifhment, or with death, he fhall, in the laft place, be brought before the magiftrate together with his neareft relations and family, and informed of the offence whereof he ftands convicted, and of the fentence intended to be pronounced upon him in confequence; their acknowledgment of its juftice, or proteft againft its injuftice, as the cafe may be, fhall then be taken down in writing: and, in every cafe of their refufing to admit the juftice of the fentence, their proteft fhall be made the ground of another and more particular inveftigation.

The magiftrate who, in a cafe of banifhment, refufes to receive fuch a proteft, fhall be punifhed with 40 blows, and in a capital cafe with 60 blows. — In all cafes however, in which the relations of the prifoner

soner are at any distance beyond 300 *lee*, it shall be sufficient to summon the prisoner singly, and to proceed as aforesaid, according to his individual protest or individual avowal.

No clause.

SECTION CCCCXVII. — *Misapplication or Disregard of an Act of Grace and Pardon.*

Whenever any tribunal of government, on the occasion of an act of grace and pardon, pronounces a sentence of punishment in a case in which, conformably to such act, it should have been remitted; or a sentence of punishment in its full extent, instead of the mitigated one; or lastly, mitigates the punishment in a case not entitled to the benefit of the act, the determination and execution in each case shall, as far as is practicable, be rectified: if the deviation arises from error, it shall be pardonable by the existing act of grace, but if intentional, the officers of the tribunal shall not have the benefit of such act of grace, although the general remission of punishment should even extend to all other offences of the same description, namely, a wilful deviation from justice.

Five clauses.

SECTION CCCCXVIII. — *Offending designedly in the Expectation of Impunity through an Act of Grace and Pardon.*

All those who, having previous knowledge and information of an act of grace and pardon, designedly transgress the laws, in the expectation of being able to escape with impunity, shall not only be excluded from the benefit of such act of grace and pardon, but shall moreover suffer punishment one degree more severely than in ordinary cases.

On the other hand, any magiſtrate who is adviſed or informed of the intended iſſue of an act of grace and pardon, and neverthelefs directs the execution of puniſhment upon thoſe offenders who are, in ſuch caſes, pardonable, ſhall be liable to puniſhment according to the law againſt an unjuſt aggravation in pronouncing ſentence.

No clauſe.

SECTION CCCCXIX. — *Services to be performed by temporarily baniſhed Offenders.*

All thoſe temporarily baniſhed offenders, who, when deſtined to perform ſervice in the iron or ſalt works of government, do not perform the ſame; and thoſe who, having obtained leave of abſence on account of ſickneſs, do not, after their recovery, work an additional number of days, correſponding to the number of thoſe during which they were abſent, ſhall, in each caſe, be puniſhed (as alſo the police officer having authority over them, who ſuffers ſuch neglect) with 20 blows for the firſt three days, and one degree more ſeverely, as far as 100 blows, for every additional three days, in which they are deficient in the performance of their duty. — If the conſtable or officer having authority over a baniſhed criminal, permits him to hire a ſubſtitute, and upon that pretext to return, previous to the expiration of the period declared in his ſentence, from his baniſhment, ſuch conſtable or officer ſhall ſerve in his ſtead, during the time that remains to be completed; and if guilty of bribery, ſhall ſuffer aggravated puniſhment, according to the law againſt bribery for an unlawful purpoſe.

The criminal returning from baniſhment, ſhall be puniſhed and ſent back, according to the law upon the caſe already provided.

No clauſe.

SECTION CCCCXX.—*Punishment of Female Offenders.*

Female offenders shall not be committed to prison except in capital cases, or cases of adultery.

In all other cases, they shall, if married, remain in the charge and custody of their husbands, and if single, in that of their relations, or next neighbours, who shall, upon every such occasion, be held responsible for their appearance at the tribunal of justice, when required.

All magistrates committing women to prison contrary to the provisions of this law, shall suffer the punishment of 40 blows.

If any female who is condemned to corporal punishment, or to the question by torture, is discovered to be with child, she shall be sent back to the custody of the responsible persons aforesaid, and not be subjected to punishment or to the question by torture, until 100 days complete are elapsed from the period of her delivery.

If, by a neglect of this law, the infliction of torture or of punishment should destroy the child in the womb, the officers of the tribunal responsible for such neglect, shall suffer punishment within three degrees of the severity of that which is incurred by law for inflicting such an injury in ordinary cases. — If the woman with child should die in consequence of the infliction of torture, or of punishment of any kind, under such circumstances, the punishment of the officers of justice shall be increased to 100 blows and three years banishment; the punishment of the officers of justice shall however be less severe than the aforesaid by one degree, when death is occasioned by the infliction of punishment or torture, not previous, as in the cases above stated, but within the hundred days after parturition.

When any woman who is condemned to be executed for a capital offence, proves to be with child, she shall be attended in prison by a midwife, and be reprieved from the execution of the sentence of the law, until 100 days are expired from the period of her being delivered.

The officers of juftice who execute any criminal fo circumftanced, previous to her delivery, fhall be punifhed with 80 blows; if within the faid period of one hundred days after her delivery, with 70 blows; and if, after the expiration of fuch period, they delay any longer to execute the criminal, they fhall be punifhable with 60 blows.

In all the cafes here defcribed, the officers of juftice are fuppofed to offend wilfully: — when merely offending through an error of judgment, the punifhment fhall, in every inftance, be proportionably lefs fevere by three degrees.

Six claufes.

Section CCCCXXI. — *Execution of Criminals without waiting for the Emperor's Ratification.*

All magiftrates who authorife the execution of any capitally convicted offender, without waiting for the Imperial refcript, containing the ratification of the fentence grounded upon their final report of the cafe, fhall be punifhed, at the leaft, with 80 blows.

After the warrant of execution is received, a further delay fhall be allowed, of three days, during which if the criminal is executed, or after which, if he is not immediately executed, the refponfible officer of government fhall be liable to the punifhment of 60 blows. — Neverthelefs, in the cafe of robbers, and thofe who are fentenced to be executed for any of the ten treafonable offences, a breach of this law fhall only be punifhed with 40 blows.

Three claufes.

SECTION CCCCXXII. — *Execution of a Sentence by a false Construction of the Laws.*

If, after a sentence is pronounced against an offender in a tribunal of justice, he is permitted to redeem himself from banishment or corporal punishment, in a case that is not by law redeemable; or if he is banished or corporally punished, in a case that is redeemable, the punishment of such false construction of the laws, shall be only one degree less severe than that of an entirely unjust and groundless sentence, under similar circumstances.

If an offender who, conformably to the laws, ought to be strangled, is beheaded; or beheaded, when he ought to have been strangled; such deviation, if wilful, shall be punished with 60 blows; if committed by mistake, with 30 blows.

Moreover, the offence of mangling or disfiguring the body of a capitally executed criminal, in any manner not prescribed by law, shall be punished with 50 blows.

If a magistrate, charged with the execution of the laws against the relations and dependants of traitors and rebels, in any instance dismisses those, whom he ought to have retained in a state of perpetual servitude to government, or retains, with that design, those whom he ought to have dismissed; he shall be liable to the same punishment as those magistrates who are guilty of improperly condemning, or improperly omitting to condemn, persons accused of offences punishable with perpetual banishment.

The distinction between the offence by design and by mistake shall be attended to in this, as in other similar cases.

No clause.

SECTION CCCCXXIII. — *Clerks of Tribunals altering the Statements of Informers.*

In all tribunals of government in which crimes are investigated, and punishments inflicted, the proceedings of the magistrates must necessarily depend upon the nature of the depositions made by the parties concerned. — If therefore, in any such tribunal, the clerks thereof transcribe falsely, add any thing to, or take away any thing from, such documents and writings, so as to mislead the magistrates by a concealment or perversion of the truth, such clerks shall, conformably to the extent of the false judgment awarded in consequence, suffer the punishment provided by law in ordinary cases of injustice to such an extent.

When a prisoner upon trial is really ignorant of letters, it shall be allowable to employ some indifferent and uninterested person to write down his deposition; but the clerks of the court shall not presume, even in such a case, to undertake to write a deposition in behalf of any person under examination, on pain of being punished as in a case of disobedience*, although a false judgment should not be the consequence of their interference.

One clause.

---

* According to the law in Section CCCLXXXV.

END OF THE SIXTH DIVISION.

SEVENTH DIVISION,

Laws relative to Public Works.

BOOK I.

PUBLIC BUILDINGS

SECTION CCCCXXIV.— *Ordering Public Works without sufficient Authority.*

ALL civil and military officers of tribunals, within the limits of whose respective jurisdictions public works are occasionally requisite, shall, in every instance, according to the nature of their offices, and the circumstances of each particular case, either give information thereof to their superiors, or await the report of their inferiors; and if, instead of so doing, they proceed immediately to employ labourers and others, on such service, the wages of the persons so employed shall be estimated at 8 *fen 5 lee 5 hao per* man *per* day *, and according to the amount of a sum, produced by computing their number, and the number of days they were employed, the responsible officer of government shall be liable to punishment, conformably to the scale provided by law in ordinary cases of pecuniary malversation.

Moreover, when labourers and others are employed otherwise than in the legal manner, and at the legal period, then, although the

---

* Not quite seven-pence sterling.

proper information should have been given, or the customary report awaited, the responsible officer of government shall be liable to punishment, according to an estimate made upon the same principles as in the preceding case.

Nevertheless, when any of the walls of cities or other fortifications, or of any inclosures in public buildings, happen to fall down, and when any of the public granaries, treasuries, offices or residences, are injured and damaged, the officer in charge thereof, who thereupon immediately appoints proper superintendants, and employs proper labourers, in order to restore or repair the same, shall be subject to none of the penalties of this law.

If any officer of government, when soliciting aid from his superior to enable him to carry into effect any public works, does not truly state the extent of the labour and quantity of the materials required, he shall be punished with 50 blows; and, if in consequence, any materials are injured or wasted, or any labour unnecessarily expended, the value of the former, and amount of the hire of the latter, shall be estimated, and these sums taken together shall be held to be the amount of the pecuniary malversation attributable to the responsible magistrate, conformably to which he shall be punished, agreeably to the law respecting that offence, the punishment not exceeding however in its utmost extent, the limit of 100 blows, and three years banishment.

Six clauses.

SECTION CCCCXXV. — *Unnecessary and unserviceable Works.*

If any of the officers of government, or other persons who have the immediate superintendance of any public works, employ stone or timber, or burn bricks or tiles, so as to occasion an unnecessary waste of materials and of labour, or employ the same in such a manner as to be unserviceable, the amount and value of such misemployed labour and materials shall be estimated, and the responsible person punished in
proportion

proportion thereto, according to the law againſt pecuniary malverſation in general; the puniſhment in no caſe exceeding 100 blows, and three years baniſhment.

If, through ſuch aforeſaid miſmanagement, or want of due diligence and precaution, houſes or walls fall down, or any other accident happens, by which ſome perſon is killed, the ſuperintendant of the work, or other perſon who is reſponſible by virtue of his office, ſhall pay a fine to the relations of the deceaſed, in the ſame manner as in ordinary caſes of accidental homicide.

No clauſe.

SECTION CCCCXXVI.— *Public Works and Manufactures to be conformable to Rule and Cuſtom.*

If a perſon ſerving in, and belonging to, any department of the public ſervice, performs, or cauſes to be performed, any public work or manufacture, contrary to the eſtabliſhed rule and cuſtom, he ſhall be puniſhed, at the leaſt, with 40 blows; and in the caſe of any ſuch deviation being made in the manufacture of military weapons, ſilks, ſtuffs, and the like valuable articles, the puniſhment ſhall be increaſed to 50 blows: if the deviation is ſo confiderable, as to render the manufactured articles totally unſerviceable, or to render it neceſſary to employ additional labour and expence in adapting them for uſe, the ſaid labour and expence attending the repair, or re placing of the articles, ſhall be eſtimated, and the reſponſible perſon puniſhed in proportion to the amount, according to the law reſpecting pecuniary malverſation in ordinary caſes.

If ſuch improperly prepared or manufactured articles, had been deſtined for the immediate uſe of His Majeſty, the puniſhment ſhall, in each caſe, be more ſevere by two degrees, and extend accordingly in extreme cafes, as far as the limit of perpetual banifhment, to the diftance of 2500 *lee*.

The perfon immediately concerned in the manufacture, fhall, in general, be efteemed the principal offender; the punifhment of the fuperintending officer of the eftablifhment fhall be lefs by one degree; and that of the officer fuperintending the fupplies, by two degrees; and the refponfible perfons fhall, moreover, always reimburfe government to the extent of the additional expence occafioned by their mifconduct.

One claufe.

SECTION CCCCXXVII. — *Mifapplication of Public Stores.*

If, in any government manufactory, or upon the occafion of any work being conducted or undertaken at the public charge, the principal or managing workman obtains upon falfe pretences more than the neceffary quantity of raw materials, in order to apply the fame, or the produce thereof, to his own private ufe or emolument, the quantity and value of the public ftores thus fraudulently applied, fhall be eftimated, and the offender punifhed in proportion thereto, according to the law applicable to the embezzlement of ftores belonging to government, in ordinary cafes.

The officer fuperintending the manufacture, or (if there fhould be no fuperintendant) the officer in whofe immediate department it lies, fhall, if convicted of knowing, and agreeing to connive at the perpetration, of fuch fraud, be liable to the fame punifhment as the aforefaid offender, except only in capital cafes, when he fhall be allowed the ufual mitigation of one degree.

If the fraud is perpetrated without the knowledge or concurrence, and therefore attributable merely to the neglect of fuch officer, his punifhpunishment shall be three degrees less severe than that of the principal offender, and not in any case exceed 100 blows.

Nine clauses.

Section CCCCXXVIII. — *Misapplication of the Public Looms.*

If any officer, or other person in the employ of government, who possesses authority or jurisdiction over any government manufactory, unduly avails himself of such authority, by sending raw materials of his own, to be manufactured into silks and stuffs in the public looms, for his own private use, he shall be punished with 60 blows, and the silks or stuffs so manufactured shall be forfeited to government: the workman who is concerned therein, shall be punished with 50 blows; the superintending officer of the manufactory, if acquainted with the transaction, and failing to give information thereof, shall suffer the same punishent as the officer of government principally offending: but if chargeable with neglect only, not having been actually privy to the transaction, his punishment shall be less severe by three degrees.

No clause.

Section CCCCXXIX. — *Working Silks or Stuffs according to prohibited Patterns.*

Any private individual who shall be convicted of manufacturing for sale, silks, satins, gauzes, or other similar stuffs, according to the prohibited pattern of the *lung* (dragon), or the *fung whang* (phœnix), shall be punished with 100 blows, and the goods so manufactured, shall be forfeited to government.

Any individual who is guilty of purchasing, and actually wearing such prohibited stuffs, shall be punished with 100 blows, and three years banishment; but if guilty of purchasing only, with 30 blows. — The working weaver, and the embroiderer of such stuffs, shall be condemned as equal participators of the offence of the master of the house or manufactory, by whose order they were prepared.

No clause.

SECTION CCCCXXX. — *Irregularity in the Supplies of Raw Materials, and in the Issue of manufactured Goods.*

A determinate quantity of silks and stuffs, and of military weapons, shall be annually manufactured and prepared for the public service, in each subdivision of the department of public works; and if any of the workmen fail to provide in due season their assigned proportion, they shall be liable, at the least, to a punishment of 20 blows; and the punishment shall be increased as far as 50 blows, at the rate of one degree for every additional tenth deficient: the punishment of the superintending officer of the work, shall be one degree less severe, and that of the officer superintending the supplies, two degrees less severe, than that of the workman.

On the other hand, if the raw materials are not delivered to the workmen in sufficient quantities, and at proper times, the superintending officer of the manufactory shall suffer a punishment of 40 blows, and the superintendants of supplies a punishment 30 blows; the workmen shall, in such cases, be excused.

No clause.

SECTION CCCCXXXI. — *Due Preservation and Repair of Public Buildings.*

When any of the government residences, granaries, treasuries, manufactories, or other buildings, are in a defective or ruinous condition,

dition, the officer having charge thereof, shall immediately report the same to his superior, and state the nature of the repairs that are required; and he shall be liable to a punishment of 40 blows, whenever he neglects to do so: if, in consequence of such neglect, any public property should happen to be injured or destroyed, he shall, besides the aforesaid punishment to which he is liable, be obliged to make good the same to government.

On the other hand, if, a regular notice having been given to the superior officer, the latter neglects to authorize the necessary repairs, he alone will be liable, both to the punishment, and to the obligation of making good the amount of the contingent damages.

One clause.

Section CCCCXXXII. — *Officers of Government not residing in the Habitations allotted to them.*

If any of the governors of cities of the first, second, or third order, or of any other provincial sub-divisions, instead of inhabiting the public buildings expressly allotted to their use, hire, and reside in private houses belonging to the inhabitants of the districts under their authority, they shall, for every such offence, be punishable with 80 blows.

Likewise, if an officer, or other person employed in the public service, is convicted of concealing any furniture, utensils, or other articles belonging to government, and of finally withdrawing them altogether from the public service; or in any way losing or destroying, without in due time replacing them, he shall be punished according to the law which is applicable in ordinary cases of losing or destroying public stores,

stores, and is already provided; namely, if wilfully deſtroying ſuch articles, the officer ſhall be puniſhed two degrees more ſeverely than in the caſe of a common theft, except that the branding ſhall be omitted; and if loſing, three degrees leſs ſeverely than when wilfully deſtroying to the ſame amount.

One clauſe.

END OF THE FIRST BOOK OF THE SEVENTH DIVISION.

BOOK II.

PUBLIC WAYS.

SECTION CCCCXXXIII. — *Damaging Embankments of Rivers.*

ANY perfon who damages or breaks down by ftealth, any of the embankments of great rivers, which are maintained at the expence, and by the authority of government, fhall be punifhed with 100 blows; and any perfon who damages or breaks down the embankments of fifh-ponds, or of fmall rivers, fuch as are maintained by private individuals at their own expence, fhall be punifhed with 80 blows, although no mifchief fhould enfue in either cafe; but if the waters overflow in confequence, and fuch an inundation takes place, as is injurious to, or deftructive of the houfes, goods, or cultivated lands in the neighbourhood, the amount of the damage fhall be eftimated, and the offender punifhed in proportion thereto, according to the law concerning pecuniary malverfation.

If the effects of the inundation fhould extend fo far as to do bodily injury to, or oecafion the death of any perfon, the offender fhall be punifhed one degree lefs feverely than in the cafe of killing or wounding in an affray.

If any perfon, from vengeful or interefted motives, fhould openly and daringly damage or break down any of the embankments, maintained as aforefaid by government, he fhall be punifhed with 100 blows, and three years banifhment; and punifhed two degrees lefs feverely, in the cafe of damaging under fimilar circumftances the embankments maintained by private individuals.

If, in either of these cases, the waters overflow and are destructive as aforesaid; the person who openly and daringly offends, shall be punished in proportion to the estimated amount of the damage sustained, according to the law in the case of a common theft to the same extent; except that he shall not be branded in the manner there provided.

Lastly; if the destruction ensuing from the offence openly and daringly committed, extends to the loss of any lives or the bodily injury of any person, the offender shall be punished according to the law against killing or wounding designedly.

Four clauses.

SECTION CCCCXXXIV.—*Neglecting duly to Repair and Maintain Embankments.*

When the embankments of great rivers are not duly repaired and maintained, or repaired unseasonably, the superintending officer in that department shall be punished with 50 blows; if any lands, goods, or other articles of property of any kind, are damaged by an inundation in consequence of such neglect and misconduct, the punishment shall be increased to 60 blows; and if any persons are killed or injured, to 80 blows.—In the case of private embankments, the responsible persons neglecting to repair them at the proper seasons, shall be liable to a punishment of 30 blows; and if any damage ensues, in consequence of such neglect, to a punishment of 50 blows.

Nevertheless, in respect to those sudden and impetuous inundations, which are produced by heavy rains, or other similar causes, and which sometimes wash away, and break down irresistibly, all ordinary embankments; as it is not in the power of man always to foresee

and

and guard against such accidents, the parties usually held responsible, shall not be liable in such cases to any punishment.

Three clauses.

Section CCCCXXXV. — *Encroaching upon Public Highways.*

Any person who encroaches upon the space allotted to public streets, squares, high-ways, or passages of any kind; that is to say, who appropriates a part of any such space to his own use, by cultivating it, or building on it, shall be punished with 60 blows, and obliged to level and restore the ground to its original state.

Any person who opens a passage through the wall of his house, to carry off filth or ordure into the streets or high-ways, shall be punished with 40 blows; but in the case of a passage being opened to carry off water only, no penalty or punishment shall be inflicted.

No clause.

Section CCCCXXXVI. — *Repair of Roads and Bridges.*

The repair and preservation of all bridges, whether permanent or formed for temporary use, of boats only; and also of all roads and high-ways, shall come under the cognizance and jurisdiction of the governors of the cities of the different orders, their assessors, and deputies; and there shall be a special examination of the same, during the interval between the harvests of each year, in order to ascertain that the bridges are maintained in a firm and complete condition, and that the roads are solid and even: when the regular communication by any of the said established roads and bridges is interrupted, for want of due attention to the necessary repairs, the responsible magistrate shall suffer a punishment of 30 blows for his neglect:

also in places of customary communication, where bridges ought to be built, or ferry-boats stationed for the accommodation of the inhabitants, a failure to do so in either case, shall be punished with 40 blows*.

No clause.

* The original work, it is proper to notice, concludes with two supplemental books, containing fifty-seven articles each, relating, however, almost wholly to the Tartar subjects of the empire; these books therefore, upon the same principle that has been acted upon in respect to the other supplemental parts of the work, has been omitted in the present translation.

END OF THE PENAL CODE.

APPENDIX.

APPENDIX.

No. I.

[Referred to from the Translation of the Third prefatory Edict.]

Translation of the Testamentary Edict of KIEN-LUNG *Emperor of China* *.

ON the seventh day of the second moon of the fourth year of KIA KING †, is recorded the testamentary edict of His late Majesty, by the grace and appointment of Heaven, THE MOST HIGH EMPEROR, in these words.

We ‡ have remarked that all those sovereign princes on whom the decrees of Heaven have conferred a long and uninterrupted enjoyment of prosperity, have been distinguished by their exemplary conduct, and by an innate integrity of disposition, which bears a resemblance to the excellence of the Divine perfection. Virtues like these attending them through life, failed not to secure a lasting and abundant felicity. With this persuasion, it has been most constantly our endeavour to guard against every such want of application or want of energy on our part, as might counteract the execution of the gracious designs of Heaven.

We were at the same time fully sensible how arduous it is to poize with an unerring hand an overflowing fulness, how arduous, to preserve entire the harmony and integrity of a vast empire; nor were we unconscious that to persevere from the

---

* The history of this Emperor is too well known to need any comment. He succeeded his father *Yong-tching*, in 1736, resigned the throne after a reign of sixty years, to his son *Kia King*, the present Emperor, and died the seventh of February, 1799, aged eighty-seven years four months and thirteen days;—according, however, to the Chinese mode of computing, he was in the eighty-ninth year of his age.

† Twelfth of March 1799.

‡ The plural is here introduced, not solely in conformity to European usage, but also as the nearest approximation to the pronoun exclusively appropriated in the Chinese language to sovereignty. The phrase " *I the Emperor*" might perhaps be more strictly correct, but its adoption would have been in many places very inconvenient.

begin-

beginning to the end, with unabated attention, is an undertaking still more difficult of performance.

Chiefly we are indebted to the all-powerful protection of Heaven, and to the sublime instructions which have been left by our ancestors for the guidance of their posterity; we have likewise gratefully to acknowledge the rare affection shewn towards us in our early youth by our Imperial grandfather, as well as the wise and provident selection of ministers which was made by our Imperial father, from whom also we received the sacred sceptre of this realm.

From the very commencement of our reign we noted the progress of each day with careful solicitude; we beheld an era of profound tranquillity and glorious prosperity; but we never dared to give way to exultation or to indulge in the full enjoyment of these advantages: we rather engaged our attention in the contemplation of the grand duties of a prince; namely, on the one hand, a reverent observance of the laws of Heaven, together with a due veneration for the memory of his forefathers; and on the other, a diligent and benevolent administration of his people. These maxims are, indeed, easily acquired and retained in remembrance; but their execution is not therefore the less arduous or perplexing. During the long course of years, however, which has elapsed since our accession, we certainly have strictly adhered to the observance of the duties of our station, and have forborne to relax in our attention, from the earliest dawn to the close of day, to any of our various avocations.

In the practice of devotion, we have sedulously observed the appointed sacrifices and occasional oblations to the Divinity, and have always personally assisted at each ceremonial, in order to testify the purity of our heart and the unfeigned piety by which we were actuated, even at a time when our extreme age had a claim to some degree of relaxation and indulgence.

Four times in the course of our reign we personally undertook a journey to our city of Mougden, in order to pay our humble adorations at the tombs of our Imperial ancestors.

When the administration of this empire was committed to our charge, we indeed beheld before us a task of serious difficulty, but we were rendered thereby, only more earnest and solicitous in avoiding all deviation from the strict line of conduct we had prescribed to ourselves. All parts of our various and widely extended domains shared equally our attention, and frequently during the darkness of the night, as well as at the middle hour of the day, we have attended, unconscious of fatigue, in the councils of our ministers, for the purpose of communicating our decisions on their reports, and of issuing new ordinances for the public weal, that thus no day might be permitted to pass away, without having been duly filled and employed.

The abundance or scarcity of rain, the favourable or deficient harvests, and the other casualties which influence the prosperity of our various provinces, are objects in which we have been always most deeply interested. Six times, therefore, we have visited our provinces of *Kiang-nan* and *Kiang-see*, with the view of directing the embankment of the rivers, and the construction of dykes and causeways to repel the encroachments of the sea.

Regarding the people also as our children, and as looking up to us their father for support and protection, we have taken occasion five times to grant a universal remission of all the taxes that are usually received in specie; and thrice have granted a similar remission of all such duties as are payable in kind. On other occasions, likewise, we granted a remission of taxes to the inhabitants of particular provinces, especially when afflicted by an inundation, drought, or other partial calamity; and, in such cases, we frequently superadded a bountiful distribution of millions to the poor, in order to alleviate their distresses; being persuaded, that in thus providing for the happiness and prosperity of our subjects, we accomplished the most important duty of an upright administration.

Through the protecting influence of Heaven, and the wise counsels left us by our ancestors, we have succeeded in establishing peace and tranquillity throughout our dominions. The bordering countries, we have placed in a state of cultivation and improvement; we have established order and restored tranquillity throughout the states of *Eli* *, *Whee-poo* †, and the greater and lesser *Kin-tchuen* ‡. The tribe of *Mien-tien* ‖ has submitted to our authority; the King of Cochinchina had acknowledged himself our vassal; and we have lastly dictated a peace to the nation of *Ko-ur-ke* §.

Even those nations who visit this country by navigating their ships across the ocean, have bowed down before our throne, and brought presents for our acceptance.

With respect to the inhabitants of the interior of the empire, who have excited commotions and disorders among themselves, we may shortly expect that this evil will be eradicated, and that the tranquillity of the provinces will be re-established.

The reports, however, of the advantages obtained by our generals over these internal enemies, clearly indicate that the employment of troops against them was unavoidable.

---

* The Eleuth Tartars.
† Little Boucharia.
‡ Countries inhabited by tribes of Tartars, immediately bordering on the province of *Se-chuen*.
‖ This people inhabit the countries immediately bordering on the province of *Yun-nan*.
§ Probably Napaul.

Thus

Thus, during the long and eventful period of our reign, the weighty affairs of government have been the objects of our constant regard; and, deeply impressed with the critical importance of the charge, we never ventured to pronounce the objects of government to have been so completely attained, or the peace of the empire so immutably established, as to admit of our relaxing our efforts or indulging in repose.

Ultimately, however, we recalled to our recollection the mental prayer which we had addressed to the Supreme Being on our accession to the Imperial dignity, and in which we had made a solemn intimation of our intention to resign to our son and successor the sovereignty of the realm, if the Divine Will should grant to our reign a sixty years continuance; forasmuch as we were unwilling to exceed in any case, the duration of our Imperial grandfather's government *.

Our years had indeed already amounted to twenty five, when we thus provided for the event of a sexagenary reign, as if we were gifted with a prescience to enable us to anticipate so protracted a period; it is under the guardian auspices of our Imperial progenitors that this inestimable favor of a reign so glorious, and so happily prolonged, has been extended to us.

While surrounded with numerous relations, and witnessing at once five generations of our family and descendants, we finally observed the progressive revolution of a cycle to be accomplished since the empire had been committed to our hands; and when we then reflected on our original wishes and designs, the contemplation of the corresponding event impressed us with the warmest sensations of joy and gratitude.

Accordingly, on the first day of the year *Ping-shin* † we transferred to our son, the present Emperor, the seals of the sovereign authority, reserving to ourself the title of MOST HIGH EMPEROR, as a distinctive appellation, thus accomplishing in the end, what in our solemn invocation to Heaven we had originally proposed.

We did not, indeed, conceive this arrangement with a view to obtain a respite from fatigue, or to indulge ourself in repose, by terminating the labours of an active and eventful reign with that ease and tranquillity, which our numerous and declining years seemed to warrant and require; we were rather influenced in our resolution of resigning the more immediate duties of government, by the consideration of our being enabled thenceforward to be more immediately occupied in aiding and instructing our successor in the guidance of public affairs, as long as our strength and ability remained unexhausted.

* The Emperor *Kaung-hee* reigned sixty one years.
† The eighth of February 1796.

To retire from the cares of government, merely with a view to our perfonal eafe and convenience, would, indeed, be an ungrateful requital for the favor and protection of Heaven and of our anceftors; an act repugnant to our feelings, which we could neither wifh nor dare to commit.

Upwards of three years have fince paffed away, during which we have diligently devoted our attention to the inftruction, and direction of the government of our fucceffor.

We have witneffed of late the operations of an active campaign againft the rebels of *Se-chuen*, and have obferved, with fatisfaction, the numerous advantages and repeated victories which have been obtained by the diligent exertions of our Imperial troops; we are even in the immediate expectation of the furrender of all the rebellious leaders, and anticipate the day on which hoftilities will ceafe, and univerfal tranquillity be re-eftablifhed in thefe dominions.

Being arrived therefore at an era fo juftly to be deemed aufpicious, and fo peculiarly diftinguifhed by the happinefs and welfare of our people, we might certainly venture at length to relax from our ufual folicitude; but to a mind accuftomed to look forward to the feafon of difficulty, in order to meet its approach with eafe and promptitude, it is impoffible to unbend altogether from care.

As upon the year *Keng-fhin**, which is the next following to the prefent, would occur the ninetieth anniverfary of our age, laft year, the Emperor, our fon, in concert with the princes and great officers of ftate, was defirous of determining upon the celebration of that event by a congratulatory feftival, and earneftly requefted our confent to the carrying the fame into effect; to which we, fhortly after, in confideration of the meritorious motives which actuated them in their proceedings, replied by an edict expreffive of our approbation and concurrence.

Viewing, indeed, the advanced age of upwards of fourfcore years, which we had then attained in the full enjoyment of every profperity, the Emperor, our fon, and the inhabitants of our vaft domains, were naturally filled with joy and exultation: no event could certainly have been more ardently defired by our fon and the great officers of the empire, than an opportunity of celebrating fuch an anniverfary.

The grandeur, however, and profufion attendant on a general rejoicing were by no means the objects of our defire; we were fatisfied with the contemplation of the maxim of antiquity, which enumerates a life prolonged to an advanced age amongft the five inftances of human felicity: for although among our ancient monarchs, fome have likewife attained a very advanced period of life,

* The year 1800.

according to the testimony of the annals of the empire, yet it may be observed, that within the full period of an hundred years, the longevity to which they had aspired has in every instance received its termination.

We have already attained the eighty-ninth year of our age; therefore but a few short years are wanting to complete the utmost period of longevity: it then only further behoves us reverently to employ the remaining days of our life, and patiently to await the hour which is to conclude it. For shall we not doom the portion of life allotted to us sufficient, nor ever cease to indulge hopes, however immoderate, of prolonging our existence!

A strong constitution and temperament of body have happily preserved us from indisposition until this winter, when, in the course of the twelfth moon of the last year, we were suddenly attacked by a disorder proceeding from cold, and though we were apparently restored to health by the aid of medicine, we perceived that the disease had left our strength of body materially impaired, and, shortly after we had received the congratulations of our ministers in the hall of audience in the palace of *Kan-tsing-kung* on the first day of the new year, our appetite wholly failed us; we are now also sensible that our faculties of sight and hearing are declining apace.

The Emperor, our son, has indeed been piously engaged in procuring medical assistance, and assiduously attentive in seeking the means most likely to conduce to our recovery, but we feel that at our advanced period of life, medicine can prove of very little avail, and therefore make this preparation previous to the last mortal paroxysm of disease. After a long succession of years we are about to close a reign sustained with caution and assiduity, and invariably favoured by the distinguished protection of Heaven and of our ancestors. We are now about to resign for ever the administration of this empire; but shall leave it in the hands of the Emperor, our son, whose eminent abilities and pious disposition are in every respect conformable to our wishes, and will, doubtless, ensure to him a felicity like ours in his future undertakings; an idea which furnishes us with the most grateful consolation.

To all the nobility and magistrates, from the highest to the lowest rank, in the exterior as well as interior departments of the empire, we especially recommend, diligently to execute their respective employments, and to preserve their hearts free from all taint and corruption, that they may worthily and effectually serve the Emperor and promote the objects of his government, and finally, that their conduct may ensure to the millions of people subjected to his authority, univeral prosperity and peace.

We shall then depart hence, and associate in Heaven with the souls of our glorious ancestors, without leaving a wish that is not satisfied, or a desire that is not fulfilled.

With

With respect to the solemnization of mourning, we direct, that it may be observed for twenty-seven days, in the first instance, and in all other respects conformably with the sacred institutions of the empire; we have lastly, and especially to enjoin our posterity, that the respect and oblations due to the spirits of Heaven and Earth, to our ancestors, and to their sacred monuments, be ever diligently and faithfully observed.

This our last will and pleasure, we hereby publish and declare, that it may be generally known and respected.

No. II.

[Referred to from the Translation of the Third prefatory Edict.]

Translation of the Edict extraordinary of the present Emperor of China, by which the Death of His Father, the Emperor KIEN-LUNG, *was first officially made public**.

HIS Majesty the Emperor, by the grace and appointment of Heaven, issues this Edict extraordinary.

With feeble virtues, and inspired with awe by a sense of our own insufficiency, we have held the vast inheritance of these dominions, since it pleased our Imperial Father, THE MOST HIGH EMPEROR, on the first day of the year *Ping-shin*, (the 8th of February 1796,) to transfer the seals of the empire to our charge.

We applied with unremitting diligence and attention to the discharge of the high duty then imposed on us, that we might not frustrate the gracious designs that were executed in our favour, though our firmest reliance was placed in the protection of Heaven and of our illustrious ancestors.

Our Imperial Father, however, continued to enjoy his wonted health, accompanied by such vigour of mind as well as of body, as enabled him to continue to direct us in the administration of the empire. We daily attended his royal presence, listened to the instructions he was graciously pleased to communicate, and submitted the various affairs of government to his consideration. In the annual visitation which His Majesty was pleased to make through different parts of

* The Edict forms a kind of supplement to the preceding; and though in itself less important, may not be found altogether uninteresting.

the empire, the people were exhilarated by his prefence, and thronged from all quarters to behold his auguft perfon.

After making our accuftomed enquiries concerning his health, and affifting at his Imperial repaft, we had always the fatisfaction to obferve, that time had not materially affected the hale conftitution of body, and animated fpirits of our Imperial Father; a view that penetrated the utmoft receffes of our heart with the moft delightful confolation.

Laft year, having refpectfully confidered, that on the approaching year *Keng-fhin* (A. D. 1800) the glorious anniverfary would occur of the 90th year of the age of THE MOST HIGH EMPEROR, we fummoned an extraordinary council of the princes and great officers of ftate, in order jointly to folicit His Majefty's confent to a due celebration of that event; this he was gracioufly pleafed foon after to grant to our defire, and we were ready to call Heaven and Earth to witnefs the lively fatisfaction and gaiety of heart which we experienced in anticipation of that event.

Viewing with veneration the exalted age of our Imperial Parent, and the unparalleled felicity by which, as it were a birth-right, he has been attended from his infancy, until the latter days in which he is furrounded by relatives of five generations, every one would doubtlefsly concur in expreffing by words and actions their congratulations on a fubject fo juftly entitled to their praife, as his profperous reign and ineftimable virtues.

We have ourfelves addreffed the moft fervent prayers to Heaven ftill to prolong his days, and to crown them as heretofore with uninterrupted felicity: indeed, we complied with the facred precept only, where it faith, " Thou fhalt " rejoice;" yet were unwilling to obferve it, when it proceeds to fay, " and " thou fhalt tremble alfo."

Freedom from indifpofition and peaceful repofe, however, continued to blefs the declining years of our Imperial Father; the peculiar protection of Heaven preferved his happy conftitution from the approaches of infirmity during a long fucceffion of years, like the tranfition of a fingle day, until this winter, when, in the laft moon of the year juft concluded, he met with an indifpofition arifing from cold, and occafioned by a fudden expofure to wind.

Medical aid feemingly reftored his health; but his wonted ftrength was evidently impaired by the attack, though he ftill continued to impart to us his gracious advice and inftruction, as he had done previous to his indifpofition.

The various *Mon-gou*, and other tributary princes, as well as the ambaffadors of foreign ftates, ftill continued therefore, as laft year, to anticipate their introduction to his Imperial prefence, for the purpofe of receiving the gracious communications, which he might be pleafed to make to them upon the occafion; nor were they unprepared, on their part, to celebrate with due honours His Majesty's almost centenary age.

On the first day of the new year we waited on his august person, in company with the princes of the blood and great officers of state of civil and military rank, in order to offer our humble congratulations upon that festive day, after which we flattered ourselves that the entire re-establishment of his health would be accomplished in the progress of the ensuing spring.

But our expectations were deceived; on the 8th hour of the morning of the 3d day of the first moon, (February 7, 1799,) our Imperial Father suddenly departed from among his ministers and people. The Imperial Spirit ascended to the regions above.

We may strike the earth with our feet, lift our voices to Heaven, rend our hearts, and shed tears of blood, but we can never repay the vast debt of gratitude we owe; it is all of no avail.

Respectfully reviewing the period of sixty years during which our Imperial Father swayed the sceptre of these dominions, we see that the people were constantly animated by his virtues and benevolence, as the earth is gladdened by refreshing showers. The very vitals and inmost recesses of their hearts were conscious of the benign influence of his government.

All creatures that breathe the air, and possess blood in their veins, must acknowledge the ties of kindred, and surely will mourn the loss now sustained, like that of a father or of a mother, of whom they had recently been bereft.

As for ourself, to whom by his gracious goodness the Imperial succession had previously been granted, the grief by which we are penetrated upon this awful event, is more cutting than sharp instruments.

But what avail our words and lamentations; we rather ought to meditate on the weighty and important charge which our Imperial Father has assigned us, and endeavour to practise the virtuous maxims and institutions, as well as to seek to fulfil the wishes and designs, of our illustrious predecessor.

These are the duties, which, however weak and inadequate, we are now called on to discharge, and anxiously as we may now wish for the gracious aid and instruction of our Imperial Father, we know that that resource has irrecoverably failed us, and in this hour of affliction and distress, we have yet more especial reason to apprehend ourselves unequal to the burthen.

It is therefore upon the upright and faithful conduct of the various officers and magistrates in the interior and exterior departments of our dominions that we must chiefly rely; we do indeed confide in their utmost exertions for the support of our government, and the dignity of our person, and expect that they will thereby testify the sense with which they are impressed of the gracious benefits conferred on them

by

by our Imperial Father. The commanders in chief, and other officers ferving in our armies, fhould alfo recollect with gratitude, the important and fignal favours conferred by the Sovereign who appointed them to their refpective ftations and commands; they fhould likewife recal to their minds the wife inftructions and advice by which he aided and directed their proceedings; and thus, renewing in themfelves a fpirit of energy and activity, finally clear the country from all enemies whatever of the public peace.

They will thereby afford a grateful confolation to the facred fpirit which is afcended, and which, though now become a bleffed inhabitant of Heaven, will not be unconfcious of their exertions.

With regard to the due obfervance of the rites and ceremonies of mourning upon this occafion, we appoint their highneffes *Chun-ying* prince of *Jui-ching*, *Tun-fing* prince of *Ching-ching*, and *Tung-fiun* prince of *Yee-kiun*; the minifters of ftate, *Ho-quen* and *Vang-kie*; the prefidents of tribunals, *Foo-kaung-gan*, *Te-ming*, *King-quee*, *Tung-tcho*, and *Ping-yung-fing*, to form a council for adminiftering the fame in the public department; we likewife appoint the great officer of ftate *Wun-pu-ching-chu*, to fuperintend the ceremonial thereof in the private department; and we efpecially direct, that they do carefully examine the ancient regulations, and after diligently confulting and deliberating upon each queftion, regularly inform us of the refult.

This edict and notification extraordinary we now publifh for general information and obedience. *Khin-tfe*.

No. III.

[Referred to from the Tranflation of the Third Prefatory Edict.]

NOTE.

THE following are titles of articles of preliminary matter which are prefixed to the original work, but which it has not been deemed neceffary to introduce into the tranflation.

Second prefatory edict of the Emperor YONG-TCHING, dated the 9th day of the 9th moon of the 3d year of his reign, A.D. 1725.

Prefatory edict of the Emperor KIEN-LUNG, dated the 5th year of his reign, A.D. 1740.

Firft refcript of the fupreme court for the execution of public juftice, (*Hing-Poo*), dated the 21ft day of the 12th moon of the 52d year of KIEN-LUNG, A.D. 1788.

Second rescript of the same supreme court, dated the 2d day of the 2d moon of the 55th year of KIEN-LUNG, A.D. 1790.

Third rescript of the same, dated the 18th of the 3d moon of the 60th year of KIEN-LUNG, A.D. 1795.

Preface of the compilers of the present edition of the Penal Code, bearing date the 4th year of KIA-KING, A.D. 1799.

List of the names of the compilers, and others, sixteen in all, who were employed in editing the work.

Preface of the superintendant of the press.

General description of the work, of its subdivisions, and of its arrangement.

No. IV.

[Referred to from the Introductory Table of Degrees of Mourning.]

NOTE.

IN addition to the detail which has been translated of the cases in which full mourning is ordered to be worn, it may be sufficient to notice briefly, that the text then proceeds to particularize the twenty-four relationships in the first degree, in which mourning is only required to be worn from three to five months; the fourteen relationships which are comprised in the second degree; the twenty-one relationships which are comprised in the third degree; and the forty-two which are comprised in the fourth or remotest degree.

In the original text, there are likewise tables subjoined of consanguinity under various circumstances, and one table in particular, which describes those who are considered by the laws to be step-fathers and step-mothers, in the following manner:

Step-Fathers
1. Mother's second husband, if also an adopted father.
2. Mother's second husband, if not an adopted father.
3. Deceased father's second wife's second husband.

Step-Mothers
1. Father's principal wife.
2. Father's wife, substituted in the place of the principal wife, deceased.
3. Father's wife, by whom nursed or suckled.
4. Father's wife, who was substituted in the place of the natural mother.
5. Father's other wives, excepting the one who is the natural mother.
6. Father's repudiated wife, if also the natural mother.
7. Father's re-married widow, if also the natural mother.
8. Adopted mother.

The father's principal wife has diſtinct rank and privileges and is, in ſome reſpects, the legally adopted mother of all the children; but each child is alſo bound by law in a particular manner, to its natural mother, except under certain circumſtances, as in the ſixth and ſeventh caſes above deſcribed.

No. V.

[Referred to from Section I. Page 2.]

NOTE.

THE number of ſupplementary clauſes annexed to each ſection in the original is regularly noticed, and will enable the ſtudent of the Chineſe language, if deſirous of inveſtigating the ſubject of any particular ſection more cloſely, to judge how far a reference to the original text is likely to afford him ſatisfaction.

The following is a tranſlation of the moſt material among the clauſes ſubjoined to the firſt ſection.

TRANSLATION.

Inſtruments of torture of the following dimenſions, may be uſed upon an inveſtigation of a charge of robbery or homicide:

The inſtrument for compreſſing the ancle-bones, ſhall conſiſt of a middle-piece, 3 *Che* 4 *Tſun** long, and two ſide-pieces, 3 *Che* each in length; the upper end of each piece ſhall be circular, and 1 *Tſun* 8 decimals in diameter; the lower ends ſhall be cut ſquare, and, 2 *Tſun* in thickneſs:—At a diſtance of 6 *Tſun* from the lower ends, four hollows, or ſockets, ſhall be excavated, 1 *Tſun* 6 decimals in diameter, and 7 decimals of a *Tſun* in depth each: one, on each ſide the middle-piece, and one in each of the other pieces, to correſpond.—The lower ends being fixed and immoveable, and the ancles of the criminal under examination being lodged between the ſockets, a painful compreſſion is effected by forcibly drawing together the upper ends.

The inſtrument of torture for compreſſing the fingers, ſhall conſiſt of 5 ſmall round ſticks, 7 *Tſun* in length, and $\frac{45}{100}$ of a *Tſun* in diameter each: the application of this inſtrument is nearly ſimilar to that of the former.

In thoſe caſes wherein the uſe of torture is allowed, the offender, whenever he contumaciouſly refuſes to confeſs the truth, ſhall forthwith be put to the queſtion by

---

* The *Che* exceeds the Britiſh meaſure of a foot by about half an inch; the *Tſun* is its decimal part.

torture; and it shall be lawful to repeat the operation a second time, if the criminal still refuses to make a confession. — On the other hand, any magistrate who wantonly or arbitrarily applies the question by torture, shall be tried for such offence, in the tribunal of his immediate superior; and the latter shall make due enquiry into the circumstances, on pain of being himself accused before the supreme court of judicature at Pekin, if guilty of wilful concealment or connivance.

Ordinary prisoners are to be confined with the small chain: the *Cangue*, or moveable pillory is never to be used, except expressly directed by the laws; nor to exceed 25 *Kin*[*] in weight, unless otherwise specially determined and expressed.

When a sentence of banishment is passed against the relations, or others, implicated in the guilt of an offender, the corporal punishment, which is usually inflicted in different degrees, proportionate to the duration of the banishment, shall be understood to be altogether remitted.

From the 25th of the 4th moon, to the last day of the 6th moon of each year, (in consideration of the heat at that season), the punishment of the lesser bamboo shall be remitted altogether; and that of the greater bamboo shall be reduced one degree, and further mitigated, by inflicting only eight for every ten blows to which the offender is condemned[†]. — This indulgence shall not, however, be extended to any other offenders beside those who are actually to be discharged within the period above-mentioned. — During the same interval, a particular degree of relaxation shall also be allowed to prisoners in general; and offenders sentenced to wear the *Cangue* shall be permitted to lay it aside, provided they can find securities for their subsequently fulfilling the law, by resuming it at the expiration of the said period.

Offenders convicted of thieving, robbing, wounding, or assaulting, shall be excluded from the benefit of the last-mentioned regulation.

No capital execution shall take place during the period of the first or sixth moons of any year; and in the event of any conviction of a crime in a court of justice during the said intervals, for which the law directs immediate execution, the criminal shall, nevertheless, be respited until the first day of the moon next following.

The mitigation of the law concerning the infliction of corporal punishment during the summer months, shall take effect without any particular reference to the Emperor.

[*] The *Kin* exceeds the British pound by one-third.
[†] This reduction is over and above that already specified in the text of the fundamental law.

The inftruments for extorting confeffion fhall be given into the charge of the magiftrates of diftricts; but fhall in the firft inftance, be examined and approved by the governors of the cities to whofe jurifdiction they belong; fecondly, by the chief judge of the province; and laftly, by the viceroy or fub-viceroy. — Any magiftrate ufing illegal or unexamined inftruments of torture, will be liable to be accufed thereof before the fupreme court.

No. VI.

[Referred to from Section II. Page 5.]

NOTE.

THE title of this fection might be, perhaps, more literally tranflated, "*The "Ten Wickedneffes*," or "*The Ten Abominations;*" but the choice of terms is not very material, as the text fully explains the nature of the offences ranked under this clafs; as well as the reafons for introducing a defcription of them in this place, though a declaration of the punifhments incurred by fuch tranfgreffions, is referved for another part of the code. — In order to give, if poffible, the full force of the expreffions employed, this article has been tranflated with more freedom than thofe which are merely declaratory of punifhment, or lefs defcriptive of the character of the offence. — Thefe obfervations will equally apply to the fubject of the next fection, and the manner in which it has been tranflated.

No. VII.

[Referred to from Section III. Page 6.]

NOTE.

THE nature and extent of the privileges enjoyed by thefe claffes are defcribed in the two following fections. — Excepting the firft and feventh claffes, it can be fcarcely fuppofed, that this claffification has any exiftence in practice; and, in fact, the firft and feventh claffes muft, generally fpeaking, comprehend all thofe who have any claim to be ranked among the others.

Exclufive of the limited privilege of birth here noticed, there are a few hereditary dignities occafionally conferred by the Emperor, which defcend to the children in the manner defcribed in the firft fection of the next divifion of the code.

No. VIII.

[Referred to from Section VI. Page 9.]

NOTE.

A Short ftatement of the charges againft the minifter of China *Ho-chung-tong*, or more properly *Ho-quen*, and the final adjudication of his fentence, has already appeared in England; but the celebrity of his fate may render acceptable an entire verfion, as well as juftify the introduction in this place of a few obfervations regarding the hiftory of that extraordinary man.

Although he had long poffeffed eminent power in the ftate, it does not appear that the peculiar character and hiftory of this minifter had been known in Europe previous to the period of the Britifh embaffy.

The powerful influence which he difplayed on that occafion foon difcovered, that to his talents and authority the difpofal of public affairs in China was principally confided; and the difinclination which he was found to have entertained to the Britifh interefts, is conceived to have had a principal fhare in counteracting the views of that expedition.

It is obferved in the authentic account of that embaffy, that *Ho-chung-tong*, " who enjoyed almoft exclufively the confidence of the Emperor, was faid to be " a Tartar of obfcure birth, raifed from an inferior ftation about twenty years " before, when, while he was on guard at one of the palace gates, the Em-" peror paffing through it, was ftruck merely with the comelinefs of his counte-" nance; but afterwards finding him to be a man of talents and education, he " quickly elevated him to dignity; and he might be faid to poffefs, in fact, under " the Emperor, the whole power of the empire."

It is fubjoined, that " His Imperial Majefty was not, however, blindly guided " by his advice, and once on conceiving that he had attempted to impofe on his " mafter by a falfehood, he was difgraced as fuddenly as he had formerly been " raifed, and he was reduced to his original low ftation for about a fortnight; " when a fortunate accident having proved to the Sovereign, that there was no " real ground for his diffatisfaction, he reftored his late fervant to his wonted " favour, and to a power bounded only by his own."

It would thus seem, that the vigour and wisdom of the Emperor Kien-lung was, until that time, sufficient to restrain within due bounds of subordination the ambitious spirit and enterprizing genius of the favourite; but it is the general opinion in China, that he took advantage of the state of dotage, into which the aged Emperor latterly declined. — This circumstance is, indeed, strongly implied to have been the case, though not directly expressed, out of respect to the memory of Kien-lung, in the articles of accusation which the present Emperor brought forward against *Ho-chung-tong*, almost immediately after His Imperial Parent's demise.

Some of the charges may appear frivolous, and others the mere suggestion of personal enmity; but the presumptive and corroborating evidence arising from the immense and almost incalculable treasures which he was found, upon an examination of his property, to have amassed, afford a sufficiently convincing proof of his guilt and corruption. According to a statement that was received as authentic at Canton at the time of the confiscation of his effects, it appears, that besides lands, houses, and other immoveable property to an amazing amount, not less than 80 millions of Chinese ounces of silver, or about 23,330,000*l.* sterling value in bullion or gems, was found in his treasury. This sum, though immense, is not incredible, when the vast extent of the empire is considered, over the various departments of which, he had certainly for many years a very unusual, and indeed almost an unbounded influence.

A disclosure of the real character of the favourite was, however, it seems, for a considerable time prevented by the exertion and display of some estimable as well as splendid talents, for which he was remarkable. It is observed in the account of the British Embassy, that " the manners of *Ho-chung-tong* were not less pleasing
" than his understanding was penetrating and acute. He seemed, indeed, to
" possess the qualities of a consummate statesman. He was called to office and
" authority, no doubt, by the mere favour of the Sovereign, as must be the case
" in most monarchies; but he was confirmed and maintained in it by the
" approving voice of such persons of rank and eminence as have influence in the
" determinations of the most absolute governments. In those governments in
" Asia, the prince is not afraid, as is the case in Europe, to debase his dignity
" by alliances with his subjects; and the number of children of Asiatic monarchs
" by different wives and concubines, occasion so many matrimonal connections
" with the crown, that the influence arising from them is counteracted by com-
" petition. A tie, however, of this sort, added to power already acquired, in-
" creases and secures it. A daughter of the Emperor is married to a son of
" *Ho-chung-tong*. This circumstance was thought sufficient to alarm some of the
" Imperial Family, and other loyal subjects of the empire, as if they were fear-
" ful of the heights to which the ambition of that favourite might aspire."

The son, who was thus honoured, is likewise included in the sentence of condemnation; but, on account of the connection he had formed with the Imperial Family, he experienced no more than a trifling diminution of rank, and a removal from public affairs, while the other relations of the minister appear to have been prosecuted and disgraced with an almost undistinguishing severity, according to the long established maxim of the Chinese laws, which esteems a degree of criminality to be inherent in all who are in any respect connected or allied with persons guilty of heinous offences.

It was, however, at the same time prescribed to the son to confine himself to the society of his family, that he might have no opportunity of reviving any of the dangerous pretensions of his father, or of executing any schemes of revenge for the fate to which he had been condemned.

Apprehensions were also previously entertained, that the views of *Ho-chung-tong*, might lead him to attempt an open revolt, or at least to endeavour to escape from a court, in which, after the death of the late Emperor, he ceased to have any protection, except what his connections and personal resources might afford him. It was probably with the view of defeating such designs, that the new Emperor appointed him to the honourable office of one of the chief superintendants of the mourning on the occasion of his father's decease; as it thus became easy to arrest his person, while engaged in the discharge of a duty which confined him to the palace, and precluded him from taking any measures for his safety, or consulting with and assembling his adherents.

The promptitude and vigour with which the Emperor, almost at the moment of his accession to independent power, struck at the root of a dangerous combination of interests which he had good reason to suppose secretly menaced his crown and dignity; and the immediate condemnation to death of this formidable state culprit, together with the punishment or humiliation of all his connections and adherents, while they were yet disconcerted in their projects by the sudden event of the late Emperor's decease, are certainly some proofs of that political courage and sagacity which are requisite in the character of a monarch of great and powerful empire.

1. *Translation of an Imperial Edict, containing the Articles of Impeachment exhibited against* Ho-chung-tong (*otherwise* Ho-quen) *Minister of China, by the Emperor* KIA-KING, *in the 4th Year of his Reign.*

ON the 25th day of the 1st moon of the 4th year of KIA-KING, the supreme council for military affairs transmitted, by an extraordinary courier, His Imperial Majesty's decree of the 11th day of the 1st moon, which is as follows:

APPENDIX, No. VIII.

Extraordinary marks of the royal favour of our most august, and now departed Father, were granted to *Ho-quen*, by elevating him through successive degrees, from an attendant at the palace to the supreme rank of a Minister of the empire, and bestowing on him an important command in the Imperial army, the advantages of which he continued to enjoy for many years by an exertion of royal munificence, far beyond his deserts, as well as unexampled among the nobility of the court.

Since we received the important trust of the government of this empire, and particularly since we have been plunged into affliction by the awful event of the decease of our Imperial Father, we have repeatedly meditated on the passage of the *Lun-yu*, which recommends the virtue of a three-years forbearance from change when succeeding to an inheritance. But, with regard to our Imperial Father, whose profound observance of the laws of Heaven, and pious veneration for his ancestors were so conspicuous; who reigned over his people with no less vigilance than affection, and whose sincerity of heart and rectitude of government, all countries whether within or without the limits of his dominions, both knew and gratefully acknowledged; the decrees of such a prince should be observed for ten thousand years, and ever regulate the administration of his successors, instead of being extended only to a triennial duration.

Deeply impressed with these sentiments, we are most unwilling to displace any of the chosen servants of the state whom our Imperial Father had employed or honoured with his confidence; and wherein they might be found guilty, every palliation and excuse would be admitted, in order to enable us to dispense with the rigorous execution of justice.

These, we declare before the light of Heaven, are our sincere sentiments and desire. But the crimes for which *Ho-quen* now stands impeached in several distinct charges by the united voice of the principal magistrates and nobles of the state, are of such magnitude and importance as appear to exclude even the possibility of extenuation.

As soon, accordingly, as we had performed the immediate duties which were imposed on us by the demise of our Imperial Father, we issued orders that *Ho-quen* should be divested of all his dignities and employments, and committed to trial on the following charges, or articles of impeachment:

1st, When our Royal Father, on the 3d day of the 9th moon of the 60th year of his reign, elected ourself to be his heir and successor, *Ho-quen* waited on us, on the 2d of the moon previous to the disclosure of the Imperial edict, and presented us with the insignia of the rank newly conferred on us, thereby betraying an important secret of the state that had been confided to him, in the expectation that such conduct would be meritorious in our estimation.

2d, On receiving the summons of our Imperial Father, on the 1st moon of the preceding year, to attend at the palace of *Yuen-ming-yuen*, he ventured to ride in on horseback through the left gate, and by the great hall of *Ching-ta-quang-ming* as far as the bottom of the mount called *Sheu-shan*, regardless to a degree beyond example, of a Father and a Sovereign.

3d, When formerly suffering from a lameness in his feet, he went into the interior of the palace in a palanquin, and passed and repassed through the gate of *Shin-vu-men* in a wheel chair before the gazing eyes of the multitude, and without the smallest fear or hesitation.

4th, The young females that were educated for the service of the palace, he took from thence, and appropriated to himself as concubines, without any sensation of shame or regard to decorum.

5th, During the latter campaigns against the rebels in the provinces of *Se-chuen* and *Hou-quang*, when our Imperial Father waited with anxious expectation for intelligence from the army, so as to be bereft of sleep and appetite, *Ho-quen* received himself, the various reports that arrived from the troops stationed in different quarters of the empire, and detained them according to his pleasure, with a view to deceive his sovereign by misrepresentation and concealment; in consequence whereof the military operations of the campaign were for a considerable time incomplete and ineffectual.

6th, Having been appointed, by a decree of our Imperial Father, to the Presidency of the supreme board for civil affairs, and also to that of the supreme court of judicature; and afterwards, on account of some experience acquired in superintending the disburfements of the army, having been directed by another Imperial decree to officiate as secretary to the supreme board of revenue; he immediately united in his own person the power and authority which were respectively annexed to these several high offices.

7th, Last winter, when the venerable person of our Imperial Father laboured under infirmity, his signature and hand-writing were in some places confused and not easily distinguishable; whereupon *Ho-quen* had the audacity to declare, that they had " *better be thrown aside* ;" and then issued orders of his own suggestion.

8th, In the last moon of the preceding year, *Kieu-ko* reported, that in the districts of *Sin-Wha* and *Quei-Te*, a party of above a thousand of the rebels had collected, and forcibly carried away a herd of cattle belonging to the *Da-lai-la-ma's* merchants, as well as mortally wounded two persons, and that they still continued to ravage the district of *Ching-hay*. *Ho-quen* however rejected and dismissed the report, and, concealing the whole transaction, took no measures in consequence.

9th, On the late event of our Imperial Father's decease, we issued our orders, declaring that the attendance of such of the princes and chieftains of the *Mongou* tribes as had not had the small-pox would be dispensed with; but *Ho-quen*, in opposition to our commands, signified to them to attend indiscriminately, whether

having

having or not having had that difeafe; regardlefs of the intention of our government to fhew to foreign tribes our kindnefs and confideration. The motives of his conduct herein it would indeed be difficult to inveftigate.

10th, The minifter of ftate *Su-lin-go*, was entirely deaf, and worn out by age and infirmity; yet, becaufe he was connected by marrriage with *Ho-lin*, the younger brother of *Ho-quen*, his incapacity to difcharge the duties of his fituation was artfully concealed from the Emperor's knowledge.

11th, The officers *Ou-fung-lan*, *Ly-han*, and *Ly-quang-yun*, having received their education at the houfe of *Ho-quen*, have been fince promoted to the moft refpectable offices in the ftate.

12th, Many of the principal officers whofe names have been regiftered in the different civil and military departments have been, in inftances too numerous to be particularized in this place, removed and difmiffed according to his pleafure, and by his fole authority.

13th, In the late confifcation of the property of *Ho-quen*, many apartments were found to be built in a moft coftly manner of the Imperial wood *Nan-moo*, and feveral ornamented terraces and feparate inclofures were obferved to have been conftructed in the ftyle and refemblance of the Imperial palace of *Ning-fheu-kung*: the gardens were likewife laid out in a ftyle little differing from that of *Yuen-ming-yuen* and *Fung-tao-yao-tay*; but with what view or defign we cannot imagine.

14th, Among his treafures of pearls and precious ftones, upwards of two hundred ftrings or bracelets of the former were difcovered, many times exceeding in value thofe in our Imperial poffeffion. One among the pearls belonging to *Ho-quen* was of an enormous fize, and exceeded even that which adorns the Imperial crown. There were likewife found various buttons diftinguifhing princely rank, carved out of precious ftones, fuch as his fituation by no means entitled him to wear. Many fcore of thefe gems were difcovered, befides pieces of the fame kind in the rough ftate, to an incalculable amount, and in an endlefs variety, unknown even among the Imperial treafures.

15th, An eftimate of the property in gold and filver which has been confifcated is not yet completed; but the fum is already found to exceed many millions of ounces of filver.

16th, The avarice by which he appears to have been actuated, and the corruption by which his wealth has been amaffed, cannot be equalled in the hiftory of preceding ages.

Thefe articles of accufation have been thoroughly inveftigated and proved by a council of princes and minifters of ftate, affembled for the purpofe; and have alfo been acknowledged without referve in his own verbal confeffion.

Ho-quen, thus deeply criminal, blind to every virtuous sentiment, and unmindful of his Sovereign Master, perverted and injured the civil and military government of this empire, usurped the highest authority for unwarrantable purposes, and perfidiously omitted, or set aside, the execution of the laws, while his insatiable and inordinate avarice ceased not to enrich his family, by sapping the vigour of the state.

Yet these crimes are small, in comparison with the base ingratitude with which he requited the gracious bounty of our Imperial Father, who, in his royal wisdom would most certainly have withheld his favour and protection, had any one in the Imperial court possessed ability or inclination to present a timely accusation of this minister's offences.

Not one, however, of the officers of the empire, either of those attached to the court or of those employed in provincial departments, ventured to charge him with his crimes; some forbearing out of respect to the venerable age of our deceased father, and disinclination to give disquiet to his royal breast; others from the apprehension of this minister's extraordinary influence and power, which we ourself have indeed witnessed, and have known through its effects.

Now, at length, the crimes alleged against *Ho-quen* are brought to light; more especially those offences which concerned our Imperial Father. They are, indeed, more numerous than the hairs on his head, and a hundred tongues would be unable to find an excuse for them.

Supposing that we were to decline the punishment of these offences, how should we afterwards appear before the Holy Spirit that is in heaven, and reconcile such an omission to the purity of our conscience.

Be it therefore known by these presents to the officers and magistrates of our dominions, that we have resolved to refer the further trial and investigation of the above charges, to a council of the princes, nobles, and ministers of state, to be held at our court of Pekin; exclusive of which, we issue our general orders to the viceroys of the several provinces of the empire, to take singly into consideration the charges brought against the minister *Ho-quen*, and to record their real sentiments concerning the punishment such offences, or any other offences of which he may have been guilty, demand; and then report the same to us, with the utmost expedition.

Khin-Tse *.

---

* It has been omitted to notice, that a termination with these words, which may be literally translated, "*Respect this*," is, in China, one of the peculiar distinctions of an Imperial Edict.

2. *Translation of an Imperial Edict, containing the Sentence of* Ho-quen, *Minister of China, and of the other Persons who were connected with him, or implicated in the Charges against him.*

The supreme council extraordinary, consisting of the ministers, great officers of state in the civil and military departments, the presidents of the Imperial college and tribunal of censors, and others, having finally determined upon the articles of accusation exhibited against *Ho-quen*, and *Foo-chang-gan*, have now submitted to our consideration, that the said *Ho-quen* do receive sentence of a slow and painful death, according to the law against the crime of high treason; and that the said *Foo-chang-gan*, do receive sentence of decollation, according to the law against the crime of abetting, and being accessary thereto; and that therefore the sentence on the one, and on the other, be duly and immediately carried into execution, according to the said laws.

The unprincipled violence and daring usurpation, which are so manifest throughout the various criminal acts whereof *Ho-quen*, stands convicted, indeed debar him from the slightest claim to any mitigation of the rigour of lawful punishment.

On a review of the grounds of the capital condemnation of *Gao-pay*, by our Imperial ancestor KAUNG-HEE; that on *Nien-keng-yao*, under the authority of our Imperial grandfather YONG-TCHING; and lastly, that of *Na-tching*, by the orders of our Imperial Father, lately deceased; we find that the rank of these criminals corresponded with that of *Ho-quen*, but that his guilt has far surpassed theirs, by its heinous enormity. Proceeding in the investigation, we observe that the royal indulgence was extended to *Gao-pay* and *Nien-keng-yao*, by the permission which was granted to each to become his own executioner; but that *Na-tching* was immediately executed in the presence of the army, as his guilt had, in a peculiar manner, been detrimental to the military operations of the state. In the present instance, however, the wilful delays interposed to the operations of the army; the desire of impeding their success, by criminally intercepting the public reports, and communicating no more than was agreeable to himself; and lastly, the failure to provide the necessary supplies, so as to render the said operations for a long time incomplete and ineffectual, all of which appear in the articles of accusation exhibited against *Ho-quen*, involve a far greater degree of criminality, than any breach of duty in a military capacity ever could amount to.

If we should, therefore, by any consideration, be induced to remit the sentence of a slow and painful death, according to the law against high treason, his offences would, at leaſt, demand a ſentence equal in ſeverity with that paſſed on *Na-tching*, in the precedent before us; from which it would indeed be abſolutely impoſſible for us to depart, by allowing of any kind of alleviation, were the execution of the criminal not neceſſarily to take place within the limits of a three years general mourning.

Even at this moment, when the awful event of our Imperial Father's deceaſe is ſtill recent, the crimes of *Ho-quen* are ſtill ſuch as to juſtify and require an immediate and exemplary execution.

There are, nevertheleſs, ſome conſiderations upon which we are inclined to pauſe. For although the guilt of *Ho-quen* bears ſo great a ſimilarity in its conſequences with that of *Na-tching*, yet as the former did not hold a command in the army, a certain diſtinction undoubtedly exiſts in the nature of their reſpective offences, moreover, although in this realm, laws have been framed, and a power eſtabliſhed, to which ſubjects of royal blood and elevated rank are undoubtedly amenable for their offences; and although *Ho-quen*, whoſe hardneſs of heart and blindneſs to every virtuous ſentiment are diſgraceful to human nature, is a delinquent whom, as far as reſpects himſelf, we cannot redeem, and whom the preſent decree of council has condemned to undergo the unabated rigour of the law; yet, moved by the conſideration that he once held the poſt of higheſt honour and dignity in the ſervice of this empire, we reſolve, in ſpite of the unpardonable guilt which he has incurrred, to ſpare him the diſgrace of a public execution.

Ho-quen is hereby permitted, through our royal favour, to become his own executioner; but, be it known, that it is our regard for the honour and dignity of the adminiſtration of this empire, and not any perſonal conſideration for *Ho-quen*, that has influenced this our preſent determination.

Foo-chang-gan was likewiſe highly favoured by our Imperial Father, and ſecond only to *Ho-quen*, of whom he was the conſtant aſſociate, and with every article of whoſe delinquency he muſt have been intimately acquainted.

If he had, during the many private audiences to which he was admitted, laid before his Sovereign a true and faithful report of the criminal conduct of the miniſter, our Imperial Father would immediately have ſanctioned the execution of the laws againſt *Ho-quen* according to their utmoſt rigour, and certainly not have protected him, or have transferred the imputation of guilt to *Foo-chang-gan*, under the plea of his having borne falſe teſtimony.

If it is urged, that out of reſpect to the venerable age of our Imperial Father, it was feared to excite his ſacred anger, the excuſe, though in ſome degree admiſſible, is weak and unworthy of that genuine attachment and fidelity which is becoming in a miniſter; but from the time that we were appointed to the Imperial inheritance, and put in poſſeſſion of the ſeals of the empire, *Foo-chang-gan* has been a

conſtant

constant resident in the palace; what obstacle did then exist against his requesting a private audience with us during the hours of his absence from *Ho-quen*, or addressing to us a secret memorial, and setting forth his crimes?

Had *Foo-chang-gan* in any manner anticipated our present decision, by drawing up the slightest statement impeaching the conduct of *Ho-quen*, we should not now have deemed him implicated in the guilt of that minister, nor even have deprived him of any of the honours or dignities which he has acquired.

From the commencement, however, to the last moment, not a word of this tendency has ever fallen from him; upon which we cannot but infer an intention of abetting and concealing the same, an act in itself of so criminal a nature, that a hundred tongues would be unable to pronounce an excuse for it.

In the present confiscation and examination of his houses and other property, moveable as well as immoveable, many things have been discovered therein which were extremely unsuitable to his rank and station; and which he could not have acquired and collected without having evinced himself at various times both avaricious and corrupt.

It is highly just and reasonable, therefore, that the sentence conformable to law, which the ministers of state and other members of the council have awarded, should be executed against him.

In consideration, however, that the board of censors has not exhibited any specific charges of guilt against *Foo-chang-gan*; and that in the confiscation and examination of his effects, they did not appear to amount to above a fiftieth or a hundredth part of those found in the possession of the minister *Ho-quen*, whose sentence we have mitigated to a private and self-execution; we resolve likewise to extend our royal favour to *Foo-chang-gan*, by postponing the execution of his sentence to the usual season for capital punishments in the ensuing autumn; and we therefore direct that he shall remain in confinement until that period.

We likewise direct, that at the hour of the execution of *Ho-quen*, *Foo-chang-gan* shall be conveyed to his cell, in order to witness the fate of that minister; and be re-conducted after the event to confinement at his own prison.

With regard to *Ho-lin*, brother of *Ho-quen* *, no merit can justly be ascribed to his proceedings; for although upon the trial of *Foo-kaung-gan* (brother of *Foo-chang-gan*), he was principally instrumental in bringing forward the impeachment, it is evident that *Ho-lin* did not accuse him from a desire of obtaining impartial justice, but merely as an instrument in the hands of *Ho-quen*, and with a view to procure the destruction of *Foo-kaung-gan*. In the present confiscation of the property of *Ho-quen*, several buildings have been discovered of the wood *Nan-moo*, and also other illicit articles; when this is compared with the circumstance of secreting

---

* *Ho-lin* was not living at the period of this trial, as appears by the sequel.

prohibited timber, alleged in charge againſt *Foo-kaung-gan*, it is evident which ought to be deemed a heinous, and which a venial offence.

With regard alſo to the campaign of *Foo-kaung-gan* in the province of *Hou-nan*, againſt the *Miao-fee* rebels, he was to that degree thwarted and impeded in his operations by the conduct of *Ho-lin*, who was in office at court, that the expedition proved ultimately unſucceſsful, and he himſelf fell in the field of battle. From this view it appears, that, upon the charge relating to the campaign againſt the *Miao-fee*, *Ho-lin*, inſtead of deſerving any credit, is himſelf involved in the delinquency it was intended by him to impute to others.

According, therefore, to the deciſion of the council, the hereditary title of *Kung* given to *Ho-lin* ſhall be annulled. With regard, alſo, to the inſcription of his name in the ſacred temple, an honour to which few can aſpire; what can entitle *Ho-lin* thus to rank with thoſe virtuous miniſters to whom we owe the eſtabliſhment of our empire? Conformably then to the deciſion of council, the inſcription of his name ſhall be eraſed from the monuments of the ſacred temple; and, in like manner, the altar which his ſurviving family have erected to his memory ſhall not be permitted to remain in exiſtence.

Fung-ſhin-yn-te (ſon of *Ho-quen*) has acquired by marriage a princely rank, and the princeſs his wife ever enjoyed the parental affection of our Imperial Father, and was peculiarly the object of his royal kindneſs. By utterly degrading *Fung-Shin-yn-te* from his rank and dignity, his family would be reduced to a level with the loweſt populace; an extreme diſgrace, which is inconſiſtent with the favour and compaſſion we are, on the above account, inclined to teſtify towards him.

According, however, to the deciſion of the council, we annul the hereditary title of *Kung*, which *Ho-quen* had obtained for his ſervices in the overthrow of the rebel *Vang-ſan-quay*, ſo as not to be inheritable by his poſterity; but to his rank as *Tſe* of the empire, which we leave unimpaired, *Fung-ſhin-yn-te* is hereby permitted to ſucceed; we direct, at the ſame time that he ſhall confine himſelf to his family, and not go abroad in order to interfere in the adminiſtration of public affairs.

Fung-ſhin-yee-mien (ſon of *Ho-lin*, and nephew of the miniſter) having been degraded from his title by inheritance, ſhall alſo be removed from his honorary command in the Imperial guards, and we forbid his attendance at the palace-gate *Kan-tſing-men*. As a mark, however, of peculiar conſideration, we confer on him the rank of hereditary *Yun-ky-wee*, and order that he do retire and diſcharge the duties thereof under his native Banner.

Su-lin (ſon of *Foo-chang-gan*) received his rank of hereditary *Yun-ky-wee* by deſcent from *Foo-lin-gan*; and, although we have annulled the hereditary rank of *Foo-chang-gan* in conſequence his crimes, yet as *Foo-lin-gan* was nowiſe

implicated

implicated therein, we grant, as a mark of our peculiar favour, our licence to *Su-lin* to inherit the inferior rank of *Yun-ky-wee*.

We remove him, however, from his honorary command in the Imperial guards; we forbid his attendance at the palace gate *Kan-tsing-men*, and desire moreover, that he do retire, and discharge the duties of his station under his native Banner.

The minister of state *Sou-lin-go* is extremely old, and totally deaf, but was nevertheless promoted to that office by *Ho-quen*, on account of his connection by marriage with *Ho-lin*, without any regard to the impropriety of the appointment. For, having passed the eightieth year of his age, and scarcely able to perform a genuflexion, how can he be presumed capable of discharging the duties of his arduous station? *Sou-lin-go* shall therefore, retaining his original rank, retire altogether from office.

With regard to *Oo-sung-lan*, and *Ly-whang*, vice-presidents of supreme courts, and *Ly-quang-yung*, officer of the household, they evidently owe their elevation solely to the interference of *Ho-quen*; *Ly-quang-yung* being incapable from sickness of discharging the duties of his appointment, shall retire from court with his original rank; and although no specific charges have been alleged against *Oo-sung-lan* and *Ly-whang*, yet, as the mode of their elevation cannot be accredited, we degrade them to their former rank, as assistants in the Imperial college; and it is hereby declared, that we dispense with the future attendance of *Oo-sung-lan* at the Imperial southern library. As for the rest, we direct the execution thereof according to the decision of the council.

Khin-Tse.

I. *Translation of an Imperial Edict, declaratory of a general Amnesty to all Persons who had been connected with, or influenced by the Minister* Ho-quen.

AFTER we had issued an extraordinary edict, to give public information of the crimes and charges for which our minister *Ho-quen* had been impeached, we received the report of the deliberate decision thereon of the council of ministers and great officers of state, and ultimately pronounced a definitive sentence on *Ho-quen*, by which he has been favoured with the permission of becoming his own executioner.

For a very considerable period *Ho-quen* held the general administration of public affairs; he was guilty of such a daring usurpation of power, and of such a fraudulent and corrupt interposition of his influence, that the concerns of the subject could not gain admittance to the knowledge of their sovereign. Unless such atrocious guilt had been speedily punished, every principle of an equitable and incorrupt administration of the people in general, and of a due dispensation of salutary ordinances and instruction for the guidance of the magistrates, must have been utterly abandoned. His guilt has been ascertained with clearness and precision; the sentence awarded against him has been duly executed.

We have still, however, to consider, that the tribunals and public boards under the influence and authority of *Ho-quen* were many; and that the appointments and promotions distributed by him must have been numerous in proportion. The provincial officers and magistrates must therefore unavoidably have incurred, in many instances, the criminality of seeking their advancement at the palace of *Ho-quen*, and of obtaining it by means of illicit and corrupt donations.

By a radical and minute investigation, we might find many persons involved in transactions that strict justice must necessarily condemn; but, on the other hand, it is necessary to guard against too great a propensity towards suggesting inquiries, which, from their nature and number, it would be difficult to unravel or determine.

We have, it is true, issued a public declaration of the criminal charges alleged against *Ho-quen*, in which the most remarkable instances of his guilt are enumerated, in order that every member of the community may possess competent information of the same. But if the officers and magistrates of our dominions should misconceive our views therein, and proceed, in consequence, to a severe scrutiny of past transactions, at the instigation of personal animosity and dislike, exposing secret and concealed actions, and the remote causes from which they arose, whereby such and such persons might be shewn to have shared in such and such transactions; although these reports should prove just and faithful, it would be inexpedient to enter into enquiries which would be almost endless in themselves, and but too probably suggested to us from unworthy motives.

When we destroyed this monstrous contriver of iniquity, we were aware that numerous adherents and connections must unavoidably have partaken in his guilt; but it was far from our intention to encourage or permit any malicious or vindictive proceedings. We condemned *Ho-quen* to condign punishment for his crimes, more especially on the ground of his having defeated and subverted the civil and military operations of the state; in comparison of which, the guilt he has incurred in various acts of corrupt peculation, and partial infringements of the laws, is indeed but trifling and unimportant. On the former account we determined to enforce the law immediately against him, without allowing any excuse or delay to intervene; but, from the commencement, we resolved to forbear to implicate in the investigation the persons who might have concurred in his other acts of criminality, confining ourself to strict and corrective admonitions for the future, and by no means intending to recommence an enquiry into abuses that are now past and done away.

The greater and lesser magistrates of our dominions may, therefore, cease to harbour any suspicions or uneasiness at a retrospect of their own conduct. We are satisfied that our magistracy still abounds with men of intrinsic worth and ability, to whom it is yet very possible to regain the path of integrity, and to amend their past errors, so as to prove themselves hereafter active and valuable servants to the state. Although in a season of critical difficulty, they may not have withstood the pressure of the times, and may have slipped from the right way, it is still in their power to purify the heart, to cleanse the thoughts, to resolve firmly on an amendment, and finally to become men of approved integrity, evincing that they were very far from having been lost irretrievably in the mazes of error and iniquity.

The present clear and explicit declaration of our pleasure, we therefore issue expressly for the purpose of requiring a strict and respectful obedience, and a diligent co-operation with us in our determination to renovate and rectify the administration, by the discontinuance of all evil habits and abuses, however inveterate. If, after the instructive admonition we have now given, a disposition is not shewn to ameliorate and reform, and the utmost exertions are not made to regain the path of integrity, the transgressors will voluntarily have sought their own ruin and destruction, in a manner which is unworthy of them as men, which will undoubtedly expose them to the consequences of our severe displeasure, and against which they will not be able to plead our having failed to instruct and forewarn them: be this general edict therefore promulgated for their information.

Khin-Tse.

No. IX.

[Referred to from Section VI. Page 9.]

Translation of an Imperial Edict, extracted from the Pekin Gazette *of the 27th of 6th Moon of the 5th Year of* KIA-KING, *or the 18th of August* 1800 *.

WHEN *Quay-lung* was last year appointed to the presidency of the tribunal of civil affairs, he had constant access to our presence, and frequently took occasion to express his desire, that a military command might be given him in

* This is only the last of a series of Edicts relative to the misconduct of the viceroy of the province of *Sechuen*; but it is, at the same time, complete in itself, as it contains a summary of the charges against him, and a declaration of his definitive sentence.

the province of *Sechuen*. He fuggefted to our recollection, that he had formerly held an active fituation in that province, during the troubles excited by the rebellious *Miao-tfe*, and had affifted in reducing them to fubmiffion by his exertions. He added, that the fuppreffion of the rebellion of *Pe-lien-kiao*, actually exifting, was an undertaking of far lefs difficulty than the reduction of the *Miao-tfe*; the delays by which the prefent conteft has been for feveral years protracted, were, he declared, folely to be attributed to the negligence and inactivity of the officers to whom the command of the Imperial Armies had been entrufted. He concluded by obferving, that if a command againft the rebels was granted to him, he would engage to accomplifh their total overthrow by an appointed day.

We were, however, fully aware of the egregious vanity that prompted this declaration; and, therefore, did not, at that time, judge it expedient to grant his requeft.

When *Le-pao*, viceroy and commander in chief of the forces, proved himfelf incapable of tranfacting the united duties of thofe two ftations; and had, moreover, been criminally negligent in remaining at *Ta-cheu*, when the invafion of the province by the rebels, required that he fhould immediately have taken arms againft them, we depofed and committed him for trial, and appointed the General *Ge-le-teng-pao* to take his place as commander in chief of the forces. But as the viceroyalty of the province had likewife become vacant by his defection, and as the ftate was at that time unprovided with an officer duly qualified to fucceed to the appointment, we confidered that *Quay-lung*, having ferved for fome years in that province, and having fince held the poft of viceroy over the united provinces of *Fo-kien* and *Che-kiang*, could not be wholly unexperienced in that department, and we therefore iffued our orders that he fhould take upon himfelf the viceroyalty of *Se-chuen*; we did not, however, inveft him with any exprefs military command.

Towards the clofe of laft winter, the rebels of *Se-chuen* paffed over from that province into *Shen-fee*, and thence to *Kan-foo*; upon which the General *Ge-le-teng-pao*, defirous to guard againft falling into the errors of his predeceffor *Le-pao*, took the field in purfuit of the enemy, on the firft day of the firft moon of the prefent year, and left to the care of *Quay-lung* the reduction of the remaining parties of the rebels, which were ftill lurking in different parts of the province.

If *Quay-lung* had felt himfelf unequal to a charge of fuch importance, he ought to have prevented the departure of the General *Ge-le-teng-pao*, or immediately have reported to us the real fituation of affairs, that we might have acted accordingly.

After having, on the contrary, readily accepted the poft thus affigned to him, he loft eight days in inaction at *Ta-cheu*, under pretence of providing clothes and accoutrements for the soldiers. His subsequent operations were also tardy and undecisive; and of this the rebels did not fail to take the advantage, by fording the river *Kia-lin-kiang*; by so doing, they at once overwhelmed the inhabitants of the opposite district of *Chuen-see* with ruin and devastation.

Still, however, *Quay-lung* forebore to take the field in person, deeming it sufficient to direct the officers *O-ho-pao* and *Chu-she-teu* to proceed with a small detachment against the rebels. Upon this occasion his measures were so injudiciously taken, that the objects of the expedition were frustrated, and the officer *Chu-she-teu* actually cut off by the enemy.

The apprehensions of *Quay-lung* were so much excited by this disaster, that having encamped with his army upon the hill *Fung-whoang-shan*, he declined making any further efforts, though he repeatedly declared to us in his addresses at that conjuncture, that he was engaged in providing for the defence of the banks of the *Tung-ho*. He had not, however, once personally encountered the rebels, at the time that the General *Te-lin-tay*, in obedience to our commands, entered into that country, and engaged the rebels with promptitude and vigour. We confined ourselves, on this occasion, to a simple declaration to *Quay-lung*, that his life and fortune should depend upon the successful defence of the river *Tung-ho*; adding that, as a mark of our especial favour, although we degraded him to the third degree of rank, on account of his criminal negligence in permitting the rebels to gain a passage over the *Kia-lin-kiang*, we, at the same time, assigned him the the post of guarding the banks of the *Tung-ho*, to afford him an opportunity of redeeming his credit.

If *Quay-lung* had used effectual exertions for the protection of that boundary, *Te-lin-tay* would have been able to have met and engaged the rebels in the eastern side. The good conduct of the former in a successful defence of the banks of the *Tung-ho* would in such a degree have contributed to efface the recollection of his previous neglect at the *Kia-lin-kiang*, that even if we had not restored him to the first degree of rank, we certainly should not have hesitated to have permitted him to continue to exercise his functions in the viceroyalty.

So improvident, however, was *Quay-lung* in his measures of defence, that when the petition of *Lieu-tsing*, suggesting the detention of the provincial troops of *Honan* for a further security, was laid before him, he issued orders rejecting their assistance: shortly after, the rebels passed the *Tung-ho*, without opposition, and after having landed on the western bank, were suffered to spread rapine and devastation throughout that district, and to ruin or extirpate its unresisting inhabitants; even the districts in the vicinity of *Ching-too-fu*, the capital of the province, were laid open to the destructive progress of the rebels. The arrival of of the General *Te-lin-tay* at this juncture was eminently fortunate. With force and intrepidity he led his troops to the charge, and having first checked the progress of the assailants, he finally drove them back acrofs the *Tung-ho*, and has since confined them entirely to its eaftern banks. *Quay-lung*, in the mean time, was content with having affifted the General *Le-pao* in one or two engagements with another party of the rebels, and then led off his troops by a circuitous route to the diftrict of *Lung-gan*. The people of the province are no lefs grateful for the fervices rendered by *Te-lin-tay*, than difcontented and exafperated at the conduct of *Quay-lung*, whofe daftardly and fpiritlefs retreat from the enemy had proved him fo unworthy of command.

If exemplary punifhment is not inflicted upon this occafion, what refpect will hereafter be fhewn to martial laws, or fubmiffion to military difcipline. The calamities which the inhabitants of the weftern diftricts of the province of *Se-chuen* have experienced are beyond the reach of calculation. Were we to perfift in extending to *Quay-lung* our indulgence and compaffion, the much injured people would look upon him with averted eyes, and lend to his words an unwilling ear; in fhort, the purpofes of our adminiftration would be defeated by committing it to fuch guilty hands.

Our royal authority was therefore iffued for his degradation and commitment for trial, at the tribunal of his appointed fucceffor *Lee-pao*, and before fpecial judges whom we named for the purpofe.

The refult of their inveftigation of his crimes, was a fentence of death by decollation. The princes of the blood and great officers of ftate were likewife convened for the purpofe of inveftigating and deliberating upon this fubject, and have come to a fimilar decifion.

Quay-lung, therefore, ought to undergo the unabated rigour of the law, by a public execution in the prefence of the troops.

Upon confideration, however, of the impending trial and execution of the leaders of the *Pe-lien-kiao*, who are fubjects of this empire, and have incurred the guilt of rebellion; we were apprehenfive, that the execution of an officer of exalted rank, who had failed in the difcharge of the duties of his ftation, might induce an affociation in the minds of the inhabitants, derogatory to that refpect and fubmiffion which is due to all magiftrates, from the people under their jurifdiction.

We iffued our commands, therefore, for the prifoner to be conveyed to Pekin, and directed the princes of the blood and minifters of ftate to renew their inveftigation for two days, and revife the fentence they had given. The unreferved acknowledgment obtained from *Quay-lung* of his guilt, has precluded the neceffity of a more severe scrutiny. The additional charge of having killed the officer *Ma-liang-Cheu*, by a random shot from his bow, and which action he had concealed by reporting the deceased to have fallen in battle, he now likewise confesses with equal readiness. The council of princes and ministers of state, therefore, persist in supporting their former opinion, that punishment should be inflicted conformably to the utmost rigour of the laws; they have also, in obedience to our commands, laid before us a statement of the decisions that have heretofore been passed against officers of rank, under similar circumstances of delinquency.

In respect to the case of the four officers, *Ma-ur-kiun*, *Na-ching-chang*, *Quang-se*, and *Ya-ur-ho-shin*, who were executed according to the rigour of the laws, on account of their misconduct at *Ye-Kin-chuen*, in the exterior provinces; we find, on comparison, that the conduct of *Quay-lung* is more seriously criminal.

The statement of the trial of *Lee-che-yao* records, that the sentence of instant execution by decollation was changed to a sentence of execution in the following autumn, by the favour of our Imperial Father. The guilt of *Lee-che-yao*, in not taking measures against the rebels called *Whey-fee*, and permitting their leader *Tien-fu* to raise the standard of rebellion, and collect his adherents, before he proceeded with his army against them, may be compared with the timidity and irresolution of *Quay-lung* in seeking to avoid the rebels, and suffering them to ravage the country and ruin the inhabitants of *Se-chuen*; but still the crime of the latter appears of a deeper dye.

With regard to the proceedings against *Tang-yng-kiay*, viceroy of the provinces of *Yun-nan* and *Quei-cheu*, during the rebellion of the *Mien-fee*, we find that his circuitous marches in order to avoid an encounter with the enemy, and the deceptive reports which he addressed to court, in order to gloss over his misconduct, drew upon him a sentence of immediate death by decollation, according to the law against a general who injures the state by misleading his troops. By our Imperial Father's gracious favour he was nevertheless permitted to become his own executioner.

The rank of *Quay-lung* corresponds with that of *Tang-yng-kiay*, each being entrusted with the government of a province. With regard to the circuitous marches which they practised in order to avoid the rebels, and prevent a general engagement, they appear equally guilty. The conduct of *Quay-lung*, in reporting himself to be engaged in defending the bank of the *Tung-ho*, while actually seeking for a pretence to avoid the enemy, and his false statement of the circumstances of the death of the officer *Ma-liang-cheu*, may likewise be placed in comparison with the deceptive reports presented to court by *Tang-yng-kiay*.

The

The charges substantiated against *Quay-lung*, on the whole, fully justify the sentence which has been awarded against him; but as some palliation may be conceived to arise from the circumstance of his voluntary offer to serve in the war against the rebels, we are induced to admit the case of *Tang-yng.kiay* as a precedent, and shall, therefore, spare to *Quay-lung* the ignominy of a public execution.

It is our pleasure that the officers of the supreme criminal court make known this our resolution, and carry it into effect. We grant to *Quay-lung* to become his own executioner; a sentence to which it would be absolutely impossible for us to admit the most trifling alleviation, without becoming ourselves guilty of dangerous and criminal partiality. It is our firm resolution never to suffer the military discipline and martial laws of this realm to be degraded or impaired by the licensed impunity of any magistrate, who fails to protect the people of the district under his authority from the cruelty and rapine of rebellious invaders.

Yuen-yen and *Cha-la-fen*, the sons of the magistrate *Quay-lung*, shall proceed to their place of banishment at *Elee* in Tartary, as an expiation for the guilt in which they are involved. Having decided upon this case, and explained the causes and motives upon which our judgment is founded, we direct that this edict extraordinary may be issued throughout all the provinces for general information.

Khin-tse.

No. X.

[Referred to from Section VI. page 9.]

1. *Translation of the Address of* Pe-ling, *Sub-Viceroy of the Province of* Quang-tung. (1805.)

I HUMBLY address Your Imperial Majesty for the express purpose of charging certain magistrates of districts with a flagrant neglect and delay in the execution of justice; in consequence of which the ordinary places of confinement are no longer adequate to contain the multitude of unexamined prisoners. I charge them also with connivance at the all-devouring rapacity of their followers and attendants. And, lastly, with the illegal and improper employment of female curators:

curators * : by which several offences, the lives of many of Your Majesty's subjects have been sacrificed. I have accordingly to solicit an Order from Your Imperial Majesty, confirming the degradation and removal of the said magistrates; that your sacred authority may be respected and enforced by the due punishment of offences of such serious magnitude.

My first inquiries enabled me to discover, that in the hands of the officers of justice in this province of *Quang-tung*, the authority of the laws had been, in some cases, abused, and, in others, neglected, and relaxed: the prisons were full, and informations had accumulated; but the dusty records of unfinished causes sufficiently evinced that very remote must be the day of their final adjustment, and no less remote the day, on which the wrongs of the injured parties could be redressed.

The crafty scribes and the lawless attendants of the courts of justice, had not scrupled to combine and concert with thriving profligates in forming plans of deceit and extortion; and the country in general has but too deeply felt the injurious consequences.

On my arrival at the government allotted to me by Your Majesty, it was my first care to seek for, and to remove successively, the most obnoxious of the official attendants, by whose misconduct the town and country had been disturbed. Two of the most notorious among the attendants of the courts, by name *Me-liang* and *Ly-yue-quang*, have already undergone a rigorous examination and punishment.

The removal of the delinquents who had been the most distinguished by their rapacity and extortion, contributed much to ease and tranquillize the minds of the people; I proceeded, nevertheless, in my investigation, and had occasion to notice, that in the divisions of the city, under the government of the *Nan-hay-fien* and *Pun-yu-fien*, exclusive of the legal prisons already full of persons in lawful confinement, everal subsidiary buildings had been engaged, with the acquiescence of the said magistrates, and under the sanction of various names, but uniformly for the sole purpose of imprisonment.

The officer whom I appointed to investigate this affair, has reported three such places of confinement in the district of *Nan-hay*, namely *Tay-heu-so*, *Ky-yun-tsang*, and *Hoei-foo-hang*, containing upwards of one hundred prisoners: and in the district of *Pun-yu* likewise, a place denominated *Tay-heu-so*, in which also above an hundred persons were found in connnement. Among the prisoners, many had been brought up from the country, under charges of theft, murder, and the like, accompanied by the witnesses and accusers respectively concerned; the cognizance of their offences having been referred to the magistrates of the provincial capital: but, whether the parties were more or less implicated, the charges serious

* The peculiar sense in which this word is employed will appear from the sequel.

or trifling, it was ufual to expofe them for many months, or even a year, to the hardfhip of a tedious and indifcriminate confinement, in thefe unauthorized places of detention.

Exclufive of the legal and the fubfidiary prifons here defcribed, it has appeared, moreover, that the attendants or officers of police attached to the court of the *Nan-hay-fien*, had not lefs than ten places of private detention, in which alfo, taken together, upwards of an hundred perfons were difcovered. The attendants of the court of the *Pun-yu-fien* were provided in a fimilar manner with twelve places, which were found to contain above ninety perfons.

It was found that thefe places were inclofed with a wooden railing, difpofed like a cage, but at the fame time, attached, on one fide, to the wall of the contiguous building, and fubdivided into cells by means of beams and rafters.

Thus conftructed, thefe dark dungeons have been, in fact, employed to enforce, by oppreffive and arbitrary confinement, nothing lefs than a fyftem of fraud and extortion.

I haftened, after inveftigating, to remedy this grievance, but already many perfons had perifhed under confinement; and the inhuman, nefarious practice has been fo long eftablifhed, that it is difficult to afcertain the year in which it originated, or to conjecture how many lives have been facrificed by its continuance. The people were either chilled with defpair, or murmuring with indignation at the exiftence of fuch an abufe.

I have, in the next place, to animadvert on the appointment of female curators, under the authority of the faid magiftates, the *Pun-yu-fien* and *Nan-hay-fien*.

Thefe women had become the confidential agents of traders, whom they enabled to carry on a difgraceful and illicit commerce of female flaves, and they often affifted in obtaining a certificate from the magiftrates, when the original right to the flave was not free from fufpicion. To the cuftody of thefe women, all the female prifoners who had not yet received fentence, or been difcharged, were committed; and the younger part of them were not unfrequently let out for proftitution, and the wages thereof received by the curators as a part of their regular profits.

An accurate inveftigation is now taking place, under the direction of an officer efpecially appointed for that fervice, of the feveral prifoners of each denomination, with the view of difcharging at once, all fuch as are able to find fecurity, or againft whom the charges cannot be fubftantiated.

The feveral places of detention, which the officers of the above-mentioned courts, had illegally employed, I have caufed to be appropriated to other ufes, the wooden enclofures to be removed, and the cells rafed from the foundations. The number of the perfons found therein, and the circumftances that occafioned their detention, remains to be afcertained by a fpecific inveftigation,

and

and will be accurately recorded for the information of the supreme court of judicature at Pekin. The female curators, who had so shamefully abused their trust, have been dismissed for ever; and the female culprits, formerly under their charge, remanded to the families to which they respectively belonged; competent security having been given for their re-appearance at the period of trial.

Lastly, after giving the subject mature consideration, I cannot hesitate to declare the use and appointment of subsidiary places of confinement, altogether illegal; more especially, as the law requires an annual and accurate report to be made of the goal-deliveries in each province, to the supreme court.

It having thus appeared that *Vang-Shee*, chief magistrate of *Nan-hay-sien*, and *Tiao-hing-vu*, chief magistrate of *Pun-yu-sien*, to whom these, which are in fact, the most important districts in the province, have been confided, have proved themselves unfaithful, and unworthy of their trust, by audaciously erecting subsidiary prisons in defiance of the law, and unjustly confining divers persons therein: that they have, in general, shewn an utter contempt of the laws of the empire, and the happiness of the people, by the full licence they have given to the destructive rapacity of their followers; by the criminal misemployment of female curators; and by the false imprisonment, and various other grievances, to which they have exposed the people either directly by their orders, or indirectly by their consent, or connivance: is it possible that their conduct should be tolerated one day longer?

I am in duty bound, therefore, to request that Your Majesty will sanction their degradation and removal; and in the mean time, I have made temporary nominations to the vacant offices, and have directed an account of the treasure and grain for which each of these magistrates stood responsible, to be accurately drawn out and compared with the actual state of the treasuries and granaries, under their respective jurisdictions, at the period of their suspension; and an exact report in due time will be made of the result.

I must further submit to Your Majesty's consideration, that the *Quang-cheou-foo*, the *Leang-tao*, and the *An-cha-sse*, being the immediate superiors of these guilty magistrates, are liable to censure, for their supineness and neglect of due examination; which, therefore, ought to become a distinct subject of investigation, on the part of the supreme court: also, that as soon as the various persons are ascertained by reference, who officiated as magistrates of the above districts, and as *Quang-tcheou-foo*, *Leang-tao* and *An-cha-sse*, when these corrupt practices originated, their delinquencies will likewise be deserving of investigation and punishment; as indeed, that of any magistrate of the province under whose jurisdiction such abuses may be found at any time to have existed.— With a view to a comprehensive enquiry of this nature, I have directed an investigation of all the facts, which it is necessary previously to ascertain; that no measure may be omitted for effectually preventing the repetition of these grievances, and that the feelings of the injured multitude, may be appeased and tranquillized.

These several measures, I have thought it necessary to adopt for the good government of the province; and having respectfully set them forth in this address, they are now humbly submitted to your Majesty's Imperial consideration.

Your Majesty will finally decide upon my conduct; and will be pleased to issue your gracious orders and instructions in regulation of my further proceedings.

2. *Translation of an Imperial Edict, issued in reply to the preceding Address, on the 22d day of the Intercalary 6th Moon of the 10th Year of* KIA KING, (*August the 16th 1805.*)

We have received the addresses of *Na-yen-tching* and *Pe-ling*, charging certain magistrates of districts with neglect and delay in the execution of justice, in consequence of which, the prisons had become inadequate to contain all the culprits successively committed for trial; secondly, with connivance at the rapacity and extortion of their attendants; and lastly, with the illegal employment of female curators: by which several offences, the lives of many of our subjects had been endangered or sacrificed. — We are accordingly solicited to degrade and remove the said magistrates.

The magistrates of districts are undoubtedly forbidden by existing regulations, to employ any subsidiary places of confinement; and in the event of an increase in the number of informations against delinquents in those large districts which include the capital of the province, absolutely requiring such an expedient, it would have been the duty of the magistrates thereof to have represented the exigency to the supreme officers of government, in order that the adoption of the measure, as far as it was necessary, should receive the sanction of the laws.

It has now appeared, upon investigation, that three subsidiary prisons had, nevertheless, been employed in the district of *Nan-hay*; and that the attendants of the tribunal, in the said district, made use of fifty other occasional places of confinement. In the district of *Pun-yu*, one subsidiary prison was found, called *Tay-heu-so*, and also twelve places of occasional confinement. It was moreover discovered, that the attendants had been very culpably suffered to divide those places of confinement into cells, and to enclose them with a railing, whereby dark dungeons were formed, with the view of practising fraud and extortion upon the unfortunate perfons who were confined therein, among whom many became fick, and died from the feverity of the imprifonment.

Laftly, it has appeared that the female prifoners, previous to their being difcharged or receiving fentence, were ufually entrufted to the cuftody of female curators, by whom it frequently happened that the younger women were expofed to proftitution, and the wages thereof received by the curators as a part of their regular profits.

The conduct of the magiftrates who permitted thefe abufes is no lefs odious than extraordinary; they feem utterly to have neglected the laws of the empire, and the happinefs of the people, with whom, by occafion of their inferior jurifdiction, they were more intimately connected than other officers of government.

On thefe grounds, the viceroy and fub-viceroy have folicited their degradation and removal; and accordingly we decree that *Vang-fhy*, magiftrate of *Nan-hay*; and *Leao-hing-vu*, magiftrate of *Pun-yu*; be divefted of their refpective employments, and expiate their guilt by an immediate banifhment to *Elee* in Tartary.

And, as it is evident from the exiftence of thefe abufes, that the fuperintending officers of the province have been guilty of fupinenefs, and neglect of due examination in their refpective departments, we direct that the fupreme court do deliberate on the cenfurable conduct of *We-fhe-poo*, the late viceroy; and on that of *Sun-yu-ting* and *Hoo-tu-lee*, fucceffively fub-viceroys of the province of *Quang-tong*; and likewife on the conduct of the *Gan-cha-ffe* (judge), *Leang-tao*, and *Quang-cheou-foo* (governor of the city), who by virtue of their refpective offices, poffeffed a jurifdiction over, and a power to control the faid guilty magiftrates.

We order that *Na-yen-tching* alfo proceed to afcertain by inveftigation, at what period, and under the government of what magiftrates, thefe abufes commenced; and that he do fpeedily report the fame for our confideration, fhewing the degree of mifconduct with which fuch magiftrates and their refpective fuperiors, are chargeable.

With regard to *Na-yen-tching* and *Pe-ling*, who have fo lately fucceeded to the government of the province; we highly applaud the vigour and ability they have fhewn in the adminiftration of public affairs, and it is our pleafure that the fupreme court for civil affairs, do take their merits into confideration.

Khin-Tfe.

No. XI.

[Referred to from Section XXXIV. page 36.]

NOTE.

THE application of the laws of China to the case of British subjects trading to, and residing at Canton, concerning which a reference has been made to this article of the appendix, is a subject which might deserve, as well as afford scope for, a distinct treatise. A trade which employs annually, upon an average, upwards of 20,000 tons of English, and 10,000 tons of Indian shipping; which carries off, every year, more than a million sterling in value, of our manufactures and productions; and which alone can supply us with an article so universally in use as to be almost a necessary of life in this country, must, even without estimating how much it contributes to the revenue of the state, as well as to that of the East India Company, be obviously of great national importance.

It is one of the necessary, but embarrassing consequences of the footing upon which foreigners are at present received in China, that they can neither consider themselves as wholly subject to, or as wholly independent of the laws of the country they live in. When unfortunately involved in contentions with the government, there is generally a line, on one side of which submission is disgraceful, and on the other, resistance unjustifiable; but this line being uncertain and undefined, it is not surprising that a want of confidence should sometimes have led to a surrender of just and reasonable privileges; or that at other times, an excess of it should have brought the whole of this valuable trade, and of the property embarked in it, to the brink of destruction.

The plan and limits of this work will not admit of any regular enquiry into a subject of this nature; but it is hoped that the four following translations of public and official documents, will contribute in some degree to illustrate the professed sentiments of the Chinese government in this respect, and be found in other points of view, not uninteresting.

1. The first relates to the Portuguese at Macao. — A Chinese had been killed by a Portuguese subject; and the crime having been fully brought home to the murderer, the authority to which he was amenable under the circumstances of the case, was the only question in dispute. In this instance the Portuguese ultimately prevailed, and the culprit was executed by their authority, and within the limits of their jurisdiction.

2. The second is a translation of an edict issued on the occasion of an attempt made by the Russians, to open a trade at Canton, in the year 1806. The Emperor's interdiction did not arrive in time to prevent the departure of the ships

with full cargoes, but will probable prove effectual in difcouraging fimilar adventures in future.

3. The third relates to a fmall Englifh veffel, which was ftranded in the courfe of the year preceding, upon the coaft of China. The crew were faved, and conveyed to Canton by land; but no part of the cargo was ever recovered.

4. The fourth and laft, is a tranflation of an Imperial Edict iffued in the year 1808, and containing the Emperor of China's conclufive and very favourable determination of a queftion which had previoufly involved the Eaft India Company's reprefentatives at Canton, in very embarraffing, and for a long time, ineffectual negotiations with the provincial government.

The tenor of this edict, and the circumftances under which it is known to have been publifhed, are calculated, it muft be acknowledged, to convey more unfavourable ideas of the adminiftration of the laws in the Chinefe empire, than almoft any other public act of that government upon record. In this cafe, all the proceedings were founded on a ftory fabricated for the purpofe; a ftory, in which the Europeans did not concur, though afferted to have done fo; which, in fact, the Chinefe magiftrates themfelves, or the merchants under their influence, invented; which the Chinefe witneffes, knowing to be falfe, adopted; and which, laftly, the fovereign himfelf appears to have acquiefced in, without examination.

The fact was fimply as follows: a number of Englifh feamen had been engaged in a fcuffle with the Chinefe populace at Canton; in the courfe of which, one of the natives unluckily received a blow that terminated in his death. The actual perpetrator of the deed not being known, one of the feamen, who had taken an active fhare in the fcuffle, was fingled out by the officers of the Chinefe government as a proper perfon to anfwer for the homicide, and at the fame time, this fictitious account of the affair was concerted, in order to juftify his acquittal.

In defence of the Chinefe government, as far as its general character may be fuppofed to be affected by thefe proceedings, it may be faid:

Firft, that the cafe in queftion being confidered to have been almoft unparalleled, cannot juftly be made the ground-work of any general inference.

Secondly, that as the Chinefe merchant, who, according to the cuftom of the port, had undertaken a general refponfibility for the fhip to which the failors who had been riotous belonged, is faid to have purchafed the acquiefcence of the parties interefted, by a divifion amongft them of a fum little fhort of 50,000l.; it muft be admitted, that the witneffes, and other agents on the occafion, were expofed to more than ordinary temptations, and fuch as could be but feldom held out to perfons in their fituations in any country, or under any circumftances.

Thirdly, that the facilities which encouraged an attempt at the fubornation of the witneffes, and corruption of the judges, were greater, and the danger of detection less, in a case in which a foreigner, than in one in which a native, was the object of the prosecution.

Lastly, that although the falsehood in which so many persons concurred, was, no doubt, base and criminal in itself, it neither produced, nor was intended to produce, the slightest deviation from substantial justice in respect to the person accused; he was well known to be innocent, or at least unconvicted, of the murder; but the strictness of the laws unfortunately rendered it impossible for the magistrates to ground a verdict of acquittal upon a true statement of the case, without, at the same time, in some degree implicating and condemning themselves; they, therefore, under these difficult circumstances, contrived to do that which was just in itself, though they certainly resorted to means which were far from defensible.

As to the Emperor's acquiescence in an acquittal, founded upon so plausible and well concerted a story, it certainly cannot be fairly considered as any impeachment of the judgment and impartiality of his government.

1. *Translation of an Edict of the Governor of the Town and District of* Hiang-shan, *addressed to the Chinese and Portuguese Inhabitants of* Macao.

WHEREAS the European Andreas struck and mortally wounded *Chin-a-lien*, a Chinese; although the relations of the deceased, instead of duly reporting, have endeavoured to conceal the fact, I have taken into custody one of the relations *Chin-ky-yen*, together with *Ly-a-voo*, the man who had apprehended the European.

These persons having undergone examination at my office, and the wounds on the body of the deceased having been inspected and legally verified, I proceeded to issue an order to the procurador of Macao to deliver up to me the said Andreas, that his trial might take place according to law; but this procurador deceitfully, and under colour of false pretences, seeks to suppress the enquiry, and is unwilling to give up the culprit.

Considering that these foreigners, who live and reside at Macao, enjoy, through the generous goodness of the Imperial government, the food which they consume, and the ground which they occupy, exactly on the same footing as its natural subjects, it is but just, that they should respectfully obey and submit to the laws and institutions of the country, and comply readily, in this instance, with what our judicial proceedings require.

Now, these foreigners, by persisting to conceal the culprit, do indeed betray such malice and obstinacy, that I ought at once to represent their conduct to the viceroy,

viceroy, preparatory to the meafure of cutting off all communcaition with them, by clofing the gates of the diftrict. Reflecting, however, that there is at Macao a great mixture of Europeans and Chinefe, and that the inhabitants of the latter defcription are very numerous, fo as to render the execution of fuch a meafure inconvenient, I fhall only for the prefent addrefs this edict, efpecially to the the faid Chinefe inhabitants, whether traders, labourers, or perfons employed in any other capacity, to inform them, that I hereby prohibit every defcription of traders from fupplying the foreigners with their refpective commodities; and alfo all labourers, carpenters, bricklayers, and other artificers, from working for them in any manner, until the faid foreigners confent to deliver up the culprit, after which permiffion will be given to refume and carry on trade and bufinefs with them as heretofore.

Whoever difregards this prohibition fhall be taken into cuftody, and feverely punifhed, without admitting of any mitigation or abatement. All perfons, therefore, will do well to obey and refpectfully conform thereto.

26th of the 7th Moon of the 10th year of KIA-KING. 18th of September, 1805.

2. *Tranflation of an Imperial Edict, dated the 9th of the 12th Moon of the 10th Year of* KIA-KING, *addreffed to the Viceroy of the Provinces of* Quang-tung *and* Quang-fee.

WE are juft apprized by the Hoppo *Yen*, that in the courfe of the 10th moon, two Ruffian fhips had fucceffively anchored in the roads of Macao, and that on board of thefe fhips two foreign merchants, named Krufentern and Lyfianfkoy, had arrived, and had brought with them a fum of money, and a cargo of furs, with the intent of opening a trade at the port of Canton: That the Hong merchants had, upon an inveftigation, found thefe Ruffians to belong to the nation termed by the Chinefe *Go-lo-fe*, and had tranflated and laid before him their petition for leave to trade at the port; upon which he, the faid Hoppo, having confulted with the viceroy *Na*, and the fub-viceroy *Sun*, had iffued the ufual orders, directing the merchants to trade honeftly and fairly with them.

This is a very negligent and fummary mode of proceeding; for it ought to have been recollected, that the trade with foreign nations is reftricted within certain limits, which it is never permitted to violate or tranfgrefs. It is true, that all fuch foreign nations as are accuftomed to frequent the ports of Canton and Macao and the neighbouring iflands, are likewife allowed the liberty of trading in thofe parts, but amongft thefe, the name of the Ruffian nation has never yet been obferved by us: wherefore, their fudden appearance at this time, and defign of opening a trade at the port of Canton, cannot be confidered otherwife, than as a very novel and extraordinary circumftance.

Now, all affairs connected with the intercourfe with foreigners, fhould be inveftigated and acted upon with peculiar circumfpection; it was, therefore, the duty of the Hoppo either to have refufed their requeft, not finding it fanctioned by any precedent, and thus at once to have difmiffed them; or at leaft, to have granted a fhort ftay to the firft fhip only. And as there had been a petition received from the foreigners, it ought to have been faithfully reported to us, and no further proceedings allowed until our pleafure was known, inftead of permitting them to trade unconditionally, upon the mere report and ftatement of the Hong merchants. Befides, as the name of Ruffia appears to be nothing more than the foreign pronunciation of *Go-lo-fe*, of which nation there never have been any interpreters employed at Canton, the Hoppo has not fhewn how their petition could have been tranflated, and explained to him; nor do we find in his report, of what fort of furs the cargoes of their fhips confifted; nor the amount of the money they brought with them to trade with; nor laftly, what returning cargoes they were defirous of purchafing. The omiffion of all thefe things, which fhould have been feverally defcribed and explained, is highly reprehenfible; we have therefore directed an enquiry to be held on the conduct of the Hoppo *Yen*, who was principally culpable in this affair; and we have further directed, that the proper board fhould deliberate and report to us, whether the viceroy *Na* and fub-viceroy *Sun*, are not likewife cenfurable for their concurrence.

The viceroy *Vu* and the Hoppo *Oe*, fhall, immediately on the receipt of thefe commands, in the firft inftance, fufpend for a time, all tranfactions at the cuftom-houfe, on behalf of the faid fhips, provided they are not already laden; if they fhall have completed their lading, but not have quitted the port, the viceroy and the Hoppo fhall proceed, without delay, accurately to enquire and inveftigate, whether thefe Ruffians really came from the nation of *Go-lo-fe*; and if fo, how the natives of the *Go-lo-fe* nation, who have hitherto always traded by way of *Ha-ke-htu* (Kiachta) in Tartary, and never before vifited the coaft of *Quang-tung*, have now been able to navigate their fhips thither, and have become acquainted with the fhoals and iflands with which that coaft abounds. Alfo, whether they have not paffed by fome other kingdoms in their way from Ruffia, and what kingdoms; whether they were not from fome, and from what kingdoms, directed and informed how to proceed to this country.

Laftly, they are to enquire whether the Ruffian merchants embarked in thefe fhips, brought their cargoes with them for their own private emolument and advantage, or were difpatched to China to trade, by the orders of their King. The viceroy and Hoppo having taken meafures for collecting full and diftinct information on

all

all these subjects, shall transmit the same to us by express. In reply we shall issue to them our final instructions for their guidance.

But should these ships, having taken in and completed their cargoes, have been permitted to depart, and no channel remain, through which this subject may be investigated, we, in that case, do direct that, in the event of any ships visiting for the future the ports of Canton and Macao, or their vicinity, belonging to any other nation besides those which have customarily frequented those ports, they shall on no account whatever be permitted to trade, but merely suffered to remain in port, until the viceroy and Hoppo, having reported to us every circumstance respecting them, shall have been apprised in return of our determination.

We now dispatch this edict by an express, that the viceroy and the Hoppo may know our pleasure, and duly conform to it. *Khin-Tse.*

3. *Translation of an Extract of an Edict of the Viceroy of* Quang-tung *and* Quang-see, *communicated to the Senior Captain of His Britannic Majesty's Ships on the Coast of China.*

The Celestial Empire (China) is provided with strict and numerous laws, according to which, whenever an act of robbery or theft is committed in the country, orders are immediately issued for rigorously enquiring after and pursuing the criminals; when they have been taken into custody, it becomes necessary, by a legal process, to investigate and verify their guilt, and also to identify the property recovered, in order that in the end, a just and equitable sentence may be awarded.

When a ship of your nation was stranded last year, near *Ping-hay*, and you represented to this government that it had been afterwards plundered, his excellency, my predecessor, immediately issued strict orders for the discovery and seizure of the offending parties.

In like manner, since I came into office, I have repeatedly and urgently given instructions to the same effect; but, on account of the remote and maritime situation of the place where the offence is alleged to have been committed, it is impracticable to declare positively any precise period, within which the guilty individuals may be expected to be traced and brought to justice: however, I shall again give orders for persevering in the investigation, and whenever the criminals, and the property plundered by them can be found, a trial and sentence strictly conformable to law, will undoubtedly follow.

9th of the 8th moon of the 11th year of KIA KING. 20th September 1806.

APPENDIX, No. XI.

4. *Translation of an Edict of the Hoppo or Superintendant of the Port of Canton, addressed to the Chinese Merchants licensed to engage in Foreign Trade.*

I have received information from His Excellency the vice-roy to the following effect:

"On the 26th of the first moon of the 13th year of KIA KING, I received the following dispatch from the supreme criminal tribunal at Pekin, relating to a case that had been tried in this province:

"A decision having taken place upon a case which we had laid before his Imperial Majesty for ratification, it is now fit and necessary that we should communicate the same to your excellency, as viceroy of *Quang-tung* and *Quang-see*, to the end that the same may be duly carried into effect under your excellency's direction.

"His Majesty's inner council having, in the first instance, issued a transcript of the report of the vice-roy of *Quang-tung* and *Quang-see*, stating his investigation of the case of a foreigner, Edward Sheen, opening a window-shutter in an upper story, and dropping a stick so as to hit and occasion the death of *Leao-a-teng*, a native of this empire; His Majesty was pleased, on the 8th of the 11th moon of the 12th year, to direct that our tribunal should revise the same and pronounce judgment thereon.—In obedience to orders, we accordingly on the 10th day of the moon, took the said transcript into consideration; and we found that the viceroy's report was grounded, in the first instance, on a statement of the magistrate of *Nan-hay-sien*, a district of Canton, which was to the following effect:

"On the 18th day of the first moon of the present year, *Leao-a-teng*, a native
" of the district *Pun-yu-sien*, went with his wife's brother *Chao-a-sse*, to buy
" goods in a street within the said district, called *She-fan-hang*, and happened to
" pass along the stone pavement under a warehouse called *Fung-tay-hong*. at the
" same time an Englishman named Edward Sheen, who was in the upper story
" of the said warehouse, in attempting to open the window, slipped his hand
" and dropped a stick, which, *Leao-a-teng* not expecting, could not avoid,
" and was therefore struck therewith on the left temple, so that he fell to the
" ground.

" *Chao-a-sse* acquainted *Leao-a-lun*, the brother of *Leao-a-teng*, with the acci-
" dent, who being thus informed of the particulars thereof, came and assisted
" the said *Leao-a-teng* to return to his home, and procured him medical assistance,
" which however had no effect, and the wounded man expired on the evening of
" the following day, the 19th of the moon;— the brother of the deceased then re-

" ported the cafe to the head-man of the diftrict; and by him, information was
" laid at the tribunal of the *Nan-hay-fien*, where the witneffes of the fact
" having been, in confequence, affembled and examined, the chief of the faid
" nation was called upon to deliver up the faid criminal Edward Sheen, for ex-
" amination and trial ".

The viceroy proceeded to ftate, that repeated orders were, in confequence, iffued to the *Hong* merchants on the fubject, and through them to the chief of the faid nation; in reply to which it was alleged, that the faid criminal was fick of an ague and fever, and undergoing medical treatment for his recovery: at length, after repeated applications, it was reported that he had recovered from his ficknefs, whereupon the magiftrates of the diftrict confronted the criminal with the relations of the deceafed, and having finifhed the inveftigation in due form, referred the confideration of the proceedings to the chief judge, by whom the fame procefs was renewed, and the refult finally tranfmitted to the vice-regal office.

His excellency having concluded the enquiry, by perfonally and ftrictly exa-mining into the affair himfelf, afcertained that " that Edward Sheen is a native of England, engaged for hire to perform the duty of a feaman, on board the fhip of Captain Buchanan, a merchant of the fame nation: the faid fhip having been laden with a cargo of goods for trade, in the faid kingdom of England, had arrived at the port of Canton and anchored in the reach of *Whampoa*, in the courfe of the 12th moon of the 11th year of KIA KING, after which the cargo was landed, and depofited in a warehoufe or factory called *Fung-tay-hong* in the fuburbs of the city of Canton: Edward Sheen had immediately thereupon, accompanied captain Buchanan and others to the upper ftory of the faid ware-houfe or factory, in order to dwell therein, until, the returning cargo having been received, the period of departure fhould arrive:—This upper ftory was alfo contiguous to, and overlooked the ftreet and path-way, towards which a window was opened with moveable fhutters.

On the morning of the 18th day of the 1ft moon of the 12th year of KIA-KING, Edward Sheen employed a wooden ftick in an oblique direction to keep open the fhutter of the abovementioned window; but in doing this, the wooden ftick flipped and fell downwards:

It happened alfo, that *Leao-a-teng*, a native of China, accompanied by his wife's brother *Chao-a-ffe*, went to the ftreet called *She-fan-hong*, to buy goods; and paffing at the fame moment under the faid upper ftory, was ftruck and wounded by the end of the ftick falling, as aforefaid, upon his left temple; and he thereupon fell to the ground. *Chao-a-ffe* acquainted *Leao-a-lun*, the brother of *Leao-a-teng*, with the accident, who, upon being informed thereof, immediately came and affifted *Leao-a-teng* to return to his home; and afterwards pro-

cured

cured him medical affiftance; all which, however, proved of no avail; and the wounded man died on the evening of the following day, the 19th of the moon.

"Now, the aforefaid criminal, Edward Sheen, having been repeatedly examined, has acknowledged the truth of all the facts here ftated, without any refervation.— Confequently, in this cafe, there is no appeal againft the conviction of this offender, Edward Sheen; who, having been proved guilty of accidental homicide, may be fentenced to pay the ufual fine, to redeem himfelf from the punifhment of death by ftrangulation"

The foregoing being the fubftance of the report of the viceroy to his Imperial Majefty, we have deliberated thereon, and have afcertained that, according to the preliminary book of the penal code, all perfons from foreign parts, committing offences, fhall undergo trial and receive fentence according to the laws of the empire:— Moreover, we find it declared in the fame code, that any perfon accidentally killing another, fhall be allowed to redeem himfelf from punifhment, by the payment of a fine; laftly, we find, that in the 8th year of KIEN-LUNG (1743) it was ordered, in reply to the addrefs of the viceroy of Canton then in office, that thenceforward, in all cafes of offences by contrivance, defign, or in affrays happening between foreigners and natives, whereby fuch foreigners are liable, according to law, to fuffer death by being ftrangled or beheaded, the magiftrate of the diftrict fhall receive the proofs and evidence thereof, at the period of the preliminary inveftigation, and after having fully and diftinctly inquired into the reality of the circumftances, report the refult to the viceroy and fub-viceroy, who are thereupon ftrictly to repeat and revife the inveftigation.— If the determination of the inferior courts, upon the alleged facts, and upon the application of the laws, is found to have been juft and accurate, the magiftrate of the diftrict fhall laftly receive orders to proceed, in conjunction with the chief of the nation, to take the offender to execution, according to his fentence. *In all other inftances of offences committed under, what the laws declare to be palliating circumftances, and which are therefore not capitally punifhable, the offender fhall be fent away to be punifhed by his countrymen in his own country* *.

The cafe of the Englifhman, Edward Sheen, opening a window-fhutter in an upper ftory, and the wooden ftick which fupported it, flipping and falling down fo as accidentally to hit *Leao-a-teng*, a native, who was paffing by, and by ftriking him to occafion his death, appears to be, in truth, one of thofe acts, of the confequences of which, neither fight, hearing, or reflection could have given a

* This paragraph is particularly important, as it announces an exemption in favour of foreigners, which, however effential to their well-being and fecurity in China, was never before fo diftinctly declared and underftood.

previous warning; there was therefore, no pre-difpofition to injure, and the cafe is evidently agreeable to the conftruction ftated in the commentary upon the law of accidental homicide. The faid Edward Sheen ought therefore, conformably to the provifional fentence fubmitted by the viceroy to his Majefty, to be allowed to redeem himfelf from the punifhment of death by ftrangulation, (to which he would otherwife have been liable, by the law againft homicide by blows,) by the payment of a fine of 12 *leang* 4 *fen* and 2 *lee*, (about 4l. 3s. fterling), to the relations of the deceafed, to defray the expences of burial; and then be difmiffed to be governed in an orderly manner in his own country.

We thus refpectfully laid before his Imperial Majefty, our deliberate judgment upon this cafe, with the confiderations whereupon it is founded, and humbly folicited a declaration of his Majefty's pleafure regarding the fame.

On the 17th day of the 10th moon of the 12th year (January 1808) the addrefs was laid before his Majefty, and received his Majefty's anfwer in thefe words " we ratify your judgment."

The above communication of the fupreme criminal court, having reached the vice-regal office, I, in the firft inftance, directed the provincial judge to attend to the ftrict execution of the Imperial decree, by forthwith taking the faid Edward Sheen and delivering him to the chief of his nation, in order to his being fent back to be governed in an orderly manner in his own country;— the ufual fine being at the fame time duly recovered, for the re-imburfement of the relatives of the deceafed for the expences of his interment:— the exact time of difmiffion of the faid foreigner, and of the reimburfement of the faid relatives, are to be duly afcertained and reported to me; but I think fit, moreover, to communicate thefe things to your excellency, that you likewife may co-operate in attending to the due execution thereof."

His Excellency the viceroy's communication having been tranfmitted to me, as Hoppo, at my office, I determine to make it known to you alfo *Hong* merchants, that you may, agreeably to thefe my orders, attend to the due execution of all things therein required.— May you refpectfully conform to thefe orders.

The 7th of the 2d moon of the 13th year of the Emperor KIA-KING (February 1808).

No. XII.

[Referred to from Section LII. Page 55.]

Translation of an Imperial Edict, extracted from the Pekin Gazette of the 30th of the 3d Moon of the 5th Year of KIA-KING, (*the 23d of April* 1800.)

WHEREAS we have respectfully considered the decisions of our Imperial Father, deceased, on the subject of a petition now presented to us, for permitting the establishment of colleges in various districts of Tartary, where the youth of those provinces might be examined, and receive their literary degrees without the inconvenience of undertaking a journey to Pekin for that purpose. Though we are aware of the advantages that might result from such a measure, yet as the profession of arms is most congenial to the disposition of the inhabitants, as well as of the greatest local necessity in those countries, it would be a matter of just regret, that too great an encouragement given to literary pursuits should ever divert the Tartar youth from the more active employments of the military and equestrian exercises. It might also be reasonably apprehended, that partiality and corruption would gradually insinuate themselves in to examinations, which should be carried on in such remote and unfrequented stations.

It is therefore our pleasure, that the examinations and distribution of literary degrees among the Tartars, should be continued solely at Pekin as heretofore; and at the same time we strongly recommend to the Tartar officers, civil and military, to instruct and exhort their sons, and the younger branches of their families, to consider the art of riding, and the use of the bow, as the most desirable and appropriate objects of their emulation, and which they cannot practice or cultivate with too much assiduity.

Khin-Tse.

No. XII. A.

[Referred to from Section LXXVIII. Page 84.]

Translation of an Extract from the Clauses annexed to Section 78.

A Man having no male issue, shall chuse an heir and representative from among those who are of the same name, and known to be descended from the same ancestors, beginning with his father's issue, next with his relations in the first degree, next with those in the second degree, next with those in the third degree; and, lastly, with those in the fourth degree; upon the failure of these, he is at liberty to chuse whomsoever he may prefer among those of the same name. — If afterwards a son should be unexpectedly born to him, such son and the appointed heir, shall participate equally in the family property.

A widow having no children, and not marrying, shall be allowed to remain in possession of the family property, but shall duly summon the next heir to the succession.

When there is an open enmity subsisting between a man who has no male issue, and the family of his lawful heir, the former shall be at liberty to chuse the one whom he esteems most among his relations, descending from the same known ancestors, If, in such a case, the excluded heir endeavours to compel the proprietor to admit his claim to the inheritance, the magistrates shall interfere and protect the right of the heir whom he had elected.

No. XIII.

[Referred to from Section LXXXVIII. Page 92.]

NOTE.

IT has long been a disputed, and is still perhaps to be considered as a doubtful question, whether the tenure by which the land is in general held in China, is of the nature of a freehold, and vested in the landholder without limitation or controul, or whether the Sovereign is, in fact, the universal and exclusive proprietor of the soil, while the nominal landholder is like the Zemindar in India, no more than the steward or collector of his master. The truth probably lies, in this instance, between the two extremes. It is well known, that several of the

merchants

merchants who trade with Europeans at Canton have confiderable landed poffeffions, and that they efteem thofe poffeffions to be the moft fecure, if not the moft important portion of their property. The miffionaries refident at Pekin, under the protection of the court, have likewife their eftates in land, granted them by different Emperors, for the fupport of their eftablifhments. Befides; the ordinary contribution of the landholder to the revenue is fuppofed not to exceed one-tenth of the produce; a proportion very different from that which is required from the Ryots, or actual cultivators of the foil in India, and which leaves enough in the hands of the landholder, to enable him to referve a confiderable income to himfelf, after difcharging the wages of the labourer, and the intereft of the capital employed in the cultivation of his property. It is chiefly upon this income that all the fuperannuated, fuperfeded, and unemployed officers of government; all merchants retired from, and no longer engaged in bufinefs; all thofe Tartar families who hold their property in China under a fpecies of feudal vaffalage; and, laftly, all farmers and other not actually labouring agriculturifts, muft be fuppofed to fubfift. — As there are no public funds in China, the purchafe of land is the chief, if not the only mode of rendering capital productive with certainty and regularity, and free from the anxiety and rifk of commercial adventure.

On the other hand, it muft be admitted, that the Penal code clearly evinces that there are confiderable deductions to be made from the advantages juft mentioned; that the proprietorfhip of the landholder is of a very qualified nature, and fubject to a degree of inteference and controul on the part of government, not known or endured under the moft defpotic of the monarchies of Europe. By the LXXVIIIth Section, the proprietor of land feems to be almoft entirely reftricted from difpofing of it by will. By the LXXXVIIIth Section, it appears that the inheritors muft fhare it amongft them in certain eftablifhed proportions. By the XCth Section, thofe lands are forfeited, which the proprietors do not regifter in the public records of government, acknowledging themfelves refponfible for the payment of taxes upon them. Allotments of lands even appear to be in fome cafes liable to forfeiture, merely becaufe they are not cultivated when capable of being fo. — By the XCVth Section, no mortgage is lawful unlefs the mortgagee actually enters into the poffeffion of the lands, has the produce thereof conveyed to him, and makes himfelf perfonally refponfible for the payment of all taxes, until the lands are redeemed by the proprietor. It will alfo be perceived that, except in the cafe of a lawful mortgage, no perfon other than the actual proprietor of the land, is allowed to engage for the payment of taxes upon it, and that therefore fuch engagement is, in fome degree, a teft of property.

No. XIV.

No. XIV.

[Referred to from Section XCI. Page 96.]

1. Extract of a Letter from a Missionary at Pekin, dated the 9th of September 1801.

"DEPUIS deux mois que j'ai finie mes lettres, il m'a été impossible de les faire partir : une inondation dont on n'a pas d'exemple, ayant rendus les chemins impraticables. A la première cruë d'eau, le gouverneur du district de Pekin a annoncé vingt mille morts, dont il avoit pris connaissance dans l'étendue de son gouvernement, qui n'est qu'une petite partie de la province ; il ajoutoit, ce que tout le monde scait, qu'il devoit nécessairement y en avoir beaucoup d'autres qu'il ignoroit. Ces premières eaux s'étant écoulées en partie, les pluies vinrent derechef, et les eaux allerent toujours en augmentant pendant un mois. — Tous les rapports qui nous viennent de dehors, s'accordent à confirmer qu'il ne reste plus de moisson en terre plate. Depuis un mois, que les pluies ont cesseés, les chemins sont à peine praticables à cheval ; on ne peut pas encore voyager en voiture : heureusement la récolte de bled étoit a peu près finie, mais les autres grains qu'on appelle ici grandes moissons, et qui font la principale ressource de la province, sont presque toùs perdues ; on n'en excepte que les endroits élevés."

2. Extract of a Letter from a Chinese Christian, dated at Lu-gan-fu, *in the Province of* Shan-sy, *30th July*, 1803.

" HIC vitam traho liberam quidem, sed a congressibus hominum alienam ; quid hic aut alibi geratur, me latet omnino : unum scio, penuriam omnium rerum, ob infinitam populi multitudinem, in his regionibus reperiri ; cibaria duplo carius vendi quam venderentur in Europa ; pauperes sustentari, immo rusticos omnes, furfuribus, corticibus arborum et leguminum, vesci panibus rarissime, eosque inter cibos lautissimos habere, carnibus vero nunquam, nisi ad convivium, adhibitos, earum mirandi potius, quam gustandi copiam apponi : quod fames his annis ingentem mortalium stragem non fecerit, fertilis annona auxilio fuit ; ceterum paupertate industriam gignente, hominesque laboribus addictissimos, victum non aliunde magis quam ab agricultura parari ; furta, et homicidia nusquam rarius, quam in hac provincia audiri *."

* This extract is given *verbatim*. — The writer of the letter is the person of whom honourable mention is made in the Authentic Account of the British Embassy, vol. II. p. 594.

No. XV.

[Referred to from Section XCV. Page 101.]

Abstract of some of the principal Clauses annexed to the XCVth Section.

NO mortgage, or redemption of lands mortgaged, shall be reversed or set aside, after it has been signed by all the parties interested, or after it has been acquiesced in by them for five years.

When it is expressly declared in the preamble of a deed of sale, that the land is sold absolutely, and not by way of pledge or mortgage, and there is no subjoined clause providing for the contingency of a further payment to the seller, as a consideration for his making the sale absolute at a subsequent period; such a deed of sale shall be an effectual bar against all claims whatsoever of redemption. But if the sale is not expressly declared to be absolute, or if there is a general clause of redemption, or a specific one of redemption at any time after the expiration of a certain period, the original proprietor shall, according to the terms of the agreement, be entitled to recover his land, upon repayment of the consideration for which it was pledged or mortgaged. If the original proprietor, at the end of the period specified in the contract, is still unable to discharge the mortgage, it shall be at his option, either to retain his right to a recovery of his land, at any future period, or to surrender it, and make the sale absolute, in consideration of a receipt of a further sum to be agreed upon between him and the mortgagee, or between arbitrators duly appointed by the parties. If they cannot agree upon the terms, the mortgagee shall have the option of either continuing in possession, or of re-imbursing himself, by re-mortgaging the land to some other person, the right of redemption remaining as before with the actual proprietor.

It is however provided, that all deeds of sale which are doubtful, or imperfect, owing to the tenor of the preamble, but which contain no clause of redemption, shall, if not questioned or objected to for thirty years from the date thereof, become to all intents and purposes absolute.

Those lands which have been allotted on the tenure of military service, cannot be pledged or mortgaged, but may be let for any term, not exceeding three years.

No. XVI.

[Referred to from Section CXXIX. Page 136.]

Translation of an Imperial Edict, extracted from the Pekin Gazette of the 21st of the 4th Moon of the 5th Year of KIA-KING, *(25th of April,* 1800.)

WHEREAS the Army Commissioner *Tsung-tay* is found guilty of the crime of fraudulently suppressing part of the supplies which had been destined for the troops at *Kia-lin*, and of applying the same to his private use and advantage; it is hereby ordered, that 40 blows with the bamboo shall be inflicted upon him, and that he shall be banished for life to *Elee* in Tartary.

It is further ordered, that the lieutenant *Tang-lin*, who connived at, and encouraged the corrupt practices of the said commissioner, shall likewise suffer 40 blows, but continue to serve in his regiment, holding, however, one of most laborious and least honourable situations in it, as a further mark of disgrace.   *Khin-Tse.*

No. XVII.

[Referred to from Section CXLIX. Page 158.]

NOTE.

THE exorbitance of the interest of three per cent. per mensem, and thirty per cent. per annum, upon either of which rates, according to this code, a contract for a pecuniary loan may be lawfully made, is a peculiarity in the Chinese laws, which it may be difficult entirely to account for. However, it is by no means to be understood, that the ordinary interest of money, considered strictly as such, in any part of China, ever attains that extent. At Canton, for instance, the rate is generally considered to be from 12 to 18 per cent.; which, although subject to no controul from the laws, does not, it will be perceived, materially exceed, upon an average, the legal rate of 12 per cent. per annum, established by ourselves in British India.

The

The rate of intereſt upon a pecuniary loan muſt, indeed, generally ſpeaking, be influenced by a twofold conſideration. Beſides what is conſidered to be ſtrictly equivalent to the advantage ariſing from the uſe of the money, the lender muſt be ſuppoſed, in moſt caſes, to receive likewiſe a certain compenſation for the riſk to which he expoſes his principal. The former conſideration will always be limited by, and bear a certain ratio to, the peculiar ſtate and degree of the general proſperity of the country; but the latter can evidently be determined by no rule or proportion, which does not include the conſideration of the relative ſituation and circumſtances of the parties intereſted in the tranfaction. In England, indeed, where the ſecurity of property, and the excluſive rights of individuals are ſo well underſtood, and ſo effectually protected by the laws, it may, in general, be almoſt as eaſy to guard againſt riſk, as to compenſate for it. But in China, where the rights connected with property are comparatively vague and undefined, and being diſtinct from the ſource of power and influence, are leſs the object of the law's regard; where, owing to the ſubdiviſion of property, there are few great capitaliſts; and where alſo there is but little individual confidence, except between relations, who, holding their patrimony in ſome degree in common, can ſcarcely be conſidered as borrowers or lenders in the eye of the law; it is not ſo ſurpriſing that it ſhould be deemed expedient to licenſe, in pecuniary tranfactions, the inſertion of ſtipulations for very ample intereſt; and, in point of fact, there is no doubt that the law in this reſpect, indulgent as it is, is frequently infringed upon.

In a ſtate of things ſo unfavourable to the accumulation and transfer of property, there cannot at any time be much floating capital; and the value of that capital, as far as it is denoted by the intereſt which it bears, it is natural to expect, will be high in proportion to its ſcarcity. In other words, where there are many borrowers and few lenders, and where it forms no part of the ſyſtem of the government to grant to the former any peculiar degree of protection or encouragement, it ſeems a neceſſary confequence, that the latter will both demand and obtain a more than ordinary compenſation in return for the uſe of his property. Trade, therefore, as far as it requires ſuc haid, cannot be ſo extenſively carried on, as it is in thoſe countries, in which there being more available capital, that capital is procurable at a cheaper rate, and accordingly a ſmaller return of profit found adequate to the charges of commercial adventure.

Excluſive of loans made ſimply on perſonal ſecurity, and thoſe which are made upon landed ſecurity, as already noticed under the title " Mortgage," it is a no leſs frequent practice in China, to lend upon pledges; and accordingly, the ſhops of money lenders, where depoſits may be made of any kind of perſonal property, are extremely numerous in all parts of the empire, and, in general, upon a ſcale of greater reſpectability than eſtabliſhments of a ſimilar nature in Europe.

The intereſt required upon loans thus made is uſually from 1½ to 2 per cent. per menſem; whereas that upon landed ſecurity, eſtimated on an average of the net returns of the land which is pledged or mortgaged, is ſaid not to exceed from 1 to 1¼ per cent. per menſem. It is neceſſary, in this place to obſerve, that, in converting monthly into annual intereſt, the Chineſe make it a general rule of computation to exclude the firſt and ſixth month of every year, ſo that 1 per cent. per menſem is only equivalent to 10 per cent. per annum, and the reſt in proportion.

When an article offered in pledge has been valued, and the rate of intereſt agreed on, a loan is negotiable, on the condition of the pledge being forfeited, unleſs redeemed while its eſtimated value continues to be ſufficient to cover both the principal and intereſt of the ſum lent. The ſubject of this note is very fully diſcuſſed in the *Memoires ſur les Chinois*, vol. iv. p. 299 to 391.

No. XVIII.

[Referred to from Section CLXII. Page 176.]

Tranſlation of Two Imperial Edicts concerning the Propagation of Chriſtianity in China, dated in the Year 1805.

FIRST EDICT.

THE ſupreme criminal tribunal has reported to us the trial, inveſtigation, and ſentence of that court, upon the caſe of *Chin-yo-vang*, a native of the province of Canton, who had been diſcovered to have received privately a map and ſundry letters from the European *Te-tien-tſe**; and alſo in regard to ſeveral others, who had been found guilty of teaching and propagating the doctrines of the Chriſtian religion.

The Europeans who adhere to the Chriſtian faith, act conformably to the cuſtoms eſtabliſhed in thoſe countries, and are not prohibited from doing ſo by our laws. Their eſtabliſhments at Pekin were originally founded with a view to the advantage of adopting the weſtern method in our aſtronomical calculations; and Euro-

* The real name of this European was Adeodato. He was a miſſionary of reſpectable character, and had been many years reſident at Pekin in the Imperial ſervice.

peans of every nation, who have been defirous of ftudying and practifing the fame at this court, have readily been permitted to come and refide in the above eftablifhments; but, from the beginning, they were reftricted from maintaining intercourfe with, and exciting troubles among our native fubjects.

Neverthelefs, *Te-tien-tfe* has had the audacity fecretly to propagate and teach his doctrines to the various perfons mentioned in the report; and he has not only worked on the minds of the fimple peafantry and women, but even many of our Tartar fubjects have been perfuaded to believe and conform to his religion; and it appears, that no lefs than thirty-one books upon the European religion have been printed in Chinefe characters. Unlefs we act with feverity and decifion on this occafion, how are thefe perverfe doctrines to be fuppreffed, how fhall we ftop their infinuating progrefs!

The books of the Chriftian religion were originally compofed in the European languages, and, in that ftate, were incapable of influencing the minds of our fubjects, or of propagating their doctrines in this country; but the books lately difcovered are all of them printed in the Chinefe character, with what view, it is needlefs to enquire; for it is enough that our fimple peafantry, and more efpecially our Tartar fubjects, ought not to be inveigled in this manner; and that fuch books are capable of producing the moft ferious effects on the hearts and minds of the people.

With refpect to *Chin-yo-vang*, who had taken charge of the letters; *Cheu-ping-te*, a private in the Chinefe infantry, who was difcovered teaching the doctrine in one of their churches; *Lieu-chao-tung Siao-chin-ting*, *Chu-chang-tay*, and the private foldier *Vang-meu-te*, who feverally fuperintended congregations of Chriftians; as they have been convicted of conveying letters, or employing other means for extending their fect and doctrine, it is our pleafure to confirm the fentence of the court, according to which they fhall feverally be fent into banifhment to *Elee*, and become flaves among the *Eleuths*; and previous to their departure, wear each of them the heavy cangue for three months, that their chaftifement may be both corrective and exemplary.

The conduct of the female peafant *Chin-yang-fhee*, who undertook to fuperintend a congregation of her own fex, is ftill more odious; fhe, therefore, fhall likewife be banifhed to *Elee*, and reduced to the condition of a flave at the military ftation, inftead of being indulged with the female privilege of redeeming the punifhment. The peafant *Kien-hen*, who was employed in diftributing letters for the congregation, and in perfuading others to affift in his miniftry; and alfo the foldier *Tung-hen-fhen*, who contumacioufly refifted the repeated exhortations made to him to renounce his errors, fhall refpectively wear the common cangue

for

for three months; and, after the expiration of that term, be banished to *Elee*, and become slaves among the *Eleuths*. The soldiers *Cheu-ping-te*, *Vang-meu-te*, and *Tung-hen-shen*, who have gone astray, and willingly become proselytes to the European doctrine, are unworthy to be considered as men; their names shall be erased from the lists of those serving under our banners.

The countrymen *Vang-shy-ning*, *Ko-tun-fo*, *Ye-se-king*, and *Vu-se-man*; and the soldiers in the Chinese infantry, *Tung-ming*, *Tung-se*, and *Chee-yung-tung*, have each of them repented, and renounced their errors, and may be discharged from confinement; but as the fear of punishment may have had more effect than any sincere design to reform, it is necessary, notwithstanding their recantation, that the magistrates and military officers, in whose jurisdiction they may be, should keep a strict watch over them, and inflict a punishment doubly severe, if they should relapse into their former errors.

Te-tien-tse, who is an European retained in our service at court, having so far forgotten his duty, and disobeyed the laws, as to print books and otherwise contrive to disseminate his doctrines, is guilty of a very heinous offence. The alternative proposed by the court, of dismissing him to his native country, or remanding him from the prison to his station at Pekin, is very inadequate to his crime. We, therefore, direct, that the supreme military tribunal appoint an officer to take charge of the said *Te-tien-tse*, and conduct him to *Ge-ho* in Tartary, where he shall remain a prisoner in the guard-house of the *Eleuths*, and be subject to the superintendence and visitation of the magistrate *King-kie*, who must carefully prevent him from having any correspondence or communication with the Tartars in that neighbourhood.

The noble officer *Chang-so*, appointed to superintend the European establishments, having been ignorant of what was going forward, and having made no investigation or inquiries during the time that *Te-tien-tse* was writing letters, printing books, and spreading his religion, has proved himself incapable and unworthy of his station; wherefore, we direct the interior council of state to take cognizance of his misconduct.

In like manner, it is our desire, that the council of state do take cognizance of the neglect and inattention of the military commanders who suffered the soldiers under their orders to be corrupted with these doctrines, and report to us the result of their deliberations, in order that we may refer the adjudication of their punishment to the proper tribunal.

The council of state shall further, in concurrence with the supreme criminal court, appoint proper officers to examine all the books of the Christian doctrine which have been discovered; after which the said books shall, without exception,

be

be committed to the flames, together with the blocks from which the impreſſions had been taken.

The governor and other magiſtrates of Pekin, and alſo the commanders of troops ſtationed thereat, ſhall ſtrictly attend to the ſubject of theſe inſtructions, and ſeverally addreſs edicts to the ſoldiers and people in their reſpective juriſdictions; they are to inform them, that all perſons who frequent the Europeans, in order to learn their doctrine, will, without exception or abatement, be puniſhed with the utmoſt rigour of the law, for thus acting in defiance of the preſent prohibition; as for the reſt, we confirm the ſentence of the court. *Khin-Tſe.*

SECOND EDICT.

IT having been diſcovered, that the European reſidents at Pekin have maintained a correſpondence with our Tartar ſubjects, for the purpoſe of inſtructing them in the doctrines of their religion, and have likewiſe cauſed books to be printed in the Chineſe and Tartar languages, with a view to facilitate the propagation of their tenets, we iſſued an edict, ſtrictly prohibiting the ſame, and alſo directed that all the books containing their doctrine, which ſhould be found in the different European eſtabliſhments at Pekin, ſhould be immediately ſeized for the purpoſe of being deſtroyed. The contents of ſeveral of their books have been already inveſtigated by our council for ſtate affairs, and having by our deſire been ſubmitted to our inſpection, we think fit to notice ſome particular paſſages.

In "*the uſeful introduction to the doctrine*" it is ſaid, "*Tien-chu* (i. e.) *the maſter* "*of heaven, is the great king of all the nations;*" but, in "*the Calendar of Saints,*" it is ſaid, that "*Jeſus the incarnate is the great king of the earth, and of all crea-* "*tures.*" Again; "*Infidelity is the left road: without meditation it is hardly* "*poſſible to purſue the ſtrait road, and obey the will of the Lord.*" Is this truth, or good ſenſe? Then we are informed, that "*all creatures are ſubordinate to the* "*great maſter of heaven and earth: kings, princes, learned, and the people in* "*general, ſhould all renounce their errors, and ſeek truth;—when the holy religion* "*prevails, it will ſoon produce the permanent benefits of order and tranquillity.*" Again; "*The maſter whom I adore is the true maſter of heaven and earth, and of* "*all created things;—through him is the way to the kingdom to come; but the* "*ways of this world are the ways of the fleſh.—Holy men were deſirous of em-* "*bracing the opportunity of propagating the doctrine in China.*"

In the "*Inſtructions concerning the Inſtitution of Marriage,*" it is ſaid, that "*thoſe who are not of the religion are no better than ſlaves of the devil.*"

The foregoing paſſages are ſufficiently abſurd and extravagant; but this is not all; there are other obſervations ſtill more falſe and irrational, making light of the obedience due to parents, and declaring, that " *the highest degree of impiety* " *consists in disobeying the will of the Tien-chu ;*" a story is related of a *Saint Ursula* *, *who, refusing to obey a command, was killed by the hands of his cruel father, whereupon the Tien-chu being incensed, struck him dead with lightning; and this is announced as a warning to all parents, relations, and friends, who attempt to obstruct the designs of their children; and so forth.*

This is surely as contradictory to reason and social order, as the wild fury of a mad dog.

In another place we are told, that *there was a Pei-tse,* (i. e.) *a Tartar prince, who used to commit many bad actions, and never attended to the expostulations of the Fo-tsin,* (i. e.) *Tartarian princess, his wife, who endeavoured to dissuade him from his wickedness. One day, a legion of devils seized the Pei-tse, and carried him to hell, and the Tien-chu, seeing that the Fo-tsin was a good and virtuous woman, privately informed her, that her husband was suffering everlasting torments in a sea of fire.* From which it is inferred, that those who neglect pious exhortations, cannot possibly escape the everlasting punishment inflicted by the *Tien-chu.*

Now this is absurd and extravagant in the highest degree: where did the Europeans become acquainted with the appellatives *Pei-tse,* and *Fo-tsin,* except it was in their interviews and conversation with the natives of Tartary, from whom they have adopted them in order to fabricate this idle tale!

We do not now mean rigorously to investigate what has been done heretofore; but, it is obvious, that this account of a *Pei-tse* carried to hell by devils, is given without any kind of evidence, and does not possess the least shadow of truth or credibility. It would appear, in short, to be a tale which their ingenuity has contrived; and, upon this principle, what is there that we may not readily expect them to say or to write!

If, instead of an early prohibition, we suffer them to go on diffusing their tenets and fabricating their stories, still more egregious falsehoods and absurdities will be obtruded upon us.

Nothing, indeed, but a severe and exact execution of the laws, can prevent the most dangerous consequences; it is better, therefore, to take salutary and efficient precautions, and we have thought fit to direct *Loo-kang,* the noble officer superintending the European establishments at Pekin, to deliberate with his colleagues on an adequate mode of procedure; as well as to examine and strictly investigate every case of the kind that may occur. In the mean time, we have selected the preceding passages out of their books for general information.

For the future, we earnestly exhort our Tartar subjects, to attend to the language and admonitions of their own country and government; to practise riding and

---

* The name is here evidently incorrectly stated.

archery; to study the works of the learned and virtuous, and to observe the social duties. If the sects of *Foe* and *Tao-fse* are unworthy of belief, how much more so is that of the Europeans? Let it be their care to wash away this foul stain, and to beware of giving ear to these sinister and fallacious doctrines.

Those who will not awake from their delusions; who neglect the truth in order to follow what is false and perverse, are unworthy to be considered as men, and ill requite the care and instructions anxiously bestowed on them by their sovereign. We here declare our sentiments, that they may be generally known.

Khin-tse.

No. XIX.

[Referred to from Section CXCI. page 201.]

Translation of an Imperial Edict, issued in the 8th Year of the Emperor KIA-KING, (1803.)

THE extraordinary council of great officers of state appointed by our command on the 20th of the intercalary 2d moon, to try the atrocious malefactor *Chin-te*, have concluded their investigation.

When we returned to the palace by the gate *Shun-ching*, on the 20th instant, in order to observe the solemn fast appointed for that day, it is unquestionably true, that some person rushed forth; although we, being in our palanquin, and already considerably advanced towards the inner court, did not distinguish his features, and only learned the circumstances that had occurred, through the eunuchs of the palace, whom we had sent out to obtain information on the subject.

On the same day, we directed the members of the supreme court of judicature, and of the council for state affairs, to institute a strict and judicial enquiry upon the case; but the confession which was made to them by the criminal, on that occasion, was highly inconsistent and unreasonable*. On the following day, we directed the ministers of state, and the presidents of supreme tribunals, to assist in the investigation; but the criminal pertinaciously refused to swerve from his original deposition. We, lastly, added the officers of the nine departments, and the

* It appears that the criminal, upon his examination, endeavoured to charge some of the principal officers of state, and members of the Imperial family, with a participation in a treasonable conspiracy to assassinate the Emperor, of whom he declared himself to have been only the agent.

prefidents of the fubordinate tribunals, forming, with the other officers of the court, a full council of ftate; before this council he repeated, without any variation, his original confeffion.

In a cafe of this treafonable nature, which both excited our attention and provoked our refentment, we were naturally defirous to difcover, by every method of inveftigation, the original contriver, the confederates, and the nature of the confpiracy, if any, which had been formed on the occafion. The fcrutinizing enquiries and examination of the council, and their earneft defire to obtain information, did not certainly exceed a faithful and patriotic difcharge of their duty; a duty which required of them to fpare no exertion, and to proceed without referve; and which acquitted them of any imputations arifing from the implications or difclofures their enquiries tended to produce.

We, indeed, who hold the univerfal fovereignty of the earth, (*i. e.* China,) furely have governed with candour and integrity! That our actions are neither equivocal or fufpicious, muft be obvious to all our fubjects, the neareft as well as the moft remote from our prefence. During thefe laft eight years, though we make no claim to the perfection of political virtue, at leaft, we have not dared fo far to forget ourfelves, as to take away a life unjuftly. Where, therefore, is there a ground for malice, or an excitement to revenge? The nobles and magiftrates who compofe our court, are efteemed by us with fraternal regard. Our fons and nephews are united to us by the clofeft ties of blood: fhall we allow a wretched criminal to injure them by his wicked afperfions? In fact, we do not fear or harbour a fufpicion againft any one. Among the inhabitants of the earth, there may furely be fome who rufh on wildly like mad dogs, and who commit acts of violence, which no one had previoufly fuggefted or contrived. The bird *Cheekiao* even devours its mother; yet who are its confederates?

If, in confequence of the confeffion extorted from this criminal, we were to proceed again thofe, whom, with the blind fury of a mad dog, he has charged with criminality, they would hardly efcape with life. We renounce, therefore, altogether, an inveftigation of fuch a malignant tendency. Our chief mortification at prefent arifes from obferving, that the influence of our government and example is not more effectual; and this leads us to infer that we have been guilty of fome failure in our duty, which we muft endeavour to rectify, that there may be no blemifh in our conduct, to render it inconfiftent with our affection for our people.

With regard to the atrocious criminal *Chin-te*, and his two fons, we direct that the council do pronounce the fentence of the law refpecting them, and report the fame for our ratification. But we direct, at the fame time, that all other perfons who may have been detained on the fame account, be fet at liberty, left the

innocent

APPENDIX, No. XIX.

innocent should be, in any manner, made to participate in the punishment of the guilty.

On the other hand, the conduct of *Mien-gen*, Prince of *Ting-ching*, who first laid hold of the criminal, and whose clothes were torn while exerting himself to repel his onset; the exertions of *La-vang-to-ur-chee*, Prince of *Ku-lun-ge-fu*, and of the officers in waiting *Tan-pa-to-ur-chee*, *Chu-ur-kang-go*, *Cha-ke-ta-ur*, and *Sang-kee-se-ta-ur*, by whom the criminal was ultimately secured, especially that that of *Tan-pa-to-ur-chee*, who received three wounds in the struggle, all deserve our warmest admiration and praise. On the last of these we confer the dignity of *Pei-le*; and to the two Princes, and the above-mentioned officers in waiting, we shall not omit to bestow distinguished marks of our favour and approbation.

But, at the time of this accident, the officers in waiting, together with the other individuals in our train, were certainly not less than an hundred persons; among whom six only, regardless of danger, stepped forward, in order to seize the villain. It is true, that the Princes *Mien-gen* and *La-vang-to-ur-chee*, and the four officers in waiting, have long enjoyed our distinguished favour; but among so many who calmly looked on with their hands in their sleeves, were there none whom we had in like manner favourably distinguished? The Prince *Mien-gen* is indeed our nephew, and the Prince *La-vang-to-ur-chee* our cousin by marriage; and the exertions of those who are so nearly connected with us by kindred or alliance is highly grateful to our feelings; but were there not many of the unmoved bye-standers as nearly related to us? Is it thus they testify their gratitude and affection to the Sovereign and to the state? If, on such occasions as this, we experience these tokens of indifference and insincerity, we can have but little reason to hope, that on more ordinary occasions, they will exert themselves for the good of their country.

It is *this*, and not *that*, (*i.e.* the dagger of the assassin) which fills us with apprehension and uneasiness. Heaven has given worth and understanding to our nobles and magistrates; let them enquire of their own hearts, whether they ought not to feel shame and remorse on this occasion. This edict we issue for general information.

Khin-tse.

SENTENCE.—By His Majesty's command, *Chin-te* to suffer death by a slow and painful execution; his sons *Lou-eur* and *Fong-eur*, being of a tender age, to be strangled; and the decision of the council to be observed in all other respects.

No. XX.

[Referred to from Section CXCIX. Page 208.]

Translation of an Extract from the Pekin Gazette *of the 23d of April* 1800.

T*E-lin-tay*, general of the Imperial forces, humbly presents his Report to inform His Majesty of the operations of the army against the rebels, during several days successively, in which the enemy was attacked, and the divisions led by *Tsay-tien-yuen* and *Kiay-Ky-siun* entirely routed, and the remainder pursued with great slaughter and effect. The circumstances will be found detailed in the following report, which is forwarded by express: —

The engagements that took place at *Pe-Kia-tsin*, with the five columns of the rebels who attempted to ford the river at that place, the slaughter that ensued, the capture of the leaders *Chin-te-fung* and *Tsay-tien-hiun*, and the subsequent retreat of the enemy, though continuing to watch our motions, have already been stated to Your Majesty.

I lost no time in leading the troops, according to the traces left by the rebels, from *Tse-tung* towards *San-mu-quan*, and reached that station on the 2d of the 3d moon. The scouts whom I had appointed to reconnoitre the position of the enemy then gave us notice, that they were lodged in considerable force in the wood of *Kiang-yeu*. Having advanced thither, pursuant to the information received, we were suddenly attacked by a body of the rebels, consisting of cavalry and infantry, who rushed upon us from four different quarters, with much clamour and impetuosity. The onset was received with firmness and courage by our troops, and upwards of three hundred of the enemy fell in the first encounter. Four hundred suffered the same fate in the skirmishes and partial engagements which ensued, and which lasted for four hours, until the rebels seemed no longer capable of opposing any resistance. In the course of the action, the colonel *Ly-tsung-tsu* was wounded by a spear, and fell from his horse. He nevertheless continued to lead the troops on foot, and greatly contributed towards the victory that ensued The force of the rebels being much broken by this defeat, they hastily dispersed to their fastnesses and concealed stations. During the action, several officers, and one hundred and twenty three privates of the enemy, were taken alive. The officers were put to death in torments, as the law directs; but such of the country people, to the number of several hundred, who appeared to have been

forcibly

forcibly detained by the rebels, and on that account to have fallen into our hands, we suffered to depart unmolested.

On the following day, I reconducted the troops to their former station at *Chung-wha*, and immediately after learned from the reconnoitering party, that a large body of the rebels was collected on the hill *Ma-ti-kang*. I encamped, therefore, the next day, with the army, in a spot 20 or 30 *lee* (two or three leagues) nearer to the station of the rebels, whose force we now learned to exceed, in cavalry and infantry, taken together, ten thousand men; this army we found to be regularly disposed on the opposite declivity of the hill.

I then determined to divide the Imperial army into four principal divisions; the first consisting of the Chinese and Tartar cavalry, under the command of the officers *Tsay-Chung-ho*, *Ly-chao-tse*, and others, to attack the enemy from the bridge at *Lo-yang*, towards *Tao-kai-keu*. The second division, consisting exclusively of regular troops, cavalry and infantry, and commanded by *O-ho pao*, *Ma-ur-quen*, and others, to engage the enemy from *Hay-chang-pu* towards *Ho-she-pu*. The third division, consisting partly of the regulars and partly of the provincial volunteers, under the command of the officers *Wun-chun*, *O-meu-le-tay*, and others, to engage from the village *Pay-fang-shy*, towards *Lung-tse-quan*. The fourth and last division, consisting of the remainder of the regular troops, together with the country militia, and commanded by myself, in conjunction with the officers *Ta-le-ching-o*, *O-te-she* and others, to attack the enemy by the direct road.

[*After relating in detail the various skirmishes and partial encounters that ensued in each division, in consequence of the rebels having avoided a regular engagement, the general proceeds to state, that*] at this time, a man who announced himself to be a native of the district, and to have just escaped from the hands of the rebels, professed to give information that the rebel post at *Tse-lin-koo*, was not defended by more than three hundred and fifty men, and that those few were wholly unprovided with fire-arms.

He offered also to conduct the army to the spot. The channel through which we received this intelligence rendering it extremely doubtful and suspicious, I ordered the informer to be detained, but nevertheless proceeded with the army towards the place that he had indicated to us.

On a nearer approach to *Tse-lin-koo*, I sent a detachment to explore the surrounding country, in order to guard against a surprise from troops in ambush. The rebels indeed received us with a brisk fire of musketry and cannon, accompanied with vollies of stones; and their attack was altogether uncommonly savage and impetuous. Our troops, however, kept their ground, without being in the smallest degree disordered or intimidated.

At the same time, all the other parties of the rebels, whose stratagems had been likewise discovered by the troops I had detached for that purpose, rushed out from their lurking places, and joined in the attack. A severe conflict ensued, in which the officers *Ly-chao-tsee*, *Mey-yn*, and others, behaved with great gallantry and intrepidity. In this action upwards of five hundred of the enemy were killed, several taken prisoners, and the rest driven back to the mountains. Upwards of four hundred of those who retreated were afterwards killed in the pursuit. Two or three leaders of rebels, and many others of a meaner rank, were captured, together with two pieces of cannon and a large assortment of standards, scymetars, swords, and the like, and many horses, asses, and other animals. But the most important advantage obtained, was that of taking alive the general of the rebels *Tsay-tien yuen*, whom we afterwards discovered to be one of their principal leaders and instigators. The prisoner being interrogated, confessed that about two months ago, finding his army to be ill supplied with the means of subsistence in the province of *Se-chuen*, he resolved to pass over with his adherents into the provinces of *Shen-sy* and *Kan-foo*, and that having collected a sufficient number of boats for that purpose, he had crossed the intervening river in the night time with an army of between thirty and forty thousand men, little expecting the vigorous resistance which was afterwards opposed to his progress. In subsequent engagements all his brothers fell in the field of battle, and he was himself once wounded with an arrow. He added, that not above five generals of the rebels still kept the field, and that those were destitute both of talents and of experience.

By this confession our opinion is confirmed, that this is the same leader who has so notoriously been at the head of the troops of the rebels for these last five years, to the great detriment and depopulation of the provinces of *Shen-sy* and *Se-chuen*, and to the sacrifice of the lives of many valuable officers and men belonging to the Imperial armies. But Heaven no longer permits the perpetration of these enormities, and is pleased to deliver him up to our hands; an event that must have been earnestly desired by all ranks of Your Majesty's faithful subjects.

I have not failed repeatedly to publish Your Majesty's Imperial manifesto, addressed to all the well disposed inhabitants, who may have had the misfortune to have been compelled or seduced to associate with the rebels, and declaring a free pardon to all such as awake from their delusion, and renounce their errors; and likewise promising to furnish them with the means of returning to their former habitations and professions.

I have

I have, moreover, thought it expedient to send the rebel chieftain to *Quay-lung* * viceroy of the province, that by His Excellency's orders, he might be sent round with a strong escort, and exposed to public view at all the principal towns and places of public resort in this part of the empire, in order that on the one hand, Your Majesty's faithful subjects may be henceforward relieved from the terror and alarm which the known cunning and ferocity of this man were calculated to excite; and that on the other hand, the hopes and reliance which the malcontents were wont to place on the talents and sagacity of their former leader, may every where be blasted and overthrown.

I finally recommend to Your Majesty's gracious favor and bounty, all those who have honourably distinguished themselves by their valour and abilities, in the late engagements; and I am happy at the same time to observe, that the loss of lives which these victories have cost to Your Majesty's officers and troops is extremely inconsiderable.

IMPERIAL REPLY.

The gracious favor of Heaven, the protecting influence of our ancestors, the fidelity and unanimity of our officers, and the valour of our troops, have all conspired in obtaining for us these victories, and in effecting the overthrow of a most dangerous and wicked leader of the rebellion: the prospect this affords of a speedy pacification of the provinces of *Se-chuen* and *Shen-sy*, is highly consolatory to us, and diminishes our self-condemnation, for the previous sufferings of our faithful subjects in those parts. *Khin-Tse.*

No. XXI.

[Referred to from Section CCXXV. Page 239.]

Translation of Two of the Clauses annexed to this Section.

ILLICIT EXPORTATION OF MERCHANDIZE.

1. ALL officers of government, soldiers, and private citizens, who clandestinely proceed to sea to trade, or who remove to foreign islands for the purpose of inhabiting and cultivating the same, shall be punished according to the law against communicating with rebels and enemies, and consequently suffer death by

* An account of the charges subsequently brought against this officer, and of his condemnation to suffer capital punishment, is inserted in the Appendix No. IX.

being beheaded. The governors of cities of the second and third orders, shall likewise be beheaded, when found guilty of combining with, or artfully conniving at the conduct of such persons. When only a neglect of their duty, in not taking measures to prevent the same, is the offence imputable to them, they shall not suffer death, but be degraded and dismissed for ever from the public service. Governors of cities of the first order, and other officers having the same rank, when guilty of a similar neglect, shall be degraded three degrees, and removed from their stations. — Viceroys and other great magistrates of provinces, shall in similar cases of imputed neglect, be degraded two degrees, but retain their offices.

Nevertheless, the neglect of all such officers shall be pardoned, if they afterwards succeed in securing the offenders, and in bringing them to condign punishment.

2. In general, only a limited number of persons shall be admitted into the empire in the suite of foreign embassies, excepting in the instance of the embassy from Corea. — The embassy from Siam shall be limited to twenty-six persons; those of European nations, in general, to twenty-two persons; and those of any other nation, to twenty persons only.

Those viceroys and sub-viceroys, who, in any case, instead of announcing to the Emperor the arrival of a ship bringing to the empire an embassy from a foreign country, and requesting His Majesty's decision thereon, undertake privately, and of their own accord, to dismiss such embassy, shall be deprived of their offices.

No. XXII.

[Referred to from Section CCLIV. Page 272.]

The following is a Translation of the Clauses annexed to this Section.

HIGH TREASON.

ALL Persons who are banished on account of their connexion, either by blood or by marriage, with persons convicted of high treason, shall be accompanied by their wives: the wives of such implicated persons shall not, however, be liable to banishment, when the husbands happen to die childless, previous to the execution of the principal offender.

The relations of all criminals found guilty of high treason shall, in general, be liable to punishment and execution, conformably to the tenor of the fundamental law;

law; yet, in the inftance of ignorant or defigning perfons attempting to eftablifh a corrupt fect and doctrine, for the fake of obtaining money under falfe and nefarious pretences, and thereby influencing and feducing the minds of the people; although this crime is conftructively high treafon, and punifhable accordingly, it does not neceffarily involve the relations of the criminal, unlefs they are convicted of having been actually concerned in the perpetration of the offence. — Any perfon malicioufly inventing a charge of high treafon, with a view to injure particular individuals, is punifhable according to the law concerning falfe accufations; but the relations of fuch perfon fhall not participate in the punifhment, as fuch relations may be endangered, and cannot be benefited by the perpetration of the offence.

All the male relations of criminals guilty of high treafon, at or above the age of fixteen, fhall be executed in the manner directed by the fundamental law; the remaining male children, if proved to be totally innocent of, and unacquainted with the commiffion of the offence, fhall be fuffered to live, but rendered eunuchs, that they may be employed for the public fervice, in the exterior buildings of the palace. — Among thefe, fuch as are under ten years of age, fhall remain in prifon until they attain that age, and then be fent to court to ferve as above-ftated.

No. XXIII.

[Referred to from Section CCLV. page 273.]

The following is a Tranflation of the Claufes annexed to this Section.

REBELLION AND RENUNCIATION OF ALLEGIANCE.

THE wives and children of perfons liable to be banifhed, as relations of criminals convicted of crimes punifhable by this law, fhall be banifhed likewife, provided the faid perfons are living at the time of conviction, but not otherwife.

The grand-children of criminals under this law, when of too tender an age to be feparated from their parents, fhall remain with them, fubject to the charge and direction of the fuperintending magiftrates.

In every trial of offences of this nature, the prefiding magiftrate fhall diligently afcertain the number, refidence, and employment of the relations of the criminal, or criminals, as well as the extent and amount of his or their property within the province; and if it fhall appear that the criminals have any relations, connexions, or property in any other province, notice fhall be immediately given to the chief magiftrate thereof, that he may duly take cognizance of the fame: — All magiftrates failing in this duty, fhall be liable to profecution by an accufation laid before the Emperor.

The Tartarian fubjects of the empire fhall be equally punifhable under this law. — When their property is fubject to confifcation, their flaves fhall be at the difpofal of the fupreme court for affairs of revenue.

All perfons who, without being related or connected by intermarriages, eftablifh a brotherhood or affociation among themfelves, by the ceremonial of tafting blood, and burning incenfe, fhall be held guilty of an intent to commit the crime of rebellion; and the principal or chief leader of fuch an affociation fhall, accordingly, fuffer death by ftrangulation, after remaining for the ufual period in confinement. — The punifhment of the acceffaries fhall be lefs by one degree. — If the brotherhood exceeds twenty perfons in number, the principal offender fhall fuffer death by ftrangulation immediately after conviction; and the acceffaries fhall fuffer the aggravated banifhment into the remoteft provinces. — If the brotherhood be formed without the aforefaid initiatory ceremonies of tafting blood and burning incenfe, and according to the rules of its conftitution, be fubject to the authority and direction of the elders only, but exceed forty perfons in number, then the principal fhall ftill fuffer death by ftrangulation, as in the firft cafe, and the acceffaries a punifhment lefs by one degree.

If the authority and direction of the affociation is found to be vefted in the ftrong and youthful members, that circumftance alone fhall be deemed a fufficient evidence of its criminality; and the principal fhall accordingly fuffer death by ftrangulation immediately after conviction: the acceffaries, as in the preceding cafes, fhall undergo aggravated banifhment.

If the affociation is fubject to the authority and direction of the elder brethren, and confifts of more than twenty, but lefs than forty members, the principals fhall be punifhed with 100 blows, and fent into perpetual banifhment to the diftance of 3000 *lee*. If the affociation under the laft mentioned circumftances, confifts of any number lefs than twenty perfons, the principal fhall fuffer 100 blows, and wear the cangue for three months. — In both cafes, the punifhment of the acceffaries fhall be one degree lefs fevere than that of the principals.

Whenever

APPENDIX, No. XXIII.

Whenever vagrant and disorderly persons form themselves into a brotherhood by the initiation of blood, as aforesaid, and endeavour to excite factious or leading men to join them, or tamper with the soldiers and servants of public tribunals, with the same intent, having for their ultimate object, to injure the people, and disturb the peace of the country; and further, when such criminal practices have been duly reported by the country-people and heads of villages, to the magistrates and governors of the division or district; if the said magistrates and governors refuse or neglect to take measures for suppressing such proceedings; or in any other manner countenance or connive at them, so that in the end an open sedition breaks out, and rapine and devastation ensue, such culpable officers of government shall be forthwith deprived of their dignities and employments, and prosecuted for their misconduct, by accusation laid before the supreme court of judicature. — Nevertheless, if, after such associations had been suffered to take place through the neglect or connivance of the magistrates, those magistrates exert themselves successfully in stopping the progress of the evil, and in preventing the commission of any act of open violence, sedition, and rapine, and are, moreover, active in seizing the criminals, and bringing them to justice, their former neglect and omission shall, in such cases, be pardoned.

All those inhabitants of the neighbourhood, and heads of villages, who, when privy to these unlawful practices, omit to give information thereof to government, shall be punished according to the degree of their responsibility, and the other circumstances of the case; but, on the other hand, those who give timely notice and information, shall be proportionably rewarded: — If, however, the charges are found to have been made under frivolous pretexts, the informers will be subject to punishment as calumniators.

The punishment of the brotherhood associated by the initiation with blood, which exists in the province of *Fo-kien*, shall be conformable to the afore-mentioned regulations; and further, when the persons thus guilty, take up arms in order to resist the magistrates, and a tumult ensues, all who are concerned in such resistance, shall, if considered as principals, suffer death by being beheaded; and by strangulation, if considered as accessaries to the offence.

All associations connected together by secret signals, whatever be their extent, are obviously instituted with the design of oppressing the weak, and injuring the solitary and unprotected. — Wherefore the leaders or principals of all such societies, shall be held to be vagabonds and outlaws, and accordingly be banished perpetually to the most remote provinces: the other members of such associations shall be considered as accessaries, and punished less severely by one degree.

Those persons who, though not regularly belonging to, had suffered themselves to be seduced to accompany such associated persons, shall not be banished, but shall suffer the punishment of 100 blows, and wear the cangue for three months. — All persons who, after having been employed as soldiers or civil servants of government, enter into any of the said unlawful associations, shall be punished as principals.

Any inhabitants of the neighbourhood, or heads of villages, who may be convicted of being privy to, and not reporting these practices to government, shall be punished more or less severely, according to the nature of the case. — Magistrates neglecting to investigate and take cognisance of the like offences; or from corrupt and sinister motives, liberating and pardoning offenders after examination, shall be punished as the law applicable to similar cases directs.

Notwithstanding the aforesaid, persons assembling for the sole purpose of doing honour, or returning thanks to a particular temple or divinity, and immediately afterwards peaceably dispersing, shall not be punished by any construction of these prohibitions.

All those vagaband and disorderly persons who have been known to assemble together, and to commit robberies, and other acts of violence, under the particular designation of "*Tien-tee-whee*," or, "the Association of Heaven and Earth," shall, immediately after seizure and conviction, suffer death by being beheaded; and all those who have been induced to accompany them, and to aid and abet their said practices, shall suffer death by being strangled.

This law shall be put in force whenever this sect or association may be revived

No. XXIV.

[Referred to from Section CCLVI. Page 273.]

The following is a Translation of the Clauses annexed to this Section.

SORCERY AND MAGIC.

WHOEVER is guilty of editing wicked and corrupt books, with the view of misleading the people; and whoever attempts to excite sedition by letters or hand-bills, shall suffer death by being beheaded: the principals shall be executed immediately after conviction, but the accessaries shall be reserved for execution at the usual season.

All perfons who are convicted of printing, diftributing, or finging in the ftreets, fuch diforderly and feditious compofitions, fhall be punifhable as acceffaries.

The conftituted authorities at Pekin, and the viceroys or fub-viceroys of the provinces, fhall not fail to take due cognizance, in their refpective jurifdictions, of the offence of introducing and offering for fale, any fpecies whatever of indecent and immoral publications. — All the copies of fuch books, and the blocks with which they fhall have been printed, fhall be deftroyed. The author, compiler, or editor thereof, if a magiftrate, fhall be degraded and deprived of his appointment; and if a private citizen, fhall receive 100 blows, and be fent into perpetual banifhment to the diftance of 3000 *lee*. — The venders of any fuch book or writing, fhall be punifhed with 100 blows, and banifhed for three years. — The purchafers and readers thereof fhall fuffer feverally the punifhment of 100 blows. — If the magiftrates do not take cognifance of, and endeavour to reftrain the fale of fuch unlawful publications, they fhall be liable to profecution, by accufation before the fupreme authorities, and punifhed more or lefs feverely according to the circumftances of the cafe. Thofe, however, who charge others with a breach of this law, under frivolous pretexts, fhall be punifhed according to the law againft falfe accufations.

Whoever wilfully publifhes a falfe and malicious report of any public acts and proceedings, which had taken place at Pekin, or in the provinces, fhall, if a magiftrate, or other officer of government, be forthwith degraded, and difmiffed from all his employments; and if a private citizen, fhall fuffer 100 blows, and be fent into perpetual banifhment to the diftance 3000 *lee*. — All magiftrates of diftricts, neglecting to take cognifance of fuch offences, fhall be liable to profecution, by accufation before the fupreme authorities.

Whenever the fons, connections, or dependent inmates of the families of any of the great officers of ftate are convicted of affociating with, or in any manner frequenting the company of perfons guilty of any of the aforefaid offences, or of perfons otherwife criminal and diforderly, they fhall be punifhed according to this law; and the heads of the families fhall likewife be brought to trial, for their criminal negligence, in fuffering perfons under their controul to participate in fuch unlawful tranfactions.

No. XXV.

No. XXV.

[Referred to from Section CCLXIII. Page 277.]

The following is a Translation of the most material Clauses annexed to this Section.

STEALING TIMBER FROM A BURYING GROUND.

1. ALL civil and military officers, and their attendants, having charge of the Imperial cemetery, shall, whenever approaching the same, dismount from their horses at the distance of one hundred paces. A breach of this regulation, being a great instance of disrespect, shall be punished with 100 blows.

2. Whoever cuts down and removes the cypresses, or other similar trees, growing within the innermost inclosure of the Imperial cemetery, shall, if a principal in the offence, be held guilty of sacrilege, and receive sentence to suffer death by being beheaded, but the case shall be, at the same time, recommended to His Imperial Majesty's consideration; the accessaries shall be banished to the frontiers of the empire. Digging the ground, removing stones, and committing other similar trespasses, shall be punished according to the extent of the offence.

3. Any son or grandson who privately cuts down and fells one or more of the trees which grew in the burying-ground of his father or grandfather, shall receive a punishment of 100 blows, and wear the cangue for three months. When the value of the wood so disposed of is considerable, it shall be estimated, and the unabated punishment of an ordinary theft to the same amount shall be inflicted on the offender. When the number of trees cut down exceeds ten, the offender, if a Tartar, shall be employed in servitude in the district of *Ningouta*; if a Chinese, he shall be perpetually banished beyond the frontier. Any son or grandson, who cuts down the dead or decayed wood belonging to such burying-grounds, without previously giving notice thereof to the magistrate of the district, shall be punished with 80 blows.

Slaves or other persons who, being appointed to watch a burying-ground, steal and fell the timber thereof, shall be punished with 100 blows, and wear the cangue for one month. When the amount stolen is considerable, it shall be estimated, and the offender shall be punished one degree more severely than in the ordinary cases of stealing from a burying-ground. When the purchaser of fuch timber knows it to have been ftolen, he fhall fuffer the punifhment of ftealing from a burying-ground in ordinary cafes. The purchafer, when ignorant of the property having been ftolen, will not be punifhable.

Stealing grave-ftones, bricks, dry wood, or other articles belonging to, and depofited in a burying-ground, is punifhable in the following manner: if the offender was the flave, fon, or grandfon of the individual whofe tomb or burying-place had been thus violated, the ftolen articles fhall be valued, and the punifhment rated one degree more feverely than in the ordinary cafes of theft.—If the offender was an indifferent perfon, the punifhment fhall be the fame as in ordinary cafes of theft. The purchafer, if aware of the goods having been ftolen, fhall be punifhed one degree lefs feverely than the feller, and the feveral articles fhall be delivered up to the charge of the magiftrate of the diftrict, in order to their being reftored to the owner.

4. Idle perfons and vagrants privately purchafing timber ftolen from burying-grounds, however fmall the quantity, fhall; for the firft offence, be punifhed with 100 blows, and the cangue for one month; for the fecond offence, with 100 blows, and the cangue for three months; and for the third offence, with perpetual banifhment beyond the frontier.

5. All perfons cutting down and ftealing the trees of a burying-ground fhall, for the firft and fecond offence, be punifhed as already ftated; but, for the third offence, fhall be punifhed in the fame manner as for a third offence in a cafe of ordinary theft.

When the offence is repeated fix times within ten days, or twenty or thirty trees are cut down within the fame period, all the parties concerned fhall be perpetually banifhed, according to the law againft theft by combination. — If the theft be committed during three fucceffive days, it fhall be confidered as one offence; and when it is the firft, the punifhment fhall be one degree lefs than it would have have been conformably to the law againft theft by combination. The parties fhall be branded with proper marks, as in ordinary cafes.

No. XXVI.

[Referred to from Section CCLXIV. Page 278.]

The following is a Translation of the first Seven Clauses annexed to this Section.

EMBEZZLEMENT OF PUBLIC PROPERTY.

1. ANY person having the charge and superintendance of the grain vessels of government, when found guilty of embezzling grain to the amount of sixty stone*, shall be banished perpetually beyond the Chinese frontier: if the grain embezzled amounts to six hundred stone, the offender shall suffer death by being beheaded, after remaining in prison until the usual period.

2. In the different provinces through which the grain vessels of government are navigated, more especially that of *Kiang-nan*, it shall be the duty of all the governors of districts to be on their guard, and to be particularly vigilant in detecting and punishing all clandestine and fraudulent sales and purchases of grain within their respective limits. All persons offending in these respects shall, when discovered, wear the cangue for one month, and be confined until the return of the grain vessels; upon which the superintending officers of such vessels shall be made acquainted with the circumstances, and the offenders punished in their presence with 40 blows each, previous to their being dismissed. All magistrates neglecting to take cognizance of such offences, will be subject to prosecution by accusation laid before the supreme authorities.

3. All proprietors of the small boats which shall be found to have been let out for the purpose of stealing and clandestinely selling the grain laden in the Imperial barges as aforesaid, shall wear the cangue for one month, in the same manner as the offenders described in the last clause; but the subsequent punishment shall be less severe by two degrees. The pilots of the Imperial barges, when privy to such fraudulent and clandestine transactions, and failing to inform the officers of government thereof, shall be punished with 80 blows; but if they also share in the plunder, their punishment shall be proportionate to the amount, as in other cases.

4. In cases of embezzlement of public stores or bullion, to the amount or value of one thousand ounces of silver or upwards, the offenders are punishable with

---

* A stone weight in China is considered to be equal to one hundred and twenty *kin*, or one hundred and sixty British pounds.

death, by being beheaded; but when the value does not exceed one thousand ounces, they may be eventually liberated by an act of grace and general pardon.

When the value exceeds the latter sum, the sentence must be executed, unless it is set aside by the Emperor's special command. No civil or military officers of government, when guilty of embezzlement, shall be branded in the manner ordered with respect to other persons.

5. In every case of embezzlement, the names of the wives and unmarried children of the offender shall be registered, that they may be held answerable for the value of the stores embezzled.

If the superintending magistrate is satisfied, after an accurate examination, that the family of the offender possesses no property, applicable to the liquidation of the demands of government, beyond what had been surrendered for that purpose, he shall sign and deliver to them a quittance and full discharge; but such magistrate shall be liable to degradation and other punishment, if it is afterwards discovered that the parties did actually possess other property; all of which, notwithstanding such quittance, shall thereupon be confiscated. No demand or assessment shall, however, be levied, on the more distant relations of any offender; and any magistrate who arbitrarily attempts to enforce the like, shall be degraded. Any magistrate, likewise, who refuses a quittance when due, will be liable to prosecution by accusation laid before the highest authorities.

6. When any offender, after having been convicted under this law, has been pardoned, or indulged with any mitigation of his sentence, the legal punishment shall be aggravated one degree, if he should ever be convicted of a repetition of the offence.

7. Although an officer or magistrate who had been guilty of embezzlement should happen to die before conviction, his sons shall still be answerable for the amount of the loss sustained by government.

No. XXVII.

[Referred to from Section CCLXV. Page 279.]

The following is a Translation of the Clauses annexed to this Section.

THEFT OF PUBLIC PROPERTY.

1. WHOEVER steals rice or other grain from the public barges, to the amount of one hundred stone, will be punishable with death by strangulation, after the usual period of confinement: when the amount is under one hundred

stone, the punishment shall be according to the scale of stealing any quantity not exceeding in value one hundred ounces of silver from a public granary.

2. Thieves and their accomplices undermining, or otherwise secretly attempting to gain access to a public storehouse, in order to steal, shall be punished in the following manner: the principal offender shall suffer 100 blows and three years banishment; and the punishment of the rest shall be one degree less, as accessaries.

When the theft is actually committed, and to the extent of one hundred ounces of silver in value, the principal offender shall suffer death by strangulation: if less than one hundred ounces value, he shall be banished to one of the most remote provinces.

Accessaries to such a theft, when not exceeding eighty ounces in value, shall be banished for five years.

Accessaries to a theft of eight-five ounces in value shall suffer 100 blows, and perpetual banishment to the distance of two thousand *lee*: if ninety ounces in value, the accessaries shall suffer one hundred blows, and perpetual banishment to the distance of two thousand five hundred *lee*: if ninety-five ounces in value, 100 blows, and perpetual banishment to the distance of three thousand *lee*: the punishment in the case of the theft amounting to, or exceeding one hundred ounces, has been already stated.

No. XXVIII.

[Referred to from Section CCLXVI. Page 281.]

The following is a Translation of some of the most material Clauses annexed to this Section.

ROBBERY.—HIGHWAY ROBBERY.

1. IF, in attempting to commit a robbery, any individual is killed, a house burned, a female violated, a prison, tribunal, or fortification broken into, or damaged; or, lastly, if an hundred persons are assembled, and aiding and abetting the same; in all such cases, each of the criminals shall be beheaded immediately after conviction; even although the party should have obtained no booty;—and the heads of the criminals, as soon as struck off, shall be fixed on pikes, and exhibited as a public spectacle.

2. Perſons armed, and on horſeback, guilty of robbing on the public highways, ſhall, in all caſes, be beheaded immediately after conviction, and their heads exhibited as a public ſpectacle.

All thoſe who are guilty of committing piracies on the high ſeas, or on great rivers, ſhall likewiſe ſuffer according to this law.

3. Whereas there are certain practiced villains who frequent taverns for the purpoſe of adminiſtering ſtupefying drugs to travellers, and afterwards riſe by break of day and way-lay them; — whenever ſuch offenders are apprehended, they ſhall not be removed to a diſtance, but a diligent ſearch and enquiry ſhall be immediately made upon the ſpot, with a view to the ſeizure and conviction of the whole gang or aſſociation; when they are all collected and convicted, they ſhall be beheaded at the ſame time; notice of their execution being given by a public edict duly authenticated by the magiſtrate of the diſtrict.

4. Any robber who has been likewiſe guilty of rapes, murders, burning of houſes, ſeverely wounding the perſon plundered, or any other ſimilar aggravation of his offence, ſhall derive no benefit or indulgence by ſurrendering himſelf. Such robbers as have ſlightly wounded the perſon plundered, whether they ſurrender themſelves before the circumſtances of the robbery are made public, or after the order had been iſſued for their apprehenſion, ſhall, if principals, ſtill ſuffer death, by being beheaded; but not until after remaining in priſon during the uſual period. In caſes wherein no perſon has been wounded, the principals ſurrendering themſelves before the offence has been reported to the magiſtrates, ſhall be baniſhed beyond the Chineſe frontiers. If, in the latter caſes, the offenders do not ſurrender themſelves until after the warrant for their apprehenſion had been iſſued, they ſhall ſuffer conformably to the law relative to a mere remiſſion of the capital part of the ſentence; and accordingly be condemned to perpetual ſlavery in the garriſoned forts on the banks of the *He-lung-kiang*, near the extreme frontier of Tartary.

If the acceſſaries to a robbery, when it is their firſt offence, ſurrender themſelves before information had been given thereof to any magiſtrate, they ſhall be pardoned. If they voluntarily ſurrender themſelves, but not before the warrant had been iſſued for their apprehenſion, they ſhall ſuffer each 100 blows, and three years baniſhment. If they do not ſurrender until after having committed the ſame offence more than once, but previouſly to the report of the laſt offence having been made to any magiſtrate, they ſhall be baniſhed beyond the Chineſe frontier; but if the warrant for their apprehenſion had been previouſly iſſued, they muſt be baniſhed, and undergo perpetual ſlavery in the manner aforeſaid.

Houſe-breakers ſurrendering themſelves, ſhall be baniſhed or capitally executed in the ſame manner as robbers, according to the circumſtances ſtated. The punishment of robbers attempting to escape after condemnation to banishment, shall be aggravated one degree; and if the banishment had been previously decreed to be of the severest kind; that is to say, perpetual slavery on the banks of the *He-lung-kiang*, in Tartary, they shall, in consequence of the aggravation of their guilt, be beheaded, immediately after the sentence pronounced conformably to the law, receives the Emperor's ratification. Persons setting fire to outhouses, and other untenanted buildings, shall suffer banishment according to the law against wilful burning; but if the property destroyed is considerable, the offender shall be banished beyond the Chinese frontier.

5. All persons who, after having been engaged by government as servants of the police, betray their trust, and are concerned in the commission of any robbery, although not actually the principals and instigators thereof, shall, nevertheless, be punished as such, and accordingly be beheaded immediately after conviction. Those magistrates, to whose want of vigilance the opportunity to commit such a crime is imputable, shall be prosecuted by an accusation laid before the Emperor. — If such magistrates attempt to falsify the evidence, and allege that they had previously dismissed from the public service the supposed offenders, their superior officers shall investigate and ascertain the truth of the case, on pain of a similar enquiry being instituted against themselves. — If any of the servants of the police as aforesaid, are convicted of maintaining a correspondence with the robbers, and divulging to them the plan by which they were to have been seized, either by themselves or any other persons in the service of the police, so that the culprits are enabled to defeat such plans, and effect their escape, the persons guilty of such criminal correspondence, whether sharers in the plunder or not, shall suffer the same punishment as had been legally due to those who had fled from justice.

6. Servants of the police, when engaged as aforesaid in the pursuit of the perpetrators of a robbery, shall, in general, suffer equal punishment with the robbers, if convicted of having corresponded with them, and shared their booty. — If only guilty of wilful connivance at the robbery, they shall be punished according to the law against receiving stolen goods, knowing them to have been stolen. If the connivance is not proved, but the police officer is convicted of a designed want of exertion in the pursuit of the criminals, he shall suffer punishment reduced according to the circumstances of the case.

7. The individual who had sustained a robbery, and, in due form, complained of it to a magistrate, shall only be required to attend at the tribunal of government, during the actual trial of the criminals, and the identification of the property recovered; all which property shall, at the conclusion of the trial, be restored to the owner, without subjecting him to delay or molestation: any superintending

intending magiſtrate who fails in theſe points, will be liable to an accuſation laid before the Emperor.

8. The individual plundered, when giving in a ſtatement of his loſſes, ſhall deſcribe the ſame in a clear and diſtinct manner: If the loſs has been conſiderable, and he has omitted to inſert any of the articles, through an overſight, he ſhall be allowed a period of five days for preparing a ſupplementary report. The original and ſupplementary reports ſhall remain thenceforward in the cuſtody of the magiſtrate of the diſtrict, that they may be referred to in all the ſucceſſive proceedings, until the criminals are ſeized, and the property recovered. — When any part thereof has been traced and diſcovered, an officer of government ſhall be ſent immediately to the ſpot, for the purpoſe of having the ſame examined and identified in his preſence. — If the police officers preſume of their own accord to condemn property ſeized by them, or, under the pretext of ſearching for and recovering plunder, make vexatious domiciliary viſits; if they maliciouſly ſuggeſt to the robbers in cuſtody, to make falſe depoſitions concerning the places in which, and the perſons by whom, they had been harboured; if they ſeize and condemn as plunder, any articles honeſtly belonging to the priſoners; if they purchaſe articles to be ſubſtituted in the place of thoſe obtained by unlawful means; or, laſtly, if in any caſe, they report the recovery of plunder, falſely or prematurely, they ſhall, in all ſuch caſes, be puniſhed with the utmoſt ſeverity of the law: — The ſuperintending magiſtrate who has neglected to prevent ſuch abuſes, and the viceroys and ſub-viceroys who had omitted to notice them to the Emperor, will be reſpectively liable to an enquiry into their conduct, and to a trial by accuſation before the ſupreme court.

9. When any member of an aſſociation of robbers has been ſeized, the individual who led the way, and ſuggeſted the plan of the robbery, ſhall, in general, be conſidered, and puniſhed, as the principal; and the reſt only as acceſſaries. — Neverthelefs, if there be one amongſt them, who neither ſuggeſted the plan, nor perſonally aſſiſted in perpetrating the crime, and yet led the way, was poſſeſſed of a previous knowledge of the place intended to be viſited, and of the perſon intended to be plundered, and laſtly, participated in the booty obtained; he alſo ſhall be conſidered, and puniſhed as a principal offender, and accordingly excluded from the benefit of the laws applicable to caſes under palliating circumſtances.

10. If any individual complaining of a robbery, makes a falſe or fraudulent report, by repreſenting that to have been robbery which was merely a theft; or by falſely charging an adulterer with having alſo committed a robbery, ſuch individual ſhall be puniſhed with 100 blows. — If, in a caſe of homicide, or of an aſſault,

assault, a robbery is pretended to have been also committed, the accusing party shall be punished with 100 blows, as before; but if he is implicated himself in the crime, his punishment shall be conformable to the utmost rigour of the law upon the case: — When the crime in which he is implicated, is not considerable, his punishment shall be less than that of the chief perpetrator, by one degree. — If any persons, confiding in their rank and influence, falsely accuse others of robbery, and deceive the superintending magistrates, with the intent to injure and distress particular individuals by such charges, they shall suffer the punishment to which false accusers of a capital offence are liable, when the charges made by them are disproved in time to prevent the execution of the innocent person. — All persons aiding and abetting such false accusers, shall be punished as accessaries.

11. Any civil or military officer of a district, wishing to avoid the difficulties and inconveniencies of carrying the laws into effect in the case of a robbery, and with that view, threatening the complainant, and compelling him to suppress the circumstances of the robbery, or obliging him to represent it as a simple theft, shall be deprived of his office, and a punishment of 100 blows shall be inflicted on each of the clerks of the tribunal, who had participated in such misconduct. — If the compulsion and oppression practised, had been carried to such lengths as to occasion the death of the complainant, or the punishment unjustly inflicted upon him, had been such as to deprive him of the use of his limbs, the magistrate guilty thereof, shall be punished according to the law applicable to the case of an intentionally unjust capital condemnation of an innocent person. — The magistrates of superior tribunals, if they neglect to report such conduct, and the viceroys and sub-viceroys, if they neglect to accuse the offenders, as they are bound to do by their office, will respectively be liable to be charged with such omission before the Emperor.

12. In every case of a theft or robbery, it is the duty of the *Ty-pao*, or head man of the civil division, and of the soldier on duty in the military division, to report the occurrence to the civil and military tribunal to which they respectively belong, in order that prompt and active measures may be jointly pursued by those tribunals for bringing the offenders to justice. — If the *Ty-pao* and the soldier agree together in concealing the fact, or the *Ty-pao* reports it to the civil magistrate, while the soldier on duty omits to make a corresponding report to the military officer on the station, or *vicê versâ*, the parties offending shall be punished in the same manner as the neighbours of persons guilty of robbery, when knowing, and failing to report the same; namely, with 100 blows. — When only very dilatory in transmitting their reports, the punishment shall be limited to 80 blows.

APPENDIX, No. XXVIII.

13. When any robbers, after having surrendered themselves voluntarily, endeavour to satisfy the laws by substituting borrowed articles in the place of those which they ought to have restored; or accuse innocent persons of being in league with them; or plot against any persons out of revenge; or, are guilty of any kind of extortion for the purposes aforesaid; they shall, on conviction of such practices, whether as principals or as accessaries, in possession or not, of the plunder, be immediately beheaded.

14. If a leader in a robbery, although he may have wounded some person and made his escape, afterwards voluntarily surrenders himself, and has likewise the merit of delivering into the hands of justice some other robber, his punishment shall be one degree less than if he had simply surrendered himself at first, that is to say, he shall receive 100 blows, and be banished for a term of three years.

15. When the leader and contriver of a robbery has made his escape; but one of the association who had been taken into custody, offers to indicate the place of the concealment of such leader, so that within the period of a year it may be possible to trace and apprehend him, the trial of the offenders shall stand over until the year is expired; when, if the ring-leader is still undiscovered, the rest of the gang or association shall be executed, or otherwise punished as the laws direct, without further delay; but if the ringleader should have been apprehended in consequence of the information received, the informer, although by law capitally punishable, shall save his life, but be sent into banishment and perpetual slavery in the garrisoned forts on the banks of the *He-lung-kiang*.

If the life of the informer had not been previously forfeited by law, he shall receive 100 blows, and undergo the ordinary perpetual banishment to the distance of 3000 *lee*.

16. When reporting the proceedings in cases of theft and robbery for the Emperor's consideration, if more than one charge of the kind is under investigation, and more than one person has been thereupon capitally convicted, separate reports shall be made upon the case of each individual; but if the capital part of the charges all center in one person, and are similar in their nature, the different charges against that person shall be stated in the same report, clearly, however, and distinctly enumerated.

All the charges against the accomplices, and all such other charges as are not capital, shall be reserved for a separate statement, to be communicated in the ordinary manner to the supreme court of judicature.

No. XXIX.

[Referred to from Section CCLXXXII. Page 304.]

The following is a Translation of Part of the Clauses and Commentary annexed to this Section.

PRECONCERTED HOMICIDE — MURDER.

1. IN the trial and investigation of a case of pre-concerted homicide, the artifice and preconcerted plan must be clearly proved, in order to warrant the condemnation of any person to suffer death by being beheaded, as an original contriver. In like manner, the act of striking and wounding must have been proved against those on whom sentence of death by strangulation is pronounced, as accessaries contributing to the perpetration of the crime. Further, a preconcerted scheme, and the prospect of booty, must be proved with the same certainty, in order to warrant a general sentence of death by being beheaded, against all the parties, whether principals or accessaries, in a case of premeditated homicide for the sake of obtaining booty.

2. If any magistrate presumes to pass sentence of death in any of the aforesaid cases of premeditated homicide, without having proof, in each case respectively, of the previous design, concurrence in the perpetration, or acquisition of booty, as the case may be, he shall be answerable for the lives of the individuals whose condemnation he pronounces.

3. Where a homicide is devised for the sake of obtaining booty, a distinction shall be made between those cases in which a robbery was only attempted, and those in which it was accomplished.

If the homicide had been perpetrated, and the booty likewise secured, the principal and all those accessaries who had contributed to the perpetration of the murder, shall suffer death by being beheaded immediately after conviction. All the other accessaries shall likewise suffer death by being beheaded, but not till the usual period of capital executions. Other individuals subsequently sharing in the booty, shall be banished perpetually to the banks of the river *He-lung-kiang* in Tartary.

When a wound is inflicted with the intent to commit murder, and for the sake of obtaining plunder, the object being also accomplished; then, although the wound should not prove mortal, the principal offender shall suffer death by being beheaded immediately after conviction: accessaries striking a blow, or otherwife directly aiding and abetting, shall likewise suffer death by being beheaded at the customary period.

All other accessaries shall, as aforesaid, be banished perpetually to the banks of the *He-lung-kiang* in Tartary. Those who were not concerned in the crime, but subsequently shared in the division of the booty, shall each suffer 100 blows, and be banished perpetually to the distance of 3000 *lee*.

When the murder is effected, but no plunder obtained, the principal offender shall suffer death by being beheaded at the customary period. When the blow struck does not produce a mortal wound, and no plunder is obtained, the principal only, shall suffer death by strangulation at the customary period; — the accessaries shall suffer punishment proportionably reduced, according to the rule already exemplified.

4. When any individual, upon becoming acquainted with a concerted plan against his life, endeavours to escape, but is drowned, or killed by a fall or other accident, in the attempt, the principal agent in such concerted scheme shall be banished perpetually to the distance of 3000 *lee*; and the accessaries shall, each of them, be punished with 100 blows.

If the murder was on the point of being committed when such accident ensued in the manner aforesaid, the principal offender shall suffer death by being strangled at the customary period; and the accessaries, after receiving 100 blows each, shall be banished perpetually to the distance of 3000 *lee*.

5. In all cases of murder committed by the people called *Miao-tse*, for the sake of obtaining booty, all the parties to the crime shall suffer death by being beheaded, immediately after conviction; and their heads shall be exhibited as a public warning.

6. Any person in priest's orders seizing and murdering a child under 12 years of age, shall suffer death by being beheaded, immediately after conviction: — Other persons committing the same crime, shall be punished as in ordinary cases of murder.

7. In all cases of piracy committed by trading vessels belonging to the island of *Tay-wan* (Formosa,) the offenders shall suffer death by being beheaded, immediately after conviction; and their heads shall be exposed to public view at the port of *Hia-men* (Emouy,) together with a written account of their crimes, as a warning to others.

8. Whoever, from an impulse of anger, kills a child under 10 years of age, shall, if a principal in the offence, suffer death by being beheaded, immediately after conviction. The accessaries who were directly aiding and abetting, shall be strangled as soon as convicted; and all other accessaries shall be banished perpetually to the distance of 3000 *lee*.

COMMENTARY.

When a homicide has been planned by a person, who was not apparently under the influence, either of resentment or of deep-rooted hatred against the party whose life he had designed to take away, a further object must have been in view, such as the gratification of lust or avarice: — Cases of the former kind are less difficult to investigate than the latter, as the actuating motive may sometimes be so carefully concealed, as to be almost undiscoverable.

Homicide by device, although resembling the crime of intentional homicide, which is the subject of another section of the code, is distinguished by peculiar traits of premeditation and contrivance, whereas the latter is simply understood to imply an intent to kill at the time the attempt was made.

When contrivance and premeditation are proved against any person by competent testimony, such proof will be sufficient to convict such person, as one of the original contrivers, and such contrivance will be considered to amount to a personal concurrence in the perpetration of the crime: those who afterwards concur in the actual commission of the murder, will be severally punishable as accessaries aiding and abetting the previous contrivance, although not personally privy thereto: — Thus, under a charge of this nature, for the destruction of one man, the lives of many may happen to be legally forfeited.

In order to convict any person of the crime of a preconcerted homicide, it must be proved that death has actually ensued; but it shall make no difference whether death ensued instantly, or after any lapse of time, provided there be always sufficient evidence of a previous contrivance.

Although preconcerted homicide necessarily implies the existence of some previous contrivance, the crime itself may be perpetrated in various ways; as by poisoning, burning, drowning, way-laying, stabbing, or any other mode which admits of a previous design.

It has been already stated, that a blow producing a wound must be proved, in order to convict an individual capitally, as an accessary directly aiding and abetting the crime: to this it may be added, that any one who menaces the person whose life is attacked, or who defeats the precautions he had taken for his security, is simply punishable as an accessary; whereas, in a case of a premeditated homicide effected by poison, the person who prepares and administers the same, is not a simple accessary, but capitally punishable as an accessary directly aiding and abetting.

If *Kia* consults with *Yee* concerning a plan of murdering a third person, against whom he *Kia* has an enmity, and *Yee*, in consequence, invents or devises a scheme for effecting the same, *Kia* will still be deemed, and punished as the original contriver.

Accessaries to a homicide by contrivance, cannot redeem by a fine any part of the corporal punishment, or banishment, to which they may have been condemned by law; nor will the length of the survivance of the deceased, after he had been wounded, procure them any indulgence; but as the life of an individual under this charge, may often depend on the discovery of the most secret operations of the mind, more than ordinary care and accuracy ought to be employed in the investigation and elucidation of the facts and circumstances upon which the conviction of offenders in these cases depends.

No. XXX.

[Referred to from Section CCXCV. Page 317.]

Translation of an Extract from a Volume of Law Reports; containing the Trial, revisal of Proceedings, and final Sentence, in the Case of an Offender charged with Homicide by Gun-firing.

AT a criminal court held in the province of *Kiang-see*, *Whang-chang-whay*, a native of *King-kao-sien*, was tried upon an information, setting forth, that he had fired a musket at a deer, and by mischance had mortally wounded a man named *Yao-wun-kuey*.

According to the report of *Mey-ching-tu*, sub-viceroy of the province of *Kiang-see*; it appeared in evidence, that *Whang-chang-whay* and *Yao-wun-kuey* were hunters by profession, and had always lived upon good terms with each other.

On the 21st day of the 11th moon of the 38th year of KIEN-LUNG, *Yao-wun-kuey* desired *Whang-chang-whay* to accompany him, and two others, named *Tang-fung-chiang* and *Kuo-pee-meu*, to hunt on the hills called *Pao-Kiu-shan*, and to meet for that purpose at the foot of the hills, on the following day.

Whang-chang-whay assented to the proposal, and on the 22d, equipped himself with a musket for the purpose, and likewise invited *Whang-tien-tsung* to accompany him, and to take a musket and dogs in order to join in the chace.

Yao-wun-kuey had previously set out with his dog and a musket; *Tang-fung-chiang* and *Kuo-py-meu* were also ready with their guns and dogs, and soon joined the party; so that there were five persons in all, assembled upon the hills.

When they opened the chace, *Yao-wun-kuey* took a foutherly ftation, *Whang-chang-whay* took his place to the eaftward in a wood called *Yeu-fhoo-lin*, and *Tang-fung-chiang* with *Kuo-py-meu* watched towards the fummit of the hills; *Whang-fien-tfung* led the dogs upon the fcent; and foon after, a deer was ftarted, and ran to the fouth-eaftward. *Tang-fung-chiang* fired his mufket, but without fuccefs, upon which the animal turned directly fouth, when *Yao-wun-kuey* fired, but having likewife miffed his aim, he took up his gun and ran in purfuit of the animal.

Whang-chang-whay, who ftill remained in the wood of *Yeu-fhoo-lin*, hearing the firing of mufkets in the fouth and fouth-eaft directions, immediately loaded his gun, and made ready for firing. When he advanced from the wood, he faw the deer in the fouth-eaft running leifurely along the hills, and inftantly fired, but perceiving the deer ftill running, found that he had miffed his object.

At the moment that *Whang-chang-whay* fired, *Yao-wun-kuey* accidentally came forward, and in confequence the fhot which had miffed the deer wounded him in the face: on receiving the fhot, he ftaggered, and, falling down, hit his left temple and eye-brow againft the rock. *Whang-chang-whay*, greatly alarmed on the difcovery of the accident, threw down his mufket and fled up the hills. *Tang-fung-chiang* and his companions, being in an elevated fituation, obferved what had paffed below, and immediately came down to give affiftance; but *Yao-wun-kuey* having received a mortal wound, in a fhort time expired.

Upon this, *Tang-fung-chiang* and the others prefent, wifhed to make known the accident to the relations of the deceafed, but *Whang-chang-whay* fearing the confequences of a difcovery of his crime, befought them to conceal the truth, and to report that *Yao-wun-kuey* muft have killed himfelf accidentally, by a fall from the rocks.

Tang-fung-chiang and the others, feeling at the fame time apprehenfive that an enquiry into the affair, might involve them likewife in trouble, agreed to comply with his requeft.

Whang-chang-whay then hid the mufket that had belonged to *Yao-wun-kuey* in the long grafs, and departed with the reft from the fpot, taking with him the dogs that *Yao-wun-kuey* had brought to the chace.

Yao-wun-hing, the elder brother of the deceafed, knew that his younger brother had taken a gun and dogs with him that morning, in order to hunt with *Whang-chang-whay* and *Tang-fung-chiang*. Finding, therefore, in the evening, that he did not return, he went out to make enquiries concerning his brother at different houfes in the neighbourhood. *Whang-chang-whay* and his companions anfwered him according to the deceit which had been concerted between them, and added that they had not feen any thing of the deceafed.

On the 25th day of the moon, however, *Yao-wun-king* found the dead body, and immediately reported the affair to the magistrates of the district. A strict enquiry and examination of the circumstances being made thereupon, *Whang-chang-whay* finally confessed the fact of his having shot the man by mistake while hunting, as related above; but it did not appear from the most minute investigation, that any dispute or other previous cause had contributed to the event.

It appeared clearly on examination, that *Whang-chang-whay*, upon seeing the deer, had taken aim at the animal with his gun, and that, at the same instant, the deer had ran past him, followed by *Yao-wun-kuey*. *Whang-chang-whay* had however already lighted the match of the gun, which accordingly went off, and mortally wounded *Yao-wun-kuey*, before he was able to change its direction. The aim had taken effect before sight or hearing could notice, or any thought or consideration ward off the fatal blow. No injury, therefore, to any one, could have been proposed or thought of by him, when he thus unfortunately gave a mortal wound to *Yao-wun-kuey*.

Whang-chang-whay may be, therefore, esteemed guilty of homicide by mischance, which our laws assimilate in punishment with a homicide committed in an affray, but determine to be redeemable by the payment of 12 *leang*, 4 *tsien*, and 2 *fen*, (4l. 2s. 10d.) to the relations of the deceased, in order to defray the expences of his burial.

With regard to *Tang-fung-chiang*, *Kuo-py-meu*, and *Whang-sien-tsung*; they being privy to the firing of the musket by *Whang-chang-whay*, and to the consequences thereof in respect to the wound received, as well as in respect to the subsequent death of *Yao-wun-kuey*, their conduct in acquiescing in the concealment of the affair, and failing to refer it to the magistrates, is highly culpable; though it does not appear by the investigation, to have been aggravated by the receipt of a bribe, as an inducement to compliance.

They are, therefore, severally punishable with 80 blows of the bamboo. The muskets of *Whang-chang-whay* and *Yao-wun-kuey*, the laws condemn to be destroyed and broken up; but the guns of *Tang-fung-chiang*, *Kuo-py-meu*, and *Whang-sien-tsung*, which were deposited in the hands of the magistrate, may be returned to their respective owners.

The trial of *Whang-chang-whay* for mortally wounding *Yao-wun-kuey* by the firing of a musket, having been revised by us, members of the supreme court of judicature, we make the amendment in the sentence, which appears to us requisite, according to the law in cases of homicide committed when shooting with bows and arrows or otherwise; which law directs a punishment of 100 blows of the bamboo, and banishment for three years; as for the rest, we confirm the sub-viceroy's decision.

The

566   APPENDIX, No. XXXI.

The supreme court quotes various precedents, and institutes a comparison between this and former cases of similar offences, in justification of the amendment, and the Emperor finally confirms their decision on the 17th day of the 10th moon of the 39th year of KIEN-LUNG, by the following words:—" Pursuant to sentence be this obeyed."

No. XXXI.

[Referred to from Section CCCXIV. page 341.]

Translation of an Extract from a Collection of Law reports, Book XXI. Page 15, containing the Trial, Revisal of Proceedings, and final Sentence upon a Case of a Master charged with the Murder of his Servant.

THE case, according to the statement of the sub-viceroy of *Kiang-see*, was as follows:

Lieu-hoey-kuey hired the services of *Pan-kiun-ting*, a slave of government, for a period of ten years. — It happened, that on the 9th of the first moon of the 45th year of KIEN-LUNG, *Lieu-she*, a married sister of *Lieu-hoey-kuey*, came home to visit her father *Lieu-kuen-fung* and her mother *Chang-she*; and one day, it being cold weather, her father sent her into the chamber of the servant *Pan-kiun-ting*, to fetch fire-wood. — *Pan-kiun-ting* being at the time intoxicated, laid hold of her clothes, and endeavoured to prevail on her to lie with him—*Lieu-she* resisted, but finding herself unable to escape him, cried out, and was heard by her mother *Chang-she*, who immediately came to her assistance; upon which the slave *Pan-kiun-ting* relinquished his hold, and was struck twice by the mother, *Chang-she*: *Pan-kiun-ting*, fearing punishment, soon after ran away from the house, and took away with him some bread and 120 *lee* (about nine-pence) in money.

Lieu-she having complained to her brother of the attempt of the slave, and having likewise solicited him to lay an information before a magistrate in order to have the offender punished, returned the next day to her own home, and imparted the circumstance to her husband *Puon-kiun-ye*. — As it was a disgraceful affair, he

merely

merely endeavoured to confole her, and took no further notice of the circumstance, until the 14th of the second moon, when the absconded slave *Pan-kiun-ting*, being unable to gain a livelihood elsewhere, returned to his master *Lieu-hoey-kuey*, acknowledging himself guilty. — *Lieu-hoey-kuey* did not, however, take any steps in consequence, until the next day, when his father *Lieu-kuen-fung* ordered him to bind the offending slave, and carry him to a magistrate, that he might be punished. — *Lieu-hoey-kuey* fearing that one or two persons might not be sufficient to accomplish the object, sent his servant *Lieu-tsing-ta* the same evening to his sister's husband *Puon-kiun-ye*, begging him to come immediately, and give his counsel and assistance.

Puon-kiun-ye having arrived, and the slave *Pan-kiun-ting* being again intoxicated and asleep, *Lieu-hoey-kuey* took a bamboo cord, and, accompanied by his brother-in-law *Puon-kiun-ye*, and his servant *Lieu-tsing-ta*, went into the chamber of *Pan-kiun-ting*, before the lamp was extinguished: having begun to tie the cord in a knot about the neck of *Pan-kiun-ting*, he awoke; and, discovering their intention, endeavoured to rise from the bed. Upon this, *Lieu-hoey-kuey* desired *Lieu-tsing-ta* to hold him down by the head, and *Puon-kiun-ye* by the feet, while he proceeded himself to tie his hands. — At this time *Pan-kiun-ting*, whose body was uncovered, (having previously taken off his clothes,) turned about, and kicked with his legs, abusing them all, in the following terms: " If you carry " me to the magistrate, I shall only be beaten or pilloried, and then sent home; " after which, I will surely take your lives in revenge."—*Lieu-hoey-kuey* being enraged at this language, took up a small knife used for cutting tobacco, which happened to lay at the head of the bed, and wounded *Pan-kiun-ting* with it in the lower part of the belly, so that he died very soon afterwards.

The parties present then became fearful of the consequences of the murder, and covered up the body with the bed-clothes. —After the first watch of the night, *Lieu-hoey-kuey* desired *Puon-kiun-ye* and *Lieu-tsing-ta* to take away the corpse, and throw it into the water, which they did accordingly; but soon after, *Pan-kiung-tching*, and others, related to the deceased, found the body, and lodged a complaint with the magistrate of the district. — *Lieu-hoey-kuey*, being in consequence brought to trial, and examined, confessed that the foregoing statement of the circumstances was correct.

The facts being thus substantiated, the sub-viceroy pronounced the offence to be the wilful murder of an hired slave, and to be equivalent to the wilful murder of a serving-man, which, according to the penal code, is punishable with death by strangulation, at the next general execution and gaol delivery.

The supreme criminal court remarks thereupon, that, according to the penal code, if a master strikes his servant, so that he dies in consequence of the blows

blows received, he shall be punished with 100 blows, and three years banishment:—again, if a master designedly kills his serving-man, he shall be strangled:—lastly, if any man unauthorizedly kills an offender after he has seized him, the punishment shall be conformable to the law in the case of killing in an affray.—Now, because unauthorizedly killing, manifestly comprehends both designed and malicious killing, designedly killing an apprehended offender will be punishable in the same manner as the offence of killing an innocent person in an affray, that is to say, killing, without a positive design to kill:—this precisely applies to the case in question; except that the deceased was not the equal, but the servant of the person who killed him: the punishment therefore ought to be conformable to the law against a master killing his servant in an affray, which is 100 blows and three years banishment; or practically, 40 blows inflicted at the place of banishment.

The sub-viceroy altered the sentence of *Lieu-hoey-kuey* conformably to the suggestion of the supreme court, and added, that as *Puon-kiun-ye* and *Lieu-tsing-ta* threw the corpse away, they ought to be punished only one degree less severely, as accessaries; that is to say, with 90 blows, and banishment for two years and a half.

The supreme court again remarked, that there is a specific regulation applicable to those less serious cases of homicide, for which no man is made legally answerable with his life; which regulation declares, that whoever throws away the corpse in such cases, shall only be punished as in any case of secretly interring a corpse of an individual whose decease has been concealed; which punishment amounts to 80 blows. Now, in the present case, the offence of killing the slave not being determined to be capital, that of throwing away the corpse cannot be punished with more than 80 blows as aforesaid:—and as *Lieu-hoey-kuey* directed the corpse to be thrown away, those who executed the same were only accessaries to the offence, and, accordingly, subject to the punishment reduced one degree;—*Puon-kiun-ye* and *Lieu-tsing-ta* ought therefore to be sentenced each to receive 70 blows; or practically, 25 blows.

The supreme court lastly notices the edict of the 38th year of Kien-Lung, by which it is ordered that all magistrates of cities of the first, second, and third order, who concur in pronouncing a sentence of death, which is afterwards set aside as erroneous, and is exchanged for banishment, are subjected to a diminution of one degree of rank, and removal to an inferior office. It is thereupon suggested, that the several magistrates who concurred in the erroneous sentence adopted and reported by the sub-viceroy, should be degraded accordingly.

On the 25th day of the 5th moon of the 46th year of Kien-Lung, the above proceedings were laid before the Emperor, and on the 29th, they received the ratification of His Imperial Majesty.

No. XXXII.

APPENDIX, No. XXXII.

No. XXXII.

[Referred to from Section CCCLXVI. Page 405.]

The following is a Translation of some of the principal Clauses annexed to this Section.

INCEST AND ADULTERY.

ALL persons, whether in official situations or not, when guilty of committing adultery with the principal wife of any civil or military officer of government, shall suffer death by strangulation; the adultress shall likewise suffer death in the same manner.

All civil and military officers committing adultery with the wife of a private individual, shall be degraded, and punished with 100 blows; and shall wear the Cangue for one month.

In all ordinary cases of adultery amongst the people, the guilty parties shall each receive 100 blows, and wear the Cangue for one month.

When the parties to an act of adultery are both slaves, whether in the service of the same master or not, they shall receive 100 blows, but suffer no further punishment.

2. Persons aiding and abetting the parties guilty of the crime of adultery, shall be punished one degree less, as accessaries.

3. Depraved and disorderly persons conspiring together, and seizing on the son or relative of an honest family, in order to commit an unnatural crime, shall, whether their guilt be aggravated by the subsequent crime of murder or not, suffer death, by being beheaded immediately after conviction, as in the case of vagabond outlaws. — Accessaries to such crimes shall suffer death, by being strangled at the usual period of executions, and all other persons concerned in such a criminal association, shall be banished perpetually.

If no conspiracy had been formed, but the additional guilt of murder incurred, or if a boy under ten years of age had been seduced away for such purpose, the criminal shall be punished with death as a vagabond outlaw, by being beheaded immediately after conviction.

Whoever forcibly commits the said crime with a boy under twelve and not above ten years of age, shall suffer death by being beheaded at the usual period for capital executions: and although the party within the age aforesaid, should have consented, the crime shall still be punished as a rape, that is to say, with death, by strangulation at the usual period.

An assault, with intent to commit the said crime, shall be punished with 100 blows, and perpetual banishment to the distance of 3000 *lee*.

Persons committing this crime by mutual consent, shall be punished respectively, as in ordinary cases of criminal connexion between different sexes, that is to say, with 100 blows, and the Cangue for one month.

Endeavouring to injure any person by charging him with the commission of such a crime, is punishable in the same degree, as the accused person would have been had he been convicted; nevertheless, in capital cases, the punishment of the false accuser shall be less by one degree: — In a case punishable with death by being beheaded immediately after conviction, the false accuser shall be banished perpetually beyond the Chinese frontier.

GENERAL INDEX.

A

	PAGE
ABSTINENCE prescribed previous to certain religious ceremonies	170
Abusive Language, between equals	354
to an officer of government	ibid.
between officers of the same tribunal	355
from a slave to his master	356
to an elder relation	ibid.
to a parent	357
from a wife to her husband's relations	ibid.
from a widow to her deceased husband's parents	358
Accessaries, how distinguished from principals	32
to a theft, how distinguished from accessaries to a robbery	299
Accident, definition of, in cases of homicide	314
Act of Grace or Pardon, how carried into effect	19
misapplication or disregard of	457
Addresses to government, intercepting	254
Adeodato, an Italian missionary, sentenced to be imprisoned for attempting to propagate the Christian religion	532
Adoption of Children, to what extent allowed	84
Adultery, see *Criminal Intercourse*.	
Affrays, punishment of the parties concerned in	311, 326
Aged and infirm, exceptions in favour of	25
care of	93
establishments for the benefit of	ibid.

	PAGE
Anonymous informations	360
Appeals, right of making, note upon	ibid.
encouraging such as are groundless	438
generally to be received and taken cognizance of	451
Army, government of	208
Arrests and escapes	420
Associations, whether secret or public, strictly prohibited	546
Astronomers, punishment of offences committed by	21
neglecting to observe the celestial appearances	187
Astronomical Board at Pekin, commonly called Tribunal of Mathematics, *note*	21

B

	PAGE
Banishment, temporary is the third, and perpetual, the fourth degree of punishment	2
places of	44
extraordinary or military	45
returning from, prematurely	423
delay in executing a sentence of	425
services to be performed during	458
Barrow, Mr. his account of Travels in China, reference to	318
Bodily injuries, punishment for inflicting, proportionate to the injury sustained	325
Books, possession and concealment of such as are prohibited	179

GENERAL INDEX.

Books, editing such as are dangerous and corrupt 548
Branding in the arm, what offenders liable to, and the mode of application . 278
    the effects of, not to be defaced . 301
Bribes, accepting 379
    table of reference in cases of . . 381
    contracting for and agreeing to accept 384
    offering 385

C

Cabals and state intrigues . . . 60
Cangue, or *Kia*, a species of punishment 12
Canton, foreign trade carried on at, *note* upon 515
Capital offences of a miscellaneous nature, meaning of the term; *note* . . 68
Cattle, belonging to government, responsibility of persons in charge . . 241
    breeding of 242
    examination of, when purchased by contract 243
    improper usage and neglect of . 244
    concealing the increase of . 249
    privately lending . . . 250
    killing without a licence . . 245
    vicious and dangerous, how to be treated 248
Censorate, a public board in China, *note* upon 182
Chastisement of a slave or hired servant, to what extent allowed . . . 340
    of a disobedient child or grandchild 347
Christianity in China, state of, *note* upon 176
    edict against the propagation of . 532
Coinage, regulations concerning . . 124
Colleges, literary, edict relative to the establishment of in Tartary . . 525
Commercial agents, appointment of . 163
Compromise and concealment of offences 415
Confiscation of the property of *Ho-chung-tong*, minister of China, notice of . 496
Confronting offenders together . . 442
Convicts and their relations never to be employed near the Imperial presence . 203
Counterfeiting any official seal, or the Imperial almanac 396

Counterfeiting the current coin of the realm 397
Court Kalendar, Chinese, *note* on 14
Creditors not allowed to reimburse themselves by seizing the property of their debtors 160
Criminal intercourse, generally . . 404
    conniving at, or consenting to, in others 405
    between relations . . . 406
    between slaves or servants and their masters' wives . . . 407
    between officers of government and females under their jurisdiction . 408
    during a period of mourning . 409
    between free persons and slaves . *ibid*.
    with prostitutes and actresses . 410
    supplementary clauses concerning . 569
Criminal laws . . . . 269—462
Criminals resisting the police-officers . 421
    assistance and concealment of . . 428

D

Death, punishment of, by strangulation or decollation 2
Debtors, regulations concerning . . 158
Desertion, crime of, generally described 3
    punishment of 35
    from military service . . . 228
    assisting the escape of the relations of persons guilty of . . . 236
    of families or relations . . 92
Dilapidation of property in trust . 161
Disciples and apprentices, the gratitude which they owe to their masters . 335
Dispatches, public, tearing, suppressing, or breaking open 253
    intercepting 254
Divorce, regulations respecting . . 120
Duties and *Customs*, generally . . 148
    on salt . . . . . *ibid*.
    arrears of, to be paid within the year 156
Duties, official, when entrusted to a particular individual, not to be transferred to another 74
Dwelling-houses, strangers entering by night 297

Edicts,

GENERAL INDEX.

E

	Page
Edicts, imperial, non-execution of,	65
falsification of	392
destroying or discarding	ibid.
delay in expediting	71
Embankments of rivers, damaging or destroying	471
neglecting duly to repair and maintain	472
superintended by the Emperor in person	479
Embassies, foreign, no trade allowed with persons belonging to	259
to consist of a limited number of persons	544
to be duly announced by the viceroy of the province in which they arrive	ibid.
Embezzlement of public property	277
supplementary clauses concerning	552
Enrolment of the people, mode of	79
to correspond with their professions	82
Errors and failures in public proceedings	31
in military operations	215
Errors and informalities in public documents	67
Eunuchs, restriction in the employment of	412
Examination, judicial, to correspond with the charges received	444
Execution, slow and painful, *note* concerning	269
instances of	539, 540
Expresses and public posts	252
Express-messengers guilty of delay	256
exceeding their allowances	257
Express-post, reserved for important dispatches	260
Extorting property by threats	288
loans and unfair sales	386

F

False weights and measures	165
pretences, obtaining property under	289
and deceitful addresses to the sovereign	395

	Page
False and malicious accusations	364
reports of public proceedings	549
reports of robberies	557
Falsification of an Imperial edict	392
of verbal orders	394
Family property, disposal of, without leave	92
Female offenders, punishment of	459
curators, misconduct of	510
Festivals and days of ceremony, observance of	180
provincial	191
Fetters and handcuffs, description of	lxxv
to be used in securing prisoners	431
Fines, tables of	lxxii
Foreigners, application of the laws in cases of offences committed by	36, 515
communication with, clandestinely beyond the boundaries	232, 237
important exemption in favour of	523
Forfeited property, concealment or denial of	145
appropriation of	note 271
Forgeries and frauds	392—403
Fortified places, scaling the walls of	206
regulations concerning the gates of	ibid.
Fraud, an instance of, punished	530
Frontiers, the protection of	232
Funerals, regulation of	190

G

Gaming, punishment of	412
Gates of cities and fortified places, to be closed and bolted at regular periods	206
Graves, disturbing	293
Great officers of state not authorised to confer appointments	51
addresses in favour of	62

H

Harbouring thieves and robbers	297
Harvests, destroying or damaging	104
Hau-kiou-choaan, a Chinese Novel, edited by the Bishop of Dromore, *note* upon	107

Heat

GENERAL INDEX.

Heat of summer-months, indulgence to prisoners and convicts in consideration of 489
Hereditary rank, instances of its being annulled 501
    not to be solicited . . 52
    rule of succession to . . 49
High treason . . . 269, 544
    trial and sentence of persons guilty of 493
Ho-chung-tong, minister of China, his history 491
Homicide (see *Killing, Murder*) 304—323
    examination of the body in cases of 452
    trials of persons charged with 521, 563, 566
Hoppo, or superintendant of the port of Canton, his edict . . . 521
House-breakers, punished as robbers . 555
House-burning, accidental . . 415
    malicious 417

I

Imperial almanac, counterfeiting . 396
    barges, stealing from . . 552
    blood, how privileged . . 5
    edict, non-execution of . . 65
    equipage and furniture, charge of . 178
    guards, failing in their duty . 195
    manifesto, announcing a pardon to all persons who, after having been seduced to associate with the rebels, return to their duty . . 542
    medicines and provisions, preparation of 177
    palaces, entering unauthorizedly . 194
    labourers in 198
    gates of, passing through irregularly 199
    passports and certificates of persons employed in . . . 200
    carrying weapons into . *ibid.*
    shooting or throwing missile weapons against . . . 202
    soldiers on guard in, to be armed *ibid.*
    convicted persons not to be employed in 203

Imperial palaces, passing through gates leading to 205
    presents, delivery of . . 180
    rank, how privileged . . 39
    retinue, failing in its attendance . 196
    intrusion into space allotted to . 204
    roads, trespass on . . 197
    temple, entering unauthorizedly . 193
Impostors, pretending to be officers of government 398
    pretending to be great officers of state 399
Imprisonment, unlawful and forcible . 335
    as a punishment, note upon - 431
    of innocent and unimplicated persons 433
Improper conduct, such as is not specifically provided against by any existing law . 419
Incest, or criminal intercourse between relations 406
Indulgence to offenders, for the sake of their parents 20
    in consideration of their age, youth, or infirmities . . . 23
Infanticide, note upon . . . 347
Informations, irregularity in presenting . 359
    anonymous . . . 360
    neglecting or declining to receive . 361
    such are not to be received, but transferred to others - . 364
    false and malicious . . *ibid.*
    table of reference in cases of . 367
    of offences punishable with extraordinary punishment . . 378
    against relations . . . 371
    presented by prisoners . . 374
    upon subjects affecting civil as well as military affairs . . . 376
    on behalf of the private concerns of officers of government . . 377
    fraudulent alterations in . . 462
    in cases of robbery, how to be presented 557
    magistrates suppressing, or compelling others to suppress . . 558
Inheritance, regulations respecting 84, 525
Injuries, neglecting to prevent those which are known to be designed, or to give information of such as are known to have actually been committed . . 323

Insurrection,

GENERAL INDEX.

	PAGE
Insurrection, proceedings in cases of	209
Interest of Money, legal rate	158
note upon	530
Inundations, precautions to prevent	472
instances of their destructive effects	528
Justice, delay in the execution of, instanced in charges against certain officers of the Canton government	509

K

Kaung-hee, Emperor of China, his prefatory edict	lxvii
Kia-king, reigning Emperor, his edicts,	483
493—509. 513. 518. 525. 530. 532—539	
Kidnapping, or the unlawful seizure and sale of free persons	290
Kien-lung, Emperor of China, his last will, or testamentary edict,	477
Killing, see *Homicide*, *Murder*.	
a stranger entering a dwelling-house by night	297
in execution of a pre-concerted scheme	303. 560
for the sake of plunder	304
an officer of government	ibid.
a parent	305
a relation or a master	306
an adulterer	307
a deceased husband's relation	ibid.
three or more persons in one family	308
with an intent to mangle the corpse for magical purposes	309
by means of venomous animals, or of poisons	310
by magical writings or imprecations	ibid.
with an intent to kill	311
in a quarrel or affray, without any express or implied design to kill	ibid.
by depriving of food or raiment, or by any indirect means	312
in play, by error, or purely by accident	313
a culpable wife	315
a son, grandson, or slave, and attributing the crime to an innocent person	316

	PAGE
Killing, by shooting arrows, or similar weapons	317
by riding carelessly or otherwise, on horses or in carriages	318
by administering improper medicines	319
by means of traps or springes	320
by the effects of violent and fearful threats	321
a slave or hired servant	340
a son or grandson	347
a criminal who is endeavouring to make his escape	422
by illegal severities in the course of a judicial examination	434
a condemned prisoner, by his own desire, in order to prevent a public execution	441
Khin-tse, meaning of the term	497

L

Lands of the nobility and officers of government	98
unoccupied, to be allotted to persons disposed to cultivate the same,	95
sowing and tilling those of strangers without authority	102
uncultivated and neglected	103
Lands and tenements	94
fraudulent sale of	99
mortgage of	101, 529
tenure by which held, note upon	526
not to be purchased by officers of government within the limits of their jurisdiction	100
Land-tax, fraudulent evasion of	94
supposed general rate of	note 527
Laws, general	47
how executed when appearing contradictory	37
when retrospective, and when not	43
civil	49—78
due knowledge of	64
fiscal	79—167
ritual	169—191
sumptuary, relative to dress and habitations	185

Laws,

GENERAL INDEX.

	Page
Laws, military	193—267
criminal	269—462
seducing persons to transgress	403
delay in the execution of	435
how to be observed in framing a judicial sentence	455
false construction of	461
relative to public works	463—474
supplementary	489. 525. 529. 543—563
Licences of priests	83
of salt-merchants	148
of commercial agents	163
of labourers in the Imperial palace	200
Licences and passports, crossing a barrier without	232
granting or obtaining under false pretences	233
Literary degrees, partiality in conferring	55
Litigation, exciting and promoting	375
Lost and forgotten property	161

M.

	Page
Magical arts, practice of, prohibited	175
Manufactures not equal to standard	167
for the public service	465. 468
Marriages, how regulated	107
during the period of mourning	112
during the imprisonment of parents	114
between persons having the same family name	ibid.
between persons related by marriage	115
between persons related by blood	ibid.
of officers of governments with females within the limits of their jurisdiction	116
with absconded females	117
forcible, with freemen's wives or daughters	ibid.
with female musicians and comedians	118
of priests of Foe or Tao-sse	ibid.
between free persons and slaves	119
dissolution of, see *Divorce*.	
on occasions in which the bride is given away unlawfully	122
Medicine, practitioners of, killing or injuring their patients	519

	Page
Merchandize, false manifests of	156
valuation of	164
illicit exportation of	238
Meu, a Chinese measure of land, *note* upon	94
Military affairs, expresses concerning	212
breach of secrecy upon	213
arms and accoutrements, clandestine sale of	222
destroying or casting away	223
prohibition of to private citizens	224
theft of	276
duties, relaxation of, and absence from	ibid.
exercise and discipline	220
forces, employing without authority	208
how to be employed in cases of insurrection	209
not to be employed by princes or hereditary nobles	229
horses and cattle	241
clandestine sale of	221
officers, not taking the field according to their instructions	215
unfaithful to their trust	217
conniving at depredations committed by the soldiers	218
favour shewn to the relatives of	230
interference of in civil affairs	77
operations, to be regularly reported	210
errors and failures in	215
extract of an official report of	540
service, desertion from	228
supplies, application for, and transmission of	214
Monopolizers and unfair traders	164
Monuments, public, not to be constructed except on suitable occasions	183
defacing and destroying	411
Mortgages, regulations concerning	101, 529
Mourning, for deceased relations, how enforced	188
degrees of	lxxv, 487
for the Emperor *Kien-lung*, directions concerning	486
Murder, (see *Homicide* and *Killing*)	303
compromising and concealing, in the case of a relation deceased	322
Musicians, exceptions in favour of	22

Naval

GENERAL INDEX.

N

	PAGE
Naval force, Chinese destitute of	note 238

O

	PAGE
Offences, of officers of government	9
public	10
private	11
committed previous to their elevation	15
of persons not liable to banishment	12
of persons of the military class	13
of astronomers	21
of artificers, musicians, and women	22
of persons already under sentence of punishment	23
of persons surrendering voluntarily	27
of persons charged with several offences	29
of members of public departments, in their official capacity	30
committed by foreigners	36. 515
who are participators in	40
committed by persons seduced by others	403
miscellaneous	411
compromise and concealment of	415
against propriety	419
against nature	569
Officers of government, such as are removed without being disgraced	14
such as are disgraced as well as removed	16
limitation to their liability to punishment	note 51
enumeration of the principal, extracted from the Chinese Court Calendar	54
dismissal of, for misconduct	56
quitting their stations without leave	57
to proceed to their stations as soon as appointed	58
attendance of, at court	59
irregular interference of, with their inferiors	ibid.
combination and collusion among	62
to have generally free access to the Emperor	181
Officers of government, honorary attendance upon, limited	184
neglecting their parents	189
guilty of exciting and causing rebellion by oppressive conduct	221
when deceased, their families to be conveyed home at the public expence	264
not to perform allotted services by substitutes	ibid.
interference with public affairs without authority	401
to reside in the official buildings allotted to them	469
statement of crimes and misdemeanours committed by	491—514
Official dispatches, how transmitted	54
alteration of the contents of	74
conveyance of	252
on public affairs, proper style and tenor of	182
Ordinary cases, explanation of the term,	note 305

P

	PAGE
Palanquin, or sedan-chair of the Chinese, note upon	263
Paper-currency, unknown in China	note 124
Parents, their power over their children	note 292
disobedience to, and neglect of	374
Parricide, crime of, generally described	3
punishment of	305
Pecuniary malversation	382
table of reference in cases of	383
Period within which deserters may obtain pardon by surrendering	229
of responsibility for the consequences of a wound	327
Perjury, wilful and corrupt	note 364
Personal services to be levied impartially	86
to be allotted impartially	87
evasion of, generally	88
by concealment or desertion	89
excessive demand of	91
Piracies on the high seas	555
Police, nocturnal, regulation of	230

578   GENERAL INDEX.

	PAGE		PAGE
Police officers, duty of	420	*Proceedings*, judicial, in cafes in which all the offenders have efcaped	29
resiftance to, when performing their duty	ibid.	in cafes in which only fome of the offenders have abfconded	34
periods allowed them in purfuing thieves and robbers	ibid.	in cafes in which the laws appear contradictory	37
how punifhed when guilty of confpiring with thieves and robbers	556	in refpect to the application of new laws	43
Portuguefe at Macao, edict addreffed to	515	falfe and deceitful report of	396
Poft-houfes, to be kept in repair	255	againft fuperior magiftrates	455
principal apartments of, referved for particular perfons	262	*Prognoftics*, pretending to difcover	401
Precious metals muft be paid to government free from alloy	140	*Propofals*, making fuch as are illegal	413
Prefents, acceptance of	387	*Prophecies*, on public affairs, prohibited	187
from the great hereditary nobles	391	*Profecutors* not to be detained after the trial is concluded	445
Pretending ficknefs or death	401	*Public* buildings	463
Priefts of Foe and Tao-ffe, laws relative to	42	due prefervation and repair of	468
privately affuming the character of	83	looms, mifapplication of	467
marriage of, interdicted	118	pofts and expreffes	252
drefs and behaviour of	186	property	124
Principals and acceffaries, diftinction between	32	privately lending and employing	133
Prifoners, efcaping and rifing againft their keepers	422	fraudulent appropriation of	135
efcaping through the connivance of the keepers	426	regulations refpecting the receipt and iffue of	139
fecuring the perfons of	431	vexatious proceedings, in the receipt and iffue of	140
ill treatment of	ibid.	refponfibility for the damage or lofs of	141
not to be allowed fharp inftruments	ibid.	regular tranfmiffion of, from inferior to fuperior jurifdictions	142
making groundlefs appeals	438	intermediate charge of	145
fupplies of food and clothes to	439	embezzlement of	277
occafional indulgences to	ibid.	mifapplication of	466
indulgence to, when diftinguifhed by their rank or former fervices	440	ways, regulations concerning	471
committing fuicide	441	encroachment upon	473
at liberty either to plead guilty, or to proteft againft the charges againft them	456	works, regulations concerning	463
		ordering, without authority	ibid.
Prifons, remark upon	431	unneceffary and unferviceable	464
guards and attendants of	90	to be conformable to rule and cuftom	465
refcue from	281	*Punifhments*, table of degrees of	lxxiv. 1
abufes committed in, a ftatement of	509—514	variation of, in refpect to the Tartars	12
Privileged claffes, defcribed	5	how mitigated	13
exceptions in favour of	7	rule for increafing and diminifhing	38
note upon	490	infliction of, in an illegal manner	453
		mitigation under particular circumftances	489

Quarrel-

Q

	Page
Quarrelling and fighting, between equals	324
within the Imperial palace	329
between slaves and free persons	336
between husbands and wives	341
see Striking, Killing, &c.	

R

	Page
Rape, definition and punishment of	404
Rebellion, crime of, described	3
punishment of	272. 545
in the provinces of Se-chuen and Shen-see, notices of	496. 540
Records, official, examination of	72
re-examination of	73
Recrimination upon innocent persons	445
Relations, how far allowed to assist each other	34
in the first degree	39
of exiles	17
Relationship, degrees of	lxxv. 345. 487
Religion of the Chinese	note 169
Reports, official, neglecting to make when requisite	68
of officers on detached service	69
Rescue from prison	281
Responsible superintendants	41
of storehouses, to attend at their respective posts in cases of fire	416
Restitution of goods, rule of	25. 144
Revenue, public, vicarious contributions to	128
contributors to, not to be discharged prematurely	129
excess of, its suppression or misapplication	131
privately lending or employing	132
receipt, transfer, and expenditure	133
of supposed total amount of,	note 143
see Public Property, Fiscal Laws, &c.	
Revenue officers, misconduct of supernumeraries	145
reciprocally answerable for each other	136
Revenue officers, responsibility of, in cases of theft	137
responsibility of, as receivers and distributors	138
Revenues in kind, periods of collecting	125
to be collected with fairness and impartiality	126
concealing or wasting	127
Reward, receiving money corruptly by way of	384
Ritual laws	169—192
Robbery, highway robbery	280. 554
ordinary, in open day	283
how distinguished from a theft	300
or theft, when considered to be completed, and when attempted only	ibid.
Rules and orders, transgression of	419
Russians, their unsuccessful attempt to establish a trade at Canton	515
edict relative to the same	518

S

	Page
Sacred rites, administration of	169
provincial	172
Sacrilege, crime of, generally described	4
punishment of	274
Sale, deed of, either absolute or conditional	529
Sales and markets	163
Scarcity of food in China, instance of	528
Seal, official, destroying or discarding	65
use of	76
omitting to use, or imperfectly using	ibid.
Sectaries prohibited	175
Sentence, judicial, execution of, not to be delayed	435
execution of, generally	451
to be founded on all the laws, statutes, and precedents applicable	455
not to executed without the Emperor's ratification	460
execution of, by a false construction of the laws	461
Sepulchral monuments, care of	173
Shun-chee, first Tartar Emperor, his prefatory edict	lxv

GENERAL INDEX.

Slavery in China, peculiar character of, *note* 293
Smuggling of salt . . . 148
    of tea . . . 154
    of allum . . . 155
    in general . . . *ibid.*
    instance of rigorous sentence against *ibid.*
Soldiers, (see *Military*)
    serving by substitutes . 216
    connivance at the depredations of . 218
    exercise and discipline of . 220
    and labourers, care of, when sick 411
Sorcery and magic . . 273. 548
State secrets, divulging . . 213
Stealing edicts and ordinances of government 274
    seals and stamps of office . 275
    from an Imperial palace . *ibid.*
    the keys of the gate of a fort or city *ibid.*
    military weapons and accoutrements 276
    timber from a burying ground . 277. 550
    public property . 279. 553
    private property in ordinary cases . 284
    horses, or other domesticated animals 285
    corn, or other produce in the open field 286
    from relations or connections . . 287
    crime of, committed by servants or slaves 288
    clothes from a corpse . . 297
Stolen goods, purchasing, knowing to have been stolen . . . 299
    suppressing the discovery of . 390
Stray children, regulations concerning . 85
Striking an individual of Imperial blood . 330
    an officer of government 331. 332. 333
    any person employed in the public service . . . 334
    disciples and apprentices, their masters 335
    slaves, their masters . 338
    a husband . . . 341
    a wife . . . 342
    a relation . 343—345
    a parent . . . 346
    wives, their husbands' relations . 349
    husbands, their wives' children by former husbands . . 351
    widows, the parents of their deceased husbands . . . 351
    in defence of a parent . 352

Strolling players . . . 410
Suicide, prisoners committing . . 441
Supernumerary officers of government . 52
    district officers . . . 88
Supplementary laws, or clauses 489. 525. 529 543—563
Surgery, practice of, in China . *note* 319
Suspected persons, detection and examination of . . . 237
Swindling, or obtaining property under false pretences . . . 289

T

Tartars, enrolled for military service, *note* 12
    military and equestrian exercises recommended to . . 525
Ta-tsing-hoei-tien, a voluminous Chinese work, notice of, . *note* 52
Taxes and personal services to be levied impartially . . . 86
    see *Land-Tax*
Tenure of land in China . *note* 526
Theatrical representations . . 418
Theft, see *Stealing.*
Time, legal division of . . 41
    mode of announcing successive periods of . . *note* 231
Torture, application of, in judicial examinations . . . 441
    instruments of, described . 488
Trade, circumstances which are unfavourable to, in China . *note* 531
Traps and springes, not to be laid without giving sufficient warning . 320
Travellers, vexatious treatment of, and detention, at the barrier stations . 235
    way-laying and robbing . 555
Travelling equipage of officers of government limited . . . 266
Treasonable offences, generally described, *note* 490
Trial and sentence of *Ho-chung-tong*, minister of the late Emperor *Kien-lung* 491
    of *Quay lung*, vice-roy of the province of *Se-chuen* . . 504

Trial

GENERAL INDEX.

	PAGE
Trial and sentence of several officers of the province of Canton	509
— of a British seaman, upon a charge of homicide	521
—— remarks on the foregoing	515
— of certain Chinese and Tartars convicted of embracing the Christian religion	532
— of *Chen-te*, a Chinese, who entered the Imperial palace with the supposed intent to assassinate the Emperor	537
— of *Whang-chang-whay*, a Chinese, upon a charge of homicide by gun-firing	563
— of *Lieu-hoey-kuey*, a Chinese, upon a charge of having killed his hired servant	566
Tribunals, why so named	note 22
— responsibility of the constituent officers of	note 30

V & U

Vaccination in China, its introduction by the surgeon of the English factory	note 319
Veterinary art, exercise of	243
Vicious and dangerous animals, to be marked and secured	248
Visitation of lands, suffering from any calamity	96

	PAGE
Unjust sentences, consequences of the declaration and execution of	447
— table exemplifying cases of	449
— reversal of	450
Usury, definition of	158
— *Note* upon	530

W

Warrant of execution, proceedings on the receipt of	460
Witnesses, prevarication of	446
Wives (see *Marriages*)	
— lending for hire	110
— regard to rank and priority among	ibid.
— distinction between inferior and principal	ibid.
Worship, forms of, among the Chinese, different opinions respecting	note 169
— certain forms of, prohibited	174
Wounds, Wounding, see *Killing, Striking*, &c.	
— periods of responsibility for the consequences of	327

Y

Yong-tching, Emperor of China, his prefatory edict	lxix

THE END.

ERRATA.

Page   4, line 4, *for* adminftering, *r.* adminiftering.
—— 10, — 18, *for* his fituation, *r.* their fituations.
—— —, — 20, *for* his fituation, *r.* their fituations.
—— 27, — 4, *for* orignal. *r.* original.
—— 30, — 8, *for* claue, *r.* claufe.
—— 51, — 16, *dele* he.
—— 53, — 27, *for* tieng, *r.* tien.
—— 54, — 29, *for* enumeration, *r.* enumerations.
—— 104, — 26, *for* drural eities, *r.* rural dieties.
—— 111, — 15, *for* and to other. *r.* and other.
—— 113, — 17, *for* his, *r.* their.
—— 134, — 29, *for* officer, *r.* officers.
—— 209, — 14, *for* a, *r.* their.
—— 313, — 1, *for* texten, *r.* extent.
—— 343, — 1, *for* ftrking, *r.* ftriking.
—— 448, — 20, *for* oi, *r.* or.
—— 474, — 8, *for* has, *r.* have.
—— 510, — 26, *for* everal, *r.* feveral.
—— 522, — 17, *dele* that.
—— 531, — 30, *for* fuc haid, *r.* fuch aid.

For EU product safety concerns, contact us at Calle de José Abascal, 56–1°,
28003 Madrid, Spain or eugpsr@cambridge.org.

www.ingramcontent.com/pod-product-compliance
Ingram Content Group UK Ltd.
Pitfield, Milton Keynes, MK11 3LW, UK
UKHW050800060825
461487UK00021B/1752